Vocab Victory

Barkha Agrawal

Published by :

Invincible Publication Pvt. Ltd.

Published by:

Invincible Publication Pvt.Ltd.

201A, SAS Tower, Sector 38, Gurugram, Haryana – 122003

Phone: +91-124-4034247, +91 9599066061

Website : www.invinciblepublishers.com

Sales Office : - 4760-61/23, Basement, Pratap Street, Ansari Road,

Daryaganj, New Delhi - 110002

Phone: +91-11-40198405

Email: invinciblepublishers@gmail.com

ISBN : 978-93-58860-05-4

Book Name : Vocab_Victory

First Edition: September 2023

Disclaimer

This book is meant for educational purposes only and is not a substitute for professional, financial or legal advice. Bearing the individual differences, it is of utmost importance that before making any financial decisions one must conduct thorough research, seek professional guidance, and consider their individual circumstances. The authors and publishers do not and cannot guarantee the accuracy or timeliness of the information provided, and disclaim any liability for any loss or damage resulting from its use. Cryptocurrency markets are volatile, and past performance is not indicative of future results. Stated by governmental authorities, crypto products and NFTs are unregulated and can be highly risky. There may be no regulatory recourse for any loss from such transactions. Thus, by reading this book, you agree to proceed with caution and take responsibility for your own financial decisions.

Contents

Chapter - One

One Word Substitution

All One word substitution in Alphabetical Order

➢ List of one word substitution start with word A

Word	Meaning	Hindi Meaning (Simple Terms)
Abattoir	Place where animals are killed for food	मांस खाने के लिए जानवरों को मारने की जगह
Abbot	A man who is the head of a monastery or an abbey	मठ या आश्रम के प्रमुख पुरुष
Abbreviation	A shortened form of a word or phrase	शब्द या वाक्य का संक्षेप रूप
Abdication	To formally give up	सरकार या पद से त्यागपत्र देना
Ablution	Ritual washing of the body	शरीर का धार्मिक धोन
Abstruse	Hard to understand	समझने में कठिन
Abundance	A quantity that is more than enough	प्रचुरता
Accentuate	Give more force or importance to	जोर देना या महत्त्व देना
Accomplice	Helper in a wrong deed or crime	ग़लत काम में सहायक
Acronym	Word formed from initial letters of a name	नाम के प्रारंभिक अक्षरों से बना शब्द
Addendum	Thing to be added at the end of a book, document, etc.	किताब के अंत में जोड़ा जाने वाला अंश

Word	Meaning	Hindi Meaning (Simple Terms)
Advertisement	A public notice offering or asking for goods, services, etc.	सार्वजनिक सूचना जिसमें माल, सेवाएं, आदि की पेशकश हो
Afforestation	The act of forestation by planting many trees	अनेक पेड़ लगाकर वृक्षारोपण का कार्य
Agenda	Items of business for consideration at a meeting	बैठक में विचार के लिए विषयों की सूची
Aggressor	Someone who attacks first	पहले हमला करने वाला व्यक्ति
Agnosticism	Doubtful about the existence of God	भगवान के अस्तित्व पर संदेहशीलता
Alien	One who belongs to a different country, race, or group	एक ऐसा व्यक्ति जो एक अलग देश, जाति या समूह का है
Alimony	Allowance fixed after divorce to a spouse	तलाक के बाद पत्नी को निर्धारित राशि की भत्ता
Allegory	Story in which ideas are symbolized as people	कहानी जिसमें विचारों को लोगों के रूप में प्रतीत किया जाता है
Alliteration	Commencement of adjacent words with the same sound	समान ध्वनि के साथ संबंधित शब्दों का प्रारंभ
Altruist	One who lives and works for the welfare of others	वह व्यक्ति जो दूसरों के कल्याण के लिए जीता और काम करता है
Amateur	Lacking professional skill or expertise	पेशेवर कौशल या विशेषज्ञता की कमी वाला

Word	Meaning	Hindi Meaning (Simple Terms)
Ambassador	A diplomatic representative of one country in another country	एक देश के बाहरी देश में राजनयिक प्रतिनिधि
Ambidextrous	Equally skillful with each hand	दोनों हाथों से बराबर कौशलवान
Ambiguous	Having more than one possible meaning	एक से अधिक संभव अर्थ रखने वाला
Amnesia	Partial or total loss of memory	स्मृति की आंशिक या संपूर्ण हानि
Amnesty	A general pardon of political offenders	राजनीतिक अपराधियों के लिए सामान्य क्षमा
Amphibian	Animals which live both on land and in water	जीवों का जो जल और थल दोनों पर रहता है
Amphitheatre	A designated section of seats in any part of a circular building	किसी वृत्ताकार इमारत के किसी भाग में सीटों का निर्दिष्ट सेक्शन
Analgesia	The loss of ability to feel pain while still conscious	अभी भी संज्ञानात्मक रूप से दर्द महसूस करने की क्षमता का हानि
Anarchist	One who wishes to destroy all established government's law and order	वह व्यक्ति जो सभी स्थापित सरकार के कानून और व्यवस्था को नष्ट करना चाहता है
Anarchy	The absence of government or order in a country	एक देश में सरकार की अनुपस्थिति

Word	Meaning	Hindi Meaning (Simple Terms)
Anecdote	Short amusing story about some real person or incident	किसी वास्तविक व्यक्ति या घटना के बारे में एक छोटी हंसी मजाकीय कहानी
Anniversary	Yearly return of the date of an event	एक घटना की तारीख का वार्षिक वापसी
Annual	That which happens once in a year	जो एक वर्ष में एक बार होता है
Anomaly	Deviation or departure from common rule or standard or what is normal	सामान्य नियम या मानक या सामान्यता से हटकर या अलग होने का विचलन
Anonymous	A book or a work of art whose author is not known	एक पुस्तक या कला का कार्य जिसके लेखक के बारे में नहीं पता हो
Antagonist	One that opposes another	जो दूसरे के खिलाफ होता है
Antidote	A medicine to cure the effects of poison	जहर के प्रभाव को ठीक करने की दवा
Aphasia	Loss of the ability to understand speech	भाषा को समझने की क्षमता का हानि
Apostate	One who abandons his religious faith	जो अपने धार्मिक विश्वास को छोड़ देता है
Aquatic	Animals which live in water	जल में रहने वाले जीवों
Arbitrator/ Arbiter	Someone chosen to judge and decide a disputed issue	विवादित मुद्दे का न्याय करने और निर्णय देने के लिए कोई चुना गया व्यक्ति

Word	Meaning	Hindi Meaning (Simple Terms)
Aristocracy	A government by the nobles	अभिजात वर्गों द्वारा चलाया जाने वाला सरकार
Armistice	The cessation of warfare before a treaty is signed	संधि पर हस्ताक्षर किए जाने से पहले युद्ध का निवर्तन
Ascetic	One who practices self-denial as a spiritual discipline	एक व्यक्ति जो आध्यात्मिक अनुशासन के रूप में आत्म-त्याग का अभ्यास करता है
Assassination	Killing or murder for political reasons	राजनीतिक कारणों के लिए हत्या
Astrology	Science of the influence of the stars on human life	तारों के प्रभाव पर आधारित विज्ञान
Astronomy	Science of the universe with the sun, moon, stars, and planets	सूर्य, चंद्रमा, तारे और ग्रहों के साथ ब्रह्मांड का विज्ञान
Atheist	A person who does not believe in the existence of God	भगवान के अस्तित्व में विश्वास न करने वाला व्यक्ति
Audience	An assembly of listeners or watchers	सुनने वालों का एक समूह
Autobiography	The life-history of a person written by themselves	एक व्यक्ति की जीवन-कथा जिसे उन्होंने खुद लिखा है
Avaricious	One who is greedy	लालची व्यक्ति

➢ List of one word substitution start with word B

Word	Meaning	Hindi Translation
Bachelorhood	The state of being unmarried (of a man)	अविवाहित होने की स्थिति (पुरुष की)
Bankrupt/Insolvent	A person unable to pay his debts	दिवालिया/दिवालियापन (कर्जों का भुगतान न कर पाने वाला व्यक्ति)
Bay	A part of the sea/lake enclosed by a wide curve of the shore	खाड़ी (समुद्र/तालाब का विस्तारित भाग)
Beach	A stretch of sand/stones along the edge of the sea/lake	समुद्र/तालाब के किनारे की रेत/ पत्थरों की खंड
Bellicose	A person who is fond of fighting	युद्ध करने का शौक रखने वाला व्यक्ति
Belligerent	Engaged in war/fight	युद्ध में लिप्त/युद्ध करने वाला
Benefactor	One who gives financial help to a school, hospital, etc.	परोपकारी (एक व्यक्ति जो स्कूल, अस्पताल आदि को आर्थिक सहायता देता है)
Bibliophile	One who loves and collects books	पुस्तकों के प्रेमी

➢ List of one word substitution start with word C

Word	Meaning	Hindi Translation
Cabaret	A series of cabre dance/ acts at a night club	कैबरेट (रात क्लब में कैब्रे नृत्य/ क्रियाएँ का संग्रह)
Cabby, Cabdriver	The driver of a taxi cab	कैबी, कैब चालक
Cacophony	A mix of unpleasant sounds	कर्णध्वनि
Cajole	Persuade by flattery	मना लेना
Calligraphy	Art of beautiful handwriting	खूबसूरत हस्ताक्षर कला
Capsize	Overturn in water	पालट देना
Carnage	Killing of large numbers of people	हत्या, नरसंहार
Carnival	Public merrymaking and feasting	कार्निवल
Cartographer	A person who draws maps and charts	मानचित्रकार
Cartography	Art of map-making	मानचित्र निर्माण कला
Catalogue	List of books and other articles	सूची, पुस्तकों और अन्य वस्त्रों की सूची
Celibate	One who has taken a vow not to have sex	अविवाहित, ब्रह्मचारी
Cemetery	The place for corpses to be buried	कब्रिस्थान, मकबरा
Centenary	Hundredth anniversary	शताब्दी
Chronological	According to sequence of time	कालानुक्रमिक
Circumlocution	A roundabout way of expression	परिभाषावाद

Word	Meaning	Hindi Translation
Cloakroom	The place for luggage at a railway station	रेलवे स्टेशन पर सामान के लिए जगह
Coerce	Compel to a course of action	दबाव डालना
Cognate	Having the same source or origin	सम्बद्ध, संबंधित
Colleagues	Persons working in the same department	सहकर्मी, सहयोगी
Collusion	Secret agreement for a fraudulent purpose	साजिश, मिलीभगत
Conflagration	Huge destructive fire	महामारी, महाघातक आग
Congregation	Gathering of worshippers	सभा, जमात
Congruent	Identical or coinciding in all respect	समान, एकसार
Connoisseur	One who is well-versed in any subject/ art	सुश्रवण
Conscription	Compulsory enlistment for military or other services	भर्ती, संविधानी लेना
Contagious	Which spreads by physical touch or contact	संक्रामक
Contemporary	Of the same time	समकालीन
Contiguous	sharing a common border; touching	संयुक्त, समयुक्त
Contrite	Showing deep sorrow for wrongdoing	पश्चातापी, पछतावा करने वाला

Word	Meaning	Hindi Translation
Convalescence	The period of gradual recovery of health after illness	स्वास्थ्य वापसी की धीरे-धीरे होने की अवधि
Conventicle	Secret and illegal religious meeting	अवैध धार्मिक सभा
Coquette	A seductive woman who uses her sex appeal to exploit men	मोहक महिला, जो अपने लोकप्रियता का उपयोग पुरुषों पर करती है
Coronation	Ceremony of crowning a king or queen	राज्याभिषेक
Cosmopolitan	A person who regards the whole world as his country	विश्वनागरिक
Credulous	One who is simple and easily believes whatever is told	विश्वासपूर्ण
Crematory	The place for corpses to be burnt	संस्कारघाट, अंतिम संस्कार का स्थान
Cripple	Someone who is unable to walk normally because of an injury or disability to the legs or back	अपंग, पंगु
Curfew	An order that certain activities/movements are prohibited	गायनकाल
Cynosure	Centre of attraction	आकर्षण केंद्र, प्रधान आकर्षण बिंदु

➢ List of one word substitution start with word D

Word	Meaning	Hindi Translation
Deist	One who believes in the existence of God	देववादी
Demagogue	Political leader who delivers sentimental speeches	जनप्रिय, भावनात्मक भाषण देने वाला राजनेता
Democracy	A government by the people, of the people, and for the people	लोकतंत्र
Denizen	A person, animal, or plant that lives in a particular place	निवासी
Depraved	Morally bad or evil	अशिष्ट, नरकी
Deprecate	Express earnest disapproval of	अस्वीकार करना
Dermatology	The medical study of the skin and its diseases	त्वचा विज्ञान, त्वचा का चिकित्सा अध्ययन
Despondency	Loss of complete hope	निराशा
Destitution	Lacking basic necessities of life	अभाव, दरिद्रता
Detrimental	Causing harm or damage	हानिकारक
Dexterous	Skilful at handling things	कुशल, निपुण
Diatribe	Bitter and violent attack in words or writing	निन्दा, तिरस्कारजनक भाषण, कटु टिप्पणी
Dictatorship	Government carried on by an absolute ruler	तानाशाही

Diplomacy	The skill and policy of a country's statesmen and politicians	कूटनीति
Discrepancy	Difference between two things that should be the same	अंतरविरोध
Dissimulate	To hide or disguise	छिपाना, छलकरना
Diurnal	Of the daytime	दैवी
Draper	A shopkeeper selling cloth and clothing	वस्त्रविक्रेता
Draw	The result of a match where neither party wins	खिचना
Dwarf	A person, plant, or animal who/which is below the usual size	बौना, अत्यल्प, बौना पौधा
Dynasty	Succession of rulers belonging to one family	राजवंश

➢ List of one word substitution start with word E

Word	Meaning	Hindi Translation
Eavesdropper	One who witnesses secretly to private conversations	खिसकने वाला, खुलेआम बातचीत में छिपकर खड़ा रहने वाला व्यक्ति
Economical	One who is careful in the use of money/fuel, etc.	अर्थव्यवस्थापक, संयमी
Edible	That which is fit to be eaten	खाद्य, भोज्य, खाने योग्य
Effeminate	A man who is womanish in his habits	महिलायी, स्त्रीसंगी, स्त्रीलिंग
Egalitarianism	Belief that all people are equal and have the same rights and opportunities	समानितावाद
Egoist	A lover of oneself/ supercilious	अहंकारी, आत्मारामी
Eligible	Fit to be chosen; qualified	योग्य, चयन के लिए योग्य
Emergency	A sudden serious situation requiring immediate action	आपत्ति, आपातकालिक
Emeritus	One who is honorably discharged from service	प्रतिष्ठित, मान्यता प्राप्त
Emigrant	A person who goes to another country to live	प्रवासी, देशांतरगामी
Emissary	A person sent on a mission (usually official)	दूत, राजदूत
Epicure	Person fond of delicious food	भोजन प्रेमी, भोजन स्वाद का प्रेमी

Epidemic	A disease affecting many people at the same place and time	महामारी
Epilogue	A speech or a poem recited at the end of a play	अंतिम भाषण, काव्य पठन, प्रस्तुति भाषण
Episode	Part of a story (especially TV or radio show story)	भाग, कथा का अध्याय, अध्याय, दौर
Episodic	Happening only sometimes and irregularly	छुट्टा चलनेवाला, अनियमित
Epistle	A letter	पत्र
Epitaph	Words which are inscribed on the grave	स्मरणीय प्रशस्ति, मृतक के समाधि पर लिखी जाने वाली बातें
Epithet	Adjective added to a person's name, usually to criticize or praise him	उपनाम, सम्मानजनक या आलिंगनकारक विशेषण
Epitome	A perfect example	उदाहरण, संक्षेप, सार, संक्षेपरूप
Epitomize	To be a perfect example	संक्षेप करना, चिह्नित करना
Equanimity	Calmness of mind and temper	समभाव, स्थिरता
Erotica	Books, pictures, etc. intended to arouse sexual desire	कामातुर्भाषा
Erudite	A learned or scholarly person	पंडित, विद्वान, प्राणीसम्बन्धी
Espionage	The practice of spying	जासूसी, गुप्तचर विद्या
Eternal	Existing forever—without any beginning or end	अविनाशी, अनंत, सनातनी

Etymology	The science which deals with the derivation of words	उत्पत्तिशास्त्र, शब्दशास्त्र
Euphemism	A mild or indirect expression substituted for a harsh or blunt one	सुगमभाषा, शोभायमान शब्दसम्पूर्ण
Euphonious	Sounding pleasant	सुस्वर, मधुरध्वनि
Euphoria	A strong feeling of happiness	प्रफुल्लता, उत्कण्ठ, आनंदी भाव
Evanescent	Of very short duration or period; ephemeral, transient	क्षणिक, अल्पकालिक, अस्थायी
Explicable	That which can be explained	स्पष्ट किया जा सकनेवाला
Extempore	A speech delivered without any preparation	तत्काल, बिना तैयारी के
Extravaganza	A public activity that takes place in a very elaborate, colorful, and expensive way	शानदार प्रदर्शनी

➤ List of one word substitution start with word F

Word	Meaning	Hindi Meaning (Simple)
Fallacy	False or mistaken belief	तर्कभ्रष्टता, ग़लत या भ्रामक विश्वास
Fanatic	One who is filled with excessive and mistaken enthusiasm	उन्मत्त, अतिरंजक, अति उत्साही व्यक्ति
Fastidious	One who is hard to please	कठिनाई से प्रसन्न होने वाला व्यक्ति
Fatal or mortal	Resulting in death	मृत्युप्रद, जानलेवा
Fatalist	One who believes in destiny	भाग्यवादी
Fauna	Animals of a certain region	प्राणिसंघ
Feminist	One who works for the welfare of women	महिलाओं के हित में काम करने वाला व्यक्ति
Fiasco	Complete failure	विफलता, असफलता
Flagstaff	A long pole on which a flag is flown	झंडा स्तंभ
Flora	All the plants of a particular area or period of time	वनस्पतिसंख्या, वनस्पति जगत
Fluke	Stroke of good luck	सौभाग्यपूर्ण संयोग
Forgery	Counterfeiting of document	जाली, नकली
Frenzy	A state of extreme excitement	उन्माद, पागलपन
Frostbite	Injury to the nose, fingers or toes, caused by extreme cold	हिमशोणित, ठंड से होने वाले घाव या नुकसान

➢ List of one word substitution start with word G

Word	Meaning	Hindi Meaning
Gallery	A room or building for showing works of art	गेलरी, कला प्रदर्शन के लिए कमरा या इमारत
Gamble	To play games of chance, etc. for money	जुआ, पैसे के लिए जुआ खेलना
Gastronomy	Science and art of preparing and appreciating good food	भोजन विज्ञान, स्वादिष्ट भोजन की तैयारी और सराहना करने की कला
Genocide	Extermination of a race or community	नरसंहार, एक जाति या समुदाय का विनाश
Geology	The science of earth's history and rocks	भूविज्ञान, पृथ्वी के इतिहास और पत्थरों का विज्ञान
Germicide	A substance that kills germs	जीवाणुनाशक, जीवाणुओं को मारने वाली एक पदार्थ
Glutton	One who eats too much	भुक्खड़, अत्यधिक खाने वाला व्यक्ति
Gobble	Eat fast, noisily and greedily	भोक भरपूरता से खाना, खुरचाते हुए और लोभपूर्वक खाना
Gratis/Gratuitous	Done or obtained with nothing expected in return	निःशुल्क, भावी, मुफ्त
Gregarious	Animals that live in flocks	झुण्ड में रहने वाले जीव

➢ List of one word substitution start with word H

Word	Meaning	Hindi Meaning
Hallucinogen	A drug that causes one to hallucinate	मोहक द्रव्य, एक ऐसी दवा जो मनोहारी अनुभव कराती है
Hedonism	Belief that the most important thing in the world is pleasure	हेडोनिज़म, यह विश्वास कि दुनिया में सबसे महत्वपूर्ण चीज़ आनंद है
Henchman	Faithful supporter	निष्ठावान समर्थक, नेतृत्व में सहायक
Herbivorous	Animals which feed on vegetation	शाकाहारी, जीवाणुओं जो वनस्पति पर आहारार्थी होते हैं
Herculean	Having enormous strength or size	बहुत ताकतवर, विशाल
Heterogeneous	Things which contain elements of different	विविधतापूर्ण, अनेक प्रकार के तत्वों को समायोजित करने वाली वस्तुएं
Hexagon	A plane figure with six sides and angles	षट्कोण, छहों सिरों और कोणों वाली एक समतल आकृति
Holocaust	Large-scale destruction by fire	महाघात, आग द्वारा विशाल-स्तरीय विनाश
Homicide	Murder or murderer of a man	हत्या, किसी आदमी की हत्या या हत्यारा
Homogeneous	Things which contain elements of the same	समरूप, एक ही प्रकार के तत्वों को समायोजित करने वाली वस्तुएं
Honorary	A post for which no salary is paid	सम्मानित, जिसके लिए कोई वेतन नहीं दिया जाता
Horticulture	Art of growing vegetables, fruit, etc.	उद्यानिकी, सब्ज़ी, फल आदि का उत्पादन करने की कला

Word	Meaning	Hindi Meaning
Hospitable	Fond of entertaining guests	आतिथ्यप्रिय, मेहमानों का सत्कार करने में रुचि रखने वाला
Hypochondria	Imaginary ailments	ज़ाहिरी बीमारी, काल्पनिक रोग

List of one word substitution start with word I

Word	Meaning	Hindi Meaning
Iconoclast	One who opposes established institutions or traditions	मूर्तिपूजा विरोधी
Idolatry	The worship of idols or images	मूर्तिपूजा
Illegal	Contrary to law	अवैध
Illegible	Incapable of being read	अपठनीय
Illicit	A trade or act prohibited by law	गैरकानूनी
Illiterate	One who does not know reading and writing	निरक्षर
Imaginary	Existing only in the mind	काल्पनिक
Immigrant	A person who comes to one country from another to settle	प्रवासी
Immune	Free from infection	प्रतिरक्षाशील
Impalpable	Incapable of being perceived by touch	अस्पृश्य
Impenetrable	That which cannot be penetrated	अप्रवेश्य
Imperceptible	That which cannot be perceived by the senses	अदृश्य
Imperialism	Policy of extending a country's empire and influence	साम्राज्यवाद
Impertinent	Not showing proper respect	अयथार्थ

Word	Meaning	Hindi Meaning
Impiety	Lack of respect or religious reverence	अपवित्रता
Imponderable	That which cannot be guessed or calculated	अकथनीय
Imposter	One who assumes a character or title not his own to deceive	ढोंगी
Impracticable	Incapable of being practiced	अव्यवहारिक
Impregnable	Too strong to be overcome or defeated	दुर्गम
Impresario	A manager or director of a ballet, concert, theatre, or opera	प्रबंधक
Impromptu	Something said or done without preparation	तत्काल
Impudent	Rude and not respectful	असभ्य
Impunity	Freedom from punishment	माफ़ी
Inaccessible	Incapable of being reached	पहुँच से दूर
Inadmissible	That which cannot be admitted or allowed	ग्रहण न करने योग्य
Inaudible	A sound that cannot be heard	अश्रव्य
Incendiary	Designed to cause fire or likely to cause violence	आगजनक

Word	Meaning	Hindi Meaning
Incombustible	That which cannot be burned	अग्निधर्मी
Incomparable	That which cannot be compared	अद्वितीय
Incorrigible	Incapable of being corrected	सुधार योग्य नहीं
Incredible	Which cannot be believed	अविश्वसनीय
Incurable	Which cannot be cured	अच्छुक
Indefatigable	Incapable of being tired	अथक
Indefensible	Which cannot be defended	अरक्षणीय
Indelible	Which cannot be erased or forgotten	अमिट
Indemnity	Compensation for loss	हरजाना
Indestructible	That which cannot be destroyed	अविनाशी
Indignant	Angry at injustice	रोषग्रस्त
Indispensable	That without which one can't do	अपरिहार्य
Indivisible	That which cannot be divided	अविभाज्य
Ineligible	Not suitable to be elected or selected under the circumstances	अयोग्य
Inevitable	Incapable of being avoided	अपरिहार्य
Inexcusable	That which cannot be excused	अक्षम्य

Word	Meaning	Hindi Meaning
Inexplicable	Which cannot be explained	अव्यख्यायित
Inexplicit	Not definitely or clearly expressed	अस्पष्ट
Inexpressible	That which cannot be expressed in words	अकथ्य
Infallible	Never wrong	अप्रमाणिक
Infanticide	Killing of an infant	शिशुहत्या
Infectious	A disease which spreads through air and water	संक्रामक
Inflammable	Which catches fire easily	सुस्त
Inimitable	Incapable of being imitated	अनुकरणीय
Insecticide	A substance that kills insects	कीटनाशक
Insolvent	A person who is unable to pay his debts	दिवालिया
Insurrection	Rising against established authority or government	विद्रोह
Intercede	Plead to obtain a favor or save someone else	मध्यस्थता करना
Intercept	To check or stop on the way	रोकना
Intrigue	Make or carry out secret planning, arouse the curiosity or interest	षड्यंत्र

Word	Meaning	Hindi Meaning
Introspection	Examination of self-thought or feeling	स्वांगालोचना
Invincible	That which cannot be defeated	अजेय
Invisible	That which cannot be seen	अदृष्य
Invulnerable	Incapable of being harmed	अभेद्य
Irreconcilable	Impossible to find agreement between	अमिलनीय
Irrecoverable	That which cannot be recovered	पुनःप्राप्त नहीं
Irreparable	Incapable of being repaired	अपरिचार्य
Irrevocable	That which cannot be altered	अपरिवर्तनीय
Itinerant	One who travels from place to place	यात्रागामी

➢ List of one word substitution start with word J

Word	Meaning	Hindi Meaning
Journal	A newspaper or magazine that deals with a specific activity	पत्रिका

➢ List of one word substitution start with word L

Word	Meaning	Hindi Meaning
Lagoon	Saltwater lake separated from the sea by sand	लैगून समुद्रान्त झील"
Lexicographer	A person who compiles a dictionary	शब्दकोशकारी
Linguist	One who speaks many foreign languages	भाषाविद्
Logic	The science of reasoning	तर्कशास्त्र

➢ List of one word substitution start with word M

Word	Meaning	Hindi Meaning
Maidenhood	The state of being unmarried (of a girl)	कुमारिका/अविवाहितता
Mammals	Animals which give birth to babies and feed them with their milk	स्तनधारी
Manuscript	Matter written by hand	हस्तलिखित मसीही/लिखित ग्रंथ
Martyr	One who dies for a noble cause	शहीद
Masque	A play or a dramatic performance in verse, with music, dance, and fine costumes	मास्क/नाटक
Massacre	Killing of large numbers of people	नरसंहार/हत्याकांड
Materialist	A person for whom money is the most important	भौतिकवादी/वस्तुवादी
Matins	Morning prayer	सुबही/प्रातःकालीन प्रार्थना
Matricide	Killing of one's own mother	मातृहत्या
Matrimony	Marriage	विवाह/विवाहिता
Maxim	A short statement of a general truth	नीतिमत्र
Memento	Something kept to remember a place or event	स्मरणीय/यादगार

Word	Meaning	Hindi Meaning
Mercenary	One who acts only for money	पैसे के लिए काम करने वाला/ भ्रष्टाचारी
Metamorphosis	Complete change in appearance	परिवर्तन/रूपांतर
Meticulous	Very particular about small details	अत्यंत सावधान/अति सूक्ष्म
Migration	Movement from one country to another	प्रवास/प्रवासन/प्रवाह
Misandrist	One who hates males	नारीद्वेषी
Misanthrope	A hater of mankind	मानवद्वेषी/मानवद्वेषी व्यक्ति
Misogamist	Hater of marriage	विवाहविरोधी/विवाह नकारी व्यक्ति
Misogynist	A hater of womankind	स्त्रीद्वेषी/स्त्रीद्वेषी व्यक्ति
Misologist	Hater of learning or reasoning	अशिक्षावादी/अज्ञानवादी
Misoneist	Hater of new things	नवीन वस्तुओं के विरोधी/ नवीनतावादी
Missionary	A person sent to teach the Christian religion	प्रचारक/मिशनरी
Monastery	Place where monks live	मठ/मोनास्ट्री/विहार
Monogamy	The practice of keeping only one wife or partner	एकपत्नीत्व/एकपत्नी विवाह
Mortal	Subject to death	मानव/नाशवान
Mortuary	A place where dead bodies are kept before post-mortem examination	मरघट/शवघर/शववाहिनी
Mutilation	Cutting off body parts	अंगभंजन/काटन/कटाव

➢ List of one word substitution start with word N

Word	Meaning	Hindi Meaning
Numismatics	The study of coins	सिक्कों का अध्ययन
Naïve	showing a lack of experience, wisdom, or judgement	सरल/भोला/अनुभवहीन
Narcotics	a drug that relieves pain and induces drowsiness	मादक/नशीली
Naturalism	Adherence or attachment to what is natural	प्राकृतिकता/स्वाभाविकता
Neogamist	One who is recently married	हाल ही में विवाहित
Nepotism	Undue favor shown to one's own relatives	भतीजावाद/भांजावाद
Neurotic	Excessively sensitive, anxious, or obsessive	तंत्रिका/मानसिक बीमारीग्रस्त
Newfangled	Newly developed and unfamiliar	नवीन/नवीनता भरा/नविन
Nonentity	Person of no importance	नीरवता/अस्तित्वहीन/महत्वहीन
Nonpareil	Person or thing which has no equal	अनुपम/अद्वितीय/अनोखा
Notorious	Having an evil reputation	बदनाम/प्रसिद्ध बुराईयों के कारण प्रसिद्ध
Nuance	Subtle difference in color, meaning, etc.	अल्पभेद/सूक्ष्म अंतर/तारा-तोड़ बहुत कम
Nuptial	Relating to marriage	विवाहित/वैवाहिक
Nurture	The care and protection given to someone or something	पोषण/प्रोत्साहन
Nutriment	Food or nourishment	पोषण/आहार

List of one word substitution start with word O

Word	Meaning	Hindi Meaning
Obscurantist	Person who is opposed to enlightenment or disclosure or information	अंधविश्वासी/ज्ञानविरोधी
Obsequies	Funeral rites	शोक संस्कार/अंत्येष्टि अनुष्ठान
Obsolete	That which is no longer in use	अप्रचलित/पुराना
Octagon	A plane figure with eight sides and angles	अष्टकोण
Oligarchy	A government by a small group of powerful	अल्पाधिकार/बहुशक्तिशाली समूहाधिकार
Omniform	Being of every form, or capable of taking any shape or figure	सर्वाकारी/सब रूपी
Omnigenous	Comprising all kinds or varieties	सर्वविद्यमान/सब प्रकार का
Omnipotent	All-powerful	सर्वशक्तिमान (ईश्वर)
Omnipresent	Present everywhere	सर्वव्यापक (ईश्वर)
Omniscient	Knowing everything	सर्वज्ञ (ईश्वर)
Opaque	That which cannot be seen through	अपारदर्शी/अस्पष्ट
Optimist	A person who looks at the bright side of things	आशावादी
Orator	One who makes an eloquent public speech	प्रवक्ता
Orchard	A garden of fruits	बगीचा
Orphan	A child whose parents are dead	अनाथ
Ostracize	To exclude out of society	समाज से निकाल देना
Oviparous	Bearing eggs and not young ones	अंडदानी/अंडे देने वाला

➢ List of one word substitution start with word P

Word	Meaning	Hindi Meaning
Pacifist	A person who believes in the total abolition of war	शांतिवादी
Pageant	Elaborate public spectacle, beauty contest	पेजेंट
Palatable	Food or drink that has a pleasant taste	स्वादिष्ट
Panacea	A remedy for all kinds of diseases	सर्वचिकित्सा/सर्वरोगहर औषधि
Pandemonium	A wild and noisy disorder	हड़बड़ाहट/हंगामा
Panegyric	Piece of writing or speech full of praise	स्तुतिरचना/महिमा गान/प्रशंसापात्र
Pantomime	Dramatic performance with dumb show	मूकनाटक
Paramour	Sexual partner or lover	प्रेमी/प्रेमिका
Parasite	One who entirely depends on another	परजीवी/परशुराम/निर्जीव
Parasol	A lady's umbrella	छतरी
Patrimony	Inherited from father or male ancestor	पैतृक धन
Patriot	One who loves one's country	देशभक्त/प्रेमी
Patronymic	Name derived from that of father or ancestor	उपनाम/गोत्रज
Pauper	One who has no means of livelihood	गरीब
Peculation	Use of public money for one's own benefit	खानगशी/धन कस्ट/मालव्यय

Word	Meaning	Hindi Meaning
Pedantic	excessively concerned with minor details or rules; over-scrupulous	शूद्रीकरण
Pedestrian	One who walks on foot	पदचारी
Peninsula	Area of land almost surrounded by sea	द्वीपांश/उपद्वीप
Pentagon	A plane figure with five sides and angles	पंचभुज
Perceptible	That can be perceived by the senses	अनुभवनीय/सज्ज्ञ/प्रत्यक्ष
Peroration	Concluding part of a speech	समापन/संभाषण का अंतिभाग
Perseverance	Constant efforts to achieve something	धैर्य/सहनशीलता/स्थिरता
Perspicacious	Quick in judging and understanding	बुद्धिमान/विचारशील/विवेकी
Perversion	Change to something abnormal or unnatural	विपरीतीकरण
Pessimist	A person who looks at the negative side of things	निराशावादी/अशांतिवादी
Philanderer	A man who amuses himself by lovemaking	आनंद लेने वाला/कामभोगी/लघु विषयों में आनंद लेने वाला
Philanthropist	A lover of mankind	परोपकारी/मानवहितैषी
Philatelist	Collector of stamps	डाक टिकटों का संग्राहक
Philistine	Person who is indifferent to art and literature	अशिष्ट/क्षुद्र/साहित्यालोचक का अनादरी
Philogynist	A lover of womankind	स्त्रीप्रेमी

Word	Meaning	Hindi Meaning
Philology	study of language, especially its history and development	भाषाविज्ञान/भाषा विज्ञान
Pilgrim	One who travels to a sacred place	तीर्थयात्री/पीलग्रिम
Pioneer	One who leads others in any field	पथप्रदर्शक/पथिका
Piquant	Pleasant or sharp to the taste/interesting	रुचिकर/तीक्ष्ण/रोमांचक
Placard/Poster	Written or printed notice pasted in public	पोस्टर/पट्टी/विज्ञापन आदि
Plagiarism	The practice of borrowing words and ideas from other authors and using them as one's own; literary theft	अनुलभ्यानुकृति/चोरी
Platitude	Statement that is obviously true and hence dull or not stimulating	गीतोच्चार/जनहित या लोककल्याण का सामान्य निदान
Polyandry	The custom of having more than two husbands at the same time	एक समय में एक से अधिक पतियों का प्रयोग
Polygamy	The custom of having more than two spouses at the same time	एक समय में एक से अधिक पत्नियों का प्रयोग
Polyglot	Person having command over many languages	बहुभाषी/अनेकभाषी

Word	Meaning	Hindi Meaning
Polygon	A figure with many angles or sides	बहुभुज/बहुकोणी आकृति
Posthumous	Received after death	मरणोपरान्त मिलनेवाला/मृतक के बाद आया
Postscript	Anything written in a letter after it is signed	अनुलग्नक/अनुप्रासंगिक लेख
Predicament	Difficult or dangerous situation	दुर्गति/विपत्ति/कठिन परिस्थिति
Prejudiced	Be biased against	पक्षपाती/पूर्वधारित
Premonition	Forewarning of an impending danger	पूर्वसूचना/पूर्वभान
Prerogative	Absolute right	विशेषाधिकार
Prodigy	A child with unusual or remarkable talent	विलक्षण/अद्वितीय या अद्वितीय प्रतिभा वाला
Prognostication	Act of forecasting by examining present	भविष्य विज्ञान/पूर्वानुमान
Prologue	A speech or a poem at the beginning of a play or a book	प्रस्तावना/प्रारंभिक पद/समर्थन पद/प्रस्तावना
Promiscuous	Having a lot of different sexual partners	अनवितर्कित/सभी अप्राप्य
Proponent	Person who proposes something	प्रयोजक/समर्थक
Propriety	State of being correct in behavior or moral	यथायोग्यता/उचितता

Word	Meaning	Hindi Meaning
Protagonist	An important supporter of an idea or political /Chief actor or character in a story or drama	मुख्य किरदार/प्रमुख अभिनेता
Protectorate	Country under the protection of a more powerful country	संरक्षित राज्य/संरक्षित क्षेत्र
Prudent	good judgment in avoiding risks and uncertainties; careful	विवेकी/सावधान/बुद्धिमान
Pseudonym	Name taken by an author instead of his real name	उपनाम/विकल्प नाम
Punctitious	Very careful to behave correctly	सतर्क/सावधान/ठीक होने की अवधारणा रखने वाला
Pyrotechnic	Art of making fireworks	पटाखों का निर्माणकः/ आगबन्दीकार/प्यरोटेक्निशियन

➢ **List of one word substitution start with word Q**

Word	Meaning	Hindi Meaning
Quadruped	Four-footed animal	चौपाया पशु

➢ List of one word substitution start with word R

Word	Meaning	Hindi Meaning
Rebel	One who takes up arms against the government or any authority	विद्रोही
Recapitulate	Repeat and state the main points	मुख्य बिंदुओं को दोहराना
Recluse	One who lives alone and avoids company	संन्यासी
Reconcile	Bring about harmony or agreement	मिलाप करना
Reconnaissance	Information gathering activity about the enemy	गुप्तचर जांच
Red tapism	Too much official formality	अधिक आधिकारिकता या प्रक्रियाकर्म
Redundancy	When something is unnecessary because it is more than needed	बहुलता
Regicide	Killing of a king	राजहत्या
Relegate/Demote	Reduce to a lower position	निम्न स्थानान्तरित करना/ अवमानित करना
Reluctant	Unwilling	अनिच्छुक
Remission	Pardon or forgiveness for breaking religious laws or for a debt, charge, or penalty.	क्षमा या माफी धार्मिक नियमों का उल्लंघन करने के लिए
Rendezvous	Place fixed for meeting or assembling	मुलाक़ात के लिए निर्धारित स्थान

Word	Meaning	Hindi Meaning
Renegade	Person who changes his religious belief/support	धर्मान्तरित/पक्ष बदलने वाला
Repartee	Witty and clever answers	तानाबाना, तुकबंदी"
Repercussion	Effect of some event, action, or decision	प्रतिध्वनि/प्रतिक्रिया
Replica	an exact copy or model of something	प्रतिलिपि/नकल
Repository	Place where things are stored for safety	भंडार/गोदाम
Republic	A political system in which the supreme power lies in a body of citizens who can elect people to represent them	गणतंत्र
Requiem	Prayer for the dead	मरे हुए के लिए प्रार्थना
Restitution	Return of an object stolen or lost	प्रतिपूर्ति/वापसी
Retaliate	Return the same sort of ill-treatment	प्रतिशोध करना
Reticent/Taciturn	Person who does not speak too much	मौन व्रती/अल्पबोध
Retrospective	An effect which has a reference to the past	पूर्वदृष्टि
Rumour/Hearsay	Unverified information	अफ़वाह/सुनी हुई बातें

➢ List of one word substitution start with word S

Word	Meaning	Hindi Meaning
Sacrilege	Treating something holy without respect	पवित्र सम्मान के बिना किसी चीज़ का व्यवहार करना
Sarcasm	Bitter and ironical remark	व्यंग्य
Savage	Violent and uncivilized	जंगली/असभ्य
Scapegoat	One who is blamed for the mistakes of others	बलि का बकरा
Sceptic	One who is doubtful	संदेहवादी
Screech	Cry out in a shrill voice	चीख़
Scrimmage	Confused struggle or fight	संघर्ष
Scurry	Move hurriedly with short steps	जल्दी में चलना
Sedition	Act or speech inciting public against the government	राज-द्रोह/विद्रोह
Senility	Extreme old age when a man behaves like a fool	बूढ़ापा/बुढ़ापे की स्थिति
Siesta	Period of rest or sleep after lunch	दोपहर की नींद/आराम
Simultaneous	Occurring at the same time	समवर्ती/एक साथ
Sinecure	An office for which high salary is paid for little or no work	सनिमित्त आदेशक
Smother	Kill by suffocation (especially by covering the face with something)	दम घुटना/साँसों की रुकावट डालना
Sojourn	Stay for a short time	क्षणिक निवास

Word	Meaning	Hindi Meaning
Soliloquy	Speaking aloud while alone	एकांत भाषण
Somnambulist	One who walks in sleep	नींद में चलने वाला
Somniloquist	One who talks in sleep	नींद में बोलने वाला
Sonorous	Having a deep and pleasant sound	गहरी और सुंदर ध्वनि
Sorocide	Killing of one's own sister	भगिनीहत्या
Spendthrift	One who spends money recklessly	उड़देबाज़
Spinster	An unmarried woman	अविवाहित स्त्री
Spiritualist	A person who believes in spiritual things	आध्यात्मिकता वादी
Sporadic	Occurring irregularly	खण्डित/विरल
Stoic	A person who is indifferent to pleasure and pain	निर्लिप्त
Strangulate	Kill by putting pressure on the throat	गर्दन दबाने से मारना
Subdue	To bring under control	नियंत्रित करना
Subjugate	To bring under control	वशीकरण करना
Suicide	Taking one's own life	आत्महत्या
Supercilious	Thinking oneself superior to others	घमण्डी
Sycophant	Person who tries to win a favor by flattering	खुशामद करने वाला
Synagogue	Place where Jews worship	यहूदी मंदिर

➢ List of one word substitution start with word T

Word	Meaning	Hindi Meaning
Talkative/Garrulous	Person who is fond of talking	बातूनी/बातचीत पसंद करने वाला
Tantrum	Fit of bad temper or anger	क्रोध/गुस्सा
Teetotaller	One who abstains from alcoholic drinks	मद्य से परहेज़ करने वाला
Theist	A person who believes in the existence of God	ईश्वर के अस्तित्व में विश्वास रखने वाला
Theocracy	A government by religious leaders	धार्मिक नेताओं द्वारा संचालित सरकार
Thermometer	An instrument for measuring temperature	तापमान मापने का यंत्र
Traitor	One who betrays one's country	गद्दार
Transgressor	One who violates a rule or law	कानून तोड़ने वाला
Transmigration	The passage of the soul after death from one body to another	पूर्वजन्मान्तर
Transmogrification	Complete change in appearance or character (especially in a magical or surprising way)	रूप में पूर्ण परिवर्तन
Transparent	That allows the passage of rays of light	पारदर्शी

Word	Meaning	Hindi Meaning
Truant	One who stays away from school/work without permission	बाग़ी
Truism	A truth that is often repeated	सत्यवचन/स्वत्यंत्रता
Turncoat	Disloyal person who changes sides	दलबदलू

➢ **List of one word substitution start with word U**

Word	Meaning	Hindi Meaning
Unanimous	Consent of all	सर्वमत से मान्य
Unavoidable	That which cannot be avoided	अटल
Unique	The only one of its type	अद्वितीय
Universal	Belonging to all parts of the world	सर्वव्यापी
Usurper	One who grabs somebody else's property or title	अधिकृत
Uxoricide	Killing of one's wife	पत्नीहत्या
Uxorious	Foolishly fond of one's wife	पत्नी-प्रेमी/पत्नी के बाणस्वामी

➢ List of one word substitution start with word V

Word	Meaning	Hindi Meaning
Vacuous	Suggesting absence of thought or intellect	खाली
Vendetta	Feud in which the relatives of the dead or injured take revenge	बदला
Verbatim	Repetition of a writing, word for word	शब्दशः
Verbose	Using or containing more words than necessary	प्रलापी
Versatile	One who possesses many talents or skills	बहुमुखी
Verso	Any left-hand page of an open book	पीछे का पन्ना
Vespers	Evening prayer in the church	संध्या आराधना
Veteran	One who has grown old in or has long experience of (especially military) service or occupation	अतिरिक्त अनुभवी
Vincible	That which can be conquered	जितने योग्य
Vindictive/Vengeful	Having or showing a desire for revenge	प्रतिशोधी/प्रतिकारी
Virulent	Highly poisonous or harmful effect	विषैला
Viviparous	Bearing living young ones and not eggs	जीवोत्पन्न

Word	Meaning	Hindi Meaning
Volte-face	Sudden change from one set of beliefs to another	अचानक मतान्तर
Voluntary	Of one's own free will	स्वैच्छिक
Voyage	Journey by water or sea	यात्रा
Vulnerable	That which can be easily damaged or hurt	संकटमय

➢ List of one word substitution start with word W

Word	Meaning	Hindi Meaning
Widow	A woman whose husband is dead	विधवा
Widower	A man whose wife is dead	विधुर
Wreathe	Flowers fastened in a circle	फूलों की माला

➢ List of one word substitution start with word Z

Word	Meaning	Hindi Meaning
Zealot	Person who shows great and uncompromising enthusiasm for religion, party, cause, etc.	उत्साही

Past year questions Exercise

PRACTICE SET - 1

DIRECTIONS: Select the word which means the same as the group of words given.

1. **A person with a long experience of any occupation.**
(a) Veteran (b) Genius
(c) Seasoned (d) Ambidextrous

2. **Words written on a tomb.**
(a) Epithet (b) Epigraph
(c) Soliloquy (d) Epitaph

3. **Stealthily done**
(a) Devious (b) Nefarious
(c) Surreptitious (d) Villainous

4. **Something no longer in use**
(a) Desolate (b) Absolute
(c) Obsolete (d) Primitive

5. **One not concerned with right or wrong**
(a) Moral (b) Amoral
(c) Immoral (d) Immortal

6. **A person who opposes war or use of military force**
(a) Fascist (b) Pacifist
(c) Narcissist (d) Fatalist

7. **Severely abusive writing in journals**
(a) Imaginary (b) Speculative
(c) Scurrilous (d) Sarcastic

8. **Call upon God or any other power (like law) etc. for help or protection.**
(a) Invocation (b) Involution
(c) Inundation (d) Revocation

9. **Fear of being enclosed in a small closed space**
(a) Agoraphobia (b) Claustrophobia
(c) Xenophobia (d) Paranoia

10. **One who has become dependent on something or drugs is**
(a) Adamant (b) Edict
(c) Addict (d) Derelict

11. **That which lasts for a short time**
(a) Regular (b) Transitory

(c) Rotatory (d) Repository

12. **Ready to believe anything**
(a) Credible (b) Incredible
(c) Credulous (d) Incredulous

13. **A four footed animal**
(a) Tetrapod (b) Quadruped
(c) Polyped (d) Double-paired

14. **A factory, where workers are employed at very low wages for long hours and under poor conditions.**
(a) Impalpable (b) Outset
(c) Bloomy (d) Sweatshop

15. **Constant efforts to achieve something**
(a) Patience (b) Vigour
(c) Attempt (d) Perseverance

16. **One who collects coins.**
(a) Archeologist (b) Numismatist
(c) Philatelist (d) Connoisseur

17. **A system of Government in which only one political party is allowed to function**
(a) Oligarchy (b) Dictatorship
(c) Totalitarianism (d) Theocracy

18. **Customs and habits of a particular group**
(a) Mores (b) Traditions
(c) Rites (d) Rituals

19. **A body of persons appointed to hear evidence and give their verdict in trials**
(a) Association (b) Council
(c) Bar (d) Jury

20. **Indifference to pleasure or pain**
(a) Perseverance (b) Tolerance
(c) Stoicism (d) Reticence

21. **21. The worship of idols or images**
(a) Atheism (b) Theism
(c) Idolatry (d) Iconoclasm

22. **Something that is poisonous or unhealthy**
(a) Trivial (b) Toxic
(c) Torpid (d) Tragic

23. **A remedy for all diseases**
(a) Amnesia (b) Panacea
(c) Intelligentsia (d) Parasol

24. **Make something seem less important, significant or trifling.**
(a) Superintend (b) Optimality
(c) Trivialize (d) Dumb down

25. **Irresistible craving for alcoholic drinks**
(a) Megalomania (b) Dipsomania
(c) Kleptomania (d) Pyromania

26. One who deserts his principles or party
(a) Apostle (b) Proselyte
(c) Renegade (d) Critic

27. One who intervenes between two or more parties to settle differences
(a) Neutral (b) Intermediary
(c) Judge (d) Connoisseur

28. The habit of always admiring oneself
(a) Psychosis (b) Neurosis
(c) Narcissism (d) Paranoia

29. To take back, withdraw or renounce
(a) Repent (b) Retrace
(c) Refuse (d) Recant

30. A pen for small animals
(a) Hutch (b) Lair
(c) Den (d) Cage

31. Belief that God is everything and that everything is God
(a) Atheism (b) Pantheism
(c) Scepticism (d) Animism

32. A picture of a person or a thing drawn in such a highly exaggerated manner as to cause laughter
(a) Cartoon (b) Cacography
(c) Cartography (d) Caricature

33. The state of being miserable bereft of all possessions
(a) Dependant (b) Complacent
(c) Destitute (d) Omnipresent

34. That which cannot be called back
(a) Irresponsible (b) Irrevocable
(c) Irredeemable (d) Incalculable

35. One who journeys from place to place
(a) Quack (b) Cannibal
(c) Itinerant (d) Courier

36. Obtain something by force, threats, or other unfair means.
(a) Regret (b) Extort
(c) Resent (d) Encompass

37. Careful in the spending of money,time,etc.
(a) Punctual (b) Economical
(c) Miserly (d) Calculative

38. Reproducing or memorizing word for word
(a) Verbatim (b) Verbose
(c) Verbiage (d) Verbalism

39. That which cannot be captured
(a) Unbreakable (b) Ungrippable
(c) Impregnable (d) Slippery

40. One who breaks the law

(a) Aggressor (b) Politician

(c) Transgressor (d) Pedestrian

41. Speed of an object in one direction

(a) Pace (b) Tempo

(c) Velodrome (d) Velocity

42. Work extremely hard or incessantly

(a) Job (b) Craft

(c) Toil (d) Activity

43. Theft of another person's writings or ideas and passing them off as one's own

(a) Plagiarism (b) Burglary

(c) Piracy (d) Pilferage

44. Express a proposition,theory,etc in clear or definite terms

(a) Publish (b) Postulate

(c) Proclaim (d) Enunciate

45. List of issues to be discussed at a meeting

(a) Schedule (b) Agenda

(c) Time-table (d) Plan

46. The process of deciding the nature of a disease by examination

(a) Test (b) Perusal

(c) Diagnosis (d) Operation

47. That which cannot be easily read

(a) Illegible (b) Incomprehensible

(c) Unreadable (d) Unintelligible

48. One who finds nothing good in anything

(a) Critic (b) Satirist

(c) Cynic (d) Slanderer

49. A person who pretends to be what he is not

(a) Explorer (b) Prompter

(c) Imposter (d) Diviner

50. In a threatening manner

(a) Ominously (b) Sprightly

(c) Ghastly (d) Terribly

ANSWERS-

1 - (1)	2 - (4)	3 - (3)	4 - (3)	5 - (2)
6 - (2)	7 - (3)	8 - (1)	9 - (2)	10 - (3)
11 - (2)	12 - (3)	13 - (2)	14 - (4)	15 - (4)
16 - (2)	17 - (3)	18 - (1)	19 - (4)	20 - (3)
21 - (3)	22 - (2)	23 - (2)	24 - (3)	25 - (2)
26 - (3)	27 - (2)	28 - (3)	29 - (4)	30 - (1)
31 - (2)	32 - (4)	33 - (3)	34 - (2)	35 - (3)
36 - (2)	37 - (2)	38 - (1)	39 - (2)	40 - (3)
41 - (4)	42 - (3)	43 - (1)	44 - (4)	45 - (2)
46 - (3)	47 - (1)	48 - (1)	49 - (3)	50 - (3)

Practice Set

Exercise 2

1. **Provide one word substitution for the following expression.**
One who does not make mistakes
(a) Infallible (b) Enlightenment
(c) Practical (d) Omnipotent

2. **Select the most appropriate word for the given group of words.**
One who makes and sells sweets and chocolates.
(a) barber (b) grocer
(c) confectioner (d) cobbler

3. **Select the most appropriate word for the given group of words.**
A person who is skilled at writing beautifully
(a) cartoonist (b) calligrapher
(c) painter (d) artist

4. **Select the most appropriate word for the given group of words.**
The statistical study of the population
(a) anthropology (b) sociology
(c) demography (d) psychology

5. **Select the most appropriate word for the given group of words.**
Place for collection of dried plant specimens
(a) herbarium (b) warehouse
(c) green house (d) nursery

6. **Select the most appropriate word for the given group of words**
A strong and fast moving stream of water
(a) Trickle (b) Torrent
(c) Creek (d) Rivulet

7. **Select the word which means the same as the group of words given.**
People living at the same time
(a) Cosmopolitans
(b) Contemporaries
(c) Comrades
(d) Friends

8. **Select the word which means the same as the group of words given.**
One who can use both hands efficiently
(a) skillful (b) ambivalent
(c) ambidextrous (d) genius

9. **Select the most appropriate word for the given group of words.**
A raised place on which offerings are made to God.
(a) Temple (b) Shrine
(c) Altar (d) Pilgrimage

10. **Select the most appropriate word for the given group of words.**
A van which carries the dead body of

a person

(a) coffin (b) ambulance
(c) hearse (d) cortege

11. **Find the most appropriate word that can be substituted for the given words.**

Record of the historical events of a 'year' in time

(a) Anniversary (b) Annual
(c) Annals (d) Biennial

12. **Find the most appropriate word that can be substituted for the given words.**

The treasury of a college or monastery

(a) Bursary (b) captivating
(c) exchequer (d) depository

13. **Find the most appropriate word that can be substituted for the given words.**

Total devastation, especially by fire

(a) Holocaust (b) Sabotage
(c) massacre (d) Demolition

14. **Find the most appropriate word that can be substituted for the given words.**

The treatment of irregularities in the teeth and jaws

(a) Periodontics
(b) Orthodontics
(c) Ophthalmologist
(d) Orthopaedics

15. **Choose the option that best substitutes the underlined phrase in the given sentence without changing the meaning of the sentence.**

The man was accused of murdering his own father.

(a) Fratricide (b) Suicide
(c) Matricide (d) Patricide

16. **Choose the option that can be substituted for the given phrase.**

Action of reviewing past events in one's life

(a) Retrospection (b) Reflection
(c) Introspection (d) Meditation

17. **In the following question, out of the four alternatives, select the alternative which is the best substitute of the phrase.**

An expert judge in matters of taste.

(a) Cannibal (b) Cynic
(c) Connoisseur (d) Convalescent

18. **In the following question, out of the four alternatives, select the alternative which is the best substitute of the phrase.**

A large group of people or things of a particular kind.

(a) Bevy (b) Conspiracy
(c) Posse (d) Flotilla

19. **Select the word which means the same as the group of words given a rabbit's dwelling.**

(a) burrow (b) den
(c) lair (d) sty

20. **Select the word which means the same as the group of words given.**

Rapid increase in the number or amount of something

(a) proliferation (b) promotion
(c) propensity (d) paucity

21. Select the most appropriate word for the given group of words.
A person or thing that has the same name as another

(a) Relative (b) Pseudonym
(c) Successor (d) Nameless

22. Out of the four alternatives, select the alternative which is the best substitute of the phrase.
The essential or characteristic custom, habits and convention of a society or community.

(a) Mores (b) Tenet
(c) Syzygy (d) Vogue

23. In the following question, out of the four alternatives, select the alternative which is the best substitute of the phrase.
The state of being unaffected or not intoxicated by alcohol

(a) Quandary (b) Invincible
(c) Sobriety (d) Preponderance

24. Choose the correct word for
'An act of officially charging someone with a crime'

(a) Felony (b) Indictment
(c) Summon (d) Dictum

25. Choose the correct word for:
Defeating easily and thoroughly

(a) Recital (b) Trounce
(c) Redress (d) Valour

26. Select the word, which means the same as the group of words given.
method of talking in a roundabout way

(a) talkative
(b) circumlocution
(c) elocution
(d) convoluted

27. Select the most appropriate word for the given group of words.
a decision on which one cannot go back

(a) intractable (b) invincible
(c) invulnerable (d) irrevocable

28. Select the most appropriate word for the given group of words.
causing no harm

(a) integral (b) inorganic
(c) innocuous (d) insolvent

29. Select the word which means the same as the group of words given.
Splendid and expensive-looking

(a) peculiar (b) curious
(c) malicious (d) sumptuous

30. Select the most appropriate word for the given group of words.
a room where medicines are prepared and provided

(a) surgery (b) dispensary
(c) infirmary (d) hospital

31. Select the word which means the same as the group of words given.
Making a show of being morally superior to others

(a) sanctum (b) profligate

(c) approving
(d) sanctimonious

32. Select the word which means the same as the group of words given.
The belief that events are predetermined and therefore cannot be changed
(a) fatalism (b) autism
(c) prism (d) chasm

33. Select the word which means the same as the group of words given.
The act of compelling or forcing authority on others.
(a) aspersion (b) volition
(c) coercion (d) scion

34. Select the word which means the same as the group of words given.
Consisting of many things or parts
(a) singular
(b) numeral
(c) multitudinous
(d) few

35. Select the word which means the same as the group of words given.
proceeding in a gradual way and secretly intending to cause harm
(a) benevolent (b) insidious
(c) malevolent (d) solvent

36. Select the word which means the same as the group of words given.
found everywhere
(a) rare (b) scarce
(c) unusual (d) omnipresent

37. Select the word which means the same as the group of words given.
a private conversation between two people
(a) sermon (b) dialogue
(c) tête-à-tête (d) monologue

38. Select the word which means the same as the group of words given.
Instrument used to measure relative humidity.
(a) Hydrometer (b) Hygrometer
(c) Tachometer (d) Barometer

39. Choose the most appropriate word that can substitute the given group of words.
A group of Lions
(a) Herd (b) Pack
(c) Flock (d) Pride

40. Select the most appropriate word for the given group of words.
One who abstains from alcoholic drinks
(a) Non-vegetarian
(b) Drunkard
(c) Vegetarian
(d) Teetotaller

41. Select the most appropriate word for the given group of words.
The fear of being enclosed in a small space or room
(a) Hydrophobia (b) Aerophobia
(c) Acrophobia (d) Claustrophobia

42. DIRECTIONS: Find the word which can be replaced for the given sentence.
A person who pretends to be what he/she is not.

(a) Altruist (b) Hypocrite
(c) Atheist (d) Theist

43. From the options given below choose the one that means the same as the below word:
Paleontology

(a) the study of birds
(b) the study of insects
(c) the study of fossils
(d) the study of soils

44. DIRECTIONS: Find the word which can be replaced for the given sentence.
Vehicle to carry dead bodies.

(a) Dissection (b) Hearse
(c) Equipment (d) Swing

45. DIRECTIONS: Find the word which can be replaced for the given sentence.
Seeking and enjoying the company of others.

(a) Alien (b) Immigrant
(c) Hostile (d) Sociable

46. Choose the word that can substitute the given sentence.
Loss of memory

(a) Syndrome
(b) Remembrance
(c) Immobile
(d) Amnesia

47. When your office requires the services of a person who can fit and repair water pipes, you contact a ________.

(a) plumber (b) plover
1. (a) carpenter
2. (a) turner

48. Select the option that can be used as a one-word substitute for the underlined group of words.
Human beings are usually ones who are naturally able to eat both, plants and flesh.

(a) Cannibals (b) Herbivorous
(c) Carnivorous (d) Omnivorous

49. Select the option that can be used as a one-word substitute for the given group of words.
One who gives money or help to another person or cause.

(a) Anarchist (b) Agnostic
(c) Benefactor (d) Amateur

50. Select the option that can be used as a one-word substitute for the given group of words.
A small organized dissenting group within a larger one.

(a) Band (b) Set
(c) Faction (d) Cluster

51. Select the option that can be used as a one-word substitute for the underlined group of words
Geeta is doubtful about getting hired as she is inexperienced at this job.

(a) Professional (b) Expert
(c) Ace (d) Novice

ANSWERS-

1 - (1)	2 - (3)	3 - (3)	4 - (3)	5 - (1)
6 - (2)	7 - (2)	8 - (3)	9 - (3)	10 - (3)
11 - (3)	12 - (1)	13 - (1)	14 - (2)	15 - (4)
16 - (1)	17 - (3)	18 - (1)	19 - (1)	20 - (1)
21 - (4)	22 - (1)	23 - (3)	24 - (2)	25 - (2)
26 - (2)	27 - (4)	28 - (3)	29 - (4)	30 - (2)
31 - (4)	32 - (1)	33 - (3)	34 - (3)	35 - (2)
36 - (4)	37 - (3)	38 - (4)	39 - (4)	40 - (4)
41 - (4)	42 - (2)	43 - (3)	44 - (2)	45 - (4)
46 - (4)	47 - (1)	48 - (4)	49 - (3)	50 - (3)
51 - (4)				

Top 300 MOST REPEATED OWS asked in SSC Exam

- **Aqueduct - जलस्रोत** - A channel or bridge-like structure that carries water over a long distance - **7 times**
- **Alimony - परत्यक्ता पत्नी के लिये निवार्मह निधि** - An allowance made to a wife by her husband, when they are legally separated - 8 times
- **Allegory - नीति कथा** - A story, play, picture, etc. in which each character - **7 times**
- **Altitude - ऊंचाई** - The height above sea level - 8 times
- **Amateur - शौकीन व्यक्ति** - One who plays for pleasure rather than as a profession - 8 times
- **Amoral - नीतिहीन** - Not following any moral rules and not caring about right/wrong - **7 times**
- **Anesthetist - बेहोशी लाने वाला** - A medical specialist who administers drugs for relieving pain during surgery - **7 times**
- **Anonymous - बेनाम** - With a name that is not known or not made public - 8 times
- **Antidote - विषहर औषध** - A medicine to nullify the effect of poison - 8 times
- **Apartheid - रंगभेद** - A policy that segregates people on the basis of race - **7 times**
- **Apiary - मधुमिक्खयों के पालने का स्थान** - A place where bees are kept - **7 times**
- **Aquatic - जलीय** - Growing or living in, or near water - **7 times**
- **Arbitrator - पंच** - A person who is chosen to settle a disagreement - 8 times
- **Arsenal - शस्त्रगार** - A military structure where arms and ammunition and other military equipment are stored, and training is given in the use of arms - **7 times**
- **Articulate - सुस्पष्ट** - Good at expressing ideas/feelings clearly in words - **7 times**
- **Artist - कलाकार** - One who practices one of the fine arts - 9 times
- **Asylum - शरणस्थाल** - Place that provides refuge - 4 times
- **Auditor - लेखा परीक्षक** - One who makes an official examination of accounts - 5 times
- **Auditorium - सभागार** - A building where an audience sits - 4 times
- **Avarice - लोभ** - Insatiable desire for wealth - 6 times
- **Avicide - पक्षियों को मारना** - Killing of birds - 3 times
- **Bald - गंजा** - A man having no hair on the scalp - 6 times
- **Bale - गट्ठा** - A large bundle bound for storage or transport - 6 times
- **Barrel - पीपा** - A wooden drum in which beer or oil is stored - 4 times
- **Omnipresent - सवत्रर्म** - One who is

present everywhere - 9 times

- **Omnipotent** - सवशिक्तमान - One who is all-powerful - 9 times
- **Omniscient** - सवज्ञर्म - One who knows everything - 12 times
- **Anthology** - काव्य संग्रह - A collection of poems - 11 times
- **Bouquet** - पुष्पगुच्छ - A collection of flowers - 10 times
- **Opaque** - अपारदशर्शी - Which cannot be seen through - 9 times
- **Philanthropist** - मानव प्रेमी - A lover of mankind - 14 times
- **Misanthrope** - मनुष्य द्रोही - A hater of mankind - 12 times
- **Altruist** - परोपकारी - A lover of others - 11 times
- **Hanger** - विमानशाला - A place for housing airplanes - 10 times
- **Dormitory** - शयनशाला - The sleeping rooms in a college or public institution - 9 times
- **Cosmopolitan** - विश्विमत्रय - A person who regards the whole world as his country - 13 times
- **Optimist** - आशावादी - A person who looks at the bright side of things - 11 times
- **Pessimist** - निराशावादी - A person who looks at the dark side of things - 13 times
- **Atheist** - नास्तिक - A person who does not believe in God - 14 times
- **Mercenary** - भाड़े पर काम करने वाला - One who does something for the sake of money - 11 times
- **Ephemeral** - अल्पजीवी - Lasting one day - 11 times
- **Incognito** - गुप्त/वेश बदले हुए - Traveling under another name than one's own - 10 times
- **Epitaph** - समाध-लेख - Inscription on a tombstone in memory of the deceased - 12 times
- **Obsolete** - अप्रचलित - Something no longer in use - 11 times
- **Stoic** - सहनशील व्यक्ति - A person who can endure pain or hardship without showing his feelings/complaining - 10 times
- **Altruist** - परोपकारी - Someone who makes charitable donations intended to increase human wellbeing - 11 times
- **Claustrophobia** - छोटे जगह में होने का अत्यधिक डर - An extreme fear of being in a small confined place - 10 times
- **Fastidious** - ढीठ, हठी - One who is difficult to please - 8 times
- **Illegible** - अपठनीय - Handwriting which is difficult or impossible to read - 10 times
- **Inaudible** - अश्राव्य - Something that cannot be heard - 9 times
- **Accomplice** - सह-अपराधी - A person who helps another to commit a crime or to do something morally wrong - 10 times
- **Brittle** - भंगुर - Hard but easily broken/ liable to break easily - 9 times
- **Chauffeur** - मोटर-चालक - A person

employed to drive a private or hired car - 10 times

- **Emigrant** - देशत्यागी - A person who leaves his country to live in another - 8 times
- **Exonerate** - दोषमुक्त करना - To free somebody from all blame - 8 times
- **ncorrigible** - असंशोधनीय - One who cannot be corrected/One who is beyond reform - 6 times
- **nevitable** - अटल - Something that cannot be avoided - 12 times
- **Lexicographer** - शब्दकोश के लेखक - A person who writes and edits dictionaries - 12 times
- **Misogynist** - स्त्री द्वेषी - A person who dislikes women - 10 times
- **Abdicate** - त्यागना - To give up one's authority or throne - 11 times
- **Amphibians** - उभयचर जन्तु - Animals that can live on land and water - **7 times**
- **Anarchy** - अराजकता - A situation in a country, an organization, etc., in which there is no government, order, or control - **7 times**
- **Archaeology** - पुरातत्व - The study of human history and prehistory through the excavation of sites - 8 times
- **Aviary** - पक्षीशाला - A place where birds are kept - 10 times
- **Bibliophile** - पुस्तक प्रेमी - One who is a great lover of books - 10 times
- **Cannibal** - नरभक्षक - A person who eats human flesh - 11 times
- **Contemporary** - समकालीन - Belonging to the same time - 10 times
- **Epilogue** - उपसंहार - A short speech at the end of a play - 8 times
- **Extempore** - बिना तैयारी के - A speech or presentation made without previous preparation - 9 times
- **Glutton** - खाऊ, पेटू - One who eats too much - 10 times
- **Gregarious** - झुण्ड में रहने वाला - An animal that lives in a group/Tending to associate with others of one's kind - 10 times
- **Gullible** - आसानी से धोखा खाने वाला - One who is easily deceived - 11 times
- **Hydrophobia** - पानी से भय - Extreme fear of water - 8 times
- **Illiterate** - निरक्षर - A person who cannot read or write - 6 times
- **Insatiable** - लालची - That which cannot be satisfied - **7 times**
- **Intestate** - बिना वसीयत मरा हुआ - One who dies without a will - 9 times
- **Itinerary** - यात्रा कायक्रम - A plan of a journey, including the route and the places that you visit - 9 times
- **Nepotism** - भाई-भतीजावाद - Giving undue favors to one's own kith and kin - 8 times
- **Notorious** - कुख्यात - Well-known for being bad - 9 times
- **Opaque** - अपारदर्शी - That through which light cannot pass - 8 times
- **Philatelist** - डाक के टिकट का संग्रहक - A person who collects or studies stamps - 9 times

- **Sacrilege** - अपवित्रीकरण - Violation of something holy or sacred - 10 times
- **Adolescence** - किशोरावस्था - The period between the beginning of puberty and adulthood - 11 times
- **Agenda** - कार्यसूची - A list of items to be discussed at a meeting - 9 times
- **Ambidextrous** - उभयहस्त - Able to use the left hand and right hand equally well - 9 times
- **Amnesia** - भूलने की बीमारी - A partial or total loss of memory - 12 times
- **Amnesty** - राज-क्षमा - An official pardon/the formal act of liberating someone - 11 times
- **Archipelago** - द्वीप समूह - A large body of water with many islands - 8 times
- **Archives** - अभिलेखागार - The place where public, government, or historical records are kept - 8 times
- **Ascetic** - तपस्वी - One who denies oneself ordinary bodily pleasures - 10 times
- **Atheist** - नास्तिक - A person who doesn't believe in God - 8 times
- **Autobiography** - आत्मकथा - An account of a person's life written by oneself - 8 times
- **Blasphemy** - ईश्वर की निन्दा - Words uttered impiously about God - **7 times**
- **Cartographer** - मानचित्रकार - A person who draws or makes maps - 10 times
- **Choreographer** - नृत्य-निर्देशक - One who plans the steps and moves in a dance - 10 times
- **Connoisseur** - विशेषज्ञ - A man who knows a lot about things like food, music, and art - 9 times
- **Convalescent** - बीमारी से ठीक होना - A man who is recovering from illness - **7 times**
- **Dermatology** - त्वचाविज्ञान - The scientific study of skin diseases - **7 times**
- **Effeminate** - नारी जैसा - Man behaving more like a woman than as a man - 6 times
- **Elegy** - शोकगीत - A poem that expresses lament for the dead - 6 times
- **Embezzlement** - गबन - An act of misappropriation of money - **7 times**
- **Entomology** - कीटविज्ञान - The scientific study of insects - 8 times
- **Fatal** - घातक - Causing or ending in death - 9 times
- **Genocide** - जातिसंहार - The murder of a whole race or a group of people - 11 times
- **Hypochondriac** - रोगभ्रमी - A person who suffers from an imaginary illness - 13 times
- **Hypocrite** - पाखंडी - A person pretending to be somebody he isn't - 12 times
- **Inaccessible** - दुर्गम - Incapable of being approached - 9 times
- **Incredible** - अविश्वसनीय - That which cannot be believed - 5 times
- **Indefatigable** - अथक - Incapable of feeling tired or exhausted - **7 times**
- **Infallible** - अपराधी - One who cannot

make a mistake - 10 times

- **Insomnia** - अनिद्रा - The condition of being unable to sleep - 9 times
- **Irrevocable** - अपरिवर्तनीय - That which cannot be called back - 10 times
- **Mercenary** - पासी - A soldier who will fight for any country/group that offers payment - 8 times
- **Misanthrope** - मानवद्वेषी - A person who hates and avoids other people - 7 times
- **Numismatist** - मुद्राशास्त्री - A person who collects coins - **7 times**
- **Octagon** - अष्टभुज - A geometrical figure with eight sides - 10 times
- **Oligarchy** - अल्पतंत्र - Government or rule by a small group of people - 11 times
- **Optimist** - आशावादी - One who sees the bright side of things - 10 times
- **Pacifist** - शांतवादी - A person who opposes war or the use of military force - 14 times
- **Polyglot** - बहुभाषी - A person who knows and is able to use several languages - 12 times
- **Reticent** - अल्पभाषी - A person very reserved in speech - 13 times
- **Secular** - धर्मनिरपेक्ष - Government not connected with religious or spiritual matters - 11 times
- **Shoal** - मछलियों का समुदाय - A large number of fish swimming together - 10 times
- **Sinecure** - आराम की नौकरी - An office with high salary but no work - 8 times
- **Teetotaler** - पूर्णतया मद्यत्यागी - A person who never takes alcoholic drinks - 9 times
- **Universal** - सर्वव्यापी - Found all over the world - **7 times**
- **Usurer** - सूदखोर - One who lends money on high rates of interest - 13 times
- **Veteran** - अनुभवी - A person who is long experienced or practiced in an activity - 11 times
- **Wreath** - पुष्पांजलि - A decorative ring of flowers and leaves - **7 times**
- **Acronym** - अक्षरों से बना एक शब्द - A word formed from the first letters of the words that make up the name of something - 8 times
- **Aesthetic** - सौंदर्य संबंधी - Concerned with beauty or the appreciation of beauty - 5 times
- **Alien** - अजनबी - A person belonging to a foreign country - 3 times
- **Ambiguous** - अनेकार्थी - Capable of being understood in either of two or more possible senses, and therefore not definite - 12 times
- **Anarchist** - अराजकतावादी - A person who believes that laws and governments are not necessary - 15 times
- **Anniversary** - सालगिरह - The date on which an event happened in some previous year - **7 times**
- **Anthropology** - मानवशास्त्र - The study of the human race, especially its origin, development, customs, and beliefs - 6 times

- **Apprentice** - **शिक्षार्थी** - A person who works for an expert to learn a trade - 6 times
- **Aquarium** - **मछलीघर** - A glass tank where fish and water are kept - 5 times
- **Aristocracy** - **श्रेष्ठ जनों के द्वारा राज्यशासन** - The rule by nobles/government by persons of the highest social order - 5 times
- **Barometer** - **वायु-दाब-मापक** - An instrument used for measuring atmospheric pressure - **7 times**
- **Barracks** - **सैनिकों के लिए बने घर** - Place given to soldiers to live in - 5 times
- **Bigot** - **कट्टर व्यक्ति** - A person who is intolerant towards those holding different opinions - **7 times**
- **Bilingual** - **द्विभाषक** - A person who can speak only two languages - 4 times
- **Bureaucracy** - **नौकरशाही** - A government run by officials in a state - **7 times**
- **Burrow** - **बिल** - Hole excavated by an animal as a dwelling - 5 times
- **Calligraphy** - **सुलेख** - Beautiful handwriting that you do with a special brush - 4 times
- **Carnivorous** - **मांसाहारी** - Animal that eats meat - 5 times
- **Cartography** - **मानचित्रकारी** - The art or process of drawing or making maps - 6 times
- **Catalogue** - **सूची** - A complete list of items, for example, books that people can look at/buy - 5 times
- **Chapel** - **छोटा गिरजाघर** - A small building/room used for Christian worship in a school, prison, large private house, etc. - **7 times**
- **Choir** - **गायक-मण्डली** - A group of singers in a church - **7 times**
- **Chronology** - **कालक्रम** - An arrangement of events or dates in the order of their occurrence - 6 times
- **Circumlocution** - **शब्द-बहुल्य** - The use of many words where only a few are necessary - 12 times
- **Colleague** - **सहकर्मी** - A person that one works with at the same place, in a profession or a business - 10 times
- **Congregation** - **धार्मिक सभा** - An assembly of worshippers - 8 times
- **Cosmopolitan** - **सर्वविदेशी** - A person who can make himself at home anywhere - **7 times**
- **Credulous** - **विश्वासपूर्ण** - A person who readily believes others - 6 times
- **Curator** - **संग्रहालय अध्यक्ष** - A person in charge of a museum - 12 times
- **Draw** - **अनिर्णीत करना** - A game in which no one wins - 4 times
- **Eccentric** - **विचित्र** - A man with abnormal habits - 8 times
- **Edible** - **खाद्य** - A thing fit to be eaten - 4 times
- **Egoist** - **आत्महत्यार** - One who is preoccupied with his own interests - 6 times
- **Empathy** - **संवेदना** - Understanding another person's feelings, experience, etc. - 5 times
- **Eternal** - **अनंत** - Something which

lasts forever - 5 times

- **Eulogy** - प्रशंसा भाषण - A formal expression of praise for someone who has died - 6 times
- **Euthanasia** - इच्छामृत्यु - Bringing about gentle and painless death from incurable disease - 5 times
- **Extravagant** - फजूल खर्ची - A person who wastes his money on luxury - 6 times
- **Fable** - किस्सा - A short story with a moral, usually with animals as characters - 6 times
- **Fanatic** - कट्टरपंथी - A person motivated by irrational enthusiasm - **7 times**
- **Flora** - फसल - The plants and vegetation of a region - 6 times
- **Fragile** - नाज़ुक - Something which gets broken easily - **7 times**
- **Fratricide** - भ्रातृहत्या - An act of murdering one's brother - 6 times
- **Hallucination** - माया - A perception without objective reality - 8 times
- **Honorary** - माननीय - Given as an honour without the normal duties - 4 times
- **Horticulture** - उद्यान-विज्ञान - The study of growing garden plants - 8 times
- **Iconoclast** - मूर्तिभंजक - One who destroys images or attacks popular beliefs - **7 times**
- **Incomprehensible** - समझ से बाहर - Something that is difficult to understand - 5 times
- **Insolvent** - दिवालिया - Being unable to pay one's debt - 5 times
- **Juxtaposed** - पास-पास रखना - Placing different things in order to create an interesting effect - 6 times
- **Kleptomania** - चोरी करने की बीमारी - A person with a strong desire to steal - 5 times
- **Manuscript** - हस्तलेख - A copy of a book, piece of music, etc. before it has been printed - **7 times**
- **Martyr** - शहीद - Someone who is killed fighting for the cause of religion or faith - 8 times
- **Mint** - टकसाल - A place where money is coined by the authority of the government - **7 times**
- **Miser** - कंजूस - A person who loves money and hates spending - 5 times
- **Monarchy** - राजतंत्र - A system of government by a king/queen - **7 times**
- **Mortuary** - शवगृह - A place for keeping dead bodies before burial or cremation - 5 times
- **Namesake** - हमनाम - A person or thing that has the same name as another - 8 times
- **Nostalgia** - अतीत की याद - Sentimental longing for a period in the past - 7 times
- **Obituary** - शोक सन्देश - A notice of a person's death - 6 times
- **Omniscient** - सर्वज्ञ - One who knows everything - 9 times
- **Omnivorous** - सर्वाहारी - One who eats both vegetables and meat - 8 times
- **Pantheism** - सर्वभाववाद - The belief that God is in everything, including

nature - **7 times**

- **Patrimony** - विरासत - Property that is given to somebody when his father dies - 6 times
- **Patriot** - देशभक्त - One who loves his country - 8 times
- **Pedant** - रूढ़वादी - A person who insists on adherence to formal rules or literary meaning - 8 times
- **Pedestrian** - पैदलयात्री - A person who walks on foot and travels - 6 times
- **Philanthropist** - दानशील - A person who makes an effort to promote human welfare - **7 times**
- **Plagiarism** - साहित्यिक चोरी - Stealing of ideas or writings of someone else - **7 times**
- **Plagiarist** - साहित्यिक चोर - One who copies from other writers - **7 times**
- **Predator** - शिकारी - An animal that lives by killing and eating other animals - 8 times
- **Psephology** - चुनाव विज्ञान - The study of how people vote in elections - 8 times
- **Pseudonym** - उपनाम - A fictitious name, especially one assumed by an author - 8 times
- **Recluse** - वैरागी - A person who withdraws from the world to live in seclusion and often in solitude - 9 times
- **Red-tapism** - लालफीताशाही - A process involving too much official formality - 9 times
- **Repatriation** - स्वदेश लौटना - The return of someone to their own country - 6 times
- **Somnambulist** - नींद में चलने वाला - Someone who walks about in sleep - 8 times
- **Stoicism** - सहिष्णुता - Indifference to pleasure and pain - 8 times
- **Theology** - धर्मशास्त्र - The study of the nature of God and religious beliefs - **7 times**
- **Truant** - गैरहाजिर रहने वाला - A student who daily or without excuse absents themselves from school - 5 times
- **Versatile** - सवगुण सम्पन्न - Someone having many skills - 6 times
- **Zealot** - कट्टरपंथी - A person who is fanatical and uncompromising in pursuit of religious, political, or other ideals - **7 times**
- **Fragile** - भंगुर - Easily broken - **7 times**
- **Nostalgia** - गहा प्रेम - A strong desire to return home, homesickness - **7 times**
- **Versatile** - चंचल/चपल - Able to adapt oneself readily to many situations - 9 times
- **Monogamy** - एक विवाह प्रथा - The practice of marrying one at a time - 6 times
- **Bigamy** - द्विविवाह - The practice of having two wives or two husbands at a time - **7 times**
- **Polygamy** - बहुपत्नी - The practice of marrying more than one wife at a time - 8 times
- **Polyandry** - बहुपत्नीकरण - The practice of marrying more than one

husband at a time - 8 times

- **Misogynist - स्त्री द्वेषी** - A hater of womankind - **7 times**
- **Philogynist - स्त्री प्रेमी** - A lover of womankind - **7 times**
- **Bibliophile - पुस्तक प्रेमी** - A lover and collector of books - 6 times
- **Plebiscite - नवार्मचन** - A decision made by voting - 8 times
- **Effeminate - नारीत्व** - A person who is womanish in his habits - 6 times
- **Philanderer - प्रेमालापी** - One who amuses himself by lovemaking - 9 times
- **Veteran - अनुभवी** - One who has a long experience of any occupation - 9 times
- **Amateur - शौकीन** - A man who does a thing for pleasure and not as a profession - **7 times**
- **Loquacious - वाचाल** - One who talks continuously - 6 times
- **Anarchist - अराजकतावादी** - One who is out to destroy all government, law, and order - 6 times
- **Philistine - अशिक्षित मनुष्य** - One who does not care for art and literature - 8 times
- **Plutocracy - धनीप्रशासनक तंत्र** - Government by the rich - 8 times
- **Aristocracy - अभिजात तंत्र** - Government by the nobles - 8 times
- **Bureaucracy - नौकर शाही** - Government by the officials - 8 times
- **Pseudonym - उपनाम/छद्म नाम** - An imaginary name assumed by an author for disguise - 8 times
- **Aquatic - जलीय/जल से संबंधित** - Animals which live in water - 8 times
- **Martyr - शहीद** - One who dies for a noble cause - 6 times
- **Novice or Tyro - नौसिखाया** - One new to anything - 6 times
- **Autobiography - आत्मकथा** - The life history of a person written by himself - 6 times
- **Maiden speech - प्रथम भाषण** - The first speech delivered by a person - 8 times
- **Carnivorous - मांसाहारी** - One who lives on flesh - **7 times**
- **Cannibal - नरभक्षी** - One who feeds on human flesh - **7 times**
- **Contemporaries - समकालीन** - Persons living at the same time - **7 times**
- **Insolvent/Bankrupt - दिवालया** - A person who is unable to pay his debts - **7 times**
- **Inaudible - जो सुना ना जा सके** - A sound that cannot be heard - 5 times
- **Inaccessible - दुर्गम्य** - That cannot be easily approached - 5 times
- **Theocracy - धर्मराज्य** - Government by religious principles - 8 times
- **Sacrilege - पवित्र वस्तु को दूषित करना** - Violating or profaning religious things/ places - 9 times
- **Incorrigible - अशोध्य** - Incapable of being corrected - 11 times

- **Irreparable** - अपरतकार्य - Incapable of being repaired - 8 times
- **Illegible** - अपठनीय - Incapable of being read - 8 times
- **Horticulture** - बागवानी - The art of cultivating and managing gardens - 8 times
- **Numismatics** - मुद्राशास्त्र - The study of coins - 8 times
- **Rhetoric** - शब्दों की प्रभावशाली कला - The art of elegant speech or writing - 6 times
- **Infallible** - अभ्रान्त - One who is free from all mistakes and failures - 6 times
- **Teetotaler** - मादक पदार्थो का बहिष्कारी - One who does not take any intoxicating drink - **7 times**
- **Indelible** - अक्षय - That cannot be erased - **7 times**
- **Orphan** - अनाथ - One who has lost parents - 5 times
- **Potable** - पीनेयोग्य - Fit to drink - **7 times**
- **Narcotic** - नींद कारक नशेकारी - A medicine for producing sleep - 5 times
- **Amputate** - हाथ या पैर काटना - To cut off a part of a person's body which is infected - **7 times**
- **Post mortem** - मरणोपरांत परीक्षण - An examination of a dead body - 5 times
- **Obituary** - मृत्यु समाचार - An account in the newspaper of the funeral of the deceased - **7 times**
- **Abdication** - त्याग - Voluntary giving up of the throne in favor of someone - 11 times
- **Portable** - वहनीय - That can be carried easily - 9 times
- **Uxoricide** - पत्नी हत्या - Murder of a wife - **7 times**
- **Genocide** - जाति हत्याकुल हत्या - Murder of a race - **7 times**
- **Sororicide** - बहन हत्या - Murder of a sister - 6 times
- **Heretic** - नास्तिक / पाखण्डी - One who acts against religion - 4 times
- **Sot, Toper** - मदोन्मत्त / पेयक्कड़ - One who is a habitual drunkard - 5 times
- **Paleography** - पुरावलेखशास्त्र - The study of ancient writing - **7 times**
- **Orphanage** - अनाथालय - A home for orphans - 6 times
- **Lunatic Asylum** - पागलखाना - A home for lunatics - 5 times
- **Infirmary** - अस्थायी या दिवंगत लोगों का आवास स्थान - A home for old persons - 5 times
- **Fatal** - घातक - Causing death - 5 times
- **Fatalist** - भाग्यवादी - One who believes in fate - 3 times
- **Transparent** - पारदर्शी - That which can be seen through - 2 times
- **Arsenal** - शस्त्रागार हथियारघर - A place for ammunition and weapons - 6 times
- **Cloak Room** - जमा कक्ष - A place for luggage at the railway station - 6 times

- **Granary - धान्यगार -** A place for grains - 5 times
- **Hive - मधुमक्खी का छत्ता -** A place for bees - 4 times
- **Hedonist - आनंदजीवी -** One who believes that pleasure is the chief good - 8 times
- **Somnambulist - निद्राचारी -** A person who walks in sleep - **7 times**
- **Somniloquy's - नींद में बातें करने वाला -** A person who talks in sleep - 8 times
- **Epitaph - स्मरण लेख -** Words that are inscribed on the grave or tomb in memory of the buried - 5 times
- **Facsimile - प्रतिलिपि / नकल -** An exact copy of handwriting, printing, etc. - 9 times
- **Plagiarism - ग्रंथ चोरी -** Literary theft or passing off an author's original work as one's own - 9 times
- **Elegy - शोकगीत -** A poem of lamentation - 10 times
- **Infanticide - शिशुहत्या -** Murder of an infant - 8 times
- **Morgue - शव पहचानगृह -** A place where dead bodies are kept for identification - 5 times
- **Inevitable - अनिवार्य / अवश्यंभावी -** Incapable of being avoided - 8 times
- **Impracticable - असाध्य / दुष्कर -** Incapable of being practiced - 8 times
- **Herbivorous - शाकाहारी -** One who lives on herbs - 9 times
- **Venial - क्षम्य -** A fault that may be forgiven - **7 times**
- **Ephemeral - अल्पजीवी -** Lasting for a short time - **7 times**
- **Altruist - परोपकारी -** One who has an unselfish concern for the welfare of others - **7 times**
- **Hanger - विमानशाला -** A place for housing airplanes - **7 times**
- **Dormitory - शयनशाला -** The sleeping rooms in a college or public institution - **7 times**
- **Cosmopolitan - विश्ववादी -** A person who regards the whole world as their country - **7 times**
- **Optimist - आशावादी -** One who looks at the bright side of things - **7 times**
- **Pessimist - निराशावादी -** One who looks at the dark side of things - **7 times**
- **Atheist - नास्तिक -** One who does not believe in God - **7 times**

One Word Substitution

(Based on Categories)

➢ ONE WORD SUBSTITUTION FOR PHOBIAS (भय से सम्बन्धी)

Word	Meaning	Hindi Meaning
Acrophobia	Fear of high places	ऊँचाइयों से डर
Aerophobia	Fear of air	हवा से डर
Aglophobia	Fear of pain	दर्द से डर
Altiphobia	Fear of altitude	ऊँचाई से डर
Anorexia	Obsessive desire to lose weight	वजन घटाने की आवेशयकता
Agoraphobia	Fear of public places or open spaces	सार्वजनिक स्थानों से डर
Androphobia	Fear of males	पुरुषों से डर
Autophobia	Fear of being alone	अकेलापन से डर
Bathophobia	Fear of depths	गहराई से डर
Bibliophobia	Fear of books	किताबों से डर
Cacophobia	Fear of ugliness	बदसूरती से डर
Catrophobia	Fear of doctors	डॉक्टर से डर
Cellophobia	Fear of beauty	सुंदरता से डर
Chronophobia	Fear of time	समय से डर
Cynophobia	Fear of dogs	कुत्तों से डर
Claustrophobia	Fear of being confined to a small place	छोटे स्थान में बंद रहने से डर
Dipsophobia	Fear of alcohol	शराब से डर

Word	Meaning	Hindi Meaning
Dipsomania	Strong need to drink alcohol	शराब पीने की मजबूरी
Demonomania	Delusion of being under evil spirits	बुरे आत्माओं के अधीन होने की भ्रांति
Entomophobia	Fear of insects	कीटों से डर
Ergophobia	Fear of work	काम से डर
Gamophobia	Fear of marriage	शादी से डर
Genophobia	Fear of sexual intercourse or intimacy	सेक्स या आपसी संबंध से डर
Geraphobia	Fear of old age	बुढ़ापे से डर
Gnosiophobia	Fear of knowledge	ज्ञान से डर
Graphophobia	Fear of writing	लेखन से डर
Gynaephobia	Fear of women	महिलाओं से डर
Haematophobia	Fear of blood	रक्त से डर
Hedonophobia	Fear of pleasure	सुख से डर
Hodophobia	Fear of travel	यात्रा से डर
Hydrophobia	Fear of water	पानी से डर
Kleptophobia	Fear of theft	चोरी से डर
Kleptomania	Strong urge to steal	चोरी करने की मजबूरी
Lipophobia	Fear of getting fat	मोटा होने से डर
Logophobia	Fear of words	शब्दों से डर
Logomania	Obsession with words or talking	शब्दों के लिए मानसिक उत्सुकता
Maicusiophobia	Fear of childbirth	प्रसव से डर
Metrophobia	Fear of poetry	कविता से डर
Menemophobia	Fear of old memories	पुरानी यादों से डर
Monophobia	Fear of loneliness	अकेलापन से डर

Word	Meaning	Hindi Meaning
Mysophobia	Fear of dirt or contamination	गंदगी या संक्रमण से डर
Megalomania	Delusion about one's power or importance	अपनी शक्ति या महत्व के बारे में मिथ्याभिमान
Nyctophobia	Fear of darkness	अंधेरे से डर
Ophthalmophobia	Fear of eyes	आँखों से डर
Ochlophobia	Fear of crowds or mobs	भीड़ या भीड़तंत्र से डर
Paedophobia	Fear of children	बच्चों से डर
Pathophobia	Fear of disease	बीमारी से डर
Peniophobia	Fear of poverty	गरीबी से डर
Pharmacophobia	Fear of medicine	दवा से डर
Pyrophobia	Fear of fire	आग से डर

➢ ONE WORD SUBSTITUTION FOR SCIENCE AND ARTS (विज्ञान और कला से सम्बन्धी)

Word	Meaning	Hindi Meaning
Acoustics	Study of sound	ध्वनि शास्त्र
Aeronautics	Science of flight	विमान-विज्ञान
Aesthetics	The philosophy of art	कला-दर्शन
Agronomy	Science of soil management	कृषि-शास्त्र
Alchemy	Medieval chemical science	रसायन शास्त्र (मध्यकालीन)
Anatomy	Science dealing with the structure of organisms and their parts	शरीर रचना विज्ञान
Anthropology	Scientific study of humanity and human behavior	मानवशास्त्र
Arboriculture	Cultivation of trees and vegetables	वृक्षारोपण और सब्जियों की खेती
Astrology	The study of patterns and relationships of planets in motion, birth charts, etc.	ज्योतिष शास्त्र
Bacteriology	The study of bacteria	जीवाणु-विज्ञान
Bibliography	The study of books as physical and cultural objects	पुस्तक-सूची विज्ञान
Botany	The study of plants	वनस्पति-विज्ञान
Calligraphy	The art of beautiful handwriting	ख़ूबसूरत हस्ताक्षर कला
Ceramics/Pottery	The art and technology of making objects from clay, etc.	मृदा से बनी वस्तुओं की कला
Chronobiology	The study of the duration of life	जीवन-काल विज्ञान
Chronology	The science of arranging events or dates in the order of their occurrence	घटनाक्रम विज्ञान
Chromatics	The art of making fireworks	आभाविकता की कला

Word	Meaning	Hindi Meaning
Cosmogony	The science of the nature of heavenly bodies	ब्रह्मांड की स्वभाव विज्ञान
Cosmography	The science that deals with the main features of the universe	ब्रह्मांड का मुख्य विशेषताओं का अध्ययन
Cosmology	The science of the nature, origin, and history of the universe	ब्रह्मांड की स्वभाव, उत्पत्ति और इतिहास की विज्ञान
Cryogenics	The science of dealing with the production and behavior of materials at very low temperatures	बहुत कम तापमान पर पदार्थों के उत्पादन और व्यवहार की विज्ञान
Cypher	The art of secret or coded writings	गुप्त या कोडेड लेखन की कला
Cytology	The study of cells	कोशिका विज्ञान
Dactylography	The study of fingerprints	अंगुलिमुद्रा विज्ञान
Dactylology	The technique of communication by signs made with the fingers	उंगलियों से बनाए गए संकेतों का संचार विधि
Demography	The study of the human population	जनसंख्या विज्ञान
Ecology	The study of the relationship of animals and plants to their surroundings	प्राणी और पौधों के संपर्क का अध्ययन
Entomology	The study of insects	कीट-विज्ञान
Epigraphy	The study of inscriptions	लिपिका विज्ञान
Ethnology	The study of human races	नस्लों का अध्ययन
Ethology	The study of animal behavior	पशुव्यवहार विज्ञान
Etymology	The study of the origin and history of words	शब्दों की उत्पत्ति और इतिहास का अध्ययन
Eugenics	The study of improving the human species by selectively mating people	ऐच्छिक रूप से लोगों के योग्यता का अध्ययन

Word	Meaning	Hindi Meaning
Ergonomy	The study of people in their work environments	कार्यालय वातावरण में लोगों का अध्ययन
Genealogy	The study of family ancestries	परिवार के वंशावली का अध्ययन
Genetics	The study of genes, genetic variation, and heredity	जीनों, आनुवंशिक विविधता और आनुवंशिकता का अध्ययन
Geology	The science that deals with the physical history of the Earth	धरती के भौतिक इतिहास का अध्ययन
Gymnastics	The art of performing acrobatics requiring balance, strength, and flexibility	तानाशाही, बल और लचीलापन की आवश्यकता वाले आक्रोबेटिक्स कला

➢ ONE WORD SUBSTITUTION FOR PERSONS (इंसानो से सम्बन्धी)

Word	Meaning	Hindi Meaning
Atheist	One who does not believe in God	ईश्वर में विश्वास न करने वाला व्यक्ति
Ascetic	One who leads an austere life	तपस्वी, तपस्या में रहने वाला व्यक्ति
Altruist	One who is a believer/ lover of mankind	मानवतावादी, मानवजाति के प्रेमी व्यक्ति
Agnostic	One who is unsure about God's existence	ईश्वर की मौजूदगी के बारे में अनिश्चित व्यक्ति
Anarchist	One who wants to destroy governments	अराजक, सरकारों को नष्ट करना चाहने वाला व्यक्ति
Amateur	One who does something for pleasure and not as a profession	प्रेमी, अव्यवसायिकता से कुछ करने वाला व्यक्ति
Apostate	One who has changed his faith	धर्म परिवर्तन करने वाला व्यक्ति
Arbitrator	One who solves a dispute between two parties	मध्यस्थ, दो पक्षों के बीच विवाद को हल करने वाला व्यक्ति
Bigot	One with excessive obsession for religious matters	पक्षपाती, धार्मिक मामलों के लिए अत्यधिक आकर्षण रखने वाला व्यक्ति
Bohemian	One with an unconventional style of living	असामान्य जीने की आदत वाला व्यक्ति
Cannibal	One who feeds on human flesh	मानव शरीर का भोजन करने वाला व्यक्ति

Word	Meaning	Hindi Meaning
Chauvinist	One who holds extreme political or religious views	प्रगटावादी, राजनीतिक या धार्मिक दृष्टिकोण रखने वाला व्यक्ति
Connoisseur	One who judges any art and craft critically	महारसिक, कला और शिल्प का मूल्यांकन करने वाला व्यक्ति
Contemporaries	Persons living at the same time	समकालीन, एक समय में रहने वाले व्यक्ति
Cosmopolitan	One who considers the whole world as his own country	सर्वविश्व नागरिक, पूरी दुनिया को अपना देश मानने वाला व्यक्ति
Cynosure	One who is a center of attraction	आकर्षण का केंद्र होने वाला व्यक्ति
Cynic	One who sneers at the beliefs of others	नकारात्मक, दूसरों के विश्वासों पर उपहास करने वाला व्यक्ति
Coquette	A girl/woman who likes to flirt with men	मनमोहिनी, पुरुषों के साथ फ्लर्ट करने वाली महिला
Demagogue	A leader who persuades his followers with his oratory	जनप्रिय नेता, अपने भाषण के जरिए अनुयायियों को प्रभावित करने वाला नेता
Debonair	A confident, charming, or stylish person	आत्मविश्वासी, प्रियकर या स्टाइलिश व्यक्ति
Dilettante	One who develops an interest in art, science, and literature without any knowledge or commitment	उपेक्षापूर्वक, कला, विज्ञान और साहित्य में रुचि विकसित करने वाला व्यक्ति

Word	Meaning	Hindi Meaning
Effeminate	A man who has characteristics of a woman	स्त्री जैसी गुणधर्मों वाला पुरुष
Egoist	One who is a lover of oneself	अहंकारी, अपने आप से प्यार करने वाला व्यक्ति
Egotist	One who is excessively self-absorbed and conceited	आत्मसमर्पी, अत्यधिक अपने आप में खोया हुआ और अभिमानी व्यक्ति
Emigrant	One who leaves his country and settles in another one	प्रवासी, अपने देश को छोड़कर किसी अन्य देश में बसने वाला व्यक्ति
Fastidious	One who is hard to please	कपटी, संतुष्टि प्राप्त करने के लिए कठिन व्यक्ति
Fatalist	One who believes in fate	भाग्यवादी, भाग्य पर विश्वास रखने वाला व्यक्ति
Fugitive	One who escapes from justice	पलायक, न्याय से बचने वाला व्यक्ति
Gourmand	One who is a lover of food	भोजन के प्रेमी, भोजन का प्रेम करने वाला व्यक्ति
Gourmet	A connoisseur of good food	स्वादिष्ट भोजन का ज्ञान रखने वाला व्यक्ति
Hedonist	One who believes in sensual/sexual pleasure	सुखवादी, भौतिक/लैंगिक आनंद में विश्वास रखने वाला व्यक्ति
Heretic	One who opposes religions	धर्मविरोधी, धर्मों के खिलाफ विरोध करने वाला व्यक्ति

Word	Meaning	Hindi Meaning
Honorary	One who works for something or holds a post without any salary	सम्मानित, कुछ के लिए काम करने वाला या बिना किसी वेतन के पदभार संभालने वाला व्यक्ति
Hypochondriac	One who overthinks about his health	निराशावादी, अपने स्वास्थ्य के बारे में अधिक सोचने वाला व्यक्ति
Iconoclast	One who breaks customs and traditions	मूर्तिपूजा के विरोधी, परंपराओं और रीति-रिवाजों को तोड़ने वाला व्यक्ति
Immigrant	One who comes to a country from his country and settles there	प्रवासी, अपने देश से किसी दूसरे देश में आने और वहां बसने वाला व्यक्ति
Impregnable	Cannot be entered by force	अजेय, बलपूर्वक प्रवेश नहीं किया जा सकता
Indefatigable	One who does not get tired	अविचलित, थक नहीं जाने वाला व्यक्ति
Introvert	One who does not express his feelings freely	अंतर्मुखी, अपनी भावनाओं को स्वतंत्र रूप से व्यक्त नहीं करने वाला व्यक्ति
Insolvent	One who is unable to pay his debts	दिवालिया, अपने कर्जों का भुगतान नहीं कर सकने वाला व्यक्ति
Itinerant	One who travels from place to place	भ्रमणकारी, एक स्थान से दूसरे स्थान की यात्रा करने वाला व्यक्ति
Invincible	One who is too strong to be defeated	अजेय, हार नहीं मानने वाला व्यक्ति

Word	Meaning	Hindi Meaning
Martyr	One who dies for a noble cause	शहीद, एक महान कारण के लिए मर जाने वाला व्यक्ति
Misanthrope	One who hates mankind	मानवद्वेषी, मानवता से नफरत करने वाला व्यक्ति
Misogamist	One who hates marriage institutions	विवाह विरोधी, विवाह संस्था से नफरत करने वाला व्यक्ति
Narcissist	One who has an excessive interest in or admiration of themselves	अहंकारी, अपने आप में अत्यधिक रुचि या प्रशंसा रखने वाला व्यक्ति
Novice	One who is a beginner, inexperienced in any field	अनुभवहीन, किसी भी क्षेत्र में शुरुआत करने वाला व्यक्ति
Numismatist	One who collects coins	सिक्कों का संग्रह करने वाला व्यक्ति
Optimist	One who looks at the positive side of life	आशावादी, जीवन के सकारात्मक पहलू को देखने वाला व्यक्ति
Philanthropist	One who loves mankind	परोपकारी, मानवता से प्यार करने वाला व्यक्ति
Philogynist	One who works for the welfare of women	महिलाओं के कल्याण के लिए काम करने वाला व्यक्ति
Polyglot	One who can speak many languages	बहुभाषी, कई भाषाएं बोलने वाला व्यक्ति
Pacifist	One who hates violence, war	शांतिवादी, हिंसा और युद्ध से नफरत करने वाला व्यक्ति
Philanderer	One who amuses oneself by lovemaking	व्यंगपूर्ण, प्रेम रस के द्वारा मनोरंजन करने वाला व्यक्ति
Posthumous	An award received after the death of the recipient	मृत्युपश्चात, प्राप्तकर्ता की मृत्यु के बाद पुरस्कार

Word	Meaning	Hindi Meaning
Philistine	One who does not care for art and literature	नकारात्मक, कला और साहित्य का ध्यान नहीं रखने वाला व्यक्ति
Philatelist	One who collects stamps	डाक टिकट संग्रह करने वाला व्यक्ति
Recluse	One who lives in seclusion	वैज्ञानिक, अलगावच्छ की जिंदगी बिताने वाला व्यक्ति
Sadist	One who feels pleasure by hurting others	नरसंहारी, दूसरों को चोट पहुंचाने से आनंद मिलने वाला व्यक्ति
Samaritan	One who helps the needy and helpless	समर्पी, गरीब और बेसहारा लोगों की मदद करने वाला व्यक्ति
Somnambulist	One who walks in sleep	नींद में चलने वाला व्यक्ति
Somniloquist	One who talks in sleep	नींद में बोलने वाला व्यक्ति
Stoic	One who is indifferent to pain and pleasures	स्थैर्यशील, दर्द और सुख के प्रति उदासीन व्यक्ति
Teetotaller	One who does not take any intoxicating drugs	सुस्त, किसी भी मादक दवा लेने वाला व्यक्ति
Truant	One who remains absent from school or duty without permission	छुट्टी, अनुमति के बिना स्कूल या कर्तव्य से अनुपस्थित रहने वाला व्यक्ति
Veteran	One who has a long experience in any field	अनुभवी, किसी भी क्षेत्र में लंबे समय तक अनुभव रखने वाला व्यक्ति
Verbose	Using or containing more words than necessary	शब्दाडंबरपूर्ण, आवश्यकता से अधिक शब्दों का प्रयोग करने वाला व्यक्ति

➢ ONE WORD SUBSTITUTION FOR TYPES OF GOVERMENTS (सरकार से सम्बन्धी)

Word	Meaning	Hindi Meaning
Anarchy	Absence of government	शासन अभाव
Autocracy	Government by one person	एकाधिकारिता
Autonomy	Right of self-government	स्वशासन
Aristocracy	Government by the nobles	उच्च वर्गीयता
Bureaucracy	Government by the officials	अधिकारियों द्वारा शासन
Democracy	Government by the people	लोकतंत्र
Gerontocracy	Government by the old people	वृद्धावस्था के लोगों द्वारा शासन
Kakistocracy	Government by the worst citizen	सबसे बुरे नागरिक द्वारा शासन
Neocracy	Government by the inexperienced persons	अनुभवहीन व्यक्तियों द्वारा शासन
Ochlocracy	Government by the mob	जनसमूह द्वारा शासन
Oligarchy	Government by a few persons	कुछ के द्वारा शासन
Panarchy	Government run universally	वैश्विकता में चलाया जाने वाला शासन
Plutocracy	Government by the rich	धनी लोगों द्वारा शासन
Secular	Government not by the laws of religion	धर्म के नियमों से अस्थायी शासन
Monarchy	Government by a King/ Queen	राजतंत्र

Theocracy	Government by the laws of religion	धर्म के नियमों द्वारा शासन

➢ ONE WORD SUBSTITUTION FOR MARRIAGES (शादी से सम्बन्धी)

Word	Meaning	Hindi Meaning
Adultery	Practice of having an extra-marital affair	वैवाहिक संबंध के बाहरी संबंध
Alimony	Financial support paid to spouse on divorce	तलाक पर पत्नी को दिया जाने वाला आर्थिक सहायता
Bigamy	Practice of having two husbands or two wives	दो पतियों या दो पत्नियों के साथ शादी करने की प्रथा
Celibacy	State of abstention from marriage	विवाह से विरति
Misogamist	Who hates marriage	शादी से नफरत करने वाला व्यक्ति
Matrimony	State of being married	विवाहित स्थिति
Monogamy	Practice of marrying one person at a time	एक समय में एक व्यक्ति से विवाह करने की प्रथा
Polygamy	Practice of marrying more than one wife at a time	एक समय में एक से अधिक पत्नियों से विवाह करने की प्रथा
Polyandry	Practice of marrying more than one husband	एक समय में एक से अधिक पतियों से विवाह करने की प्रथा
Spinster	An older woman who is not married	एक वयस्क महिला जो विवाहित नहीं है

➢ ONE WORD SUBSTITUTION FOR TIME PERIOD (समय से सम्बन्धी)

Word	Meaning	Hindi Meaning
Annual	Happening once a year	सालाना
Biennial	Happening in two years	द्विवार्षिक
Triennial	Happening in three years	त्रिवार्षिक
Quadrennial	Happening in four years	चतुर्वर्षिक
Quinquennial	Happening in five years	पाँचवर्षिक
Decennial	Happening in ten years	दशवर्षिक
Semicentennial	50th anniversary	अर्धशताब्दी
Centennial	100th anniversary	शताब्दी
Century	A period of hundred years	सदी
Millennium	A period of 1000 years	हज़ार वर्षों का अवधि

➢ ONE WORD SUBSTITUTION FOR PLACES (जगह से सम्बन्धी)

Word	Meaning	Hindi Meaning
Abattoir	A place where animals are slaughtered for the market	मांस विक्रय के लिए पशुओं का कटाई करने का स्थान
Arena	A place for wrestling	कुश्ती के लिए स्थान
Arsenal	A place for ammunition and weapons	गोली और हथियारों के लिए स्थान
Apiary	A place where bees are kept	मधुमक्खियों को रखने का स्थान
Aviary	A place where birds are kept	पक्षियों को रखने का स्थान
Asylum	A place for lunatics and political refugees	पागलों और राजनीतिक शरणार्थियों के लिए स्थान
Aquarium	A tank for fishes	मछलियों के लिए टैंक
Archives	A place for government records or official documents	सरकारी रिकार्ड या आधिकारिक दस्तावेज़ों के लिए स्थान
Burrow	Dwelling place of a wild animal	जंगली जानवर का निवास स्थान
Cage	A structure of bars or wires to confine animals	जानवरों को रोकने के लिए पट्टियों या तार का ढांचा
Cemetery	A graveyard where the dead are buried	मकबरा
Convent	A residence for nuns	संन्यासिनियों के लिए आवास
Creche	A nursery where children of working parents are cared for	नर्सरी

Word	Meaning	Hindi Meaning
Crematorium	A cremation ground where the last funeral rites are performed	शवदहन ग्राउंड
Dormitory	Sleeping rooms in a college or public institution	कॉलेज या सार्वजनिक संस्थान में सोने के कमरे
Gymnasium	A place where athletic exercises are performed	एथलेटिक व्यायाम करने का स्थान
Granary	A place for storing grains	अनाज रखने का स्थान
Hangar	A place for housing airplanes	विमानों को रखने का स्थान
Hive	A place for bees	मधुमक्खियों का आवास
Hutch	A wooden fox with a front of wire for rabbits	खरगोशों के लिए लकड़ी की एक ढांचा
Infirmary	A place for the care of the infirm, sick, or injured	अस्पताल
Kennel	A house of shelter for a dog	कुत्ते के लिए शरण का घर
Den/Lair	Resting place of a wild animal	जंगली जानवर की आराम करने की जगह
Monastery	A residence for monks or priests	मठ
Mint	A place where money is coined	सिक्के बनाने का स्थान
Morgue	A place where dead bodies are kept for identification	मृतक शरीरों को पहचान के लिए रखा जाने वाला स्थान

Word	Meaning	Hindi Meaning
Mortuary	A place where dead bodies are kept for post-mortem	मृतक शरीरों को पोस्टमार्टम के लिए रखा जाने वाला स्थान
Orchard	A place where fruit trees are grown	फलों के पेड़ उगाए जाने वाला स्थान
Pantry	A room or closet for storage of provisions, food, etc.	भंडार
Stable	A house of shelter for a horse	घोड़े के लिए शरण का घर
Sty	A place where pigs are kept	सुअरों को रखने का स्थान
Scullery	A place where plates, dishes, pots, and other utensils are washed up	बर्तन धोने का स्थान
Scabbard	A case in which the blade of a sword is kept	तलवार का धार जिसमें रखा जाता है
Sanatorium	A place for the sick to recover health	आरोग्य उपचार का स्थान

➢ ONE WORD SUBSTITUTION FOR PROFESSIONS (काम से सम्बन्धी)

Word	Meaning	Hindi Meaning
Anchor	A person who presents a radio or television program	प्रस्तुतकर्ता
Astronaut	A person who travels in spacecraft	अंतरिक्ष यात्री
Anthropologist	A person who studies the evolution of mankind	मानवशास्त्रज्ञ
Calligraphist	A person who writes beautiful writing	ख़ूबसूरत लेखन करने वाला
Cartographer	A person who draws maps	मानचित्रकार
Choreographer	A person who teaches the art of dancing	नृत्य-निर्देशक
Chauffeur	A person employed to drive a private or hired car	चालक
Curator	A person who is in charge of a museum	संग्रहालय का प्रबंधक
Invigilator	A person who supervises in the examination hall	परीक्षा हॉल में पर्यवेक्षक
Lexicographer	A person who compiles a dictionary	शब्दकोश संकलक
Psephologist	A person who studies the pattern of voting in elections	मतगणना विज्ञ
Sculptor	A person who gives shape to stone or clay	मूर्तिकार
Usurer	A person who lends money at very high rates	ब्याजवाला

➢ ONE WORD SUBSTITUTION FOR Killing and Mania

Word	Meaning	Hindi Meaning
Mariticide	The killing of one's husband	पतिकत्ल (पति की हत्या)
Parricide	The killing of parents	मातृहत्या (माता-पिता की हत्या)
Genocide	The killing of a whole race	जनसंहार (पूरे जाति की हत्या)
Infanticide	The killing of a newborn child	शिशुहत्या (नवजात शिशु की हत्या)
Regicide	The killing of a king	राजहत्या (राजा की हत्या)
Homicide	The killing of a human being	मानवहत्या (मानव की हत्या)
Suicide	The killing of oneself	आत्महत्या (खुद की हत्या)
Patricide	The killing of a father	पितृहत्या (पिता की हत्या)
Matricide	The killing of a mother	मातृहत्या (माता की हत्या)
Fratricide	The killing of one's brother or comrade	भ्रातृहत्या (भाई या साथी की हत्या)
Sororicide	The killing of one's sister	बहिनहत्या (बहन की हत्या)
Uxoricide	The killing of one's wife	पत्नीहत्या (पत्नी की हत्या)
Dipsomania	Morbid compulsion to keep on consuming alcohol	नशामुक्ति (अल्कोहल के सेवन की मनोवृत्ति)
Kleptomania	Morbid compulsion to steal	चोरीक्लेप्टोमेनिया (चोरी की मनोवृत्ति)
Bibliokleptomania	Morbid compulsion to steal books	पुस्तक चोरीक्लेप्टोमेनिया (पुस्तकों की चोरी की मनोवृत्ति)
Pyromania	Morbid compulsion to start a fire	अग्निक्लेप्टोमेनिया (आग लगाने की मनोवृत्ति)

Word	Meaning	Hindi Meaning
Megalomania	Morbid delusion of power, importance, or godliness	विशेषमान्यतावाद (अधिकार, महत्व या देवत्व की मनोवृत्ति)
Nymphomania	Morbid, uncontrollable sexual desire on the part of a woman	स्त्रीसंगीनि (महिला की अयम्य सेक्सुअल इच्छा)
Satyromania	Morbid, uncontrollable sexual desire on the part of a man	पुरुषसंगीनि (पुरुष की अयम्य सेक्सुअल इच्छा)
Monomania	A person with a one-track mind	एकतरफा मनोमानिया (एकमात्र विचारों वाला व्यक्ति)
Mythomania	The compulsion to tell lies	झूठ बोलने की मनोवृत्ति
Mania	Madness with an obsession with something	पागलपन (किसी चीज़ के प्रति भक्ति की पागलपन)

Chapter - Two

Idioms and Phrases

All Idioms asked in SSC Exam [from 2012 till date]

Idioms	English Meaning	Hindi meaning
ABC	Basic knowledge of.	(प्राम्भिक ज्ञान)
Above board	Openly.	(स्पष्ट एवं प्रकटत:)
A big gun	An important person.	(महत्वपूर्ण व्यक्ति)
A fancy price	High price.	(ऊंची कीमत)
A freelance	An independent journalist.	(स्वतन्त्र लेखक)
A gala day	A jovial day.	(खुशी का दिन)
A going concern	A well-run business.	(व्यापार की सुचारू स्थिति)
To A Tee	Quite same, exactly.	(वैसा ही समान, पूर्णत:)
A Lady's habit	Riding dress of a lady.	(स्त्रियों के लिये घुड़सवारी के वस्त्र)
To A man	Everyone without exception.	(बिना कोई छूटे सभी)
A scapegoat	One who is made to suffer for another.	(दूसरे के लिए कष्ट उठाने वाला)
To A hair	Exactly.	(बिल्कुल)
Abide by	To obey the rule.	(नियम पालन करना)
Above all	At the highest point.	(सर्वोपरि)
A bad lot	A dishonest or of bad qualities.	(बेईमान अथवा बुरा आदमी)
Abscond from	To run away, to avoid the arrest.	(गिरफ्तारी से बचने के लिए भागना)
Absolve from	To release from (blame, duty, law, etc.).	(छुटकारा प्रदान करना)
Access to	To approach.	(पहुँच होना)
Acquainted with	To meet someone.	(किसी व्यक्ति से मेल-जोल करना, मिलना)
Act for	To do on behalf of someone.	(किसी के लिए कार्य करना)
Act on/upon	To have an effect.	(प्रभाव डालना)
Act up to	To satisfy, to fulfil.	(सन्तुष्ट करना, पूर्ण करना)
Adam's ale	Pure water.	(शुद्ध जल)
Add fuel to the fire	To make the situation worse.	(हालात को बदतर बनाना, आग में घी डालना)
Add insult to injury	To harm as well as humiliate.	(जले पर नमक छिड़कना)
Add up to	To be understood.	(समझ में आना)
Add zest to	To make interesting.	(मनोरंजक बनाना)
Adept in	To be an expert.	(निपुण होना)
Adhere to	To stick to.	(से सम्बद्ध, पालना करना)

Idioms	English Meaning	Hindi meaning
Addicted to	To indulge in a bad habit.	(बुरी आदत का शिकार होना)
Affiliated to	To be connected, an associate of.	(से सम्बद्ध, सहायक होना)
After a fashion	To a certain degree, not satisfactorily.	(एक सीमा तक, सन्तोषजनक नहीं)
Against the clock	Against the time.	(समय के विपरीत)
Against the grain	Contrary to one's natural inclination or feeling.	(की प्राकृतिक प्रवृत्ति या भावना के विरुद्ध)
Against the hair	Without pleasure.	(प्रसन्नता रहित)
Against the law	To be illegal.	(कानून के विरुद्ध होना)
Against the rainy days	An arrangement for hard days.	(बुरे दिनों के लिए व्यवस्था)
Against time	With utmost speed.	(तीव्रतम गति के साथ)
Aghast at	To be filled with fear.	(भयभीत होना)
Agree to differ	To give up efforts to convince each other.	(एक-दूसरे को समझाने के प्रयत्नों का त्याग)
Agree with	To make friends again.	(पुन: मित्रता करना)
All along	Throughout.	(लगातार)
All at once	Suddenly.	(अचानक)
All but	Very nearly.	(लगभग)
All day long	For the whole day.	(दिनभर)
All eyes	To watch eagerly.	(ध्यान से, उत्सुकतापूर्वक देखना)
All for	In favor of.	(पक्ष में)
All Greek	Beyond comprehension, understanding.	(न समझ में आने योग्य)
All in	To be exhausted.	(प्रयोग होना)
All in all	Of exclusive importance.	(सर्वस्व)
All moonshine	Talks without reality.	(कपोलकल्पित बातें)
All one	Just the same.	(कोई फर्क न पड़ना)
All out	Giving maximum effort, using all available resources, or putting forth one's best performance	(पूर्ण शक्ति अथवा गति से)
All over	Everywhere.	(सभी स्थान पर)
All over with	Finished, done with.	(समाप्त होना)
All right (alright)	Satisfactorily.	(सन्तोषपूर्वक)
All the rage	Very popular.	(अधिक प्रचलित)

Idioms	English Meaning	Hindi meaning
All the same	Nevertheless.	(तथापि, तो भी)
All the while	During the time.	(पूर्ण समयावधि में)
All there	To be mentally alert.	(सावधान होना, रहना)
All up with	Beyond any hope for, dead.	(कोई उम्मीद न होना, मृत्यु होना)
An apple of discord	A cause of quarrel.	(झगड़े का कारण)
An apple of one's eye	Very dear.	(बहुत प्यारा, आँख का तारा)
An axe to grind	To have some personal motives.	(स्वार्थ रखना)
An old flame	A former romantic partner.	(पूर्व प्रेमी)
And so on	Et cetera, etc.	(आदि, इत्यादि)
Angle at	Attempt to get by hint.	(संकेत द्वारा प्राप्ति हेतु यत्न करना)
Anything but	Far from.	(दूर)
Arm-chair critic	A criticizer without posing him/herself.	(अपरोक्ष रूप से आलोचना करने वाला)
Arouse from	To wake up.	(जगना या जगाना)
As a matter of fact	In reality.	(वास्तव में)
As a result of	Due to.	(के फलस्वरूप)
As a rule	According to rules.	(नियमानुसार)
As for	In connection with.	(संबंध में)
As good as	Compare or equate something to a high standard of quality	(वास्तविक रूप से)
As good as gold	Very good.	(बहुत अच्छा)
As good as one's word	To keep one's promise.	(वादा निभाना)
As if	As though.	(जैसे कि)
As long as	Up until.	(जब तक)
As regards	With regard to.	(के संबंध में)
As soon as	No sooner.	(जैसे ही)
As such	Therefore.	(इसलिए)
As sure as gun	To be quite sure.	(निश्चित होना)
As the crow flies	In a straight line.	(सीधे)
As usual	In the usual manner.	(जैसा सामान्यतः होता है)
As well as	In addition to.	(के अतिरिक्त)

Idioms	English Meaning	Hindi meaning
Ask after someone	To inquire about someone.	(किसी के संबंध में जानकारी प्राप्त करना)
Ask somebody in	To invite someone into the house.	(किसी के प्रवेश हेतु अनुमति देना)
At a cross purpose	To have conflicting intentions or goals.	(एक-दूसरे के विपरीत इरादों के साथ)
At a discount	Below the usual price.	(सामान्य मूल्य से कम)
At a loss	To be puzzled.	(घबरा जाना)
At a low ebb	Decreasing.	(घटता हुआ)
At a pinch	In case of necessity.	(आवश्यकता पड़ने पर)
At a snail's pace	A very slow speed.	(बहुत मंद चाल)
At a standstill	Motionless.	(गतिहीन)
At a stone's throw	At a little distance.	(थोड़ी दूर पर)
At a stretch	Constantly.	(निरन्तर)
At a tender age	very young age.	(बाल्यावस्था अथवा किशोरावस्था)
At a time	In one time.	(एक बार में)
At all	In any way.	(किसी भी प्रकार से, तनिक भी)
At all events	No matter what happens.	(चाहे कुछ भी हो)
At all hazards	Inspite of all the obstacles.	(सभी बाधाओं के बावजूद)
At an arm's length	At a distance.	(दूरी पर)
At any cost	Anyhow.	(किसी भी प्रकार)
At bay	Keep something or someone under control	(किसी के पक्षपातियों से सामना होना)
At best	At most.	(अधिकाधिक)
At dagger's drawn	To have enmity.	(दुश्मनी रखना)
At discretion	A decision or action is left to the judgement or choice of a person or authority	(बिना किसी शर्त के)
At ease	Easily.	(सुविधापूर्वक)
At enmity with	At hostility.	(शत्रुतापूर्ण)
At first sight	Seeing for the first time.	(पहली नजर में)
	B	
Bad blood	Ill feelings.	(द्वेषभाव, बुरे विचार)
a Bad egg	A useless, worthless fellow.	(बेकारआदमी)
a Bad patch	A period of difficulties.	(कष्टदायक अवधि, स्थिति)
a Bad quarter of an hour	A short but painful experience.	(क्षणिक दर्दयुक्त अनुभव)

Idioms	English Meaning	Hindi meaning
Bags of	Plenty of, great deal of.	(अधिकता होना)
Bald as a Coot	Totally bald.	(पूर्णत: गंजा)
Barge into	To force inside.	(बलपूर्वक किसी वस्तु को दूसरे स्थान में डालना)
to Be about	To be busy.	(व्यस्त होना)
Be above the law	Not to obey the rule.	(नियन पालन न करना)
Be afraid of one's own shadow	Be very timid.	(अत्यधिक कायर होना)
Be after	In search.	(खोज में)
Be all ears	To listen attentively.	(ध्यानपूर्वक सुनना)
Be at fault	At a loss.	(हानि होना, नुकसान होना)
Be at pains to do	Pay much care	(पर्याप्त धन देना)
Be at the zenith of	Be at the peak of.	(चोटी पर पहुँचना)
Be back bone	A main support.	(मुख्य आधार)
Be born with a silver spoon in one's mouth	To born in a rich family.	(धनाढ्य परिवार में जन्म लेना)
Be drawn	To be attracted.	(आकर्षित करना)
Be even with	To have revenge upon.	(बदला चुकाना)
Be foursquare	To be frank, honest.	(स्पष्टवादी, ईमानदार होना)
Be given to going	Have the habit of something.	(किसी वस्तु की आदत होना)
Be going strong	Be still flourishing.	(फलते-फूलते रहना)
Be hard done by	To treat unfairly.	(उचित व्यवहार न करना)
Be hard up for	To need something direly.	(किसी वस्तु की बहुत जरूरत होना)
Be hung up	Be emotionally upset.	(भावात्मक रुप से परेशान होना)
Be in a brown study	To be absent-minded because of deep thoughts.	(गहन विचारों में डूबे होने के कारण ध्यान न देना)
Be in a false position	To be in misunderstanding	(गलतफहमी में पड़ना)
Be in bad books of	To be bad in somebody's eye.	(किसी की नजर में बुरा होना)
Be in bad odour of	To be out of favour.	(किसी की दृष्टि में अच्छा न होना)
Be in good books of	To be good in someone's opinion.	(किसी की दृष्टि में अच्छा होना)
Be in good odour of	To be in kind favour.	(कृपापात्र होना)

Idioms	English Meaning	Hindi meaning
Be in hot water	To be in troubles.	(परेशानियों में होना)
Be in labour	To be going to give birth.	(प्रसव अवधि)
Be in one's element	To be in agreeable company.	(समान विचारधारा वाला साथ)
Be intimately with	To have close relation with.	(घनिष्ठ सम्बन्ध रखना)
Be lead by the nose	To follow submissively.	(नम्रता से अनुसरण करना)
Be laden with	To be filled with.	(लदा होना, परिपूर्ण होना)
Be on about	To talk about.	(.... के सम्बन्ध में बात करना)
Be on edge	To be in a state of tension, anxiety, or nervousness	(उत्तेजित होना)
Be on one's own kneel	To kneel down to pray.	(प्रार्थना के लिए झुकना, घुटने के बल)
Be on the go	Be very busy.	(अधिक व्यस्त होना).
Be one's own fair hand	By oneself.	(स्वयं के द्वारा)
Be oner	To be an expert or a big lie.	(निपुण अथवा बड़ा झूठा होना)
Be out of one's wits	To be mad.	(पागल हो जाना)
Be quick at	To be fast at.	(फुर्ती से, तेजी से)
Be quit of	To be free from.	(से छुटकारा प्राप्त होना)
Be short sighted	Unable to see or think about the future.	(अदूरदर्शी)
Be unfair to	Not to be good to.	(न्यायसंगत न होना)
Be unsuited to	To be unfit to.	(अनुपयुक्त होना)
Be upset by	To be puzzled by.	(घबरा देना, उलझन में डाल देना)
Be well to do	To be prosperous.	(साधन सम्पन्न होना, अच्छा होना)
Be zero	To end, esp without implementation.	(कार्यान्वयन के पूर्व ही योजना समाप्ति)
Bear a charmed life	To be invulnerable, magically.	(रहस्यमय शक्ति से अभिपूरित)
Bear a hand	To help.	(सहायता करना)
Bear away the palm	To win	(जीतना, पुरस्कार प्राप्त करना)
Bear fruits	Become successful.	(सफल होना)
a Bear garden	A place full of noise and quarrels.	(हंगामायुक्त स्थान)
Bear in mind	To keep in memory.	(याद रखना)
Bear the brunt of	To endure the calamities.	(विषमताओं का हिम्मत से सामना करना)
Bear the cross	To endure adversity, suffering.	(कष्ट सहन करना)

Idioms	English Meaning	Hindi meaning
Bear the palm	To win, to be victorious.	(जीतना)
Beat a retreat	To go back.	(लौटना)
Beat about the bush	To stray from the main point.	(मुख्य विषय से भटक जाना)
Beat black and blue	To beat severely.	(बुरी तरह पीटना)
Beat hollow	A resounding or overwhelming victory or defeat	(परेशान होना)
Beat into	To expound a dull fellow.	(मन्दबुद्धि को समझाना)
Beat off	To face boldly.	(साहसपूर्वक सामना करना)
a Beauty sleep	To sleep before midnight.	(मध्यरात्रि से पूर्व सोना)
a Bed of roses	A comfortable life or place.	(सुखद जीवन या स्थान)
Beef up	To add strength to.	(... को शक्ति प्रदान करना)
Before long	Recently.	(शीघ्र ही)
Beggar description	Beyond description.	(अवर्णनीय)
Behind the scene	Not openly, indirectly.	(अप्रत्यक्ष रूप से)
Below the mark	Not upto the standard.	(स्तरहीन)
Bend down	To bow or incline.	(झुकना)
Bereft of	To be deprived of.	(वंचित होना)
Beside himself	To be puzzled.	(परेशान होना)
Beside the mark	Not to the point.	(असंगत होना)
Best foot foremost	To do one's best.	(उत्तम प्रयास करना)
Between Scylla and Charybdis	Between two great dangers.	(दो मुसीबतों के बीच फँस जाना)
Between the devil and the deep sea	To be in two great difficulties.	(दो कठिनाइयों के मध्य झूलना)
Between two lights	Under cover of darkness.	(अन्धकार की चादर लपेटे हुए)
Beyond all questions	Undoubtedly.	(नि:सन्देह)
Beyond measure	Without limit.	(असीमित)
Beyond the veil	After death.	(मृत्यु के उपरांत)
Bid against	To pay more.	(अधिक भुगतान करना)
Bid debble	Ready to obey.	(आदेश पालन हेतु तत्पर)
Bid fair	To seem likely.	(सम्भाव्य प्रतीत होना)

Idioms	English Meaning	Hindi meaning
Bid goodbye	Farewell	(जाते समय अभिवादन करना, नमस्कार करना)
Bid welcome	To welcome.	(स्वागत सत्कार करना)
Bide one's time	To wait for the right opportunity.	(अनुकूल अवसर की प्रतीक्षा करना)
a Big cheese	An important person.	(महत्वपूर्ण व्यक्ति)
a Bird of passage	A person who doesn't stay in a country.	(परदेशी)
Birds of the same feather	People of the same nature and taste.	(समान प्रकृति एवं पसन्द के लोग)
Bite one's lips	To show hatred.	(घृणा प्रदर्शित करना)
a Bitter pill to swallow	To accept something unpleasant	(अनिच्छित वस्तु स्वीकार करना)
Black art	Use of magic for evil purposes.	(बुरे कार्य हेतु प्रयुक्त जादू)
Black comedy	A pessimistic or tragic comedy.	(निराशापूर्ण या दुःखपूर्ण हास्य)
Black leg	A person who offers to work while the others are on strike	(अन्य लोगों द्वारा हड़ताल पर जाने पर किसी कर्मचारी द्वारा काम करने का प्रस्ताव)
Black ox	Bad luck, misfortune.	(बदकिस्मती)
Black Sheep	Good for nothing fellow.	(व्यर्थ आदमी)
Black tidings	Depressing news.	(हताशाजनक समाचार)
Blessings in disguise	Intrinsically good news but having a bad appearance.	(ऊपर से बुरी दिखने वाली अच्छी बात)
Blood is thicker than water	Strong tie of the blood.	(घनिष्ठ रक्त-सम्बन्ध)
Blood on one's hand	To be responsible for the death of a person.	(किसी व्यक्ति की मृत्यु के लिए उत्तरदायी होना)
Blood run cold	To be horrified.	(भयभीत होना)
Blow one's own trumpet	To praise oneself.	(अपनी ही शेखी बघारना)
Blue blood	To belong to an aristocratic family.	(उच्च परिवार से सम्बद्ध होना)
Blue pencil	To correct, edit or censor.	(संशोधन व सम्पादन करना)
Bolt from the blue	A sudden calamity.	(अनायास आया हुआ संकट)
Bone of contention	The reason of quarrel.	(झगड़े का कारण)
Bone to pick with	Some cause of quarrel.	(झगड़े का कुछ कारण)
Bosom friend	Fast or close friend.	(अभिन्न मित्र)

Idioms	English Meaning	Hindi meaning
Box someone's ears	To wring or twist the ears.	(कान मरोड़ना)
Break even point	No profit - No loss position.	(न लाभ-न हानि)
Break the ice	To break the silence.	(सन्नाटे को तोड़ना)
Break the news	To inform someone about important or significant information	(अचानक चहुँओर समाचार फैलना)
Breathe one's last	To die.	(मर जाना)
Bring down the house	To call forth general and loud applause.	(घर को सिर पर उठाना, नाज-नखरे दिखाना)
Bring home	To make something understood or clear to someone	(समझाना)
Bring into play	To give an opportunity for the exercise of...	(योग्यता प्रदर्शन का अवसर प्रदान करना)
Bring to book	To give punishment.	(दण्ड़ देना)
Bring to light	To reveal.	(प्रदर्शित करना, उजागर करना)
Bring up by hand	To bring up by feeding-bottle.	(जन्म होते ही बच्चे का पालन-पोषण करना)
Bring up the rear	To come last.	(सबसे बाद में आना)
Broke to the wide	Completely bankrupt	(पूर्णत: धनविहीन)
Broken reed	An unbelievable person.	(अविश्वासी व्यक्ति) E
Buckle down to	To prepare for action.	(कार्य के लिए तैयार, तत्पर होना)
Bull in China shop	A heedless destroyer.	(विध्वंसकारी व्यक्ति)
Burn a hole in the pocket	To spend money fast.	(शीघ्रता से अपव्यय करना)
Burn one's fingers	To put oneself into trouble.	(स्वयं को मुसीबत में डालना)
Burn the candle at both ends	To work excessively hard or engage in activities that consume a lot of energy	(एक समय में दो प्रकार से नष्ट करना या उपयोग करना, फिजूलखर्ची करना)
Burn the midnight oil	To study late into the night.	(देर रात्रि तक पढ़ना)
Burn to ashes	To reduce to ashes.	(जलकर राख हो जाना)
Burning topic	Current and hot topic.	(ज्वलन्त विषय)
Burst into tears	To weep heavily, suddenly.	(अचानक जोर-जोर से रोना)
Bury the hatchet	End the quarrel.	(झगड़ा खत्म होना)
But for	Without	(के बिना)
Buy dearly	To make sacrifice to get something.	(... की प्राप्ति हेतु कुछ त्याग करना)

Idioms	English Meaning	Hindi meaning
Buy pig in a poke	Buy something without knowing its value.	(बिना मूल्य अथवा उपयोगिता जाने कोई वस्तु खरीदना)
By a long chalk	By a considerable degree.	(पर्याप्त रूप से, पूर्णत:)
By all means	In every possible way.	(प्रत्येक सम्भव तरीके से)
By degrees	Gradually.	(धीरे-धीरे)
By dint of	By means of.	(... के द्वारा)
By fair or foul means	By any means.	(किसी भी विधि से, चाहे गलत या सही)
By hook or by crook	Any how, at all the costs.	(किसी भी प्रकार, किसी भी कीमत पर)
By long odds	By far, without fail.	(नि:सन्देह)
By no means	In no way.	(किसी भी तरह नहीं)
By oneself	Alone.	(अकेले ही)
By return of post	Immediately.	(तुरन्त)
By the sweat of one's brows	Hard labour.	(कठिन परिश्रम)
By the way	Incidentally.	(फिर भी)
By virtue of	By dint of.	(के बदौलत)
By words of mouth	Orally.	(मौखिक, मुँहजबानी)
C		
Call a meeting	To convey a meeting.	(सभा आयोजित करना)
Call a spade a spade	To talk clearly.	(स्पष्टत: बोलना)
Call attention	To point out.	(इशारे से बताना)
Call forth	To evoke	(आमन्त्रित करना, उभारना)
Call in question	To be doubtful.	(शंकायुक्त या शंका करना)
Call it a day	Stop working.	(काम बन्द कर देना)
Call names	To abuse.	(अपशब्द कहना)
Call to account	To reprimand, scold.	(डाँटना)
Call to mind	To recall.	(स्मरण करना)
Call to order	To call upon to observe the rules of debate.	(वाद-विवाद के नियम आदि के पालन हेतु आगाह करना)
Can of worms	Complicated problem.	(उलझी हुई समस्या)
Cap in hand	With the submissive attitude.	(नम्रता अधीनता का भाव रखना)

Idioms	English Meaning	Hindi meaning
Capable of	Able to do a certain task.	(कार्य को करने की योग्यता)
Caper about	To make merry by playing and jumping.	(खेल में उछल-कूद मचाना)
Capital punishment	Death penalty.	(मृत्यु दण्ड़)
Care a fig	Not to care.	(ध्यान न देना)
Carry all before	To be completely successful.	(पूर्णत: सफल होना)
Carry coals to New Castle	To do unnecessary and useless work.	(उल्टे बाँस बरेली को)
Carry conviction	To be persuasive or convincing in one's words, actions, or arguments	(उचित या सत्य प्रतीत होना)
Carry fortress	To win the fortress.	(किले पर विजय प्राप्त करना)
Carry no weight	Have no influence.	(प्रभावित न करना)
Carry off one's feet	To be in anger, excitement.	(क्रोध, उत्तेजना से अभिभूत होना)
Carry one's point	To persuade others.	(दूसरे लोगों को मनाना, समझाना)
Carry the can	To accept the blame or responsibility.	(आरोप या उत्तरदायित्व स्वीकार करना)
Carry the day	To win.	(जीतना)
Carry through	To accomplish, complete.	(सम्पन्न करना)
Carry too far	To go far.	(दूर तक जाना या ढोना)
Cast a glance at	To look or see.	(देखना)
Cast a slur	To bring discredit.	(बदनामी कराना)
Cast a spell	To put under an enchantment.	(मन्त्रमुग्ध करना)
Cast an aspersion	To defame.	(बदनाम करना)
Cast light upon	To reveal.	(उजागर करना)
Cat nap	To sleep for a while.	(अल्पावधि के लिए सोना, झपकी लेन)
a Cat's paw	Someone used as a tool by another.	(किसी अन्य व्यक्ति को अपने हथियार के रूप में उपयोग करना)
Catch a Tartar	To face a great adversity.	(महान परेशानी, शत्रु से सामना)
Catch a whiff of	To smell.	(सूँघना)
Catch at a straw	A help in dire need.	(आवश्यकता के समय प्राप्त साधन या सहायता)
Catch fire	To be aflamed.	(आग लगना)
Catch one's breath	To stop suddenly.	(अचानक ठहर जाना)
Catch red-handed	To capture someone doing wrong etc.	(रंग हाथों पकड़ना)
Catch sight of	To get glimpse suddenly.	(अचानक किसी पर नजर पड़ना)

Idioms	English Meaning	Hindi meaning
Catch someone's imagination	To rouse interest.	(दिलचस्पी उत्पन्न होना)
Catch the fancy of	To be attractive.	(आकर्षक लगना)
Catch unaware	To surprise.	(आश्चर्यचकित करना)
Catch up with	To reach one's destination.	(किसी को पकड़ना)
Cavil at	To raise captious objection.	(व्यर्थ आपत्ति करना, झगड़ा करना)
Cease one's anxiety	To relieve from worries.	(चिन्तामुक्त करना)
Chalk for cheese	A negligible price for a valuable article.	(नगण्य मूल्य पर बहुमूल्य वस्तु प्राप्त करना)
Change colour	To be turned pale.	(अनुत्तरित हो जाना, पीला पड़ जाना)
Change hands	To be in other's possession.	(अन्य व्यक्ति के कब्जे में होना, जाना)
Change one's tune	To alter one's attitude or way of talking.	(व्यवहार अथवा वार्ताशैली में परिवर्तन)
Chase after	To go or run after.	(पीछे जाना या दौड़ना)
Cheek by jowl	Side by side, close together.	(निकटस्थ होना)
Cheer to the echo	To cheer at heart.	(हार्दिक रूप से प्रसन्न होना)
Chicken-hearted	Timid.	(डरपोक)
Child's play	A very easy task.	(अत्यन्त सरल काम, बच्चों का खेल)
Chip of the old/same block	Worthy son of a worthy father.	(यशस्वी पिता का यशस्वी पुत्र)
Cleanse the Augean stables	To abolish long accumulated evils.	(संचित बुराइयों को समाप्त करना)
Clear a fence	To cross the fence.	(बाड़ या रोक को कूदकर पार करना)
Clear from debt	To pay the debt fully.	(ऋण से मुक्ति प्राप्त होना)
Clear land	To cut down the trees of jungle.	(जंगल के पेड़ काट डालना)
Clear one's throat	To clear the throat by coughing.	(खाँसकर गला साफ करना)
.Clear the decks	To remove obstructions.(बाधाओं को हटाना)	
Clip the wings	To deprive of the means of rising.	(उन्नति के मार्ग में रोड़ा अटकाना)
Close fisted	Miser.	(कंजूस)
a Close shave	A narrow escape.	(बाल-बाल बचना)
Cog in the machine	A person in a big organisation.	(बड़े संस्थान में अमहत्वपूर्ण व्यक्ति)
Coin money	To make large money rapidly, easily.	(तेजी से सुगमता से अधिक धन कमाना)
Cold blooded murder	Murdered brutally, cruelly.	(निर्मम हत्या)

Idioms	English Meaning	Hindi meaning
Cold nip in the air	A feeling of chillness.	(शीतलता का अनुभव होना)
Cold reception	A dry welcome, without enthusiasm.	(रूखा स्वागत)
Cold war	Costile mutual relations.	(पारस्परिक खराब सम्बन्ध)
Come a cropper	To fall again and again.	(बार-बार गिरना)
Come again ?	What did you say? Pardon?	(क्या कहा? क्षमा कीजिए ?)
Come apart	To break into pieces.	(टुकड़े-टुकड़े होना)
Come back to earth	To stop daydreaming.	(दिवास्वप्न देखना, रोकना)
Come clean	To confess.	(अपराध स्वीकार करना, पश्चाताप करना)
Come cropper	Fall heavily.	(जोर से गिरना)
Come hell or high water	Even in difficulties.	(कष्टों में भी, चाहे जो भी हो)
Come home	To understand..	(समझ में आना)
Come in one's way	To interrupt.	(बाधा या विघ्न डालना)
Come into sight	To be visible.	(दिखाई पड़ना)
Come of age	To reach at full legal age, i.e., .	(बालिग होना)
Come off second best	To be defeated.	(परास्त होना. दूसरे स्थान पर रहना)
Come off with flying colours	To achieve extraordinary results.	(असाधारण उपलब्धि प्राप्त करना)
Come on the scene	To come or seen.	(आना, दिखाई पड़ना)
Come out in one's true colours	To appear in one's real character	(अपने असली रूप में आना)
Come to a head	To come into a crisis.	(कठिनाई में पड़ना)
Come to a standstill	To stop moving	(रूक जाना, बन्द हो जाना)
Come to blows	To fight.	(हाथापाई पर उतरना)
Come to grief	To meet with disaster.	(दु:ख की स्थिति में पड़ना)
Come to light	To be revealed.	(प्रकाशित हो जाना)
Come to oneself	To return to normal state of mind.	(पूर्ववत: मनःस्थिति में आना)
Come to pass	To happen.	(घटित होना)
Come to the front	To attain prominence.	(प्रमुख स्थान प्राप्त होना)
Come to view	To be seen.	(दिखाई पड़ना)
Come upto	To be equal to.	(बराबर होना)

Idioms	English Meaning	Hindi meaning
Come up with	To get hold of.	(कब्जे में लेना)
Commit suicide	To do self-murder.	(आत्महत्या करना)
Commit to memory	To learn by heart.	(याद करना)
Cook the account	To falsify the books etc.	(खातों में गड़बड़ी करना)
Cool one's wheels	Kept waiting for.	(प्रतीक्षारत रखना)
Corporal punishment	Bodily punishment.	(शारीरिक दण्ड)
Count chickens before they are hatched	To anticipate huge profit before hand.	(शेखचिल्ली का ख्वाब)
Crocodile's tears	Showy, false tears.	(दिखावा करना)
Cross one's mind	To flash across the mind.	(दिमाग में कौंधना)
Crow over	To triumph over.	(विजय प्राप्त करना)
Cry ditto to	To support someone's statement.	(... के कथन का अनुमोदन करना)
Cry for the moon	To desire for unattainable.	(अप्राप्य की आकांक्षा रखना)
Cry in the wilderness	An ineffective demand.	(प्रभावहीन माँग)
Cry over spilt milk	To repent.	(पश्चाताप करना, हाथ मलना)
Cumber with	To hamper, hinder.	(बाधा डालना)
Curl one's lips	To show hatred.	(घृणा प्रदर्शित करना)
Curry favour	To win favour by flattery.	(चापलूसी करके कृपापात्र बनना)
Cut a fine figure	To influence well.	(अच्छी तरह प्रभावित करना)
Cut a poor figure	To produce a poor impression.	(उचित प्रभाव न डालना)
Cut a sorry figure	Not to get on properly.	(ठीक प्रयास न करना)
Cut above	To be shown higher in position than others.	(स्वयं को दूसरों से श्रेष्ठ समझना, या सिद्ध करना)
Cut corners	To achieve success by the quickest way.	(सीधे रास्ते न जाना)
Cut no ice	To be in effective.	(प्रभावहीन होना)
Cut of one's job	Personal appearance.	(व्यक्तित्व दर्शन)
Cut one dead	To insult deliberately.	(जानबूझकर अनादर, उपेक्षा करना)
Cut one into the quick	To feel badly.	(बुरा लगना, चुभ जाना)
Cut one off with a shilling	To disinherited by bequeathing a trifling sum.	(थोड़ा-सा धन देकर उत्तराधिकार से वंचित करना)

Idioms	English Meaning	Hindi meaning
Cut one's coat according to one's cloth	To accommodate within the available means.	(उपलब्ध साधनों में ही गुजारा चलाना)
Cut one's own throat	To harm oneself.	(स्वयं को हानि पहुँचाना)
Cut short	To silence by interruption.	(बीच में टोककर चुप करा देना)
Cut the gordian knot	To solve difficult situation/problem.	(दुष्कर समस्या का हल करना)
Cut-throat competition	Destructive competition.	(गलाकाट प्रतियोगिता)
	D	
Dampen down	To make weaker.	(शक्तिहीन बनाना या करना)
a Damsel in distress	A helpless woman.	(बेसहारा स्त्री)
Dance attendance upon	To flatter.	(चापलूसी करना)
Dance to someone's tune	Do as one say.	(किसी के हुक्म पर चलना)
a Dark horse	One who suddenly comes into light.	(अचानक ख्याति प्राप्त करने वाला)
Dash off	To leave in haste.	(शीघ्रता में प्रस्थान करना)
Dawdle away	To be slow.	(धीमे होना, करना)
Dawn on/upon	To be clear to the mind.	(स्पष्टत: समझ में आना)
Dead beat	Extremely exhausted, tired.	(पूर्णत: थका हुआ)
Dead hand on/of	Oppressive instincts of someone.	(अत्याचारी प्रवृत्ति)
a Dead letter	To be no longer in force.	(वर्तमान में प्रभावी न होना)
a Dead silence	Immense quietness.	(अत्यधिक शान्ति)
Descant on/upon	To criticize.	(आलोचना करना)
Descent on/upon	To attack suddenly.	(अचानक आक्रमण करना)
Diddle somebody	To deceive, cheat.	(धोखा देना)
Die in harness	To die at workplace.	(सेवा-कर्तव्य करते हुए मरना)
Die in one's bed	To die during sickness.	(रोगावस्था में मृत्यु होना)
Die with one's boots on	To die during war.	(युद्ध में मरना)
Differ from	To have disagreement, difference.	(असहमत होना, भिन्न होना)
Diffident about	Lacking self-confidence.	(आत्मविश्वास की कमी होना)
Dig one's grave	To bring one's ruin.	(स्वयं को तबाह करना)

Idioms	English Meaning	Hindi meaning
Dilly-dally	To dawdle, waste time.	(कुछ कहने/करने में विलम्ब करना, हिचकिचाना)
Dish out	To serve, to share.	(दे देना, बाँटना)
Do for somebody	To manage.	(प्रबन्ध करना)
Do great lengths	Do a great deal.	(कठिन परिश्रम करना)
Do not (don't) mind someone	Not to be bothered, worried.	(चिन्ता न करना)
Do one's best	To put forth one's best efforts.	(श्रेष्ठ यत्न करना)
Do one's damnedest	To do one's very best.	(अपनी ओर से सर्वश्रेष्ठ यत्न करना)
Do one's nuts	To get very angry.	(अत्यन्त क्रोधित होना)
Do or die	To make a final desperate attempt to do.	(अन्तिम महा-प्रयास)
Do somebody	To cheat.	(धोखा देना या छल करना)
Do somebody in	To kill.	(मारना)
Do somebody over	To assault.	(प्रहार करना)
Do someone down	To speak ill of.	(गाली देना)
Do someone well	To provide good food and amenities.	(उत्तम भोजन एवं सुविधाएँ प्रदान करना)
Do something out	To clean out or put in order.	(सफाई करना अथवा स्थान / सामान को व्यवस्थित करना)
Do something over	To refurnish.	(पुन: साज-सज्जा करना)
Do the handsome things	To behave in a magnanimous manner.	(उत्कृष्ट व्यवहार करना)
Do the thing on the sly	To do surreptitiously.	(छल-कपटपूर्ण कार्य करना)
Do to death	To kill.	(मार देना)
Do violence to	To oppose, go against.	(विरोध करना)
Do well out of	To take profit.	(लाभ प्राप्त करना)
Do with something	To make loss.	(नुकसान पहुँचाना)
Dog in the manger	A selfish person.	(स्वार्थी व्यक्ति)
a Dog's life	Very miserable life.	(कष्टमय जीवन)
Done to a turn	Well cooked.	(भली-भाँति पका हुआ)
Done up	Tired or fatigued.	(थका हुआ)
Done with	Finished.	(समाप्त)
Double dealing	Deceitful action.	(धोखाधड़ी पूर्ण कार्य)

Idioms	English Meaning	Hindi meaning
Double Dutch	Illegible or not to be understandable.	(अस्पष्ट अथवा न समझ में आने वाली)
Double-edged sword	An action which can harm others as well as harm oneself.	(अन्य लोगों के साथ ही स्वयं के प्रति हानिप्रद कार्य)
Double-minded	Confused, have different opinions.	(संशय युक्त भिन्न मत का)
Down in the mouth	Out of spirits.	(उत्साहहीन)
Drain the cup of misery to the dregs	To suffer a lot of misery.	(अत्यधिक संकट या कष्ट झेलना)
Draw a bead on	To aim at.	(निशाना लगाना या निशाने पर रखना)
Draw a parallel	To compare.	(तुलना करना)
Draw a veil over	To avoid discussion.	(बहस की उपेक्षा करना)
Draw near	To come near.	(नजदीक आना)
Draw on one's memory	Try to recall.	(याद करने का यत्न करना)
Draw one out	To elicit informations.	(सूचनाएँ प्राप्त करना)
Draw the line	To fix a limit.	(सीमा निश्चित करना)
Drawn match	a position in which no party wins.	(बराबर की बाजी होना)
Drawn in the dumps	To be in bad spirits, depressed.	(हताश, निराश होना)
Drink in	To think over deeply.	(गहन विचार करना)
Drink off	To drink the entire quantity in a gulp.	(एक ही साँस, धूट में पी जाना)
Drink to	To have wine with good wishes.	(विशेष अवसर पर, शुभकामनावश पीना)
Drink up	To finish with drink.	(मदिरापान द्वारा सम्पन्न करना)
Drive one out of one's sense	To madden	(पागल करना)
Drive somebody home	To impress, influence deeply.	(गहरा प्रभाव छोड़ना)
Drive someone in a corner	To drive someone in an inescapable position during discussion.	(वार्तालाप के दौरान अप्रिय स्थिति में पहुँचना)
Drive something into	To hammer something into.	(किसी में कुछ ठोकना)
Drive to the wall	To crush.	(कुचल देना)
Drop a hint	To intimate an inner information.	(आन्तरिक सूचना प्रदान करना)
Drop a letter	To send letter by post.	(डाक द्वारा पत्र भेजना)
Drop a subject	To abandon or omit a matter.	(विषय का त्याग करना)
Drop by drop	One at a time.	(एक-एक करके, बूँद-बूँद से)
Drop in the ocean	Very insignificant amount.	(अत्यल्प मात्रा)

Idioms	English Meaning	Hindi meaning
Drop on one's knees	To bow, humble.	(झुकना)
Drop someone off at	To leave or deliver.	(छोड़ना)
Drown out	Driven out by flood.	(बाढ़ द्वारा बहा के ले जाना)
Dry as dust	Very lazy.	(बहुत आलसी, सुस्त)
Due to	Owing to, because of.	(के कारण)
Due 'to'	To be paid.	(जो भुगतान करना है)
Duck diamond	Beloved.	(प्रेमिका)
During the joint lives	While all alive.	(जबकि सभी जीवित हों)
Dutch courage	Courage inspired by drinking alcohol.	(शराब के नशे से प्राप्त साहस)
	E	
Eager to	To have strong passion.	(तीव्र आकांक्षा रखना)
Eagle eyed	Sharp-sighted.	(दूरदर्शी)
Ear-mark	To set aside for particular purpose.	(विशेष उद्देश्य हेतु सुरक्षित करना)
Earnest money	Security money given in advance.	(जमा की गई धरोहर राशि)
Ear-shot	Hearing distance.	(श्रवण-क्षमता की दूरी)
Early bird gets the worm	One who starts early can be more successful.	(जो पहले प्रारंभ करता है, सफल होता है)
Earth up	to cover with mud, soil.	(पौधों पर मिट्टी चढ़ाना)
Earth-worm	a gravelling fellow.	(औंधेमुँह व्यक्ति)
Easy circumstances	Having influence.	(प्रभावी होना).
Easy come, easy go	Money acquired without efforts is spent mercilessly.	(हराम की कमाई का व्यर्थ जाना)
Easy going	Inactive, indolent.	(चैन का जीवन)
Easy money	Bribe.	(रिश्वत)
Easy virtue	Of loose character.	(चरित्रहीन)
Eat crow	to force to accept unwillingly.	(अनिच्छा से स्वीकार करने को बाध्य करना)
Eat humble pie	To be submissive	(विनम्र होना)
Eat one's head off	To gormandise, gluttony.	(खाते समय जल्दी - बाजी करना)
Eat one's heart Out	to endure peacefully.	(शान्तिपूर्वक सहन करना)
Eat one's salt	To be guest of someone.	(किसी का मेहमान होना)
Eat one's words	To take statement back.	(शब्द वापस होना)

Idioms	English Meaning	Hindi meaning
Eat out of someone's hand	To have complaint against some	(किसी के प्रति शिकायत होना)
Economy of truth	Untrue, false.	(झूठा)
Edge in a word	To get a word in with difficulty.	(किसी शब्द को कठिनाई से समझना)
Eject from	To oust.	(बाहर करना, निष्कासित करना)
Eke out	To make up.	(कमी को पूरा करना)
Elbow room	Having enough space.	(पर्याप्त स्थान होना)
Elf struck	To charm, bewitch.	(जादू-सा करना)
Elixir of life	life giving, saving medicine.	(जीवनवर्द्धक, राक्षक औषधि)
Encumber someone to	to prevent moving freely.	(स्वतन्त्र रूप से चलने से रोकना)
Ended in smoke	To end in nothing.	(कोई परिणाम न निकलना)
Endue with	Be of noble virtues.	(गुण सम्पन्न होना)
Engrossed into	To be absorbed completely.	(विचारमग्न या कार्य में व्यस्त रहना)
Equip with	To provide with.	(उपलब्ध कराना)
Escape from	To be free from somebody's control.	(किसी से बचना, जान छुड़ाना)
Even-handed	To be just.	(ठीक प्रकार से)
Even if	Though.	(यद्यपि, हालांकि)
Even	Minded-To be of calm mind.	(शान्त चित्त)
Evening of life	The old age.	(बुढ़ापा)
Evening star	At the decline.	(अवनति की ओर)
Ever-green	Be fresh always.	(सदाबहार)
Ever-lasting	The omnipotent, the God.	(सर्वशक्तिमान, ईश्वर)
Ever-more	For ever, for always.	(सदैव के लिए)
Every inch	Entirely.	(सम्पूर्ण)
Every inch a gentleman	A well-brought up person.	(कुलीन व्यक्ति)
Everything under the sun	Everything in this world.	(सब कुछ इस संसार में)
Evil eye	Malicious look.	(बुरी नजर)
Exchange blows	To quarrel verbally or physically.	(झगड़ा करना)
Exert on / upon	To apply or put forth effort	(प्रयोग में लाना)
Expatiate about	To dictate in detail.	(विस्तार से श्रुतलेखन करना)

Idioms	English Meaning	Hindi meaning
an Eye for an eye	Tit for tat, to be bad for bad.	(बुराई के बदले बुराई)
Eye-wash	An ineffective remedy.	(आँसू पोंछना)
	F	
Fabian Policy	The slow and cautious strategy to wear out the opposition.	(विपक्ष को समाप्त करने की सावधानीपूर्वक मन्दगतिज नीति).
Face the music	To face the consequences.	(परिणाम को झेलना)
Face to face	In the presence.	(सामना होना)
Fact of the matter	A simple truth.	(वास्तविकता, सत्य)
Fag end	Worthless ramnant	(व्यर्थ अवशेष)
Fair fame	Good name.	(सुप्रसिद्ध)
Fair field and no favour	Equal conditions in a contest.	(प्रतियोगिता में समान स्थिति होना).
Fair hand	Legible writing.	(साफ सुथरा लेख)
Fair means	With honesty.	(ईमानदारी से)
Fair play	Without cheating.	(बिना धोखाधड़ी के)
Fair promise	Better chance.	(अच्छा, अनुकूल अवसर)
Fair sex	A lady.	(महिला)
Fair trade	Just and honest business or bargain.	(उचित एवं ईमानदारी से पूर्ण व्यापार या सौदेबाजी).
Fair weather friend	Friends of good days only.	(अच्छे दिनों के मित्र)
Fairy tale	An incredible story.	(अविश्वसनीय कहानी)
Fall back on	To make the last attempt.	(अन्तिम प्रयास करना)
Fall down to	To hang down to.	(लटकना)
Fall flat	To prove ineffective.	(अप्रभावी होना)
Fall flat on one's face	To fall down on the ground.	(मुंह के बल गिरना)
Fall from the grace	To back slide.	(प्रतिष्ठा कम होना)
Fall foul	To make an attack.	(आक्रमण करना)
Fall in love with	To be in love.	(प्रेम में पड़ जाना)
Fall into a rage	To become angry.	(क्रोधित होना)
Fall into error	To make a mistake.	(त्रुटि करना)
Fall on deaf ears	To be passed unnoticed.	(ध्यान न देना)
Fall on easy prey	To be victim easily.	(सुगमता से शिकार हो जाना)

Idioms	English Meaning	Hindi meaning
Fall on one's feet	To be fortunate.	(भाग्यशाली होना)
Fall over oneself	To be very eager.	(अत्यधिक आकांक्षी होना)
Fall short of	To be of inferior.	(निकृष्ट होना)
Fall to pieces	To slashed or crumble.	(टुकड़े हो जाना)
Fall within	Come in purview of.	(अन्तर्गत होना)
False coin	Counterfeit coin.	(जाली सिक्के)
Fan the flame	To aggravate.	(उत्तेजित करना)
Far cry	A long way or distance.	(पर्याप्त दूरी)
Far fetched	Of a distant meaning.	(दूर का अर्थ रखना)
Far sighted	Viewing to a great distance.	(दूरदर्शी)
Fast friend	Good, bosom friend.	(पक्का दोस्त)
Fast with gout	To be confined.	(एक क्षेत्र या कर्म तक सीमित होना)
Fat brained (or headed or witted)	A stupid fellow.	(मन्द बुद्धि या मुर्ख)
Fatal blow	A death causing blow.	(मृत्युजनक चोट)
A Feather of one's cap	Something to be proud of.	(जिस पर गर्व हो)
Feather one's own nest	To earn by unfair means.	(अनुचित ढंग से पैसा कमाना)
Feel at home	To feel comfortable.	(सुविधाजनक अनुभव करना)
Feel one's ears burning	To feel one is being talked about.	(अपनी बात सुनने का सुख)
Feel the pulse	To find out the opinion of.	(किसी के विचार जानना)
Fiddle	Faddle to trifle.	(छिछोरापन करना)
Fight shy of	To be hesitant.	(सकुचाते हुए कर्म करना)
Fight to the finish	to fight up to the end.	(अन्तिम साँस तक लड़ना)
Fight with their back to the wall	Fight desperately.	(भयानक रूप से लड़ना)
Figure out	To have the solution	(समाधान या हल करना)
Finger in the pie	To be mixed up in the affair.	(किसी कार्य कलाप में शामिल रहना)
First born	First child.	(प्रथम शिशु)
Fish in troubled waters	To take advantage of a chaotic or turbulent situation for personal gain or benefit	(प्रतिकूल अवसर से भी लाभ उठाना)
Fish out of waters	To be like one out of one's element.	(दुविधा में पड़ जाना).

Idioms	English Meaning	Hindi meaning
Fit in with	To suit.	(अच्छा लगना, जँचना)
Flair for	Natural ability to do something.	(कुछ करने की प्राकृतिक देन)
Flake out	Fall asleep due to tiredness.	(थकावट के कारण नींद आना)
Flare up	To intensify the flame of the fire.	(आग को दहकाना)
Flush up-to fill-up	to the level of surface.	(ऊपरी सतह तक भरना)
A Fly in the ointment	A little thing that spoils everything.	(पूर्णतः बर्बाद करने वाली कोई छोटी वस्तु).
Fly into a passion	To be in anger, enrage.	(क्रोधित होना)
Follow suit	To follow the example.	(बड़ो के पदचिन्हों पर चलना)
Fool's paradise	Foolish ideas.	(मूर्ख विचारधारा)
Foot about	To kill time.	(समय नष्ट करना)
Foot the bill	To pay up.	(भुगतान करना)
For good	For good and all, forever.	(सदैव के लिए)
For keep	Forever, always.	(सदैव के लिए)
For long	For many days, longer time.	(अधिक समय तक)
For the best	With the best of intention.	(उत्तम भावनाओं सहित)
For the sake of	for one's sake.	(किसी के लिए)
For the time being	in the present time.	(वर्तमान अवधि में)
For want of	Short of.	(के अभाव में)
Force somebody's hands	To force one to do unwillingly.	(इच्छा विरुद्ध कार्य करने हेतु दबाव डालना).
Forewarn	To warn of danger etc. to be happen in near future.	(भविष्य में होने वाली घटना के सम्बन्ध में सूचित करना)
Forty winks	A siesta	(दिन में, दोपहर को अल्प-निद्रा)
Foul play	Cheating.	(धोखाधड़ी)
Freak out	Make someone angry (or happy).	(किसी को अप्रसन्न या प्रसन्न करना)
From A to Z	From the beginning to the end.	(प्रारम्भ से समाप्ति तक)
From hand to hand	From one person to another.	(एक व्यक्ति से दूसरे व्यक्ति तक)
From hand to mouth	Bare existence.	(निर्धनता का जीवन बिताना)
From pillar to post	From one difficulty to another, one place	(एक कठिनाई से दूसरी कठिनाई में पड़ना, एक स्थान से दूसरे स्थान को दौड़ना).
From sun to sun	Between sunrise and sunset.	(सूर्योदय एवं सूर्यास्त के मध्य)

Idioms	English Meaning	Hindi meaning
From the bottom of one's heart	Very sincerely.	(अन्त: करण से)
From time immemorial	From very ancient times.	(प्राचीनकाल से)
From time to time	Sometime.	(कभी - कभी)
Fuck all	Nothing at all.	(कुछ भी नहीं)
Fuck off	To go away, be off.	(चले जाना)
Fuck up	To spoil.	(बरबाद करना)
Fuck well	Definitely.	(निश्चित)
Fuddy-duddy	Old fashioned people.	(पुराने जमाने के लोग)
	G	
Gain ends	to succeed in purpose	(उद्देश्य में सफलता प्राप्त करना)
Gain on	to be nearer to someone.	(करीब होना या करीब आना)
Gallop ahead of	to progress rapidly.	(शीघ्रता से प्रगति की ओर अग्रसर)
Get a knife into	to kill.	(मार देना)
Get above oneself	have high opinion about oneself.	(स्वयं के सम्बन्ध में ऊँचे विचार रखना).
Get at able	to be accessible.	(अभिगम्य उपयोगी)
Get away (Noun)	to escape after committing a crime.	(अपराध करके भाग जाना).
Get away with	to not be punished.	(दण्डित होना).
Get back in	to return back (of a political party) in power.	(राजनीतिक दल का पुनः शक्ति में आना)
Get back to somebody	to write or speak again to.	(पून: लिखना या बोलना).
Get back to something	to return.	(वापस आना, करना)
Get behind with something	not to proceed with required pace.	(आवश्यकतानुसार गति से आगे न बढ़ना).
Get by on	to manage to survive.	(जीवनयापन हेतु प्रबन्ध करना)
Get down to something	to start to do.	(आरम्भ करना).
Gung-ho	to be excessively or irrationally enthusiastic or zealous	(अप्रत्याशित रूप से उत्साहित होना)
Get in on something	to participate, take part in.	(भाग लेना).
Get in with someone	to become friendly with someone.	(मित्रता होना)

Idioms	English Meaning	Hindi meaning
Get into mess	to make things difficult, disorderly.	(मुश्किल बढ़ाना, अव्यवस्थित करना).
Get into good grace	to gain friendship or favour.	(मित्रता होना, अथवा कृपापात्र होना).
Get Left	to avoid.	(अनदेखा करना)
Get off easy	to get a easy sentence.	(सुगम दण्ड प्राप्त होना).
Get off something	to stop discussion.	(वार्तालाप करना)
Get on one's feet	to stand.	(खड़े होना).
Get on one's nerve	to be worrisome.	(दुःखी या चिन्तित होना).
Get on to	to be prosper.	(सम्पन्न होना).
Get one's back up	to be annoyed.	(परेशान होना, खीझना).
Get over somebody	to forget somebody.	(किसी को भूल जाना).
Get rid of	to become free from.	(छुटकारा प्राप्त होना).
Get something across	to be understood.	(समझ में आना).
Get something back	to receive back the lost thing.	(वस्तु प्राप्त होना).
Get somebody by the short hair	to have complete control over.	(किसी पर पूर्ण नियन्त्रण होना).
Get something down	to swallow something with difficulty.	(कठिनाई से निगलना) .
Get somebody in	to call somebody to serve in home.	(घर में सेवा हेतु बुलाना).
Get something in	to buy something.	(खरीदना).
Get somebody off	to leave a place and go far.	(स्थान छोड़कर कहीं जाना).
Get something off	to remove.	(हटाना).
Get something up	to arrange.	(व्यवस्था करना).
Get the better of	to overcome.	(काबू में करना).
Get the hang of	to understand a thing.	(किसी वस्तु को समझना).
Get up (N)	set of dress.	(वस्त्र संयोजन).
Get up to something	to reach on specific point.	(बिन्दु विशेष पर पहुँचना).
Get wind of	to know the secret.	(रहस्य जान लेना).
Get wise to	to be aware of, alert to.	(सचेत होना).
Ghost of	very faint, faded.	(अस्पष्ट).
Gibble-gabble	a senseless chatter.	(मूर्खतापूर्ण वार्तालाप).
Gibe at	mock at, make fun of.	(हंसी उड़ाना).
Gifted at	a God gift to do something extraordinary.	(असाधारण कार्यों को करने वाली दैवीय भेंट).

Idioms	English Meaning	Hindi meaning
Gift of the gab	ability or art of speaking fluently.	(धाराप्रवाह बोलने की क्षमता या कला).
Gift from the gods	an unearned or unexpected receipt.	(अनपेक्षित वस्तु की प्राप्ति).
Giggle at	to laugh in a silly way.	(मूर्खों की तरह हँसना).
Gird up the loins	to be well prepared for some task.	(कार्य के लिए कमर कस लेना).
Give a damn	to pay attention, to care.	(ध्यान देना).
Give a handle to	to provide an occasion for.	(के लिए अवसर प्रदान करना).
Give a piece of one's mind	to scold someone.	(किसी को डाँटना-फटकारना).
Give a wide berth	remain at a safe distance.	(सुरक्षित दूरी पर रहना).
Give away (M)	a present.	(बिना मूल्य दिये प्राप्त वास्तु).
Give false colours	to misrepresent.	(गलत प्रस्तुतीकरण करना).
Give free reign to	give complete freedom.	(पूर्ण स्वतंत्रता देना).
Give in charge	to handover to police.	(पुलिस को सौंप देना).
Give into someone	to force to surrender.	(समर्पण हेतु बाध्य करना).
Give it to somebody	to criticise.	(आलोचना करना).
Give on	to something-have a view of.	(किसी वास्तु का नजर आना).
Give one's ears	to make sacrifice.	(त्याग करना).
Give oneself airs	to behave arrogantly.	(आक्रामक रवैया अपनाना).
Give oneself over to	to sink into.	(व्यस्त होना, मग्न होना).
Give oneself up	to protect.	(रक्षा करना)
Give somebody away	to escort, esp. bride to the bride- groom.	(दुल्हन को दूल्हे के पास ले जाना, कन्यादान करना).
Give somebody to believe	to convince.	(समझाना).
Give somebody the go-by	to ignore.	(उपेक्षा करना)
Give somebody up	to leave the hope of someone's recovery.	(...का पता मिलने की आशा त्याग देना).
Give something away	to distribute.	(बांटना)
Give something for	to exchange	(विनिमय करना, अदला-बदली करना).
Give something to someone	to pass on an infection.	(संक्रमित करना).
Give the cold shoulder	to discourage a person.	(निराश करना).

Idioms	English Meaning	Hindi meaning
Give the devil his dues	even the wicked should be given praise.	(दुष्ट व्यक्ति की भी उचित प्रशंसा करना).
Give up the ghost	to die.	(मरना).
Give up on somebody	not to believe in somebody's success.	(किसी की सफलता के सम्बन्ध में विश्वास न रहना)
Give vent to	to express one's feelings or thoughts.	(अपने विचारों अथवा भावनाओं को प्रदर्शित करना).
Glad about	to be happy with.	(...से प्रसन्न होना)
Glad of	to be grateful for.	(...हेतु कृतज्ञ होना).
Glad to do	eager to do.	(कुछ करने की आशंका).
Go a wool gathering	to become lunatic.	(पागल हो जाना).
Go about something	to manage.	(प्रबन्ध करना)
Go after	try to win.	(पीछे पड़ जाना).
Go along	go ahead, proceed.	(आगे बढ़ना).
Go back on	to withdraw, break the promise.	(वादा तोड़ना).
Go behind something	to search.	(खोज करना).
Go berserk	to become mad.	(पागल हो जाना).
Go broke	to become moneyless.	(निर्धन होना).
Go bust	to become bankrupt.	(दिवालिया हो जाना).
Go by someone	to trust upon someone as correct.	(सत्य विश्वास करना).
Go by something	to assess about the truthfulness from one's statement.	(किसी के कथन से सच-झूठ का पता लगाना).
Go down before someone	to be defeated.	(हराया जाना).
Go down like a nine-pin	to fall with a bang, heavy sound.	(जोर से गिरना).
Go for nothing	to be considered of no value.	(कोई मूल्य न होना).
Go forward	to proceed.	(आगे बढ़ना).
Go hard with	to prove a serious matter.	(गंभीर मामला सिद्ध होना).
Go haywire	to be destructed.	(विक्षिप्त होना)
Go home	to appeal deeply.	(गहराई से अपील होना, करना).
Go in for the kill	to kill the opponent.	(विरोधी को मार देना).
Go it alone	act by oneself.	(स्वयं कार्य करना).

Idioms	English Meaning	Hindi meaning
Go leeward	to move in the direction of blow.	(हवा के रुख की ओर चलना)
Go out of the way	to take extra trouble.	(अतिरिक्त कष्ट सहना).
Go phut	to collapse (of car, machine etc.).	(कार, मशीन आदि खराब होना).
Go scot free	to be free from punishment.	(दण्ड से छुटकारा प्राप्त होना).
Go spare	to become furious or frenzied.	(उत्तेजित या विक्षिप्त होना).
Go the whole hog	to do something thoroughly.	(ठीक प्रकार सम्पन्न करना).
Go through a bad patch	to be a bad luck, have bad days.	(कष्टों में पड़ना).
Go through the mill	to undergo training or sufferings.	(प्रशिक्षण प्राप्त करना या कष्ट उठाना).
Go to all lengths	to do all the best.	(हरसंभव प्रयत्न करना).
Go to one's heart	to touch deeply.	(गहराई तक स्पर्श करना).
Go to roost	to retire for the night.	(सो जाना).
Go to the dogs	to be destroyed.	(बरबाद हो जाना).
Go to the wall	to be defeated.	(पराजित हो जाना).
Go west	to be destroyed.	(बरबाद हो जाना).
a Golden mean	neither too much nor too little.	(पर्याप्त मात्रा, साधन).
a Golden opportunity	a very favourable chance.	(स्वर्ण अवसर)
Good at	doing nicely.	(अच्छा कार्य करना).
a Good egg	an excellent person.	(उत्कृष्ट व्यक्ति).
Good for nothing	of no use.	(बेकार)
a Good hand at	an expert.	(निपुण, दक्ष).
Good money	earned genuinely, with honesty.	(ईमानदारी से अर्जित).
Grand slam	the winning of all major championships in a season.	(सत्र के सभी प्रमुख पुरस्कार जीतना).
Grapes from thorns	to fetch good even from bad.	(अच्छा प्राप्त करना).
Grasp the nettle	to deal a problem firmly.	(समस्या को दृढ़तापूर्वक सुलझाना).
Grass on somebody	to inform the police.	(पुलिस को मुखबिरी करना).
Grass roots	initial stage.	(प्रारम्भिक अवस्था).
Grass over	to cover with turf.	(घास से ढँकना).
Graze on	to be teased by.	(तंग करना या होना).
Grease the palm	to bribe or give tip.	(रिश्वत देना).
Great a hand at	to be expert at.	(निपुण होना).

Idioms	English Meaning	Hindi meaning
Great for	an ideal person.	(आदर्श व्यक्ति).
a Great gun	an important person.	(महत्वपूर्ण व्यक्ति).
Greek gift	to give to harm.	(क्षतिजनक उपहार लेना).
Green eye	have jealousy.	(द्वेष भाव रखना).
Green fingers	expert in gardening.	(बाकवानी में निपुण).
Green harm	an inexperienced person.	(अनुभवहीन व्यक्ति).
Green with envy	be envious.	(ईष्यालु होना).
Grind one's own axe	to think about one's own self.	(अपना उल्लू सीधा करना).
Grind one's teeth	to grind teeth with anger.	(प्रतिक्रिया स्वरूप, गुस्से से दाँत पीसना).
Grow away from	have less relationship.	(सम्बन्ध या मिलन कम करना).
Grow from- into	of developing nature.	(विकासशील प्रकृति का होना).
Grow into	to be with passage to time, gradually.	(धीरे-धीरे होना).
a Guiding light/star	one who leads.	(नेतृत्व करने वाला).
Guilty of	offender of.	(अपराधी).
	H	
Habeas Corpus petition	a writ to produce the prisoner in court.	(कैदी को न्यायालय में प्रस्तुत करने हेतु रिट, प्रार्थना).
Hail from	belong to, come from.	(सम्बद्ध होना, से आना).
a Hair	breadth escape narrow escape.	(बाल-बाल बचना).
Half hearted	to try with less efforts.	(अधूरे मन से कार्य करना)
Half the battle	anything that brings one well on the way of success.	(सफलता की ओर सुचारु रूप से अग्रसर होना).
Hammer something into	to force one to learn by repeating again and again.	(याद करने हेतु बाध्य करना).
Hands to be full	to be very busy.	(बहुत व्यस्त होना)
Hang around	to be around someone.	(किसी के चारों तरफ मँडराना).
Hang by a thread	a critical condition.	(गम्भीर स्थिति).
Hang fire	to be hesitated, reluctant.	(असमंजस में पड़ना)
Hang in balance	undecided matter.	(अनिर्णीत या बिना निष्कर्ष के अधर में लटकना)
Hang on one's lips	to listen eagerly.	(उत्सूकता से सुनना)
Hang on to	to.hold.	(पकड़ना)

Idioms	English Meaning	Hindi meaning
Hang over one's head	to be in danger.	(खतरे में होना, पड़ना)
Hang up one's hat	to take up one's abode.	(निवास बनाना या शरण लेना)
Hanker after	to have intense desire.	(तीव्र इच्छा रखना या होना)
Hard as nails	cruel person.	(क्रूर व्यक्ति)
Hard of hearing	to be somewhat deaf.	(कम सुनाई पड़ना)
Hard nut to crack	a difficult problem to solve.	(कठिन समस्या समाधान हेतु)
Harp on the same string	to repeat tediously.	(रट लगाये रखना)
Hatchet job	destructive attack.	(सर्वनाशजन्य आक्रमण).
Haul over the coals	to scold, chide.	(डॉटना - फटकारना).
Have a go	to try.	(प्रयत्न करना).
Have a hand	to be concerned.	(सम्बन्धित होना).
Have a screw loose	disturbed mentally.	(मानसिक रूप से असन्तुलित).
Have an ear to the ground	to be alert about happenings secretly.	(गुप्त बातों की भी जानकारी रखना).
Have an eye to the main chance	to have one's own interests.	(केवल अपना स्वार्थ रखना).
Have bats in the belfry	to be crazy, slightly mad.	(विक्षिप्त होना).
Have done with	to lose interest in.	(रुचि नष्ट होना).
Have itching ear	to be desirous to listen.	(सुनने को उत्सूक)
Have kittens	to be worried.	(चिन्तित होना).
Have no truck with	to avoid dealings.	(दूर रहना या व्यवहार समाप्त करना).
Have one's eyes on	to want or desire.	(चाहना).
Have someone's ears	to win favour of.	(किसी व्यक्ति का हृदय जीतना).
Have something on	to put on.	(वस्तू, परिधान धारण करना).
Have the blues	to be depressed, gloomy.	(कष्टमय, चिन्तित होना).
Have the checks	to presume.	(सम्भावना होना).
Have the whip-hand of	to be in a position to control.	(नियन्त्रण करने की स्थिति में).
Have to do with	to have connection with.	(सम्बन्ध रखना या होना).

Idioms	English Meaning	Hindi meaning
Have too many irons in the fire	to be engaged in too many things.	(अनेक कार्यों में संलग्नता रखना).
Have two strings to one's bow	to have two sources of income.	(आय के दो साधन होना).
Heads I win, tails you lose	to win in any case.	(हर हाल में जीतना).
Heap coals of fire on/upon one's head	to one's enmity by kindness.	(सद्भाव से शत्रुता का अन्त करना).
Hear someone out	to listen upto the end.	(अन्त तक सुनना).
Heart in the right place	to be faithful and true hearted.	(निष्ठावान एवं सहृदय होना).
Heart to heart	very openly.	(खुले दिन से).
Heave in sight	to be in sight.	(दृष्टिगोचर होना).
Heels of Achilles	the weak point of a person.	(व्यक्ति की कमजोरी).
Helter skelter	in haste and puzzle.	(घबराते हुए जल्दबाजी में).
Herculean task	work which requires extraordinary strength to accomplish at	(श्रमसाध्य कर्म, कठिन काम).
Himalayan blunder	a serious mistake.	(महान गलती).
Hit below the belt	to take advantage by unfair means.	(अनुचित उपायों से लाभ उठाना).
Hit or miss	success or failure.	(सफलता या असफलता).
Hit the high spots	to be excess of.	(अधिकता होना).
Hit the mark	to achieve one's object.	(उद्देश्य पूर्ति करना, होना).
Hit the nail on the head	do exactly the right thing.	(सही निशाने पर चोट मारना).
Hit upon something	to get ideas by chance.	(संयोगवश विचार आना).
Hobson's choice	to be selected to take.	(किसी वस्तु का चयन करना अथवा लेना या न लेना).
Hocus pocus	a deception, to cheat.	(धोखा).
Hold good	remain valid.	(जारी रहना).
Hold one's ground	to be firm.	(दृढ़ रहना).
Hold one's jaws	to stop talking.	(वार्तालाप बन्द करना)
Hold one's peace	keep silence.	(शान्त, चुप रहना).
Hold the fort	to be firm on one's position.	(अपने स्थान पे जमे रहना).

Idioms	English Meaning	Hindi meaning
Hold the scales even	to be impartial.	(निष्पक्ष रहना).
Hold water	to prove sound.	(ठीक सिद्ध होना).
Hope against hope	to hope even when the case seems hopeless.	(व्यर्थ की आशा रखना).
Horse trading	hard bargaining.	(कठिन सौदेबाजी करना).
House of ill fame	place of prostitution.	(वेश्यालय).
How come ?	how does it happen?	(यह कैसे हो गया?).
Human powder keg	to be like a bullet.	(बंदूक की गोली के समान तेज होना) .
Hung up	in the state of anxiety.	(व्यग्रता की स्थिति में).
Hush money	to give bribe to keep silence.	(शान्त रहने के लिए रिश्वत, घूस देना).
	I	
Ill at ease	to be uncomfortable, disturbed.	(अशान्त, चिन्तित होना).
Ill blood	enmity.	(शत्रुता).
I'll buy that I shall accept that	explanation though it seems surprising	(अविश्वसनीय तथ्य या बात को भी स्वीकार करने हेतु तत्पर).
Impinge upon	to affect.	(प्रभाव डालना).
Implicit in	to be firm, uncontroversial.	(पक्का एवं निर्विवाद).
Impose on/upon	try to make one accept.	(लादना).
Improve on/upon	to achieve a better standard.	(बेहतरी प्राप्त करना).
Impulsion to	strong urge to do something.	(कुछ करने के लिए प्रबल आकांक्षा).
Impute to	to give responsibilities to.	(उत्तररदायित्व सौंपना).
In a body	together.	(साथ-साथ).
In a daze	in a fix.	(प्रतिकूल, कष्टप्रद स्थिति में).
In a fix	in puzzling state.	(घबराहट की स्थिति में).
In a jiffy	to be in a hurry.	(शीघ्रता में).
In a measure	upto some extent.	(किसी सीमा तक).
In a nutshell	concisely briefly, in a few words.	(संक्षेप में).
In a state of	in condition of.	(...की दशा में)
In a state of nature	naked.	(नग्न अवस्था में होना).
In abeyance	in suspension.	(असमंजस में, दुविधा में).
In absentia	in the state of absence.	(अनुपस्थिति, अनुपलब्धि की स्थिति में).

Idioms	English Meaning	Hindi meaning
In accordance with	according to.	(...के अनुसार).
In addition to	along with.	(.....के साथ, के अतिरिक्त).
In all	in total, altogether.	(सबको जोड़कर).
In an instant	within a wink.	(पलभर में).
In bad nick	not to be in good health, ill.	(अस्वस्थ होना).
In brief	in short.	(संक्षिप्त में).
In case	if.	(यदि).
In character	in keeping.	(सामंजस्य रखना).
In cold blood	with cruelty.	(निर्दयता के साथ).
In common with	along with.	(साथ-साथ),
In consideration of	due to, for.	(... के कारण)
In deep waters	in great difficulties.	(अत्यधिक कठिनाई में).
In embryo-immature, in under	developing stage.	(अविकसित अवस्था).
In excess	more than.	(अधिक).
In exchange of	in return of.	(के बदले में).
In fact	indeed.	(वस्तुत:).
In favour of	take side of.	(...के पक्ष में).
In fine	in short.	(संक्षिप्त में).
In force to be	in operation, going to.	(लागू होना).
In front of	in face of	(के समक्ष, सामने).
In full swing	in full glory, at a fast pace.	(पूरे जोरों पर).
In good nick	to be in sound health.	(स्वास्थ्य का अच्छा होना)
In good part	in good faith, without offence.	(सद्भावना से ग्राह्य करना).
In hand	under control.	(नियंत्रण में).
In high feather	be full of spirits.	(उत्साहित होना).
In high spirits	enthusiastic and jovial.	(उत्साह से एवं प्रसन्नता से ओत-प्रोत).
In hot haste	in a hurry.	(शीघ्रता में)
In infancy	the beginning of, childhood.	(प्रारम्भिक अवस्था में, बचपन में).
In jest	not seriously.	(गम्भीरता रहित).
In keeping	to be of same in nature, homogenous.	(समान प्रकृति का होना).
In kind	in the same way.	(उसी प्रकार, समान रूप में).

Idioms	English Meaning	Hindi meaning
In lieu of	in place of, instead of.	(के बदले में).
In meal or malt	in one way or the other way.	(किसी न किसी प्रकार).
In merry pin	in joke.	(मजाक में).
In no time	at once.	(तुरन्त).
In no way	not at any cost.	(किसी भी तरह नहीं).
In on	participating in.	(हिस्सा लेना).
In one's element	in state of being congenial.	(स्वभावत: अनुरूपता).
In one's teens	in between and years.	(किशोरावस्था).
In order to	'to' or 'for'.	(के लिए).
In points of	from the point of view.	(...के दृष्टिकोण से).
In proportion to	in the ratio of.	(...के अनुपात में).
In pursuance of	to effort constantly to achieve.	(उपलब्धि हेतु निरन्तर प्रयास).
In queer street	in debt.	(कर्ज में डूबा हुआ).
In quest of	in search of.	(खोज मे).
In rags	in worn out dress.	(फटे-पुराने वस्त्रों में).
In regard to	in comparison with.	(...की तुलना में).
In respect of	in opinion of, in the eye of.	(... के दृष्टिकोण से).
In response to	in reply of.	(..... के उत्तर में)
In retrospect	to recall the past event.	(पिछली घटना को याद करना).
In round numbers	approximately, roughly.	(लगभग).
In search of	in quest of	(... की खोज में, तलाश में).
In short	in brief,	(संक्षिप्तत:).
In spite of	notwithstanding.	(....... के बावजूद भी).
In sum	briefly, in summary.	(संक्षेप में).
In the act of	in between.	(... के मध्य में).
In the air	not decided so far.	(अनिश्चित होना).
In the ascendent	to upwards.	(ऊँचे उठते हुए).
In the cotton line	to follow the trade.	(कार्य का अनुसरण करना).
In the dark	keep ignorant about.	(अन्धकार में रखना).
In the driver's seat	to have control.	(नियंत्रण में रखना).
In the egg	in the early stage.	(प्रारम्भिक अवस्था में).
In the event of	in case of.	(यदि ऐसा हो तो).

Idioms	English Meaning	Hindi meaning
In the face of	in despite of.	(...के बावजूद).
In the family way	to start a family	(गर्भवती होना).
In the guise of	in false dress, in disguise.	(भेष बदलकर, छिपकर).
In the heart of	at the centre place.	(मध्य में).
In the hope of	to be in hope.	(आशा में).
In the jaws of	in the grip of.	(कब्जे में, शिकंजे में).
In the long run	ultimately.	(अन्ततः).
In the know of	to be informed.	(सूचित रहना).
In the making	in developing stage.	(प्रगतिशील अवस्था में).
In the mean time	meanwhile, at the sometime.	(समय विशेष में).
In the melting pot	in a confused state.	(अनिश्चित स्थिति में).
In the midst of	in the middle of.	(...के बीच में).
In the nick of time	just in time, at the critical moment.	(बस समय से).
In the prime of life	best part of life.	(जीवन का श्रेष्ठ भाग, यौवनावस्था).
In the rear of	in behind.	(पीछे).
In the red	in loss or debt.	(हानि में अथवा कर्ज में).
In the running	to have good prospects.	(उत्तम परिणाम रखना).
In the same boat	in the same condition.	(समान स्थिति में):
In the teeth of	to be against.	(विरुद्ध होना).
In the twinkling of an eye	in a moment, in no time.	(पलक झपकते ही).
In the vicinity of	on the campus of.	(... के क्षेत्र में, परिसर में).
In the wake of	immediately after.	(...के तुरन्त पश्चात).
In the wars	to hurt oneself.	(स्वयं को चोट पहुँचाना).
In toto	entirely.	(पूर्णतः).
In touch with	in communication or direct relation with.	(सीधे सम्बद्ध होना)
In two ticks	in moments.	(क्षणभर में).
In unions with	in confidence, with approval.	(विश्वास में, सहमति से).
In vain	of no use.	(व्यर्थ होना).
In view of	having regard to.	(दृष्टिकोण से).
In vogue	to be in fashion, popular.	(लोकप्रिय, प्रचलित होना).
Indebted to	owing money to.	(कर्जदार होना).

Idioms	English Meaning	Hindi meaning
Inhibit somebody from	to put obstacle.	(अवरोध उत्पन्न करना).
Inkling of	a little knowledge.	(अल्प ज्ञान).
Into the bargain	besides, in addition to.	(साथ ही).
Inveigh against	to argue violently.	(वाद-विवाद करना या शब्द प्रहार करना).
Iron hand	with strictness.	(कड़ाई से).
Iron out	to settle.	(घर बसना, बसाना).
Iron will	strong conviction.	(दृढ़ विश्वास).
Itching palm	habit of taking bribe.	(रिश्वत लेने की आदत).
Itsy Bitsy	very small.	(अत्यंत छोटा).
	J	
Jack of all trades	one who can turn his hand to anything.	(हर काम में माहिर).
Jail bird	a hardened criminal.	(नियमित कैदी).
Jar upon	to irritate.	(चिढ़ाना).
Jaundiced eye	to have prejudice or jealousy.	(पूर्वधारणा या ईर्ष्या रखना).
Jaw at	someone to annoy with words.	(बोलकर चिढ़ाना).
Jib at	to express no desire.	(इच्छा प्रकट न करना).
Jiggered up	to be exhausted, tired, worn out.	(थका हुआ).
Jiggery- pokery	in a magical way.	(जादू-मन्तर होना).
Jim-Jams	restlessness, unease.	(उलझन, घबराहट).
Jitter bug	habit of dancing.	(नृत्य करने की आदत).
Job's news	bad news.	(बुरा समाचार).
Jog trot	slow but walk regularly.	(धीमा परन्तु लगातार चलना).
Join battle	to start fighting.	(झगड़ा शुरू करना).
Join issue with	to be differ with.	(मतभेद होना, भिन्न विचार रखना).
Join the majority	to die.	(मरना).
Jolly foot	a happy fellow.	(प्रसन्नचित्त व्यक्ति).
Jolly well	certainly, surely.	(नि:सन्देह).
Jot down	to write down.	(लिखना).
Juda's kiss	any act of treachery under the guise of kindness.	(दया प्रदर्शन में छिपा हुआ विश्वासघात, झूठा प्रेम).
Just so exactly,	I agree.	(पूर्णत: सहमत होना)

Idioms	English Meaning	Hindi meaning
	K	
Kangaroo Court	non-government court.	(गैर-सरकारी कचहरी).
Keen as mustard	extremely eager.	(अत्यन्त आकांक्षा रखना)
Keen eye	fully alert.	(पूर्णत: जागरुक).
Keen on	to be interested in.	(... में रुचिवान होना)
Keen set	to be hungry of.	(भूखा होना).
Keep a good table	to serve sumptuous dishes.	(स्वादिष्ट भोजन परोसना).
Keep a thing dark	to keep a thing secret or to conceal.	(... छिपाये रखना, गुप्त रखना).
Keep an eye	to be alert.	(सावधान रहना).
Keep an open table	to entertain all the visitors.	(सभी आगन्तुकों का स्वागत करना).
Keep at bay	to keep the enemy at a distance.	(दुश्मन को दूर ही रखना).
Keep body and soul together	for survival.	(जीवन-यापन हेतु).
Keep early hours	early to bed and early to rise.	(रात्रि में शीघ्र सोना, प्रातः शीघ्र उठना).
Keep house	to maintain house.	(आर्थिक रूप से घर सँभालना)
Keep in touch	to remain in contact.	(सम्पर्क रखना)
Keep in with	to maintain relation.	(सम्बन्ध बनाये रखना).
Keep one guessing	to put in doubt.	(शक में डालना).
Keep one's balance	to remain stable.	(स्थिर रहना).
Keep one's hair on	to lose temper, to break out in anger.	(क्रोधित हो जाना)
Keep one's hand above water	to keeps out of debt.	(ऋण से मुक्त होना).
Keep one's own counsel	to keep a discreet silence.	(विचारशील शान्ति रखना)
Keep one's powder dry	to keep one's energy for action.	(सदैव तत्पर रहना)
Keep pace	to forward with equal, constant speed.	(समान गति से बढ़ना).
Keep quiet	about to say nothing about.	(चुप रहना).
Keep sake	cheap small gift.	(सस्ता एवं छोटा उपहार).
Keep the ball rolling	to keep conversation going on.	(लगातार बात किये जाना).
Keep the wolf from the door	to avoid starvation.	(भुखमरी से बचने के लिए).
Keep the world from the door	keep away from poverty.	(निर्धनता से दूर रखना) .

Idioms	English Meaning	Hindi meaning
Keep up appearance	to keep one's prestige, image.	(अपनी इज्जत बनाये रखना).
Kick the bucket	to die.	(मर जाना).
Kick up a row	make a great noise.	(अत्यधिक शोरगुल करना).
Kill the fatted calf for	to arrange a lavish reception.	(धूमधाम से स्वागत करना).
Kill the time	to waste time.	(समय नष्ट करना).
Kill two birds with one stone	to serve two purposes at one time.	(एक तीर से दो शिकार करना).
Kill with kindness	to harm by pretending to be kind to.	(भलाई करने का दिखावाकर हानि पहुँचाना)
Kindle with	to shine.	(चमकना).
King of terrors	the death.	(मृत्यु).
Kingdom come	the life after death.	(मृत्यु के पश्चात् जीवन).
Kip down	to go to bed.	(सो जाना).
Kiss the dust	to be humiliated.	(अपमानित होना).
Kiss the rod	accept the punishment.	(दण्ड स्वीकार करना)
Kit out	to equip with, to supply.	(आपूर्ति करना).
Knee deep in	to be busy in.	(व्यस्त होना)
Knit the brows	to frown.	(भौंहें चढ़ाना, त्यौरियाँ चढ़ाना).
Knock against	to collide with.	(टकरा जाना).
Knock down price	auction price.	(नीलाम में बोली गई कीमत)
Knock one's head against a brick wall	to get nothing.	(भी प्राप्त न होना).
Knock the bottom out of	to make ineffectual, bring to nothing.	(अप्रभावी बनाना, कोई परिणाम प्राप्त न होना).
Knock the living day lights out of	to beat severely.	(पिटाई करना).
Knotty problem	a difficult problem, situation.	(जटिल समस्या, स्थिति).
Know on which side the bread is buttered	to recognise the benefits.	(लाभ की जानकारी रखना या पहचानना).
Know what one is about	to be farsighted and prudent.	(दूरदर्शी एवं बुद्धिमान होना).
	L	
Labour of love	work undertaken without a hope of emolument.	(मेहनताने की आशा किए बिना काम करना).

Idioms	English Meaning	Hindi meaning
Lack of	to be short of.	(कमी होना).
Languish in	to live wretchedly, in poor condition.	(अभावों में जीवन व्यतीत करना).
Lapped in luxury	brought up in luxury.	(विलासिता में पलना).
Last cast	the last venture.	(अन्तिम प्रयास).
Last enemy	the death.	(मृत्यु).
Late for	to be late.	(विलम्ब करना, होना).
Laugh into someone's face	to contempt someone.	(आलोचना करना).
Laugh like a drain	to laugh aloud.	(जोर-जोर से हँसना).
Laugh somebody down	to silence by laughing at.	(हँसी उड़ाकर चुप कराना).
Laugh up one's sleeves	to laugh in disguise.	(मन ही मन हँसना-मुस्कराना).
Launch into	to start.	(किसी कार्य को प्रारम्भ करना).
Lay a ghost	to drive off so called evil spirit.	(तथाकथित). भूत-प्रेत उतारना).
Lay an idea	to put idea before.	(... के समक्ष विचार-प्रस्तूति).
Lay at one's door	to be charged for.	(दोषारोपण करना).
Lay down the specks	to search.	(शोध, खोज करना).
Lay hands on	to seize.	(अधिकार में लेना).
Lay into	to attack.	(आक्रमण करना).
Lay one's head together	to consult together.	(एक साथ विचार मग्न होना) .
Lay something on	to bet.	(शर्त लगाना).
Lead by the nose	to control absolutely and unduly.	(पूर्ण व अनुचित अधिकार जमाना).
Lead someone on	to persuade.	(प्रेरित करना).
Lead to the altar	to marry.	(विवाह करना).
Leap in the dark	uncertainty about outcome.	(परिणाम की अनिश्चितता).
Leave for	to go, depart.	(जाना, प्रस्थान करना).
Leave it at that	to take no further action.	(कोई कार्यवाही न करना).
Leave no stone unturned	to make all possible efforts.	(हर सम्भव यत्न करना).
Leave one in the lurch	to leave one in difficulties.	(कठिनाई में किसी का साथ छोड़ना).

Idioms	English Meaning	Hindi meaning
Lend an ear	to listen.	(सुनना).
Let alone	not to mention, much less.	(वर्णन न करना).
Let bygones be bygones	let past quarrels be ignored.	(पुराने झगड़ों को भुलाना).
Let drive at	to aim a blow at.	(किसी पर निशाना लेना).
Let someone off	to give pardon.	(क्षमा करना).
Let the grass grow under one's feet	to procrastinate.	(अवलम्बित करना, टालना) .
Letter (to the)	in order, accordingly.	(भली-भांति).
Lick into shape	to be in discipline, esp. by means of drill and instructions.	(निर्देशों आदि की सहायता से अनुशासन में रहना) .
Lick one's lips	to be impatient to eat.	(खाने के लिए लालायित होना) .
Lick the dust	to accept defeat.	(हार मान लेना).
Lie back	to enter, come into.	(प्रवेश करना)
Lie in one's teeth	to tell a lie without shy.	(बेशर्मी से झूठ बोलना)
Lie in the bed one has made	to suffer for one's own misdeeds.	(अपने दुष्कर्मों के कारण हानि उठाना).
Lie in wait	to keep waiting for the victim.	(घात लगाकर बैठना).
Lie to someone about	to tell a lie.	(झूठ बोलना).
Like a bat out of hell	very quickly.	(तीव्रता, शीघ्रता से).
Like greased lighting	very fast.	(बहुत तेज).
Like the wind	very fast.	(बहुत तेज).
Like wildfire	very quickly.	(बहुत तेजी से).
Lion's share	the biggest share.	(सबसे बड़ा हिसा).
Live by one's wits	to earn livelihood by deceit or fraud.	(धोखाधड़ी करके धन कमाना).
Lock, stock and barrel	entirely.	(पूर्णत:).
Long drawn agony	great sufferings.	(अत्यधिक कष्टदायक).
a Long purse	abundance of money.	(पर्याप्त धन होना).
Look back on	to recall, remember.	(याद करना).
Look black at	to look with anger.	(गुस्से से देखना).
Look daggers	to look with anger.	(क्रोध से देखना या क्रोधित दिखना)
Look down upon	to regard as inferior.	(तुच्छ समझना).

Idioms	English Meaning	Hindi meaning
Look in the face	to be bold.	(साहसी होना).
Look nifty	to do quickness, hurry up.	(जल्दी, शीघ्रता करना).
Look nippy	to be quick, in haste.	(शीघ्रता में).
Look sharp	to make haste.	(जल्दबाजी करना).
Look to one's laurels	to take care not to lose one's pre eminence.	(अपने गर्व को यथावत बनाये रखना).
Look you	take notice of this.	(इसका ध्यान रखना).
Loose ends	unsettled matter.	(विवादास्पद, अनसुलझे मामले).
Lord it over	to domineer over.	(धौंसा जमाना).
Lose one's grip	to lose control.	(नियन्त्रण खो देना).
Lose the day	to be defeated.	(पराजित होना).
Lose the face	to be humiliated.	(अपमानित होना).
Lots of	many.	(अनेक).
Loud mouthed	one who talks too much or too offensively, a boaster.	(अत्यधिक, आक्रामक रूप में बोलने वाला, शेखी खोर).
Lumber up with	fill up with.	(भरा हुआ).
Lump in the throat	an emotional state.	(भावात्मक, उत्तेजित अवस्था).
Lump someone together	to consider people together.	(सभी के बारे में सोचना).
	M	
Mad as a March hare	to be disturbed.	(किसी विशेष परिस्थिति में विक्षिप्त होना).
Mad with	much excited.	(अत्यधिक उत्तेजित होना).
Maiden speech	first speech.	(प्रथम भाषाण)
Mailed fist	force's strength, military might.	(सैन्य शक्ति).
Main stay	main support.	(मुख्य आधार, सहायता).
Make a bid for	try to obtain.	(प्राप्त करने हेतु यत्न करना).
Make a clean breast of	to confess.	(सच्चे दिल से कार करन).
Make a dead set at	to combine to attack by arguments.	(तर्क-प्रहार हेतु एकत्र होना).
Make a face of	to grimace.	(मुंह बनाना, चिढ़ाना).
Make a fortune	to become rich.	(धनवान बन जाना).
Make a go of	to make a success of.	(को सफल बनाना).
Make a mark	to achieve distinction.	(विशेषता, विशेष योग्यता प्राप्त करना).
Make a motion	to make an appeal	(एक अपील करना)

Idioms	English Meaning	Hindi meaning
Make a mountain out of a molehill	make a trifle a big issue	(बात का बतंगड़ बनाना, तिल का ताड़ बनाना)
Make a move	start action, be active	(कार्रवाई शुरू करना, सक्रिय रहना)
Make a pass at	to be attracted	(आकर्षित होना)
Make a pile of	to make a fortune, to earn	(मालामाल करना, कमाई करना)
Make against	to militate, tell against	(विपरीत प्रभाव डालना, हानि पहुंचाना)
Make amends	to compensate	(हर्जाना देना, त्रुटि के लिए क्षमा माँगना)
Make an end of	to end	(समाप्त करना)
Make an example of	to punish	(दंड देना)
Make an exemption	to object	(आपत्ति करना)
Make an exhibition of oneself	to behave foolishly	(बेवकूफ़ाना व्यवहार करना)
Make aware of	to make cautious, informed of	(सतर्क करना, जागरूक करना)
Make both ends meet	to earn to just meet out the necessities	(आवश्यकता पूर्ति योग्य आय)
Make good	to compensate	(मुआवज़ा देना)
Make head or tail of	to understand	(समझना)
Make inroads on	to encroach, interfere	(आक्रमण करना, हस्तक्षेप करना)
Make light of	to treat lightly	(छिपाना, हल्का महसूस करना)
Make merry	to hold festival, be jovial	(उत्सव मनाना, प्रसन्न रहना)
Make mincemeat of	to destroy utterly	(पूरी तरह नष्ट करना)
Make much ado about nothing	to make much of little things	(बात का बतंगड़ बनाना)
Make one's blood/ flesh creep	to be filled with horror	(भयभीत होना)
Make one's mark	to be distinguished	(पहचान बनाना)
Make one's mouth water	to have a strong desire for	(तीव्र इच्छा होना)
Make oneself scarce	to go away, be off	(गायब होना, दूर चला जाना)
Make out	to understand	(समझना)
Make shift	a temporary expedient or substitute	(चलानेवाला व्यवसाय)
Make the most of	to make complete use	(पूरी तरह से उपयोग करना)
Make up one's mind	to determine	(निर्धारित करना)
Malice towards	desire to harm others	(दूसरों को हानि पहुंचाने की इच्छा)

Idioms	English Meaning	Hindi meaning
Man in the moon	a very rare person	(बहुत ही दुर्लभ व्यक्ति)
Man in the street	a common person	(साधारण व्यक्ति)
Man of iron	a strong man	(एक मजबूत आदमी)
Man of letters	a scholar	(विद्वान)
Man of mark	a renowned person	(प्रसिद्ध व्यक्ति)
Man of parts	a man of talent	(प्रतिभाशाली व्यक्ति)
Man of straw	good for nothing	(बेकार व्यक्ति)
Man of the world	an experienced man	(अनुभवी व्यक्ति)
Mania for	to lean towards	(विषयासक्त होना)
Many men, many minds	as many persons, so many opinions	(जितने व्यक्ति उतने विचार)
Mare's nest	a false rumor	(एक झूला झूला)
Marry off	to find a spouse for one's son or daughter	(पुत्र या पुत्री के लिए जीवनसाथी ढूंढ़ना)
Marry money	the dowry	(दहेज)
Mass of (the)	the majority in number	(अधिकांश)
Mean business	to be in earnest	(गंभीर होना)
Meet halfway	to be prepared for compromise	(मध्यमार्ग ढूंढ़ना)
Meet the case	to be satisfactory	(संतुष्ट करना)
Meet the ear	to be audible	(सुनाई देना)
Mend or end	to improve or ruin	(सुधारना या नष्ट करना)
Milk of human kindness	human compassion	(मानवीय दयालुता)
Mince matters/ words	to speak of things with affected delicacy or to soften an account unduly	(बातें बहुत धीमे या अनुचित रूप से करना)
Miss the mark	to fail	(असफल होना)
Money for jam	money for nothing	(बिना कुछ किए पैसे पाना)
Mother wit	common sense	(सामान्य समझ)
Much cry and little wool	disappointing outcomes	(निराशाजनक परिणाम)
	N	
Nail a lie	Expose a lie	(झूठ का पर्दाफ़ाश करना)
Nail one's colours to the mast	Declare one's beliefs or loyalty openly and firmly	(अपने विश्वास या निष्ठा को स्पष्ट और पक्के तरीके से घोषित करना)

Idioms	English Meaning	Hindi meaning
Narrow circumstances	hard days, poverty.	(संकीर्ण परिस्थितियाँ)
Natter on about	to chatter, talk aimlessly.	(कुछ के बारे में बातचीत करना)
Needle woman	a lady tailor.	(एक महिला सिलाईदार या दर्जी)
Neither chick nor child	no child.	(न तो बच्चा है और न जवान, एक मध्यवर्ती चरण में होने वाला को दर्शाने के लिए)
Neither head nor tail	have nothing.	(किसी चीज को समझने में असमर्थ, स्पष्टता या सहजता की कमी)
Neither here nor there	to be irrelevant.	(यहां नहीं और वहां नहीं, अप्रासंगिक या महत्वहीन होना)
a Nig-nog	a fool.	
Nigger in a wood pile	something that mess good thing.	(अच्छी वस्तु को नष्ट करने वाला).
Night	side of the dark, gloomy side of.	(रात के समय की ओर जो अंधकारशील होती है)
Niminy-piminy	be affected.	(प्रतिकूल)
Nine day's wonder	a short-lived glory.	
Nip cheese	a stingy fellow.	(छोटे - छोटे टुकड़े चीज़ चुराना)
Nip in the bud	to hinder the development.	(पहले ही चरण में किसी चीज़ को रोकना या समाप्त करना)
Nit-witted	innocent.	(मूर्ख या मूर्खतापूर्ण)
Nitty-gritty	the gist, main point.	(किसी चीज़ के सबसे महत्वपूर्ण या मौलिक पहलुओं या विवरण)
No end	having no limit.	(सीमा या निष्कर्ष के बिना, अनंत)
No love lost	having no love.	(दो लोगों के बीच आपसी अनबन या शत्रुता)
No way	under no circumstances, absolutely not	(बिल्कुल नहीं, असंभव)
Nose about (or around/into)	to search out	(किसी के मामलों में घुसना या खोजना)
Not fit to hold a candle to	not to be in comparison with.	(किसी दूसरे की तुलना में उत्कृष्ट या क्षमताशाली नहीं होना)
Not in one's line	to be out of one's province.	(अपने विशेषज्ञता या रुचि के क्षेत्र में नहीं होना)

Idioms	English Meaning	Hindi meaning
Not in voice	unable to sing well.	(मौजूद नहीं होना या नहीं होने के रूप में गणना नहीं होना)
Not one's cup of tea	an unwanted thing.	(किसी की पसंद नहीं होना या उससे रुचि नहीं होना)
Not worth one's salt	to be quite worthless.	(सम्मान या विचार के पात्र नहीं होना)
Notch up	to get something.	(कुछ प्राप्त करना या स्कोर करना)
Nuclear family	the basic family unit consisting of the mother and father with their children.	(बच्चों सहित माता-पिता का परिवार).
O		
Object to	have objection to.	(आपत्ति, एतराज होना).
Obtain from	to get from.	(किसी से प्राप्त होना).
Of a kind	somewhat, to some extent, as it were.	(कुछ सीमा तक).
Of a piece	as if of the same piece, the same in nature.	(समान गुण-धर्म सहित).
Of course	certainly, definitely.	(निश्चय ही)
Of late	recently.	(हाल ही में).
Of no avail	of no use, useless.	(बेकार).
Of no use	useless.	(व्यर्थ).
Of one mind	to have agreement.	(सहमति रखना).
Of the first order	to have eminent position, highest degree.	(सर्वोच्च, प्रमुख स्थान रखना).
Of the first water	of rare excellence.	(असाधारण).
Off one's own bat	by one's own efforts.	(अपने प्रयासों से).
Off scouring	to refuse.	(मना करना).
Off the map	no account of.	(बेकार व्यक्ति या वस्तु).
Off the record	out of record, not to publish.	(रिकार्ड से बाहर, न छपने योग्य).
Ogle at	to look curiously.	(उत्सुकता सहित देखना).
Oil one's hands	to bribe.	(घूस देना).
Old as the hills	very old.	(प्राचीन).
Old head on young shoulders	more intelligent and experienced than age.	(उम्र से अधिक बुद्धिमान).
On account of	because of.	(कारणवश).
On all fours	to be analogous, strictly comparable.	(समानता होना) .
On no account	not at all.	(बिल्कुल नहीं).
On no occasion	on no time.	(किसी भी अवसर पर नहीं)

Idioms	English Meaning	Hindi meaning
On one's last legs	come to close.	(समाप्ति की ओर, नजदीक आना)
On one's mettle	to rouse to do best.	(श्रेष्ठता प्राप्ति हेतु तत्पर होना)
On patrol	on security watch.	(सुरक्षा - चौकसी पर) .
On the alert	to be aware.	(सावधान रहना).
On the bad nick	in ill health.	(अस्वस्थ रहना).
On the brain	to be constantly in thoughts.	(निरन्तर विचारों में रहना).
On the brink of	to be near to.	(नजदीक होना, किनारे पर होना).
On the cards	on plan, likely.	(विचारणीय, संभवत:)
On the carpet	under consideration.	(विचाराधीन).
On the credit	on delayed payment.	(उधार).
On the dot	within time.	(समय से).
On the drink	drunken.	(मदिरापान किये हुए).
On the eve of	at the time of.	(के अवसर पर).
On the horns of a dilemma	to face a difficult situation between two problems.	(मुसीबत में फँसना) .
On the job	in action.	(क्रियाशील होना).
On the occasion of	on the opportunity of, eve of.	(अवसर पर).
On the point	strike the actual thing.	(के बिन्दु पर, नजदीक).
On the pretence of	to make an excuse.	(बहानेबाजी करना).
On the rack	towards destruction, collapse.	(बरबादी की ओर).
On the rebound	to start a new bonding.	(नये सम्बन्ध बनाना).
On the right side	one's age being less than.	(किसी संख्या से कम आयु होना).
On the rocks	to be penniless.	(धन रहित होना)
On the score of on the	ground of.	(के आधार पर)
On the sly	secretly.	(गुप्त रूप से).
On the spur of the moment	at once.	(तुरन्त).
On the tenterhooks	in impatient suspense or anxiety.	(अत्यधिक संशय या बेचैनी में होना) .
On the tip of tongue	to be difficult to recall something during the speech.	(बोलते समय कुछ याद न आना) .
On the upgrade	towards progress.	(उन्नति की ओर, स्वस्थ्य में सुधार की ओर).

Idioms	English Meaning	Hindi meaning
On the verge of	on the point of.	(नजदीक, किनारे पर)
On the wane	to decline gradually.	(शनैः-शनैः कम होना या समाप्त होना).
On the watch	to be under vigil.	(निगरानी के अन्तर्गत)
On the whole	generally speaking, all things considered.	(सब ध्यान में रखते हुए).
On the wrong side	one's age being more than.	(किसी संख्या से अधिक उम्र का होना).
On tiptoe	to be greatly excited.	(अत्यधिक उत्साहित या उत्तेजित होना).
Once again	once more.	(एक बार फिर).
Once for all	forever.	(हमेशा के लिए).
Once in a blue moon	very rarely, seldom.	(बहुत कम).
Once in a way	very rare.	(बिरले).
One foot in the grave	about to die.	(धीघ्र मरने वाला).
One on one	face to face.	(आमने-सामने).
One or two	a few.	(थोड़ा-सा, कुछ).
One to one	corresponding each one uniquely to other.	(एक-दूसरे से विलक्षण होना) .
Oodles of	great amount, much.	(अधिक).
Open-mouthed wonder	a great surprise.	(अत्यधिक आश्चर्यजनक).
Open out	to lose one's shyness.	(लज्जाहीन होना).
Open secret	known to all.	(सर्वविदित).
Open to somebody	to be available to someone.	(सुलभ होना).
Open up	to start up a business.	(व्यापार प्रारम्भ करना).
Order of the day	popular thing of the age.	(कोई प्रचलित बात)
Other than	except, apart.	(के अतिरिक्त).
Out cry	loud cry, shout.	(चीख, तेज शोर).
Out from under	out of a difficult situation.	(कठिन परिस्थिति से बाहर निकलना).
Out growth	natural growth, development.	(प्राकृतिक विकास)
Out-Herod	to be cruel.	(निर्दयी होना).
Out of date	obsolete.	(पुरानी).
Out of elbow	poor.	(गरीब).
Out of gear	in worse condition.	(खराब हालत में).

Idioms	English Meaning	Hindi meaning
Out of joint	out of order.	(खराब हो जाना).
Out of one's grasp	beyond someone's reach.	(वश से बाहर होना) .
Out of order	out of course.	(ठीक स्थिति में न होना).
Out of pocket	without money.	(बिना धन के, पैसों के).
Out of question	not possible.	(असम्भव).
Out of sorts	not being well.	(अस्वस्थ होना).
Out of spirits	be gloomy .	(उत्साहहीन, निढाल होना).
Out of the blue	unexpectedly.	(संयोगवश).
Out of the way	to be not in proper order.	(गलत ढंग से होना).
Out of the wood	free from problems.	(कठिनाइयों, समस्याओं से मुक्त).
Out of work	to be unemployed.	(बेरोजगार होना).
Out to out	overall, altogether.	(सर्वोपरि).
Outside one's ken	out of knowledge.	(जानकारी में न होना).
Outstay ones welcome	to stay too long.	(अधिक देर या दिनों तक ठहरना).
Overt act	something obviously done in execution of a criminal intent.	(अपराध भाव से कुछ कार्य करना).
Owing to	due to.	(कारणवश)
	P	
Pace something of	To measure by steps.	(कदमों से चलकर नापना)
Pack away	To keep, pack in a box.	(सन्दूक में रख देना)
Pack in	To give something up.	(त्याग देना)
Pack of fools	A company of idiots.	(मूर्खों का समूह)
Pack one's bag	To be ready to go.	(प्रस्थान के लिए तत्पर रहना)
Pack out	To fill completely.	(पूर्णरूपेण भरना)
Paint a lily	To attempt to beautify that which is already beautiful.	(सुन्दरतम को अधिक सुन्दर बनाने का यत्न)
Painted lady	A butterfly.	(तितली)
Pandora's box	A source of evil powers.	(बुराईयों का भण्डार)
Paradise on earth	A heaven on land.	(पृथ्वी पर स्वर्ग)
Pass into	Be a part of.	(अंग बन जाना)
Pass muster	To accept as satisfactory.	(सन्तोषजनक स्वीकृति)
Pass out	To give away.	(देना, बाँटना)

Idioms	English Meaning	Hindi meaning
Put up with	To tolerate.	(सहन करना)
Past master	An expert.	(विशेषज्ञ)
Pat oneself on the back	To pay congratulation.	(शाबासी देना)
Patch up	To mend, to fill.	(पेंच लगाना, भर देना)
Patient with	To have content.	(सन्तुष्ट होना)
Pay lip service	To give word, make promise.	(वादा करना)
Pay off old scores	To have one's revenge.	(बदला चुकाना)
Pay one back in one's own coin	Tit for tat.	(जैसे का तैसा)
Pay one's way	To be not in a debt.	(कर्जदार न होना)
Peak a boo	Game for amusing little ones.	(नन्हे-मुन्नों को बहलाने हेतु खेलना)
Pell mell	In confusion or fix.	(उलझन, घबराहट में)
People of quality	Of high class.	(उच्चवर्गीय)
Pester with	To be troubled with.	(से परेशान होना)
Petticoat government	The undue influence of women.	(स्त्रियों का अनुचित दबाव, प्रभाव)
Pick holes in one's coat	To find the fault.	(गलतियाँ खोजना)
Pick up a quarrel	To seek opportunity to fight.	(झगड़ने हेतु अवसर तलाशना)
Pick up the tab	To pay the bill.	(बिल का भुगतान करना)
Pin drop silence	Unexpected peace.	(गहन खामोशी)
Pin one's faith	To place full reliance upon.	(पूर्ण विश्वास रखना)
Pin prick	Little troubles.	(छोटी-मोटी परेशानियाँ)
Pine away	to be ill and die.	(बीमार पड़ना और मृत्यु हो जाना)
Platonic love	A love that is only spiritual and, therefore, devoid of sensuality.	(आध्यात्मिक, पवित्र प्रेम)
Play a double game	To act dubiously.	(धोखाधड़ी करना)
Play a second fiddle	To take a subordinate part.	(गौड़ भूमिका निभाना)
Play one false	To deceive, act deceitfully.	(धोखा देना)
Play one's cards well	To play an intelligent role.	(समझदारी से कार्य करना)
Play the fool	To act foolishly.	(धोखा खा जाना)

Idioms	English Meaning	Hindi meaning
Play the game	To act honourable according to rules of conduct.	(नियमानुसार उचित रूप से कार्य सम्पादन करना)
Play truant	To remain absent from duty or from the class.	(कार्य स्थल या कक्षा से भाग जाना)
Play with fire	To trifle ignorantly with matters liable to cause suffering.	(अनजाने में हानिप्रद मामलों में हाथ डाल देना)
Pocket an insult	To bear insult.	(अपमान सहना)
Pocket an affront	To receive or submit to without showing resentment.	(बिना प्रतिवाद प्रदर्शन के प्राप्त करना या प्रस्तुत करना)
Pocket/swallow one's pride	To be humble oneself to accept the situation.	(परिस्थितिवश नम्र बनना या अपमान सहना)
Point blank	Directly, clearly.	(सीधे साफ तौर पर)
Point of view	In the opinion.	(विचार, राय में)
Poison one's ears	To speak ill, untrue of someone.	(कम भरना)
Poke one's nose into	To interfere with.	(हस्तक्षेपर करना)
Poles apart	Widely separated.	(काफी दूर, मतभेद)
Pour oil on troubled water	To calm down the anger.	(क्रोध को शान्त करना)
Prick up one's ears	To become suddenly attentive.	(अचानक सचेत होना)
Prima facie	On the first consideration.	(प्रथम दृष्टया देखने पर)
Pull a long face	To look dismal.	(मुहँ लटकाना, दु:खी दिखना)
Pull one's leg	To harass, to cut the jokes.	(तंग करना, मजाक उड़ाना)
Pull the wire	To exercise secret indirect influence.	(अप्रत्यक्ष रूप से प्रभाव डालना)
Pull the wool over one's eyes	To deceive.	(धोखा देना)
Pull to pieces	To criticise adversely.	(कटु आलोचना करना)
Pull together	To cooperate, help.	(सहयोग करना)
Pull well with	To live in amity.	(प्रेमपूर्वक जीवन व्यतीत करना)
Put a good face on	To be happy.	(प्रसन्न रहना)
Put a jinx on	To bring one's bad luck, bad days.	(कठोर समय, बुरे दिन आना)
Put a new face on	To change the aspect of.	(पहलू को बदलना या प्रभावित करना)
Put a person through one's paces	To testify someone.	(व्यक्ति की परीक्षा लेना)

Idioms	English Meaning	Hindi meaning
Put a quart into a pint pot	To attempt the impossible.	(असम्भव यन करना)
Put a question	To ask.	(पूछना)
Put a spoke in one's wheel	To obstruct the progress.	(उन्नति में रोड़े अटकाना)
Put an end to	To finish.	(समाप्त कर देना)
Put hands in pocket	To give charity.	(दान देना)
Put in cold storage	To neglect something.	(.... की उपेक्षा करना)
Put on the market	To offer for sale.	(विक्रय हेतु प्रस्तुति)
Put one in mind	To keep in memory.	(स्मृति में रखना)
Put one's foot down	To refuse to yield.	(कुछ करने या विचार करने से मना कर देना)
Put one's foot in	To do blunder.	(भारी भूल करना)
Put one's head together	To consult with each other.	(एक-दूसरे से सलाह करना)
Put one's shoulder	To the wheel to do work with one's own efforts.	(स्वयं अपने प्रयासों से किसी कार्य को करना)
Put paid to	To finish, to destroy chances of success in.	(सफलतादायक अवसरों को नष्ट कर देना)
Put pen to paper	To start writing.	(लिखना शुरु करना)
Put the cart before the horse	To do something in a wrong way.	(गलत ढंग से कार्य करना)
Put the saddle on the right horse	To blame the actual guilty person.	(वास्तविक अपराधी को पहचान लेना)
Put the screw on	To bring pressure to.	(...के लिए दबाव डालना)
Put to the sword	To kill.	(मार देना)
Put two and two together	To reason logically.	(तर्कसम्मत निष्कर्ष निकालना)
	Q	
Quail at/before	Feel of fear.	(भय अुभूति होना)
Qualify for	To be entitled to.	(पात्र होना)
Queer fish	Eccentric person.	(सनकी व्यक्ति)
Queer one's pitch	To upset, puzzle.	(घबरा देना)
Quibble about/over	To argue over small, trifling thing.	(तुच्छ वस्तु के लिए लड़ना)

Idioms	English Meaning	Hindi meaning
Quid pro quo	To give or receive something in return.	(बदले में विनिमय में देना अथवा लेना)
Quids in	In a very favourable or profitable situation.	(अत्यन्त अनुकूल अथवा लाभप्रद स्थिति में)
Quiet as the grave	To be of extreme quiet.	(श्मशान शान्ति)
Quite the thing	To be fashionable.	(फैशन के योग्य होना)
	R	
Rabid hate	A great hate.	(अत्यधिक घृणा)
Rack one's brain	To think too much.	(अत्यधिक सोच-विचार करना)
Rack rent	The exorbitant rent.	(अत्यधिक किराया)
Radical errors	Basic or fundamental mistakes.	(आधारभूत त्रुटियाँ).
Radical idea	Basic or fundamental principle.	(आधारभूत सिद्धांत)
Rain down	To flow in large quantity.	(अधिक मात्रा में बहना)
Raise from the dead	To restore life.	(जीवन लौट आना)
Raise hell	To create hell.	(शंका उत्पन्न होना)
Raise the banner	To lead.	(नेतृत्व करना)
Raise the temperature	To increase hostility, enmity.	(द्वेष भाव बढ़ाना)
Raise the veil	To remove cover.	(पर्दा हटाना, उठाना)
Rake over old ashes	To recall the past.	(बीती बातों को याद करना)
Rally round	To prompt to help.	(सहायता हेतु तत्पर होना)
Rapt in	To spell bound.	(तल्लीनता से)
Rate soundly	To criticise severely.	(कड़ी निन्दा करना)
Rather better than	To be in excess than.	(से कहीं अधिक)
Rave up	Lively party, get together.	(जीवन्त पार्टी)
React against	To do or speak against.	(के विरूद्ध प्रतिक्रिया करना)
Read between the lines	To hit at the real meaning.	(वास्तविक मतलब पता करना)
Reason with	To try to convince.	(समझाने को यत्न करना)
a Red letter day	A memorable day.	(अविस्मरणीय, यादगार दिवस)
Red rag to a bull	Something that irritates.	(उत्तेजनात्मक बात, कार्य)
Red tape	Excessive and unnecessary adherence to formalities.	(लालफीताशाही)
Redolent of	Having a smell.	(गन्ध अनुभव करना)
Reel something off	To repeat or say without pause.	(बिना रूके बोलते जाना)

Idioms	English Meaning	Hindi meaning
Reek with	To be covered with.	(से सना हुआ, ढ़ँका हुआ)
Rescue from	Save from.	(बचाना, रक्षा करना)
Resolve on/upon	To take firm decision.	(पक्का निर्णय लेना)
Rest on	To rely on, count on.	(भरोसा करना)
Rest on one's laurels	To retire from active life.	(सक्रिय जीवन से अवकाश लेना)
Rest on one's oars	To stop working for a while and to take rest.	(कुछ क्षणों के लिए कार्य रोक देना तथा विश्राम करना)
Result from	Due to, conclusion of.	(का परिणाम)
Revolt against	To rebel against.	(बगावत करना, क्रान्ति करना)
Rich as jews	Very wealthy.	(अत्यन्त धनी)
Rift in the lute	Any action or thing that causes discord or disharmony.	(एक छोटा सा काम या बुराई जिससे गड़बड़ उत्पन्न होना, काम खराब होना)
Right-hand man	A very helpful person.	(अच्छा सहायक)
Ring out	To celebrate the departure of, farewell.	(विदाई समारोह आयोजित करना)
Rip up old sores	Reopen the quarrel.	(पुन: झगड़ा करना)
Rise to the occasion	To help at the hour of need.	(आड़े वक्त पर मदद करना)
Roll up one's sleeves	To be ready for contest.	(मुकाबले के लिए तैयार रहना).
A Rolling stone	A man not sticking to his job.	(अपने काम में न जमने वाला व्यक्ति)
Rope of sand	Something seems effective but actually worthless.	(दिखने में प्रभावशाली, परन्तु वास्तव में व्यर्थ)
Royal road	An easy and popular way.	(आसान रास्ता)
Rub shoulders	To mix up.	(मिलना-जुलना)
Rub the wrong way	To annoy, to irritate by tactless handling.	(गुस्सा दिलाना, खीझ उत्पन्न करना)
Rule the roost	To dominate, govern.	(शासन करना)
Run about	To shuttle from one place to another in hurry.	(तेजी से इधर-उधर दौड़ना)
Run against	To fight.	(लड़ना)
Run along	To be of.	(चले जाना)
Run amuck	Rush to in a frenzy.	(उत्तेजनावश दौड़ना)
Run at	To attack.	(आक्रमण करना)
Run down	To kill.	(मार देना)
Run in the same groove	To maintain relations in good spirits.	(सम्बन्धों को उत्तम भावना से बरकरार रखना)

Idioms	English Meaning	Hindi meaning
Run it fine	To allow very little margin, as of time.	(समय आदि का अत्यल्प अंश प्रदान करना)
Run out	To run short.	(कमी पड़ना, कम हो जाना)
Run short	Shortage of.	(कमी होना)
Run sore	A continuous source of problems.	(समस्याओं का निरन्तर माध्यम)
Run to earth	To search out.	(तलाश करना)
Rush one's fences	To act precipitately.	(प्रबलता से, साहसपूर्वक कार्य करना)
Rustle up	To arrange, gather together.	(व्यवस्था करना, एकत्र करना)
	S	
Sail close to the wind	To take risk.	(जोखिम उठाना)
Salt of the earth	An Ideal person.	(आदर्श व्यक्ति)
Satisfy the examiner	Pass the examination.	(परीक्षा में सफलता प्राप्त करना)
Saturate something with	To soak or make wet.	(सोख लेना, या भिगो देना)
Save one's skin	To protect oneself.	(स्वयं को बचाना)
Saw down	To cut down by the help of saw.	(आरी से काटकर गिराना)
Say a good word for	To recommend.	(सिफारिश करना)
Scale down	To lessen.	(कम करना, घटाना)
School-master is abroad	Education and intelligence are now widely spread.	(शिक्षा एवं ज्ञान अब चहुँ ओर फैल रहा है)
School of adversity	In worse circumstances.	(बुरी स्थिति में)
Scrap through	To pass just now.	(अभी-अभी गुजरना)
Scratch one's head	To be perplexed.	(परेशान हो जाना)
Screw up one's courage	To have courage.	(साहस अथवा धैर्य रखना)
Seal of love	A kiss.	(चुम्बन)
See day light	To reach at expected point.	(लक्ष्य तक पहुँचना)
See eye to eye	To think alike, to be agreed.	(समान विचारधारा रखना, सहमत होना)
See red	To be very angry.	(अत्यन्त क्रोधित होना)
See the back of	To get rid of	(मुक्ति प्राप्त करना, छुटकारा पाना)
See the light	To be born.	(जन्म लेना)
See the world	To be highly experienced.	(अत्यधिक अनुभवी होना)

Idioms	English Meaning	Hindi meaning
Send one about one's business	To dismiss peremptorily.	(अन्ततः कार्यमुक्त कर देना, निकाल देना)
Send round the hat	To take up a contribution.	(चन्दा माँगना, उगाहना)
Send someone packing	To dismiss summarily.	(पदच्युत करना)
Serve one out	To retaliate upon.	(से बदला लेना, चुकाना)
Serve one's right	To get one's reward.	(अपना पुरस्कार, उपहार प्राप्त करना)
Serve one's time	To be an apprentice, trainee.	(प्रशिक्षु के रूप में सेवा करना)
Set at naught	To ruin.	(नष्ट कर देना, हो जाना)
Set by the ears	Be a mischief maker.	(शैतानी करना, तंग करना)
Set on foot	To inaugurate, to start.	(शुभारम्भ करना)
Set one's face against	To oppose sternly.	(तीव्र विरोध करना)
Set price on one's head	To offer a reward for killing or help in arresting a criminal.	(अपराधी को मारने या पकड़वाने हेतु इनाम की घोषणा)
Set teeth on edge	To irritate.	(खीझ उत्पन्न करना)
Set Thames on fire	To do extraordinarily or exceptionally.	(असाधारण कार्य करना)
Seventh day (the)	The Saturday.	(शनिवार)
Shake in one's shoes	To tremble with fear.	(भय से काँपना)
Sharp practice	Cheating.	(धोखाधड़ी)
Sheet of anchor	The place of protection or shelter.	(आश्रय स्थल)
Shell out	To pay.	(चुकाना)
Shot in the arm	a boost or stimulus that provides encouragement, motivation	(थर्रा भरना)
Shot in the locker	Without money in pocket.	(खाली जेब)
Show a clean pair of heels	To flee away.	(भाग जाना)
Show one's face	To appear.	(उपस्थित होना)
Show one's hand	To reveal one's intentions.	(आश्रय, अभिप्राय प्रदर्शित करना)
Show one's teeth	To threat.	(धमकी देना)
Show one's true colour	To show one's real character.	(असली रूप दिखाना)
Show the white feather	To run away.	(भाग जाना)

Idioms	English Meaning	Hindi meaning
Sign of wonder	A miracle.	(चमत्कार)
Sinews of war	The money.	(धन)
Single combat	A fight between two persons.	(दो व्यक्तियों के बीच झगड़ा होना)
Sit on the fence	To hesitate between two opinions.	(दुविधा में पड़ जाना)
Skin of one's teeth	To escape narrowly.	(बाल-बाल बचना)
Sleeping partner	An inactive partner in business.	(निष्क्रिय साझेदार)
Slip of the pen	A small unintentional mistake in writing.	(लिखते समय गलती हो जाना)
Slip of the tongue	A mistake of speech.	(बोलते समय त्रुटि होना)
Small purpose	Having no much practical benefit.	(व्यवहारिक उपयोगिता या लाभ न रखना)
Smell a rat	To have reason to suspect.	(आशंका, संदेह होना)
Snake in the grass	A hidden enemy.	(छिपा हुआ दुश्मन)
Snap one's finger at	To defy, with arrogance.	(अवहेलना या अवज्ञा करना)
Softsoap	Flattery.	(चापलूसी)
Sow one's wild oats	To engage, involve in lust.	(यौन सम्बन्ध बनाना)
Speak volumes for	To serve as a strong testimony to.	(श्रेष्ठ प्रमाण होना)
Spill the beans	To tell the secrets.	(भेद, रहस्य खोलना)
Spin a yarn	To tell a story.	(मनगढ़न्त कहानी सुनाना)
Split hairs	To argue unnecessarily about trivial matters.	(साधारण मामलों पर अनावश्यक तर्क-वितर्क करना)
Square meal	Full meal.	(पेटभर भोजन)
Square peg in a round hole	To be misfit.	(कार्य या पद हेतु उचित न होना)
Stand in good stead	To be of great services,	(अत्यधिक सहायक होना)
Stand in one's own light	To hinder one's own advantage.	(अपने लाभ के रास्ते में रोड़े अटकाना)
Stand on ceremony	To behave in a stiff, correct way.	(अनुशासित तौर-तरीकों से व्यवहार करना)
Stand on one's own ground	To maintain one's own position.	(स्थिति बरकरार रखना)
Stand on one's own legs	To become independent.	(अपने पैरों पर खड़े होना)
Stand pat	Stick to one's decision.	(अपने निश्चय पर अडिग रहना)
Stand sam	To treat the company, esp. to drinks.	(संगी साथियों की आवभगत करना)

Idioms	English Meaning	Hindi meaning
Stand to one's guns	To maintain one's own opinion.	(विचारधारा पर दृढ़ रहना)
Stand to reason	To be quite clear.	(पूर्णत: स्पष्ट होना)
Stand to win	To be in a position to win or gain.	(जीत अथवा प्राप्ति की स्थिति में होना)
Stand well with	To be well thought of.	(के साथ वतैक्य होना)
Stands are running out	Nearly end of point of time.	(समाप्ति की ओर, समय सीमा)
Star in the ascendent	To have favour of fortunes.	(भाग्य का साथ देना)
Stave off	To avert, prevent.	(रोकना)
Steal a march	To surpass.	(से आगे निकल जाना)
Stick at nothing	To be unscrupulous and selfish.	(सिद्धान्तहीन एवं स्वार्थी होना)
Stick to one's colours	To be faithful to the cause.	(के प्रति निष्ठा बनाये रखना)
Stick to one's guns	To remain faithful to.	(के प्रति निष्ठावान बने रहना)
Stir up a hornet's nest	To excite the hostility of the mass.	(अधिसंख्यक वर्ग को उत्तेजित कर देना)
Stone deaf/blind	Completely deaf/blind.	(पूर्णत: अन्धा/बहरा)
Storm in a tea-cup	Greatly excited on a petty matter.	(छोटी सी बात पर अत्यधिक उत्तेजना)
Straight from the horse's mouth	Information direct from a trustworthy person.	(विश्वसनीय व्यक्ति से प्राप्त सूचना)
Strain at a gnat	To fuss about things that are not important and disregard tlfose that are	(छोटी सी बात का बतंगड़ बनाना)
Strain every nerve	To make every possible effort.	(हर प्रकार का यत्न करना)
Strike a light	To express surprise.	(आश्चर्य व्यक्त करना)
Stretch a point	Giving undue elaboration.	(विषय के व्यर्थ ही लम्बा खींचना)
Strike the iron while it is hot	To make the best of an opportunity when it comes.	(प्राप्त अवसर का सर्वोत्तम लाभ उठाना)
Summer friends	Friends of prosperity.	(खुशहाली के मित्र)
Suppress query	To hide the facts.	(तथ्यों को छिपाना)
Switched on	Under the influence of drugs.	(नशे के प्रभाव में होना)
Swollen headed	To be conceited.	(अभिमान करना)
Sword of Damocles	An imminent danger.	(सिर पर तलवार लटकना)
	T	
Tace up	To be silent.	(शान्त रहना)

Idioms	English Meaning	Hindi meaning
Tag along with	To follow.	(अनुसरण करना)
Take a leaf out of other's book	To imitate another person.	(अन्य व्यक्ति की नकल करना)
Take a rain check	First decline a offer, then accept it.	(पहले अस्वीकार करना तत्पश्चात स्वीकार करना)
Take an exception to	To object to something.	(किसी की बात का बुरा मानना)
Take away one's breath	To surprise extremely.	(अत्यधिक चकित करना)
Take delivery of	To receive.	(प्राप्त होना, करना)
Take hard	To be upset, puzzle someone.	(को घबरा देना)
Take heart	To have courage.	(साहस रखना)
Take into account	To take into consideration.	(ध्यान में रखना)
Take into one's head	To think or to believe.	(सोचना या विश्वास कर लेना)
Take it easy	Not to be in hurry.	(जल्दीबाजी में न होना)
Take leave of one's senses	To become irrational.	(विवेक खो देना)
Take notice of	To heed.	(ध्यान देना)
Take off weight	To be slim.	(दुबला होना)
Take one to task	To rebuke, to scold.	(विरोध करना या डाँटना)
Take one's ease	To stop working.	(कार्य को रोक देना)
Take one's life in one's hands	To undergo great risks.	(अत्यधिक जोखिम उठाना)
Take one's medicine	To suffer punishment.	(दण्ड भुगतना)
Take pains	Take great care.	(अधिक ध्यान देना)
Take pot luck	Have a chance.	(अवसर प्राप्त होना)
Take shape	To be real.	(वास्तविक सच्चा होना)
Take someone aback	To surprise.	(आश्चर्योचकित करना)
Take someone up on	To put a person's statement to the test.	(व्यक्ति के कथन की जाँच करना या कराना)
Take stock of	To survey.	(निरीक्षण करना)
Take the air	To walk in the open air.	(खुली हवा में सैर करना)

Idioms	English Meaning	Hindi meaning
Take the bull by the horns	To face difficulty, boldly.	(कठिन स्थिति का साहसपूर्वक सामना करना)
Take the edge off	To make blunt, ineffective.	(अप्रभावी बनाना)
Take the wind out of one's sails	To make words or action ineffective by anticipating them.	(मुँह की बात छीनना)
Take things easy	Not to work hard.	(कठोर परिश्रम न करना)
Take time by the forelock	To do one's work in time.	(समय के अन्दर कार्य करना)
Take to one's bed	To lie in bed due to illness.	(रोगावस्था में बिस्तर पकड़ना)
Take to one's heels	To run away.	(भाग जाना)
Take to town	To mystify, bewilder.	(घबराना, व्यग्र करना)
Take up the cudgels	To defend someone.	(किसी को बचाना)
Take up the gauntlet	To accept a challenge.	(चुनौती स्वीकार करना)
Take up the quarrel	To settle down the dispute, quarrel.	(झगड़ा समाप्त करना)
Take with a grain of salt	To have doubt.	(सन्देह होना)
Talk shop	To talk exclusively about one's business or professional affairs.	(अपने व्यापार या अध्यवसाय सम्बन्धी बातें करना)
Tall talk	To boast.	(शेखी बघारना)
Tarred with the same brush	To commit the same mistake.	(किसी गलती को दोहराना)
Tart up	To make showy, shining.	(भड़कीला, प्रदर्शन करना)
Tax one's patience	To test one's patience.	(धैर्य की परीक्षा लेना)
Team up	To work together.	(साथ-साथ कार्य करना)
Tear one's hair	To express sorrow.	(खेद प्रकट करना)
Tell tales	To report discreditable facts about others.	(दूसरों के विरुद्ध अनर्गल तथ्य या वार्ता करना)
Thick skinned person	A shameless person.	(निर्लज्ज व्यक्ति)
Thin down	To dilute, make thinner.	(द्रव को अधिक पतला करना)
Thin end of the wedge	A bright future with small beginning.	(स्वर्णिम भविष्यमय छोटी-सी शुरूआत)
Thin out	To make more scattered.	(बिखरा देना)
a Thing or two	To be wise or cunning.	(बुद्धिमान अथवा चालाक होना)

Idioms	English Meaning	Hindi meaning
Think better of	To think carefully and to reach at wiser decision.	(भली-भाँति विचारकर उत्तम निर्णय पर पहुँचना)
Think lightly	Not to be serious about something.	(गम्भीर न होना, मजाक के रूप में लेना)
Think something out	To ponder over.	(ध्यान से विचार करना)
a Thorn in one's side	A constant source of annoyance.	(खीझ अथवा गुस्से का निरन्तर कारण)
Throw a fit	To be an opponent.	(शत्रुता निभाना)
Throw cold water	To discourage.	(हतोत्साहित करना)
Throw down the gauntlet	To challenge.	(चुनौती देना)
Throw light on	To explain.	(प्रकाश डालना, स्पष्ट करना)
Throw mud at	To rebuke or provoke.	(उकसाना, क्रोधित करना)
Throw someone off the scent	To mislead someone.	(कुमार्ग पर ले जाना, बहकाना)
Throw out of gear	To disturb the working.	(कार्यों में बाधा उत्पन्न करना)
Throw up the sponge	To abandon the efforts.	(प्रयास को तिलांजलि देना)
Thrust one's nose into	To meddle officiously.	(धौंस सहित बाधा पहुँचाना)
Tidy up	To keep clean.	(साफ-सुथरा रखना)
Tie of blood	Blood relationship.	(रक्त-सम्बन्ध)
Tom, Dick and Harry	Ordinary people.	(साधारण, आमलोग)
Tool in the hands of	Under someone's authority.	(दूसरों के हाथ में कठपुतली की भाँति)
Top of the tree	To be head of one's profession.	(अपने अध्यवसाय में उच्च स्थान पर पहुँचना)
Tower of Strength	Main force, support.	(मुख्य आधार, शक्ति-स्तम्भ)
Toy with	To dally amorously.	(उटपटांग कार्यों में समय व्यर्थ करना)
Track back	To find out the origin, roots.	(आधार, जड़ का पता लगाना)
Trade at	To buy or sell at any special shop.	(दुकान विशेष से खरीदारी करना)
Trade on	To take advantage of.	(लाभ उठाना)
Tread on one's toes	To give offence to.	(....को आक्रमण का अवसर देना)
True to one's salt	To be faithful to someone.	(नमकहलाल होना)
Try one's hand	To make an attempt.	(सद्प्रयास करना)
Try out	To experiment to test.	(प्रयोग द्वारा जाँच करना)

Idioms	English Meaning	Hindi meaning
Turn a deaf ear	To pay no attention.	(कोई ध्यान न देना)
Turn end for end	To reverse.	(उलटना, उलट देना)
Turn one's coat	To change one's party.	(दल-बदल करना)
Turn one's hand to	To adapt to.	(कुशलता, दक्षता हासिल करना)
Turn one's head	To make one quite vain.	(......को पूर्णत: अभिमानी बना देना)
Turn over a new leaf	To start a new life.	(नवजीवन प्रारम्भ करना)
Turn the corner	To pass the crisis.	(संकट से मुक्त होना)
Turn the tables	To change the situation completely.	(स्थिति को पूर्णतः बदल देना)
Turn to account	Take benefit from.	(लाभ उठाना)
Turn up one's nose at	To regard with contempt.	(उपेक्षा करना)
Twist the lion's tail	To irritate immediate boss.	(बॉस को, मालिक को नाराज कर देना)
Two can play at the game	To retaliate in the same way.	(समान व्यवहार करना, जैसे को तैसा)
Two or three	A few.	(कुछ-थोड़े से)
	U	
an Ugly customer	a formidable person.	(उपेक्षा योग्य व्यक्ति).
Unaccustomed to	not to be in habit of.	(...की आदत न होना).
Unaware of	to be careless.	(लापरवाह होना).
Under a cloud	in suspicion.	(शंकायुक्त)
Under one's nose	in the presence of.	(किसी के सामने)
Under the embargo	under impediment.	(दुविधा में).
Under the nose	in close vicinity.	(आस-पास).
Under the rose	secretly.	(गुप्त रूप से).
Under the sun	anywhere.	(कहीं भी).
Under the thumb of	under the authority of.	(... के अधिकार में).
Under the wing	under the protection.	(सुरक्ष में).
Uneasy about for	to be anxious about.	(बेचैनी होना).
Unfaithful to	not faithful to.	(नमकहराम).
Unfamiliar to	unknown to.	(अपरिचित).
Unfold something to	to disclose a secret.	(भेद उजागर करना).
Unsure about of	not sure of.	(अनिश्चित).

Idioms	English Meaning	Hindi meaning
Upper hand	to dominant, control.	(नियन्त्रक प्रभाव रखना).
Upto date	complete till date.	(तिथि तक पूर्ण).
Upto the elbow	completely engrossed.	(पूर्णत: व्यस्त).
Upto the eyes	to be deeply engaged or involved.	(अत्यधिक सम्बद्ध होना).
Upto the knocker	upto the required standard of excellence or fashion.	(उत्कृष्टता या फैशन के वांछित स्तर तक).
Upto the mark	upto standard.	(उचित स्तर का).
Upto time	punctual, not later than the due time.	(निश्चित समय से).
Usher in	to lead upto	(तक साथ जाना, पहुँचाना).
Ut infra/ut supra	as below/as above.	(निम्नानुसार/उप्युक्तानुसार).
Utter failure	extreme failure.	(पूर्णत: असफल).
	V	
the Vestige of	the evidence of.	(प्रमाण).
Vet for	to examine someone's record.	(किसी का रिकॉर्ड जॉचना).
a Vexed question	a complicated problem.	(कठिन समस्या).
Via tria, via tuta	safe path, beaten path.	(सुरक्षित मार्ग, सुविधाजनक तरीका).
Vice versa	the other way round.	(विलोमत:).
Vis a vis	in relation to.	(के सम्बन्ध में, तुलना में).
View with	to complete.	(पूरा करना).
	W	
Wag a war	to launch a war.	(युद्ध आरम्भ करना).
Walk the streets	to be a whore, prostitute.	(वेश्या हो जाना).
Walls have ears	to listen by someone in disguise.	(कोई अन्य भी छिपकर सुन सकता है).
War of element	a great storm.	(तेज अन्धड़-तूफान).
War to the knife	a bitter and deadly struggle.	(कटु एवं कठोर संघर्ष).
Wash dirty linen in public	to discuss unpleasant domestic affairs in public.	(व्यक्तिगत बातों को उजागर करना, उछालना) .
Wash one's hand off	to be free from.	(किसी बात से मुक्ति प्राप्त होना).
Watch how the wind blows	to watch and see how the things are developing.	(घटनाक्रम पर तीक्ष्ण दृष्टि रखना).
Wear a long face	to look gloomy.	(उदास दिखाई पड़ना).
Well balanced	be reasonable.	(सुयोग्य होना).
Well off	in good circumstances.	(अच्छी स्थिति में).

Idioms	English Meaning	Hindi meaning
Wet behind the ears	to be naive and inexperienced.	(अनुभवहीन होना).
Wet blanket	one who acts like a damper on the enthusiasm or jovility of others.	(हतोत्साहित करने वाला).
What's to do	what is the matter?	(क्या मामला है?).
What's what	the true position of affairs.	(किसी कार्य की सही स्थिति).
Where the shoe pinches	where the problem lies.	(जहां समस्या खड़ी हो).
Where you're ?	What you are saying or getting at?	(आप क्या कह रहे हैं ?).
While away	to waste time.	(समय व्यर्थ करना).
White elephant	a very expensive thing.	(बहुत खर्चीली वस्तू).
White lie	a blunt lie.	(सफेद झूठ).
Whittle down	to lessen the force or scope of.	(शक्ति या क्षेत्र में कमी करना).
Wild goose chase	unfruitful efforts.	(व्यर्थ का प्रयत्न).
Win laurels	to distinguish oneself.	(उत्कृष्टता प्राप्त करना).
Win one's spur	to make one's reputation as a politician.	(राजनेता के रूप में ख्याति प्राप्त करना).
Win someone's hand	to be promised to get marry with.	(विवाह हेतु वचनबद्धता).
Wipe off	to clean by rubbing with cloth.	(कपड़े से रगड़कर साफ करना).
Wipe one's eyes	to console, comfort.	(सान्तवना देना).
Wipe the slate clean	to remove grievances etc.	(कष्ट,परेशानी,शिकायत का निराकरण करना)
Wise as an owl	an utter stupid.	(महामूर्ख).
With a high hand	to be oppressively.	(निर्दय होना).
With a view to	for the purpose of.	(........के उद्देश्य से).
With ease	without difficulty.	(बिना कठिनाई के)
With flying colours	to be successful with eclat.	(विशिष्ट सफलता प्राप्त करना).
With good	grace;willingly.	(इच्छानुसार).
With one accord	agreeing together.	(सहमति से, एक स्वर में).
With one voice	unanimously.	(पूर्ण सहमति से).
With open arms	jubilant reception.	(उत्साहपूर्ण स्वागत).
With the exception	except of .	(... के अतिरिक्त, अलावा).
With young	with small one, Child.	(बच्चे के साथ).

Idioms	English Meaning	Hindi meaning
Within a stone's throw	within a short distance.	(पास ही, नजदीक ही) .
Within an ace of	within a hairs breadth of.	(बाल बराबर दूरी से).
Without an exception	for everyone.	(प्रत्येक के लिए).
Without fail	definitely.	(निश्चित रूप से).
Without reserve	absolutely, wholly.	(पूर्णरूपेण).
Without rhyme or reason	without any justification.	(अकारण).
Without the source	of having no interest.	(बिना दिलचस्पी लिए).
Wolf in sheep's clothing	an enemy posing as a friend.	(मित्र के रूप में दुश्मन).
a Word in one's ears	to say in private.	(व्यक्तिगत रूप से, गुप्त रूप से कहना).
World apart	completely different.	(पूर्णत: भिन्न).
Worm out	to discover by persistent questioning.	(खोद-खोदकर पूछना).
Worth a jew's eye	most precious.	(बेशकीमती).
Wrong shop	the wrong place to look for help etc.	(सहायता आदि की व्यर्थ आशा करना).
	X	
To X ray	to examine thoroughly.	(सूक्ष्म निरीक्षण, परीक्षण करना).
	Y	
Yawning gap	a wide gap	(विस्तृत अन्तर, दूरी).
Year by year	yearly.	(साल-दर-साल).
Yellow boy	a gold coin.	(सोने की मोहन-मुद्रा).
Yellow brick road	a path to fame, wealth etc.	(यशस्वी मार्ग).
Yellow press	sensational journalism.	(पीत पत्रकारिता).
Yeoman service	an excellent work.	(उत्कृष्ट कार्य).
Yet again	once more.	(फिर एक बार).
Yoke of opinion	force of public opinion.	(जन-विचार-शक्ति).
	Z	
Zig zag	not straight.	(टेड़ा-मेड़ा).

Top 300 most Repeated Idioms asked in SSC

Idioms	Meaning	Hindi meaning	No of times repeated
A Wet blanket	A person who discourages enjoyment or enthusiasm	कबाब में हड्डी.	8
A wolf in sheep's clothing	Hypocrite	भेड़ की खाल में भी भेड़िया	7
Acid test	Definitive proof of truth or falsehood	अग्नि परीक्षा	8
Add insult to injury	To further a loss with mockery to worsen an unfavourable situation	जले पर नमक छिड़कना	9
All and sundry	Everybody without distinction	हर कोई बिना भेद क	7
All our might and main	Full force	एड़ी चोटी का जोर लगाना (पूरी ताकत से)	6
Apples and oranges	Two unlike things or people	दो अलग चीजे	12
Alphabet soup	A metaphor for an abundance of abbreviations or acronyms	शब्दों के लघुत्तम का जरुरत से ज्यादा प्रयोग	13
Alpha and omega	Beginning and end	शुरुआत और अंत	14
As daft as a brush	Extremely silly	बेहद मूर्खतापूर्ण	10
As fit as a fiddle	Strong and healthy	बहुत अच्छे स्वास्थ्य में	11
At large	A criminal escaped or not yet captured	भागा हुआ अपराधी	7
At loggerheads	In conflict with someone	असहमति के कारण हिंसक	7
At sixes and sevens	In disorder or confusion	अव्यवस्था या भ्रम में	7
Back to square one	To return to the starting point	जहाँ के तहाँ	7
Back to the drawing board	Plan it all over again	नये सिरे से बनाना	7
Be going places	Talented and successful	सफल होना	10

Top 300 most Repeated Idioms asked in SSC

Idioms	Meaning	Hindi meaning	No of times repeated
A Wet blanket	A person who discourages enjoyment or enthusiasm	कबाब में हड्डी.	8
A wolf in sheep's clothing	Hypocrite	भेड़ की खाल में भी भेड़िया	7
Acid test	Definitive proof of truth or falsehood	अग्नि परीक्षा	8
Add insult to injury	To further a loss with mockery to worsen an unfavourable situation	जले पर नमक छिड़कना	9
All and sundry	Everybody without distinction	हर कोई बिना भेद क	7
All our might and main	Full force	एड़ी चोटी का जोर लगाना (पूरी ताकत से)	6
Apples and oranges	Two unlike things or people	दो अलग चीजे	12
Alphabet soup	A metaphor for an abundance of abbreviations or acronyms	शब्दों के लघुत्तम का जरुरत से ज्यादा प्रयोग	13
Alpha and omega	Beginning and end	शुरुआत और अंत	14
As daft as a brush	Extremely silly	बेहद मूर्खतापूर्ण	10
As fit as a fiddle	Strong and healthy	बहुत अच्छे स्वास्थ्य में	11
At large	A criminal escaped or not yet captured	भागा हुआ अपराधी	7
At loggerheads	In conflict with someone	असहमति के कारण हिंसक	7
At sixes and sevens	In disorder or confusion	अव्यवस्था या भ्रम में	7
Back to square one	To return to the starting point	जहाँ के तहाँ	7
Back to the drawing board	Plan it all over again	नये सिरे से बनाना	7
Be going places	Talented and successful	सफल होना	10

Idioms	Meaning	Hindi meaning	No of times repeated
Be in the red	To be in a loss or debt	हानि में होना	12
Be out of order	A device not working properly or at all	उपकरण का काम नहीं करना	10
To turn over a new leaf	To change one's behaviour of better	नया जीवन शुरु करना	12
Turn down	Reject	अस्वीकार कर देना	10
A bird's eye view	A general view from above	ऊंचाई से विस्तृत दृश्य	13
A blue eyed boy	One who is favourite	आंखो का तारा (बहुत ब्यारा	12
A bull in a China	An extremely awkward, clumsy person	अनाड़ी व्यक्ति	12
A carrot and stick approach	Reward and punishments that influence someone's behaviour	साम दाम दंड भेद	10
A child's play	Something that is very easy	बच्चों का खेल (आसान काम)	16
A cut above something	Superior to	बेहतर	9
A damp squib	A disappointing result	ऊंची दुकान फीका पकवान	16
A drop in the ocean	A very small amount compared with what is needed or expected	ऊंट के मुंह में जीरा (बहुत कम	14
A golden mean	Middle course between two extremes	बीच का रास्ता	13
A hornet's nest	An unpleasant situation	अप्रिय स्थिति	11
A laughing stock	An object of laughter	हंसी का पात्र	6
A left handed compliment	An ambiguous compliment	प्रशंसा के रुप में अपमानजनक टिप्पणी	11
A live wire	Lively and active	जिन्दादिल व्यक्ति	13

Idioms	Meaning	Hindi meaning	No of times repeated
A lot on your plate	To have a large number of problems to deal with	बहुत सारी जिम्मेदारियां	6
A mare's nest	A difficult situation	जटिल या भ्रामक स्थिति	6
A needle in a haystack	Something that is very difficult to locate	घास के ढेर में सुई	5
A penny for your thoughts	A way of asking what someone is thinking	कोई क्या सोच रहा है यह पूछने का तरीका	7
A sea change	A profound or notable	पूर्ण परिवर्तन	12
A shot in the arm	An encouraging stimulus	उत्साहवर्धक प्रोत्साहन	10
A storm in a teacup	Big fuss over a small matter	बात का बतंगड़	11
Soft option	Easy and agreeable option	आसान विकल्प	4
Spick and span	Clean and tidy	साफ-सुथरा	8
Stick to his guns	Maintain his own opinion	बात पर अड़े रहना	6
Take the bull by the horns	To face a difficulty courageously	साहसपूर्वक मुसीबतों का सामना करना	8
The last straw	Final problem in the series	स्थिति को असहनीय बनाने वाली आखिरी परेशानी	11
The man in the street	Simple man	आम आदमी	16
The pros and cons	For and against	नफा नुकसान	6
The salt of the earth	A good, reliable, honest person	विश्वनीय और ईमानदार व्यक्ति	7
To be on cloud nine	To be extremely happy	सातवें आसमान पर (अत्यंत प्रसन्न होना)	14
To be taken aback	To be surprised	हक्का - बक्का होना (चकित होना	12

Idioms	Meaning	Hindi meaning	No of times repeated
To beat about the bush	Speak in a roundabout manner	घुमा फिराकर बात करना	10
To fight tooth and nail	To make every possible effort	जी जान से लड़ना	10
To have something up one's sleeve	To have secret plan	गुप्त योजना	10
To jump on the bandwagon	To follow popular trends	बहती गंगा में हाथ धोना	12
To keep someone at arm's length	To be at a distance with someone	दूर से सलाम तकना (दूरी बनाना	12
To make both ends meet	To live within one's income	किसी तरह से गुजारा करना	`14
To put a spoke in one's wheel	To put a difficulty in the way of progress	टाँग अड़ाना	14
To take French leave	Absenting oneself without permission	बिना अनुमति के अनुपस्थित रहना	10
To throw dust in one's eyes	To deceive	आँखो में धूल झोंकना (धोखा देना)	11
Hobson's choice	No real choice at all	कोई विकल्प नहीं	6
In a pickle	In trouble	कठिन परिस्थिति में	6
In the good books	In favour with	पक्ष में होना	7
In the long run	Eventually	आखिरकार	6
In the teeth of	Directly against	प्रत्यक्ष विरोध मे होना	6
Ins and outs	Full details	पूरा विवरण	5
Kill two birds with one stone	To serve two purposes at one time	एक तीर से दो शिकार करना	5
Lend me your ear	To pay attention to	कान लगाकर सुनना	8

Idioms	Meaning	Hindi meaning	No of times repeated
Let the grass grow under one's feet	To remain idle	निष्क्रिय रहना	5
Made a clean breast of	Confessed his crime	अपराध स्वीकार करना	3
No love lost between	Not on good terms	बहुत नफरत	6
On tenterhooks	Anxious	चिंता में	8
Over head and ears	Completely	पूरी तरह	5
Part and parcel	Essential element	अनिवार्य अंग	7
Played ducks and drakes	Spent lavishly	आवश्यकता से अधिक खर्च करना	3
Pull a long face	Look dejected	मुंह लटकाना (दुखी होना)	12
Putting the cart before the horse	Doing a thing in the wrong way	गलत तरीके से काम करना	10
Raining cats and dogs	Raining extremely heavily	मूसलाधार बारिश होना	10
Rule to roost	To dominate	हावी होना	6
Run out of stream	To lose impetus	उत्साह खत्म होना	5
Shake off	Forget	भूल जाना	4
At sea	At a loss	परेशान	15
At snail's pace	Do something very slowly	बहुत धीरे - धीरे	12
Backseat driver	Interfering in affairs without having knowledge	बिना ज्ञान के मामलों में दखल देना	12
Be in the air	Still to be settled	व्यक्ति के जाने से खुश होना	9
Bite the dust	Suffer a defeat	धूल चाटना (हार जाना)	9
Carry the day	Win a victory	जीत हासिल करना	8
Couch potato	A lazy person	आलसी व्यक्ति	9
Died in harness	Died while working	सेवा में रहते हुए मर जाना	6
Draw a blank	To be unsuccessful	खाली हाथ लौटना	6
Fair weather friends	Friends in good times	स्वार्थी मित्र	5

Idioms	Meaning	Hindi meaning	No of times repeated
Fall flat	To have no effect	असफल होना	4
Feather in one's cap	A new and additional distinction	चार चाँद लगाना	9
For good	Permanently	सदा के लिए	6
Gave vent to something	Expressed forcefully	किसी पर भड़ास निकालना	4
Get on somebody's nerves	To be an irritant	हाथ से निकलना	5
Get out of hand	To become uncontrollable	जानबूझकर नजरअंदाज करना	7
Give someone the cold shoulder	Deliberately ignore someone	जान बूझकर नजरअंदाज करना	12
Hard and fast	That cannot be altered	अपरिवर्तनीय	11
Have a finger in every pie	To be meddlesome	एक से अधिक काम में फंसा होना	13
Hit the nail on the head	Say or do something exactly right	सटीक जबाव देना	10
A wee bit	A little amount	थोड़ी मात्रा	6
Under his thumb	Under his control	उसके नियंत्रण में]	9
At one's wits end	In a state where one does not know what to do	ऐसी दशा जहाँ पता न हो की क्या करना है और क्या नहीं]	10
At daggers drawn	Bitterly hostile	दुश्मनी	10
Between the devil and the deep sea	Between two dangers situation	दो खतरनाक स्थिति के बीच	12
To get rid of	Dispose of	[निपटा देना]	9
play ducks and drakes	acting foolishly or inconsistently[	मूर्खता से काम करना]	9

Idioms	Meaning	Hindi meaning	No of times repeated
To take the bull by the horns	tackle a problem in a bold and direct fashion	एक बोल्ड और प्रत्यक्ष तरीके में एक समस्या से निपटने]	6
Rain cats and dogs	Raining heavily	भारी बारिश	10
Keep one's fingers crossed	The anxiety in which you hope that nothing will upset your plans	कुछ बुरा ना होने की उम्मीद करना	7
By hook or by crook	By fair or foul means /by any how	किसी भी तरह से]	8
Throw out of gear	Disturbing the work	काम में बाधा	8
Take to one's heels	Run away	भागना	8
In the nick of time	Just at the last moment	अंतिम क्षण में]	8
Spread like wildfire	Spread quickly	फैलाना	8
Tooth and nail	With all one's power	सभी एक की शक्ति के साथ	8
Die in harness	Die while in service	सेवा में रहते हुए मर जाना	6
Take a leaf out one's book	Imitate one	नक़ल करना	7
Like a fish out of water	In a strange situation	एक अजीब स्थिति में]	8
At one's beck and call	to be ready to react to their commands without a delay	—-	6
To make both ends meet	To live within one's income	आय में गुज़ारा करना	10
In hot water	In trouble	मुसीबत में	4
Nip in the bud	Destroy in the early stage	शुरुआत में ही रोक देना या नष्ट कर देना	7
Stick to one's guns	Remain faithful to the cause	वफादार रहना	3

Idioms	Meaning	Hindi meaning	No of times repeated
To eat humble pie	To apologise humbly and to yield under humiliating circumstances	नाक रगड़ना	5
Harp on the same string	Dwelling on the same subject	एक ही बात पर अड़े रहना]	3
Bury the hatchet	End the quarrel and make peace	झगड़ा खत्म करना]	6
Leave one in the lurch	Desert one in difficulties; leave one in a helpless condition	एक असहाय हालत में छोड़ देना	6
In high spirits	Very happy	बहुत खुश	5
Put the cart before the horse	Put or do things in the wrong order	वस्तुओं को उल्टे-सीधे क्रम में रखना]	4
To all names	To abuse	गाली देना	2
On tenterhooks	In a state of suspense and anxiety	सस्पेंस और चिंता की स्थिति में	5
Kill two birds with one stone	To achieve two results with one effort	एक प्रयास के साथ दो परिणाम प्राप्त करना	8
Take one to task	rebuke	डांटना	8
A bosom friend	A very close friend	बहुत करीबी दोस्त	6
A brown study	Dreaming	सपना देखना	5
Turn over a new leaf	Change for the better	एक नए रुप में	6
Wash one's dirty linen	Discuss unpleasant in public-private matters before strangers	—	3
To bell the cat	To face the risk	जोखिम का सामना करना	4
A hard nut to crack	A difficult problem	कठिन समस्या	9
Let the cat out of the bag	Disclose/Reveal a secret	खुलासा	6
A big gun	An important person	एक महत्वपूर्ण व्यक्ति	4

Idioms	Meaning	Hindi meaning	No of times repeated
Make up one's mind	Decide	निश्चय करना	2
In the long run	over or after a long period of time; eventually	अंततः	5
Pay off old scores	Take revenge	बदला लेना]	5
Hard and fast rules	very Strict rules	बहुत सख्त नियम	4
At the eleventh hour	At the last moment	आखिरी वक्त	12
Above board	Honest and open	ईमानदार	4
Through thick and thin	Under all conditions	सभी शर्तों के तहत	10
Put a spoke in one's wheel	To upset one's plans	किसी की योजनाओं को खराब करना	5
At sixes and seven	In a disordered/disorganised manner	अस्त व्यस्त तरीके से	11
To cut a sorry figure	To make a poor show	नाटक करना	8
With a high hand	Oppressively	अत्याचारपूर्ण	6
Burn one's fingers	Get into trouble by interfering in others affairs	दूसरे के मामलों में हस्तक्षेप करके मुसीबत में पड़ना	8
Laugh one's head off	to Laugh heartily	खुल के हसना	5
Chew the cud	Pondering over something	किसी बात पर विचार करना	5
Apple of one's eye	Be cherished	दुलारा	12
Beating around the bush	Avoid the main topic	मुख्य विषय से बचना	10
Cry over spilled milk	Complaining about a loss or failure from the past	व्यर्थ पछताना	10
Chip on your shoulder	When someone is upset about something that happened a while ago	पुरानी बातों पर दुखी होना	9
Golden handshake	big sum of money given to a person when he/she leaves a company or retires	—	6

Idioms	Meaning	Hindi meaning	No of times repeated
Icing on the cake	Something that turns good into great	सोने पे सुहागा	7
Cost an arm and a leg	very expensive	बहुत महंगा	8
To be in the doldrums	be in low spirits	उदासी में होना	`10
sit on the fence	avoid making a decision	दुविधा में होना	6
Hear it on grapevine	hearing rumours about something or someone	किसी वस्तु या व्यक्ति के बारे में अफवाहें सुनना]	7
Can't judge a book by its cover	Can't judge something/ someone primarily on appearance	सूरत से सीरत नहीं पता चलती	8
A litmus test	A method that helps to know if something is correct or not	एक विधि जो यह जानने में मदद करती है कि कुछ सही है या इसका अर्थ नहीं है	4
A house of cards	A very poor plan	एक बहुत ही खराब योजना	8
Fool's paradise	False sense of happiness	हवाई महल	8
Get a raw deal	To not be treated as well as other people	अनुचित व्यवहार	5
Give cold shoulder	To ignore or neglect	रूखा व्यवहार करना	8
It takes two to tango	Actions or communications need more than one person	एक हाथ से ताली नहीं बजती	7
Black and blue	Bruises	चोट से नीला पड़ा हुआ	6
Last straw	The final problem in a series of problems	बर्दाश्त से बाहर	4
A bird's eye view	View from a very high place that allows you to see a very large area[	—	9
A red letter day	An important day	महत्वपूर्ण दिन	12
Face the music	Get reprimanded	कियो का परिणाम भुगतान	10

Idioms	Meaning	Hindi meaning	No of times repeated
To smell a Rat	Suspect a trick or deceit	दाल में काला होना (संदेह होना)	7
A wild goose chase	Futile search	निर्थक खोज	9
By fits and starts	Unsteady	अनियमित रुप से	11
A hard nut to crack	Difficult task	लोहे का चने चबाना	10
Blow one's own trumpet	Praise oneself	अपने मुंह मियाँ मिठ्ठू बनना	8
By leaps and bounds	Very quickly	बहुत तेजी से	11
Once in a blue moon	Rarely and infrequently	कभी कभार	11
A bolt from the blue	A complete surprise	आकस्मिक घटना	10
At one's wit's end	To be puzzled	समस्याओं से इतना चिंतित होना कि पता नहीं आगे क्या करना है	10
At the drop of a hat	Without any hesitation	तुरन्त	9
Break the ice	Initiate something	चुप्पी तोड़ना	8
Bury the hatchet	To make peace	झगड़ा खत्म करना	11
Cock and bull story	Absurd story	बे-सिरपैर की बात	7
Feather one's own nest	Promote their own interest	बेईमानी करके धनी होना	12
Leave no stone unturned	To make all possible efforts	खून पसीना एक करना	9
Spill the beans	To leak the secret	अनजाने में भेद खोल देना	9
To be under the weather	To not feel well	बीमार होना	7
To end in smoke	Yielded no result	धुवें में उड़ना (कोई परिणाम न निकलना)	7
To flog a dead horse	To attempt to do the impossible	असंभव काम करना	11
To have the gift of the gab	Talent for speaking	वाक्यपटुता	10

Idioms	Meaning	Hindi meaning	No of times repeated
To read between the lines	Understand the hidden meaning	छिपा हुआ अर्थ निकालना	8
To turn a deaf ear	Disregard	कान पर जूँ तक न रेंगना	9
A dark horse	An unexpected winner	अप्रत्याशित विजेता	10
A snake in the grass	A treacherous person	आस्तीन का साँप	10
A stone's throw away	At a short distance	थोड़ी दूरी पर	9
At the eleventh hour	At the very last moment	आखिरी मौके पर	8
Barking up the wrong tree	Trying to do something in a way that will not work	निर्रथक प्रयास	8
Give a piece of one's mind	To rebuke someone strongly	डाँटना	10
In a nutshell	Briefly and concisely	संक्षेप में	8
Sailing in the same boat	Being in the same difficult situation	उसी कठिन परिस्थिति में होना	9
See eye to eye	Be in full agreement	पूर्णत: सहमत होना	10
Through thick and thin	Support under all circumstances	हर हाल में	6
To add fuel to the fire	Make things worse	आग में घी डालना	7
To eat a humble	To accept defeat	हार मानना	5
To keep the wolf away from the door	To keep off starvation	भुखमरी से बचना	9
To take to task	Punished	बुरी तरह फटकारना	7
Under a cloud	Under suspicion	शक के दायरे में	8
A bone of contention	Cause of dispute	झगड़े की जड़	8
A close shave	Narrow escape from danger	बाल-बाल बचना	5
A fish out of water	An uncomfortable position	असहज परिस्थिति	7
Bad blood	Angry feeling	आपसी दुश्मनी	7

Idioms	Meaning	Hindi meaning	No of times repeated
Be wet behind the ears	Young and inexperienced	अनुभवहीन	8
Beat around the bush	Avoiding the main topic	घुमा-फिराकर बात करना	8
Best of both worlds	All the advantages	दोनो हाथों में लड्डू	7
Call it a day	To give up work and go back to home	संन्यास लेना	8
Catch red handed	To catch someone doing something illegal	रंगे हाथ पकड़ना	8
Cost an arm and a leg	Very expensive	बहुत महंगा पड़ना	8
Cry over spilt milk	To complain about a loss from the past	अब पछताए होत क्या जब चिड़िया चुग गई खेत	6
Grease the palm	Bribe	रिश्वत देना	7
Hand in glove	In close association	घनिष्ठ सम्बन्ध	9
In black and white	In writing	लिखित रुप में	9
Live from hand to mouth	Consuming daily what little is earned	जैसे तैसे गुजर बसर करना	7
Put one's foot down	Take a firm stand	दृढ़तापूर्वक विरोध करना	6
Sit on the fence	Remain undecided and unsure	दुविधा में होना	5
To be all at sea	Puzzled	असमंजस की स्थिति	3
To pay through the nose	Pay an extremely high price	भारी कीमत देना	5
All moonshine	Far from reality	दिखावटी	6
An axe to grind	Have a selfish interest	निजी स्वार्थ	4
Ball is in your court	To be responsible for further action	जिम्मेदार होना	5
Bite off more than one can chew	To take on a task too big for oneself	अपनी क्षमता से अधिक काम लेना	5
Build castles in the air	Daydream	हवाई किले बनाना	4

Idioms	Meaning	Hindi meaning	No of times repeated
Chicken hearted	Timid	डरपोक	5
In high spirits	Joyful	उत्साह से भरपूर	4
In the nick of time	Just in time	सह समय पर	5
Leaves you in the lurch	Leave someone in a helpless condition	बिच मजधार में छोड़ देना	4
Maiden speech	First speech	पहला भाषण	5
Off and on	Occasionally	कभी - कभी	6
Strain every nerve	Work very hard	खून पसीना एक करना	4
Takes after	To resemble	एक जैसा होना	5
Throw in the towel	Acknowledge defeat	हार मान लेना	6
To bring to light	To reveal	उजागर करना	3
To get into hot water	To get into trouble	मुसीबत में पढ़ना	3
To miss the boat/bus	To miss an opportunity	मौका गवाँ बैठना	3
To put up with	Tolerate	बर्दाश्त करना	4
To take to heart	To grieve over	दिल पर लेना	7
Turn a blind eye	To ignore a situation	अंधा बन जाना	4
A blessing in disguise	A hidden favour	दुख के भेद में सुख	7
A cakewalk	Extremely easy	अत्यंत सरल	8
A chip off the old block	Reminds them of one's father	जैसा बाप वैसा बेटा	5
A fool's paradise	Being happy for foolish reasons	हवाई महल	7
A man of letters	Proficient in literary art	विद्वान	6
A piece of cake	A very easy task	बच्चों का खेल	5
Above board	Honest and frank	ईमानदार	5
Achilles' heel	A weakness or vulnerable point	कमजोरी	6
All ears	Listening intently	गौर से सुनना	6

Idioms	Meaning	Hindi meaning	No of times repeated
An iron will	A firm opinion	मजबूत दृढ़ संकल्प	7
An open book	One that held on secrets	खुली किताब	7
As hard as a nail	Emotionless	भावनाहीन	8
At daggers drawn	Enemies	दुश्मनी	8
Look up	Search	खोजें	8
Look upto	Respect someone	सम्मानित करना	7
Look into	Investigate	जांच पडताल करना	8
Look for	Search for something	ढूंढना	6

IDIOMS BASED ON 'ANIMAL'

Idioms based on 'Fish'

Fish out of water

Meaning - Feeling uncomfortable or out of place in a new or unfamiliar environment.

Hindi meaning of the Idiom - नयी या अनजानी वातावरण में असहज महसूस करना।

Sentence - After living in a small town her whole life, moving to the bustling city made her feel like a fish out of water.

A big fish

Meaning - An important or influential person.

Hindi meaning of the Idiom - महत्वपूर्ण या प्रभावशाली व्यक्ति।

Sentence - The CEO of the company is considered a big fish in the business world.

Fish in troubled water

Meaning - To willingly involve oneself in a risky or dangerous situation for personal gain.

Hindi meaning of the Idiom - अपने लाभ के लिए खुद को जोखिम में डालना।

Sentence - The corrupt politician was a fish in troubled water, exploiting the chaos for personal profit.

Drink like a fish

Meaning - To consume alcohol excessively or habitually.

Hindi meaning of the Idiom - अत्यधिक मात्रा में शराब पीना।

Sentence - Jake has a serious drinking problem. He drinks like a fish every night.

A cold fish

Meaning - Someone who lacks emotions or is unresponsive in social situations.

Hindi meaning of the Idiom - जिसके पास भावनाओं की कमी होती है या सामाजिक परिस्थितियों में अक्रिय होता है।

Sentence - Despite being surrounded by friends, she always appears distant and aloof. She's a real cold fish.

A fishy story

Meaning - A story or explanation that seems suspicious or not entirely believable.

Hindi meaning of the Idiom - एक ऐसी कहानी या व्याख्या जो संदिग्ध लगती हो या पूरी तरह से अविश्वसनीय

Sentence - His explanation for being late seemed like a fishy story to me. I think he's hiding something.

Fish for a compliment

Meaning - Seeking or trying to elicit praise or compliments from others.

Hindi meaning of the Idiom - दूसरों से प्रशंसा या सराहना प्राप्त करने का प्रयास करना।

Sentence - Sarah always dresses up nicely when she's fishing for a compliment.

Neither fish nor fowl

Meaning - Something or someone that is not easily categorised or falls into a clear classification.

Hindi meaning of the Idiom - कुछ ऐसा या कोई ऐसा जिसे आसानी से श्रेणीबद्ध नहीं किया जा सकता है या स्पष्ट वर्गीकरण में नहीं आता है।

Sentence - The new hybrid car is neither fish nor fowl. It doesn't fit into the traditional categories of vehicles.

Shooting fish in a barrel

Meaning - Referring to an extremely easy task or action.

Hindi meaning of the Idiom - एक बड़े आसान कार्य या कार्रवाई को दर्शाते हैं।

Sentence - With all the evidence we have against him, proving his guilt will be like shooting fish in a barrel.

To have other/a bigger fish to fry

Meaning - To have more important or pressing matters to attend to.

Hindi meaning of the Idiom - ज्यादा महत्वपूर्ण या तत्परता वाले मामलों का समर्पण करना।

Sentence - I can't join you for lunch today. I have other fish to fry, like finishing this urgent report.

Idioms based on ' Horse'

Idioms: **To beat a dead horse**

Meaning: To waste time or energy on something that is already finished or hopeless and will not produce any desired results.

Hindi meaning: ऐसे मुद्दे पर समय या ऊर्जा व्यर्थ खर्च करना जो पहले से ही समाप्त हो चुके हों

Sentence: Continuing to argue about the issue is like beating a dead horse It's time to move on and focus on more productive matters .

Idioms: **To flog a dead horse**

Meaning: To persistently or futilely try to revive interest or support in a matter or cause that is already considered hopeless or unproductive.

Hindi meaning: निराशाजनक विषय में रुझान या समर्थन को जीवंत करने की कोशिश करना।

Sentence: His attempts to gather funding for the failing project are like flogging a dead horse. It's time to accept the reality and move on to new opportunities.

Idioms: **To put the cart before the horse**

Meaning: To do things in the wrong order or prioritise incorrectly.

Hindi meaning: गलत क्रम में काम करना या गलती से क्रम बदल देना।

Sentence: Buying new furniture before finding a house would be putting the cart before the horse. It's essential to secure a place first and then consider furnishing it.

Idioms: **Eat like a horse**

Meaning: To eat a large amount of food or to have a hearty appetite.

Hindi meaning: घोड़े की तरह खाना

Sentence: After playing sports all day, I was so hungry that I ate like a horse at dinner.

Idioms: **Straight from the horse's mouth**

Meaning: Information or news that comes directly from a reliable or authoritative source.

Hindi meaning: मुँह से सीधा

Sentence: I heard from a friend who heard it straight from the horse's mouth that the concert is going to be rescheduled.

Idioms: **Hold your horses**

Meaning: To be patient and wait, to restrain oneself from acting hastily or impulsively.

Hindi meaning: जल्दबाजी या बिना सोचे-समझे कार्रवाई से अपने आप को रोकना।

Sentence: Before making any decisions, let's hold our horses and gather all the necessary information.

Idioms: **Horse trade**

Meaning: To engage in skillful bargaining or negotiations, especially shrewdly or strategically

Hindi meaning: योग्यतापूर्वक मोल-भाव करना

Sentence: The two businessmen engaged in a horse trade to finalize the terms of the contract.

Idioms: **Horse sense**

Meaning: Practical or common sense, practical intelligence or judgement.

Hindi meaning: अविद्यावान अच्छा बुद्धि

Sentence: It doesn't require much education to understand that saving money for emergencies is just horse sense.

Idioms based on 'Dog'

Idiom: **A dog in the manger**

Meaning: A person who tries to keep others from having, using, or enjoying something that they themselves do not want or cannot use.

Hindi meaning: जो चीज़ों का लाभ लेने या इस्तेमाल करने से दूसरों को रोकने का प्रयास करता है, जो खुद चाहता नहीं है या उसे उपयोग नहीं कर सकता है।

Sentence: He's a dog in the manger when it comes to sharing his toys with other children.

Idiom: **Let sleeping dogs lie**

Meaning: Not to talk about things that have created problems in the past, to avoid further trouble.

Hindi meaning: पिछले मसलों के बारे में बात न करना, और आगे की मुसीबतों को उत्पन्न करने से बचने के लिए।

Sentence: I decided to let sleeping dogs lie and not bring up the issue during the family gathering.

Idiom: **Fighting like cats and dogs**

Meaning: To fight or argue vehemently and constantly.

Hindi meaning: बहुत खराब तरीके से लड़ना या झगड़ना।

Sentence: The siblings are always fighting like cats and dogs, but deep down, they still care for each other.

Idiom: **Raining cats and dogs**

Meaning: To rain heavily, usually with large and heavy drops.

Hindi meaning: बहुत तेज़ी से बारिश होना, आम तौर पर बड़े और भारी बूंदों के साथ।

Sentence: We had to cancel our picnic plans because it was raining cats and dogs outside.

Idiom: **Lead a dog's life**

Meaning: To live a miserable or difficult life.

Hindi meaning: एक दुखद या कठिन जीवन जीना।

Sentence: After losing his job, he ended up leading a dog's life, struggling to make ends meet.

Idiom: **Top dog**

Meaning: Someone who is important or dominant in a particular field or organisation.

Hindi meaning: किसी विशेष क्षेत्र या संगठन में महत्वपूर्ण या प्रमुख व्यक्ति।

Sentence: As the CEO, she is the top dog in the company and makes all the major decisions.

Idiom: **Underdog**

Meaning: A person or group in a disadvantaged position.

Hindi meaning: व्यक्ति या समूह जिसे हारने की उम्मीद

होती है या असुरुचित स्थिति में होता है।

Sentence: Despite being the underdog, the team put up a great fight and surprised everyone by winning the championship.

Idiom: In the doghouse

Meaning: In a situation where someone is angry or upset with you for some reason.

Hindi meaning: ऐसी स्थिति में जहां कोई आपसे किसी कारण से नाराज़ या उदास है।

Sentence: After forgetting their anniversary, he found himself in the doghouse with his wife.

FOOD BASED IDIOMS

Piece of cake -

Meaning: Something that is very easy to do.

Hindi meaning: बहुत आसान काम

Sentence: Don't worry about the exam. It's a piece of cake.

Spill the beans -

Meaning: To reveal a secret or confidential information.

Hindi meaning: राज़ खोलना

Sentence: John accidentally spilled the beans about the surprise party.

Full of beans -

Meaning: To be full of energy and enthusiasm.

Hindi meaning: ऊर्जा से भरा होना

Sentence: The children were full of beans after playing at the park.

Bring home the bacon -

Meaning: To earn a living or provide financial support for one's family.

Hindi meaning: पारिवारिक आय कमाना

Sentence: Sarah works two jobs to bring home the bacon.

Like two peas in a pod -

Meaning: Two people who are very similar or closely related.

Hindi meaning: दोनों में बहुत बड़ी समानता

Sentence: Mary and her sister are like two peas in a pod, they even finish each other's sentences.

Bread and butter -

Meaning: A person's main source of income or livelihood.

Hindi meaning: रोज़ी-रोटी

Sentence: His small business is his bread and butter.

Cool as a cucumber -

Meaning: To remain calm and composed, especially in a difficult or stressful situation.

Hindi meaning: ठंडा दिमाग़

Sentence: Despite the chaos around her, she remained cool as a cucumber.

Sour grapes -

Meaning: To disparage something that one but cannot have.

Hindi meaning: नाखुशी दिखाना

Sentence: After losing the competition, he called it sour grapes and pretended he didn't want to win anyway.

Big cheese -

Meaning: A person of importance or high authority.

Hindi meaning: महत्वपूर्ण व्यक्ति

Sentence: The CEO is the big cheese of the company.

Take something with a grain of salt -

Meaning: To not completely believe or trust something.

Hindi meaning: किसी बात को पूरी तरह न मानना

Sentence: He tends to exaggerate, so take his stories with a grain of salt

Idioms based on 'Apple'

Apple of discord -

Meaning: Referring to something or someone that triggers or intensifies a disagreement or conflict among people.

Hindi Meaning: झगड़े का कारण - लोगों के बीच एक असहमति या विवाद को प्रेरित या अधिकतम करने वाली किसी चीज या किसी को छेड़ने का कारण।

Sentence: The disputed property became the apple of discord among the family members, leading to frequent arguments.

Apple pie order -

Meaning: Describing something that is neatly organised or arranged in a systematic manner.

Hindi Meaning: बिल्कुल ठीक ढंग से व्यवस्थित किया हुआ - कुछ जो ठीक ढंग से व्यवस्थित हो या एक व्यवस्थापन तंत्र में व्यवस्थित हो।

Sentence: Her books were always in apple pie order, arranged alphabetically on the shelves.

Apple of one's eye

Meaning: Referring to a person who is cherished, loved, or considered as someone's favourite.

Hindi Meaning: आँखों का तारा - किसी को सम्मानित, प्यार और पसंदीदा माना जाने वाला व्यक्ति।

Sentence: His daughter is the apple of his eye, and he can't imagine life without her.

Comparing apples and oranges -

Meaning: Attempting to compare or evaluate two things that are fundamentally different and cannot be compared.

Hindi Meaning: दो बिल्कुल अलग चीजों का तुलना करना - दो चीजों की तुलना करने का प्रयास करना जो मूल रूप से भिन्न हैं और तुलना नहीं की जा सकती है।

Sentence: Comparing the intelligence of humans and animals is like comparing apples and oranges, as they have different cognitive abilities.

Adam's apple -

Meaning: Referring to the visible protrusion in the neck, specifically the laryngeal prominence, which is more prominent in males.

Hindi Meaning: गले का गुटथिला - गले का दिखाई देने वाला उतक, विशेष रूप से स्त्री पुरुषों में अधिक प्रमुख।

Sentence: He cleared his throat, and his Adam's apple moved visibly as he swallowed.

Bad apple -

Meaning: Referring to someone or something that is negative, problematic, or has a detrimental influence on a group or situation.

Hindi Meaning: खराब सेब - व्यक्ति या चीज़ जो किसी समूह या स्थिति पर नकारात्मक, समस्यात्मक या हानिकारक प्रभाव डालती है।

Sentence: The team worked well together, except for one bad apple who always caused conflicts.

An apple doesn't fall far from the tree -

Meaning: Referring to the idea that children often display similar characteristics or behaviours as their parents.

Hindi Meaning: एक सेब वृक्ष के बहुत दूर नहीं गिरता - बच्चे अक्सर अपने माता-पिता की सामान्य गुणधर्म या आचरण का प्रदर्शन करते हैं।

Sentence: The child's talent in painting is not surprising; after all, an apple doesn't fall far from the tree.

IDIOMS BASED ON 'COLOR'

Based On Red Color

Red alert -

Meaning: A state of emergency or heightened alertness, often indicating a dangerous or critical situation.

Hindi Meaning: चेतावनी या उच्चतम सतर्कता की स्थिति, जिससे अक्सर खतरनाक या महत्वपूर्ण स्थिति का संकेत होता है।

Sentence: The military received a red alert about a possible terrorist attack.

A red letter day -

Meaning: A memorable or significant day, often associated with a special event or occasion.

Hindi Meaning: एक यादगार या महत्वपूर्ण दिन, जिसे अक्सर एक विशेष घटना या अवसर से जोड़ा जाता है।

Sentence: Graduation day was a red letter day in her life.

To paint the town red -

Meaning: To go out and have a lively, extravagant, or enjoyable time, often involving celebration or partying.

Hindi Meaning: उमंग, आनंद या खुशी करने के लिए बाहर जाना और मजेदार, अतिरंजनात्मक या मनोरंजक समय बिताना, अक्सर जश्न या पार्टी के साथ।

Sentence: After winning the championship, they decided to paint the town red and celebrate all night.

Red- handed -

Meaning: Caught in the act of doing something wrong or illegal.

Hindi Meaning: किसी ग़लत या अवैध काम करते हुए पकड़ा गया।

Sentence: The thief was caught red-handed while stealing from the jewelry store.

In red ink -

Meaning: To have financial losses or owe money.

Hindi Meaning: वित्तीय हानि होना या पैसे उधार में होना।

Sentence: The company's accounts were in red ink due to poor financial management.

Red tape/tapism -

Meaning: Excessive bureaucracy or administrative procedures that cause delay or inefficiency. Hindi Meaning: अत्यधिक नियमों और प्रशासनिक प्रक्रियाओं का उपयोग, जो देरी या अप्रभावकारिता का कारण बनता है।

Sentence: The project was delayed due to all the red tape involved in obtaining permits and licences.

In the red -

Meaning: Having negative financial balance or being in debt.

Hindi Meaning: नकदी का अभाव या कर्ज में होना।

Sentence: The company has been struggling financially and is currently in the red.

Red carpet -

Meaning: To give someone a special and warm welcome, often involving VIP treatment.

Hindi Meaning: किसी को विशेष और गर्म स्वागत देना, अक्सर वीआईपी व्यवहार के साथ।

Sentence: The celebrity was greeted with a red carpet reception at the movie premiere.

Red in the face -

Meaning: To feel or display embarrassment or shame.

Hindi Meaning: शर्मिंदा या लज्जित महसूस करना या प्रदर्शित करना।

Sentence: After tripping and falling in front of everyone, she turned red in the face.

To see red -

Meaning: To become extremely angry or furious with someone or something.

Hindi Meaning: किसी व्यक्ति या वस्तु के प्रति बहुत गुस्सा या क्रोध करना।

Sentence: When he heard the news, he saw red and stormed out of the room.

Based On Blue Color

A bolt from the blue -

Meaning: An unexpected and surprising event or news that is often unpleasant or shocking.

Hindi Meaning: अप्रत्याशित और चौंकाने वाली घटना या समाचार जो अक्सर अप्रिय या चौंकाने वाला होता है।

Sentence: The sudden announcement of layoffs came as a bolt from the blue for the employees.

Out of the blue -

Meaning: Without any warning or preparation; unexpectedly.

Hindi Meaning: बिना किसी चेतावनी या तैयारी के; अप्रत्याशित रूप से।

Sentence: She received a job offer out of the blue while she was not actively looking for employment.

Blue blood -

Meaning: Coming from a noble or aristocratic family; having high social status or pedigree.

Hindi Meaning: किसी महाराजी या आदिकारी परिवार से संबंधित; उच्च सामाजिक स्थान या वंशवाद होना।

Sentence: The princess was born with blue blood and had all the privileges of royalty.

Feel blue -

Meaning: To feel melancholy, sad, or downcast.

Hindi Meaning: उदास, दुखी या मनहूस महसूस करना।

Sentence: After her breakup, she started to feel blue and found it hard to enjoy anything.

Beat black and blue -

Meaning: To severely beat or bruise someone, either physically or emotionally.

Hindi Meaning: किसी को गंभीरता से पीटना या घायल करना, चाहे यह शारीरिक रूप से हो या भावनात्मक रूप से।

Sentence: The victim was beaten black and blue by the assailants.

Blue-eyed -

Meaning: Someone who is favoured or regarded with special attention or affection.

Hindi Meaning: कोई व्यक्ति जिसे विशेष ध्यान या प्रेम के साथ प्राथमिकता दी जाती है।

Sentence: The boss's blue-eyed employee always gets the best opportunities and perks.

Blue collar -

Meaning: Relating to manual labour or industrial work, typically associated with the working class.

Hindi Meaning: हाथी-कर्मी या औद्योगिक कार्य से संबंधित, जो आमतौर पर कार्यवर्ग से जुड़ा होता है।

Sentence: He comes from a blue-collar background and has worked as a factory worker his whole life

Blue stockings -

Meaning: A woman who is highly educated or intellectual, often associated with scholarly pursuits.

Hindi Meaning: एक महिला जो उच्च शिक्षित या बौद्धिक होती है, जिसे विद्यार्थी गतिविधियों से जोड़ा जाता है।

Sentence: She was known as a blue stocking in her time, being one of the few women pursuing higher education.

Once in a blue moon -

Meaning: Something that happens very rarely or on rare occasions.

Hindi Meaning: कुछ जो बहुत कम या दिन-ब-दिन घटनात्मक होता है।

Sentence: I only see my childhood friends once in a blue moon since we all live in different countries now.

Based On White Color

White collar job -

Meaning: A job or occupation that typically involves professional or managerial work, often performed in an office setting.

Hindi Meaning: व्यावसायिक कौशलों की आवश्यकता वाली नौकरी या व्यवसाय, जिसे आमतौर पर कार्यालय स्थान में किया जाता है।

Sentence: He works in a white-collar job as an accountant at a prestigious firm.

Wave a white flag -

Meaning: To indicate surrender or submission, often by waving a white flag.

Hindi Meaning: हार या समर्पण का संकेत देना, अक्सर एक सफेद झंडा लहराकर।

Sentence: Realizing they were outnumbered, the troops waved a white flag and surrendered.

As white as a ghost -

Meaning: To become extremely pale, often due to fear, shock, or illness.

Hindi Meaning: भय, आघात या बीमारी के कारण बहुत ही पीला हो जाना।

Sentence: When she saw the car accident, she turned as white as a ghost.

As white as a sheet -

Meaning: To become extremely pale, usually from fear, shock, or extreme anxiety.

Hindi Meaning: डर से, आघात से या अत्यधिक चिंता से बहुत ही पीला हो जाना।

Sentence: He was so frightened by the horror movie that he turned as white as a sheet.

Put something down in black and white -

Meaning: To express or document something in writing, making it clear and unambiguous.

Hindi Meaning: कुछ लिखित रूप में व्यक्त करना, जिससे यह स्पष्ट और सुस्पष्ट हो जाए।

Sentence: The agreement should be put down in black and white to avoid any misunderstandings.

White elephant -

Meaning: Something that is expensive or burdensome to maintain, but has little or no practical value.

Hindi Meaning: कोई ऐसी चीज़ जो रखरखाव के लिए महंगी होती है लेकिन उपयोग की दृष्टि से नहीं होती है।

Sentence: The mansion they bought turned out to be a white elephant because it required extensive renovations and upkeep.

To show white feather -

Meaning: To display fear or cowardice; to act timidly or in a way that shows a lack of courage.

Hindi Meaning: डर या कायरता प्रदर्शित करना; कायरता या साहस की कमी दिखाने के रूप में डरपोकी या हयाहूयाही से काम करना।

Sentence: When faced with a difficult challenge, he showed white feather and refused to confront it.

White lie -

Meaning: A minor lie told with good intentions, often to spare someone's feelings or prevent unnecessary harm.

Hindi Meaning: छोटी सी झूठ जो अच्छे इरादों के साथ कही जाती है, अक्सर किसी के भावनाओं को बचाने या अनावश्यक हानि से बचाने के लिए।

Sentence: She told a white lie to her friend by saying she had already eaten, even though she was hungry

Based On Black Color

Black and white -

Meaning: A clear and straightforward choice between two contrasting options.

Hindi Meaning: दो विपरीत चीजों के बीच एक सरल चुनाव।

Sentence: The instructions were given in black and white, leaving no room for interpretation.

Black as night -

Meaning: Extremely dark or lacking light, often used metaphorically to describe something mysterious or ominous.

Hindi Meaning: बहुत ही काला या प्रकाशहीन, अक्सर किसी रहस्यमय या भयानक चीज़ को वर्णित करने के लिए इस्तेमाल किया जाता है।

Sentence: The room was as black as night, making it difficult to see anything inside.

Black and blue -

Meaning: To inflict physical injury on someone, resulting in bruising or discoloration.

Hindi Meaning: किसी को शारीरिक रूप से घायल करना, जिससे शारीर पर नीले निशान या रंग का बदलाव हो।

Sentence: The victim was beaten black and blue, with bruises covering his body.

To blackball someone -

Meaning: To vote against or reject someone's membership or inclusion in a group, often due to personal bias or disapproval.

Hindi Meaning: किसी की सदस्यता या समूह में शामिली के खिलाफ मतदान करना या अस्वीकार करना, अक्सर व्यक्तिगत पक्षपात या अस्वीकृति के कारण।

Based On Green Color

Green eyed -

Meaning: Feeling or showing jealousy or envy towards someone.

Hindi Meaning: किसी के प्रति ईर्ष्या या अभिमान भाव दिखाना या महसूस करना।

Sentence: She couldn't hide her green-eyed jealousy when she saw her ex-boyfriend with his new girlfriend.

Be green -

Meaning: To lack experience or knowledge in a particular field or situation. Hindi Meaning: किसी विशेष क्षेत्र या स्थिति में अनुभव या ज्ञान की कमी होना।
Sentence: As a fresh graduate, he may be green in the corporate world, but he is eager to learn and grow.

Get the green light -

Meaning: To receive approval or permission to proceed with a particular plan or action.

Hindi Meaning: किसी विशेष योजना या कार्रवाई के लिए मंजूरी या अनुमति प्राप्त करना।

Sentence: After thorough deliberation, the project was finally given the green light to commence.

Green thumb -

Meaning: Someone who has a natural talent or ability for gardening; someone who is skilled at growing plants.

Hindi Meaning: उद्यानिकी में कुशलता रखने वाला व्यक्ति; पौधों को उगाने में माहिर व्यक्ति।

Sentence: My neighbour has a green thumb. Her garden is always thriving with beautiful flowers and plants.

Green belt -

Meaning: A designated area of land, typically surrounding an urban area, that is kept undeveloped and preserved with fields and trees.

Hindi Meaning: फसलों और पेड़ों के साथ अविकसित रखा जाने वाला क्षेत्र, आमतौर पर एक शहरी क्षेत्र के चारों ओर स्थित।

Sentence: The city planned to designate a green belt around its outskirts to maintain the natural beauty of the area.

To go/look green -

Meaning: To appear pale or sickly, often due to illness or discomfort.

Hindi Meaning: बीमारी या अस्वस्थता के कारण पीले या बीमार दिखाई देना।

Sentence: He went green after eating the spoiled food, and we knew he was not feeling well

IDIOMS BASED ON 'FEATHER'

Idiom - **To show a white feather**

Meaning - Behave like a coward

Hindi meaning - भीगी बिल्ली बनना

Sentence - He was afraid to confront his opponent and showed a white feather by backing out of the argument.

Idiom - **A feather in one's cap**

Meaning - An achievement/success to be proud of

Hindi meaning - अपने सिर पर ताज

Sentence - Winning the competition was a feather in his cap and he celebrated his victory with joy.

Idiom - **To feather one's nest**

Meaning - To look after one's own interests, especially material ones

Hindi meaning - अपने अधिकारों का ध्यान रखना

Sentence - The corrupt official used his position to feather his own nest, accumulating wealth through illegal means.

Idiom - **Birds of the same feather**

Meaning - Two people who are very similar to each other in any way

Hindi meaning - एक जैसी प्रकृति के लोग

Sentence - John and Peter are birds of the same feather as they both have a passion for adventure sports.

Idiom - **In fine feather**

Meaning - Well-dressed

Hindi meaning - भद्र तरीके से सजा हुआ

Sentence - She attended the gala event in fine feather, wearing an elegant gown and stunning jewellery.

Idiom - **Ruffles one's feathers**

Meaning - To annoy/irritate someone

Hindi meaning - किसी को चिढ़ाना/चिढ़ाना

Sentence - His sarcastic remarks always ruffled her feathers, making her feel uncomfortable in his presence.

IDIOMS BASED ON 'SEA/OCEAN'

At sea -

Meaning: In a state of confusion or dilemma.

Hindi meaning: भ्रमित अवस्था में

Sentence: After receiving conflicting instructions, she was completely at sea about what to do next.

A sea change -

Meaning: A significant or substantial change.

Hindi meaning: बड़ा बदलाव

Sentence: The company went through a sea change after the new management took over.

Between the devil and the deep sea -

Meaning: In a very difficult situation, having to choose between two equally undesirable options.

Hindi meaning: आपदा में पड़ना

Sentence: She was caught between the devil and the deep sea when both job offers she had were undesirable.

A drop/spit in the ocean -

Meaning: A small amount of something in comparison to the whole.

Hindi meaning: छोटी सी मात्रा

Sentence: The amount of money raised so far is just a drop in the ocean compared to what we need.

An ocean of something -

Meaning: A large amount or quantity of something.

Hindi meaning: किसी चीज़ की अस्थायी ज़रूरत

Sentence: She had an ocean of patience when dealing with difficult customers.

Boil the ocean -

Meaning: To attempt or undertake an impossible or excessively difficult task.

Hindi meaning: असंभव कार्य करना

Sentence: Don't waste your time trying to boil the ocean. Focus on achievable goals

IDIOMS BASED ON 'CONFUSION'

At sixes and sevens -

Meaning: Confusion or disorder.

Hindi meaning: भ्रमित या व्यवस्थित न होना

Sentence: After the renovation, the furniture was all at sixes and sevens.

At one's wits' end / out of one's wits -

Meaning: Extremely worried or frustrated, not knowing what to do.

Hindi meaning: बेचैन या परेशान होना

Sentence: She was at her wits' end trying to solve the difficult maths problem.

At sea / at a loss -

Meaning: Confused or uncertain, not knowing what to do or how to proceed.

Hindi meaning: भ्रमित या संकोच में होना

Sentence: When the power went out, he was at a loss as to how to continue his work.

In a fix / in a quandary / in a muddle / in a dilemma / in a flutter -

Meaning: Being in a difficult or uncertain situation.

Hindi meaning: परेशानी या संकट में होना

Sentence: She was in a fix when she realised she had lost her wallet.

Blow hot and cold -

Meaning: To have contradictory or inconsistent opinions or feelings about something.

Hindi meaning: स्पष्ट रूप से अभिप्रेत करना

Sentence: He keeps blowing hot and cold on whether he wants to go on the trip or not.

Alphabet soup -

Meaning: A confusing or complex mixture of letters or acronyms.

Hindi meaning: वर्णमाला का दाल

Sentence: The manual was filled with technical terms and alphabet soup that made it difficult to understand.

All Greek to someone -

Meaning: Something that is completely incomprehensible or unintelligible.

Hindi meaning: समझ में न आने वाली चीज़

Sentence: When it comes to advanced calculus, it's all Greek to me.

Clear as mud -

Meaning: Something that is unclear, confusing, or difficult to understand.

Hindi meaning: मिट्टी के जितना स्पष्ट

Sentence: The professor's explanation of the topic was clear as mud; nobody understood it.

Scratch one's head -

Meaning: To be puzzled or confused about something.

Hindi meaning: मस्तक कसना

Sentence: I've been scratching my head trying to figure out how to solve this problem.

On the horns of a dilemma -

Meaning: Being faced with a difficult choice between two equally undesirable options.

Hindi meaning: मुसीबत की दो धारों में

Sentence: She found herself on the horns of a dilemma when she had to choose between her career and her family.

Get/have one's wires crossed -

Meaning: To have a misunderstanding or miscommunication with someone.

Hindi meaning: समझ न आने की स्थिति

Sentence: We got our wires crossed and ended up going to different restaurants for dinner.

IDIOMS BASED ON 'HARD WORK'

Burn the midnight oil -

Meaning: To work late at night, especially to study or complete a task.

Hindi meaning: रातोंरात काम करना

Sentence: He had to burn the midnight oil to finish his project before the deadline.

Go the extra mile -

Meaning: To put in additional effort or do more than what is expected.

Hindi meaning: अतिरिक्त प्रयास करना

Sentence: She always goes the extra mile to provide excellent customer service.

A hard nut to crack -

Meaning: Something or someone that is difficult to understand or solve.

Hindi meaning: कठिन समस्या

Sentence: Solving this maths equation is a hard nut to crack.

Keep nose to the grindstone -

Meaning: To work hard and diligently.

Hindi meaning: मेहनत करना

Sentence: If you want to succeed, you have to keep your nose to the grindstone.

Herculean task -

Meaning: A task that requires tremendous effort and strength.

Hindi meaning: बड़ा कठिन काम

Sentence: Cleaning the entire house in one day was a Herculean task.

Work your fingers to the bone -

Meaning: To work very hard, often to the point of exhaustion.

Hindi meaning: काम में बाहुत मेहनत करना

Sentence: She worked her fingers to the bone to provide for her family.

Pull your socks up -

Meaning: To make an effort to improve or work harder.

Hindi meaning: मेहनत या सुधार करना

Sentence: If you want to pass the exam, you need to pull your socks up and study more.

Bend over backwards -

Meaning: To make a great effort or go to extreme lengths to achieve something.

Hindi meaning: पूरी कोशिश करना

Sentence: The company bent over backwards to accommodate the needs of their clients.

IDIOMS BASED ON 'EASY TASK'

Shooting fish in a barrel -

Meaning: a task or situation that is very easy.

Hindi Translation: बड़ी आसानी से काम करना

Sentence: For a skilled archer, hitting the target was like shooting fish in a barrel.

As easy as ABC/123 -

Meaning: extremely easy or simple.

Hindi Translation: ABC/123 की तरह आसान

Sentence: After studying for hours, solving the maths problem felt as easy as ABC.

Cup of tea -

Meaning: something that one enjoys or is interested in.

Hindi Translation: मनपसंद चीज़

Sentence: Reading novels is not his cup of tea; he prefers non-fiction books.

Child's play -

Meaning: something that is very easy to do.

Hindi Translation: बच्चों का खेल

Sentence: For a skilled pianist, playing that piece was child's play.

Like a cakewalk

Meaning: something that is extremely easy and effortless.

Hindi Translation: आसान और आरामदायक काम

Sentence: After months of practice, the final exam

felt like a cake walk for him.

Piece of cake -

Meaning: something that is very easy.

Hindi Translation: आसान काम

Sentence: Fixing the broken shelf was a piece of cake for the experienced carpenter.

Walking in the park -

Meaning: a task or activity that is very easy.

Hindi Translation: पार्क में चलने जैसा आसान

Sentence: After mastering the dance routine, performing on stage was like walking in the park.

It is no rocket science -

Meaning: It is not a complex or difficult task.

Hindi Translation: यह रॉकेट साइंस नहीं है

Sentence: Figuring out the solution to that problem is no rocket science; anyone can do it with a little effort

IDIOMS BASED ON TIME

At the eleventh hour -

Meaning: at the last moment or just before a deadline.

Hindi Translation: अंतिम समय पर

Sentence: He submitted his assignment at the eleventh hour.

In the nick of time -

Meaning: just in time or at the last possible moment.

Hindi Translation: समय के अंतिम में

Sentence: She arrived at the airport in the nick of time to catch her flight.

Turn back the hands of time -

Meaning: to travel backwards in time, into the past.

Hindi Translation: समय की घड़ी पलट देना

Sentence: If I could, I would turn back the hands of time and change my decisions.

A hard time -

Meaning: hardship, suffering, or problems.

Hindi Translation: कठिन समय

Sentence: She went through a hard time after losing her job.

Beat the clock -

Meaning: to perform a task quickly or within a fixed time limit.

Hindi Translation: समय से पहले पूरा कर लेना

Sentence: He managed to beat the clock and finish the project before the deadline.

In the long run -

Meaning: over an extended period of time.

Hindi Translation: लंबे समय तक

Sentence: Saving money regularly can benefit you in the long run.

Dog's age -

Meaning: a very long time.

Hindi Translation: कुत्ते के युग

Sentence: We haven't seen each other in a dog's age.

Donkey's year -

Meaning: a very long time.

Hindi Translation: बहुत लंबा समय

Sentence: I haven't been to the beach in a donkey's year.

A month of Sundays -

Meaning: after a very long time.

Hindi Translation: बहुत लंबे समय बाद

Sentence: She finally completed her book, but it took a month of Sundays.

A Penelope's web -

Meaning: an endless work or task.

Hindi Translation: अनंत कार्य

Sentence: Cleaning the garage felt like unraveling a Penelope's web.

Around the clock -

Meaning: throughout an entire 24-hour day.

Hindi Translation: घड़ी के आस-पास

Sentence: The hospital staff works around the clock to take care of patients.

Fullness of time -

Meaning: an appropriate amount of time.

Hindi Translation: समय की परिपूर्णता

Sentence: Success will come in the fullness of time, so be patient.

Once in a while -

Meaning: occasionally.

Hindi Translation: कभी-कभी

Sentence: I treat myself to ice cream once in a while.

Every now and then -

Meaning: occasionally.

Hindi Translation: कभी-कभी

Sentence: He still visits his hometown every now and then

IDIOMS BASED ON FIGHT/DISPUTE

Bad blood -

Meaning: feeling of ill will arousing active hostility.

Hindi Translation: बुरी दुश्मनी

Sentence: There has been bad blood between them ever since the argument.

No love lost -

Meaning: nothing but animosity for one another.

Hindi Translation: आपस में नफ़रत

Sentence: There's no love lost between those two - they can't stand each other.

Be at loggerheads -

Meaning: in conflict with someone.

Hindi Translation: मतभेद होना

Sentence: The two political parties are at loggerheads over the new policy.

At daggers drawn -

Meaning: ready to fight or be in a state of hostility.

Hindi Translation: लड़ने के लिए तैयार

Sentence: The two rival gangs are at daggers drawn with each other.

Cross swords -

Meaning: in conflict or opposition to someone.

Hindi Translation: टकराव करना

Sentence: The lawyer and the prosecutor crossed swords during the trial.

Hammer and tongs -

Meaning: engaging in a vigorous or heated argument.

Hindi Translation: बहुत जोर-शोर से बहस करना

Sentence: The siblings were going at it hammer and tongs over the remote control.

Bone of contention -

Meaning: a cause of dispute or dislike.

Hindi Translation: विवाद का कारण

Sentence: Money has become a bone of contention in their relationship.

An apple of discord -

Meaning: a small matter that could lead to a big fight.

Hindi Translation: विवाद का कारण बनने वाला छोटा मुद्दा

Sentence: The distribution of inheritance became the apple of discord among the siblings.

Cat and dog life -

Meaning: a quarrelsome life.

Hindi Translation: झगड़ालू जीवन

Sentence: They live a cat and dog life, constantly bickering with each other

Fight like cat and dog -

Meaning: to fight or argue fiercely.

Hindi Translation: बिल्ली और कुत्ते की तरह लड़ना

Sentence: Whenever they get together, they fight like cat and dog.

Bury the hatchet -

Meaning: to end a quarrel or conflict and become friendly.

Hindi Translation: झगड़ा समाप्त करना

Sentence: After years of feuding, they finally decided to bury the hatchet and reconcile.

Gloves are off -

Meaning: to have decided to compete or fight aggressively.

Hindi Translation: मुकाबला या लड़ाई करने का निर्णय लिया होना"

Sentence: The competitors entered the ring, and the gloves were off.

Let bygones be bygones -

Meaning: to forgive someone and end a quarrel.

Hindi Translation: बीते वक्त को बीता होने दें

Sentence: It's time to let bygones be bygones and move on from the past.

Olive branch -

Meaning: to show someone that you want to end a quarrel.

Hindi Translation: दोस्ताना संकेत देना

Sentence: He extended an olive branch to his estranged friend, hoping to mend their relationship.

IDIOMS BASED ON 'FRIENDSHIP'

On good terms -

Meaning: friendly relationships.

Hindi Translation: अच्छे संबंध

Sentence: Despite their differences, they managed to stay on good terms with each other.

To build bridges -

Meaning: promote friendly relations between groups.

Hindi Translation: संबंध बढ़ाना

Sentence: The diplomat's mission was to build bridges between the two warring nations.

To hit it off -

Meaning: be naturally friendly.

Hindi Translation: सहमत हो जाना

Sentence: They met for the first time at the party and immediately hit it off.

Bosom friend -

Meaning: very close friend.

Hindi Translation: गहरी मित्रता

Sentence: She's not just a friend; she's my bosom friend whom I can trust with anything.

Through thick and thin -

Meaning: under all circumstances (both good and bad).

Hindi Translation: अच्छे और बुरे समय में

Sentence: He has been by my side through thick and thin, always supporting me.

Close-knit -

Meaning: close friend.

Hindi Translation: घनिष्ठ

Sentence: Their group of friends is very close-knit and always there for each other.

Have a shoulder to cry on -

Meaning: friends who understand you.

Hindi Translation: रोने के लिए कंधा होना

Sentence: It's comforting to know that I have a shoulder to cry on whenever I'm feeling down.

Kith and kin -

Meaning: close friends/relatives.

Hindi Translation: नजदीकी रिश्तेदार और मित्र

Sentence: The family gathering was filled with kith and kin, all coming together to celebrate.

To be as thick as thieves -

Meaning: very close or friendly.

Hindi Translation: बहुत घनिष्ठ

Sentence: Those two are as thick as thieves; they do everything together.

Fair-weather friend -

Meaning: a person who is only there for you in good times.

Hindi Translation: अच्छे समय में ही साथ देने वाला मित्र

Sentence: Don't rely on him; he's just a fair-weather friend who disappears when things get tough.

IDIOMS BASED ON ANGER

Up in arms -

Meaning: very angry.

Hindi Translation: बहुत नाराज़

Sentence: The citizens were up in arms over the government's decision.

Blow your top -

Meaning: suddenly become angry.

Hindi Translation: अचानक गुस्सा हो जाना

Sentence: He blew his top when he found out about the broken vase.

To blow a -

Meaning: lose temper.

Hindi Translation: गुस्सा निकलना

Sentence: The boss blew a gasket when he saw the unfinished report.

To flip out -

Meaning: become very angry.

Hindi Translation: बहुत गुस्सा हो जाना

Sentence: My sister flipped out when she saw her phone was missing.

Pissed somebody off / cheesed somebody off -

Meaning: to make someone angry or annoyed.

Hindi Translation: किसी को नाराज़ करना

Sentence: His constant interruptions really pissed off his colleagues.

Get someone's nerves -

Meaning: become extremely angry.

Hindi Translation: किसी को बहुत गुस्सा दिलाना

Sentence: The constant noise from the construction site got on her nerves.

The last straw -

Meaning: the final irritation that causes a person to lose patience and become angry.

Hindi Translation: अंतिम झटका

Sentence: The constant delays were the last straw for him, and he lost his temper.

Rub the wrong way -

Meaning: to annoy or irritate someone.

Hindi Translation: किसी को परेशान करना

Sentence: His arrogant attitude always rubbed me the wrong way.

To drive someone up the wall -

Meaning: to make someone extremely annoyed or angry.

Hindi Translation: किसी को बहुत गुस्सा दिलाना

Sentence: Her constant complaining drove me up the wall.

To be like a red rag to a bull -

Meaning: to cause someone to become very angry or irritated.

Hindi Translation: बहुत गुस्सा दिलाना

IDIOMS BASED ON CALMNESS

Pull yourself together -

Meaning: to regain composure and calmness.

Hindi Translation: अपने आप को संयमित करो

Sentence: After receiving the shocking news, she took a deep breath and pulled herself together.

Keep one's hair on / Let your hair down -

Meaning: to ask someone to remain calm or relax.

Hindi Translation: शांत रहो / बढ़ा ले अपने बाल

Sentence: When he started getting angry, his friend told him to keep his hair on and not overreact.

Hold one's nerve -

Meaning: to remain calm and composed in a challenging situation.

Hindi Translation: शांतिपूर्वक बने रहो

Sentence: Despite the pressure, he held his nerve and delivered an excellent presentation.

Smooth someone's ruffled feathers -

Meaning: to calm or pacify someone who is angry or upset.

Hindi Translation: किसी को शांत करना

Sentence: She tried to smooth her colleague's ruffled feathers after the disagreement.

Keep your cool -

Meaning: to remain calm and composed in a challenging or stressful situation.

Hindi Translation: ठंडा रहो

Sentence: Even though the situation was tense, he managed to keep his cool and handle it calmly.

Take it easy -

Meaning: to relax and not worry or stress about something.

Hindi Translation: धीरे रहो

Sentence: After a long day at work, he decided to take it easy and spend the evening watching a movie.

Cool as a cucumber -

Meaning: to remain calm and composed, especially in stressful situations.

Hindi Translation: ठंडा जैसा

Sentence: Despite the chaos around her, she stayed cool as a cucumber and handled the situation calmly.

Hold your fire -

Meaning: to wait or refrain from taking action or making a comment.

Hindi Translation: आग को रोको

Sentence: Before making a decision, it's better to hold your fire and gather more information.

Still waters run deep -

Meaning: quiet or calm people often have a strong and complex character.

Hindi Translation: चुप चाप लोगों की गहरी बातें होती हैं

Sentence: He may seem quiet, but still waters run deep, and he has a lot of depth and wisdom.

IDIOMS BASED ON ENTHUSIASM

Live wire -

Meaning: someone who is enthusiastic.

Hindi Translation: उत्साही इंसान

Sentence: She's a live wire, always full of energy and enthusiasm.

All agog -

Meaning: excited or enthusiastic, eager to know or see more.

Hindi Translation: उत्साहित

Sentence: The children were all agog to open their presents on Christmas morning.

Let one's hair down -

Meaning: to relax and enjoy oneself.

Hindi Translation: आराम करना

Sentence: After a long week of work, she decided to let her hair down and have a fun weekend.

All one's might and main -

Meaning: full of capability and energy.

Hindi Translation: पूरी ताकत और ऊर्जा से

Sentence: He put all his might and main into completing the project on time.

Full of beans -

Meaning: very energetic.

Hindi Translation: बहुत ऊर्जावान

Sentence: The children were full of beans, running and playing in the park all day.

Go bananas over -

Meaning: to be excited about something.

Hindi Translation: कुछ पर बहुत उत्साहित होना

Sentence: The fans went bananas over the arrival of their favourite celebrity.

In high spirits -

Meaning: full of enthusiasm.

Hindi Translation: उच्छवास में

Sentence: Despite the setbacks, they remained in high spirits and were determined to achieve their goal

IDIOMS BASED ON LAZINESS

Couch potato / mouse potato -

Meaning: Someone who spends a lot of time sitting or lying down, typically watching television or using a computer.

Hindi Meaning: एक सुस्त व्यक्ति जो बैठकर या लेटकर बहुत समय बिताता है, आमतौर पर टेलीविजन देखते हुए या कंप्यूटर का उपयोग करते हुए।

Sentence: He has become a couch potato, spending most of his day watching TV and not engaging in any physical activity.

To slack off -

Meaning: To not put in the necessary effort or diligence, resulting in decreased productivity or quality of work.

Hindi Meaning: काम में आलस्यपूर्ण या कम प्रयास करना।

Sentence: Instead of studying for the exam, he decided to slack off and play video games all day.

To bum around -

Meaning: To be idle or loiter around without any specific purpose or productive activity.

Hindi Meaning: आलस्यपूर्ण रूप से व्यतीत समय बिना किसी विशेष उद्देश्य या उत्पादक गतिविधि के।

Sentence: During his vacation, he decided to bum around and just relax without doing any work.

Watching the grass grow

Meaning: Used to describe a very slow or uneventful activity or process.

Hindi Meaning: बहुत धीमी या अक्रांति रहित गतिविधि या प्रक्रिया को वर्णित करने के लिए इस्तेमाल किया जाता है।

Sentence: Waiting for the bus feels like watching the grass grow, it's taking forever.

To get off one's tail -

Meaning: To cease being idle or lazy and start being active or productive.

Hindi Meaning: आलस्यपूर्ण और सुस्त होना छोड़कर सक्रिय या उत्पादक बनना।

Sentence: It's time for you to get off your tail and start working on your assignments.

IDIOMS BASED ON MAN

Man of few words -

Meaning: someone who doesn't speak too much or is reticent.

Hindi Translation: कम शब्दों का इंसान

Sentence: He was a man of few words, but his actions spoke louder than his words.

Man of words -

Meaning: someone who keeps his promises or is trustworthy.

Hindi Translation: वचनबद्ध इंसान

Sentence: John is a man of words; if he says he will do something, he always follows through.

Man of letters -

Meaning: someone who is scholarly or erudite.

Hindi Translation: विद्वान इंसान

Sentence: The professor was a renowned man of letters in the field of literature.

Man in the street -

Meaning: the common man or ordinary person.

Hindi Translation: आम आदमी

Sentence: The policies of the government affect the man in the street the most.

A man of straw -

Meaning: a weak person or someone lacking strength.

Hindi Translation: कमजोर इंसान

Sentence: He proved to be a man of straw when faced with adversity.

A man of substance -

Meaning: a very rich person or someone of importance.

Hindi Translation: अहमियती या धनी इंसान

Sentence: He is a man of substance, known for his wealth and influence

IDIOMS BASED ON HEART

Chicken hearted -

Meaning: a coward.

Hindi Translation: कायर

Sentence: He didn't stand up for himself; he was too chicken hearted to confront the bullies.

By heart -

Meaning: to memorise something.

Hindi Translation: याद करना

Sentence: She learned the poem by heart and recited it flawlessly in the competition.

Heavy heart -

Meaning: feeling sad or sorrowful.

Hindi Translation: दुखी मन से / भारी दिल से

Sentence: She delivered the news with a heavy heart, knowing it would disappoint many.

Wear your heart on their sleeves -

Meaning: to openly express one's feelings or emotions.

Hindi Translation: अपनी भावनाओं को खुलकर बयां करना

Sentence: She wears her heart on her sleeve and is always honest about her emotions.

Heart in one's mouth -

Meaning: feeling nervous and excited about something.

Hindi Translation: घबराहट और उत्साह से भरा होना

Sentence: As she stood on the stage to deliver her speech, her heart was in her mouth.

Eat your heart out -

Meaning: to feel jealous of someone's achievement.

Hindi Translation: इन्हें ईर्ष्या होना

Sentence: He won the championship, so you can eat your heart out with envy.

To lose heart / Sinking heart / Sick at heart -

Meaning: feeling disappointed or hopeless.

Hindi Translation: उम्मीदों खो देना / डूबते हुए मन / उदास मन से

Sentence: After facing continuous failures, he started to lose heart and doubted his abilities.

IDIOMS BASED ON HONESTY

Good Samaritan -

Meaning: a person who selflessly helps others; an honest individual.

Hindi Translation: नेक इंसान / ईमानदार इंसान

Sentence: The stranger who helped the accident victim on the road proved to be a Good Samaritan.

A safe pair of hands -

Meaning: a trustworthy and reliable person.

Hindi Translation: एक भरोसेमंद इंसान

Sentence: When it comes to handling important tasks, John is known to be a safe pair of hands.

IDIOMS BASED ON DISHONESTY

Bad egg -

Meaning: a person who is morally bad or dishonest.

Hindi Translation: बुरा इंसान

Sentence: We found out that he was a bad egg when he cheated on his friends.

Bad hats -

Meaning: evil individuals who intentionally cause trouble.

Hindi Translation: बुरे लोग

Sentence: The gang of bad hats vandalised the neighbourhood and caused chaos.

Black sheep -

Meaning: a cunning or troublesome person within a group.

Hindi Translation:

Sentence: Amongst the family members, he was considered the black sheep due to his constant mischief.

Broken reed -

Meaning: an unreliable or untrustworthy person.

Hindi Translation: अविश्वसनीय इंसान

Sentence: I can't rely on him to complete the project; he is a broken reed.

Gather roses only -

Meaning: to seek only personal happiness and pleasure.

Hindi Translation: सिर्फ खुशियाँ चाहना

Sentence: She was criticised for being selfish and always wanting to gather roses only.

Trumped-up -

Meaning: a person who fabricates falsehoods or makes up false accusations.

Hindi Translation: झूठा / बेबुनियाद

Sentence: The defendant's lawyer argued that the charges against his client were trumped-up.

Wolf in sheep's clothing -

Meaning: a person who appears harmless but is actually dangerous or deceitful.

Hindi Translation: कोई व्यक्ति जो प्रतिभाशाली, हानिकारक या निर्दोष दिखता हो, लेकिन वास्तविकता में खतरनाक, धोखेबाज या दुरुपयोगी होता है।

Sentence: Be cautious of him; he may seem friendly, but he is a wolf in sheep's clothing.

All moonshine -

Meaning: complete lies or falsehoods.

Hindi Translation: झूठ

Sentence: Don't believe his promises; it's all

moonshine.

Take someone for a ride -

Meaning: to deceive or trick someone through dishonesty.

Hindi Translation: किसी को ठगना

Sentence: He took his unsuspecting friend for a ride by selling him a fake product.

Hand in glove -

Meaning: closely associated with someone, often in something dishonest.

Hindi Translation: मिलीभगत करना

Sentence: The corrupt politician and the businessman were hand in glove in their fraudulent activities.

Crocodile tears -

Meaning: an insincere or fake display of grief or sympathy.

Hindi Translation: मगरमच्छ की आँसू

Sentence: She pretended to cry at the funeral, but everyone could see through her crocodile tears.

IDIOMS BASED ON EYE

Bird's eye view -

Meaning: a general view or overview.

Hindi Translation: सामान्य दृष्टिकोण

Sentence: From the top of the mountain, we had a bird's eye view of the entire valley.

Eagle view -

Meaning: having the ability to notice even the smallest details or mistakes.

Hindi Translation: बहुत ध्यान से देखने की क्षमता

Sentence: The supervisor has an eagle view and can easily spot errors in the work.

Turn a blind eye -

Meaning: to ignore something wrong or unethical.

Hindi Translation: अनदेखा करना

Sentence: The teacher turned a blind eye to the student's cheating during the exam.

Hit the bull's eye -

Meaning: to achieve or accomplish something precisely or accurately.

Hindi Translation: लक्ष्य को पूरा करना

Sentence: His arrow hit the bull's eye right in the centre of the target.

Catch someone's eye -

Meaning: to attract someone's attention.

Hindi Translation: किसी का ध्यान आकर्षित करना

Sentence: The colourful display caught everyone's eye at the art exhibition.

Keep an eye on -

Meaning: to watch or monitor carefully.

Hindi Translation: सतर्क रहना

Sentence: Please keep an eye on the kids while I'm away.

See eye to eye -

Meaning: to agree with someone on something.

Hindi Translation: मेल खाना

Sentence: They finally saw eye to eye on the best way to solve the problem.

In the public eye / In the limelight -

Meaning: to be noticeable or in the focus of public attention.

Hindi Translation: लोगों की नजर में / सार्वजनिक ध्यान केंद्र में

Sentence: As a celebrity, she is constantly in the public eye and has to deal with media attention.

IDIOMS BASED ON HEALTH

Under the weather -

Meaning: feeling unwell or sick.

Hindi Translation: अस्वस्थ

Sentence: I can't come to the party tonight; I'm feeling a bit under the weather.

As fit as a fiddle -

Meaning: in very healthy condition or state.

Hindi Translation: बहुत स्वस्थ

Sentence: After regular exercise and a balanced diet, he is now as fit as a fiddle.

In the pink -

Meaning: in good health or excellent condition.

Hindi Translation: अच्छे स्वास्थ्य में

Sentence: Despite his age, he is still active and in the pink of health.

At death's door -

Meaning: so ill that one may die.

Hindi Translation: मृत्यु की ओर

Sentence: After the accident, he was in critical condition and at death's door.

Get back on your feet -

Meaning: to recover or become well again after an illness or setback.

Hindi Translation: फिर से खड़े हो जाना

Sentence: After a week of rest, he finally got back on his feet and returned to work

IDIOMS BASED ON OPPORTUNITY

Cross one's mind -

Meaning: a thought occurs to one.

Hindi Translation: मन में खयाल आना

Sentence: It never crossed my mind that he would quit his job.

Have something in mind -

Meaning: to be thinking of doing something.

Hindi Translation: मन में कुछ सोचना

Sentence: I have a few ideas in mind for our next vacation.

Give it a shot / Take a shot -

Meaning: to try something.

Hindi Translation: इसे कोशिश करें

Sentence: I've never played golf before, but I'm willing to give it a shot.

Seize the opportunity -

Meaning: to act quickly in order to use an opportunity.

Hindi Translation: मौका पकड़ो

Sentence: When the job opening came up, she seized the opportunity and applied immediately.

Miss the boat -

Meaning: to miss the opportunity.

Hindi Translation: मौका हाथ से निकल जाना

Sentence: I missed the boat on investing in that company, and now it's become very successful.

Open the door -

Meaning: to make something possible by making it easier.

Hindi Translation: रास्ता खोलना

Sentence: The new technology has opened the door for advancements in medical research.

Kill two birds with one stone -

Meaning: achieve two aims at once.

Hindi Translation: एक पथर से दो तीर मारना

Sentence: By studying while commuting, she kills two birds with one stone

IDIOMS BASED ON PRICES

As cheap as chips -

Meaning: very inexpensive.

Hindi Translation: बहुत सस्ता

Sentence: I bought this dress on sale, and it was as cheap as chips.

Cost an arm and a leg -

Meaning: extremely expensive.

Hindi Translation:

Sentence: The price of that luxury car is so high, it costs an arm and a leg.

Cost a fortune -

Meaning: extremely expensive.

Hindi Translation: बहुत महंगा पड़ना

Sentence: The designer handbag she bought cost a fortune.

Worth the money -

Meaning: having good value for the price paid.

Hindi Translation: मूल्यवान

Sentence: The quality of the service made it worth the money I spent.

Rolling in money -

Meaning: having a large amount of something, usually money.

Hindi Translation: पैसे में डूबा हुआ

Sentence: The millionaire was rolling in money and could afford anything he desired.

Bring home the bacon -

Meaning: to earn the money needed to live.

Hindi Translation: परिवार का पेट भरना

Sentence: He works hard to bring home the bacon and support his family

IDIOMS BASED ON PLACE

Hustle and bustle -

Meaning: a large amount of activity and work, usually in a noisy surrounding.

Hindi Translation: गहन व्यापार

Sentence: The city streets were filled with hustle and bustle during rush hour.

A stone's throw away -

Meaning: nearby, at a short distance.

Hindi Translation: बहुत करीब

Sentence: The café is just a stone's throw away from our office.

Heaven on earth -

Meaning: a very pleasant or enjoyable place.

Hindi Translation: पृथ्वी पर स्वर्ग

Sentence: Spending time with my loved ones makes me feel like I'm in heaven on earth

IDIOMS BASED ON HAPPY AND SAD

Based On Happiness

On cloud nine -

Meaning: To feel elated or euphoric, experiencing a state of extreme happiness or joy.

Hindi Meaning: बहुत खुश या आनंदित होना, अत्यंत खुशी या हर्ष की स्थिति में होना।

Sentence: Winning the competition put her on cloud nine; she couldn't stop smiling.

On top of the world -

Meaning: To feel ecstatic or on a pinnacle of happiness and contentment.

Hindi Meaning: आनंदित या खुशी और संतोष की शिखर पर होना।

Sentence: After receiving the promotion, he felt on top of the world, proud of his accomplishments.

Over the moon -

Meaning: To be extremely delighted or thrilled about something.

Hindi Meaning: किसी चीज़ के बारे में अत्यंत प्रसन्न या उत्साहित होना।

Sentence: She was over the moon when she found out she got accepted into her dream university.

Walking on air

Meaning: To feel extremely happy or elated, as if walking on a cloud or in a state of euphoria.

Hindi Meaning: बहुत खुश या आनंदित होना, जैसे कि बादलों पर चल रहे हो या उत्साह की स्थिति में होना।

Sentence: After receiving the good news, she felt like she was walking on air.

In seventh heaven

Meaning: To be in a state of extreme happiness, bliss, or joy.

Hindi Meaning: अत्यधिक खुशी, आनंद, या परमानंद की स्थिति में होना।

Sentence: Winning the championship put him in seventh heaven; he couldn't believe his success.

Music to one's ears -

Meaning: Information or news that is highly satisfying, comforting, or enjoyable to hear.

Hindi Meaning: सुनने के लिए बहुत प्रसन्नदायक, शानदार या आनंददायक सूचना या खबर।

Sentence: Hearing that she got the job offer was music to her ears; she had been waiting for it eagerly.

Belly laugh -

Meaning: A hearty, deep, and uninhibited laugh that originates from the belly or abdomen.

Hindi Meaning: गहरा, अनियंत्रित और मोटापे से उत्पन्न हंसी।

Sentence: The comedian's jokes had the audience in fits of belly laughter; they couldn't stop laughing.

Smiling from ear to ear -

Meaning: To be smiling very broadly, with the corners of one's mouth reaching from one ear to the other.

Hindi Meaning: चेहरे पर बड़ी मुस्कान होना, जिसमें मुंह के

कोने एक कान से दूसरे कान तक जाते हैं।

Sentence: When he saw the surprise party, he couldn't help but smile from ear to ear.

Laugh one's head off -

Meaning: To laugh loudly, energetically, or without restraint.

Hindi Meaning: जोर-जोर से हँसना, ऊर्जावानी से या नियंत्रण के बिना हँसना।

Sentence: The comedian's jokes were so funny that the audience laughed their heads off throughout the show.

Based On Sadness

Long face / straight face -

Meaning: To have a facial expression that shows sadness or disappointment.

Hindi Meaning: दुख या निराशा जताने वाला चेहरा होना।

Sentence: She had a long face after hearing the bad news about her friend.

Weal and woe -

Meaning: Referring to the experiences of both joy and sorrow, the ups and downs of life.

Hindi Meaning: खुशी और दुःख के अनुभवों को दर्शाने का संकेत देता है, जीवन के उछल-कूद को।

Sentence: They have been together through weal and woe, supporting each other in both good and bad times.

Ill at ease -

Meaning: Feeling uncomfortable, uneasy, or troubled, often accompanied by sadness or anxiety.

Hindi Meaning: असहज या चिंतित महसूस करना, जो अक्सर दुख या चिंता के साथ साथ होता है।

Sentence: She appeared ill at ease during the meeting, her sadness and anxiety evident in her demeanour.

Eat one's heart out -

Meaning: To experience intense sadness or grief, usually due to longing or unfulfilled desires.

Hindi Meaning: गहरे दुख या व्यथा को महसूस करना, आमतौर पर इच्छाएं या पूरी न होने के कारण।

Sentence: He ate his heart out when he realised he had missed his chance of a lifetime.

Down in the dumps -

Meaning: Feeling unhappy, depressed, or low in spirits.

Hindi Meaning: दुखी, उदास या मनोविकार से युक्त महसूस करना।

Sentence: She has been down in the dumps since her pet passed away.

Cry over spilt milk -

Meaning: Regretting or feeling upset about something that has already happened and cannot be undone.

Hindi Meaning: उस चीज़ पर खेद करना जो पहले हो चुकी है और पलट नहीं सकती।

Sentence: There's no point crying over spilt milk; it's better to focus on finding a solution.

Out of sorts -

Meaning: Feeling unwell, irritable, or in a state of discomfort, often resulting in a sad or unhappy mood.

Hindi Meaning: अस्वस्थ, चिढ़चिढ़ा या असहज स्थिति में होना, जो अक्सर दुखी या उदास मन की स्थिति में परिणामित होता है।

Sentence: She has been feeling out of sorts lately, and her sadness is evident in her behaviour

IDIOMS BASED ON START AND END

Based On Starting

From scratch -

Meaning: Starting something from the very beginning, without using any existing resources or progress.

Hindi Meaning: शुरुआत से, किसी मौजूदा संसाधन या प्रगति के बिना कुछ शुरू करना।

Sentence: She built her business from scratch, starting with just a small loan and a lot of determination.

Maiden speech -

Meaning: The first public speech or address given by someone, typically in a formal setting or on a specific occasion.

Hindi Meaning: किसी का पहला सार्वजनिक भाषण या प्रस्तावना, आमतौर पर एक औपचारिक स्थिति या विशेष अवसर पर।

Sentence: The new politician delivered her maiden speech with confidence and eloquence.

Seed money -

Meaning: The initial capital or funds provided to start a business or project.

Hindi Meaning: व्यापार या परियोजना की शुरुआत के लिए प्रदान की गई प्राथमिक पूंजी या धन।

Sentence: They used their savings as seed money to start their own company.

The alpha and omega -

Meaning: Referring to the very beginning and the ultimate end of something, encompassing the entire scope or range.

Hindi Meaning: किसी चीज़ की बहुत प्रारंभिक और अंतिम सीमा, पूरी क्षमता या श्रेणि को समेटने के लिए।

Sentence: Love is the alpha and omega of his existence; it is the beginning and end of everything for him.

Zero hour -

Meaning: The designated time at which a planned activity, event, or operation is scheduled to begin.

Hindi Meaning: किसी योजनित गतिविधि, आयोजन या संचालन की शुरुआत के लिए निर्धारित समय।

Sentence: The soldiers were instructed to be ready for action at zero hour.

Back to the drawing board -

Meaning: To start over again, usually due to a failed attempt or unsatisfactory outcome, requiring a fresh approach or plan.

Hindi Meaning: फिर से शुरू करें, आमतौर पर असफल प्रयास या अप्रसन्नजनक परिणाम के कारण, जो एक नयी दृष्टिकोण या योजना की आवश्यकता को संकेत करता है।

Sentence: After the project failed to meet the expectations, they decided to go back to the drawing board and come up with a new strategy.

Based On Ending

In the long run -

Meaning: Referring to the ultimate outcome or result over a longer period of time, considering the overall effects or consequences.

Hindi Meaning: अंत में, बड़े समयावधि में परिणाम या परिणाम को सोचते हुए, सामान्य प्रभाव या परिणाम को ध्यान में रखकर।

Sentence: It may seem difficult now, but in the long run, all your hard work will pay off.

Swan song -

Meaning: Referring to a final performance, act, or achievement before retirement or the end of something.

Hindi Meaning: रिटायरमेंट या किसी चीज़ के समाप्त होने से पहले की अंतिम प्रदर्शन, कार्य या उपलब्धि को संकेत करता है।

Sentence: The legendary actor's final movie was considered his swan song, showcasing his exceptional talent one last time.

The I and end all -

Meaning: The most important or essential thing, often regarded as the ultimate goal or result.

Hindi Meaning: सबसे महत्वपूर्ण या आवश्यक चीज़, जिसे आमतौर पर परम लक्ष्य या परिणाम के रूप में माना जाता है।

Sentence: For him, success in his career was the be all and end all; it was the ultimate goal he strived for.

Lock, stock, and barrel -

Meaning: Referring to the entirety or completeness of something, including all its components or aspects.

Hindi Meaning: किसी चीज़ की पूरी या संपूर्णता को संकेत करता है, जिसमें इसके सभी घटक या पहलू शामिल हैं।

Sentence: When they moved, they took everything with them, lock, stock, and barrel

IDIOMS BASED ON CAREFUL AND CARELESS

Based on Careful

Argus eyed -

Meaning: Being watchful, observant, and attentive, often to a high degree.

Hindi Meaning: सतर्क, संवेदनशील और ध्यानवान होना, अक्सर एक उच्च स्तर पर।

Sentence: The security guard was argus-eyed, keeping a close watch on the premises throughout the night.

All ears -

Meaning: Being fully attentive and receptive, eagerly listening to what someone has to say.

Hindi Meaning: पूर्ण ध्यानवान और संप्रेषणशील होना, जो किसी के कहने को उत्सुकता से सुनने में लगा होता है।

Sentence: When the teacher announced a surprise, the students were all ears, eager to hear what it was.

Eagle eyes -

Meaning: Being highly observant and watchful, paying close attention to details and surroundings.

Hindi Meaning: बहुत ध्यानपूर्वक और सतर्क होना, विवरणों और आसपास की चीजों पर ध्यान केंद्रित करना।

Sentence: The detective had eagle eyes, noticing even the slightest of changes in the crime scene.

Walk on eggshells -

Meaning: Being cautious and careful in one's behaviour or interactions, avoiding anything that could cause offence or conflict.

Hindi Meaning: अपने शब्दों या क्रियाओं के प्रति सतर्क और सतर्क रहना, जो किसी भी चीज़ के कारण अपमान या संघर्ष का कारण बन सकता है।

Sentence: After their argument, they had to walk on eggshells around each other, trying to avoid any further conflict.

Keep a weather eye on -

Meaning: Being vigilant and observant, keeping a close watch or monitoring a situation.

Hindi Meaning: सतर्क और सतर्क रहना, एक स्थिति का करीबी ध्यान रखना या निगरानी करना।

Sentence: The captain instructed the crew to keep a weather eye on the approaching storm to ensure their safety.

Based on careless

Fast and loose -

Meaning: Referring to someone who behaves in a careless, reckless, or irresponsible manner without considering the consequences.

Hindi Meaning: एक ऐसे व्यक्ति के बारे में जो बिना परिणामों को ध्यान में रखे बेपरवाह, लापरवाह या असत्यापित ढंग से व्यवहार करता है।

Sentence: He played fast and loose with his finances, spending extravagantly without considering his debts.

Hand over head -

Meaning: Acting or behaving in a reckless and careless manner without considering the consequences.

Hindi Meaning: परिणामों को ध्यान में न रखते हुए बेहतरीन और लापरवाह ढंग से कार्य करना।

Sentence: He made a hand over head decision without thinking it through and later regretted the consequences.

Like a bull in a china shop -

Meaning: Describing someone who is enthusiastic and energetic but lacks finesse or carefulness, often causing accidents or damage due to their lack of caution.

Hindi Meaning: वह व्यक्ति जो उत्साही और ऊर्जावान होता है, लेकिन सजगता या सतर्कता में कमी होती है, जिससे उनकी सतर्कता की कमी के कारण दुर्घटनाएँ या क्षति होती हैं।

Sentence: He entered the delicate antique store like a bull in a china shop, knocking over valuable items due to his lack of caution

IDIOMS BASED ON INTELLIGENCE AND FOOLISHNESS

Based On Intelligence

Sharp as a tack -

Meaning: Describing someone who is extremely intelligent, clever, and mentally sharp.

Hindi Meaning: वह व्यक्ति जो बहुत ही बुद्धिमान, चतुर और मानसिक रूप से तेज़ होता है।

Sentence: She solved the complex math problem effortlessly; she's as sharp as a tack.

Brainiac -

Meaning: Referring to someone who is exceptionally intelligent and knowledgeable.

Hindi Meaning: वह व्यक्ति जो अत्यधिक बुद्धिमान और ज्ञानवान होता है।

Sentence: He was known as a brainiac in his school, always scoring top marks in every subject.

Einstein -

Meaning: Using the name of Albert Einstein, a renowned physicist, to refer to someone who is highly intelligent.

Hindi Meaning: उस व्यक्ति के लिए उपयोग होने वाला एक शब्द जिससे बताया जाता है की व्यक्ति अत्यंत बुद्धिमान है।

Sentence: She's such an Einstein; she always comes up with brilliant ideas and solutions.

Whiz kid -

Meaning: Referring to a young individual who demonstrates exceptional talent or intelligence in a particular field.

Hindi Meaning: एक युवा व्यक्ति को संकेत करने के लिए, जो किसी विशेष क्षेत्र में असाधारण प्रतिभा या बुद्धिमत्ता दिखाता है।

Sentence: The twelve-year-old is a real whiz kid in computer programming; he's already developing his own apps.

Intellectual powerhouse -

Meaning: Describing someone who possesses immense intellectual abilities, expertise, and knowledge.

Hindi Meaning: वह व्यक्ति जिसके पास बहुत बड़े स्तर की बुद्धिमत्ता, विशेषज्ञता और ज्ञान होता है|

Sentence: The renowned professor is considered an intellectual powerhouse, with his extensive research and publications.

A smart cookie -

Meaning: Referring to someone who is clever, intelligent, and quick-witted.

Hindi Meaning: वह व्यक्ति जो चतुर, बुद्धिमान और तेज-दिमाग है।

Sentence: She's a smart cookie; she always comes up with innovative solutions to problems.

On the ball -

Meaning: Describing someone who is alert, attentive, and competent in their work or responsibilities.

Hindi Meaning: वह व्यक्ति जो अपने काम या जिम्मेदारियों में सतर्क, चौकस और प्रभावी है।

Sentence: Our team leader is always on the ball and ensures that projects are completed on time.

Sharp as a needle -

Meaning: Referring to someone who is exceptionally intelligent, sharp, and quick-minded.

Hindi Meaning: वह व्यक्ति जो अत्यंत बुद्धिमान, तेजस्वी और तेज-दिमाग है।

Sentence: He's sharp as a needle; he grasps new concepts quickly and easily.

Based on Foolishness

A nincompoop - a foolish person

Meaning: Referring to someone who is silly, foolish, or lacking intelligence.

Hindi Meaning: वह व्यक्ति जो मूर्ख, मूर्खतापूर्ण या बुद्धिहीन होता है।

Sentence: Don't pay attention to him; he's just a nincompoop who doesn't know what he's talking about.

Out of mind - crazy or insane

Meaning: Describing someone who is mentally unstable or irrational.

Hindi Meaning: वह व्यक्ति जो मानसिक रूप से अस्थिर या तर्कहीन होता है।

Sentence: After losing everything, he went out of his mind and started behaving erratically.

Lose one's marbles - become mentally unstable

Meaning: Referring to someone who is losing their sanity or mental clarity.

Hindi Meaning: वह व्यक्ति जो अपने समझ या मानसिक स्पष्टता को खो रहा है।

Sentence: Ever since the accident, he seems to have lost his marbles and struggles with memory loss.

Go nuts - go crazy or become very excited

Meaning: Describing someone who is acting in a wild, irrational, or overly excited manner.

Hindi Meaning: वह व्यक्ति जो एक विलक्षण, तर्कहीन या अत्यधिक उत्साहित ढंग से व्यवहार कर रहा है।

Sentence: The crowd went nuts when their favourite team scored the winning goal.

Take leave of one's senses - become irrational or act in a foolish manner

Meaning: Referring to someone who is behaving in an irrational, foolish, or nonsensical way.

Hindi Meaning: वह व्यक्ति जो तर्कहीन, मूर्ख या बेतुका ढंग से व्यवहार कर रहा है।

Sentence: He took leave of his senses and made a series of reckless decisions.

All thumbs - lacking coordination or clumsy

Meaning: Describing someone who is clumsy or lacks coordination, especially with their hands.

Hindi Meaning: वह व्यक्ति जो बेतुकी या समन्वय की कमी का सामना कर रहा है, विशेष रूप से अपने हाथों के साथ।

Sentence: I'm all thumbs when it comes to playing musical instruments; I can't seem to coordinate my fingers properly.

Daft as a brush - very silly or foolish

Meaning: Referring to someone who is extremely silly, foolish, or lacking common sense.

Hindi Meaning: वह व्यक्ति जो बहुत मूर्ख, मूर्खतापूर्ण या सामान्य समझ की कमी होती है। Sentence: He's daft as a brush; he always says the silliest things without thinking.

IDIOMS BASED ON DEVELOP AND DESTROY

Based On Development

Rise like Phoenix -

Meaning: Bouncing back and recovering from a difficult or challenging situation, becoming stronger and more resilient.

Hindi Meaning: एक आपदा से मजबूत, बुद्धिमान और शक्तिशाली रूप से बाहर आना।

Sentence: Despite facing numerous setbacks, she rose like a Phoenix and built a successful business.

Turn the corner -

Meaning: Reaching a point where a situation begins to improve or progress after a period of difficulty.

Hindi Meaning: मुख्य बिन्दु को पार करना और प्रगति करना शुरू करना।

Sentence: After months of struggling, the company finally turned the corner and started seeing positive results.

Date back to -

Meaning: Referring to something that began or existed in the past, often indicating a long history or origin.

Hindi Meaning: पहले समय में प्रारंभ होना या मौजूद होना।

Sentence: The tradition of celebrating Diwali dates back to ancient times.

Rise and shine -

Meaning: An expression used to greet someone in the morning and encourage them to wake up and start their day with enthusiasm.

Hindi Meaning: उठें और चमकें - सक्रियता के साथ उठें और अपना दिन शुरू करें।

Sentence: Come on, rise and shine! It's a brand

new day full of possibilities.

Come of age -

Meaning: Reaching a point in life where one is considered mature and responsible, often associated with legal adulthood.

Hindi Meaning: प्रौढ़ या पक्का होना - जीवन में एक ऐसा बिंदु प्राप्त करना जहां एक व्यक्ति को परिपक्व और ज़िम्मेदार माना जाता है, जिसे आमतौर पर कानूनी वयस्कता के साथ जोड़ा जाता है।

Sentence: When she turned 18, she officially came of age and took on more responsibilities in her family.

Based On Destruction

Put a nip in the bud -

Meaning: Taking action to prevent a problem or undesirable situation from developing further.

Hindi Meaning: किसी समस्या या अनुचित स्थिति को पहले ही रोकने के लिए कार्रवाई करना।

Sentence: It's important to put a nip in the bud and address the issue before it becomes more serious.

Put an end to -

Meaning: Taking action to terminate or finish something.

Hindi Meaning: किसी चीज को रोकने या समाप्त करने के लिए कार्रवाई करना।

Sentence: We need to put an end to this argument and find a solution that works for everyone.

Play havoc with -

Meaning: Creating disorder, damage, or disruption.

Hindi Meaning: हाथ में बड़ा हावोस खड़ा करना या नष्ट करना।

Sentence: The storm played havoc with the town, causing extensive damage to buildings and infrastructure.

Play with fire -

Meaning: Engaging in risky behaviour or actions that may have negative consequences.

Hindi Meaning: अनावश्यक जोखिम लेना या खतरनाक गतिविधियों में संलग्न होना।

Sentence: You're playing with fire by investing all your money in speculative stocks.

Blow out of the water -

Meaning: Overwhelmingly surpassing or defeating someone or something.

Hindi Meaning: किसी को पूरी तरह से हरा देना या किसी की उपेक्षा करना।

Sentence: The team's exceptional performance blew their opponents out of the water.

Give someone their cards -

Meaning: Terminating someone's employment or ending their working relationship.

Hindi Meaning: किसी की नौकरी खत्म करना या उन्हें निकाल देना।

Sentence: Due to the company's downsizing, they had to give several employees their cards.

Give someone the sack/boots -

Meaning: Terminating someone's employment or ending their working relationship.

Hindi Meaning: किसी की नौकरी खत्म करना या उन्हें निकाल देना।

Sentence: After repeatedly failing to meet deadlines, the employee was given the sack.

Confidence Booster Practice Sets

Exercise 1: Mark the correct meaning of the given Idioms below.

1. **What does the term "Carpe Diem" mean?**
a) Seize the day
b) Life is short
c) Time is precious
d) Live in the moment

2. **What does the idiom "Break a leg" mean?**
a) Congratulations
b) Be careful
c) Good luck
d) Perform well

3. **What does the phrase "Kill two birds with one stone" mean?**
a) Achieve multiple goals with a single action
b) Display exceptional skill
c) Cause harm unintentionally
d) Solve a difficult problem

4. **What does the expression "Let the cat out of the bag" mean?**
a) Show off
b) Reveal a secret
c) Make a mistake
d) Start an argument

5. **What does the idiom "Piece of cake" mean?**
a) A challenging task
b) A delicious dessert
c) Something easy to accomplish
d) A broken item

6. **What does the term "FOMO" stand for?**
a) Future of modern organisations
b) Friends on my own
c) Find out more often
d) Fear of missing out

7. **What does the phrase "Bite the bullet" mean?**
a) Accept a difficult situation or task
b) Experience a sudden pain
c) Have a courageous attitude
d) Injure oneself accidentally

8. **What does the idiom "The ball is in your court" mean?**
a) It's time to play a game
b) Take responsibility for a situation
c) Pass the ball to someone else
d) Make a quick decision

9. **What does the expression "Turn a blind eye" mean?**
a) Close your eyes
b) Ignore something intentionally
c) Look for a solution
d) Change your perspective

10. **What does the term "Burning the midnight oil" mean?**
a) Exercising at night
b) Lighting a fire at midnight
c) Studying or working late into the night
d) Celebrating late into the night

Answers

1.	(a)	2.	(c)	3.	(a)
4.	(b)	5.	(c)	6.	(d)
7.	(a)	8.	(b)	9.	(b)
10.	(c)				

Exercise 2: Mark the correct meaning of the given Idioms below.

1. What does the idiom "Above board" mean?

a) Hidden b) Openly
c) Underneath d) Secretly

2. What does the idiom "A big gun" refer to?

a) A large weapon
b) An important person
c) A powerful explosion
d) A skilled marksman

3. What does the idiom "A fancy price" indicate?

a) A cheap price
b) A reasonable price
c) A high price
d) A discounted price

4. What does the term "A free-lance" refer to?

a) A voluntary worker
b) A hired employee
c) A contractual agreement
d) An independent journalist

5. What does the expression "A gala day" represent?

a) A boring day b) A busy day
c) A festive day d) A routine day

6. What does the idiom "A going concern" imply?

a) A failing business
b) A closed operation
c) A new venture
d) A well-run business

7. What does the phrase "To A Tee" mean?

a) Approximately
b) Completely wrong
c) To a precise degree
d) With hesitation

8. What does the term "A Lady's habit" refer to?

a) A lady's addiction
b) A lady's routine
c) A lady's behaviour
d) A riding dress of a lady

9. What does the expression "To A man" mean?

a) Selectively
b) With reluctance
c) Only once
d) Without exception

10. What does the term "A scapegoat" describe?

a) A heroic figure
b) A neutral bystander
c) One who is made to suffer for another
d) A secret admirer

Answers

1.	(b)	2.	(b)	3.	(c)
4.	(d)	5.	(c)	6.	(d)
7.	(c)	8.	(d)	9.	(d)
10.	(c)				

Exercise 3: Mark the correct meaning of the given Idioms below.

1. **A storm in a teacup**
   (a) Disarranging the cutlery
   (b) Unnecessary tension
   (c) Lot of fuss that will soon be forgotten
   (d) A sudden storm during teatime
2. **At the eleventh hour**
   (a) One hour before midnight
   (b) At 11: 00 p.m.
   (c) At the very last minute
   (d) At 11: 00 a.m.
3. **Herculean task**
   (a) A job that requires a lot of talking and information
   (b) A job that makes everyone feel proud
   (c) A job that only weak people are assigned
   (d) A job that requires a large amount of physical strength
4. **Pipe dream**
   (a) A dream or idea that is unlikely to happen
   (b) A dream or idea that is loudly proclaimed
   (c) A dream or idea that keeps getting repeated
   (d) A dream or idea that is nearly accomplished
5. **Spick and span**
   (a) Noisy and loud
   (b) Neat and clean
   (c) Far and near
   (d) Fast and efficient
6. **Go easy on something**
   (a) Use only a small amount of
   (b) Fill one's plate easily
   (c) Take as much as one wants
   (d) Eat slowly and liberally
7. **A stumbling block**
   (a) Removing stones on the way
   (b) Putting stones along the way
   (c) An obstacle to progress
   (d) Skipping over a hurdle
8. **A kick in the teeth**
   (a) A grave setback
   (b) Severe toothache
   (c) Removing tooth cavities
   (d) Hitting someone hard
9. **Lion's share**
   (a) The part that must be left for the guests in a party
   (b) The sound produced by a lion when it is attacking a prey
   (c) The greatest and most desirable portion of something
   (d) The strongest and richest partner in a group
10. **A live wire**
   (a) An angry and bad-tempered person
   (b) A dangerous and evil person
   (c) A very active or energetic person
   (d) An influential and powerful person

Answers

1.	(c)	2.	(c)	3.	(d)
4.	(a)	5.	(b)	6.	(a)
7.	(c)	8.	(a)	9.	(c)
10.	(c)				

Exercise 4 - Mark the correct meaning of the given Idioms below.

1. **After tripping on a rock, he _______.**
   a) fell into error
   b) fell on deaf ears
   c) fell flat on his face
   d) fell into a rage

2. **His reputation suffered, and he _______________.**
   a) fell from the grace
   b) fell foul
   c) fell in love with
   d) fell on one's feet

3. **The journalist decided to _______________ the corrupt politician.**
   a) fall into a rage b) fall short of
   c) fall foul d) fall on easy prey

4. **They spent a lot of time together and eventually _______________.**
   a) fell into error
   b) fell on deaf ears
   c) fell in love with
   d) fell on one's feet

5. **His rude behaviour made her _______________.**
   a) fall from the grace
   b) fall foul
   c) fall into a rage
   d) fall to pieces

6. **Due to his carelessness, he _______________ in the exam.**
   a) fell short of
   b) fell into error
   c) fell on deaf ears
   d) fell flat on his face

7. **The warning about the impending danger _______________.**
   a) fell on deaf ears
   b) fell on easy prey
   c) fell on one's feet
   d) fell to pieces

8. **The vulnerable animal _______ to the predator.**
   a) fell from the grace
   b) fell foul
   c) fell on easy prey
   d) fell short of

9. **Despite facing challenges, she always _______________.**
   a) fell on one's feet
   b) fell flat on her face
   c) fell short of
   d) fell into a rage

10. **He was so eager to impress that he _______________.**
   a) fell over oneself
   b) fell on deaf ears
   c) fell into error
   d) fell from the grace

Answer Key

1.	(c)	2.	(a)	3.	(c)
4.	(c)	5.	(d)	6.	(b)
7.	(a)	8.	(c)	9.	(a)
10.	(a)				

Exercise 5 Mark the correct meaning of the given Idioms below.

1. **The lawyer filed a ______________ to secure the release of the accused.**
   a) Hang around
   b) Hang fire
   c) Habeas Corpus petition
   d) Half-hearted attempt
2. **She ______________ a small town in the countryside.**
   a) Had ill blood
   b) Hung on to
   c) Hails from
   d) Hammer something into
3. **Despite the odds, he managed to have a ________________.**
   a) Half-hearted attempt
   b) Hair-breadth escape
   c) Hang on one's lips
   d) Hang fire
4. **The team's ________________ turned out to be a turning point in the game.**
   a) In a body
   b) Implicit in
   c) Impose on/upon
   d) Improve on/upon
5. **He had a strong ________________ to travel and explore new places.**
   a) Impulsion to
   b) In a body
   c) Hang by a thread
   d) Hang around
6. **The responsibility to handle the project was ______________ him.**
   a) Hung on to　　b) Hail from
   c) Implicit in　　d) Imputed to
7. **The student studied diligently to ________________ the subject matter.**
   a) Hammer something into
   b) Hail from
   c) Hang fire
   d) Hang on one's lips
8. **They all worked ________________ to achieve their common goal.**
   a) As a body　　b) In a hang fire
   c) Half-heartedly　　d) With ill blood
9. **The committee members had ______________ and could not reach a decision.**
   a) Hang around
   b) Hang by a thread
   c) Hang fire
   d) Hang on one's lips
10. **She had to ________________ to meet the demands of her busy schedule.**
   a) Hail from
   b) Hammer something into
   c) Hang around
   d) Hang on to

Answer Key:

1.	(c)	2.	(c)	3.	(b)
4.	(d)	5.	(a)	6.	(d)
7.	(a)	8.	(a)	9.	(c)
10.	(d)				

Exercise 7 Mark the correct meaning of the given Idioms below.

1. **Under wraps**
(a) underestimate
(b) double layered
(c) secretly
(d) underhand

2. **On tenterhooks**
(a) Very sad (b) Very tense
(c) Very happy (d) very angry

3. **To go red in the face**
(a) To shout at someone for doing something wrong
(b) To feel extremely irritated
(c) To feel very happy and proud
(d) To feel embarrassed

4. **His jokes [fell flat] on the audience.**
(a) failed to have an effect
(b) deeply touched
(c) irritated
(d) provoked laughter

5. **Pull something off**
(a) Drag something forcibly
(b) Take out the cover or lid
(c) Make something happen
(d) Make a lot of noise

6. **Go to the dogs**
(a) Fail miserably
(b) Deteriorate shockingly
(c) Want something badly
(d) Go crazy

7. **To have eggs on one's face**
(a) To buy eggs and break them
(b) To apply egg yolk on one's face for making it look beautiful
(c) To throw eggs on a speaker's face
(d) To be embarrassed because of one's action

8. **Thick as thieves**
(a) Having a close friendship
(b) Being very dishonest
(c) Never helping anyone
(d) Telling lies all the time

9. **Butter fingers**
(a) To be very efficient
(b) To like rich food
(c) To cook well
(d) To be clumsy

10. **Large-hearted**
(a) Corrupt (b) Unhealthy
(c) Overweight (d) Generous

Answers

1.	(c)	2.	(b)	3.	(d)
4.	(a)	5.	(c)	6.	(b)
7.	(d)	8.	(a)	9.	(d)
10.	(d)				

Exercise 8 Mark the correct meaning of the given Idioms below.

1. **To poke one's nose into**
(a) To clean one's nose with a twig
(b) To bury oneself in another matter
(c) To insert something in another's nose
(d) To take interest in others' affairs

2. **The friends quarrelled some time ago but now they are trying to [make up] with each other.**
(a) to part forever
(b) to blame each other
(c) to compete with one another
(d) to settle their differences

3. To add insult to injury

(a) to make fun of someone

(b) to work hard on making up

(c) to make something worse

(d) to wound physically

4. He is very impulsive and does things [without rhyme or reason].

(a) without proper planning

(b) without a reasonable explanation

(c) without any resources

(d) without anyone's help

5. Hard nut to crack

(a) a difficult person or problem

(b) someone who solves puzzles easily

(c) someone who needs guidance

(d) a person who likes to joke around

6. know inside out

(a) To know a little about something

(b) To know everything by rote memory

(c) To know something thoroughly

(d) To always know a lot about every topic

7. Organic food seems to be [in vogue] these days.

(a) readily available

(b) out of stock

(c) in fashion

(d) very expensive

8. To play with fire

(a) To act in a dangerous and risky way

(b) To hold a revenge against someone

(c) To fight fires like a fireman

(d) To pour oil on a burning fire

9. Cook the books

(a) To falsify financial records

(b) To be a good writer

(c) To write books on cooking

(d) To be a good editor

10. To cut corners

(a) cut something easily without spoiling it

(b) cut something into pieces

(c) be able to do a job effortlessly

(d) not do a thing to perfection in order to save money or effort

Answers

1.	(d)	2.	(d)	3.	(c)
4.	(b)	5.	(a)	6.	(c)
7.	(c)	8.	(a)	9.	(a)
10.	(d)				

Exercise 9 Mark the correct meaning of the given Idioms below.

1. Match the idiom on the left with its corresponding meaning on the right.

1. On patrol	(a) at the time of
2.On the brink of	(b) In action
3. On the carpet	(c) Secretly
4. On the eve of	(d) impatient, suspense or anxiety
5. On the horns of a dilemma	(e) On security watch
6. On the job	(f) To be aware
7. On the rocks	(g) Towards destruction, collapse
8. On the sly	(h) At the time of
9. On the tenterhooks	(i) Penniless
10. On the alert	(j) To face a difficult situation between two problems

Answer Key:

1. On patrol -	e) To security watch
2. On the brink of -	h) At the time of
3. On the carpet -	g) Towards destruction, collapse
4. On the eve of -	a) at the time of
5. On the horns of a dilemma -	j) To face a difficult situation between two problems
6. On the job -	b) In action
7. On the rocks -	i) Penniless
8. On the sly -	c) Secretly
9. On the tenterhooks	d) impatient, suspense or anxiety
10. On the alert -	f) To be aware

Exercise **10 Mark the correct meaning of the given Idioms below.**

1. **Off and on**
   (a) again and again
   (b) every day
   (c) sometimes but not regularly
   (d) not soon
2. **Hang on every word**
   (a) Speak very slowly
   (b) Listen very carefully
   (c) Stop after hearing one word
   (d) Stammer while speaking
3. **To fish in troubled waters**
   (a) To take advantage of a difficult situation
   (b) To try to find a big catch in the deep sea
   (c) To try to do something that is very difficult
   (d) To catch fish in stormy weather in the sea
4. **At a stone's throw**
   (a) Beat someone with a stone
   (b) Throw a stone at someone
   (c) At a very short distance
   (d) Like throwing a stone
5. **A dime a dozen**
   (a) common and so of little value
   (b) in great demand as not easily available
   (c) available only in bulk
   (d) not available everywhere
6. **A red letter day**
   (a) a day of fun and enjoyment
   (b) a day of horror
   (c) the worst day
   (d) a memorable day
7. **The eradication of coronavirus is still [a far cry].**
   (a) very near
   (b) very easy
   (c) very fast
   (d) very distant
8. **Living in a fool's paradise**
   (a) To believe wrongly that your situation is good
   (b) To be fooled by someone
   (c) To live in luxuriously after fooling someone
   (d) To live in a world of imagination
9. **To put one's foot in one's mouth**
   (a) To deliberately provoke someone
   (b) To accidentally embarrass or upset someone
   (c) To gather all of one's resources
   (d) To be disorderly and stupid
10. **She may be the Principal but it is the**

school administrator who [rules the roost].

(a) is dependent upon her

(b) is totally submissive

(c) is proved right

(d) is in complete control

Answer

1.	(c)	2.	(b)	3.	(a)
4.	(c)	5.	(a)	6.	(d)
7.	(d)	8.	(a)	9.	(b)
10.	(d)				

PYQs Practise sets

Exercise 1

1. **Bang for the buck**
(a) More value for money
(b) Less value for money
(c) A sorrowful heart
(d) Dash against something

2. **Raise the bar**
(a) To grow taller
(b) To win a competition
(c) To raise the price
(d) To set higher goals

3. **To walk on air**
(a) To be very rich
(b) To feel very depressed
(c) To be very happy
(d) To be completely free

4. **To take a chill pill**
(a) To ask a doctor for medication
(b) To drink cold water
(c) To gulp a tablet for a cold
(d) To calm down

5. **Be at a loss for words**
(a) Not aware of the language
(b) Not know what to say
(c) Habituated to using difficult words
(d) Lost the urge to speak

6. **Want to curl up and die**
(a) Unable to sleep well
(b) Want to die comfortably
(c) Too tired from physical labour
(d) Feel terribly ashamed and sorry

7. **To cut a long story short**
(a) Tell something briefly
(b) Like to tell long stories
(c) Tell something in a roundabout way
(d) Like to tell short stories

8. **Full of beans**
(a) A storeroom full of vegetables
(b) A dish made of French beans
(c) Full of energy
(d) Full of cowardice

9. **Apple of one's eye**
(a) Someone who plays all sports
(b) Someone very precious or dear
(c) Someone who behaves courteously
(d) Someone with great respect

10. **To the nines**
(a) To perfection
(b) To great depths
(c) To be exalted
(d) To be jealous

11. **A storm in a teacup**
(a) Disarranging the cutlery
(b) Unnecessary tension
(c) Lot of fuss that will soon be forgotten
(d) A sudden storm during teatime

12. **At the eleventh hour**
(a) One hour before midnight
(b) At 11: 00 p.m.
(c) At the very last minute
(d) At 11: 00 a.m.

13. **Herculean task**
(a) A job that requires a lot of talking and information
(b) A job that makes everyone feel proud

(c) A job that requires a large amount of physical strength
(d) A job that only weak people are assigned

14. Pipe dream
(a) A dream or idea that keeps getting repeated
(b) A dream or idea that is loudly proclaimed
(c) A dream or idea that is unlikely to happen
(d) A dream or idea that is nearly accomplished

15. Spick and span
(a) Noisy and loud
(b) Neat and clean
(c) Far and near
(d) Fast and efficient

16. Go easy on something
(a) Use only a small amount of
(b) Fill one's plate easily
(c) Take as much as one wants
(d) Eat slowly and liberally

17. A stumbling block
(a) Removing stones on the way
(b) Putting stones along the way
(c) An obstacle to progress
(d) Skipping over a hurdle

18. A kick in the teeth
(a) A grave setback
(b) Severe toothache
(c) Removing tooth cavities
(d) Hitting someone hard

19. Lion's share
(a) The part that must be left for the guests in a party
(b) The sound produced by a lion when it is attacking a prey
(c) The greatest and most desirable portion of something
(d) The strongest and richest partner in a group

20. A live wire
(a) An angry and bad-tempered person
(b) A dangerous and evil person
(c) A very active or energetic person
(d) An influential and powerful person

21. Sit on the fence
(a) Poke fun at people
(b) Protect something
(c) Create conflicts
(d) Avoid making a decision

22. Fair and square
(a) Calm and quiet
(b) Beautiful in appearance
(c) By any means available
(d) According to the rules

23. A bad egg
(a) Someone who doesn't like eggs
(b) Someone who is dishonest and unreliable
(c) Someone who likes to break eggs
(d) Someone who regularly makes mistakes

24. Tide someone over
(a) Ask someone for financial assistance
(b) Give temporary help, usually financial
(c) Get a boat ready to cross a river or water body
(d) Complete a voyage successfully

25. To pay lip service
(a) To be insincere

(b) To make loud statements

(c) To talk out of turn

(d) To ask for permission

26. To get the ball rolling

(a) To play a ball game well

(b) To begin a process

(c) To match an opponent

(d) To keep working until late

27. Through thick and thin

(a) With humility

(b) With ego and pride

(c) With all kinds of people

(d) Under all conditions

28. On the horizon

(a) A plan for the distant future

(b) The successful beginning of a business venture

(c) An event that is likely to end soon

(d) An event that is likely to happen soon

29. Draw the line at something

(a) Accept something up to a particular point

(b) Agreeing to an idea

(c) Making pencil sketches

(d) Coming to a conclusion

30. On cloud nine

(a) Extremely happy

(b) Flying with a parachute

(c) Frequently flying by air

(d) Extremely sad

31. To be light years away

(a) To be too distant for human beings to reach

(b) An extremely long time from now in the past or future

(c) When something seems like it is about to happen in the near future

(d) An unlikely event that happened suddenly

32. A fish out of water

(a) Feel uncomfortable in unfamiliar surroundings

(b) Feel as if you are unable to breathe

(c) Feel like going to an unfamiliar and new place

(d) Feel comfortable in any kind of place

33. A square deal

(a) A nice decoration

(b) A dishonest transaction

(c) A fair agreement

(d) An unfair agreement

34. On edge

(a) Keeping things safely

(b) Doing exercises regularly

(c) Playing a tiring game

(d) Nervous and unable to relax

35. Feel at sea

(a) Feel lost or confused

(b) Feel seasick

(c) Feel angry

(d) Feel comfortable while travelling by water

36. The gift of the gab

(a) Writes very well

(b) Talks well and persuasively

(c) Loves to give gifts

(d) Used to grabbing others' gifts

37. Twiddling one's thumbs

(a) Feeling angry

(b) Feeling sad

(c) Feeling hungry

(d) Feeling bored

38. Out of the blue

(a) Beat someone black and blue

(b) Loves to wear only blue colour clothes

(c) Completely unexpectedly

(d) Completely honestly

39. To fight tooth and nail

(a) To silently leave the scene of battle

(b) To fight or compete with great ferocity and intensity

(c) To use unusual weapons to fight

(d) To keep the enemy guessing about the weapons used

40. To fan the flames

(a) To call for help to solve an issue

(b) To resolve the issue amicably

(c) To make a bad situation worse

(d) To cool the situation

Answers

1.	(a)	2.	(d)	3.	(c)	4	(d)
5	(b)	6.	(d)	7.	(a)	8.	(c)
9.	(b)	10.	(a)	11.	(c)	12.	(c)
13.	(c)	14.	(c)	15.	(b)	16.	(a)
17.	(c)	18.	(a)	19.	(c)	20.	(c)
21.	(d)	22.	(d)	23.	(b)	24.	(b)
25	(a)	26.	(b)	27.	(d)	28.	(d)
29.	(a)	30.	(a)	31.	(a)	32.	(a)
33.	(c)	34.	(d)	35.	(a)	36.	(b)
37.	(d)	38.	(c)	39.	(b)	40.	(c)

Exercise 2

1. Under wraps

(a) underestimate

(b) double layered

(c) secretly

(d) underhand

2. On tenterhooks

(a) Very sad

(b) Very tense

(c) Very happy

(d) very angry

3. To go red in the face

(a) To shout at someone for doing something wrong

(b) To feel embarrassed

(c) To feel very happy and proud

(d) To feel extremely irritated

4. His jokes [fell flat] on the audience.

(a) deeply touched

(b) failed to have an effect

(c) irritated

(d) provoked laughter

5. Pull something off

(a) Drag something forcibly

(b) Take out the cover or lid

(c) Make something happen

(d) Make a lot of noise

6. Go to the dogs

(a) Fail miserably

(b) Deteriorate shockingly

(c) Want something badly

(d) Go crazy

7. To have eggs on one's face

(a) To be embarrassed because of one's action

(b) To apply egg yolk on one's face for

making it look beautiful
(c) To throw eggs on a speaker's face
(d) To buy eggs and break them

8. Thick as thieves
(a) Having a close friendship
(b) Being very dishonest
(c) Never helping anyone
(d) Telling lies all the time

9. Butter fingers
(a) To be very efficient
(b) To like rich food
(c) To cook well
(d) To be clumsy

10. Large-hearted
(a) Corrupt (b) Unhealthy
(c) Overweight (d) Generous

11. To poke one's nose into
(a) To clean one's nose with a twig
(b) To bury oneself in another matter
(c) To insert something in another's nose
(d) To take interest in others' affairs

12. The friends quarrelled some time ago but now they are trying to [make up] with each other.
(a) to part forever
(b) to blame each other
(c) to compete with one another
(d) to settle their differences

13. To add insult to injury
(a) to make fun of someone
(b) to work hard on making up
(c) to make something worse
(d) to wound physically

14. He is very impulsive and does things [without rhyme or reason].
(a) without proper planning
(b) without a reasonable explanation
(c) without any resources
(d) without anyone's help

15. Hard nut to crack
(a) a difficult person or problem
(b) someone who solves puzzles easily
(c) someone who needs guidance
(d) a person who likes to joke around

16. know inside out
(a) To know a little about something
(b) To know everything by rote memory
(c) To know something thoroughly
(d) To always know a lot about every topic

17. Organic food seems to be [in vogue] these days.
(a) readily available
(b) out of stock
(c) in fashion
(d) very expensive

18. To play with fire
(a) To act in a dangerous and risky way
(b) To hold a revenge against someone
(c) To fight fires like a fireman
(d) To pour oil on a burning fire

19. Cook the books
(a) To falsify financial records
(b) To be a good writer
(c) To write books on cooking
(d) To be a good editor

20. To cut corners
(a) cut something easily without spoiling it
(b) cut something into pieces
(c) be able to do a job effortlessly
(d) not do a thing well in order to save

money or effort

21. A fire in someone's belly
(a) one who is energetic and enthusiastic about something
(b) one who is rich and powerful and exploits the poor
(c) one who comes from a middle class background
(d) one who continues to work without wanting a reward

22. Poke one's nose
(a) Not be careful about one's health
(b) Interfere or meddle
(c) Do unhygienic things
(d) Tease or irritate

23. A blessing in disguise
(a) something good that isn't recognised at first
(b) someone who comes disguised
(c) a person who blesses others quietly
(d) an event that is unknown

24. Needle in a haystack
(a) Someone having vast opportunities
(b) Someone in trouble
(c) Something impossible to find
(d) Something very trivial

25. My brother has decided to settle in London [for good].
(a) forever
(b) briefly
(c) for a better income
(d) for a promotion

26. Rank and file
(a) The manager of a personnel department
(b) Ordinary workers in a company
(c) Financial activities in a firm
(d) A very well-organised company

27. To come round
(a) To meet someone by chance
(b) To spend a lot of time with someone
(c) To go round and round
(d) To become conscious again

28. Burn the midnight oil
(a) burn things using oil
(b) work many nights at a stretch
(c) create problems in the night
(d) work late into the night

29. Break the ice
(a) Make a beginning or start something
(b) Cool the room for everyone
(c) Arrange for a skating show
(d) Make things available for a party

30. A lean patch
(a) Cloth that is beginning to tear
(b) A part of hair that is thin
(c) Friendship that has ended
(d) A period of poor performance

31. Off and on
(a) again and again
(b) every day
(c) sometimes but not regularly
(d) not soon

32. Hang on every word
(a) Speak very slowly
(b) Listen very carefully
(c) Stop after hearing one word
(d) Stammer while speaking

33. To fish in troubled waters
(a) To take advantage of a difficult situation
(b) To try to find a big catch in the deep sea

(c) To try to do something that is very difficult

(d) To catch fish in stormy weather in the sea

34. At a stone's throw

(a) Beat someone with a stone

(b) Throw a stone at someone

(c) At a very short distance

(d) Like throwing a stone

35. A dime a dozen

(a) common and so of little value

(b) in great demand as not easily available

(c) available only in bulk

(d) not available everywhere

36. A red letter day

(a) a day of fun and enjoyment

(b) a day of horror

(c) the worst day

(d) a memorable day

37. The eradication of coronavirus is still [a far cry].

(a) very near

(b) very easy

(c) very fast

(d) very distant

38. Living in a fool's paradise

(a) To believe wrongly that your situation is good

(b) To be fooled by someone

(c) To live in luxuriously after fooling someone

(d) To live in a world of imagination

39. To put one's foot in one's mouth

(a) To deliberately provoke someone

(b) To accidentally embarrass or upset someone

(c) To gather all of one's resources

(d) To be disorderly and stupid

40. She may be the Principal but it is the school administrator who [rules the roost].

(a) is dependent upon her

(b) is totally submissive

(c) is proved right

(d) is in complete control

Answers

1.	(c)	2.	(b)	3.	(b)	4	(b)
5	(c)	6.	(b)	7.	(a)	8.	(a)
9.	(d)	10.	(d)	11.	(d)	12.	(d)
13.	(c)	14.	(b)	15.	(a)	16.	(c)
17.	(c)	18.	(a)	19.	(a)	20.	(d)
21.	(a)	22.	(b)	23.	(a)	24.	(c)
25	(a)	26.	(b)	27.	(d)	28.	(d)
29.	(a)	30.	(d)	31.	(c)	32.	(b)
33.	(a)	34.	(c)	35.	(a)	36.	(d)
37.	(d)	38.	(a)	39.	(b)	40.	(d)

Exercise 3

1. Caught red-handed

(a) Caught by someone wearing a red wristband

(b) Caught in the act of doing something illegal

(c) Caught stealing red objects like apples and tomatoes

(d) Caught with a hand covered in blood

2. Full of beans

(a) Happy and energetic

(b) Sad and dull

(c) Being foolish

(d) Have crazy ideas

3. **To be all ears**
(a) To have extra-large ears
(b) To be inquisitive and curious
(c) To be impatient about something
(d) To be ready and eager to listen

4. **Their marriage wasn't working but they kept up appearances.**
(a) maintained an expression of well being
(b) maintained peace and harmony
(c) kept throwing parties
(d) revealed the truth

5. **Method to one's madness**
(a) Being very neat and particular about details
(b) Seeming disorderly yet having a structure
(c) Always behaving like a mad person
(d) Not following rules and conventions

6. **Get out of hand**
(a) To get irritated
(b) To become difficult to control
(c) To be able to complete a task
(d) To be anxious

7. **Not one's cup of tea**
(a) Not absolutely true
(b) Not according to one's interest
(c) Beyond one's comprehension
(d) Of no concern for someone

8. **To cross one's mind**
(a) To forget something
(b) To put a thought away from one's mind
(c) To move from one idea to another
(d) To think of something

9. **Wash your dirty linen in public**
(a) Hang Clothes outside
(b) Discuss private matters in front of others
(c) Fight with everyone unnecessarily
(d) Complain about everything

10. **Newton's work in the field of physics speaks volumes about his genius.**
(a) conveys a great deal
(b) advertises his work
(c) claims fame and honour
(d) does not gives a detailed report

11. **To run around like a headless chicken**
(a) To do things methodically one by one
(b) To be lazy and unwilling to work
(c) To do many things in a disorganised manner
(d) To be unable to catch escaping chicken

12. **To leave no stone unturned**
(a) To turn everything upside down
(b) To try everything possible to solve a problem
(c) To become furious with somebody
(d) To become accustomed to routine things

13. **In hot water**
(a) In advantage
(b) In shower
(c) In trouble
(d) In suspense

14. **Make big time**
(a) Reach earlier than expected
(b) Attain fame and success
(c) Spend more than one earns
(d) Earn more than needed

15. Read between the lines

(a) read carefully each and every word written

(b) read very slowly enjoying each line

(c) read loudly each and every word given in the sentence

(d) understand what is implied but not stated directly

16. A good turn

(a) A great opportunity

(b) A helpful act

(c) A pleasant experience

(d) A lucky chance

17. Be glad to see the back of

(a) Be happy at another's success

(b) Be relieved at another's failure

(c) Be happy to see someone again

(d) Be happy when a person leaves

18. By the skin of one's teeth

(a) With the help of someone

(b) By a very big margin

(c) By a very narrow margin

(d) Without anyone's help

19. Go back to the drawing board

(a) get started on a new job as the old one wasn't good

(b) look back at your achievements and learn from them

(c) withdraw support to someone whom you always supported

(d) start planning again because earlier plans failed

20. Provide a blueprint

(a) Propose a plan of a secret meeting

(b) Submit a printed application for a blue-collared job

(c) Give a detailed plan or scheme

(d) Have a building plan printed in blue

21. A bolt from the blue

(a) something causing a head injury

(b) something that is hotly debated

(c) a strange dream that wakes one up suddenly

(d) something that happens suddenly

22. Cost an arm and a leg

(a) Be easily available

(b) Be extremely expensive

(c) Be worthy of the cost

(d) Be rather cheap

23. Get One's Ducks in a Row

(a) have everything improperly disorganised

(b) have nothing properly organised, though ready

(c) have everything messily arranged

(d) have everything properly organised

24. Child's play

(a) Something that is very easy to do

(b) Something for a child to play with

(c) Something that everybody knows

(d) Something children have made by themselves

25. A sea change

(a) Going on a trip abroad

(b) Getting transferred overseas

(c) Complete transformation

(d) Health-related vacation

26. Getting butterflies in one's stomach

(a) To be confident of oneself

(b) To be anxious and nervous

(c) To be suspicious of someone

(d) To be very angry with someone

27. A Herculean task

(a) An important task
(b) An immediate task
(c) A task requiring great effort
(d) A task for brave people

28. A grey area

(a) An unclear situation
(b) A special part of the brain
(c) An unspoken truth
(d) An unusual spot

29. To be in the dark

(a) to always be in a bad mood about darkness
(b) to learn to face dark places without fear
(c) to be afraid of darkness and refuse to go out at night
(d) to not know something others are aware of

30. The wedding preparations are [in full swing].

(a) in great difficulty
(b) at the height of activity
(c) hard to arrange
(d) very costly affair

31. In times of economic recession, the demand for goods is on the wane.

(a) out of control
(b) at the peak
(c) on the rise
(d) on the decline

32. I cannot take up any new assignment as I have my hands full.

(a) am short of time
(b) need to seek help
(c) am very busy
(d) am very rich

33. India's problem boils down to just one thing - lack of infrastructure for health services.

(a) heats up to
(b) adapts to something
(c) fulfils something
(d) sums up to

34. He runs for two hours at a stretch to build his stamina.

(a) painfully
(b) comfortably
(c) continuously
(d) easily

35. You must seize the opportunity to make amends for your earlier curtness.

(a) to correct a mistake
(b) to make a proposal
(c) to offer a deal
(d) to give a suggestion

36. The embezzlement in the company's accounts has come to light.

(a) been concealed
(b) been revealed
(c) been rewarded
(d) been punished

37. When the miscreants saw the police they beat a retreat.

(a) ran away
(b) marched ahead
(c) protested strongly
(d) attacked fiercely

38. The new CEO is in favour of giving plenty of elbow room to the managers.

(a) leave to go on vacation

(b) freedom to do what one wants
(c) tough competition
(d) huge salaries and perks

39. He knows the ins and outs of the case and has been chosen to defend the accused.
(a) complete details
(b) time needed to complete
(c) high stakes
(d) expense involved

40. To make clean breast of
(a) To gain prominence
(b) To praise oneself
(c) To confess without of reserve
(d) To destroy before it blooms

Answers

1.	(b)	2.	(a)	3.	(d)	4	(a)
5	(b)	6.	(b)	7.	(b)	8.	(d)
9.	(b)	10.	(a)	11.	(c)	12.	(b)
13.	(c)	14.	(b)	15.	(d)	16.	(b)
17.	(d)	18.	(c)	19.	(d)	20.	(c)
21.	(d)	22.	(b)	23.	(d)	24.	(a)
25	(c)	26.	(b)	27.	(c)	28.	(a)
29.	(d)	30.	(b)	31.	(d)	32.	(c)
33.	(d)	34.	(c)	35.	(a)	36.	(b)
37.	(a)	38.	(b)	39.	(a)	40.	(c)

Exercise 4

1. By the same token
(a) In the same bus
(b) Use the same ticket
(c) Use the same password
(d) In the same way

2. To get on the nerves
(a) To irritate
(b) To give medicine
(c) To have an illness
(d) To soothe

3. Keep someone in the loop
(a) Tie a loop
(b) Save all their numbers
(c) Give them all the information
(d) Take good care of them

4. Of the old school
(a) School in an old age home
(b) School one attended long ago
(c) Old fashioned in thought
(d) Old dilapidated building

5. Close to one's heart
(a) One who is being followed
(b) One who treats heart problems
(c) One who is very emotional
(d) Dear and important to oneself

6. Go bonkers
(a) Become crazy
(b) Become wealthy
(c) Become selfish
(d) Become greedy70

7. Turn a deaf ear
(a) Pretend to listen carefully
(b) Shout to be heard by someone
(c) Be hard of hearing
(d) Ignore what someone says

8. Pull someone up
(a) Agree with someone
(b) Drag someone
(c) Criticise someone
(d) Help someone

9. Over the moon
(a) Extremely happy
(b) Highly imaginative

(c) Very ambitious
(d) Very unrealistic

10. Copycat
(a) One who loves cats and dogs
(b) One who imitates another closely
(c) One who copies all drawings of cats
(d) One who doesn't like cats as pets

11. Go off
(a) Continue or happen
(b) Stop working
(c) Leave or disappear
(d) Explain something in detail

12. Break in
(a) Enter a building illegally
(b) End a relationship
(c) Be unable to control (one's) feelings
(d) Begin to do (something) suddenly

13. Babe in the woods
(a) A wise old person
(b) A young defenceless person
(c) A pale and sickly person
(d) A foolish and stupid person

14. Be all ears
(a) Not being alert
(b) Ready to wait
(c) Eager to listen
(d) Be content

15. Raining cats and dogs
(a) Facing light rain and wind
(b) Raining very heavily
(c) Having lots of pets around you
(d) Worried about cats and dogs

16. How time flies!
(a) Time seems to stay still
(b) Difficult to pass time
(c) A clock going very fast
(d) Time seems to move quickly

17. To be off your food
(a) To have no food
(b) To help someone
(c) To give food to others
(d) To have no appetite

18. To go bananas
(a) To become nervous
(b) To feel very hungry
(c) To become very excited or angry
(d) To keep eating bananas

19. Comb through
(a) To carefully look through
(b) To be trapped somewhere
(c) To hide information
(d) To come out of a problem

20. Loudmouth
(a) One who talks well
(b) One who talks boastfully
(c) One who speaks calmly
(d) One who speaks nervously

21. Change for the better
(a) Exchange an old product for new
(b) Pretend to be someone else
(c) To keep loose change
(d) An improvement in the situation

22. Loosen the purse strings
(a) To reduce the expenditure
(b) To increase the money available for expenditure
(c) To lose a purse
(d) To be miserly

23. Fly the nest
(a) Children returning home after studying abroad
(b) To run at a very fast pace to reach

home

(c) To lose direction and not reach one's destination

(d) Children leaving their parents' home to live on their own

24. Your guess is as good as mine

(a) To have the same idea as another

(b) To have no idea of the answer

(c) To play a guessing game

(d) To have a better idea than others

25. Horses for courses

(a) Different people are suited for different jobs

(b) The same horse can run in different race courses in order to win

(c) The same person can do many jobs and give good results

(d) Horses are mainly bred for race courses and are winners

26. Many a slip between the cup and the lip

(a) The work is going as per plan and must be completed

(b) The cup is slippery and likely to break if you are not careful

(c) The tea is too hot and likely to burn the lips

(d) Bad things may happen before the task is finished

27. Fit as a fiddle

(a) To be in excellent health and good working order

(b) About to buy a good musical instrument

(c) Ready to start playing a fiddle

(d) To have an expensive musical instrument

28. Elbow grease

(a) Oil on the shirt sleeve

(b) Too much cream on hands

(c) Stain on a car glass

(d) A lot of physical effort

29. Drop in

(a) Reduce in numbers

(b) Have very little effect

(c) Go back on a promise

(d) Pay a casual visit

29. A turning point

(a) The time when people decide to give up plans

(b) The time at which an important change starts

(c) A change of destiny that is surprising

(d) A decision to turn things around

30. To be taken aback

(a) To be excited

(b) To be irritated

(c) To be nervous

(d) To be surprised

31. In the eye of the storm

(a) Be involved in discussion

(b) Be calm in difficulty

(c) Be in a controversial situation

(d) Be the centre of attraction

32. Get on like a house on fire

(a) To be angry and unfriendly

(b) To become friends quickly

(c) To end a relationship

(d) To take an instant dislike

33. Have your heart set on something

(a) To not want something at all

(b) To want something very much

(c) To be always in a nervous state
(d) To be in control of one's feelings

34. Alive and kicking
(a) To be very good in football
(b) To be active and healthy
(c) To behave childishly
(d) To be careless and unafraid

35. Chinks in the armour
(a) An old fashioned and useless weapon
(b) A weakness that can be taken advantage of
(c) A protective shield with ventilation
(d) A soldier's inner vest that protects

36. Hit the ceiling
(a) Explode in anger
(b) Reach the top
(c) Make good progress
(d) Have high hopes

37. Months on end
(a) In a month's time
(b) End of the month
(c) Last month of the year
(d) Several months in a row

38. A rotten apple
(a) A time when things are left to spoil
(b) A single bad person or thing in a group
(c) A single moment when things change
(d) A tree which gives poor produce

39. Giving a false alarm
(a) A situation when people ring an alarm bell to frighten everybody just for fun
(b) A situation when people wrongly think that something bad is going to happen
(c) A situation when people don't think that something is good and the opposite happens
(d) A situation when things go wrong and everything bad happens

Answers

1.	(d)	2.	(a)	3.	(c)	4	(c)
5	(d)	6.	(a)	7.	(d)	8.	(c)
9.	(a)	10.	(b)	11.	(b)	12.	(a)
13.	(b)	14.	(c)	15.	(b)	16.	(d)
17.	(d)	18.	(c)	19.	(a)	20.	(b)
21.	(d)	22.	(b)	23.	(d)	24.	(a)
25	(a)	26.	(d)	27.	(a)	28.	(d)
29.	(d)	30.	(b)	31.	(d)	32.	(c)
33.	(b)	34.	(b)	35.	(b)	36.	(b)
37.	(a)	38.	(d)	39.	(b)	40.	(b)

Exercise 5

1. Call off
(a) Speak to someone over the phone
(b) Visit someone
(c) Shout someone's name aloud
(d) Cancel something

2. A piece of the pie
(a) Feel humbled
(b) An unpleasant thing to accept
(c) Make a sweet dish
(d) A share in money or business

3. Follow suit
(a) To do as others have done
(b) To chase a convict
(c) To take a different path
(d) To dress as someone else

4. Put off
(a) To wear

(b) To delay
(c) To keep
(d) To suggest

5. See eye to eye
(a) Disturb
(b) Agree
(c) Quarrel
(d) Smile

6. Be over the moon
(a) Very unhappy at an incident
(b) Willing to take on a task
(c) Very pleased about something
(d) Unable to perform well

7. At beck and call
(a) Try to convince others about something
(b) Ready to do everything for someone
(c) Signal someone to approach
(d) Gain an advantage over someone

8. Bear fruit
(a) Be creative
(b) Put in hard work
(c) Produce positive results
(d) Accept the truth

9. Tighten one's belt
(a) To make efforts to be slim
(b) To cut one's expenditure
(c) To stop working full time
(d) To lose one's job

10. Be Off
(a) To switch off the light
(b) To not eat anything
(c) To be in a bad mood
(d) To go away

11. Carry on
(a) Continue doing something
(b) Throw something away
(c) Take someone or something away
(d) Put something into action

12. Fall for
(a) To be supported by
(b) To be tricked or fooled by
(c) To invite someone
(d) To fall down and injure oneself

13. Whet your appetite
(a) To want something more
(b) To find the food tasteless
(c) To feel lonely and isolated
(d) To go on a diet

14. Get something off one's chest
(a) To escape from a dangerous situation
(b) To defeat someone in a physical fight
(c) Talk about something that is worrying you
(d) To stop oneself from confiding in a friend

15. At loggerheads
(a) To agree unwillingly
(b) To disagree strongly
(c) To hit someone with a log
(d) To sit and discuss

16. At a stretch
(a) Within a month
(b) After some time
(c) Without a stop
(d) During a year

17. Bear the brunt
(a) Be first to try something
(b) Confront a powerful rival
(c) Know what is going on
(d) Suffer the worst of something

18. Behind closed doors

(a) Do something alone
(b) Be in prison
(c) Be away from others
(d) Do something secretly

19. Make out
(a) Understand someone or something with difficulty
(b) Invent an explanation for something
(c) Become friends again with someone
(d) Run away from a difficult situation

20. Pick and choose
(a) Start all over again after a crisis
(b) Select only the best from choices
(c) Question someone on a topic
(d) Start a quarrel or a fight over something

21. To be moved to tears
(a) To be mesmerised by something
(b) To be overwhelmed with emotion
(c) To be surprised or shocked
(d) To be transported to another world

22. To gain ground
(a) To make progress
(b) To be happy
(c) To grow crops
(d) To buy land

23. Lean and mean
(a) Fat and lazy
(b) Evil and selfish
(c) Thin and weak
(d) Ready and efficient

24. Keep in check
(a) To keep something safe
(b) To place an order
(c) To control something
(d) To test something

25. Play safe
(a) Avoid risks and take precautions
(b) Do something following rules
(c) Play a game steadily
(d) Play a game without getting hurt

26. Feel the pinch
(a) Maintain total silence
(b) Be in an agitated state of mind
(c) Listen carefully
(d) Face financial difficulties

27. Bull's-eye
(a) Something that is the centre of a target
(b) Something that is glassy-looking
(c) Something that scares people
(d) Something that is round

28. Off-colour
(a) Feeling slightly ill
(b) Not able to appreciate art
(c) Wearing dull-coloured clothes
(d) Not well-dressed

29. Change hands
(a) Pass from one person to another
(b) Give away something you do not need
(c) Move from one hand to another
(d) Carry something in both hands

30. Out of the question
(a) Not possible at all
(b) Very badly written
(c) Very difficult
(d) Not in the syllabus

31. Make no bones about something
(a) Insist on buying only boneless mutton
(b) Be frank and open about something
(c) Be fussy about bones in one's soup

(d) Take care of one's health

32. To go nuts

(a) To look for nuts
(b) To become crazy
(c) To become nervous
(d) To feel very hungry

33. To be on a roll

(a) To be experiencing a successful period
(b) To be experiencing setbacks
(c) To be feeling extremely unhappy
(d) To be moving from place to place

34. Back up

(a) Stand up to fight
(b) Think about the past
(c) Defend or support
(d) Withdraw

35. Work out

(a) Struggle very hard
(b) Exercise or develop a plan
(c) Do something successfully
(d) Work very hard

36. To take for granted

(a) To get a scholarship and assignment easily
(b) To apply for a loan with low rates of interest
(c) To accept without question or objection
(d) To accept a sponsorship without much fuss

37. Ritu was shocked to learn that her kids had _____________ somewhere after school.

(a) wandered off
(b) jumped at
(c) wondered at
(d) finished off

38. Vidushi liked the cake so much that she _________.

(a) pulled at it
(b) poked with it
(c) polished it off
(d) pushed it over

39. Burn the midnight oil

(a) burn things using oil
(b) work many nights at a stretch
(c) create problems in the night
(d) work late into the night

40. Break the ice

(a) Make a beginning or start something
(b) Cool the room for everyone
(c) Arrange for a skating show
(d) Make things available for a party

Answers

1.	(d)	2.	(d)	3.	(a)	4	(b)
5	(b)	6.	(c)	7.	(b)	8.	(c)
9.	(b)	10.	(d)	11.	(a)	12.	(b)
13.	(a)	14.	(c)	15.	(b)	16.	(c)
17.	(d)	18.	(d)	19.	(a)	20.	(b)
21.	(b)	22.	(a)	23.	(c)	24.	(c)
25	(d)	26.	(d)	27.	(a)	28.	(a)
29.	(a)	30.	(a)	31.	(b)	32.	(b)
33.	(a)	34.	(c)	35.	(b)	36.	(c)
37.	(a)	38.	(c)	39.	(d)	40.	(a)

Chapter - Three

Synonyms and Antonyms

All synonyms and Antonyms asked in SSC Exams[from 2000 till May 2023]

A

Word	Meaning in English	Meaning in Hindi	Synonyms	Antonyms
Abandon	Inclined to pry into or meddle in other people's affairs; overly curious	जिज्ञासु, दख़लबाज़	Nosy, curious, intrusive	Disinterested, indifferent, unconcerned
Ability	The power or capacity to do something	क्षमता	Skill, Talent, Capability	Inability, Incapacity, Disability
Absorb	To take in or soak up something	शोषित करना	Engross, Immerse, Assimilate	Release, Emit, Exude
Abundant	Plentiful, having a large quantity or supply	प्रचुर	Ample, Copious, Generous	Scarce, Limited, Insufficient
Accurate	Correct, exact, or precise	सटीक	Precise, True, Exact	Inaccurate, Incorrect, Wrong
Achieve	To successfully reach or accomplish something	प्राप्त करना	Accomplish, Attain, Succeed	Fail, Lose, Miss
Acquire	To gain or obtain something	प्राप्त करना	Obtain, Get, Procure	Lose, Give away, Release
Adapt	To adjust or change in response to new conditions	अनुकूलित करना	Adjust, Modify, Alter	Resist, Reject, Refuse
Adequate	Sufficient or satisfactory in quantity or quality	पर्याप्त	Satisfactory, Sufficient, Ample	Insufficient, Inadequate, Unsatisfactory
Admire	To regard with respect, approval, or pleasure	प्रशंसा करना	Respect, Appreciate, Esteem	Dislike, Disapprove, Despise
Adore	To love or worship intensely	पूजा करना	Love, Worship, Idolize	Hate, Detest, Abhor
Advance	To move forward or make progress	आगे बढ़ना	Progress, Proceed, Develop	Retreat, Regress, Decline
Adventure	An exciting or daring experience or activity	साहसिक अनुभव	Expedition, Journey, Quest	Boredom, Monotony, Routine

Word	Meaning in English	Meaning in Hindi	Synonyms	Antonyms
Advocate	To support or promote a cause or idea	वकील	Support, Champion, Defend	Oppose, Criticise, Attack
Affection	A gentle feeling of fondness or liking	प्यार	Love, Care, Fondness	Aversion, Dislike, Indifference
Agile	Quick and light in movement or action	प्रफुल्लित	Nimble, Quick, Spry	Clumsy, Slow, Inflexible
Alert	Watchful and ready to act or respond quickly	सतर्क	Vigilant, Attentive, Watchful	Careless, Inattentive, Unaware
Alleviate	To make suffering, pain, or burden less severe	कम करना	Relieve, Ease, Mitigate	Aggravate, Worsen, Intensify
Ally	A person or group that cooperates or supports another	सहयोगी	Partner, Associate, Friend	Adversary, Enemy, Opponent
Ambitious	Having a strong desire and determination to succeed	महत्वाकांक्षी	Driven, Goal-oriented, Aspiring	Content, Unambitious, Laid-back
Ample	Plentiful or more than sufficient in size or amount	प्रचुर	Abundant, Sufficient, Plentiful	Insufficient, Scarce, Limited
Analyze	To examine or study something in detail	विश्लेषण करना	Examine, Study, Scrutinise	Accept, Ignore, Neglect
Animate	To give life or energy to something	प्राणित करना	Energise, Vitalize, Inspire	Stagnate, Inanimate, Deaden
Appreciate	To recognize the value or significance of something	मान्य करना	Value, Treasure, Admire	Disregard, Underestimate, Dislike
Approve	To officially agree to or accept something	स्वीकृति देना	Agree, Consent, Endorse	Reject, Disapprove, Oppose
Ardent	Enthusiastic, passionate, or eager	उत्साही	Fervent, Zealous, Devoted	Indifferent, Apathetic, Cool
Ascend	To go up or climb upward	चढ़ना	Climb, Rise, Mount	Descend, Fall, Decline
Aspire	To have a strong desire or ambition for something	आकांक्षा रखना	Desire, Seek, Strive	Settle, Give up, Abandon
Assure	To give confidence or make someone feel certain	आश्वासन देना	Guarantee, Reassure, Promise	Doubt, Uncertain, Distrust

Word	Meaning in English	Meaning in Hindi	Synonyms	Antonyms
Attain	To achieve or reach something through effort	प्राप्त करना	Achieve, Obtain, Accomplish	Lose, Miss, Fail
Audacious	Bold, daring, or fearless in action or ideas	साहसिक	Courageous, Brave, Bold	Timid, Cowardly, Cautious
Authentic	Genuine, real, or true	मान्य	Genuine, Original, Legitimate	Fake, Counterfeit, Inauthentic
Authority	The power or right to give orders or make decisions	अधिकार	Power, Control, Command	Subordination, Powerlessness, Insubordination
Avid	Enthusiastic, keen, or eager	उत्सुक	Zealous, Passionate, Fervent	Indifferent, Uninterested, Apathetic
Awe	An overwhelming feeling of reverence, admiration, or fear	आदरभाव	Wonder, Astonishment, Reverence	Disgust, Apathy, Indifference
Awesome	Extremely impressive or inspiring awe	शानदार	Amazing, Spectacular, Breathtaking	Awful, Terrible, Mediocre
Awkward	Clumsy, uncomfortable, or lacking grace	बेढ़ैन	Ungraceful, Clumsy, Ungainly	Graceful, Skillful, Coordinated
Aware	Having knowledge or perception of something	जागरूक	Conscious, Mindful, Informed	Unaware, Ignorant, Oblivious
Axiom	A self-evident or universally recognized truth	सिद्धान्त	Principle, Maxim, Postulate	Fallacy, Paradox, Contradiction
Awake	To stop sleeping and become conscious	जागना	Waken, Arise, Rouse	Sleep, Slumber, Unconscious
Axiomatic	Self-evident or unquestionably true	स्वयंसिद्ध	Obvious, Incontestable, Undeniable	Questionable, Controversial, Doubtful
Asset	Something valuable or useful	संपत्ति	Advantage, Benefit, Resource	Liability, Drawback, Hindrance
Astonish	To greatly surprise or amaze someone	चकित करना	Amaze, Startle, Stun	Expect, Predict, Anticipate
Articulate	Expressing oneself clearly and effectively	स्पष्ट व्यक्त करना	Express, Enunciate, Vocalize	Mumble, Stumble, Incoherent
Assert	To state or declare confidently or forcefully	दावा करना	Affirm, Declare, Insist	Deny, Disclaim, Contradict

Word	Meaning in English	Meaning in Hindi	Synonyms	Antonyms
Anchor	A device used to secure or hold something in place	जंग	Secure, Fasten, Mooring	Release, Unfasten, Unanchor
Aggressive	Assertive, forceful, or ready to attack	प्रबल	Assertive, Bold, Militant	Passive, Timid, Peaceful
Absolve	To free someone from guilt or blame	मुक्त करना	Acquit, Pardon, Clear	Blame, Convict, Condemn
Adept	Skilled or proficient in a particular activity or subject	प्रवीण	Skillful, Proficient, Expert	Inept, Incompetent, Amateur
Adorn	To decorate or add beauty to something	सजाना	Embellish, Ornament, Beautify	Strip, Bare, Simplify
Adulate	To praise or flatter excessively	चाटुकारिता करना	Flatter, Compliment, Idolize	Criticise, Insult, Belittle
Affirm	To state or assert positively, confirm	पुष्टि करना	Confirm, Declare, Assert	Deny, Disprove, Contradict
Altruistic	Showing a selfless concern for the well-being of others	परोपकारी	Selfless, Charitable, Benevolent	Selfish, Greedy, Egoistic
Applaud	To show approval or praise by clapping hands or cheering	ताली बजाना	Praise, Cheer, Commend	Criticise, Boo, Disapprove
Artistic	Creative or skilled in the arts or aesthetic activities	कलात्मक	Creative, Talented, Expressive	Uncreative, Untalented, Inept
Assimilate	To absorb or integrate into a larger group or culture	समाविष्ट करना	Absorb, Incorporate, Integrate	Reject, Exclude, Separate
Audacity	Boldness, daring, or fearless behaviour	साहस	Boldness, Courage, Fearlessness	Timidity, Cowardice, Shyness
Authenticity	The quality of being genuine, real, or trustworthy	प्रामाणिकता	Genuineness, Veracity, Reliability	Falseness, Fraudulence, Deception
Awe-inspiring	Evoking a feeling of admiration, respect, or wonder	आदरणीय	Majestic, Breathtaking, Sublime	Ordinary, Unimpressive, Mundane

Word	Meaning in English	Meaning in Hindi	Synonyms	Antonyms
Abide	To accept or act in accordance with a rule, decision, or recommendation	पालन करना	Observe, Follow, Comply	Disregard, Violate, Break
Adroit	Skillful, clever, or resourceful in handling situations	कुशल	Skillful, Dexterous, Clever	Clumsy, Inept, Awkward
Affable	Friendly, approachable, and easy to talk to	मिलनसार	Friendly, Amiable, Genial	Hostile, Unfriendly, Rude
Amass	To gather or accumulate a large quantity or number of something	इकट्ठा करना	Accumulate, Gather, Collect	Disperse, Scatter, Distribute
Amiable	Friendly, pleasant, or likeable	सौम्य	Friendly, Affable, Pleasant	Hostile, Unpleasant, Unfriendly
Abdicate	To renounce or relinquish power or responsibility	त्यागना	Resign, Surrender, Relinquish	Assume, Retain, Claim
Abettor	A person who helps or encourages someone to commit a crime or wrongdoing	सहायक	Accomplice, Collaborator, Ally	Opponent, Adversary, Foe
Ability	The capacity or skill to do something	क्षमता	Capability, Competence, Talent	Inability, Incapacity, Disability
Ablaze	Burning fiercely; on fire	ज्वालामुखी	Burning, Fiery, Flaming	Extinguished, Dull, Dim
Ablution	The act of washing oneself, often in a religious context	स्नान	Cleansing, Washing, Purification	Filthiness, Dirtiness, Stain
Abnegation	The act of renouncing or rejecting something, often a belief or desire	त्याग	Renunciation, Denial, Rejection	Acceptance, Embrace, Approval
Abnormal	Deviating from the normal or usual standard	असामान्य	Unusual, Deviant, Anomalous	Normal, Typical, Ordinary
Abode	A place where someone resides or lives	निवास	Residence, Dwelling, Home	Departure, Vacancy, Emptiness

Word	Meaning in English	Meaning in Hindi	Synonyms	Antonyms
Abolition	The act of officially ending or abolishing something, especially a law or syst	उन्मूलन	Elimination, Eradication, Termination	Establishment, Implementation, Continuation
Abort	To terminate or stop before completion	निष्पादित करना	Terminate, Cancel, Cease	Proceed, Continue, Finish
Abortive	Unsuccessful or fruitless	निष्फल	Failed, Unproductive, Ineffective	Successful, Productive, Effective
Amplify	To make louder or stronger; to increase in size, extent, or importance	बढ़ाना	Intensify, Enhance, Magnify	Reduce, Diminish, Minimise
Annihilation	Complete destruction or obliteration	संक्षेप्ता	Destruction, Eradication, Extinction	Preservation, Conservation, Survival
Anticipated	Expected or predicted to happen	प्रत्याशित	Expected, Foreseen, Predicted	Unexpected, Surprising, Unforeseen
Antipathy	Strong dislike or aversion towards someone or something	घृणा	Aversion, Hatred, Disgust	Fondness, Affection, Liking
Arduous	Difficult and tiring; requiring great effort	कठिन	Strenuous, Laborious, Challenging	Easy, Effortless, Simple
Aroma	A pleasant or distinctive smell	सुगंध	Fragrance, Scent, Perfume	Odour, Stench, Stink
Austere	Severe or strict in manner or appearance; simple and plain	कठोर	Strict, Harsh, Spartan	Indulgent, Luxurious, Lavish
August	Respected and impressive, often due to high rank or dignity	बहुमानीय	Dignified, Noble, Grand	Humble, Ordinary, Common
Atrocity	An extremely wicked or cruel act, typically involving violence or brutality	अत्याचार	Brutality, Cruelty, Inhumanity	Kindness, Compassion, Humanity

Word	Meaning in English	Meaning in Hindi	Synonyms	Antonyms
Attract	To draw or pull someone or something towards oneself; to evoke interest or admiration	आकर्षित करना	Allure, Entice, Charm	Repel, Deter, Disinterest
Artful	Clever or skillful, typically in a cunning or deceptive way	मक्कार	Crafty, Cunning, Sly	Honest, Genuine, Naive
		B		
Balance	A state of equilibrium or stability	संतुलन	Equilibrium, Harmony, Stability	Imbalance, Instability, Disarray
Believe	To have confidence in the truth or existence of something	विश्वास करना	Trust, Have faith in, Convinced	Doubt, Disbelieve, Scepticism
Bold	Fearless, courageous, or daring	साहसिक	Brave, Courageous, Fearless	Timid, Cowardly, Fearful
Brilliant	Exceptionally intelligent, talented, or shining brightly	शानदार	Smart, Genius, Dazzling	Dull, Mediocre, Ordinary
Buoyant	Able to float or stay afloat; cheerful or optimistic	भरपूरता	Floating, Light, Optimistic	Sinking, Heavy, Pessimistic
Blissful	Full of joy, happiness, or bliss	आनंदमय	Joyful, Ecstatic, Serene	Miserable, Sorrowful, Troubled
Blossom	To bloom or flourish; the flower of a plant	खिलना	Flourish, Bloom, Flower	Wither, Fade, Decline
Bounty	Generosity, abundance, or a reward	उदारता	Generosity, Abundance, Reward	Scarcity, Lack, Stinginess
Benevolent	Kind, generous, and caring	उदार	Kind, Generous, Charitable	Malevolent, Cruel, Selfish
Bestow	To present or grant something as a gift or honour	प्रदान करना	Grant, Give, Confer	Withhold, Deny, Refuse
Benefit	An advantage or positive outcome	लाभ	Advantage, Gain, Benefit	Disadvantage, Loss, Drawback
Bountiful	Plentiful, abundant, or generous	उपहारदायक	Abundant, Plentiful, Generous	Scarce, Meagre, Limited
Boost	To increase or improve; a push or lift	बढ़ावा	Increase, Improve, Enhance	Decrease, Diminish, Reduce

Word	Meaning in English	Meaning in Hindi	Synonyms	Antonyms
Boldness	Courageous and confident behaviour	साहसिता	Courage, Fearlessness, Daring	Timidity, Cowardice, Shyness
Brave	Courageous, fearless, or not afraid to face danger	साहसी	Courageous, Fearless, Valiant	Cowardly, Timid, Fearful
Boundless	Without limits or boundaries; infinite	असीम	Infinite, Unlimited, Endless	Limited, Restricted, Finite
Beaming	Radiating happiness or joy	मुस्कानदार	Radiant, Smiling, Gleaming	Gloomy, Sad, Frowning
Beam	A ray of light or a long, sturdy piece of timber	प्रकाश किरण / बीम	Ray, Shaft, Girder	Shadow, Darkness, Dimness
Bound	To jump or leap; to be obliged or certain	कटौती / सीमित	Leap, Spring, Obliged	Stagnant, Stationary, Unbounded
Blessed	Favoured or protected by divine grace; happy or fortunate	धन्य	Fortunate, Favoured, Graced	Cursed, Unfortunate, Unblessed
Benevolence	Kindness, generosity, or a charitable act	उदारता / दयालुता	Kindness, Generosity, Charity	Cruelty, Selfishness, Greed
Bliss	Extreme happiness, joy, or spiritual joy	आनंद	Happiness, Joy, Euphoria	Misery, Sadness, Suffering
Brighten	To make or become brighter or more cheerful	चमकाना / उज्ज्वल होना	Illuminate, Cheer up, Enhance	Dim, Darken, Sadden
Brisk	Quick, active, and energetic	तेज	Lively, Vigorous, Swift	Slow, Sluggish, Leisurely
Bonanza	A situation or event that brings great prosperity or success	लाभदायक घटना	Windfall, Jackpot, Success	Misfortune, Failure, Loss
Booming	Thriving, growing rapidly or making a loud, resonant sound	बढ़ते हुए / गर्जना	Prosperous, Flourishing, Resounding	Declining, Fading, Quiet
Breakthrough	A significant development or achievement, especially in science or technology	प्रवर्तन	Milestone, Advancement, Discovery	Stagnation, Setback, Regression

Word	Meaning in English	Meaning in Hindi	Synonyms	Antonyms
Build	To construct or assemble something by putting parts together	निर्माण करना	Construct, Create, Form	Demolish, Destroy, Dismantle
Beneficial	Producing good or advantageous effects; helpful or advantageous	लाभदायक	Advantageous, Favourable, Positive	Harmful, Detrimental, Negative
Belief	A conviction or acceptance that something is true or exists	विश्वास	Faith, Conviction, Trust	Doubt, Scepticism, Disbelief
Blossom	To develop or flourish; to come into bloom	खिलना	Flourish, Thrive, Prosper	Wither, Fade, Decline
Brilliantly	In a very bright, intelligent, or impressive manner	उज्ज्वलता से	Radiantly, Excellently, Superbly	Poorly, Mediocrely, Unimpressively
Blazing	Burning with a strong flame; extremely intense or passionate	तेज़ आग से जलना / उग्र	Fiery, Fierce, Scorching	Extinguished, Cold, Subdued
Bounteous	Generously given or giving; abundant	उदार	Generous, Lavish, Plentiful	Stingy, Scanty, Miserly
Banish	To send away or exile someone; to get rid of or eliminate something	दूर करना	Exile, Expel, Oust	Welcome, Embrace, Accept
Beneath	In a lower position or place; below or underneath	नीचे	Under, Below, Underneath	Above, Over, Up
Blithe	Showing a casual and cheerful indifference; carefree and lighthearted	प्रसन्न	Carefree, Joyful, Merry	Sad, Gloomy, Miserable
Brevity	The quality of being brief or concise; using few words	संक्षिप्तता	Conciseness, Shortness, Succinctness	Verbosity, Long-windedness, Prolixity
Burnish	To polish, shine, or make smooth and glossy, especially by rubbing	चमकाना	Polish, Shine, Gloss	Dull, Dim, Tarnish
Bypass	To avoid or go around; to find an alternative route or means	चूंटी	Detour, Circumvent, Avoid	Direct, Face, Encounter

Word	Meaning in English	Meaning in Hindi	Synonyms	Antonyms
Blunder	A careless or stupid mistake; an error or misunderstanding	भूल	Mistake, Error, Fumble	Accuracy, Precision, Success
Bewilder	To confuse or puzzle someone completely; to perplex or confound	हक्का-बक्का करना	Confuse, Puzzle, Perplex	Clarify, Enlighten, Explain
Bleak	Desolate, dreary, and without any positive or hopeful features	उदास	Grim, Dreary, Desolate	Bright, Cheerful, Lively
Baffle	To frustrate or perplex; to cause someone to be completely puzzled or confused	चकरा देना	Puzzle, Confound, Perplex	Clarify, Explain, Elucidate
Blatant	Very obvious and intentional; without any attempt to hide or disguise	प्रचंड	Obvious, Flagrant, Evident	Subtle, Inconspicuous, Hidden
Bizarre	Very strange, unusual, or eccentric in style, appearance, or character	विचित्र	Strange, Unusual, Eccentric	Normal, Ordinary, Conventional
Blister	A small, raised area on the skin filled with fluid and caused by friction or burning	छाला	Sore, Vesicle, Pustule	Heal, Cure, Mend
Breakable	Capable of being broken or damaged; fragile or delicate	टूटने योग्य	Fragile, Delicate, Frangible	Unbreakable, Sturdy, Durable
Burden	A heavy load or something that is carried, usually metaphorically as a responsibility or duty	भार	Load, Weight, Encumbrance	Relief, Ease, Lighten
Blissfully	In a state of extreme happiness, joy, or contentment	आनंदित रूप से	Joyfully, Delightfully, Ecstatically	Sadly, Miserably, Sorrowfully
Bountifully	In a plentiful or abundant manner; with great generosity or richness	प्रचुरतापूर्वक	Generously, Lavishly, Plentifully	Sparingly, Scantily, Meagerly
Benevolently	In a kind, charitable, or compassionate manner; with goodwill and generosity	उदारतापूर्वक	Kindly, Charitably, Compassionately	Cruelly, Maliciously, Selfishly

Word	Meaning in English	Meaning in Hindi	Synonyms	Antonyms
		C		
Careful	cautious	सतर्क	vigilant, attentive, cautious	reckless, negligent, careless
Challenge	difficulty	चुनौती	obstacle, test, difficulty	easy task, simplicity, cakewalk
Cheerful	happy	हंसमुख	joyful, lively, happy	sad, gloomy, miserable
Comfortable	cosy	सुखदायी	relaxed, contented, cosy	uncomfortable, uneasy, restless
Commitment	dedication	समर्पण	loyalty, devotion, dedication	indifference, apathy, neglect
Compassion	empathy	दया	sympathy, kindness, empathy	indifference, cruelty, callousness
Confident	self-assured	आत्मविश्वासी	bold, assured, self-assured	insecure, unsure, doubtful
Courageous	brave	साहसी	fearless, heroic, brave	cowardly, timid, fearful
Considerate	thoughtful	सदभावपूर्ण	caring, kind, thoughtful	inconsiderate, thoughtless, selfish
Create	generate	सृजन करना	produce, invent, generate	destroy, demolish, ruin
Charismatic	magnetic	प्रभावशाली	charming, persuasive, magnetic	dull, unimpressive, uncharismatic
Consideration	Thoughtful and careful consideration of something	सोच-विचार, विचारशीलता	Reflection, Deliberation, Contemplation	Disregard, Neglect, Inconsideration
Celebratory	Pertaining to celebration or expressing joy	उत्सवपूर्ण, जश्नीला	Festive, Joyful, Commemorative	Somber, Gloomy, Mournful
Creative	Having the ability to produce or invent something new and original	रचनात्मक, नवीनतापूर्ण	Innovative, Imaginative, Artistic	Uninspired, Mundane, Conventional
Cordial	Warm and friendly in natur	सजीव, प्रिय	Affable, Amiable, Genial	Cold, Hostile, Unfriendly

Word	Meaning in English	Meaning in Hindi	Synonyms	Antonyms
Charitable	Willing to help others and show kindness	दानशील, धार्मिक	Philanthropic, Benevolent, Altruistic	Selfish, Stingy, Greedy
Coherence	Logical and consistent connection or arrangement of ideas	सुसंगतता, संगति	Consistency, Unity, Integration	Incoherence, Disarray, Disconnection
Clear-headed	Having a calm and rational mindset.	स्पष्ट-मनस्क, विचारशील	Rational, Level-headed, Sober	Confused, Distracted, Hasty
Crystal clear	Completely clear and transparent.	परम स्पष्ट, शुद्ध	Transparent, Lucid, Unambiguous	Cloudy, Opaque, Ambiguous
Cozy	Comfortable, warm, and snug.	सुखद, आरामदायक	Snug, Homely, Inviting	Uncomfortable, Cold, Uninviting
Cautious	Being careful and aware of potential risks or dangers.	सतर्क, सावधान	Prudent, Vigilant, Wary	Reckless, Careless, Inattentive
Conscientious	Diligent, thorough, and responsible in one's work.	ईमानदार, जगरिमापूर्ण	Meticulous, Attentive, Conscientious	Careless, Negligent, Irresponsible
Committed	Dedicated and loyal to a cause or belief.	प्रतिबद्ध, समर्पित	Devoted, Dedicated, Loyal	Uncommitted, Indifferent, Disloyal
Compliment	A polite expression of praise or admiration.	प्रशंसा, सराहना	Praise, Admiration, Complimentary remark	Insult, Criticism, Disapproval
Craft	Skill or expertise in a particular field or activity.	कौशल, शिल्प	Skill, Artistry, Proficiency	Incompetence, Ineptitude, Clumsiness
Captivating	Attracting and holding attention in a fascinating way.	मोहक, आकर्षक	Enchanting, Alluring, Engaging	Boring, Repellent, Uninteresting
Contribute	To give or provide support, help, or input.	योगदान, सहयोग देना	Contribute to, Participate, Donate	Withhold, Hold back, Abstain
Consistent	Acting or done in the same way over time, showing reliability.	सुसंगत, समानुपातिक	Reliable, Steady, Uniform	Inconsistent, Unreliable, Variable

Word	Meaning in English	Meaning in Hindi	Synonyms	Antonyms
Compassionate	Feeling or showing sympathy, care, and concern for others.	दयालु, करुणामय	Empathetic, Kind, Sympathetic	Cruel, Callous, Heartless
Courage	The ability to face and overcome fear or challenges.	साहस, धैर्य	Bravery, Valor, Fearlessness	Cowardice, Timidity, Fear
Cooperative	Willing to work or collaborate with others for a common goal.	सहकारी, सहयोगी	Collaborative, Supportive, Teamwork-oriented	Uncooperative, Hostile, Divisive
Competent	Having the necessary knowledge, skills, or abilities to do something well.	प्रावीण, योग्य	Skilled, Capable, Proficient	Incompetent, Inadequate, Unqualified
Charming	Pleasant and attractive in a way that captivates others.	मोहक, प्रियंकर	Enchanting, Alluring, Appealing	Repulsive, Unattractive, Disagreeable
Caring	Showing concern, kindness, and consideration for others.	परवाह करने वाला, सदभावनाशील	Compassionate, Nurturing, Thoughtful	Indifferent, Callous, Unconcerned
Calculate	Determine the value or result of a mathematical or numerical problem through arithmetic or logical reasoning.	गणना करना	Compute, Estimate	Guess, Speculate
Captivate	Attract and hold the interest and attention of someone by charm, beauty, or excellence.	मोहित करना	Fascinate, Enchant, Mesmerize	Repel, Bore, Repulse
Cherish	Hold dear, treasure, or appreciate something or someone deeply.	प्रियतम मानना	Adore, Value, Appreciate	Disdain, Despise, Neglect
Clarity	The quality or state of being clear, coherent, or easily understood.	स्पष्टता	Transparency, Clearness, Lucidity	Ambiguity, Obscurity, Vagueness
Convey	Transport or communicate a message, information, or feeling.	संचार करना	Communicate, Transmit, Transfer	Withhold, Retain, Suppress

Word	Meaning in English	Meaning in Hindi	Synonyms	Antonyms
Conquer	Overcome and take control or possession of a place or situation.	जीतना	Overcome, Triumph, Vanquish	Surrender, Yield, Submit
Courteous	Polite, respectful, and considerate in manner.	शिष्ट	Polite, Respectful, Civil	Rude, Impolite, Discourteous
Coherent	Logical and consistent, clear and easy to understand.	सुसंगत	Logical, Consistent, Rational	Incoherent, Disjointed, Illogical
Compass	An instrument used to determine directions, typically having a magnetic needle that points towards the Earth's magnetic north.	दिशा	Direction, Orientation, Bearing	Misdirection, Confusion, Lost
Consume	To eat, drink, or ingest food, drink, or other substances.	खर्च करना	Devour, Ingest, Eat	Save, Preserve, Conserve
Cope	Deal effectively with something difficult or challenging.	सामर्थ्य दिखाना	Deal, Manage, Handle	Surrender, Give up, Quit
Curious	Eager to know or learn something; inquisitive.	जिज्ञासु	Inquisitive, Interested, Nosy	Indifferent, Uninterested, Apathetic
Comprehend	To understand or grasp the meaning or nature of something.	समझना	Understand, Grasp, Fathom	Misunderstand, Misinterpret, Confuse
Congratulate	To express pleasure or joy to someone for an achievement or good fortune.	बधाई देना	Felicitate, Applaud, Compliment	Condemn, Criticise, Disapprove
Conform	To comply with rules, standards, or laws; to be in accordance or agreement.	अनुरूप होना	Comply, Obey, Follow	Defy, Rebel, Resist
Cultivate	To foster the growth or development of something; to nurture or promote.	खेती करना	Nurture, Foster, Develop	Neglect, Abandon, Ignore
Composure	Mental calmness and self-control, especially in difficult situations.	संयम	Calmness, Serenity, Equanimity	Agitation, Disturbance, Turmoil

Word	Meaning in English	Meaning in Hindi	Synonyms	Antonyms
Courtesy	Polite behaviour, manners, or acts of civility.	शिष्टाचार	Politeness, Manners, Civility	Rudeness, Impoliteness, Discourtesy
Complement	Something that completes or brings perfection to another thing.	पूरक	Supplement, Enhance, Complete	Oppose, Contradict, Nullify
Collaborate	To work together with others on a common project or goal.	सहयोग करना	Cooperate, Work together, Team up	Compete, Oppose, Disagree
Cantankerous	Bad-tempered, argumentative, and uncooperative	झगड़ालू	Quarrelsome, Contentious, Disagreeable	Agreeable, Cooperative, Amiable
Capitulate	To surrender or give up resistance; to yield	हार मान लेना	Surrender, Yield, Concede	Resist, Defy, Persist
Caricature	A picture, description, or imitation of a person that exaggerates their distinctive features or characteristics	कारिकेचर	Cartoon, Parody, Lampoon	Realistic portrayal, Serious depiction
Carnage	The killing of a large number of people, especially in a violent or bloody manner	हत्याकांड	Massacre, Slaughter, Bloodshed	Peace, Harmony, Nonviolence
Carouse	To engage in noisy, drunken revelry or partying	मस्ती मनाना	Revel, Party, Celebrate	Abstain, Restrain, Sobr
Casual	Relaxed, informal, or not formal or serious	आकस्मिक	Informal, Laid-back, Unconcerned	Formal, Serious, Careful
Catastrophe	A sudden and widespread disaster or misfortune	आपदा	Disaster, Calamity, Tragedy	Success, Triumph, Fortune
Cavort	To jump or dance around excitedly; to frolic	उछाल-कूद करना	Frolic, Gambol, Romp	Rest, Languish, Idle
Celebrate	To honour or commemorate with festivities or joyous activities	जश्न मनाना	Commemorate, Rejoice, Festive	Mourn, Lament, Grieve
Ceremonial	Relating to or used for formal or solemn occasions	सांस्कृतिक	Ritual, Formal, Solemn	Informal, Casual, Spontaneous
Certain	Having no doubt or uncertainty; confident	निश्चित	Confident, Sure, Definite	Uncertain, Doubtful, Indefinite

Word	Meaning in English	Meaning in Hindi	Synonyms	Antonyms
Chafe	To irritate or make someone impatient or annoyed	खींचना	Irritate, Frustrate, Annoy	Soothe, Calm, Pacify
Challenge	A task or situation that tests someone's abilities, skills, or knowledge	चुनौती	Test, Trial, Confrontation	Easy task, Acceptance, Avoidance
Change	To make or become different; to alter or modify	बदलना	Alter, Modify, Transform	Maintain, Preserve, Unchanged
Chaos	Complete disorder and confusion	अव्यवस्था	Disorder, Confusion, Anarchy	Order, Harmony, Organisation
Character	The mental and moral qualities distinctive to an individual; the essence of a person's identity	चरित्र	Personality, Integrity, Ethos	Dishonesty, Vice, Corruption
		D		
Disaster	A sudden event or accident causing great damage, destruction, or distress.	आपदा	Calamity, Catastrophe, Misfortune	Success, Triumph, Achievement
Delicate	Easily broken, fragile, or sensitive.	सूक्ष्म	Fragile, Tender, Sensitive	Robust, Sturdy, Resilient
Dynamic	Characterised by constant change, activity, or progress.	गतिशील	Energetic, Vibrant, Active	Static, Inactive, Lethargic
Dawn	The first appearance of light in the sky before sunrise; the beginning or start.	भोर	Sunrise, Daybreak, Morning	Sunset, Dusk, Nightfall
Dazzling	Extremely bright, impressive, or beautiful.	चमकदार	Sparkling, Radiant, Brilliant	Dull, Dim, Gloomy
Devour	To eat or consume greedily and enthusiastically.	खा जाना	Consume, Eat, Swallow	Abstain, Reject, Spit out
Divert	To change the direction or course; to redirect or distract.	मोड़ना	Redirect, Turn, Detour	Straighten, Direct, Guide
Deliberate	Done consciously and intentionally; carefully thought out.	सोच-विचार करना	Consider, Ponder, Contemplate	Impulsive, Hasty, Rash

Word	Meaning in English	Meaning in Hindi	Synonyms	Antonyms
Defiant	Showing resistance or disobedience; openly challenging or confrontational.	अवज्ञापूर्ण	Rebellious, Resistant, Obstinate	Obedient, Compliant, Submissive
Drench	To soak or wet thoroughly; to saturate.	भिगोना	Soak, Wet, Saturate	Dry, Dehydrate, Drain
Dreadful	Causing fear, shock, or terror; extremely bad or unpleasant.	भयानक	Terrible, Horrifying, Frightening	Pleasant, Delightful, Wonderful
Depict	To represent or portray something or someone in a picture or words.	चित्रित करना	Portray, Illustrate, Represent	Conceal, Hide, Cover
Diplomatic	Skilled in dealing with people or sensitive situations; tactful and discreet.	कूटनीतिक	Tactful, Polite, Discreet	Blunt, Inconsiderate, Rude
Dismantle	To take apart or dismantle a structure or object.	तोड़ना	Disassemble, Take apart, Deconstruct	Assemble, Construct, Build
Disguise	To conceal the true identity or nature of something or someone.	छिपाना	Camouflage, Mask, Conceal	Reveal, Unmask, Disclose
Disrupt	To interrupt, disturb, or cause disorder or chaos.	बाधित करना	Disturb, Interrupt, Upset	Facilitate, Maintain, Stabilise
Dwell	To live or reside in a particular place; to think, speak, or write at length about something.	निवास करना	Reside, Live, Inhabit	Leave, Vacate, Abandon
Drizzle	Light rain falling in very fine drops.	बूंद-बूंद गिरना	Sprinkle, Mist, Spritz	Pour, Downpour, Torrential rain
Dauntless	Showing fearlessness, courage, or determination; not intimidated or discouraged.	निडर	Fearless, Brave, Bold	Timid, Cowardly, Fearful
Dwindle	To diminish gradually in size, amount, or strength; to shrink or reduce.	धीमा हो जाना	Diminish, Decrease, Shrink	Increase, Expand, Grow

Word	Meaning in English	Meaning in Hindi	Synonyms	Antonyms
Disperse	To scatter, spread out, or distribute in different directions.	छितरना	Scatter, Spread, Distribute	Gather, Collect, Assemble
Delve	To explore or investigate thoroughly; to search deeply.	खोजना	Explore, Investigate, Probe	Neglect, Ignore, Disregard
Despise	To feel a strong dislike or contempt for someone or something.	घृणा करना	Detest, Abhor, Dislike	Admire, Respect, Esteem
Deteriorate	To become progressively worse or decline in quality or condition.	खराब होना	Decline, Worsen, Degrade	Improve, Enhance, Upgrade
Dire	Extremely serious or urgent; causing fear, dread, or disaster.	भयानक	Terrible, Grave, Dreadful	Mild, Slight, Insignificant
Decipher	To convert a coded or encrypted message into understandable language.	समझना	Decode, Decrypt, Interpret	Encode, Encrypt, Confuse
Dishearten	To cause someone to lose determination, confidence, or enthusiasm.	हतोत्साहित करना	Discourage, Dismay, Demoralize	Encourage, Inspire, Motivate
Dispatch	To send off or deal with promptly; to send a message or goods for delivery.	तुरंत	Send, Forward, Expedite	Receive, Retrieve, Delay
Dabble	To take part in an activity or interest in a casual or superficial way.	हाथ लगाना	Splash, Paddle, Tinker	Specialise, Focus, Master
Dormant	Inactive, sleeping, or temporarily suspended; not currently active.	सुस्त	Inactive, Sleeping, Idle	Active, Awake, Energetic
Deviate	To depart or stray from the established course, norm, or expectation.	भटकना	Stray, Wander, Veer	Follow, Stay, Adhere
Defy	To openly resist or refuse to obey; to challenge or confront boldly.	टाकना	Challenge, Resist, Oppose	Obey, Submit, Comply

Word	Meaning in English	Meaning in Hindi	Synonyms	Antonyms
Dismiss	To reject, disregard, or put aside as unworthy or irrelevant.	खारिज करना	Reject, Ignore, Exclude	Accept, Acknowledge, Consider
Disruptive	Causing disruption, disturbance, or disorder; tending to interrupt or hinder.	अव्यवस्थापूर्ण	Troublesome, Disturbing, Chaotic	Orderly, Harmonious, Peaceful
Dazzle	To impress or astonish greatly with brightness, skill, or excellence.	चकाचौंध करना	Amaze, Impress, Stun	Bore, Disappoint, Dull
Dignity	The quality of being worthy of respect, honour, or esteem; composed and serious behaviour.	मर्यादा	Honor, Respect, Prestige	Disgrace, Shame, Humiliation
Disseminate	To spread or disperse widely, especially information or knowledge.	प्रसारित करना	Spread, Circulate, Disperse	Gather, Collect, Accumulate
Dominate	To have control, influence, or power over others; to be the most important or prominent.	वश में करना	Control, Rule, Command	Submit, Yield, Surrender
Discern	To perceive, recognize, or distinguish something with the senses or intellect.	पहचानना	Perceive, Recognize, Distinguish	Overlook, Ignore, Neglect
Durable	Able to withstand wear, pressure, or damage; long-lasting and resilient.	स्थायी	Long-lasting, Sturdy, Enduring	Fragile, Temporary, Perishable
Desolate	Deserted and barren; feeling or showing great unhappiness or loneliness.	उजड़ा हुआ	Deserted, Barren, Empty	Populated, Vibrant, Thriving
Deceive	To cause someone to believe something that is not true; to mislead or trick.	धोखा देना	Mislead, Trick, Dupe	Inform, Reveal, Disclose
Devotion	Deep love, loyalty, or commitment to someone or something.	भक्ति	Dedication, Commitment, Loyalty	Indifference, Disinterest, Neglect
Drastic	Likely to have a strong or far-reaching effect; extreme or severe.	कठोर	Extreme, Severe, Radical	Mild, Gentle, Moderate

Word	Meaning in English	Meaning in Hindi	Synonyms	Antonyms
Dwelling	A place where someone lives; a residence or habitation.	आवास	Residence, Home, Abode	Departure, Evacuation, Vacancy
Dismay	A feeling of distress or despair caused by something unexpected or disheartening.	हताशा	Discouragement, Despair, Alarm	Encouragement, Hope, Reassurance
Disintegrate	To break apart or decompose into smaller parts; to crumble or disperse.	टूटना	Break apart, Crumble, Fragment	Integrate, Combine, Consolidate
Distinct	Clearly different or separate from others; easily perceptible or recognizable.	अलग	Separate, Different, Unique	Similar, Identical, Indistinct
Detest	To dislike intensely; to abhor or hate strongly.	घृणा करना	Abhor, Hate, Despise	Love, Admire, Cherish
Docile	Easily taught, managed, or controlled; obedient and submissive.	आज्ञाकारी	Obedient, Submissive, Compliant	Stubborn, Rebellious, Defiant
Discomfort	A state of physical or psychological unease or distress.	असुविधा	Unease, Distress, Inconvenience	Comfort, Ease, Relaxation
Diligent	Showing persistent and hardworking effort; attentive and thorough in work.	मेहनती	Hardworking, Industrious, Assiduous	Lazy, Idle, Negligent
Distinctive	Having a unique or recognizable quality or feature that sets someone or something apart.	विशिष्ट	Unique, Peculiar, Noteworthy	Common, Ordinary, Unremarkable
Detour	A long or roundabout route taken to avoid something or reach a destination.	घूम फिरकर जाना	Diversion, Bypass, Deviation	Direct route, Straight path, Main road
Dissolve	To become or cause to become incorporated into a liquid; to melt away or disperse.	घुलना	Melt, Disintegrate, Disperse	Solidify, Condense, Coagulate
Divulge	To make known or reveal something secret or private.	प्रकट करना	Reveal, Disclose, Expose	Conceal, Hide, Cover

Word	Meaning in English	Meaning in Hindi	Synonyms	Antonyms
Devoid	Entirely lacking or free from something; empty or without.	विहीन	Lacking, Empty, Void	Filled, Abundant, Replete
Discontent	A state of dissatisfaction, restlessness, or unhappiness with one's circumstances.	असंतुष्टि	Dissatisfaction, Displeasure, Restlessness	Contentment, Satisfaction, Happiness
Dwellers	People who reside or live in a particular place.	निवासी	Residents, Inhabitants, Occupants	Travelers, Nomads, Visitors
Dearth	scarcity or lack of something	अकाल	Scarcity, Shortage, Lack	Abundance, Surplus, Plenitude
Decimated	To destroy or kill a large portion or majority of something.	पूर्णतया नष्ट कर देना	Devastate, Annihilate, Obliterate	Restore, Revive, Preserve
Defer	To delay or postpone something to a later time.	टाल देना	Postpone, Delay, Procrastinate	Expedite, Advance, Hasten
Deference	Respectful submission or yielding to the judgement or opinion of another person.	सम्मान	Respect, Reverence, Obedience	Disregard, Defiance, Disrespect
Deficiency	A lack or shortage of something, often used to describe a condition of not having enough or being inadequate.	कमी	Shortage, Insufficiency, Inadequacy	Abundance, Surplus, Sufficiency
Deluge	A severe flood or overwhelming amount of something, typically referring to a heavy rain or an influx of information.	बाढ़	Flood, Inundation, Torrent	Drought, Scarcity, Deficiency
Despicable	Worthy of contempt or scorn, deserving to be despised.	घिनौना	Vile, Abhorrent, Disgusting	Admirable, Worthy, Respectable
Despondent	Feeling or showing extreme discouragement, dejection, or depression.	मायूस	Depressed, Disheartened, Gloomy	Hopeful, Optimistic, Encouraged
Destroy	To cause severe damage or ruin, to demolish or eradicate completely	नष्ट करना	Ruin, Devastate, Demolish	Create, Build, Preserve

Word	Meaning in English	Meaning in Hindi	Synonyms	Antonyms
Determined	Having a firm or resolute purpose, characterised by a strong will or resolve.	प्रतिष्ठित	Resolute, Persistent, Steadfast	Indecisive, Hesitant, Fickle
Detrimental	Causing harm or damage, having a negative or harmful effect.	हानिकारक	Harmful, Damaging, Adverse	Beneficial, Advantageous, Positive
Discover	To find or uncover something for the first time, to become aware of or reveal something previously unknown.	खोजना	Unearth, Uncover, Find	Conceal, Hide, Suppress
Drag	To pull or draw something along a surface, often with effort or resistance.	खींचना	Pull, Haul, Tug	Push, Propel, Glide
		E		
Eager	Having or showing keen interest, enthusiasm, or willingness.	उत्सुक	Enthusiastic, Keen, Excited	Indifferent, Reluctant, Apathetic
Early	Happening or done before the usual or expected time; occurring at the beginning.	जल्दी	Premature, Timely, Prompt	Late, Delayed, Belated
Earn	To obtain money or receive payment for work or services.	कमाना	Gain, Acquire, Achieve	Lose, Spend, Forfeit
Earth	The planet we live on; the ground or soil.	पृथ्वी	Soil, Ground, Land	Sky, Heaven, Space
Ease	The state of being comfortable, relaxed, or free from effort or difficulty.	आसानी	Comfort, Relaxation, Simplicity	Difficulty, Hardship, Struggle
East	The direction toward which the sun rises; the opposite of west.	पूर्व	Orient, Sunrise, Levant	West, Westward, Occident
Easy	Not difficult or demanding; requiring little effort or discomfort.	आसान	Simple, Effortless, Uncomplicated	Difficult, Challenging, Complex
Eat	To consume food by putting it into the mouth and swallowing.	खाना	Consume, Devour, Ingest	Abstain, Fast, Starve

Word	Meaning in English	Meaning in Hindi	Synonyms	Antonyms
Edge	The outside limit or part of something; the sharp side of a blade or cutting tool.	किनारा	Border, Boundary, Rim	Center, Interior, Middle
Educate	To teach someone knowledge, skills, or information; to provide formal instruction.	शिक्षा देना	Instruct, Teach, Train	Mislead, Ignorant, Misinform
Effect	A result or consequence of an action, process, or event.	प्रभाव	Impact, Result, Consequence	Cause, Source, Origin
Efficient	Capable of producing desired results with minimal waste of time, effort, or resources.	कुशल	Productive, Competent, Effective	Inefficient, Ineffective, Unproductive
Either	Used to indicate a choice between two alternatives.	दोनों में से कोई भी	One or the other, Any, Indifferent	Both, Neither, None
Elderly	Used as a polite or respectful way of referring to old people.	बुजुर्ग	Senior, Aged, Old	Young, Youthful, Junior
Elect	To choose or select (someone) for a position, job, or honor by voting.	चुनना	Choose, Select, Pick	Reject, Dismiss, Decline
Element	A part or aspect of something abstract, especially one that is essential or characteristic.	तत्व तत्व	Component, Ingredient, Factor	Whole, Entirety, Totality
Elevate	To raise or lift (something) to a higher position.	उच्च स्थान पर ले जाना	Raise, Lift, Ascend	Lower, Descend, Depress
Earnest	Showing sincere and intense conviction; serious and determined in intention or purpose.	गंभीर	Serious, Sincere, Genuine	Lighthearted, Insincere, Frivolous
Eccentric	Unconventional and slightly strange; deviating from conventional or accepted norms.	अद्वितीय	Quirky, Peculiar, Odd	Conventional, Normal, Typical

Word	Meaning in English	Meaning in Hindi	Synonyms	Antonyms
Echo	A sound or series of sounds caused by the reflection of sound waves from a surface back to the listener.	गूंज	Reverberation, Resonance, Repetition	Silence, Stillness, Quiet
Eclipse	The obscuring of the light from one celestial body by the passage of another between it and the observer or between it and its source of illumination.	ग्रहण	Obscure, Overshadow, Conceal	Reveal, Illuminate, Expose
Economic	Relating to the production, distribution, and use of goods and services; relating to money or finance.	आर्थिक	Financial, Monetary, Fiscal	Expensive, Costly, Wasteful
Edit	To prepare (written material) for publication by correcting, condensing, or otherwise modifying it.	संपादन	Revise, Modify, Correct	Write, Create, Compose
Educate	To give intellectual, moral, and social instruction to someone, typically at a school or university.	शिक्षा देना	Instruct, Teach, Train	Mislead, Ignorant, Misinform
Effect	A change that is a result or consequence of an action or other cause.	प्रभाव	Impact, Result, Consequence	Cause, Source, Origin
Efficacy	The ability to produce a desired or intended result.	प्रभावकारिता	Efficiency, Effectiveness, Productiveness	Ineffectiveness, Inefficiency, Ineptitude
Effort	Physical or mental exertion towards accomplishing something.	प्रयास	Endeavor, Attempt, Strive	Laziness, Inactivity, Negligence
Elaborate	To expand or explain in detail; to give more information or detail about something.	विस्तृत	Detailed, Intricate, Elaborated	Simple, Concise, Brief

Word	Meaning in English	Meaning in Hindi	Synonyms	Antonyms
Elastic	Able to resume its normal shape or size after being stretched or compressed; flexible.	लचीला	Flexible, Stretchable, Resilient	Inflexible, Stiff, Rigid
Elate	To make (someone) ecstatically happy.	आनंदित करना	Delight, Thrill, Exhilarate	Depress, Sadden, Disappoint
Elegant	Graceful and stylish in appearance or manner.	सुरुचिपूर्ण	Graceful, Stylish, Refined	Clumsy, Awkward, Unrefined
Eligible	Having the right to do or obtain something; satisfying the appropriate conditions.	योग्य	Qualified, Suitable, Appropriate	Ineligible, Unqualified, Unsuitable
Embark	To begin a course of action, especially one that is important or demanding.	प्रारंभ करना	Begin, Commence, Start	Abandon, Cease, Discontinue
Embrace	To hold (someone) closely in one's arms, especially as a sign of affection.	गले लगाना गले लगाना	Hug, Clasp, Cuddle	Reject, Avoid, Shun
Emerging	Becoming apparent or prominent.	उभरता हुआ	Rising, Developing, Evolving	Declining, Fading, Waning
Eminent	Famous and respected within a particular sphere or profession.	प्रमुख	Distinguished, Prominent, Notable	Unknown, Obscure, Insignificant
Empathy	The ability to understand and share the feelings of another.	सहानुभूति	Compassion, Understanding, Sympathy	Apathy, Indifference, Insensitivity
Employ	To give work to (someone) and pay them for it.	नौकरी देना	Hire, Engage, Use	Fire, Dismiss, Unemploy
Empower	To give (someone) the authority or power to do something.	सशक्त करना	Authorise, Enable, Strengthen	Disempower, Weaken, Impede
Empty	Containing nothing; not filled or occupied.	खाली	Vacant, Void, Blank	Full, Occupied, Filled
Enable	To give someone the authority, means, or opportunity to do something.	सक्षम करना	Empower, Facilitate, Permit	Disable, Hinder, Prevent

Word	Meaning in English	Meaning in Hindi	Synonyms	Antonyms
Encourage	To give support, confidence, or hope to someone.	प्रोत्साहित करना	Inspire, Motivate, Support	Discourage, Deter, Demotivate
Endorse	To declare one's public approval or support of (someone or something).	पुष्टि करना	Support, Approve, Validate	Reject, Disapprove, Denounce
Endure	To suffer (something painful or difficult) patiently.	सहना	Bear, Tolerate, Sustain	Abandon, Quit, Surrender
Energise	To give vitality, vigour, or enthusiasm to someone or something.	ऊर्जा प्रदान करना	Revitalise, Recharge, Invigorate	Exhaust, Drain, Deplete
Engage	To occupy, attract, or involve (someone's interest or attention).	संलग्न होना	Involve, Participate, Occupy	Disengage, Disconnect, Uninvolved
Enhance	To intensify, increase, or further improve the quality, value, or extent of something.	बढ़ाना	Improve, Augment, Boost	Diminish, Decrease, Weaken
Enjoy	To take pleasure in (something).	आनंद लेना	Delight in, Savour, Relish	Dislike, Detest, Loathe
Enrich	To improve or enhance the quality or value of something.	समृद्ध करना	Enhance, Improve, Prosper	Impoverish, Deplete, Reduce
Ensure	To make certain that something will happen or be the case.	सुनिश्चित करना	Guarantee, Assure, Secure	Jeopardise, Risk, Endanger
Entertain	To provide amusement or enjoyment.	मनोरंजन करना	Amuse, Delight, Engage	Bore, Repel, Dull
Enthusiasm	Intense and eager enjoyment, interest, or approval.	उत्साह	Passion, Zeal, Excitement	Apathy, Indifference, Lethargy
Entice	To attract or tempt by offering pleasure or advantage.	आकर्षित करना	Lure, Attract, Tempt	Repel, Deter, Discourage
Entire	Whole; complete; with no part missing or left out.	सम्पूर्ण	Whole, Complete, Full	Partial, Incomplete, Fragmented

Word	Meaning in English	Meaning in Hindi	Synonyms	Antonyms
Entrance	An opening, such as a door, passage, or gate, that allows access to a place.	प्रवेश	Entry, Access, Admission	Exit, Egress, Departure
Envelop	To wrap up, cover, or surround completely.	ढकना	Enclose, Cover, Wrap	Uncover, Expose, Unwrap
Environment	The surroundings or conditions in which a person, animal, or plant lives or operates.	पर्यावरण	Surroundings, Habitat, Ecosystem	Uninhabitable, Unfriendly, Polluted
Envision	To imagine or picture something in one's mind.	कल्पना करना	Imagine, Visualise, Picture	Disregard, Overlook, Ignore
Equal	Being the same in quantity, size, degree, or value.	समान	Same, Identical, Equivalent	Different, Unequal, Inequivalent
Equip	To provide someone with necessary items or skills for a particular purpose.	सुसज्जित करना	Prepare, Outfit, Furnish	Disarm, Strip, Deprive
Equitable	Fair and impartial; just and reasonable.	न्यायसंगत	Fair, Just, Impartial	Biassed, Unfair, Partial
Era	A period of time marked by distinct characteristics, events, or developments.	युग	Age, Period, Epoch	Antiquity, Past, Obsolete
Erase	To remove or obliterate something by wiping or scraping it out.	मिटाना	Delete, Remove, Obliterate	Write, Add, Inscribe
Essential	Absolutely necessary; extremely important.	महत्वपूर्ण	Vital, Crucial, Necessary	Nonessential, Insignificant, Dispensable
Establish	To set up or create (an organisation, system, or set of rules) on a firm or permanent basis.	स्थापित करना	Set up, Found, Institute	Disestablish, Dismantle, Abolish
Esteem	Respect and admiration for someone or something.	सम्मान	Respect, Admiration, Honor	Disrespect, Contempt, Disregard
Ethics	Moral principles that govern a person's behaviour or the conducting of an activity.	नैतिकता	Morality, Integrity, Principles	Unethical, Immoral, Dishonest

Word	Meaning in English	Meaning in Hindi	Synonyms	Antonyms
Evaluate	To assess or judge the value, importance, or quality of something.	मूल्यांकन करना	Assess, Appraise, Judge	Ignore, Disregard, Neglect
Even	Equal in degree, extent, or amount; equally matched or balanced.	समान	Equal, Level, Balanced	Uneven, Odd, Irregular
Event	A thing that happens, especially one of importance or significance.	घटना	Occasion, Incident, Happening	Non-event, Inaction, Stagnation
Evolve	To develop or change gradually over time.	विकसित होना	Develop, Grow, Progress	Regress, Decline, Devolve
Excel	To be exceptionally good at or proficient in an activity or subject.	प्रशंसायोग्य होना	Succeed, Outshine, Triumph	Fail, Underperform, Mediocre
Exclaim	To cry out or speak suddenly and vehemently, typically as an expression of strong emotion.	चिल्लाना	Shout, Cry out, Declare	Whisper, Mumble, Murmur
Execute	To carry out or put into effect (a plan, order, or course of action).	कार्रवाई करना	Perform, Accomplish, Carry out	Abandon, Neglect, Fail
Ebullient	Cheerful and full of energy	उमंगयुक्त	Enthusiastic, Energetic, Exuberant	Gloomy, Depressed, Dull
Ecstasy	An overwhelming feeling of joy or delight	आनंद	Bliss, Euphoria, Rapture	Misery, Despair, Gloom
Eliminate	To completely remove or get rid of something	समाप्त करना	Eradicate, Remove, Exterminate	Retain, Preserve, Keep
Elusive	Difficult to find, catch, or achieve	लब्धिकर्ता	Evasive, Slippery, Sneaky	Accessible, Clear, Obvious
Emancipation	The act of being set free or liberated from oppression or bondage	मुक्ति	Liberation, Freedom, Independence	Enslavement, Bondage, Subjugation
Engulf	To completely surround or cover something	घेरना	Submerge, Immerse, Swallow	Free, Uncover, Release

Word	Meaning in English	Meaning in Hindi	Synonyms	Antonyms
Enormous	Very large in size, quantity, or extent	विशाल	Huge, Gigantic, Immense	Tiny, Small, Miniature
Enthralled	Captivated or deeply fascinated by someone or something	मोहित	Enchanted, Mesmerised, Spellbound	Uninterested, Bored, Indifferent
Erroneous	Incorrect or mistaken	ग़लत	Wrong, Inaccurate, False	Accurate, Correct, True
Espionage	The practice of spying or gathering information secretly, especially for political or military purposes	जासूसी	Spying, Surveillance, Intelligence	Transparency, Openness, Honesty
Estimate	To make an approximate calculation or judgement	अनुमान	Approximation, Assessment, Evaluation	Exactness, Precision, Accuracy
Exasperated	Frustrated or irritated to a high degree	परेशान	Irritated, Annoyed, Frustrated	Calm, Composed, Content
Exempt	Freed or released from an obligation or liability	मुक्त	Excused, Immune, Dispensed	Subject to, Liable, Accountable
Extricate	To free or release from entanglement or difficulty	निकालना	Untangle, Unravel, Liberate	Entangle, Ensnare,
		F		
Fable	A short story with a moral, often involving animals as characters.	नीतिकथा	Tale, Allegory, Parable	Fact, Reality, Truth
Faint	To lose consciousness temporarily; lacking in strength or clarity.	बेहोश होना	Swoon, Pass out, Dim	Conscious, Clear, Strong
Falcon	A bird of prey, known for its swift flight and sharp beak.	बाज	Hawk, Eagle, Raptor	Pigeon, Sparrow, Finch
Fame	The state of being widely known or recognized, typically for achievements.	प्रसिद्धि	Celebrity, Reputation, Renown	Obscurity, Anonymity, Ignominy
Farewell	An act of parting or saying goodbye.	विदाई	Goodbye, Adieu, Parting	Welcome, Greeting, Arrival

Word	Meaning in English	Meaning in Hindi	Synonyms	Antonyms
Fasten	To close or secure firmly; to attach or fix in place.	बांधना	Attach, Secure, Clasp	Unfasten, Release, Detach
Fatigue	Extreme tiredness resulting from physical or mental exertion.	थकान	Exhaustion, Weariness, Tiredness	Energy, Vigor, Refreshment
Feasible	Possible to do easily or conveniently; likely to be successful.	व्यवहार्य	Achievable, Attainable, Possible	Impractical, Unrealistic, Unfeasible
Feather	One of the flat appendages growing from a bird's skin that helps in flying.	पंख	Plume, Quill, Plumage	Scale, Skin, Fur
Feign	To pretend or give a false appearance of; to fake or simulate.	बहाना करना	Pretend, Simulate, Counterfeit	Genuine, Real, Sincere
Festive	Relating to or suitable for a festival or celebration; joyous and merry.	उत्सवपूर्ण	Joyful, Celebratory, Jovial	Gloomy, Solemn, Dull
Fever	An abnormally high body temperature, usually as a result of an illness.	बुख़ार	Temperature, Heat, Pyrexia	Normal, Cool, Chills
Fierce	Having a violent or aggressive nature; intense or strong.	भयानक	Ferocious, Savage, Vicious	Gentle, Mild, Tame
Figurine	A small ornamental statue or sculpture, often depicting a human or animal.	प्रतिमा	Statue, Sculpture, Figural	Life-size, Giant, Enormous
Filter	A device or porous material used to remove impurities from a substance.	फ़िल्टर	Strainer, Sieve, Purifier	Contaminate, Pollute, Dirty
Finale	The last part of a performance, event, or composition; the conclusion.	अंतिम भाग	Conclusion, Ending, Climax	Beginning, Opening, Prologue
Fireworks	Explosive devices designed to produce a visual or auditory display for celebrations.	पटाख़े	Pyrotechnics, Firecrackers, Sparklers	Silence, Stillness, Calmness

Word	Meaning in English	Meaning in Hindi	Synonyms	Antonyms
Flair	A natural talent or aptitude; a distinctive style or elegance.	कौशल	Talent, Skill, Style	Ineptitude, Clumsiness, Awkwardness
Flaw	A mark, fault, or imperfection that mars the perfection or completeness of something.	कमी	Defect, Blemish, Imperfection	Perfection, Strength, Advantage
Fluffy	Soft, light, and airy in texture or appearance; having a lot of fur or hair.	मुलायम	Soft, Fuzzy, Puffy	Dense, Compact, Solid
Foil	To prevent the success of something; a character who contrasts with the protagonist.	बाधा डालना	Thwart, Hinder, Counter	Assist, Support, Aid
Forbidden	Not allowed or permitted; prohibited by authority or rules.	निषिद्ध	Prohibited, Banned, Taboo	Permitted, Allowed, Authorised
Foresee	To see or know beforehand; to anticipate or predict.	पूर्वदृष्टि करना	Anticipate, Predict, Envisage	Surprise, Unforeseen, Unexpected
Formulate	To create or prepare methodically; to express in precise form or language.	तैयार करना	Devise, Frame, Construct	Disorganised, Destroy, Ruin
Fragile	Easily broken, damaged, or destroyed; delicate or vulnerable.	नाज़ुक	Delicate, Frail, Brittle	Strong, Sturdy, Robust
Frantic	Wildly excited or anxious; desperate or frenzied.	व्याकुल	Hysterical, Panicked, Agitated	Calm, Composed, Collected
Frequent	Occurring or appearing often; happening at short intervals.	आसिद्ध	Regular, Common, Repeated	Rare, Infrequent, Occasional
Frigid	Very cold in temperature; lacking warmth or enthusiasm.	ठंडा	Freezing, Icy, Cold	Warm, Hot, Heated
Frugal	Practising economy; avoiding waste or extravagance; thrifty.	तितोड़	Thrifty, Economical, Stingy	Lavish, Extravagant, Wasteful

Word	Meaning in English	Meaning in Hindi	Synonyms	Antonyms
Frustrate	To prevent or hinder the achievement of a goal or purpose; to cause disappointment.	निराश करना	Thwart, Foil, Disappoint	Assist, Support, Encourage
Fuel	A material, such as coal, gas, or oil, that is burned to produce heat or power.	ईंधन	Energy source, Power, Propellant	Exhaust, Deplete, Empty
Fulfil	To carry out or bring to realisation; to satisfy or meet a requirement.	पूरा करना	Accomplish, Achieve, Complete	Fail, Neglect, Disappoint
Fundamental	Serving as a foundation or basis; essential, basic, or primary.	मौलिक	Basic, Essential, Core	Secondary, Superficial, Supplementary
Furious	Extremely angry or enraged; full of intense emotion or rage.	आक्रामक	Angry, Enraged, Fuming	Calm, Composed, Serene
Fuse	To join or blend together; to melt or blend by the application of heat.	मिलाना	Unite, Blend, Merge	Separate, Disconnect, Split
Fussy	Excessively concerned about small details; picky or particular about things.	चिढ़चिढ़ापन	Finicky, Fastidious, Choosy	Easygoing, Carefree, Unconcerned
Fusion	The process of joining or blending different things together into a unified whole.	मिश्रण	Union, Integration, Combination	Separation, Division, Disconnection
Fragrance	A pleasant or sweet smell; a distinctive scent or aroma.	सुगंध	Scent, Perfume, Aroma	Stench, Odour, Stink
Fade	To gradually lose brightness, colour, or strength; to become less visible or noticeable.	मुरझाना	Dim, Decline, Deteriorate	Intensify, Brighten, Strengthen
Flatter	To praise or compliment someone excessively or insincerely; to please or gratify.	खुशामद करना	Compliment, Adulate, Butter up	Insult, Offend, Criticise

Word	Meaning in English	Meaning in Hindi	Synonyms	Antonyms
Fluctuation	An irregular rise and fall; a variation or instability in a quantity or condition.	अस्थिरता	Variation, Oscillation, Instability	Stability, Consistency, Steadiness
Forefront	The leading or most important position or place; the forefront or vanguard.	मुख्य रेखा	Front, Lead, Cutting edge	Rear, Background, Trail
Frail	Weak or delicate in health; easily broken or damaged; fragile or infirm.	नाजुक	Weak, Delicate, Fragile	Strong, Sturdy, Robust
Fanatic	A person with an excessive and irrational enthusiasm or zeal for a particular cause.	अति उत्साही	Zealot, Enthusiast, Devotee	Indifferent, Apathetic, Unenthusiastic
Formidable	Inspiring fear, respect, or awe due to being impressively powerful, intense, or capable.	दुर्जेय	Daunting, Intimidating, Impressive	Insignificant, Easy, Simple
Fracture	A break or crack in a hard object or material; a rupture or splitting.	टूट	Break, Crack, Split	Mend, Repair, Heal
Fascinate	To attract and hold the interest, attention, or curiosity of someone.	मोह लेना	Captivate, Enthrall, Mesmerize	Bore, Repel, Disinterest
Feasible	Possible, practical, or capable of being accomplished or done.	कर्किय	Achievable, Realistic, Attainable	Impractical, Unrealistic, Unattainable
Friction	The resistance encountered when one surface or object rubs against another.	घर्षण	Rubbing, Scratching, Abrasion	Smoothness, Harmony, Peace
Fury	Extreme anger or rage; a violent or intense emotional state.	क्रोध	Wrath, Rage, Anger	Calmness, Serenity, Tranquility
Fanfare	A showy or elaborate display or celebration, often with trumpets or other instruments.	धूमधाम	Pageantry, Celebration, Pomp	Quiet, Modesty, Restraint

Word	Meaning in English	Meaning in Hindi	Synonyms	Antonyms
Fabricate	To invent or create (something), typically with deceitful intent.	झूठा बनाना	Invent, Manufacture, Forge	Disclose, Reveal, Uncover
Fickle	Likely to change or fluctuate, especially in affections or loyalties; not constant or reliable.	चंचल	Capricious, Inconstant, Unstable	Constant, Reliable, Steadfast
Forge	To shape or create with effort or skill; to form or make something, typically by hand.	कुशलता से बनाना	Craft, Fashion, Construct	Destroy, Demolish, Ruin
Foresee	To anticipate or predict (something) before it happens.	पूर्वदृष्टि करना	Anticipate, Predict, Forecast	Surprised, Unforeseen, Unexpected
Foremost	First in order or importance; leading or most important.	सबसे पहले	Primary, Principal, Leading	Last, Least, Secondary
Flourish	To thrive, prosper, or grow in a healthy or vigorous way; to be successful or flourishing.	फलना-फूलना	Thrive, Prosper, Bloom	Wither, Decline, Fail
Fierce	Having or displaying an intense or ferocious aggressiveness; strong or powerful.	उग्र	Ferocious, Savage, Violent	Gentle, Mild, Tame
Fragile	Easily broken, damaged, or destroyed; delicate or vulnerable.	नाज़ुक	Delicate, Brittle, Sensitive	Strong, Sturdy, Robust
Fluctuate	To rise and fall irregularly in number, amount, or value; to vary or change unpredictably.	अस्थिर होना	Vary, Oscillate, Waver	Stabilise, Remain steady, Persist
Fathom	To understand or comprehend (a difficult problem or an enigmatic person) after much thought.	समझना	Comprehend, Grasp, Understand	Misunderstand, Confuse, Baffle
Flawless	Without any imperfections or defects; perfect or without blemishes.	निखरा हुआ	Perfect, Impeccable, Faultless	Flawed, Imperfect, Defective

Word	Meaning in English	Meaning in Hindi	Synonyms	Antonyms
Fatuous	Silly or foolish, lacking intelligence or seriousness.	मूर्खतापूर्ण	Stupid, Inane, Senseless	Intelligent, Wise, Sensible
Flabbergasted	Astonished or greatly surprised, often to the point of being speechless.	हक्का-बक्का हो जाना	Astounded, Stunned, Amazed	Unimpressed, Unfazed, Expecting
Fleeting	Lasting for a very short time, passing quickly or swiftly.	फुर्तीला	Transient, Ephemeral, Transitory	Permanent, Enduring, Everlasting
Forbid	To prohibit or disallow something, to order someone not to do something.	निषेध करना	Prohibit, Ban, Restrict	Allow, Permit, Authorise
Forego	To give up or do without something, to precede or go before something or someone.	त्याग देना	Renounce, Waive, Sacrifice	Retain, Keep, Hold onto
		G		
Game	A form of play or sport	खेल	Sport, Recreation, Play	Work, Task, Chore
Growth	The process of developing or maturing	विकास	Development, Progress, Advancement	Decline, Stagnation, Regression
Giant	An extremely large or powerful person or thing	विशालकाय	Huge, Enormous, Massive	Tiny, Small, Miniature
Goal	An aim or objective	लक्ष्य	Objective, Target, Purpose	Hurdle, Obstacle, Barrier
Group	A collection of individuals or things	समूह	Team, Assembly, Cluster	Individual, Solo, Alone
Grace	Elegance or beauty of movement or demeanour	गरिमा	Elegance, Charm, Poise	Clumsiness, Awkwardness, Ungraceful
Guide	A person or thing that leads or directs others	मार्गदर्शक	Leader, Mentor, Instructor	Follower, Novice, Learner
Global	Relating to the whole world; worldwide	वैश्विक	Worldwide, International, Universal	Local, Regional, Domestic

Word	Meaning in English	Meaning in Hindi	Synonyms	Antonyms
Guitar	A stringed musical instrument played with the fingers or a plectrum	गिटार	Stringed instrument, Acoustic guitar, Electric guitar	None
Gallery	A room or building for the display or sale of works of art	दीर्घा	Exhibition, Museum, Showroom	None
Gift	A thing given willingly to someone without payment	उपहार	Present, Donation, Offering	Takeaway, Loss, Penalty
Graceful	Having or showing grace or elegance	सुंदर	Elegant, Refined, Polished	Awkward, Clumsy, Ungainly
Guard	A person or group that protects or watches over someone or something	रक्षक	Protector, Sentinel, Watchman	Threat, Vulnerability, Danger
Generation	All the people born and living at about the same time	पीढ़ी	Age group, Cohort, Descendants	Ancestors, Predecessors, Earlier generation
Geography	The study of the physical features of the earth and its atmosphere	भूगोल	Geology, Topography, Cartography	None
Gentle	Having or showing a mild, kind, or tender temperament or character	कोमल	Mild, Tender, Caring	Harsh, Rough, Aggressive
Glacier	A large mass of ice that moves slowly down a mountain or valley	बर्फानी	Icecap, Icefield, Iceberg	None
Graduate	A person who has successfully completed a course of study	स्नातक	Alumnus, Degree holder, Diplomate	Undergraduate, Dropout, Non-graduate
Garden	A piece of ground used for growing flowers, fruits, or vegetables	बगीचा	Horticultural area, Flowerbed, Plantation	Concrete, Asphalt, Urban area
Gain	Obtain or secure something desired, favourable, or profitable	प्राप्ति	Acquire, Attain, Achieve	Lose, Forfeit, Sacrifice

Word	Meaning in English	Meaning in Hindi	Synonyms	Antonyms
Gesture	A movement or action of the body to express an idea or meaning	इशारा	Sign, Signal, Motion	Stillness, Inactivity, Rest
Glorious	Having, deserving, or bringing fame or admiration	महिमान्वित	Splendid, Magnificent, Exquisite	Ordinary, Humble, Mediocre
Gas	An air-like substance that expands freely to fill any space available	गैस	Air, Vapour, Fumes	Solid, Liquid, Condensation
Guest	A person who is invited to visit or stay in someone's home or place	अतिथि	Visitor, Houseguest, Lodger	Host, Resident, Inhabitant
Grammar	The study and rules governing the use of language	व्याकरण	Syntax, Language rules, Grammatical structure	Ungrammatical, Incorrect, Improper
Grocery	A store that sells food and other household items	किराना	Supermarket, Market, Provision store	None
Gulf	A deep inlet of the sea, usually surrounded by land	खाड़ी	Bay, Inlet, Cove	Peninsula, Isthmus, Land bridge
Glitter	Shine with a bright, shimmering, reflected light	चमक	Sparkle, Gleam, Glimmer	Dullness, Dimness, Fade
Gap	A space or opening that is empty or unfilled	अंतर	Hole, Interval, Breach	Continuity, Connection, Closure
Grateful	Feeling or showing an appreciation of kindness or benefits received	कृतज्ञ	Thankful, Appreciative, Obliged	Ungrateful, Unappreciative, Unthankful
Glory	High renown or honour won by notable achievements	महिमा	Fame, Splendor, Prestige	Disgrace, Shame, Infamy
Goose	A large waterbird with a long neck, short legs, and webbed feet	हंस	Gander, Bird, Waterfowl	None
Grin	Smile broadly, especially in an unrestrained manner and with amusement	मुस्कान	Smile, Beam, Smirk	Frown, Scowl, Grimace

Word	Meaning in English	Meaning in Hindi	Synonyms	Antonyms
Glow	Give out steady light without flame	चमक	Shine, Radiate, Gleam	Dim, Dull, Fade
Greedy	Having or showing an intense and selfish desire for something	लालची	Avaricious, Covetous, Rapacious	Generous, Content, Satisfied
Garnish	Decorate or embellish (something, especially food) with a small amount of additional items	सजावट	Adorn, Embellish, Ornament	Undecorated, Plain, Unadorned
Grass	Vegetation consisting of typically short plants with narrow leaves	घास	Turf, Sod, Herbage	Concrete, Pavement, Flooring
Gigantic	Of very great size or extent; huge or enormous	विशाल	Massive, Colossal, Mammoth	Tiny, Small, Miniature
Groove	A long, narrow cut or depression in a hard material	धार	Furrow, Channel, Trench	Ridge, Bump, Protrusion
Guilt	The fact of having committed a specified or implied offence or crime	अपराध	Blame, Fault, Remorse	Innocence, Absolution, Acquittal
Gossip	Casual or idle talk about other people, typically involving details that are not confirmed as true	गपशप	Rumor, Chitchat, Tittle-tattle	Truth, Confirmation, Fact
Gym	A place or facility equipped for indoor sports or physical exercise	जिम	Fitness centre, Workout facility, Training studio	Sedentary lifestyle, Inactivity, Laziness
Glance	Take a brief or hurried look	झलक	Glimpse, Peek, Cursory look	Stare, Scrutinise, Examine
Generous	Showing a readiness to give more of something, especially money or time, than is strictly necessary or expected	उदार	Benevolent, Charitable, Magnanimous	Stingy, Selfish, Greedy
Gadget	A small tool or device that is often innovative or ingenious	गैजेट	Device, Appliance, Contraption	None

Word	Meaning in English	Meaning in Hindi	Synonyms	Antonyms
Gaze	Look steadily and intently, especially in admiration, surprise, or thought	घूरना	Stare, Gape, Peer	Avoid, Ignore, Disregard
Grave	A place of burial for a dead body, typically marked by a tombstone	कब्रिस्तान	Cemetery, Burial ground, Sepulcher	None
Gymnastics	A sport involving exercises that require balance, strength, flexibility, agility, and coordination	ताल मेल	Acrobatics, Tumbling, Exercise	None
Generate	Produce or create (something) from a source or by a process	उत्पन्न करना	Create, Produce, Make	Destroy, Eliminate, Annihilate
Gravel	A loose aggregation of small water-worn or pounded stones	कंकड़	Pebbles, Crushed stone, Aggregate	Smooth surface, Paved road, Concrete
Grumble	Complain or protest about something in a bad-tempered but typically muted manner	रुग्न	Mutter, Mumble, Murmur	Praise, Appreciate, Applaud
Garbage	Waste material or discarded items, especially household waste	कचरा	Trash, Rubbish, Litter	Cleanliness, Orderliness, Neatness
Growl	Make a low guttural sound in the throat, typically as a sign of anger or hostility	गरजना	Snarl, Roar, Rumble	Purr, Mew, Whimper
Genetic	Relating to genes or heredity, or the study of genes and heredity	आनुवंशिक	Hereditary, Inherited, Genomic	Acquired, Non-genetic, Environmental
Glaze	Cover with a shiny or glassy surface	शीशा	Gloss, Luster, Polish	Roughen, Dull, Fade
Glamorous	Having an attractive or exciting quality that is associated with wealth, luxury, or fashion	प्रभावशाली	Elegant, Stylish, Alluring	Plain, Unattractive, Dull

Word	Meaning in English	Meaning in Hindi	Synonyms	Antonyms
Guarantee	A formal assurance or promise, especially that certain conditions will be fulfilled	गारंटी	Assurance, Warranty, Pledge	Risk, Uncertainty, Doubt
Gear	A toothed wheel that engages with another toothed mechanism in order to change the speed or direction of transmitted motion	गियर	Equipment, Apparatus, Machinery	None
Grasp	Hold firmly, seize, or understand with clarity and certainty	पकड़	Grip, Clutch, Comprehend	Release, Drop, Misunderstand
Glider	A type of aircraft that is designed to glide through the air with no engine power	ग्लाइडर	Sailplane, Soaring aircraft, Gliding machine	Powered aircraft, Jet, Helicopter
Goodbye	A parting remark or farewell	अलविदा	Farewell, Adieu, Bye	Greeting, Welcome, Hello
Gratitude	The quality of being thankful or showing appreciation	कृतज्ञता	Thankfulness, Appreciation, Acknowledgment	Ingratitude, Unappreciation, Discontent
Garment	An item of clothing	वस्त्र	Apparel, Clothing, Attire	Nakedness, Undress, Bareness
Gallant	Brave, heroic, or chivalrous	बहादुर	Brave, Valiant, Daring	Cowardly, Timid, Fearful
Gory	Involving or showing violence and bloodshed	रक्तसंबंधी	Bloody, Gruesome, Horrifying	Bloodless, Peaceful, Mild
Gruesome	Causing horror or disgust	भयानक	Horrifying, Frightening, Shocking	Pleasant, Delightful, Enchanting
Germ	A microorganism, especially one that causes disease	कीटाणु	Microbe, Bacterium, Virus	None
Gust	A brief, strong rush of wind	झोंका	Blast, Breeze, Wind	Calm, Stillness, Stagnation
Glimpse	A momentary or partial view	झलक	Glance, Peek, Quick look	Stare, Scrutiny, Examination

Word	Meaning in English	Meaning in Hindi	Synonyms	Antonyms
Grater	A kitchen tool with sharp-edged holes, used for grating cheese, vegetables, etc.	घोरा	Shredder, Grindstone, Grinding tool	None
Gazette	An official journal or newspaper	गज़ेट	Journal, Newspaper, Bulletin	None
Governor	The elected executive head of a state in certain countries	राज्यपाल	Chief executive, Administrator, Leader	Subordinate, Deputy, Servant
Gorge	A narrow valley between hills or mountains, typically with steep rocky walls and a stream running through it	दर्रा	Canyon, Ravine, Chasm	Plain, Plateau, Flatland
Glare	An intense or harsh light	चमक	Shine, Glint, Radiance	Dullness, Darkness, Shadow
Genie	A supernatural being that fulfils wishes when summoned	जिन	Djinn, Spirit, Magical being	None
Gastronomy	The practice or art of choosing, cooking, and eating good food	रसोईयाँ	Culinary art, Food culture, Cooking	None
Gospel	The teachings or revelation of Jesus Christ	सुंदर सत्य	Good news, Truth, Doctrine	Heresy, Falsehood, Deception
Ground	The solid surface of the earth	ज़मीन	Earth, Soil, Terrain	Sky, Air, Space
		H		
Habitat	Natural environment or home of a plant or animal	प्राकृतिक आवास	Environment, Territory, Dwelling	Uninhabitable, Barren, Void
Harmony	Agreement or peaceful coexistence	सामंजस्य	Unity, Concord, Accord	Conflict, Discord, Disharmony
Healthy	In good physical or mental condition	स्वस्थ	Fit, Well, Robust	Unhealthy, Ill, Sick
Hearty	Warm and friendly; enthusiastic	हार्दिक	Cordial, Sincere, Lively	Cold, Reserved, Unenthusiastic
Heritage	Inherited or preserved from the past	विरासत	Tradition, Legacy, Ancestry	Innovation, Modernity, Novelty

Word	Meaning in English	Meaning in Hindi	Synonyms	Antonyms
Hesitate	Pause or hold back in uncertainty or unwillingness	हिचकिचाना	Waver, Vacillate, Dither	Decide, Resolve, Act
Hierarchical	Arranged in a graded or ranked order	व्यवस्थितावधान	Organised, Structured, Ordered	Chaotic, Disorganized, Unstructured
Highlight	Center of attention or emphasise	मुख्य बात	Accentuate, Spotlight, Showcase	Diminish, Understate, Downplay
Hilarious	Extremely funny or amusing	हंसी का विषय	Humorous, Comical, Laughable	Dull, Serious, Boring
Historical	Relating to the past or history	ऐतिहासिक	Past, Traditional, Ancestral	Modern, Contemporary, Futuristic
Horizon	The line where the sky and the Earth's surface appear to meet	क्षितिज	View, Perspective, Outlook	Limitation, Restriction, Boundary
Hospitality	Friendly and generous treatment of guests or strangers	मेहमाननवाज़ी	Warmth, Generosity, Reception	Hostility, Unfriendliness, Rudeness
Humanitarian	Concerned with promoting human welfare and happiness	मानवीय	Philanthropic, Benevolent, Charitable	Selfish, Cruel, Inhumane
Humble	Modest or not proud; showing a lack of superiority	विनम्र	Modest, Meek, Unpretentious	Arrogant, Proud, Conceited
Hurricane	A violent storm with strong winds and heavy rain	तूफान	Cyclone, Typhoon, Tempest	Calm, Serenity, Tranquility
Hypothesis	A proposed explanation based on limited evidence	अनुमान	Theory, Assumption, Supposition	Fact, Truth, Certainty
Habit	An acquired pattern of behaviour regularly followed	आदत	Routine, Custom, Practice	Abnormality, Anomaly, Exception
Halt	Come to a stop or pause	रुकना	Stop, Cease, Suspend	Continue, Proceed, Advance

Word	Meaning in English	Meaning in Hindi	Synonyms	Antonyms
Handy	Convenient or easily accessible	उपयोगी	Useful, Practical, Convenient	Useless, Impractical, Inconvenient
Hazard	A danger or risk	जोखिम	Peril, Threat, Jeopardy	Safety, Security, Protection
Headache	A continuous pain in the head	सिरदर्द	Migraine, Cephalalgia, Pain in the head	Relief, Comfort, Ease
Health	State of being free from illness or injury	स्वास्थ्य	Well-being, Fitness, Wellness	Illness, Disease, Sickness
Heaven	A place or state of perfect happiness or bliss	स्वर्ग	Paradise, Nirvana, Elysium	Hell, Inferno, Purgatory
Heir	A person who inherits or is entitled to inherit something	उत्तराधिकारी	Successor, Inheritor, Descendant	Ancestor, Predecessor, Donor
Herald	A messenger or a sign that announces something	संदेशवाहक	Messenger, Announcer, Harbinger	Conceal, Hide, Suppress
Herd	A group of animals that live, feed, or move together	झुंड	Flock, Pack, Swarm	Individual, Solitary, Lone
Heroic	Brave, courageous, or showing extreme valour	वीरतापूर्ण	Valiant, Gallant, Brave	Cowardly, Timid, Fearful
Hierarchy	A system or organisation in which people or groups are ranked	श्रेणीबद्धता	Ranking, Order, Structure	Equality, Anarchy, Disorganization
Hike	A long walk or trek, often in the countryside	पैदल यात्रा	Trek, Walk, Excursion	Decrease, Reduction, Decline
Hint	A clue or suggestion indicating something	संकेत	Clue, Tip, Indication	Direct, Clear, Obvious
Honest	Truthful, sincere, and free from deceit	ईमानदार	Genuine, Truthful, Trustworthy	Dishonest, Deceptive, Untruthful
Honour	High respect, esteem, or recognition	सम्मान	Respect, Dignity, Prestige	Disgrace, Shame, Dishonor
Hostile	Unfriendly, aggressive, or antagonistic	शत्रुतापूर्ण	Adversarial, Antagonistic, Inimical	Friendly, Amicable, Hospitable

Word	Meaning in English	Meaning in Hindi	Synonyms	Antonyms
Humid	Having high moisture or dampness in the air	आर्द्र	Moist, Damp, Wet	Dry, Arid, Dehydrated
Humorous	Funny, amusing, or entertaining	हास्यप्रद	Comical, Witty, Jovial	Serious, Dull, Boring
Hypnotise	To put someone into a state of hypnosis	सम्मोहित करना	Mesmerize, Entrance, Enthrall	Awaken, Rouse, Free
Hack	To gain unauthorised access to a computer system or data	हैक	Breach, Intrude, Trespass	Secure, Protect, Defend
Halve	To divide into two equal parts	आधा करना	Divide, Split, Bisect	Unify, Combine, Join
Hamper	To hinder or obstruct the progress or movement of something	बाधा डालना	Impede, Obstruct, Hinder	Aid, Assist, Facilitate
Harvest	The process of gathering crops or the season of gathering crops	फसल काटने की प्रक्रिया / फसल काटने का मौसम	Crop, Yield, Gather	Plant, Sow, Preserve
Haste	Excessive speed or urgency of movement or action	जल्दबाज़ी	Hurry, Rush, Swiftness	Slowness, Delay, Patience
Haunt	To repeatedly visit or appear in the thoughts of someone	सताना	Ghost, Visit, Torment	Forget, Ignore, Neglect
Hazardous	Involving risk or danger	जोखिमपूर्ण	Dangerous, Perilous, Risky	Safe, Secure, Harmless
Headline	A heading at the top of an article or page in a newspaper or magazine	शीर्षक	Title, Heading, Caption	Subtitle, Description, Content
Heavenly	Of or relating to heaven; delightful or perfect	स्वर्गीय / सुंदर	Divine, Celestial, Blissful	Earthly, Mundane, Infernal
Heed	To pay attention to or take notice of something	ध्यान देना	Listen, Observe, Attend	Ignore, Neglect, Disregard
Hero	A person who is admired or idealised for their courage, outstanding achievements, or noble qualities	नायक / महान व्यक्ति	Champion, Brave, Idol	Coward, Villain, Antihero

Word	Meaning in English	Meaning in Hindi	Synonyms	Antonyms
Hinder	To create difficulties or obstacles that delay or prevent something	रोकना / बाधा डालना	Impede, Obstruct, Hamper	Assist, Aid, Facilitate
Hip	Fashionable or in-the-know; the side of the body between the waist and the thigh	मोड़ / कूल	Trendy, Stylish, Cool	Outdated, Unfashionable, Square
Historic	Important or significant in history	ऐतिहासिक	Momentous, Monumental, Historical	Insignificant, Unimportant, Trivial
Hoist	To raise or lift something, often using ropes or pulleys	उठाना	Lift, Elevate, Raise	Lower, Drop, Lowering
Hollow	Having an empty space inside; lacking significance or substance	खोखला / खोखलापन	Empty, Vacant, Cavity	Solid, Full, Substantial
Homage	Respect or reverence paid or expressed publicly	श्रद्धांजलि / अभिवादन	Tribute, Respect, Adoration	Disrespect, Contempt, Insult
Hone	To sharpen or refine something, especially a skill or talent	सुखाना	Sharpen, Refine, Improve	Dull, Blunt, Hinder
Honourable	Deserving respect, admiration, or recognition; having high moral principles	माननीय / गर्वनीय	Respectable, Noble, Dignified	Dishonorable, Disgraceful, Shameful
Hood	A removable covering for the head, often part of a coat or jacket; a neighbourhood, typically characterised by a specific group or culture	टोपी / मुकुट	Cap, Bonnet, Covering	Uncover, Unhood, Expose
Horrible	Extremely unpleasant, shocking, or terrifying	भयानक / भयभीत करनेवाला	Terrible, Dreadful, Frightening	Wonderful, Pleasant, Delightful
Host	A person who receives or entertains guests	मेजबान	Hostess, Entertainer, Emcee	Guest, Visitor, Attendee
Hound	To pursue relentlessly or nag someone persistently	अड़गना / पीछा करना	Pester, Harass, Stalk	Leave alone, Ignore, Neglect
Hover	To remain suspended in the air, or linger uncertainly	टलना / विचरण करना	Float, Levitate, Drift	Land, Settle, Descend

Word	Meaning in English	Meaning in Hindi	Synonyms	Antonyms
Human	Of, relating to, or characteristic of people or human beings	मानव / मनुष्य	Person, Individual, Homo sapiens	Inhuman, Non-human, Animal
Humidify	To add moisture or increase the humidity in the air or a space	नमी बढ़ाना	Moisturize, Dampen, Wet	Dehumidify, Dry, Desiccate
Hurl	To throw with great force or violence	फेंकना / फेंक देना	Throw, Fling, Launch	Catch, Retrieve, Receive
Hybrid	Something that is a combination or mixture of different elements or types	मिश्रित / मिश्रण	Crossbreed, Mixed, Composite	Purebred, Unmixed, Homogeneous
Hypnotic	Having the ability to induce sleep or a trance-like state	सम्मोहक / हिप्नोटाइजिंग	Mesmerizing, Enchanting, Captivating	Boring, Dull, Uninteresting
Hypocrite	A person who pretends to have moral beliefs or virtues that they do not actually possess	पाखंडी / कपटी	Phoney, Pretender, Deceiver	Genuine, Sincere, Authentic
Hackneyed	Overused and lacking originality, becoming trite or cliché	पुराना / मार्कट	Overused, Stale, Banal	Fresh, Original, Innovative
Hangover	The unpleasant after-effects of excessive alcohol consumption	पेट में अस्वस्थता / नशा	Residual effects, Post-drinking syndrome, Morning after	Sobriety, Clarity, Recovery
Haughty	Arrogantly superior and disdainful, displaying an attitude of superiority.	घमण्डी	Arrogant, Snobbish, Condescending	Humble, Modest, Down-to-earth
Hoodwink	To deceive or trick someone, typically by giving false information or playing a confidence game.	धोखा देना	Deceive, Mislead, Dupe	Inform, Enlighten, Disclose
Humdrum	Lacking variety or excitement, dull and monotonous.	उबाऊ	Monotonous, Tedious, Boring	Exciting, Stimulating, Thrilling
Hurdle	An obstacle or difficulty that must be overcome in order to achieve a goal.	बाधा	Obstacle, Barrier, Obstruction	Advantage, Assistance, Support

Word	Meaning in English	Meaning in Hindi	Synonyms	Antonyms
		I		
Ideal	Perfect or most suitable	आदर्श / सर्वोत्तम	Perfect, Optimal, Model	Flawed, Imperfect, Suboptimal
Identify	Recognize or establish the identity of someone or something	पहचानना / निर्धारित करना	Recognize, Distinguish, Discern	Misidentify, Confuse, Mistake
Identity	The distinguishing characteristics or personality of an individual	पहचान / व्यक्तित्व	Individuality, Character, Self	Anonymity, Unidentified, Incognito
Idle	Not active or in use, without purpose or occupation	निष्क्रिय / आलसी	Inactive, Unused, Unoccupied	Active, Busy, Engaged
Ignite	Set something on fire, or to arouse or inflame a passion or emotion	प्रज्वलित करना / प्रभावित करना	Light, Kindle, Spark	Extinguish, Quench, Suppress
Ignorant	Lacking knowledge or awareness about something	अज्ञानी / अनजान	Uninformed, Unaware, Illiterate	Knowledgeable, Informed, Educated
Illusion	False perception or belief, something that deceives the senses	मोह / भ्रम	Delusion, Mirage, Hallucination	Reality, Truth, Certainty
Imagination	The ability to create mental images or ideas not present to the senses	कल्पना / ख्याल	Creativity, Fantasy, Invention	Reality, Fact, Literalism
Imagine	Form a mental image or concept of something not present	कल्पना करना / विचार करना	Envision, Visualise, Conceive	Disbelieve, Reject, Dismiss
Immediate	Happening or done without delay or with no intervening time	तत्काल / समीपस्थ	Prompt, Instant, Quick	Delayed, Deferred, Gradual
Immense	Extremely large or great in size, extent, or degree	अत्यधिक / विशाल	Huge, Massive, Enormous	Tiny, Small, Minuscule
Impact	The effect or influence of one thing on another	प्रभाव / असर	Influence, Effect, Consequence	Insignificance, Irrelevance, Negligible
Imperative	Absolutely necessary or essential	अनिवार्य / अत्यावश्यक	Vital, Crucial, Mandatory	Optional, Unnecessary, Dispensable

Word	Meaning in English	Meaning in Hindi	Synonyms	Antonyms
Implement	Put into effect, execute, or fulfil	कार्यान्वित करना / लागू करना	Apply, Execute, Carry out	Abandon, Neglect, Disregard
Impose	Force something to be accepted or put in place	थोपना / बाध्य करना	Enforce, Oblige, Levy	Remove, Withdraw, Relieve
Impress	Make a positive impact or influence on someone	प्रभावित करना / छापना	Influence, Affect, Inspire	Disappoint, Underwhelm, Discourage
Impressive	Evoking admiration or respect due to excellence or grandeur	प्रभावशाली / भव्य	Striking, Remarkable, Magnificent	Unimpressive, Ordinary, Mediocre
Imprint	Leave a mark, impression, or lasting effect on something	छाप / प्रभाव	Mark, Stamp, Brand	Erase, Remove, Efface
Improve	Make or become better, enhance in quality or value	सुधारना / सुधार	Enhance, Upgrade, Refine	Deteriorate, Worsen, Regress
Inaugurate	Formally commence or initiate (an event or activity)	उद्घाटन करना / समारंभ करना	Commence, Launch, Initiate	Conclude, End, Terminate
Incentive	Something that motivates or encourages someone to do something	प्रोत्साहन / प्रेरणा	Motivation, Stimulus, Encouragement	Disincentive, Discouragement, Deterrent
Incident	An event or occurrence, typically of a minor nature	घटना / घटनाक्रम	Event, Occurrence, Episode	Non-event, Insignificance, Irrelevance
Include	Contain, involve, or comprise as part of a whole	शामिल करना / सम्मिलित करना	Incorporate, Encompass, Embrace	Exclude, Omit, Remove
Income	Money received, especially on a regular basis, through work or investments	आय / इनकम	Earnings, Revenue, Salary	Expenses, Loss, Debt
Incorporate	Include or absorb something as part of a whole	शामिल करना / मिला देना	Integrate, Merge, Combine	Exclude, Remove, Separate
Increase	Become or make greater in size, amount, intensity, or degree	वृद्धि / बढ़ना	Augment, Expand, Multiply	Decrease, Reduce, Diminish

Word	Meaning in English	Meaning in Hindi	Synonyms	Antonyms
Incredible	Impossible or very difficult to believe; extraordinary	अविश्वसनीय / अद्वितीय	Unbelievable, Astonishing, Remarkable	Believable, Credible, Ordinary
Indicate	Point out, show, or suggest as a sign or evidence	इंगित करना / संकेत करना	Suggest, Signify, Demonstrate	Conceal, Hide, Mislead
Indifferent	Having no particular interest or sympathy; unconcerned	उदासीन / निर्लिप्त	Apathetic, Unconcerned, Detached	Caring, Concerned, Engaged
Individual	Single, separate, or distinct	व्यक्ति / व्यक्तित्व	Person, Human, Individualistic	Collective, Group, General
Indulge	Allow oneself to enjoy the pleasure or satisfaction of something	आनंद उठाना / आत्म-पूर्ति करना	Gratify, Pamper, Spoil	Deny, Restrain, Abstain
Inevitable	Certain to happen; unavoidable	अपरिहार्य / अनिवार्य	Unavoidable, Inescapable, Unpreventable	Avoidable, Preventable, Surmountable
Infect	Cause disease or infection by harmful microorganisms	संक्रामित करना / रोगजनक	Contaminate, Transmit, Spread	Disinfect, Cleanse, Purify
Infer	Deduce or conclude information from evidence and reasoning	निष्कर्ष निकालना / अर्थ निकालना	Deduce, Conclude, Gather	Misinterpret, Misconstrue, Disregard
Influence	The capacity to have an effect on the character, behaviour, or development of someone or something	प्रभाव / असर	Impact, Power, Control	Irrelevance, Insignificance, Impotence
Inform	Give facts or information; tell	सूचित करना / जानकारी देना	Notify, Advise, Update	Misinform, Mislead, Conceal
Infuse	Fill or pervade with a quality or emotion	देर से विचार करना / प्रवेश कराना	Imbue, Permeate, Instil	Remove, Extract, Drain
Ingenious	Clever, original, and inventive	प्रतिभाशाली / चतुर	Resourceful, Creative, Inventive	Unimaginative, Uncreative, Dull
Inhabit	Live in or occupy (a place or environment)	बसना / निवास करना	Dwell, Reside, Occupy	Abandon, Vacate, Desert

Word	Meaning in English	Meaning in Hindi	Synonyms	Antonyms
Initial	Existing or occurring at the beginning	प्रारंभिक / शुरुआती	First, Introductory, Primary	Final, Last, Concluding
Initiative	An introductory step or action taken to resolve an issue or achieve a goal	पहल / पहेली कदम	Drive, Ambition, Enterprise	Inertia, Passivity, Indifference
Injustice	Lack of fairness or justice	अन्याय / न्यायहीनता	Unfairness, Discrimination, Oppression	Justice, Fairness, Equality
Innate	Inborn, natural, or inherent	सहज / अंतर्जात	Inborn, Inherent, Natural	Learned, Acquired, Taught
Innocent	Not guilty of a crime or wrongdoing; free from sin or moral wrong	मासूम / निर्दोष	Guiltless, Blameless, Pure	Guilty, Culprit, Corrupt
Innovate	Introduce something new or make changes in an existing method, idea, or product	नवीनता लाना / नवाचार	Invent, Create, Revolutionise	Maintain, Preserve, Conserve
Input	Data or information that is entered into a computer or a system	इनपुट / दाखिल करना	Data, Information, Entry	Output, Result, Outcome
Inquire	Ask for information from someone	पूछना / जांचना	Ask, Query, Investigate	Ignore, Neglect, Disregard
Insight	The ability to understand and perceive things clearly	अंतर्दृष्टि / अंतर्ज्ञान	Understanding, Perception, Awareness	Ignorance, Blindness, Incomprehension
Inspire	Fill someone with the urge or ability to do or feel something	प्रेरित करना / प्रेरित होना	Motivate, Encourage, Stimulate	Demotivate, Discourage, Deter
Install	Set up or place something in position for use or service	स्थापित करना / इंस्टॉल करना	Set up, Fix, Establish	Uninstall, Remove, Disassemble
Instant	Occurring or done immediately; without any delay	तत्काल / तुरंत	Immediate, Prompt, Quick	Delayed, Protracted, Prolonged

Word	Meaning in English	Meaning in Hindi	Synonyms	Antonyms
Institute	An organisation or establishment having a particular purpose, especially one that is involved in education, research, or promoting a cause	संस्थान / संस्था	Organization, Establishment, Foundation	Dissolve, Disband, Abolish
Instruct	Direct or command someone to do something	निर्देश देना / शिक्षा देना	Teach, Train, Guide	Mislead, Misguide, Confuse
Integrate	Combine or bring together to form a whole	सम्मिलित करना / एकीकृत करना	Unify, Merge, Incorporate	Disintegrate, Separate, Disconnect
Intellectual	Relating to the ability to think and understand ideas and information	बौद्धिक / बुद्धिजीवी	Cognitive, Mental, Rational	Stupid, Ignorant, Unintelligent
Intense	Extreme in degree, strength, or severity	तीव्र / अत्यधिक	Fierce, Strong, Powerful	Mild, Gentle, Calm
Intent	A person's intention or purpose	इरादा / मकसद	Purpose, Objective, Goal	Indifferent, Unconcerned, Uninterested
Interact	Act in such a way as to have an effect on each other	संप्रभुता रखना / बातचीत करना	Communicate, Engage, Collaborate	Ignore, Avoid, Isolate
Interior	Situated within or inside; relating to the inside part of something	आंतरिक / अंतर्भूत	Inner, Internal, Inside	Exterior, Outer, Outside
Interpret	Explain the meaning of something or translate from one language to another	व्याख्या करना / अनुवाद करना	Explain, Understand, Translate	Misinterpret, Misunderstand, Confuse
Interval	A period of time between events or actions; a break or pause	अंतराल / विराम	Gap, Break, Pause	Continuation, Uninterrupted, Nonstop
Intervene	Come between two things or people in order to prevent or alter a result or course of events	हस्तक्षेप करना / आड़ में पड़ना	Mediate, Intercede, Interpose	Withdraw, Retreat, Stay out

Word	Meaning in English	Meaning in Hindi	Synonyms	Antonyms
Invent	Create or design something that has not existed before	आविष्कार करना / नवीनता लाना	Create, Devise, Discover	Destroy, Eliminate, Ruin
Inventory	A complete list of items or goods in stock	शेल्फ / सूची	Stock, Supply, Catalog	Shortage, Lack, Depletion
Invest	Put money, effort, or resources into something to make a profit or achieve a result	निवेश करना / लगाना	Put in, Allocate, Contribute	Withdraw, Divest, Disinvest
Investigate	Carry out a systematic or formal inquiry to discover and examine the facts of an incident, crime, or situation	जांचना / छानबीन करना	Examine, Explore, Probe	Ignore, Neglect, Disregard
Invitation	A written or verbal request inviting someone to go somewhere or to do something	निमंत्रण / आमंत्रण	Offer, Request, Bid	Rejection, Refusal, Decline
Invoke	Call upon a higher power, law, or authority for help or inspiration	आह्वान करना / आवाहन करना	Summon, Evoke, Appeal to	Dismiss, Ignore, Reject
Involvement	The state or fact of being included or involved in something	संलग्नता / शामिली	Participation, Engagement, Connection	Exclusion, Detachment, Disengagement
Irresistible	Too attractive or appealing to be resisted or refused	लुभावना / आकर्षक	Alluring, Captivating, Tempting	Resistible, Avoidable, Rejected
Irritate	Make someone annoyed, impatient, or angry	चिढ़ाना / परेशान करना	Annoy, Provoke, Aggravate	Soothe, Calm, Pacify
Isolate	Set apart or separate from others	अलग करना / पृथक करना	Separate, Segregate, Detach	Unite, Combine, Integrate
Issue	An important topic or problem for debate or discussion	मुद्दा / समस्या	Problem, Concern, Matter	Solution, Resolution, Agreement
Itch	An uncomfortable sensation on the skin that causes a desire to scratch	खुजली करना / खुजलाना	Scratch, Irritate, Tingle	Soothe, Relieve, Alleviate

Word	Meaning in English	Meaning in Hindi	Synonyms	Antonyms
Inimical	Hostile or unfriendly	शत्रुतापूर्ण	Adverse, Antagonistic, Harmful	Friendly, Favorable, Beneficial
Insane	Mentally deranged or mad	पागल	Crazy, Mad, Delirious	Sane, Rational, Normal
Intricate	Very complicated or detailed	जटिल	Complex, Elaborate, Involved	Simple, Straightforward, Basic
Isolated	Separated or set apart from others; lonely	अलग	Secluded, Remote, Solitary	Connected, Integrated, Social
		J		
Jade	A hard, typically green stone used for ornaments and jewellery.	मरकत	Emerald, Greenstone, Nephrite	None
Jam	A sweet spread or preserve made from fruit and sugar boiled to a thick consistency.	जैम	Jelly, Marmalade, Preserves	None
Jargon	Special words or expressions that are used by a particular profession or group and are difficult for others to understand.	शब्दावली	Lingo, Terminology, Slang	Plain language, Common speech, Clarity
Javelin	A light spear thrown in track and field events.	तीरंदाज़ी	Spear, Lance, Pike	None
Jealous	Feeling or showing envy or resentment toward someone else's possessions, qualities, or achievements.	ईर्ष्यापूर्ण	Envious, Covetous, Green-eyed	Content, Satisfied, Indifferent
Jelly	A soft, semisolid food substance with a gel-like consistency.	जेली	Gelatin, Jell-O, Dessert	Liquid, Fluid, Runny
Jester	A person who performs comic acts or tricks to entertain others.	हंसमुख	Clown, Fool, Comedian	Serious person, Stoic, Gravitas
Jet	A rapid stream of liquid or gas forced out of a small opening.	जेट	Stream, Spurt, Eject	Trickle, Drip, Seep

Word	Meaning in English	Meaning in Hindi	Synonyms	Antonyms
Jewel	A precious stone, typically a single crystal or pearl, used as a decoration.	मणि	Gem, Precious stone, Bejewel	Plain, Ordinary, Unadorned
Jigsaw	A puzzle consisting of a picture printed on cardboard or wood and cut into various irregular pieces that must be fitted together.	जिगसॉ	Puzzle, Brainteaser, Enigma	Solution, Answer, Clarity
Jingle	A light ringing or tinkling sound.	झंझर	Chime, Tingling, Tinkle	Silence, Mute, Quiet
Jockey	A person who rides in horse races, especially as a profession.	जॉकी	Rider, Equestrian, Horseman	None
Joint	A point where two or more bones meet, usually allowing movement.	जोड़	Connection, Junction, Link	Disconnection, Separation, Gap
Joke	A form of humour that is intended to make people laugh.	मज़ाक	Jest, Quip, Gag	Seriousness, Gravity, Sobriety
Journal	A daily record of news and events of a personal nature.	पत्रिका	Diary, Log, Chronicle	None
Journey	A long-distance travel from one place to another.	यात्रा	Trip, Voyage, Expedition	Stagnation, Standstill, Inaction
Joy	A feeling of great pleasure and happiness.	आनंद	Delight, Bliss, Elation	Sadness, Sorrow, Misery
Judge	A public official appointed to decide cases in a court of law.	न्यायाधीश	Magistrate, Justice, Arbiter	Accused, Defendant, Lawbreaker
Juggle	To continuously toss and catch objects, typically for entertainment.	जादू गर्दना	Balance, Manipulate, Perform tricks	Stumble, Drop, Fail
Jumbo	Extremely large in size or weight.	विशालकाय	Gigantic, Huge, Massive	Tiny, Small, Miniature
Jungle	A dense, tangled, and often dangerous forest or vegetation area.	जंगल	Rainforest, Wilderness, Woodland	Clearing, Open space, Field

Word	Meaning in English	Meaning in Hindi	Synonyms	Antonyms
Junior	Younger or of lower rank or status.	जूनियर	Young, Lesser, Subordinate	Senior, Superior, Elder
Jury	A group of people sworn to deliver a verdict in a legal case.	ज्यूरी	Panel, Council, Board	Judge, Magistrate, Arbiter
Justice	Fairness, righteousness, or moral rightness.	न्याय	Fairness, Equity, Impartiality	Injustice, Unfairness, Bias
Jut	To extend out or project beyond a surface or boundary.	बाहर निकलना	Extend, Protrude, Stick out	Recede, Retract, Withdraw
Jail	A place of confinement for people who have been accused or convicted of a crime.	जेल	Prison, Penitentiary, Correctional facility	Freedom, Liberation, Release
Jasmine	A fragrant flower that is often used in perfumes and teas.	चमेली	Scented flower, Fragrant blossom	None
Jealousy	A feeling of envy or resentment towards someone's possessions, qualities, or achievements.	ईर्ष्या	Envy, Resentment, Covetousness	Contentment, Generosity, Indifference
Jeep	A small, rugged vehicle with off-road capabilities.	जीप	SUV, Off-roader, 4x4	None
Jellyfish	A gelatinous marine creature with tentacles that can deliver a sting.	जेलीफ़िश	Medusa, Sea jelly, Cnidarian	None
Job	A task or piece of work done to earn money or achieve a particular purpose.	काम	Work, Occupation, Employment	Unemployment, Inactivity, Idleness
Join	To connect or link together.	जुड़ना	Unite, Connect, Combine	Separate, Disconnect, Divide
Judgment	The ability to make considered decisions or come to sensible conclusions.	निर्णय	Decision, Verdict, Assessment	Indecision, Uncertainty, Doubt
Judo	A martial art and sport that emphasises using an opponent's force and movements against them.	जूडो	Martial art, Combat technique	None

Word	Meaning in English	Meaning in Hindi	Synonyms	Antonyms
Jumble	To mix or shuffle in a confused manner.	गड़बड़ करना	Tangle, Confuse, Disarrange	Arrange, Organise, Order
Juxtapose	To place side by side for comparison or contrast.	साथ-साथ रखना	Compare, Contrast, Compare and contrast	Separate, Disconnect, Divide
Jab	To poke or thrust suddenly and forcefully.	मुड़ाना	Poke, Prod, Thrust	Withdraw, Retract, Remove
Jack	A device used for lifting heavy objects, typically with a lever and a lifting mechanism.	जैक	Lift, Hoist, Elevate	Lower, Drop, Descend
Jaguar	A large wild cat with a yellow-brown coat and black spots, native to the Americas.	जगुआर	Panthera onca, Big cat, Feline	None
Jamboree	A large celebration or party, typically outdoors with games, music, and dancing.	उत्सव	Festival, Gathering, Carnival	None
Jazz	A genre of music characterised by improvisation, syncopation, and swing rhythms.	जैज़	Swing, Blues, Improvise	None
Jellybean	A small bean-shaped candy with a soft and chewy texture.	जेलीबीन	Candy, Sweet, Confectionery	None
Jetty	A structure built out into the water to protect a shore or to serve as a landing place.	जेटी	Pier, Wharf, Dock	None
Jiffy	A very short period of time; a moment.	क्षण	Moment, Instant, Second	Eternity, Forever, Infinity
Jiggle	To move or cause to move with repeated small jerky motions.	हिलाना	Shake, Wobble, Quiver	Stabilise, Settle, Still
Jinx	A person or thing that is believed to bring bad luck.	अशुभ	Bad luck, Curse, Hoodoo	Good luck, Fortune, Blessing

Word	Meaning in English	Meaning in Hindi	Synonyms	Antonyms
Jumper	A knitted or crocheted garment that is worn over the upper body and typically has sleeves.	जंपर	Sweater, Pullover, Cardigan	None
Juno	The ancient Roman goddess of marriage and childbirth.	जूनो	Goddess, Deity, Divine	None
Justify	To provide an explanation or reason for something to make it seem right or reasonable.	न्याय स्थापित करना	Defend, Support, Vindicate	Refute, Deny, Condemn
Jeopardy	The risk or possibility of danger, harm, or failure.	जोखिम	Risk, Peril, Hazard	Safety, Security, Protection
		K		
Kaleidoscope	An optical instrument with mirrors and colourful pieces that create symmetrical patterns when rotated.	केलिडोस्कोप	Scope, Viewer, Spectacle	Monotony, Uniformity, Boredom
Keen	Having a sharp or eager intellect; showing interest or enthusiasm.	तत्पर	Eager, Enthusiastic, Alert	Indifferent, Apathetic, Disinterested
Kernel	The central or essential part of something; a grain or seed.	कर्णेल	Core, Nucleus, Essence	Periphery, Exterior, Surface
Keynote	The main or central theme or idea; an important or introductory speech.	मुख्य विचार	Theme, Highlight, Address	Side issue, Tangent, Digression
Kettle	A metal container with a handle and spout, used for boiling water or liquids.	केतली	Pot, Teapot, Boiler	No common antonyms found.
Kidnap	To unlawfully seize and hold someone captive, usually for ransom.	अपहरण करना	Abduct, Snatch, Hijack	Release, Free, Liberate
Kindle	To start a fire; to ignite or arouse a feeling or interest.	जलाना	Ignite, Spark, Enkindle	Extinguish, Quench, Douse
Kinetic	Relating to or resulting from motion; active or dynamic.	गतिज	Active, Dynamic, Energetic	Inactive, Static, Idle

Word	Meaning in English	Meaning in Hindi	Synonyms	Antonyms
Kingdom	A country or territory ruled by a king or queen; a domain or realm.	राज्य	Realm, Domain, Empire	Wasteland, barren
Kiosk	A small open-fronted hut or stall, often selling newspapers, refreshments, or tickets.	खुदरा दुकान	Stall, Booth, Stand	No common antonyms found.
Kit	A set of tools, equipment, or clothing used for a specific purpose.	किट	Set, Package, Gear	No common antonyms found.
Knead	To work or massage dough or clay by pressing, folding, and stretching.	गोंदना	Massage, Manipulate, Press	Leave, Neglect, Abandon
Knight	A mediaeval warrior who was usually mounted and served a king or lord.	योद्धा	Champion, Warrior, Crusader	Common man
Knock	To strike a surface with a knuckle, fist, or object to make a sound or gain attention.	दस्तक	Rap, Tap, Strike	Whisper, Mumble, Murmur
Knowledge	Information, understanding, or awareness gained through experience, learning, or study.	ज्ञान	Understanding, Wisdom, Expertise	Ignorance, Incomprehension, Illiteracy
Knuckle	The rounded prominence formed by the bones of a finger when the fist is closed.	मुट्ठी का अंगूठा	Joint, Knob, Node	No common antonyms found.
Knit	To create fabric by interlocking loops of yarn using knitting needles or a machine.	बुनना	Weave, Stitch, Interlock	Unravel, Undo, Unknit
Kneel	To rest or support the body on the knees, often as a sign of respect or supplication.	घुटने टेकना	Bow, Genuflect, Pray	Stand, Rise, Ascend
Keep	To have or retain possession of something; to maintain or continue a particular state.	रखना	Hold, Preserve, Maintain	Release, Let go, Abandon

Word	Meaning in English	Meaning in Hindi	Synonyms	Antonyms
Knot	A fastening made by tying a piece of string, rope, or other material upon itself or to another object.	गांठ	Tie, Bond, Loop	Unwind, uncoil, unweave
Knife	A sharp-edged utensil used for cutting or as a weapon.	चाकू	Blade, Dagger, Cutlery	No common antonyms found.
Kale	A vegetable of the cabbage family, with green or purple leaves that do not form a head.	केल	No common synonyms found.	No common antonyms found.
Ketchup	A thick sauce made from tomatoes, vinegar, sugar, and spices, used as a condiment.	केचप	Tomato sauce, Catsup, Relish	No common antonyms found.
Kiss	Touch or caress with the lips as a sign of love, greeting, or reverence.	चुम्बन	Smooch, Peck, Embrace	No common antonyms found.
Kitten	A young cat.	बिल्ली का बच्चा	Kitty, Catling, Whelp	No common antonyms found.
Kite	A toy consisting of a light frame with thin material stretched over it, flown in the wind at the end of a long string.	पतंग	Flying toy, Drachen, Delta	No common antonyms found.
Kick	Strike or propel forcibly with the foot.	ठोकर	Boot, Strike, Punt	Retract, Withdraw, Pull back
Knob	A rounded handle, often decorative, that is attached to a door, drawer, or piece of furniture.	बटन	Handle, Knocker, Grip	No common antonyms found.
Kin	One's family and relations.	रिश्तेदार	Relatives, Family, Clan	No common antonyms found.
Knack	A skill or talent for doing something easily and skillfully.	दक्षता	Talent, Ability, Expertise	No common antonyms found.

Word	Meaning in English	Meaning in Hindi	Synonyms	Antonyms
Keyboard	A set of keys, usually arranged in a particular order, used for operating a typewriter, computer, or musical instrument.	कीबोर्ड	Keypad, Piano keys, Typewriter keys	No common antonyms found.
Knapsack	A bag with shoulder straps, carried on the back, and typically made of canvas or other sturdy material.	थैला	Backpack, Rucksack, Haversack	No common antonyms found.
Kayak	A small, narrow boat propelled by a double-bladed paddle.	कायाक	No common synonyms found.	No common antonyms found.
Karate	A martial art developed in Japan, characterised by striking and kicking techniques.	कराटे	No common synonyms found.	No common antonyms found.
Karma	The sum of a person's actions in one of their successive states of existence, viewed as deciding their fate in future existences.	कर्म	Fate, Destiny, Consequence	Choice, freewill
Kiwi	A flightless bird native to New Zealand, or the edible fruit it produces.	किवी	Kiwifruit, Chinese gooseberry, Yang tao	No common antonyms found.
Kickboxing	A combat sport that combines elements of boxing and karate, involving kicking and punching.	किकबॉक्सिंग	No common synonyms found.	No common antonyms found.
Kerchief	A square of fabric worn on the head or around the neck as a covering or accessory.	रुमाल	Scarf, Bandana, Headscarf	No common antonyms found.
Kindness	The quality of being friendly, generous, and considerate.	दयालुता	Compassion, Benevolence, Goodwill	Cruelty, Malice, Unkindness

Word	Meaning in English	Meaning in Hindi	Synonyms	Antonyms
Knowledgeable	Having knowledge, well-informed or well-acquainted with facts or information.	ज्ञानी	Informed, Educated, Well-versed	Ignorant, Uninformed, Illiterate
Keenness	The quality of being eager, enthusiastic, or mentally sharp.	उत्साह	Eagerness, Enthusiasm, Zeal	Apathy, Indifference, Lethargy
Knighthood	The title, rank, or dignity of a knight.	नाइटहुड	Chivalry, Honor, Nobility	No common antonyms found.
Kneecap	The rounded bone that covers the front part of the knee joint.	घुटने का पटेला	Patella, Knee bone, Knee cap	No common antonyms found.
Knotweed	Any of various weedy plants with long, jointed stems that are difficult to eradicate.	गंटा लहरा	Bistort, Japanese knotweed, Fallopia	No common antonyms found.
Krypton	A chemical element of the noble gas group, used in certain electric lamps and fluorescent lighting.	क्रिप्टॉन	No common synonyms found.	No common antonyms found.
Kinesthetic	Relating to the perception or awareness of the position and movement of the body.	शरीरिक अनुभव संबंधी	Tactile, Sensory, Physical	Linear, Static
Kidnapper	A person who unlawfully seizes and detains another person, typically for ransom.	अपहरणकर्ता	Abductor, Captor, Kidnaper	Savior, Helper
Kerosene	A flammable hydrocarbon oil used as a fuel in lamps and heaters.	कीरोसीन	No common synonyms found.	No common antonyms found.
Knucklehead	A stupid, foolish, or dim-witted person.	मूर्ख, भोला	Idiot, Blockhead, Dolt	No common antonyms found.
		L		
Labyrinth	A complex and intricate network of passages or paths; a maze.	विकिरण	Maze, Puzzle, Network	Straightforward, Simple, Direct
Lacerate	To tear or deeply cut the flesh or skin.	दरार डालना	Tear, Mangle, Rip	Mend, Repair, Heal
Lackadaisical	Lacking enthusiasm or determination; carelessly lazy.	आलसी	Lazy, Indifferent, Apathetic	Energetic, Enthusiastic, Active

Word	Meaning in English	Meaning in Hindi	Synonyms	Antonyms
Lacquer	A protective coating or varnish made of resin dissolved in a volatile solvent.	लैकर	Varnish, Finish, Glaze	Strip, Remove, Bare
Lament	To express grief, sorrow, or regret.	विलाप करना	Mourn, Grieve, Weep	Rejoice, Celebrate, Delight
Lampoon	A satirical piece of writing or artwork that mocks or ridicules someone or something.	व्यंग्यपूर्ण लेखन	Satire, Parody, Mockery	Praise, Tribute, Admiration
Lance	A long weapon with a sharp point used for thrusting or throwing.	भाला	Spear, Javelin, Pike	Shield, Defense, Protection
Landmark	A recognizable object or feature used as a point of reference.	सीमाचिन्ह	Monument, Milestone, Signpost	Unremarkable, Insignificant, Unknown
Languid	Lacking energy or enthusiasm; weak or sluggish.	निस्तेज	Sluggish, Lethargic, Indolent	Energetic, Vigorous, Active
Lantern	A portable light source with a protective case and transparent sides.	लालटेन	Lamp, Light, Torch	Darkness, Gloom, Obscurity
Lapse	A temporary failure or cessation of continuity or activity.	गलती	Error, Mistake, Interruption	Perfection, Continuity, Success
Large	Of considerable or relatively great size, extent, or capacity.	बड़ा	Big, Huge, Massive	Small, Tiny, Miniature
Lark	A carefree or spirited adventure or activity done for amusement.	खेल	Frolic, Romp, Play	Work, Task, Chore
Latch	A fastening device that holds a door, gate, or window closed.	लैच	Lock, Clasp, Catch	Release, Open, Unfasten
Latitude	The distance north or south of the equator, measured in degrees.	अक्षांश	Freedom, Flexibility, Scope	Restriction, Limitation, Rigidity

Word	Meaning in English	Meaning in Hindi	Synonyms	Antonyms
Laudable	Worthy of praise; commendable.	प्रशंसनीय	Admirable, Exemplary, Honourable	Blameworthy, Disgraceful, Reprehensible
Laurel	A wreath of honour or distinction, especially made of bay leaves.	ताज	Award, Prize, Honor	Dishonor, Shame, Humiliation
Lavish	Rich, elaborate, or luxurious in a generous and extravagant way.	उदार	Extravagant, Opulent, Sumptuous	Simple, Modest, Frugal
Lax	Not sufficiently strict, severe, or careful; relaxed or loose.	ढीला	Slack, Careless, Negligent	Strict, Diligent, Attentive
Leverage	The power or ability to influence a person or situation to achieve a desired result.	पूर्वभास	Influence, Advantage, Control	Disadvantage, Weakness, Powerlessness
Levitate	To rise or float in the air without any physical support.	हवा में उड़ाना	Hover, Float, Glide	Descend, Fall, Sink
Lexicon	A dictionary or a complete set of words in a language.	शब्दकोश	Vocabulary, Wordbook, Glossary	Silence, Inarticulateness, Speechlessness
Liaison	A connection or relationship between different groups or individuals.	संपर्क	Connection, Link, Relationship	Disconnection, Separation, Isolation
Liberate	To set free or release from captivity or restrictions.	मुक्त करना	Free, Release, Unchain	Confine, Restrain, Imprison
Licentious	Lacking moral discipline or disregarding accepted sexual norms.	अशिष्ट	Immoral, Dissolute, Promiscuous	Virtuous, Chaste, Moral
Limerick	A humorous or nonsensical poem consisting of five lines with a specific rhyming pattern.	लिमेरिक	Verse, Poem, Rhyme	Serious, Tragic, Solemn
Limpid	Clear, transparent, or easily understood.	पारदर्शी	Clear, Transparent, Lucid	Cloudy, Murky, Opaque

Word	Meaning in English	Meaning in Hindi	Synonyms	Antonyms
Linger	To stay in a place longer than necessary, often delaying departure.	ठहरना	Stay, Remain, Delay	Leave, Depart, Go
Literal	Taking words in their usual or most basic sense, without metaphor or exaggeration.	शाब्दिक	Exact, Precise, Verbatim	Figurative, Metaphorical, Symbolic
Livid	Furiously angry; dark bluish-grey in colour, typically due to bruising.	बहुत गुस्से वाला	Furious, Enraged, Incensed	Calm, Serene, Composed
Loathe	To feel intense dislike or disgust for something or someone.	घृणा करना	Detest, Abhor, Despise	Like, Love, Adore
Locale	A place or location, especially with regard to its specific features or surroundings.	स्थान	Place, Site, Setting	None
Logic	Reasoning conducted or assessed according to strict principles of validity.	तर्क	Reasoning, Rationality, Intellect	Illogic, Irrationality, Nonsense
Longevity	Long life or the length of time something or someone lasts.	दीर्घायु	Durability, Endurance, Survival	Transience, Ephemeralness, Shortness
Loom	To appear as a shadowy form, especially one that is large or threatening.	उभरना	Tower, Rise, Dominate	Shrink, Diminish, Recede
Loquacious	Tending to talk a great deal; talkative.	बातूनी	Talkative, Chatty, Garrulous	Silent, Reserved, Taciturn
Lucid	Expressed clearly and easy to understand; mentally clear or rational.	स्पष्ट	Clear, Transparent, Comprehensible	Confused, Vague, Incoherent
Ludicrous	So foolish, unreasonable, or out of place as to be amusing; ridiculous.	हास्यास्पद	Ridiculous, Absurd, Preposterous	Serious, Sensible, Reasonable
Luminous	Emitting or reflecting light, especially in the dark; shining or glowing.	प्रकाशमय	Radiant, Bright, Glowing	Dim, Dark, Dull

Word	Meaning in English	Meaning in Hindi	Synonyms	Antonyms
Lunar	Relating to the moon or based on the moon's position or phases.	चंद्रमा संबंधी	Moonlit, Celestial, Lunar-related	Solar, Terrestrial, Earthly
Lurk	To remain hidden or in secret, especially for an evil or harmful purpose.	छिपकर रहना	Skulk, Hide, Sneak	Reveal, Show, Expose
Luscious	Having a pleasingly rich, sweet, or savoury taste or smell.	स्वादिष्ट	Delicious, Tasty, Flavorful	Tasteless, Bland, Unappetizing
Lustrous	Having a shiny or glossy surface; radiant and glowing.	चमकीला	Shiny, Glossy, Radiant	Dull, Matte, Lacklustre
Luxurious	Characterised by luxury, comfort, or abundance.	आलीशान	Opulent, Sumptuous, Lavish	Simple, Basic, Modest
Lymphatic	Relating to or carrying lymph, a fluid that circulates in the lymphatic system.	लसीका संबंधी	Lymph-related, Immune	None
Lyric	Relating to the words of a song; expressing personal emotions or feelings.	गीत का	Songlike, Melodic, Poetic	Prosaic, Unpoetic, Narrative
Lethargic	Feeling a lack of energy or enthusiasm; sluggish or apathetic.	थका हुआ	Sluggish, Drowsy, Inactive	Energetic, Active, Vigorous
Longing	A strong desire or yearning for something or someone.	आकांक्षा	Desire, Craving, Wishing	Indifference, Apathy, Disinterest
Lively	Full of life, energy, or excitement; animated and spirited.	जीवंत	Energetic, Active, Dynamic	Dull, Boring, Lifeless
Locomotive	A powered vehicle used to pull or push trains along a railway.	रेल गाड़ी	Train engine, Engine, Loco	None
Leeway	The amount of freedom or flexibility to move or act within certain limits.	मार्जिन	Latitude, Margin, Room	Restriction, Constraint, Limitation
Lurid	Sensational, shocking, or explicit in a way that is meant to be shocking or disturbing.	भयंकर	Gruesome, Shocking, Sensational	Mild, Tame, Soothing

Word	Meaning in English	Meaning in Hindi	Synonyms	Antonyms
Lavatory	A room or compartment with facilities for washing and relieving oneself; a bathroom or toilet.	शौचालय	Bathroom, Restroom, Toilet	None
Lingering	Lasting for a long time; slow to end or disappear.	टिका हुआ	Prolonged, Enduring, Persistent	Brief, Transient, Fleeting
Lethal	Causing or capable of causing death or serious harm.	घातक	Deadly, Fatal, Mortal	Harmless, Benign, Nonlethal
Lightweight	Having less weight than usual or expected; not heavy.	हल्का	Featherweight, Light, Easy	Heavy, Weighty, Bulky
Lengthy	Having a great length or extent; long or protracted.	लंबा	Long, Extended, Prolonged	Short, Brief, Concise
Locomotion	The act or ability to move from one place to another; the ability to travel.	गतिविधि	Movement, Motion, Travel	Stillness, Immobility, Inaction
Lachrymose	Tending to cause tears; tearful or given to weeping.	आँसूपूर्ण	Tearful, Weepy, Crying	Unemotional, Stoic, Dry-eyed
Likelihood	The state or fact of being likely or probable; the chance of something happening.	संभाव्यता	Probability, Chance, Possibility	Unlikelihood, Improbability, Doubt
Lecherous	Having or showing excessive or offensive sexual desire; lustful.	कामुक	Lustful, Lascivious, Licentious	Chaste, Pure, Modest
Luminosity	The quality of being bright, radiant, or full of light.	प्रकाशता	Brightness, Radiance, Brilliance	Darkness, Dimness, Dullness
Lattice	A structure or pattern consisting of crisscrossed strips forming a grid.	जालीदार संरचना	Grid, Mesh, Network	Solid, Unperforated, Seamless
Loutish	Ill-mannered, boorish, or coarse in behaviour.	असभ्य	Uncouth, Rude, Unrefined	Polite, Well-mannered, Refined

Word	Meaning in English	Meaning in Hindi	Synonyms	Antonyms
Lambaste	To criticise or reprimand harshly or severely.	कठोर आलोचना करना	Berate, Censure, Rebuke	Praise, Applaud, Compliment
Looming	Appearing as a vague, threatening, or large and indistinct shape or figure.	नजदीक आना	Emerging, Approaching, Impending	Receding, Fading, Dissipating
Lapel	The part of a garment, such as a coat or jacket, that is turned back on either side of the front opening.	आगे की दिशा में चिढ़ी हुई उच्च वस्त्र की कंगन	Collar, Revers, Flap	None
Lopsided	Uneven or unequal in size, shape, or position.	एकतरफ़ा	Uneven, Asymmetrical, Disproportionate	Symmetrical, Balanced, Even
Larceny	Theft of personal property; the act of stealing.	चोरी	Theft, Stealing, Robbery	Return, Restitution, Restoring
Luminary	A person who inspires or influences others; a notable or famous person in a particular field.	प्रसिद्ध व्यक्ति	Celebrity, VIP, Icon	Nobody, Unknown, Nonentity
Lettuce	A leafy green vegetable that is often used as a salad ingredient.	सलाद पत्ता	Salad greens, Leafy vegetables, Garden lettuce	None
Lifelike	Resembling or appearing similar to real life; realistic.	जीवित जैसा	Realistic, Naturalistic, Authentic	Unrealistic, Artificial, Fictitious
Laconic	Using few words; expressing much in few words; concise.	संक्षिप्त	Concise, Brief, Succinct	Verbose, Wordy, Long-winded
Lousy	Very poor or bad in quality; contemptible; miserable.	घटिया	Terrible, Awful, Wretched	Excellent, Wonderful, Superb
Lure	To attract, entice, or tempt someone or something.	आकर्षित करना	Attract, Entice, Tempt	Repel, Deter, Discourage
Luxuriant	Growing thickly, abundantly, or in a rich and vigorous manner.	वृद्धिपूर्ण	Abundant, Lush, Exuberant	Sparse, Barren, Scanty

Word	Meaning in English	Meaning in Hindi	Synonyms	Antonyms
		M		
Magnificent	Extremely beautiful, impressive, or grand	अत्यंत सुंदर, प्रभावशाली या गरिमामय	Splendid, Grand, Majestic	Ordinary, Common, Unremarkable
Marvellous	Extraordinary, amazing, or wonderful	अद्भुत, आश्चर्यजनक या अद्वितीय	Fantastic, Incredible, Astonishing	Terrible, Awful, Unimpressive
Melody	A sequence of musical notes that create a pleasant sound	ध्वनि का आकार जो सुरमय ध्वनि उत्पन्न करता है	Tune, Harmony, Song	Noise, Dissonance, Cacophony
Moonlight	The light from the moon	चाँद की रोशनी	Lunar light, Moonbeam, Moonshine	Darkness, Shadows, Nightfall
Majestic	Having grandeur, dignity, or beauty	शानदार, गरिमामय, या सुंदर होना	Regal, Stately, Noble	Ordinary, Common, Unimpressive
Misty	Full of mist or fog, hazy or unclear	कुहरे से भरा हुआ या धुंधला या अस्पष्ट	Foggy, Hazy, Dewy	Clear, Sunny, Bright
Mythology	A collection of myths, legends, or traditional stories	पौराणिक कथाओं का संग्रह	Folklore, Legend, Saga	Reality, Fact, Truth
Modest	Having a humble or moderate opinion of oneself, not boastful	विनम्र, संयमी, आत्मनिर्भर	Humble, Unpretentious, Simple	Arrogant, Boastful, Conceited
Monument	A structure, statue, or building that commemorates a person or event	स्मारक, स्मृति स्थल	Memorial, Statue, Memorialization	Ephemeral, Temporary, Insignificant
Motivate	To stimulate, encourage, or inspire someone to take action or achieve a goal	प्रेरित करना, प्रोत्साहित करना	Encourage, Inspire, Drive	Discourage, Demotivate, Deter
Magnify	To make something appear larger or more significant	बढ़ाना, महत्व या आकार में बढ़ाना	Amplify, Enlarge, Expand	Reduce, Shrink, Diminish

Word	Meaning in English	Meaning in Hindi	Synonyms	Antonyms
Meditate	To focus one's mind for relaxation, contemplation, or spiritual purposes	ध्यान करना, चिंतन करना	Contemplate, Reflect, Ponder	Neglect, Ignore, Disregard
Microscope	An optical instrument used for magnifying and examining small objects	माइक्रोस्कोप, सूक्ष्मदर्शक	Scope, Magnifier, Optic	Macro lens, Telescope, Binoculars
Mirage	An optical illusion caused by atmospheric conditions, making distant objects appear distorted or nonexistent	मिराज, मृगतृष्णा	Illusion, Hallucination, Phantasm	Reality, Fact, Truth
Melancholy	A feeling of sadness, gloom, or depression	उदासी, दुख, मनोविषाद	Sadness, Sorrow, Despondency	Happiness, Joy, Elation
Momentum	The force or speed of movement gained by a moving object or idea	प्रवृत्ति, गति	Impetus, Drive, Energy	Inertia, Stagnation, Sluggishness
Muscular	Having well-developed muscles or strength	मांसपेशियों वाला, मजबूत	Strong, Brawny, Powerful	Weak, Frail, Feeble
Mysterious	Difficult to understand, puzzling, or enigmatic	रहस्यमय, अपरिचित	Cryptic, Enigmatic, Uncanny	Clear, Transparent, Obvious
Monarch	A sovereign ruler, usually a king or queen	सम्राट, राजा या रानी	King, Queen, Emperor	Subject, Citizen, Peasant
Mastery	Comprehensive knowledge or skill in a particular subject or activity	प्रवीणता, निपुणता	Expertise, Proficiency, Skill	Incompetence, Ineptitude, Ignorance
Moisture	Small amounts of water or other liquid present in the air, on a surface, or in a substance	नमी, आर्द्रता	Dampness, Wetness, Humidity	Dryness, Aridity, Dehydration
Meteor	A small celestial body that enters the Earth's atmosphere and burns up, producing a streak of light	उल्का, ग्रहाणु	Shooting star, Meteorite, Falling star	Planet, Satellite, Asteroid
Manifest	To display or show a quality or feeling clearly	प्रकट करना, दिखाना	Demonstrate, Exhibit, Reveal	Conceal, Hide, Suppress

Word	Meaning in English	Meaning in Hindi	Synonyms	Antonyms
Modulate	To adjust or change the pitch, tone, or volume of something, usually sound or voice	स्वर बदलना, समायोजित करना	Adjust, Alter, Vary	Maintain, Preserve, Stabilise
Meticulous	Showing great attention to detail, extremely careful and precise	सचेत, सूक्ष्म	Thorough, Diligent, Precise	Careless, Negligent, Sloppy
Migrate	To move from one region or habitat to another, usually in search of better conditions or opportunities	प्रवास करना, वंचित होना	Move, Relocate, Transplant	Stay, Settle, Remain
Manuscript	A handwritten or typed document, especially an author's original copy of a book or a document before it is published	हस्तलिखित पाठ, मस्तिष्कगत	Document, Script, Writing	Published, Printed, Typeset
Marinate	To soak or steep food, typically meat, in a marinade to add flavour or tenderise it	मरिनेट करना, रस से भरना	Infuse, Soak, Steep	Drain, Remove, Dry
Monopoly	Exclusive control or ownership of a product or service in a particular market or industry	एकाधिकार, मोनोपॉली	Domination, Control, Supremacy	Competition, Free market, Open market
Mentor	An experienced and trusted advisor, guide, or teacher who provides support, guidance, and knowledge to someone less experienced	प्रशिक्षक, मार्गदर्शक	Coach, Tutor, Guide	Novice, Learner, Follower
Mellow	Soft, gentle, or relaxed in character or mood	मधुर, सुहावना	Laid-back, Calm, Soothing	Harsh, Abrupt, Intense
Memorial	Something, such as a monument or ceremony, that serves as a remembrance or tribute to someone or something	स्मारक, स्मृति	Monument, Remembrance, Tribute	Forgettable, Unremarkable, Unmemorable

Word	Meaning in English	Meaning in Hindi	Synonyms	Antonyms
Melodious	Pleasant-sounding, having a pleasing or musical quality	सुरीला, संगीतमय	Harmonious, Musical, Tuneful	Dissonant, Discordant, Unmelodious
Maritime	Relating to the sea or navigation, connected with seafaring or shipping	समुद्री, जहाजी	Nautical, Marine, Naval	Landlocked, Inland, Terrestrial
Merit	The quality of being particularly good or worthy, deserving praise or recognition	मान्यता, गुण	Excellence, Virtue, Worth	Flaw, Deficiency, Weakness
Morphology	The study of the form, structure, and arrangement of words and the patterns of word formation in a language	आकृतिशास्त्र, रूप-विज्ञान	Structure, Configuration, Anatomy	Formlessness, Disorder, Chaos
Meadow	A piece of grassy land, often with flowers and low-growing plants, typically used for grazing or as a scenic area	मैदान, घास का खेत	Field, Pasture, Grassland	Forest, Woodland, Thicket
Mythical	Existing only in myths or legends, imaginary or fictional	पौराणिक, काल्पनिक	Legendary, Imaginary, Fictitious	Real, Actual, Historical
Mend	To repair or fix something that is broken or damaged	सुधारना, मरम्मत करना	Repair, Fix, Restore	Break, Damage, Destroy
Multitude	A large number or a great quantity of people, things, or events	बहुतायत, असंख्य	Abundance, Plenty, Host	Few, Scarcity, Handful
Maternal	Relating to a mother or motherhood, characteristic of a mother	मातृत्व संबंधी, मातृसत्तायी	Motherly, Parental, Nurturing	Paternal, Non-maternal, Unmaternal
Mediation	The act of intervening in a dispute to help resolve it, negotiation or intervention by a neutral third party	समझौता, मध्यस्थता	Arbitration, Intervention, Conciliation	Conflict, Dispute, Hostility
Magnitude	The great size, extent, or importance of something, the degree of brightness of a star or celestial body	महत्व, परिमाण	Greatness, Immensity, Scale	Smallness, Insignificance, Negligible

Word	Meaning in English	Meaning in Hindi	Synonyms	Antonyms
Mermaid	A mythical sea creature with the upper body of a woman and the tail of a fish	मत्स्यकन्या, जलपरी	Siren, Water nymph, Sea maiden	Human, Man, Woman
Mosaic	A pattern or picture made using small coloured pieces of glass, stone, or other materials	मोजेक, टुकड़े-टुकड़े	Collage, Montage, Assemblage	Uniform, Homogeneous, Monochrome
Motion	The act or process of moving or being moved, a gesture or action used to express or convey an idea or feeling	गति, चलन	Movement, Action, Gesture	Stillness, Inaction, Immobility
Manifesto	A public declaration of principles, policies, or intentions, especially by a political party or government	प्रमाणपत्र, घोषणापत्र	Proclamation, Declaration, Statement	Secret, Concealment, Hiding
Muse	A source of artistic inspiration, especially a person or a divine being	मुसा, प्रेरणा देने वाला	Inspiration, Source, Guide	Block, Dullness, Apathy
Magnanimous	Very generous or forgiving, especially towards a rival or someone less powerful	उदार, उदारमय	Generous, Noble, Benevolent	Selfish, Mean, Greedy
Monotonous	Lacking in variety, tedious or repetitive, without change or variation	एकरस, निरंतर	Tedious, Dull, Boring	Varied, Interesting, Stimulating
Meteorology	The study of the Earth's atmosphere, weather patterns, and climate conditions	मौसम विज्ञान	Weather science, Atmospheric science, Climatology	–
Marshal	To arrange or assemble in order, to lead or direct with authority	प्रशासन, आदेश देना	Organise, Mobilise, Direct	Disorganized, Disperse, Scatter
Medley	A mixture or combination of different elements or things	मिश्रण, संयोजन	Assortment, Variety, Blend	Uniformity, Consistency, Singular

Word	Meaning in English	Meaning in Hindi	Synonyms	Antonyms
Melodrama	A dramatic or emotional situation or event that is exaggerated or sensationalised	मेलोड्रामा	Exaggeration, Theatrics, Histrionics	Realism, Naturalism, Subtlety
Marquee	A large tent or roof-like structure used as a shelter or entrance, often used for events or shows	मार्की, छतरी	Canopy, Awning, Pavilion	–
Molten	In a liquefied or melted state, usually due to high temperature	पिघला हुआ, गलते हुए	Melted, Liquid, Fluid	Solid, Frozen, Hardened
Monumental	Impressively large, significant, or enduring; related to a monument	महान, स्मारक संबंधी	Massive, Grand, Historic	Insignificant, Small, Inconsequential
Metamorphosis	A complete transformation or change in form, structure, or character	परिवर्तन, परिणामांतरण	Transformation, Change, Evolution	Stagnation, Inertia, Unchanging
Mutate	To undergo a genetic or physical change, to evolve or alter	परिवर्तित होना, मूटेट होना	Transform, Modify, Evolve	Preserve, Maintain, Unchanged
Mammal	A warm-blooded vertebrate animal that typically has hair or fur, gives birth to live young, and feeds them with milk	स्तनधारी, जन्तु	Animal, Creature, Beast	Inanimate, Plant, Invertebrate
Mischievous	Playfully naughty, causing trouble or annoyance in a playful way	शरारती, नकचड़ा	Naughty, Prankish, Rascally	Well-behaved, Obedient, Innocent
Monitor	To observe, watch, or check closely; a device or person used for observing or tracking	निगरानी करना, मॉनिटर	Watch, Supervise, Track	Neglect, Ignore, Disregard
Maneuver	A planned movement or action to achieve a particular result, often involving skill or strategy	योजना, चाल	Tactic, Plan, Strategy	Inaction, Stillness, Stagnation

Word	Meaning in English	Meaning in Hindi	Synonyms	Antonyms
Muster	To assemble, gather, or collect; to call or summon a group of people	संगठन, एकत्र	Assemble, Gather, Mobilise	Disperse, Scatter, Dissolve
Mulberry	A type of tree or shrub that produces edible berries or fruits	शहतूत	Berry, Fruit, Tree	–
Mystify	To puzzle or confuse someone, to make something mysterious or difficult to understand	उलझाना, रहस्यमय बनाना	Puzzle, Baffle, Perplex	Clarify, Explain, Unravel
Meddle	To interfere or involve oneself in someone else's business or affairs without invitation	हस्तक्षेप करना, दखल देना	Interfere, Intrude, Interlope	Mind one's own business, Stay out, Respect privacy
Majesty	Greatness, dignity, or grandeur; royal power or authority	महिमा, शानदारता	Splendor, Royalty, Greatness	Humility, Meekness, Insignificance
Mane	Long hair or fur growing on the neck of a horse, lion, or other animals	जटा, खेस	Hair, Tresses, Locks	Bald, Hairless, Shaved
Magnetic	Having the power to attract or pull objects towards itself, related to magnetism	चुंबकीय, आकर्षक	Attractive, Alluring, Captivating	Repulsive, Unattractive, Unappealing
Mutual	Shared or experienced by two or more parties, reciprocal in nature	परस्पर, आपसी	Reciprocal, Shared, Common	One-sided, Individual, Unilateral
Manicure	A cosmetic treatment for the hands and fingernails, involving trimming, shaping, and polishing	मैनिक्योर, नाखून का सुंदरीकरण	Nail care, Nail treatment, Nail grooming	–
Manifestation	The act of showing, demonstrating, or making something visible or evident	प्रकटीकरण, अभिव्यक्ति	Expression, Display, Demonstration	Concealment, Suppression, Hiddenness
Murmur	A low, indistinct, continuous sound, often made by a person speaking softly or a gentle breeze	शब्दांश, धीमी ध्वनि	Whisper, Mumble, Mutter	Shout, Roar, Yell

Word	Meaning in English	Meaning in Hindi	Synonyms	Antonyms
Morsel	A small piece or portion of food, a bite-sized amount	टुकड़ा, भोजन की थोड़ी मात्रा	Bite, Piece, Fragment	Whole, Entirety, Bulk
Mulch	A protective covering of material (e.g., straw, wood chips) spread over the soil to retain moisture, suppress weeds, and improve fertility	मलच, खाद्य पदार्थों का आवरण	Ground cover, Covering, Top dressing	Uncovered, Exposed, Bare
Merciless	Showing no mercy or compassion, cruel or unrelenting in nature	निर्दयी, निर्मर्यादा	Ruthless, Pitiless, Cruel	Merciful, Compassionate, Kind
Mystic	Relating to or characterised by mystical experiences or the belief in hidden meanings and spiritual realities	रहस्यमय, अद्भुत	Mysterious, Occult, Esoteric	Clear, Obvious, Mundane
Matrimony	The state or ceremony of being married; marriage as an institution or relationship	विवाह, पतिपरम्परा	Marriage, Wedlock, Nuptials	Divorce, Separation, Singlehood
Matinee	A daytime performance of a play, film, or concert, typically held in the afternoon	मटिनी, दोपहरी अभिनय	Afternoon performance, Daytime show, Matinee show	Evening performance, Night show, Late-night show
Memento	An object kept as a reminder or souvenir of a person, place, or event	यादगार, स्मृतिचिह्न	Keepsake, Souvenir, Remembrance	Forgetfulness, Oblivion, Disregard
Malignant	Harmful or cancerous; showing intense ill will or hatred	दुर्जन	Malevolent, Evil, Malicious	Benign, Kind, Friendly
Menace	A threat or danger; to threaten or pose a threat	ख़तरा	Threat, Peril, Intimidate	Security, Safety, Protect
Moribund	In a dying or decaying state; coming to an end	मरणासन्न	Dying, Declining, Fading	Thriving, Flourishing, Vital
Mimic	To imitate or copy the actions, speech, or appearance of someone or something	अनुकरण करना	Imitate, Copy, Replicate	Original, Genuine, Authentic

Word	Meaning in English	Meaning in Hindi	Synonyms	Antonyms
		N		
Naive	Lacking experience or wisdom; innocent	अनुभवहीन या बुद्धिहीन; मसूम	Innocent, inexperienced, unsophisticated	Experienced, worldly, sophisticated
Nautical	Relating to ships, sailors, or navigation on water	जहाजी, नौका या जलयान संबंधी	Marine, maritime, naval	Terrestrial, land-based
Navigable	Capable of being navigated or travelled by boat or ship	नाविकरण या जहाजों द्वारा यात्रा करने योग्य	Passable, traversable, sail-worthy	Impassable, unnavigable
Neophyte	A beginner or novice in a particular activity or subject	शुरुआती, नवागम्य	Novice, beginner, newcomer	Expert, veteran, professional
Nostalgia	A sentimental longing or wistful affection for the past	गुजरे हुए समय के प्रति संवेदनशील आकर्षण	Longing, reminiscence, homesickness	Indifference, apathy
Nexus	A connection or link between two or more things	संबंध, बांध	Connection, link, relationship	Disconnection, detachment
Nurturing	Providing care, support, and nourishment; fostering growth	परवरिश, संवर्धन	Fostering, fostering, cultivating	Neglecting, abandoning
Noble	Possessing honourable qualities; having high moral character	उदात्त, मानवीय	Honourable, virtuous, dignified	Ignoble, dishonourable, base
Nefarious	Wicked, evil, or criminal in nature	दुष्ट, अधर्मी	Villainous, sinful, corrupt	Virtuous, righteous, moral
Notorious	Famous or well-known, typically for something negative	बदनाम, अपयश	Infamous, renowned, infamous	Unknown, obscure, anonymous
Necessitate	To make something necessary; to require or demand	आवश्यक करना, मांगना	Require, demand, entail	Eliminate, avoid, exclude
Negligent	Failing to take proper care or attention; careless or irresponsible	लापरवाह, लापरवाहीपूर्ण	Careless, inattentive, heedless	Careful, attentive, responsible

Word	Meaning in English	Meaning in Hindi	Synonyms	Antonyms
Novel	New and original; not seen or experienced before	नवीनतम, नया	New, fresh, innovative	Familiar, old, conventional
Nomenclature	A system of naming or a set of terms used in a particular field or subject	नामकरण, शब्दावली	Terminology, classification, vocabulary	Anonymous, untitled, nameless
Nimble	Quick and light in movement or action; agile	चुस्त, फुर्तीला	Agile, quick, spry	Clumsy, sluggish, slow
Narcissistic	Having an excessive interest in oneself; self-centred	आत्मरत, अहंकारी	Egotistical, self-absorbed, vain	Humble, modest, selfless
Nuance	A subtle difference in meaning, expression, or tone	अतिसूक्ष्म अंतर, रंग	Subtlety, distinction, subtlety	Obviousness, clarity, simplicity
Neutral	Not taking sides; unbiased; neither positive nor negative	तटस्थ, मध्यस्थ	Impartial, unbiased, fair	Biassed, partial, prejudiced
Numerical	Relating to numbers or a series of numbers	संख्यात्मक, गणनात्मक	Numeric, numerical, quantitative	Non-numeric, qualitative
Nascent	Just beginning to exist or develop; in the early stages	नवजात, उदभवमान	Emerging, budding, incipient	Mature, developed, established
Notable	Worthy of attention or notice; remarkable	महत्वपूर्ण, प्रमुख	Remarkable, noteworthy, significant	Insignificant, ordinary, unremarkable
Natural	Existing in or derived from nature; not artificial or man-made	प्राकृतिक, सहज	Genuine, innate, inherent	Artificial, synthetic, unnatural
Nomad	A person who travels from place to place, often without a fixed home	घुमंतू, खानाबदोश	Wanderer, traveller, rover	Settler, resident, stationary
Noxious	Harmful, poisonous, or very unpleasant	हानिकारक, विषैला	Toxic, harmful, deleterious	Harmless, benign, non-toxic
Nurturer	Someone who nourishes, supports, and encourages growth or development	पोषक, परिपालक	Caregiver, supporter, nurturer	Neglecter, destroyer, hinderer
Navigate	To find one's way or travel a planned route	मार्गदर्शन करना, यात्रा करना	Steer, pilot, direct	Misnavigate, get lost, wander

Word	Meaning in English	Meaning in Hindi	Synonyms	Antonyms
Necessity	Something that is required or indispensable; a need	आवश्यकता, ज़रूरत	Requirement, essential, demand	Luxury, surplus, non-essential
Nourish	To provide with food, sustenance, or nurturing elements	पोषण करना, पालना करना	Feed, nurture, sustain	Starve, deprive, neglect
Nocturnal	Active or occurring during the night; opposite of diurnal	रात्रिक, रात का	Nighttime, nightly, dark	Diurnal, daytime, daylight
Needy	Lacking the necessities of life; poor or impoverished	गरीब, निर्धन	Poor, impoverished, destitute	Wealthy, affluent, prosperous
Niche	A specialised segment or position within a larger market or system	विशेषज्ञ क्षेत्र, स्थान	Specialised market, segment, position	General market, mainstream, standard
Nutrient	A substance that provides nourishment or sustenance for growth	पोषक पदार्थ, पोषणशाली	Nourishment, food, sustenance	Toxin, harmful substance
Novelty	Something new, original, or unusual; a new or unfamiliar experience	नवीनता, अद्वितीयता	Innovation, uniqueness, freshness	Familiarity, routine, commonness
Neat	Tidy, organised, and free from clutter or mess	सुस्थित, साफ़-सफ़ाईपूर्ण	Tidy, clean, orderly	Messy, untidy, disorganised
Neglect	To fail to care for, pay attention to, or give proper importance to	उपेक्षा करना, ध्यान न देना	Ignore, disregard, overlook	Attend to, care for, prioritise
Noteworthy	Worthy of attention or notice; deserving recognition	महत्वपूर्ण, उल्लेखनीय	Remarkable, notable, significant	Insignificant, ordinary, unremarkable
Nurturance	The act of nourishing, supporting, and promoting growth or development	पोषण, परिपालन	Nurturing, fostering, encouragement	Neglect, hindrance, suppression
Nutritious	Providing essential nutrients for growth, health, and well-being	पौष्टिक, आहारयुक्त	Healthy, nourishing, wholesome	Unhealthy, detrimental, nutrient-deficient

Word	Meaning in English	Meaning in Hindi	Synonyms	Antonyms
Numb	Deprived of physical or emotional sensation; unable to feel or respond	सुन्न, अनुभूति-हीन	Insensitive, unfeeling, numb	Sensitive, responsive, aware
Nasty	Disgusting, unpleasant, or offensive in nature	घिनौना, अप्रिय	Disgusting, unpleasant, repulsive	Pleasant, agreeable, enjoyable
Nasal	Relating to the nose	नाक संबंधी	Nose-related, nostril	Non-nasal, unrelated to the nose
Nauseous	Causing a feeling of sickness or disgust	उबकाई, अरुचिकर	Sickening, revolting, nauseating	Pleasing, appetising, delightful
National	Relating to a particular nation; characteristic of a nation	राष्ट्रीय, राष्ट्रवादी	Patriotic, nationalistic, citizen	International, global, cosmopolitan
Nerve	A bundle of fibres that transmits impulses between the brain and other parts of the body	नस, दमन	Courage, bravery, fortitude	Cowardice, fear, timidity
Nourishment	Food or other substances necessary for growth, health, and good condition	पोषण, पुष्टि	Nutrition, sustenance, sustentation	Malnutrition, deprivation, starvation
Naked	Not covered or clothed; without clothing or any protective covering	नंगा, निर्वस्त्र	Nude, unclothed, exposed	Covered, clothed, protected
Notion	A belief or idea about something; a concept or understanding	धारणा, विचार	Idea, concept, belief	Fact, reality, truth
Nappy	Having a rough, curly texture (especially of hair)	घने बालों वाला	Curly, frizzy, textured	Straight, smooth, sleek
Norm	A standard or pattern that is typical or expected in a particular situation	मानक, मानकीय	Standard, rule, guideline	Abnormality, deviation, exception
Nursery	A place where young plants or children are raised or cared for	नर्सरी, पौधशाला	Plantation, greenhouse, creche	Adult space, grown-up area

Word	Meaning in English	Meaning in Hindi	Synonyms	Antonyms
Nudge	To gently push or prod someone or something in order to draw attention or encourage action	स्पर्श, धक्का	Prod, poke, push	Ignore, neglect, avoid
Nominal	Existing in name only; very small or insignificant compared to the actual value or importance	नाममात्र, असली मूल्य से काफी कम	Symbolic, token, minimal	Actual, real, substantial
Notch	A V-shaped cut, indentation, or nick on an object's surface	कंटी, छिद्र	Groove, incision, cut	Flatness, smoothness, evenness
Nuanced	Having subtle differences or shades of meaning, expression, or understanding	अलौकिक, सूक्ष्म	Subtle, delicate, refined	Obvious, straightforward, blunt
Nervous	Feeling or showing anxiety, unease, or apprehension	घबराहट, चिंतित	Anxious, uneasy, worried	Calm, relaxed, composed
Nosey	Inclined to pry into or meddle in other people's affairs; overly curious	जिज्ञासु, दख़लबाज़	Nosy, curious, intrusive	Disinterested, indifferent, unconcerned
Nuclear	Relating to or involving atomic nuclei, nuclear energy, or nuclear weapons	परमाणु, नभिकीय	Atomic, atomic energy, atomic weapons	Non-nuclear, conventional, traditional
Night	The period of darkness between sunset and sunrise; the time when it is dark outside	रात, रात्रि	Darkness, nighttime, evening	Daytime, daylight, morning
Nectar	A sweet liquid secreted by flowers and collected by bees to make honey	रस, अमृत	Ambrosia, honey, sweet sap	Bitterness, sourness, unpleasant taste
Numbness	The loss or reduction of sensation or feeling in a part of the body	आवर्तन, अनुभूति का गुम होना	Insensitivity, lack of feeling, deadness	Sensitivity, feeling, responsiveness
Noon	The middle of the day; 12 o'clock in the daytime	दोपहर, मध्याह्न	Midday, lunchtime, mid-morning	Midnight, morning, evening

Word	Meaning in English	Meaning in Hindi	Synonyms	Antonyms
Neutron	A subatomic particle that has no electric charge and is found in the nucleus of an atom	न्यूट्रॉन	Particle, atomic particle	Proton, electron, charged particle
Nectarine	A type of fruit similar to a peach but with a smooth skin	अमृत आलूबुखारा	Stone fruit, peach, juicy fruit	Vegetable, savoury food
Nighttime	The period of darkness between evening and morning; the time during which it is dark outside	रात का समय, रात्रि का समय	Night, dark hours, evening	Daytime, daylight, morning
Nut	A hard-shelled fruit that does not split open to release its seed	ख़ार, मगज़	Kernel, seed, fruit	Shell, husk, outer covering
Narrative	A story or account of events, experiences, or the telling of a story	कथा, कहानी	Story, tale, account	Nonfiction, fact, reality
Nitrate	A compound containing the nitrate ion (NO3−), often used as a fertiliser	नाइट्रेट	Fertiliser, chemical compound	Organic matter, natural fertilisers
Neutrality	The state of not supporting or taking sides in a conflict or dispute	तटस्थता, मध्यस्थता	Impartiality, neutrality, objectivity	Bias, partiality, favouritism
Nobility	The quality of being noble in character, behaviour, or status	उच्चता, शानदारी	Aristocracy, gentry, high rank	Ignobility, baseness, lowliness
Nymph	In mythology, a nature spirit typically depicted as a young and beautiful maiden	अप्सरा, नदी की देवी	Fairy, sprite, goddess	Monster, ogre, demon
Nap	A short period of sleep, especially during the day	झपकी, नींद	Doze, snooze, siesta	Wakefulness, alertness, insomnia
Nib	The pointed end of a pen, pencil, or other writing instrument	कलम का नुकीला हिस्सा	Pen tip, point, writing end	Blunt end, flat end, eraser
Nincompoop	A foolish or silly person; someone lacking intelligence or common sense.	मूर्ख	Fool, Idiot, Imbecile	Genius, Intellectual, Wise

Word	Meaning in English	Meaning in Hindi	Synonyms	Antonyms
Nomadic	Roaming or moving from place to place without a fixed home; characterised by a wandering lifestyle.	ख़ानाबदोश	Wandering, Roaming, Itinerant	Sedentary, Settled, Stationary
Novice	A person who is new to or inexperienced in a certain activity, skill, or field.	अनुभवहीन	Beginner, Learner, Rookie	Expert, Veteran, Pro
		O		
Oasis	A fertile spot in a desert where water is found; a pleasant or peaceful place	ओआसिस	Paradise, haven, sanctuary	Arid land, desert, wasteland
Oath	A solemn promise, often invoking a divine witness, regarding one's future actions or behaviour	शपथ, प्रतिज्ञा	Pledge, vow, commitment	Denial, disavowal, renouncement
Obese	Extremely overweight, having an excessive amount of body fat	मोटा, मोटापा	Overweight, corpulent, plump	Thin, slim, slender
Obey	To comply with the commands, orders, or instructions of someone in authority	आज्ञा पालन करना, अनुपालन करना	Follow, heed, conform	Defy, disobey, rebel
Objective	Something that is real, concrete, tangible, or based on facts; unbiased and not influenced by personal feelings or opinions	उद्देश्य, लक्ष्य	Goal, purpose, aim	Subjective, biassed, prejudiced
Oblige	To do a favour or service for someone; to be morally or legally bound to do something	कृपा करना, मजबूर करना	Accommodate, help, assist	Refuse, deny, reject
Obnoxious	Extremely unpleasant, offensive, or annoying; deserving strong dislike or disapproval	अप्रिय, घिनौना	Repugnant, repulsive, odious	Pleasant, agreeable, likeable

Word	Meaning in English	Meaning in Hindi	Synonyms	Antonyms
Obscure	Not well-known; difficult to understand, vague, or indistinct	अस्पष्ट, अनजाना	Ambiguous, enigmatic, mysterious	Clear, evident, obvious
Observe	To watch carefully or attentively; to notice or perceive something	देखना, अनुसरण करना	Watch, behold, examine	Ignore, overlook, neglect
Obstacle	Something that blocks or hinders progress or movement; a difficulty or challenge	बाधा, अवरोध	Barrier, hindrance, impediment	Aid, assistance, help
Obtain	To come into possession of; to acquire or get something	प्राप्त करना, हासिल करना	Attain, procure, secure	Lose, forfeit, surrender
Occasion	A particular time or instance; a special event or happening	अवसर, आयोजन	Event, occurrence, ceremony	Ordinary time, everyday, routine
Occupy	To take control or possession of a place or area; to fill or engage one's time, attention, or thoughts	कब्जा करना, आवास करना	Seize, inhabit, monopolise	Vacate, abandon, leave
Ocean	A large body of saltwater that covers a significant portion of the Earth's surface	सागर, महासागर	Sea, deep, main	Land, continent, shore
Odour	A distinctive smell or fragrance, especially an unpleasant one	गंध, सुगंध	Scent, aroma, fragrance	Fragrance-free, odourless, scentless
Offend	To cause anger, resentment, or displeasure; to violate or transgress social or moral norms	आपत्ति देना, अपमानित करना	Insult, outrage, hurt	Please, flatter, compliment
Offensive	Causing anger, resentment, or displeasure; insulting or highly inappropriate	अपमानजनक, आक्रामक	Insulting, abusive, derogatory	Inoffensive, harmless, pleasant
Offering	Something that is presented or given as a gift, contribution, or sacrifice	दान, भेंट	Donation, contribution, present	Refusal, rejection, withholding

Word	Meaning in English	Meaning in Hindi	Synonyms	Antonyms
Offspring	The product of reproduction, such as a child or animal offspring; descendants or progeny	संतान, उत्पन्न होना	Descendants, progeny, children	Ancestors, forefathers, predecessors
Omen	An event or phenomenon regarded as a sign or warning of something to come	शकुन, अशुभ संकेत	Sign, portent, augury	None
Omit	To leave out or exclude someone or something; to fail to include or mention	छोड़ देना, अल्पविराम लगाना	Exclude, disregard, neglect	Include, incorporate, mention
Onset	The beginning or start of something, especially something unpleasant or harmful	प्रारंभ, आरंभ	Start, commencement, initiation	Conclusion, end, finish
Open	Not closed or blocked; allowing access, passage, or visibility	खुला, खुलना	Unlocked, accessible, unrestricted	Closed, shut, sealed
Opinion	A belief or judgement about something, formed by personal thoughts, experiences, or preferences	राय, मत	View, perspective, standpoint	Fact, truth, reality
Oppose	To be against or resist someone or something; to disagree or disapprove	विरोध करना, विपक्ष में होना	Resist, contradict, challenge	Support, agree, favour
Optimal	Best or most favourable; achieving the highest possible efficiency or effectiveness	सर्वोत्तम, श्रेष्ठ	Best, ideal, optimum	Suboptimal, unsatisfactory, inefficient
Optimise	To make the best or most efficient use of something; to improve or enhance the performance or effectiveness	अधिक्षेत्र करना, बेहतर बनाना	Improve, enhance, maximise	Degrade, diminish, minimise

Word	Meaning in English	Meaning in Hindi	Synonyms	Antonyms
Oracle	A person or thing regarded as a source of wise or prophetic knowledge; a priest or priestess acting as a medium for divine communication	मान्य विचारक, भविष्य वाणी कारक	Prophet, seer, sage	Ignoramus, fool, dunce
Orbit	The curved path followed by a celestial object or spacecraft around a star, planet, or moon	आवर्तन, मार्ग	Path, trajectory, course	Straight line, deviation
Ordinary	Common, usual, or average; not special, remarkable, or exceptional	सामान्य, आम	Common, average, regular	Extraordinary, exceptional, unusual
Organise	To arrange or plan systematically; to coordinate or manage effectively	व्यवस्थित करना, संगठित करना	Arrange, coordinate, systematise	Disorganized, scatter, disrupt
Orient	To align or position towards the east; to familiarise or adapt to a particular situation, environment, or culture	पूर्वाभिमुख करना, अभियोजित करना	Align, position, adjust	Disorient, confuse, misalign
Original	Being the first of its kind; not a copy, imitation, or translation	मूल, प्राथमिक	Authentic, genuine, unique	Derived, copied, imitation
Ornament	A decorative object or accessory used to enhance the appearance of something	सजावटी सामग्री, आभूषण	Decoration, adornment, embellishment	Plainness, simplicity, austerity
Orphan	A child whose parents are dead or have abandoned them	अनाथ, यतीम	Abandoned, parentless, fatherless	Supported, nurtured, cared for
Ounce	A unit of weight equal to 1/16 of a pound or approximately 28 grams	औंस	None	None
Outfit	A set of clothes or equipment for a particular purpose or activity	सजावट, सामग्री	Attire, clothing, ensemble	Disarray, undress, strip

Word	Meaning in English	Meaning in Hindi	Synonyms	Antonyms
Outrageous	Shockingly bad or excessive; very bold, unconventional, or unconventional	अत्याचारी, अत्यधिक	Shocking, scandalous, outrageous	Mild, moderate, reasonable
Outshine	To surpass or excel in brightness, performance, or quality	प्रकाशमान होना, अच्छा करना	Surpass, excel, outperform	Dim, fade, underperform
Outstanding	Exceptionally good; remaining unpaid or unresolved	उत्कृष्ट, अवकलित	Excellent, remarkable, unpaid	Mediocre, ordinary, resolved
Overcome	To succeed in dealing with or overcoming a difficulty or problem	परास्त करना, वश में करना	Conquer, defeat, prevail over	Succumb, surrender, yield
Overflow	To flow over the edges or limits of a container or space	ओवरफ्लो, बहना	Flood, inundate, deluge	Dryness, shortage, deficiency
Overhaul	To examine thoroughly and make necessary repairs or improvements	मरम्मत करना, सुधार करना	Repair, renovate, revamp	Neglect, ignore, worsen
Overjoyed	Extremely happy or delighted	बहुत खुश, हर्षित	Ecstatic, thrilled, elated	Depressed, saddened, disappointed
Overlook	To fail to notice or consider something or someone; to have a view of from above	नज़रअंदाज़ करना, देखना	Ignore, neglect, miss	Notice, acknowledge, observe
Overpower	To defeat or overcome with superior strength or force	मात करना, दबाना	Conquer, vanquish, overwhelm	Submit, yield, surrender
Oversee	To supervise or watch over in a responsible position	पर्यवेक्षण करना, देखभाल करना	Supervise, manage, monitor	Neglect, ignore, abandon
Overtake	To catch up with and pass by someone or something that is moving in the same direction	पीछे छोड़ देना, पास करना	Pass, surpass, outstrip	Lag behind, fall behind, trail
Overthrow	To remove forcibly from power; to defeat or bring down by force	तख़्ता पलट देना, गिराना	Topple, defeat, depose	Establish, uphold, support

Word	Meaning in English	Meaning in Hindi	Synonyms	Antonyms
Overwhelm	To overcome or bury with a great amount or intensity	घेर लेना, बहुत कुछ सामने लाना	Submerge, engulf, overpower	Underwhelm, disappoint, fail to impress
Occur	To happen or take place	होना, घटित होना	Happen, take place, transpire	Cease, stop, end
Official	Relating to an authority or public body and its duties, actions, and responsibilities	आधिकारिक, सरकारी	Formal, authorised, legitimate	Unofficial, informal, unauthorised
Omega	The last letter of the Greek alphabet (Ω, ω), often used to represent the last or final thing in a series	अंतिम, अखिरी	ending	beginning
Omnivore	An animal or person that eats both plants and other animals	सर्वभक्षक, सर्वान्न	None	None
Online	Connected to or available through the internet or computer network	ऑनलाइन, इंटरनेट से जुड़ा हुआ	Internet-based, connected, digital	Offline, disconnected, unconnected
Opaque	Not able to be seen through; not transparent or translucent	अपारदर्शी, अस्पष्ट	Nontransparent, cloudy, unclear	Transparent, clear, translucent
Operate	To control or manage the functioning of a machine, process, or system	संचालित करना, चलाना	Control, manage, run	Malfunction, fail, stop
Opponent	A person or group that is competing against or arguing with another in a contest, game, or debate	प्रतिद्वंद्वी, विरोधी	Adversary, rival, competitor	Ally, supporter, friend
Orchestrate	To organise or arrange something carefully, especially a complex event or system	योजना बनाना, व्यवस्था करना	Organise, coordinate, arrange	Disorganised, dismantle, disrupt
Organic	Relating to or derived from living matter; relating to or denoting compounds containing carbon	स्वाभाविक, कार्बनिक	Natural, biological, ecological	Synthetic, inorganic, artificial

Word	Meaning in English	Meaning in Hindi	Synonyms	Antonyms
Originate	To have a specified beginning or come into being from a source	उत्पन्न होना, उद्भव होना	Start, begin, emerge	End, finish, conclude
Outcast	A person who has been rejected or excluded from a society or group	बाहरी, निर्वस्त्र	Pariah, reject, exile	Insider, member, inclusion
Outgoing	Leaving or retiring from a position or job; friendly and sociable	निवेदन करने वाला, सामाजिक और अनुगामी	Departing, retiring, extroverted	Incoming, arriving, introverted
Outlaw	A person who has been declared illegal or outside the law; to make something illegal or prohibited	अवैध घोषित करना, बाहरी कर देना	Criminal, fugitive, bandit	Lawful, legal, permitted
Overture	An introduction or opening to something more substantial; a musical composition preceding a larger work	प्रस्ताव, पहल	Prelude, introduction, proposal	Conclusion, finale, rejection
Osteoporosis	A medical condition in which bones become brittle and fragile due to loss of tissue	ऑस्टियोपोरोसिस	Bone loss, Brittle bones, Fragile bones	Healthy bones, Strong bones
Obstreperous	Noisy, unruly, or difficult to control	शोरगुल	Disorderly, Unruly, Rowdy	Quiet, Calm, Well-behaved
Onus	Responsibility or duty	जिम्मेदारी	Burden, Obligation, Accountability	Freedom, Release, Exemption
Obligations	Duties or tasks that one is required or expected to fulfil	दायित्व	Responsibilities, Commitments, Duties	Freedoms, Discretion, Exemptions
P				
Pacify	To calm or soothe someone or something	शांत करना	Calm, appease, soothe	Aggravate, provoke, agitate
Palatable	Pleasant to the taste; acceptable or agreeable	स्वादिष्ट	Tasty, delicious, flavorful	Unappetizing, distasteful, unpleasant

Word	Meaning in English	Meaning in Hindi	Synonyms	Antonyms
Pamper	To indulge or spoil someone with excessive care or attention	बड़ाई करना	Spoil, coddle, indulge	Neglect, ignore, deprive
Panacea	A remedy or solution that is believed to cure all problems	सर्वोत्तम उपाय	Cure-all, remedy, solution	Problem, issue, trouble
Paradox	A statement or situation that appears contradictory but may actually be true	विरोधाभास	Contradiction, puzzle, enigma	Clarity, certainty, explanation
Paragon	A person or thing that is regarded as a perfect example of a particular quality	अतिशयोक्ति	Model, epitome, ideal	Flaw, imperfection, defect
Paramount	Of supreme importance or significance	प्रमुख	Supreme, primary, dominant	Insignificant, secondary, subordinate
Parched	Extremely dry, especially due to heat or lack of moisture	सूखा हुआ	Dried, dehydrated, arid	Moist, hydrated, damp
Parsimonious	Excessively frugal or unwilling to spend money	कंजूस	Stingy, miserly, tightfisted	Generous, lavish, liberal
Particular	Concerned with or attentive to details; specific or individual	विशेष	Specific, precise, detailed	General, vague, nonspecific
Passionate	Having or showing strong intense emotions or feelings	जोशीला	Enthusiastic, fervent, ardent	Indifferent, apathetic, unenthusiastic
Patience	The capacity to accept or tolerate delay, trouble, or suffering without getting angry or upset	धैर्य	Endurance, forbearance, composure	Impatience, frustration, irritability
Patronise	To treat someone condescendingly or with an air of superiority; to be a regular customer or supporter of a business or organisation	अनुग्रह करना / आश्रय देना	Condescend, support, frequent	Respect, empower, discontinue

Word	Meaning in English	Meaning in Hindi	Synonyms	Antonyms
Peculiar	Strange or unusual; distinctive or particular to a specific person, place, or thing	अजीब / विशेष	Odd, eccentric, unique	Common, ordinary, typical
Pedantic	Excessively concerned with minor details or rules; overly academic or formal	अध्ययन केन्द्रित	Nitpicking, precise, meticulous	Informal, casual, laid-back
Peerless	Unequalled or unmatched; having no equal or rival	अनुपम	Unrivalled, unparalleled, unmatched	Ordinary, average, common
Pensive	Deeply thoughtful, often with a hint of sadness or melancholy	सोचमुच	Contemplative, reflective, meditative	Carefree, lighthearted, unthinking
Perceptive	Having or showing keen insight, understanding, or intuition	सूक्ष्मदर्शी	Discerning, observant, insightful	Oblivious, unaware, clueless
Perennial	Lasting or existing for a long or seemingly infinite time; recurring or enduring	सदाबहार	Everlasting, enduring, perpetual	Temporary, transient, short-lived
Perilous	Full of danger or risk; hazardous or precarious	ख़तरनाक	Dangerous, risky, unsafe	Safe, secure, harmless
Perseverance	Persistence in doing something despite facing difficulties or obstacles	सहनशीलता / दृढ़ता	Tenacity, determination, steadfastness	Quitting, giving up, irresolution
Persistent	Continuing to exist, endure, or occur over a prolonged period; showing determination or resolve	दृढ़	Enduring, constant, steadfast	Temporary, sporadic, wavering
Perspective	A particular way of viewing or understanding something; a point of view	दृष्टिकोण	Viewpoint, outlook, perception	Narrow-mindedness, bias, prejudice
Pertinent	Relevant or applicable to a particular matter; on-topic	संबंधित	Appropriate, applicable, germane	Irrelevant, unrelated, inconsequential
Petulant	Easily irritated or annoyed; childishly sulky or bad-tempered	क्रोधी	Irritable, cranky, moody	Calm, patient, agreeable

Word	Meaning in English	Meaning in Hindi	Synonyms	Antonyms
Phenomenon	A fact or event that can be observed and studied; something that is extraordinary or impressive	घटना	Occurrence, event, marvel	Normality, commonplace, ordinary
Philanthropy	The practice of giving money, resources, or time to help improve the welfare of others, especially those in need	परोपकार	Charity, benevolence, generosity	Selfishness, greed, stinginess
Pinnacle	The highest point or peak; the culmination or highest level of achievement or success	शिखर	Summit, apex, acme	Nadir, bottom, low point
Pious	Devoutly religious; showing reverence and deep respect for religious principles	धार्मिक	Devout, religious, holy	Irreligious, impious, sinful
Placid	Calm and peaceful, with little or no disturbance or agitation	शांत	Serene, tranquil, undisturbed	Turbulent, agitated, restless
Precise	Exact, accurate, and careful in details	सटीक	Accurate, exact, meticulous	Inaccurate, imprecise, vague
Predicament	A difficult, unpleasant, or embarrassing situation from which it is hard to escape	कठिन परिस्थिति	Dilemma, quandary, crisis	Solution, ease, advantage
Prejudice	Preconceived opinion or bias formed without proper knowledge or reason, often based on stereotypes	पूर्वाग्रह	Bias, discrimination, bigotry	Fairness, impartiality, tolerance
Preoccupied	Deeply engrossed or absorbed in thoughts, ideas, or activities, making it difficult to pay attention to other things	दिलचस्पी से भरा हुआ	Absorbed, engrossed, immersed	Focused, attentive, present
Presumptuous	Failing to observe the limits of what is appropriate or allowed, especially in being too confident or forward	ढीठ	Arrogant, audacious, overconfident	Modest, humble, deferential

Word	Meaning in English	Meaning in Hindi	Synonyms	Antonyms
Pretentious	Making exaggerated claims or creating an appearance of greater importance, talent, or culture than is actually possessed	दिखावटी	Ostentatious, affected, showy	Genuine, modest, humble
Prevail	To be widespread or dominant; to prove more powerful or successful	प्रबल होना	Triumph, succeed, overcome	Surrender, yield, succumb
Primary	First or highest in rank, importance, or value; main or principal	प्राथमिक	Principal, chief, leading	Secondary, subordinate, minor
Pristine	In its original condition; pure, clean, and untouched	पवित्र	Untouched, unspoiled, immaculate	Dirty, contaminated, spoiled
Procrastinate	To delay or postpone doing something, often out of habit or reluctance	टालना	Delay, postpone, dawdle	Act, proceed, expedite
Prodigy	A person, especially a young one, who demonstrates exceptional talent or skill in a particular area	प्रतिभाशाली	Genius, virtuoso, talented	Mediocre, untalented, average
Profound	Having deep meaning or significance; intense, thoughtful, or insightful	गहरा	Deep, thoughtful, profound	Superficial, shallow, trivial
Progressive	Favouring or advocating for change, improvement, or reform, typically in social, political, or economic matters	प्रगतिशील	Forward-thinking, innovative, modern	Conservative, traditional, regressive
Prolific	Producing a large quantity or number; highly productive or fruitful	उपजाऊ	Productive, fruitful, abundant	Barren, unproductive, scarce
Prominent	Standing out, easily noticeable, or widely recognized; important or well-known	प्रमुख	Notable, significant, distinguished	Inconspicuous, obscure, insignificant

Word	Meaning in English	Meaning in Hindi	Synonyms	Antonyms
Proponent	A person who advocates or supports a particular cause, idea, or theory	प्रस्तावक	Advocate, supporter, champion	Opponent, critic, detractor
Prosperity	The state of being successful, thriving, or flourishing, often involving financial well-being	समृद्धि	Success, wealth, abundance	Poverty, adversity, misfortune
Protagonist	The main character or leading figure in a story, play, or movie; the central or primary person in a situation or event	मुख्य नायक	Hero, main character, central figure	Antagonist, villain, adversary
Prudent	Acting with or showing careful, sensible, and wise judgement in practical matters	विवेकी	Wise, cautious, sensible	Foolish, reckless, impulsive
Pseudonym	A fictitious name used by an author or person, especially to conceal their identity	उपनाम	Pen name, alias, nom de plume	Real name, true identity
Pungent	Having a strong, sharp, or tangy smell or taste; causing a sharp or intense sensation	तेज़गंधी, कटु	Strong, intense, aromatic	Mild, subtle, odourless
Purify	To remove impurities, pollutants, or contaminants; to make clean, clear, or free from anything harmful	शुद्ध करना	Cleanse, filter, refine	Contaminate, pollute, dirty
Purposeful	Having a clear intention, aim, or objective; deliberate and determined in action	उद्देश्यपूर्ण	Intentional, deliberate, focused	Aimless, random, purposeless
Puzzling	Confusing, difficult to understand or solve; causing uncertainty or perplexity	पेचीदा, उलझन	Perplexing, bewildering, enigmatic	Clear, straightforward, obvious
Prolong	To extend the duration or time of something; to lengthen or protract	बढ़ाना, लंबा करना	Extend, lengthen, elongate	Shorten, abbreviate, truncate

Word	Meaning in English	Meaning in Hindi	Synonyms	Antonyms
Proximity	Nearness in space, time, or relationship; being close or in close proximity to something or someone	निकटता	Closeness, vicinity, proximity	Distance, remoteness, separation
Pragmatic	Dealing with things practically, based on practical considerations rather than theoretical or idealistic ones	व्यावहारिक	Practical, realistic, sensible	Idealistic, theoretical, impractical
Propensity	A natural inclination or tendency to behave, think, or act in a particular way; a predisposition	प्रवृत्ति	Inclination, tendency, proclivity	Aversion, disinclination, reluctance
Posterity	Future generations, all of the people who will be alive in the future after the current generation has passed away	आने वाली पीढ़ी, भविष्यवर्ती	Descendants, future generations, progeny	Ancestors, past generations, forebears
Penchant	A strong liking or inclination for something; a preference or fondness	रुझान, रुचि	Preference, inclination, fondness	Dislike, aversion, indifference
Palpable	Able to be touched, felt, or perceived; tangible or noticeable	स्पष्ट, महसूस किया जा सकने वाला	Perceptible, tangible, evident	Intangible, imperceptible, hidden
Peccadillo	A small, minor, or slight sin or offence; a minor wrongdoing	छोटी ग़लती, छोटी अपराध	Fault, indiscretion, misdemeanour	Virtue, righteousness, innocence
Plight	A difficult, challenging, or precarious situation; a predicament or dilemma	कठिन परिस्थिति, बदस्तूरी	Predicament, dilemma, crisis	Ease, comfort, solution
Prevalent	Widely existing, occurring, or accepted; widespread or common	प्रचलित, प्रबल	Common, widespread, prevalent	Rare, uncommon, infrequent
Pretext	A false reason or excuse given to hide the true purpose or motive; a pretence	बहाना, प्रताड़ना	Excuse, pretence, cover-up	Genuine reason, truth, honesty

Word	Meaning in English	Meaning in Hindi	Synonyms	Antonyms
Palatial	Resembling or suitable for a palace; grand, luxurious, or magnificent	महल का समान, आलिशान	Luxurious, grand, opulent	Modest, humble, simple
Pompous	Having an exaggerated sense of self-importance; arrogant, self-important, or pretentious	आत्मगर्वपूर्ण, अहंकारी	Arrogant, haughty, self-important	Humble, modest, unassuming
Portray	To depict, represent, or describe someone or something in a particular way; to present or show	चित्रित करना, प्रस्तुत करना	Depict, represent, illustrate	Conceal, hide, distort
Piquant	Having a pleasantly sharp or stimulating taste or flavour; spicy or tangy	तीखा, मसालेदार	Spicy, tangy, flavorful	Bland, tasteless, insipid
Pedestrian	Lacking inspiration, imagination, or excitement; dull, ordinary, or commonplace	दरिद्र, नीरस	Ordinary, dull, unremarkable	Extraordinary, remarkable, exceptional
Palpitate	To beat rapidly or irregularly, typically referring to the heart; to throb or pulsate	दिल की धड़कन, कंपन	Pulsate, throb, pound	Calm, steady, tranquil
Preconceived	Formed or conceived beforehand, typically based on prejudice or preconception; biassed or prejudiced	पूर्वधारित, पूर्वाग्रह से निर्मित	Prejudiced, biassed, prejudged	Open-minded, unbiased, impartial
Protean	Displaying great diversity or variety; versatile or capable of assuming different forms or roles	बहुरूपी, अनेकरूपी	Versatile, adaptable, changeable	Fixed, unchanging, inflexible
Propitious	Favourable or advantageous; indicating or suggesting a good chance of success	शुभ, अनुकूल	Favourable, auspicious, advantageous	Unfavourable, inauspicious, unfavourable
Probity	Honesty, integrity, and strong moral principles; uprightness and decency	ईमानदारी, नैतिकता	Integrity, honesty, righteousness	Dishonesty, deceit, corruption

Word	Meaning in English	Meaning in Hindi	Synonyms	Antonyms
Protract	To prolong, extend, or draw out in time; to lengthen or delay	बढ़ाना, टालना	Prolong, extend, lengthen	Shorten, abbreviate, expedite
Parsimony	Extreme unwillingness to spend money or use resources; extreme frugality.	कंजूसी	Stinginess, Frugality, Thriftiness	Generosity, Liberality, Extravagance
Pathetic	Arousing pity, sympathy, or sadness; pitifully inadequate or inferior.	दयनीय	Pitiful, Miserable, Woeful	Impressive, Remarkable, Admirable
Perceive	To become aware of, to comprehend or understand through the senses or intellect.	प्राप्त करना	Detect, Recognize, Grasp	Overlook, Ignore, Miss
Perish	To die or be destroyed, typically in a sudden or violent manner.	नष्ट होना	Die, Expire, Succumb	Survive, Flourish, Thrive
Peruse	To read or examine carefully and in detail.	ध्यानपूर्वक पढ़ना	Study, Scrutinise, Analyse	Skim, Glance, Browse
Pleasant	Giving a sense of enjoyment or satisfaction; agreeable, enjoyable, or pleasing.	सुखद	Agreeable, Pleasing, Delightful	Unpleasant, Displeasing, Distasteful
Plebiscite	A direct vote in which all members of a community or electorate decide an issue or question.	सार्वजनिक मतदान	Referendum, Ballot, Poll	Dictation, Imposition, Oligarchy
Poignant	Evoking a keen sense of sadness, regret, or sympathy; deeply moving or touching.	कठोर	Touching, Moving, Heartrending	Unemotional, Indifferent, Apathetic
Primitive	Relating to an early stage of development or existence; basic, crude, or rudimentary.	प्रारंभिक	Primitive, Basic, Rudimentary	Advanced, Sophisticated, Modern
Priority	The state or condition of being regarded as more important or needing attention before something else.	प्राथमिकता	Precedence, Primacy, Preference	Secondary, Subordinate, Lesser Importance

Word	Meaning in English	Meaning in Hindi	Synonyms	Antonyms
Prodigal	Spending money or resources freely and recklessly; wastefully extravagant.	अपव्ययी	Extravagant, Wasteful, Lavish	Thrifty, Frugal, Economical
Profligate	Recklessly extravagant or wasteful in the use of resources, energy, or money.	अपव्ययी	Extravagant, Squandering, Wasteful	Thrifty, Economical, Frugal
Protest	A formal declaration or expression of objection, disapproval, or dissent against something.	विरोध	Object, Oppose, Resist	Support, Approve, Endorse
		Q		
Quaint	Attractively unusual or old-fashioned.	पुराने या अनोखे ढंग से आकर्षक।	Charming, Picturesque, Quirky	Common, Ordinary, Typical
Quake	Shake or tremble violently.	कांपना या अचंभित होना।	Tremor, Shake, Quiver	Stabilise, Settle, Still
Quandary	A state of uncertainty or perplexity.	संदेह या उलझन की स्थिति।	Dilemma, Predicament, Confusion	Certainty, Clarity, Solution
Quarry	A place where stone, minerals, or other materials are extracted.	एक स्थान जहां पत्थर, खनिज या अन्य सामग्री निकाली जाती है।	Mine, Pit, Excavation	Deposit, Stockpile, Reserve
Quaver	Shake or tremble in the voice, typically through nervousness or emotion.	आवाज में कांपना या कंपकंपी करना, आमतौर पर घबराहट या भावना के कारण।	Tremble, Quiver, Shake	Stabilise, Steady, Compose
Quench	Satisfy one's thirst by drinking.	पीकर प्यास बुझाना।	Satiate, Satisfy, Slake	Parch, Dehydrate, Dry

Word	Meaning in English	Meaning in Hindi	Synonyms	Antonyms
Quest	A long or arduous search for something.	किसी चीज़ की लम्बी या कठिन खोज।	Search, Pursuit, Expedition	Abandonment, Disinterest, Neglect
Quibble	Argue or raise objections about a trivial matter.	एक तुच्छ मुद्दे के बारे में विवाद करना या आपत्ति उठाना।	Nitpick, Cavil, Protest	Agree, Accept, Approve
Quirk	A peculiar behaviour or mannerism.	एक विचित्र व्यवहार या आचरण।	Eccentricity, Peculiarity, Oddity	Normality, Conformity, Standard
Quiver	Shake with a slight, rapid motion.	हल्की, तीव्र गति से हिलना।	Tremble, Shake, Shiver	Still, Stabilise, Calm
Quota	A fixed share or portion, especially of something that is distributed among a group.	एक निश्चित अंश या भाग, विशेष रूप से जो एक समूह के बीच वितरित होता है।	Share, Allocation, Allotment	Unlimited, Unrestricted, Abundance
Quotient	The result of dividing one quantity by another.	एक मात्रा को दूसरी मात्रा से विभाजित करने का परिणाम।	Result, Outcome, Division	Whole, Sum, Total
Quorum	The minimum number of members required to be present at a meeting to make the proceedings valid.	सभी कार्यवाही को मान्य बनाने के लिए एक बैठक में मौजूद होने के लिए आवश्यक न्यूनतम सदस्यों की संख्या।	Majority, Attendance, Quota	Minority, Insufficiency, Lack
Quack	A person who falsely claims to have medical skills or knowledge.	व्यक्ति जो मेडिकल कौशल या ज्ञान रखने का झूठा दावा करता है।	Charlatan, Impostor, Fraud	Professional, Expert, Specialist

Word	Meaning in English	Meaning in Hindi	Synonyms	Antonyms
Quadruple	Multiply by four.	चार से गुणा करना।	Multiply by four, Quadruplicate, Quadrisect	Divide by four, Halve, Quarter
Quandaries	Difficulties or dilemmas; a state of uncertainty or perplexity.	संकट या दुविधा; संदेह या उलझन की स्थिति।	Dilemmas, Predicaments, Quagmires	Solutions, Certainties, Resolutions
Quip	A witty or clever remark.	बुद्धिमान या हास्यपूर्ण टिप्पणी।	Wisecrack, Joke, Retort	Serious remark, Statement, Silence
Quicken	To make or become faster or more active.	तेज़ या सक्रिय बनाना।	Accelerate, Speed up, Hasten	Slow down, Decelerate, Delay
Quotable	Worthy or suitable for being quoted or cited.	उद्धरण या उद्धरण के लायक होने वाला।	Memorable, Noteworthy, Remarkable	Forgettable, Insignificant, Unremarkable
Qualified	Meeting the necessary requirements or standards.	आवश्यक योग्यता या मानकों को पूरा करना।	Competent, Skilled, Certified	Unqualified, Incompetent, Inexperienced
Quenchless	Impossible to satisfy or quench.	संतुष्ट या शांत नहीं करने योग्य।	Insatiable, Unquenchable, Unappeasable	Satisfiable, Quenchable, Appeasable
Quintessence	The most perfect or typical example of a quality or class.	गुण या वर्ग का सबसे पूर्ण या प्रतिष्ठित उदाहरण।	Epitome, Embodiment, Essence	Incomplete, Imperfection, Flaw
Quicklime	A white, caustic, alkaline crystalline solid used in various applications, including construction.	सफेद, कार्यकारी, एल्कलाइन बर्फीली ठोस पदार्थ जो निर्माण सहित विभिन्न उपयोगों में इस्तेमाल होता है।	Calcium oxide, Burnt lime, Calx	Water, Moisture, Hydration

Word	Meaning in English	Meaning in Hindi	Synonyms	Antonyms
Quintessential	Representing the most perfect or typical example of a quality or class.	गुण या वर्ग का सबसे पूर्ण या प्रतिष्ठित उदाहरण का प्रतिनिधित्व करना।	Epitome, Embodiment, Classic	Incomplete, Imperfection, Flawed
Quay	A concrete, stone, or metal platform lying alongside or projecting into water for loading and unloading ships.	जहाजों की लोडिंग और अनलोडिंग के लिए पानी के साथ साइडलाइन पर या आउटप्रोजेक्टिंग इंटो प्लेटफॉर्म, जो ठोस होता है।	Dock, Pier, Wharf	Open water, Shore, Land
Quotability	The quality of being quotable; worth being quoted or cited.	उद्धरण या उद्धरण के योग्य होने की गुणवत्ता।	Memorable quality, Citable characteristic, Quotable feature	Forgettable quality, Insignificant characteristic, Unquotable feature
Quoteworthy	Deserving to be quoted or worthy of being quoted.	उद्धरण करने योग्य या उद्धरण के योग्य होने योग्य।	Memorable, Remarkable, Notable	Forgettable, Insignificant, Unremarkable
Quark	A type of elementary particle and a fundamental constituent of matter.	किसी प्रकार का प्राथमिक कण और पदार्थ का मूल घटक।	Particle, Subatomic particle, Elementary particle	Composite particle, Complex particle, Compound particle
Quisling	A person who collaborates with an enemy occupying force, especially a traitor who collaborates with an invading army.	व्यक्ति जो एक दुश्मन के कब्जे में होने वाले बल के साथ मिलजुल करता है, विशेष रूप से एक ऐसा देशवासी जो एक आक्रमणकारी सेना के साथ सहयोग करता है।	Collaborator, Traitor, Turncoat	Patriot, Loyalist, Hero

Word	Meaning in English	Meaning in Hindi	Synonyms	Antonyms
Quad	A quadrilateral or quadrangle; a square or rectangular area or enclosure.	एक चतुर्भुज या चतुर्भुज क्षेत्र; एक वर्ग या आयताकार क्षेत्र या ढालन।	Quadrilateral, Square, Rectangle	Circle, Triangle, Curved
Quadrant	One of four equal parts into which something can be divided, especially of a circle.	चक्र का एक चतुर्थांश, जिसे विशेष रूप से चार बराबर भागों में विभाजित किया जा सकता है।	Quarter, Section, Segment	Whole, Complete, Full
Queer	Strange, odd, or unconventional; not in accordance with what is expected or usual.	अजीब, अनोखा, या अनुशासित नहीं; उम्मीद के अनुसार या सामान्य के अनुरूप नहीं है।	Eccentric, Peculiar, Bizarre	Normal, Conventional, Typical
Quicksilver	Mercury, a shiny, silvery-white, liquid metal.	पारा, एक चमकदार, चांदी के रंग का, तरल धातु।	Mercury, Liquid silver, Quicksilver metal	Solid, Non-metallic
Quicksand	Loose, wet sand that yields easily to pressure and sucks in anything resting on or moving through it.	ढीली, गीली रेत जो दबाव को आसानी से झुकती है और इस पर या इसके माध्यम से हो रहे किसी चीज़ को खींच लेती है।	Sinking sand, Mire, Quagmire	Firm ground, Solid soil, Stable surface

Word	Meaning in English	Meaning in Hindi	Synonyms	Antonyms
Quirky	Characterised by peculiar or unexpected traits; unconventional or eccentric.	अजीब या अप्रत्याशित गुणों से युक्त; अनौपचारिक या विलक्षण।	Eccentric, Unconventional, Peculiar	Normal, Conventional, Typical
Quotative	Indicating or functioning as a quotation or quote.	उद्धरण या उद्धरण के रूप में इंगित करना या कार्य करना।	Quotation, Quoting, Quoted	Non-quoted, Original, Unreferenced
Quaintness	The quality of being attractively old-fashioned or unusual.	पुराने ढंग से आकर्षक या असामान्य होने की गुणवत्ता।	Charm, Quirkiness, Uniqueness	Commonness, Ordinariness, Banality
Quincentenary	A 500th anniversary or the celebration of it.	500वीं वर्षगांठ या इसका उत्सव।	500th anniversary, Quincentennial, Jubilee	Non-anniversary, Non-celebration
Quaff	To drink a beverage heartily or in large quantities.	खुशी या बड़े मात्रा में पेय पिना।	Guzzle, Sip, Swig	Abstain, Refrain, Avoid
Quadrangle	A four-sided courtyard or open area, often surrounded by buildings.	चार-तरफा आंगन या खुले क्षेत्र, जो अक्सर इमारतों द्वारा घिरा होता है।	Courtyard, Square, Plaza	Enclosed space, Interior, Closed area
Quirkiest	The most peculiar or unconventional.	सबसे अजीब या अनौपचारिक।	Most eccentric, Most peculiar, Most unconventional	Most normal, Most conventional, Most typical
Qualify	To meet the necessary conditions or requirements.	आवश्यक शर्तों या आवश्यकताओं को पूरा करना।	Meet requirements, Satisfy conditions, Fulfil criteria	Disqualify, Fail, Invalidate

Word	Meaning in English	Meaning in Hindi	Synonyms	Antonyms
Quakeful	Prone to or characterised by earthquakes; tremulous, quivering.	भूकंप के लिए आवेगी या विशेषता होना; कंपन, कांपता हुआ।	Trembling, Shaking, Shivering	Stable, Unshaking, Steady
Quill	A main wing or flight feather of a bird, especially a large or primary feather.	एक पक्षी की मुख्य पंख या उड़ान वाला पंख, विशेष रूप से एक बड़ा या प्राथमिक पंख।	Feather, Plume, Pinion	Scale, Fur, Skin
Quickset	A hedge or fence made of living plants with branches that take root and grow.	जीवित पौधों से बना एक झाड़ी या बाड़, जिसमें टहनियां जड़ लेती हैं और बढ़ती हैं।	Live fence, Hedge, Hedgerow	Dead fence, Wire fence, Wooden fence
Quiche	A savoury open-faced pastry crust with a filling of savoury custard with cheese, meat, seafood, or vegetables.	एक नमकीन ओपन फेस्ड पेस्ट्री खोल के साथ, जिसमें चीज़, मांस, समुद्री खाद्य पदार्थ या सब्जियों के साथ नमकीन कस्टर्ड का भरण होता है।	Savory pastry, Savory tart, Open-faced pie	Sweet pastry, Sweet tart, Sweet pie
Qualm	A sudden feeling of doubt, fear, or unease; a misgiving.	एक अचानक संदेह, भय या असंतोष की भावना; एक संदेह।	Doubt, Unease, Misgiving	Certainty, Confidence, Reassurance

Word	Meaning in English	Meaning in Hindi	Synonyms	Antonyms
Quoin	A wedge-shaped stone or piece of timber used to secure or support the corner of a wall.	दीवार के कोने को सुरक्षित या समर्थन करने के लिए उपयोग किया जाने वाला एक कीलाकार पत्थर या टिम्बर का टुकड़ा।	Cornerstone, Wedge, Support	Center, Middle, Interior
		R		
Radiant	Emitting light or shining brightly	प्रकाशमान	Bright, Luminous, Glowing	Dull, Dim, Gloomy
Rambunctious	Noisy, wild, and uncontrollable	अशांत	Boisterous, Rowdy, Energetic	Calm, Serene, Quiet
Ravenous	Extremely hungry or voracious	भुक्खड़	Famished, Starving, Insatiable	Satiated, Full, Content
Reckless	Acting or behaving without thinking about the consequences	लापरवाह	Careless, Impulsive, Rash	Cautious, Prudent, Deliberate
Relentless	Persistent and determined, not giving up easily	अटल	Tenacious, Unyielding, Tireless	Yielding, Flexible, Indulgent
Reminiscent	Tending to remind one of something, evoking memories	स्मृति ज्ञापक	Evocative, Redolent, Recalling	Forgetful, Unrelated, Disconnected
Replicate	To reproduce or duplicate, make an exact copy of something	प्रतिलिपि बनाना	Copy, Duplicate, Mirror	Original, Unique, Different
Resilient	Able to recover quickly from difficult situations or setbacks	प्रतिरोधी	Tough, Elastic, Resistant	Fragile, Vulnerable, Delicate
Resonate	To produce a deep, full, and reverberating sound or to evoke a strong feeling or response	सहमति बढ़ाना	Reverberate, Echo, Harmonize	Dull, Silence, Disagree

Word	Meaning in English	Meaning in Hindi	Synonyms	Antonyms
Revelation	A surprising and enlightening disclosure or realisation	प्रकटीकरण	Discovery, Epiphany, Unveiling	Concealment, Secrecy, Covering
Rhapsody	An exuberant and enthusiastic expression of emotion or feeling	उत्साह	Ecstasy, Enthusiasm, Euphoria	Melancholy, Gloom, Despair
Rigorous	Extremely thorough, precise, or demanding	कठोर	Strict, Severe, Exacting	Flexible, Lenient, Relaxed
Robust	Strong, healthy, and vigorous	मजबूत	Sturdy, Fit, Hardy	Weak, Fragile, Delicate
Rogue	A dishonest or unprincipled person	नक़ली	Scoundrel, Rascal, Knave	Honest, Virtuous, Decent
Remarkable	Worthy of attention or notice, extraordinary or exceptional	अद्वितीय	Notable, Outstanding, Impressive	Ordinary, Average, Unremarkable
Rejuvenate	To make someone or something feel refreshed, revitalised, or restored	पुनर्जीवित करना	Revive, Renew, Energise	Exhaust, Drain, Deplete
Repertoire	The range or collection of skills, abilities, or performances that a person or group has	प्रदर्शन सूची	Catalog, Portfolio, Inventory	Limitation, Restriction, Scarcity
Reclusive	Preferring to live alone or withdrawn from society, seeking solitude	एकांतवासी	Solitary, Isolated, Hermetic	Social, Outgoing, Gregarious
Repentance	The feeling of remorse or regret for one's wrongdoing or sins	पश्चाताप	Remorse, Contrition, Penitence	Defiance, Unrepentance, Stubbornness
Resolute	Firmly determined, unwavering in purpose or opinion	दृढ़	Steadfast, Tenacious, Unyielding	Indecisive, Vacillating, Fickle
Rendezvous	A meeting or appointment at a prearranged place and time	मिलन स्थल	Meeting, Encounter, Tryst	Separation, Departure, Disconnection
Rustic	Relating to the countryside or rural areas, simple and unsophisticated	ग्रामीण	Rural, Countryside, Bucolic	Urban, Sophisticated, Cosmopolitan

Word	Meaning in English	Meaning in Hindi	Synonyms	Antonyms
Ruthless	Showing no mercy or compassion, cruel and without remorse	निर्दयी	Merciless, Brutal, Unrelenting	Compassionate, Merciful, Kind
Resplendent	Shining brilliantly, dazzlingly beautiful or impressive	चमकीला	Radiant, Splendid, Glorious	Dull, Plain, Unimpressive
Rigidity	The quality of being stiff or inflexible, lacking adaptability	कठोरता	Stiffness, Inflexibility, Rigour	Flexibility, Adaptability, Pliability
Reciprocate	To respond to a gesture or action by making a corresponding one	प्रतिदान करना	Return, Counter, Exchange	Ignore, Reject, Disregard
Rapture	A state of intense joy, delight, or ecstasy	आनंद	Ecstasy, Bliss, Euphoria	Misery, Sorrow, Despair
Revitalise	To give new life or energy to something or someone	पुनर्जीवित करना	Rejuvenate, Renew, Reenergize	Exhaust, Drain, Deplete
Riddle	A puzzling or enigmatic statement, question, or problem	पहेली	Enigma, Puzzle, Conundrum	Solution, Answer, Clarity
Resonance	The quality of a sound or vibration being deep, full, and reverberating	सहयोग	Reverberation, Echo, Harmonics	Dullness, Silence, Dissonance
Reconciliation	The act of making peace or restoring friendly relationships between two parties	सुलह	Resolution, Settlement, Agreement	Conflict, Dispute, Estrangement
Refurbish	To renovate, repair, or improve the condition of something	नवीनीकरण करना	Renovate, Restore, Revamp	Neglect, Deteriorate, Ruin
Rampant	Widespread and uncontrolled, growing or spreading unchecked	अनियंत्रित	Pervasive, Unrestrained, Epidemic	Controlled, Restricted, Limited
Repugnant	Extremely distasteful or offensive, causing strong aversion or disgust	घिनौना	Abhorrent, Offensive, Disgusting	Appealing, Pleasant, Agreeable

Word	Meaning in English	Meaning in Hindi	Synonyms	Antonyms
Redeem	To compensate for or make up for a past mistake or failure	मुक्त करना	Restore, Compensate, Repay	Forfeit, Lose, Abandon
Revere	To regard with deep respect, admiration, or awe	पूजा करना	Worship, Admire, Honor	Disrespect, Despise, Disregard
Refrain	To stop oneself from doing something, or a repeated line or phrase in a poem or song	बचना	Abstain, Resist, Avoid	Indulge, Engage, Participate
Replenish	To fill or make something full again, especially after it has been depleted or used up	पूरा करना	Refill, Recharge, Renew	Empty, Deplete, Exhaust
Rebirth	The act or process of being born again, renewed or revived existence	पुनर्जन्म	Regeneration, Resurgence, Revival	Death, Demise, Termination
Reimburse	To repay or compensate someone for expenses or losses incurred	प्रतिपूर्ति करना	Compensate, Refund, Repay	Charge, Bill, Collect
Rambler	A person who takes leisurely walks or wanders without a specific destination	टहल रहा होनेवाला	Wanderer, Roamer, Stroller	Settler, Stay-at-home, Resident
Relinquish	To voluntarily give up or surrender something, to let go of a possession or responsibility	त्याग देना	Surrender, Abandon, Renounce	Retain, Keep, Hold onto
Refute	To prove a statement or argument to be false or incorrect, to disprove or contradict	खण्डन करना	Disprove, Discredit, Challenge	Confirm, Validate, Support
Reproach	To express disapproval, criticism, or disappointment towards someone for their actions or behaviour	आलोचना करना	Blame, Criticise, Reprimand	Praise, Compliment, Applaud
Retrospect	A review or examination of past events, a reflection on the past	पूर्वावलोकन	Review, Examination, Assessment	Prospect, Anticipation, Outlook

Word	Meaning in English	Meaning in Hindi	Synonyms	Antonyms
Recurring	Occurring repeatedly or regularly, happening over and over again	बार-बार होनेवाला	Repeating, Reoccurring, Persistent	One-time, Singular, Occasional
Radiate	To emit or give off rays of light, heat, or energy, to spread outwards from a central point	फैलना	Emit, Shine, Glow	Absorb, Consume, Retain
Retribution	Punishment inflicted as a form of revenge or payback for a wrongdoing	प्रतिशोध	Revenge, Vengeance, Retaliation	Forgiveness, Pardon, Mercy
Regal	Having the quality or appearance of royalty, majestic or noble in character or appearance	शाही	Royal, Majestic, Grand	Humble, Common, Ordinary
Renowned	Famous, widely known, and highly regarded	प्रसिद्ध	Celebrated, Eminent, Distinguished	Unknown, Obscure, Anonymous
Reverberate	To echo or resound, to have a lasting impact or influence	प्रतिध्वनित होना	Resonate, Echo, Repercuss	Silence, Quiet, Stillness
Repress	To restrain, control, or suppress an emotion, desire, or action	दबाना	Suppress, Inhibit, Constrain	Express, Release, Unleash
Refined	Showing elegance, sophistication, and good taste, cultured or polished	परिष्कृत	Elegant, Polished, Cultivated	Crude, Unrefined, Vulgar
Ransack	To search thoroughly or vigorously through something, often causing disorder or damage	खोजना	Search, Explore, Loot	Arrange, Organise, Systemize
Resuscitate	To revive or bring someone or something back to consciousness or life	पुनर्जीवित करना	Revive, Reanimate, Restore	Kill, Destroy, Terminate
Relish	To enjoy or take pleasure in something, to savour or appreciate	आनंद लेना	Enjoy, Appreciate, Delight in	Dislike, Detest, Abhor

Word	Meaning in English	Meaning in Hindi	Synonyms	Antonyms
Revive	To bring back to life, consciousness, or activity, to rejuvenate or restore	पुनर्जीवित करना	Resurrect, Renew, Reawaken	Kill, Destroy, Terminate
Relevance	The quality of being closely connected or appropriate to the matter at hand	प्रासंगिकता	Pertinence, Applicability, Significance	Irrelevance, Inapplicability, Insignificance
Revert	To return to a previous state, condition, or subject	वापस ले जाना	Go back, Return, Regress	Progress, Advance, Evolve
Revoke	To cancel, repeal, or withdraw an official order, law, or privilege	वापस लेना	Cancel, Annul, Nullify	Confirm, Approve, Uphold
Rouse	To awaken, stir up, or excite someone from a state of sleep, inactivity, or indifference	जगाना	Stir, Awaken, Activate	Calm, Soothe, Quiet
Refine	To purify, improve, or make something more precise or elegant	परिष्कृत करना	Purify, Perfect, Polish	Coarsen, Degrade, Tarnish
Raven	A large, black, glossy bird, often associated with death or mystery	कागज़	Crow, Blackbird, Corvus	Dove, Sparrow, Finch
Repel	To drive away, ward off, or keep something or someone at a distance	विरोध करना	Deter, Resist, Reject	Attract, Entice, Welcome
Rig	To manipulate or set up something dishonestly or fraudulently, to arrange or fix	ढीठ बनाना	Manipulate, Engineer, Fix	Undo, Disassemble, Dismantle
Retaliate	To respond to an attack or harm by inflicting a similar or greater harm in return	पलटवार करना	Strike back, Revenge, Counterattack	Forgive, Pardon, Yield
Remorse	Deep regret or guilt for a past action, often accompanied by a sense of sorrow or repentance	पछतावा	Regret, Guilt, Contrition	Indifference, Unconcern, Satisfaction
Recoil	To suddenly spring or flinch back in fear, shock, or disgust	पीछे हटना	Flinch, Shrink, Retreat	Advance, Approach, Proceed

Word	Meaning in English	Meaning in Hindi	Synonyms	Antonyms
Recede	To move back or retreat, to gradually withdraw or diminish	पीछे हटना	Retreat, Withdraw, Retire	Advance, Approach, Proceed
Revamp	To renovate, redesign, or improve something, especially in a significant way	सुधार करना	Renovate, Overhaul, Upgrade	Neglect, Abandon, Ruin
Remedy	A solution or treatment for a problem or illness, a way to correct or alleviate a situation	उपाय	Cure, Solution, Treatment	Problem, Affliction, Malady
Relocate	To move or establish in a new place or position, to change one's residence or business location	स्थानांतरित करना	Move, Transfer, Resettle	Stay, Remain, Settle
Resurrect	To bring back to life or existence, to revive or restore from death or inactivity	पुनर्जीवित करना	Revive, Restore, Reanimate	Kill, Destroy, Terminate
Retaliation	The act of responding to an attack or harm with a similar or greater action in return	पलटवार	Revenge, Counterattack, Vengeance	Forgiveness, Pardon, Yield
Rejoinder	A reply or response to a remark or comment, a quick and witty comeback	जवाब	Reply, Response, Retort	Silence, Ignorance, Unresponsiveness
Ravage	To cause severe damage or destruction.	नाश करना	Devastate, Destroy, Wreck	Restore, Preserve, Protect
Realm	A kingdom or domain; a field or sphere of activity or interest.	साम्राज्य	Kingdom, Domain, Territory	N/A
Recapitulation	A summary or concise review; the act of summarising or reviewing.	संक्षेप में दोहराव	Summary, Review, Overview	Expansion, Elaboration, Detail
Regime	A system or method of government or rule; a particular administration.	शासन व्यवस्था	Government, Rule, Administration	Anarchy, Disorder, Chaos

Word	Meaning in English	Meaning in Hindi	Synonyms	Antonyms
Relevant	Closely connected or appropriate to the matter at hand; pertinent.	संबंधित	Appropriate, Pertinent, Applicable	Irrelevant, Inapplicable, Unrelated
Reliable	Able to be trusted or relied on; dependable.	विश्वसनीय	Trustworthy, Dependable, Credible	Unreliable, Untrustworthy, Inconsistent
Requisite	Necessary or essential for a particular purpose or situation.	अनिवार्य	Essential, Required, Mandatory	Optional, Unnecessary, Dispensable
		S		
Saccharine	Excessively sweet or sentimental	अत्यधिक मिठा या भावुक	Sweet, Sugary, Cloying	Bitter, Tart, Sour
Sacrifice	To give up something valuable for the sake of others or a higher purpose	बलिदान करना	Surrender, Forfeit, Forgo	Keep, Retain, Withhold
Sadistic	Deriving pleasure from causing pain or suffering to others	अत्यंत अत्याचारी	Cruel, Inhumane, Brutal	Benevolent, Compassionate, Kind
Safeguard	A measure taken to protect or preserve something from harm or damage	सुरक्षा कवच	Protect, Defend, Shield	Endanger, Jeopardise, Expose
Sagacious	Having or showing keen mental discernment and good judgement	दूरदर्शी	Wise, Insightful, Shrewd	Foolish, Unwise, Imprudent
Salient	Most noticeable or important	प्रमुख	Prominent, Conspicuous, Eminent	Insignificant, Unremarkable, Obscure
Salubrious	Favourable to health or well-being	स्वास्थ्यकर	Healthy, Wholesome, Beneficial	Unhealthy, Harmful, Detrimental
Sanguine	Optimistic, especially in a difficult situation	आशावादी	Positive, Confident, Hopeful	Pessimistic, Gloomy, Despondent
Sarcasm	The use of irony to mock or convey contempt	व्यंग्य	Satire, Mockery, Ridicule	Praise, Compliment, Flattery

Word	Meaning in English	Meaning in Hindi	Synonyms	Antonyms
Sardonic	Grimly mocking or cynical	व्यंग्यात्मक	Sarcastic, Caustic, Ironic	Sincere, Genuine, Earnest
Satiate	To satisfy fully or to excess	पूर्णतः संतुष्ट करना	Gratify, Quench, Surfeit	Deprive, Starve, Abstain
Savvy	Shrewdness and practical knowledge, especially in social or political situations	चतुर	Astute, Street-smart, Clever	Naive, Ignorant, Inexperienced
Scandalous	Causing general public outrage or disgust	अभद्र	Disgraceful, Infamous, Shameful	Respectable, Virtuous, Decent
Scathing	Severe or harshly critical	तीव्र	Cutting, Searing, Ferocious	Mild, Gentle, Praise-worthy
Scepter	An ornamented staff held by a ruling monarch as a symbol of authority	राज-सूचक छड़ी	Staff, Baton, Mace	Submission, Surrender, Obedience
Schism	A split or division between opposing factions	विद्वेष	Split, Rift, Dissension	Unity, Harmony, Agreement
Scintillating	Sparkling or shining brightly, or brilliantly clever or skillful	चमकदार	Dazzling, Brilliant, Radiant	Dull, Boring, Unimpressive
Scurrilous	Making or spreading scandalous claims about someone with the intention of damaging their reputation	अपमानजनक	Defamatory, Libellous, Abusive	Respectful, Praiseworthy, Admiring
Secluded	Sheltered or private, away from the view or access of others	छुपा हुआ	Isolated, Remote, Private	Open, Public, Accessible
Secrete	To produce or discharge (a substance) and release it from a cell or gland	छिपाना	Emit, Release, Exude	Retain, Withhold, Suppress
Sedentary	Characterised by or requiring sitting; inactive	अवकाशी	Inactive, Idle, Stationary	Active, Mobile, Energetic
Seethe	To be in a state of extreme agitation or anger	उबलना	Boil, Fume, Rage	Calm, Soothe, Relax
Segregate	To separate or set apart from others or from the main group	अलग करना	Isolate, Divide, Separate	Integrate, Unify, Combine

Word	Meaning in English	Meaning in Hindi	Synonyms	Antonyms
Seismic	Relating to earthquakes or other vibrations of the earth and its crust	भूकंपीय	Earthshaking, Tremendous, Cataclysmic	Stable, Secure, Calm
Semblance	The outward appearance or apparent form of something	प्रतिरूप	Likeness, Resemblance, Appearance	Disparity, Difference, Dissimilarity
Sensible	Showing or having good judgement or practical understanding	समझदार	Rational, Prudent, Wise	Foolish, Irrational, Unwise
Serene	Calm, peaceful, and untroubled	शांत	Tranquil, Serene, Placid	Agitated, Disturbed, Turbulent
Serendipity	The occurrence of fortunate events by chance in a happy or beneficial way	आकस्मिक सौभाग्य	Luck, Fortune, Providence	Misfortune, Unfortunate, Bad luck
Servile	Showing an excessive willingness to serve or please others	दास-मुक्त	Submissive, Obedient, Subservient	Independent, Assertive, Dominant
Shrewd	Having or showing sharp powers of judgement or astuteness	चतुर	Astute, Clever, Discerning	Naive, Gullible, Simple-minded
Simultaneous	Occurring, operating, or done at the same time	समवर्ती	Concurrent, Synchronous, Coexistent	Sequential, Consecutive, Subsequent
Sinister	Giving the impression that something harmful or evil is happening or will happen	अमांगलिक	Menacing, Ominous, Threatening	Benign, Harmless, Innocuous
Skeptic	A person inclined to question or doubt accepted opinions or beliefs	संशयवादी	Doubter, Disbeliever, Cynic	Believer, Trusting, Optimist
Skirmish	A brief and usually unplanned fight or encounter between small groups	दंगली	Clash, Conflict, Encounter	Truce, Peace, Harmony
Slander	False spoken statements intended to damage a person's reputation	अपमान	Defamation, Libel, Vilification	Praise, Commendation, Flattery

Word	Meaning in English	Meaning in Hindi	Synonyms	Antonyms
Sluggish	Lacking energy, slow, and inactive	मंदगति	Lethargic, Slow, Idle	Energetic, Active, Vigorous
Smitten	Deeply affected by feelings of love, infatuated	प्यार में पड़ा हुआ	Enamored, Infatuated, Charmed	Indifferent, Apathetic, Uninterested
Snippet	A small piece or brief extract of something	टुकड़ा	Excerpt, Fragment, Quotation	Whole, Entirety, Complete
Soothe	To make calm or relieve pain or distress	शांत करना	Comfort, Ease, Calm	Agitate, Disturb, Upset
Sophisticated	Cultured, refined, or knowledgeable about complex or advanced subjects	प्रगतिशील	Elegant, Refined, Cultivated	Naive, Simple, Unsophisticated
Spacious	Having ample space, roomy	विस्तृत	Generous, Expansive, Capacious	Cramped, Crowded, Compact
Spontaneous	Occurring or done in an unplanned or natural way	स्वतः होने वाला	Impromptu, Unplanned, Impulsive	Deliberate, Planned, Calculated
Sprightly	Full of energy and enthusiasm; lively	जोशीला	Energetic, Vivacious, Animated	Dull, Lethargic, Sluggish
Squabble	A noisy argument or disagreement	झगड़ा	Quarrel, Dispute, Altercation	Agreement, Harmony, Peace
Stagnant	Not flowing or moving; inactive or sluggish	बिना गति	Inactive, Idle, Stale	Flowing, Active, Dynamic
Staunch	Loyal, committed, and dependable	निष्ठावान	Steadfast, Devoted, Reliable	Unfaithful, Disloyal, Unreliable
Steadfast	Resolutely or dutifully firm and unwavering	दृढ़	Unwavering, Determined, Resolute	Fickle, Inconstant, Indecisive
Steeped	Immersed or soaked in a particular quality or influence	भरा हुआ	Immersed, Saturated, Drenched	Devoid, Free, Empty

Word	Meaning in English	Meaning in Hindi	Synonyms	Antonyms
Stellar	Of or relating to a star or stars; outstanding or excellent	तारा-समान	Celestial, Brilliant, Superb	Mediocre, Ordinary, Average
Stimulate	To encourage or arouse interest or enthusiasm in someone	प्रोत्साहित करना	Excite, Energise, Inspire	Suppress, Dull, Discourage
Stipulate	To specify a requirement, condition, or demand in an agreement or contract	निर्धारित करना	Specify, Prescribe, Demand	Omit, Exclude, Waive
Stoic	Enduring pain or hardship without showing emotions or complaining	निर्द्वन्द्व	Impassive, Unemotional, Calm	Emotional, Expressive, Sensitive
Strident	Loud, harsh, and grating in sound or manner	तेज और कठोर	Shrill, Piercing, Discordant	Gentle, Soft, Melodious
Stringent	Strict, precise, and exacting; rigorous	कठोर	Rigorous, Severe, Strict	Lenient, Flexible, Lax
Strive	To make great efforts or struggle in order to achieve something	प्रयास करना	Endeavor, Aspire, Work hard	Relax, Abandon, Give up
Sublime	Of such excellence, grandeur, or beauty as to inspire great admiration or awe	उत्कृष्ट	Exalted, Majestic, Transcendent	Mediocre, Ordinary, Common
Subtle	Not immediately obvious or noticeable; elusive or delicate	सूक्ष्म	Slight, Nuanced, Elusive	Obvious, Blatant, Overt
Succinct	Briefly and clearly expressed; concise	संक्षेप में	Concise, Terse, Compact	Wordy, Lengthy, Prolix
Sufficient	Adequate, enough, or satisfactory in quantity, degree, or amount	पर्याप्त	Ample, Adequate, Enough	Insufficient, Inadequate, Scant
Sullen	Showing irritation or ill humour by a gloomy silence or reserve	उदास	Moody, Gloomy, Morose	Cheerful, Happy, Pleasant
Superfluous	Exceeding what is necessary or required; extra or unnecessary	अतिरिक्त	Excessive, Redundant, Unnecessary	Essential, Necessary, Vital

Word	Meaning in English	Meaning in Hindi	Synonyms	Antonyms
Suppress	To prevent or stop something from happening; to restrain or subdue	दबाना	Inhibit, Curb, Quell	Promote, Encourage, Support
Surreptitious	Kept secret, especially because it would not be approved of	चोरी-छिपे	Covert, Stealthy, Clandestine	Open, Overt, Transparent
Susceptible	Likely to be influenced or affected by something; vulnerable	प्रभावशील	Prone, Sensitive, Predisposed	Resistant, Immune, Invulnerable
Sustenance	The process of providing nourishment or support for someone or something	पोषण	Nourishment, Support, Sustaining	Deprivation, Starvation, Neglect
Swagger	To walk or behave in a very confident and typically arrogant or aggressive way	दिखावा करना	Strut, Parade, Flaunt	Stumble, Shuffle, Cower
Sweltering	Very hot and humid, causing discomfort	बहुत गर्म	Scorching, Sultry, Roasting	Cool, Refreshing, Chilled
Swindle	To cheat or deceive someone in order to get money or gain an advantage dishonestly	ठगी	Defraud, Cheat, Trick	Honest, Fair, Genuine
Symmetry	Balanced proportions; similarity or exact correspondence between different things	सममिति	Balance, Harmony, Proportion	Asymmetry, Imbalance, Disproportion
Synergy	The combined power or cooperation of two or more elements that results in a greater effect than the sum of their individual effects	सहयोगी	Collaboration, Cooperation, Unity	Discord, Conflict, Disunity
Synthesis	The combination of separate elements or substances to form a coherent whole	संश्लेषण	Combination, Integration, Fusion	Analysis, Separation, Disintegration
Synchronise	To cause to occur or operate at the same time or rate	समकालीन	Coordinate, Align, Harmonize	Desynchronize, Desynchronize, Misalign

Word	Meaning in English	Meaning in Hindi	Synonyms	Antonyms
Systematic	Done or acting according to a fixed plan or system; methodical	व्यवस्थित	Methodical, Organized, Structured	Haphazard, Chaotic, Random
Sizable	Fairly large in size or extent; considerable	मात्रात्मक	Substantial, Ample, Large	Small, Tiny, Insignificant
Surmount	To overcome a difficulty or obstacle; to be on top of or rise above	पार करना	Overcome, Conquer, Master	Yield to, Surrender, Succumb
Synonym	A word or phrase that means exactly or nearly the same as another word or phrase	पर्यायवाची	Equivalent, Parallel, Alike	Antonym, Opposite, Different
Scrupulous	Diligent, thorough, and extremely attentive to details; having high moral standards	सावधान	Meticulous, Conscientious, Precise	Careless, Negligent, Unscrupulous
Sympathy	Feelings of pity or sorrow for someone else's misfortune; understanding and sharing the feelings of another person	सहानुभूति	Compassion, Empathy, Understanding	Apathy, Indifference, Callousness
Symposium	A conference or meeting at which experts discuss a particular topic or subject	संगोष्ठी	Conference, Seminar, Forum	Monologue, Soliloquy, Lecture
		T		
Taboo	Prohibited or forbidden by social custom or practice	पाबंदी/अनुचित मान्यता	Forbidden, Prohibited, Banned	Allowed, Permitted, Acceptable
Tact	Skill and sensitivity in dealing with others or with difficult issues	कुशलता/ वात्सल्य	Diplomacy, Politeness, Discretion	Insensitivity, Rudeness, Inconsideration
Talisman	An object believed to have magical or protective powers	चर्म/यंत्र	Amulet, Charm, Fetish	Jinx, Hex, Curse
Tangible	Perceptible by touch; clear and definite	स्पर्शनीय/ वास्तविक	Concrete, Physical, Real	Intangible, Abstract, Immaterial
Task	A piece of work to be done or undertaken	कार्य/श्रेणी	Assignment, Project, Duty	Inactivity, Idleness, Leisure

Word	Meaning in English	Meaning in Hindi	Synonyms	Antonyms
Tedious	Too long, slow, or dull; tiresome or monotonous	उबाऊ/ऊब करने वाला	Boring, Monotonous, Dreary	Interesting, Engaging, Stimulating
Temperance	Moderation or self-restraint, especially in indulgence of appetite or passion	संयम/मध्यस्थता	Self-control, Moderation, Sobriety	Indulgence, Excess, Intemperance
Temporal	Relating to time; earthly or secular rather than spiritual	कालिक/समयसाधारण	Time-based, Worldly, Secular	Eternal, Spiritual, Heavenly
Tenacious	Tending to keep a firm hold of something; persistent in maintaining or adhering to something	दृढ़/अटल	Persistent, Resolute, Steadfast	Weak, Indifferent, Fickle
Tenuous	Very weak or slight; insubstantial	अतिसूक्ष्म/तुच्छ	Thin, Flimsy, Fragile	Strong, Solid, Substantial
Terrestrial	Relating to the Earth or its inhabitants; referring to land rather than water or air	पृथ्वीय/भूत	Earthly, Land-based, Terrene	Celestial, Extraterrestrial, Heavenly
Testimony	A formal written or spoken statement, especially one given in a court of law	प्रतिवचन/गवाही	Evidence, Declaration, Statement	Denial, Refutation, Contradiction
Thorough	Complete with regard to every detail; painstakingly accurate or comprehensive	पूर्ण/व्यापक	Comprehensive, Detailed, Meticulous	Superficial, Incomplete, Shallow
Thrive	Prosper; grow or develop vigorously	फलना/उन्नति करना	Flourish, Succeed, Prosper	Decline, Wither, Fail
Timid	Showing a lack of courage or confidence; easily frightened	डरपोक/अनिश्चयी	Shy, Bashful, Cautious	Bold, Courageous, Confident
Tirade	A long, angry or vehement speech; a diatribe	निंदात्मक भाषण/कटु आलोचना	Rant, Diatribe, Harangue	Compliment, Praise, Acclaim
Tolerate	Allow the existence, occurrence, or practice of something that one dislikes or disagrees with, without interference	सहन करना/सहिष्णु होना	Endure, Bear, Accept	Disallow, Forbid, Reject

Word	Meaning in English	Meaning in Hindi	Synonyms	Antonyms
Torment	Severe physical or mental suffering; to cause severe physical or mental suffering	यातना/सताना	Agony, Torture, Distress	Pleasure, Comfort, Contentment
Torpid	Mentally or physically inactive; lethargic or sluggish	सुस्त/उदासीन	Inactive, Lethargic, Dormant	Energetic, Active, Lively
Torrential	Pouring in abundance; characterised by heavy, fast-flowing rainfall or water flow	जलप्रपाती/ बहुत जोरदार	Pouring, Deluging, Overflowing	Trickle, Dribble, Drizzle
Tranquil	Calm and peaceful; free from disturbance	शांत/निर्मल	Serene, Peaceful, Placid	Agitated, Turbulent, Chaotic
Transcend	To go beyond the limits of; to surpass or exceed	पार करना/ ऊपर निकलना	Surpass, Outstrip, Exceed	Conform, Obey, Follow
Transient	Lasting only for a short time; temporary	क्षणिक/ अस्थायी	Temporary, Fleeting, Ephemeral	Permanent, Enduring, Everlasting
Transparent	Allowing light to pass through so that objects can be clearly seen; easily understood or recognized	पारदर्शी/स्पष्ट	Clear, See-through, Obvious	Opaque, Cloudy, Ambiguous
Treacherous	Guilty of or involving betrayal or deception; hazardous or dangerous	धोखेबाज़/ अपवित्र	Deceitful, Untrustworthy, Perfidious	Trustworthy, Reliable, Loyal
Tremendous	Very large or great in amount, scale, or intensity; extraordinary	भारी/अद्वितीय	Enormous, Immense, Gigantic	Small, Insignificant, Tiny
Trivial	Of little value or importance; insignificant	तुच्छ/नगण्य	Inconsequential, Minor, Petty	Significant, Important, Crucial
Truncate	To shorten or cut off a part of something; to make something shorter or quicker	काट देना/ संक्षिप्त करना	Shorten, Cut off, Abbreviate	Lengthen, Extend, Elongate
Tumultuous	Making a loud, confused noise; characterised by disorderly commotion or agitation	उपद्रवपूर्ण/ अशांत	Turbulent, Chaotic, Riotous	Calm, Peaceful, Serene

Word	Meaning in English	Meaning in Hindi	Synonyms	Antonyms
Turbulent	Characterised by conflict, disorder, or confusion; not controlled or calm	अशांत/ उपद्रवपूर्ण	Chaotic, Unstable, Agitated	Calm, Peaceful, Stable
Tyranny	Cruel and oppressive government or rule; the arbitrary or unrestrained exercise of power	निरंकुशता/ तानाशाही	Despotism, Oppression, Dictatorship	Freedom, Liberty, Democracy
Tactile	Relating to the sense of touch; perceptible by touch or capable of being felt	स्पर्शी/ स्पर्शजन्य	Tangible, Palpable, Physical	Intangible, Immaterial, Abstract
Talented	Having a natural aptitude or skill in a particular area	प्रतिभाशाली/ प्रवीण	Gifted, Skilled, Capable	Untalented, Inept, Incompetent
Tamper	To interfere with or manipulate something without permission, especially in a harmful or unauthorised manner	छेड़छाड़/ हानिकारक हस्तक्षेप करना	Meddle, Interfere, Tinker	Respect, Adhere, Observe
Tariff	A tax or duty to be paid on a particular class of imports or exports; a schedule or system of rates or charges	शुल्क/महसूल	Duty, Levy, Tax	Exemption, Waiver, Deduction
Taunt	To provoke, mock, or insult someone with scornful or contemptuous remarks	आपत्तिजनक बातें/तिरस्कार	Mock, Ridicule, Tease	Praise, Compliment, Encourage
Teem	To be full or swarming with; to abound or overflow with	भरपूर होना/ उमड़ना	Swarm, Overflow, Thrive	Lack, Deplete, Empty
Temerity	Excessive confidence or boldness; audacity or recklessness	दिलेरी/बहुत साहसी होना	Boldness, Audacity, Impudence	Caution, Prudence, Timidity
Tepid	Lukewarm; showing little enthusiasm or passion	गुनगुना/ उत्साहहीन	Lukewarm, Indifferent, Halfhearted	Enthusiastic, Passionate, Fervent
Tether	A rope or chain with which an animal is tied to restrict its movement; to tie or fasten with a tether	सीमित करना/ रस्सी से बांधना	Restrain, Tie, Leash	Release, Free, Unleash

Word	Meaning in English	Meaning in Hindi	Synonyms	Antonyms
Theatrical	Relating to or characteristic of drama or theatre; excessively dramatic or exaggerated	रंगमंच संबंधी/थिएटरी	Dramatic, Theatric, Exaggerated	Natural, Genuine, Untheatrical
Thwart	To prevent someone from accomplishing something; to hinder or frustrate	बाधा डालना/रोकना	Hinder, Block, Obstruct	Aid, Assist, Facilitate
Tinge	A slight trace or hint of colour, flavour, or quality; to colour or affect slightly	सालना/रंग डालना	Tint, Shade, Slight	Remove, Erase, Clear
Topsy-turvy	In a state of confusion or disorder; upside down or in an inverted position	उलट-पुलट/उलट लटके	Disordered, Chaotic, Upside-down	Orderly, Organized, Systematic
Transfix	To cause someone to become motionless with awe, horror, or fascination; to pierce or impale with a sharp object	घायल कर देना/मोहित करना	Enthrall, Mesmerize, Stun	Release, Unfix, Unbind
Transitory	Lasting only for a short time; temporary or brief	अनित्य/अस्थायी	Temporary, Fleeting, Ephemeral	Permanent, Enduring, Everlasting
Tremor	A slight shaking or quivering movement; a trembling or shaking sensation	कंपन/कांप	Quiver, Shudder, Shake	Stability, Stillness, Calm
Trepidation	A feeling of fear or anxiety about something that may happen; apprehension or uneasiness	डर/घबराहट	Fear, Anxiety, Apprehension	Calmness, Courage, Confidence
Tribulation	A cause of great trouble or suffering; a state of distress or affliction	कष्ट/पीड़ा	Hardship, Adversity, Misery	Comfort, Ease, Happiness
Trite	Lacking originality or freshness; overused and consequently of little interest or impact	पुराना/घिसा-पिटा	Clichéd, Banal, Hackneyed	Original, Fresh, Innovative

Word	Meaning in English	Meaning in Hindi	Synonyms	Antonyms
Triumph	A great victory or success; the feeling or state of being victorious or successful	जीत/विजय	Victory, Success, Achievement	Defeat, Failure, Loss
Trivialize	To make something seem less important, significant, or complex than it actually is	हल्का समझना/ महत्त्वहीन ठहराना	Underestimate, Belittle, Minimise	Magnify, Emphasise, Highlight
Trove	A valuable collection or discovery of something; a treasure or store	खजाना/ बंदगिरत	Treasure, Collection, Cache	Loss, Depletion, Emptiness
Tumult	A loud, confused noise, especially caused by a large mass of people; a state of commotion or disorder	हड़बड़ी/ अशांति	Uproar, Commotion, Turmoil	Quiet, Calm, Serenity
Turmoil	A state of great disturbance, confusion, or uncertainty; chaos or upheaval	उथल-पुथल/ अशांति	Chaos, Disorder, Agitation	Order, Stability, Harmony
Tutelage	Protection, guidance, or instruction given by a mentor or guardian; the state of being under someone's guardianship	अध्यापन/ मार्गदर्शन	Guidance, Instruction, Mentorship	Neglect, Abandonment, Independence
Twig	A small, slender branch or shoot of a tree or bush	डंठल/टहनी	Branchlet, Sprig, Shoot	Trunk, Log, Stump
Tycoon	A wealthy and powerful business person or industrialist	उद्योगपति/ व्यापारी	Magnate, Mogul, Entrepreneur	Employee, Worker, Labourer
Taint	To contaminate or pollute something with a harmful or undesirable substance; to spoil or tarnish	दूषित करना/ मलिन करना	Contaminate, Pollute, Corrupt	Purify, Cleanse, Sanitize
Takeoff	The action of becoming airborne; the moment or process of leaving the ground during flight	उड़ान/उड़ान की शुरुआत	Departure, Lift-off, Launch	Landing, Arrival, Touchdown

Word	Meaning in English	Meaning in Hindi	Synonyms	Antonyms
Tangent	A straight line or plane that touches a curve or curved surface at a single point without intersecting it; a completely different or unrelated line of thought or action	स्पर्शवक्र/ आप्रत्यक्ष	Digression, Aside, Diversion	Direct, Connected, Relevant
Tardy	Delayed or late in happening or arriving; slow to act or respond	विलंबित/धीमा	Late, Delayed, Behind schedule	Punctual, Prompt, Early
Tarantula	A large, hairy spider found chiefly in tropical and subtropical regions	तरंगुला	Spider, Arachnid, Insect	-
Tease	To playfully make fun of someone or provoke them with light or playful remarks; to deliberately provoke or irritate	छेड़ना/ उलझाना	Mock, Taunt, Ridicule	Compliment, Encourage, Support
Tempest	A violent windy storm with strong winds and usually accompanied by rain, hail, or snow; a tumultuous or chaotic situation	आंधी/विप्लव	Storm, Cyclone, Tornado	Calm, Serenity, Peace
Tender	Showing gentleness, kindness, or affection; easily hurt or damaged; to offer or present something formally	कोमल/सौम्य	Gentle, Soft, Affectionate	Harsh, Rough, Callous
Tentative	Not certain or fixed; done without confidence; hesitant or uncertain	परोक्ष/अनिश्चित	Provisional, Experimental, Uncertain	Definite, Confident, Assured
Thaw	To become liquid or soft as a result of warming; to unfreeze or melt; to become more relaxed or friendly	पिघलाना/ पिघलाने का कार्य	Melt, Defrost, Unfreeze	Freeze, Solidify, Chill
Thirst	A strong desire or craving for something; a feeling of needing or wanting to drink	प्यास/तृष्णा	Craving, Longing, Desire	Satisfaction, Quenching, Fulfilment

Word	Meaning in English	Meaning in Hindi	Synonyms	Antonyms
Tickle	To touch or stroke someone lightly in a way that causes tingling or laughter; to amuse or entertain someone	गुदगुदाना/हंसी उड़ाना	Amuse, Entertain, Titillate	Bore, Sadden, Displease
Timely	Done or occurring at the right or proper time; well-timed; opportune	समयिक/समय पर	Punctual, Prompt, Well-timed	Late, Delayed, Untimely
Toil	Hard and continuous work; to work extremely hard or laboriously	कठिन मेहनत/ कठिनाई से काम करना	Labor, Work, Effort	Relax, Rest, Idle
Tonic	A medicinal substance that invigorates or strengthens; a refreshing or invigorating drink; something that gives a feeling of vigour or well-being	टॉनिक/ ताजगीदार पेय	Invigorating, Stimulating, Restorative	Depressing, Dulling, Weakening
Topple	To overbalance or cause to fall over; to remove from a position of power or authority	गिराना/खड़ा करना	Overturn, Collapse, Tumble	Stabilise, Establish, Support
Torrent	A strong and fast-moving stream of water or other liquid; a sudden, overwhelming outpouring of something	बाढ़/तेज धारा	Deluge, Flood, Rush	Trickle, Dribble, Drip
Toss	To throw something lightly or casually; to move or flip something with a quick or sudden motion	फेंकना/फेंक	Throw, Fling, Hurl	Catch, Retrieve, Keep
Traverse	To travel or move across or through an area; to cross over or through something	तर्क करना/पार करना	Cross, Travel, Navigate	Stay, Remain, Stand
Testify	To give evidence or make a statement based on personal knowledge or experience, typically in a legal or formal setting.	गवाही देना	Declare, Attest, Witness	Refute, Deny, Disclaim

Word	Meaning in English	Meaning in Hindi	Synonyms	Antonyms
Thrifty	Practising economy and frugality in the use of resources, especially money; showing careful management of finances.	टिकाऊ	Economical, Frugal, Prudent	Wasteful, Extravagant, Prodigal
Tinsel	Shiny, metallic material used for decoration, often resembling thin strips or threads.	चमकीली चीज़	Sparkle, Glitter, Luster	Dullness, Matte, Subdued
		U		
Ubiquitous	Present, appearing, or found everywhere	सर्वव्यापक	Pervasive, Widespread, Omnipresent	Rare, Limited, Scarce
Ultimate	Being the best or most extreme example of its kind	परम	Supreme, Final, Last	Initial, Preliminary, Incomplete
Unanimous	Fully in agreement or sharing the same opinion	एकमत	Consensual, Unified, Concordant	Divided, Disagreeing, Conflicting
Unassuming	Modest or humble, not attracting attention	आत्मनिर्भर	Modest, Humble, Unpretentious	Arrogant, Conceited, Pretentious
Unattainable	Impossible to achieve or reach	प्राप्य नहीं	Inaccessible, Impossible, Unachievable	Attainable, Achievable, Obtainable
Unbeknownst	Without the knowledge of someone	अज्ञात रूप से	Unaware, Unknown, Ignorant	Known, Aware, Conscious
Unbridled	Uncontrolled, lacking restraint	अनियंत्रित	Unrestrained, Wild, Rampant	Controlled, Restrained, Moderate
Uncharted	Not yet mapped or surveyed	अनजाना	Unknown, Unexplored, Unmapped	Charted, Mapped, Explored
Uncompromising	Unwilling to make concessions or compromise	अड़ियल	Inflexible, Firm, Unyielding	Flexible, Accommodating, Compromising

Word	Meaning in English	Meaning in Hindi	Synonyms	Antonyms
Unconditional	Not subject to any conditions or limitations	निर्वाधिक	Absolute, Unrestricted, Unqualified	Conditional, Limited, Qualified
Unconventional	Not conforming to accepted or traditional standards	अपरंपरागत	Nonconformist, Quirky, Unorthodox	Conventional, Traditional, Standard
Undeniable	Cannot be denied or disputed	अविवाद्य	Irrefutable, Incontrovertible, Indisputable	Questionable, Doubtful, Debatable
Underestimate	To undervalue or underestimate the importance, size, or difficulty of something	अवमूल्यन करना	Underassess, Undervalue, Underrate	Overestimate, Overvalue, Exaggerate
Underlying	Fundamental, basic, or forming the basis of something	आधारभूत	Fundamental, Subsidiary, Implicit	Surface, Superficial, Overt
Understandable	Capable of being understood or comprehended	समझने योग्य	Comprehensible, Clear, Intelligible	Confusing, Incomprehensible, Unintelligible
Understated	Subtle or restrained in style or appearance	संयमित	Subdued, Modest, Unpretentious	Bold, Dramatic, Flashy
Undertake	Commit to or begin (a task, responsibility, etc.)	उठाना	Embark on, Assume, Engage in	Abandon, Neglect, Shirk
Undisclosed	Not made known or revealed	अप्रकट	Secret, Hidden, Confidential	Revealed, Disclosed, Open
Undulate	Move with a smooth wavelike motion	लहराना	Ripple, Wave, Oscillate	Straighten, Flatten, Stabilise
Unearth	Discover or dig up something from the ground	उखाड़ना	Excavate, Uncover, Expose	Bury, Cover, Conceal
Unequivocal	Leaving no doubt, clear and unambiguous	निश्चित	Definite, Unambiguous, Explicit	Ambiguous, Vague, Uncertain
Unflappable	Calm and composed, not easily upset or excited	स्थिर	Imperturbable, Cool-headed, Collected	Nervous, Agitated, Flustered

Word	Meaning in English	Meaning in Hindi	Synonyms	Antonyms
Unforeseen	Not anticipated or expected	अप्रत्याशित	Unexpected, Unpredicted, Unanticipated	Foreseen, Expected, Predicted
Unfurl	Unroll, unfold, or spread out (something, like a flag)	खोलना	Unroll, Unwind, Expand	Roll up, Fold, Contract
Unison	Simultaneous action, agreement, or harmony	एकता	Harmony, Accord, Agreement	Discord, Disagreement, Disharmony
Unyielding	Firm, resolute, or not giving way to pressure	अड़ियल	Inflexible, Firm, Steadfast	Flexible, Yielding, Accommodating
Unanimity	Complete agreement or consensus among a group	सर्वसम्मति	Consensus, Accord, Unity	Dissent, Disagreement, Discord
Unabridged	Not shortened, condensed, or reduced	अदूर	Complete, Full, Uncut	Abridged, Condensed, Shortened
Unwind	Relax, loosen, or undo something that is wound up	धीमा होना	Relax, Unravel, Decompress	Tense, Wind up, Stress
Unique	One of a kind, unlike anything else	अद्वितीय	Distinctive, Singular, Exclusive	Common, Ordinary, Typical
Universal	Applicable or common to all cases or situations	सार्वभौमिक	Global, General, Comprehensive	Specific, Limited, Particular
		V		
Vacant	Not occupied or filled; available for use	रिक्त	Empty, Unoccupied, Vacated	Occupied, Filled, Inhabited
Vacate	To leave, give up, or abandon a place, position, or role	खाली करना	Evacuate, Abandon, Relinquish	Occupy, Fill, Retain
Vaccine	A substance used to stimulate the immune system and provide immunity against diseases	टीका	Immunisation, Inoculation, Shot	Disease, Infection, Vulnerability
Vacillate	To hesitate or be indecisive in making a choice or decision	दुविधा में होना	Waver, Fluctuate, Oscillate	Decide, Determine, Resolve

Word	Meaning in English	Meaning in Hindi	Synonyms	Antonyms
Vague	Not clear, definite, or precise; uncertain or unclear	अस्पष्ट	Indefinite, Ambiguous, Unclear	Clear, Definite, Specific
Valediction	The act of saying farewell or bidding goodbye	विदाई	Farewell, Goodbye, Parting	Greeting, Welcome, Arrival
Validate	To confirm, approve, or prove the truth, accuracy, or validity of something	पुष्टि करना	Confirm, Verify, Authenticate	Invalidate, Disapprove, Refute
Valiant	Brave, courageous, or showing valour	बहादुर	Brave, Courageous, Heroic	Cowardly, Timid, Fearful
Validity	The quality of being logical, sound, or legally binding; the state of being valid	वैधता	Legitimacy, Authenticity, Credibility	Invalidity, Inaccuracy, Illegitimacy
Valuable	Having great worth, importance, or usefulness; precious or highly esteemed	मूल्यवान	Precious, Priceless, Invaluable	Worthless, Insignificant, Disposable
Vanish	To disappear suddenly or cease to be visible	लापता होना	Disappear, Fade, Evaporate	Appear, Materialise, Reveal
Vanity	Excessive pride in one's appearance, achievements, or abilities; self-admiration	अहंकार	Ego, Conceit, Narcissism	Humility, Modesty, Simplicity
Vaporize	To convert or turn into vapor (gas) by heating or spraying	वाष्पीकरण करना	Evaporate, Dissipate, Sublimate	Condense, Solidify, Liquidize
Variable	Not consistent or having a fixed pattern; liable to change or vary	परिवर्तनशील	Changeable, Inconstant, Mutable	Constant, Fixed, Stable
Variation	A change or difference in condition, amount, or level, often within a certain range	विविधता	Fluctuation, Deviation, Diversity	Uniformity, Consistency, Sameness
Varied	Having or consisting of many different types, forms, or elements; diverse	विविध	Diverse, Multifarious, Assorted	Uniform, Monotonous, Unvaried
Variegated	Having different colours, markings, or patterns; diverse or varied	बहुरंगी	Multicolored, Motley, Dappled	Monochromatic, Uniform, Plain

Word	Meaning in English	Meaning in Hindi	Synonyms	Antonyms
Vast	Very great in size, extent, or quantity; immense or enormous	विशाल	Huge, Massive, Extensive	Small, Tiny, Limited
Vault	A secure room or compartment, typically used for storing valuables or as a burial chamber	गुप्तग्रह	Safe, Strongroom, Repository	Open, Unprotected, Vulnerable
Venerate	To regard with deep respect, reverence, or admiration	पूज्य	Adore, Honor, Worship	Despise, Disrespect, Ignore
Vengeance	Punishment or harm inflicted in retaliation for a perceived wrong or injury	प्रतिशोध	Revenge, Retribution, Retaliation	Forgiveness, Pardon, Mercy
Veracity	The quality of being truthful, honest, or accurate	सत्यनिष्ठा	Truthfulness, Authenticity, Sincerity	Falsehood, Deception, Dishonesty
Verbose	Using or containing more words than needed; excessively wordy	बातचीती	Wordy, Talkative, Prolix	Concise, Succinct, Terse
Verdict	A formal decision or judgement given by a court or jury in a legal case	फैसला	Judgement, Decision, Ruling	Acquittal, Release, Discharge
Verdant	Green with vegetation; covered in lush greenery	हरियाली भरा हुआ	Green, Leafy, Luxuriant	Barren, Desolate, Arid
Verify	To confirm the truth, accuracy, or validity of something	सत्यापित करना	Confirm, Validate, Authenticate	Disprove, Refute, Invalidate
Vernacular	The language or dialect spoken by the ordinary people in a particular country or region	लोकभाषा	Dialect, Jargon, Slang	Standard, Formal, Official
Versatile	Able to adapt or be adapted to many different functions, activities, or roles	बहुमुखी	Adaptable, Flexible, Multifaceted	Inflexible, Limited, Specialized
Version	A particular form or variant of something, typically different from the original	संस्करण	Edition, Variation, Adaptation	Original, Unchanged, Standard

Word	Meaning in English	Meaning in Hindi	Synonyms	Antonyms
Vertical	Perpendicular to the plane of the horizon; upright or straight up and down	लंबकारी	Upright, Plumb, Perpendicular	Horizontal, Slanted, Diagonal
Vestige	A trace, mark, or visible sign left behind by something that no longer exists or is lost	अवशेष	Remnant, Trace, Relic	Whole, Entirety, Absence
Vex	To irritate, annoy, or bother someone persistently	परेशान करना	Annoy, Irritate, Aggravate	Soothe, Pacify, Delight
Vibrant	Full of energy, enthusiasm, and life; bright and striking	जीवंत	Lively, Energetic, Dynamic	Dull, Lifeless, Muted
Vice versa	With the main items in a preceding statement exchanged in order	उल्टा सोचो	Reversed, Inverted, Reciprocally	Unchanged, Unswapped, As before
Vicinity	The area near or surrounding a particular place; the neighbourhood	पड़ोस	Proximity, Nearness, Surroundings	Distance, Far-off, Remote
Victorious	Having achieved victory or success; triumphant	विजयी	Triumphant, Winning, Conquering	Defeated, Unsuccessful, Losing
Viewpoint	A particular way of looking at or thinking about something; a perspective	दृष्टिकोण	Perspective, Standpoint, Opinion	Bias, Prejudice, Close-mindedness
Vigilant	Watchful, alert, and attentive to detect and avoid danger or trouble	सतर्क	Alert, Watchful, Attentive	Careless, Inattentive, Negligent
Vigorous	Strong, healthy, and full of energy and vitality; characterised by physical or mental strength	प्रबल	Energetic, Robust, Dynamic	Weak, Feeble, Lethargic
Vindicate	To clear someone from blame, suspicion, or doubt; to prove or justify	समर्थित करना	Justify, Clear, Absolve	Condemn, Blame, Accuse
Vintage	Denoting something from the past of high quality and enduring interest; classic or old-fashioned	पुराना और मूल्यवान	Classic, Retro, Antique	Modern, Contemporary, New

Word	Meaning in English	Meaning in Hindi	Synonyms	Antonyms
Violate	To disregard or break a law, rule, agreement, or principle; to infringe or trespass	उल्लंघन करना	Infringe, Transgress, Breach	Observe, Follow, Comply with
Violent	Involving or characterised by physical force intended to cause harm, damage, or destruction	हिंसात्मक	Aggressive, Fierce, Brutal	Peaceful, Gentle, Nonviolent
Virulent	Extremely severe or harmful in its effects; highly infectious or poisonous	विषैला	Toxic, Deadly, Lethal	Harmless, Benign, Mild
Visible	Able to be seen; perceptible to the eye or within sight	दृश्य	Apparent, Observable, Clear	Invisible, Hidden, Concealed
Visionary	Having or showing clear ideas and plans about what the future should be like; imaginative and forward-thinking	कल्पनाशील	Imaginative, Innovative, Creative	Practical, Realistic, Conventional
Vital	Absolutely necessary or essential; full of energy, vigour, or life	महत्वपूर्ण	Essential, Crucial, Fundamental	Insignificant, Trivial, Nonessential
Vivacious	Lively, animated, and full of enthusiasm and energy	जीवंत	Energetic, Spirited, Bubbly	Dull, Lifeless, Lethargic
Vivid	Producing clear, strong, and detailed images or impressions in the mind; bright or intense in colour	जीवंत	Graphic, Striking, Colourful	Faded, Dull, Pale
Vocabulary	A set of words within a language known and used by a particular person or group	शब्दावली	Lexicon, Wordlist, Terminology	Silence, Inarticulateness, Nonverbal
Vociferous	Expressing feelings or opinions loudly and forcefully; vehement or clamorous	शोरमग्न	Noisy, Boisterous, Outspoken	Quiet, Soft-spoken, Muted
Void	Completely empty; having no legal force or effect; invalid or without value	शून्य	Empty, Vacant, Null	Filled, Occupied, Valid

Word	Meaning in English	Meaning in Hindi	Synonyms	Antonyms
Volatile	Easily evaporating at normal temperatures; liable to change rapidly and unpredictably	अस्थायी	Unstable, Unpredictable, Fickle	Stable, Steady, Consistent
Volition	The faculty or power of using one's will; the act of making a conscious choice or decision	स्वेच्छा	Will, Choice, Decision	Coercion, Compulsion, Obligation
Volley	A simultaneous discharge of a number of missiles or firearms; a rapid succession of something	वालीबाली	Barrage, Salvo, Burst	Single, Individual, Isolated
Volume	The amount of space that a substance or object occupies; a large quantity or number	आयतन	Capacity, Size, Amount	Scant, Minimal, Insufficient
Volunteer	A person who willingly offers to do something without being compelled or paid to do so	स्वयंसेवक	Helper, Contributor, Enthusiast	Recruit, Draftee, Obliged
Voracious	Having a huge appetite; excessively eager or avid in some desire or pursuit	भूखा	Ravenous, Insatiable, Greedy	Satisfied, Contented, Moderate
Vortex	A mass of whirling fluid or air, especially a whirlpool or whirlwind	घूर्णन	Whirlpool, Cyclone, Swirl	Calm, Stillness, Stability
Vouch	To give a guarantee, assurance, or support for someone or something; to confirm or authenticate	गारंटी देना	Attest, Confirm, Authenticate	Disclaim, Deny, Refute
Voyage	A long journey, especially by sea or in space; an adventurous or exciting trip	यात्रा	Journey, Expedition, Cruise	Stay, Halt, Stop
Vulnerable	Susceptible to physical or emotional harm, attack, or damage; easily influenced or harmed	आघातयोग्य	Defenceless, Exposed, Open	Invulnerable, Protected, Secure

Word	Meaning in English	Meaning in Hindi	Synonyms	Antonyms
Vulture	A large bird of prey that feeds primarily on carrion (dead animals)	गिद्ध	Scavenger, Predator, Carrion-eater	Prey, Herbivore, Innocent
Vulcanize	To treat (rubber or similar materials) with sulphur at a high temperature to improve elasticity and durability	वल्केनाईज़ करना	Harden, Strengthen, Temper	Soften, Weaken, Deteriorate
Ventilate	To provide fresh air and remove stale air from a space; to express or discuss (thoughts, opinions, etc.)	हवा देना	Air, Refresh, Discuss	Stifle, Suffocate, Suppress
Velocity	The speed of an object in a given direction; the rate of change of position	गति	Speed, Swiftness, Rapidity	Slowness, Crawl, Inactivity
Vindictive	Having or showing a strong desire for revenge; inclined to seek vengeance.	प्रतिशोधी	Revengeful, Spiteful, Retaliatory	Forgiving, Merciful, Benevolent
Vocation	A person's occupation or profession; a strong inclination or calling to pursue a particular career or line of work.	व्यवसाय	Profession, Occupation, Calling	Avocation, Hobby, Pastime
		W		
Waffle	A batter cake with deep grids or impressions on both sides, typically eaten with syrup or fruit.	वॉफल	Pancake, Griddlecake, Flapjack	None
Wagon	A four-wheeled vehicle for transporting heavy goods or passengers, usually pulled by horses or oxen.	वैगन	Cart, Carriage, Trolley	None
Waitress	A woman who serves food and drinks to customers in a restaurant.	वेट्रेस	Server, Attendant, Hostess	None

Word	Meaning in English	Meaning in Hindi	Synonyms	Antonyms
War	A state of armed conflict between different nations or states or different groups within a nation or state.	युद्ध	Conflict, Battle, Warfare	Peace, Harmony, Truce
Wardrobe	A large, tall cupboard or cabinet typically used for storing clothes.	अलमारी	Closet, Armoire, Cupboard	None
Warehouse	A large building where raw materials or manufactured goods may be stored before their distribution for sale.	गोदाम	Storage, Depot, Repository	None
Warmth	A quality or state of being warm in temperature or feeling.	गर्मी	Heat, Hotness, Warmness	Coldness, Chilliness, Coolness
Warning	A statement or event that indicates a possible danger, problem, or other negative situation.	चेतावनी	Alert, Caution, Notice	None
Warrior	A brave and experienced soldier or fighter.	योद्धा	Fighter, Soldier, Gladiator	Pacifist, Coward, Noncombatant
Watch	To observe or keep under surveillance.	देखना	Observe, Monitor, Survey	Ignore, Neglect, Disregard
Wave	A long body of water curling into an arched form and breaking on the shore.	लहर	Ripple, Surge, Billow	Calm, Stillness, Serenity
Wealth	An abundance of valuable possessions or money.	धन	Riches, Fortune, Prosperity	Poverty, Destitution, Lack
Weather	The state of the atmosphere at a particular place and time, with regard to temperature, precipitation, and other factors.	मौसम	Climate, Conditions, Atmosphere	None
Wedding	A ceremony in which two people are united in marriage.	विवाह	Marriage, Nuptials, Matrimony	Divorce, Separation, Dissolution

Word	Meaning in English	Meaning in Hindi	Synonyms	Antonyms
Web	A complex system of interconnected elements, especially one perceived as a trap or danger.	जाल	Network, Mesh, Net	Freedom, Independence, Disconnection
Weight	The amount or quantity of heaviness of an object or person.	वजन	Mass, Load, Burden	Lightness, Unburden, Weightlessness
Welcome	To greet or receive someone with pleasure or kindness.	स्वागत	Greet, Embrace, Receive	Farewell, Reject, Exclude
Welfare	The health, happiness, and well-being of an individual or a group.	कल्याण	Well-being, Prosperity, Benefit	Suffering, Misery, Disadvantage
West	The direction toward which the sun sets, opposite to the east.	पश्चिम	Occident, Sunset, Western	East, Orient, Sunrise
Whisk	To move or take something or someone quickly and suddenly.	झटका	Dart, Sweep, Flick	Slow, Delay, Stay
Whisper	To speak or say something very quietly, using one's breath rather than one's throat.	फुसफुसाहट	Murmur, Mumble, Hush	Shout, Yell, Roar
White	The colour of milk or fresh snow, the opposite of black.	सफेद	Ivory, Snowy, Pure	Black, Dark, Colored
Wicked	Evil or morally wrong; intending to harm or cause trouble.	दुष्ट	Evil, Sinister, Malevolent	Virtuous, Righteous, Moral
Wide	Measuring a great distance from side to side; broad.	चौड़ा	Broad, Spacious, Expansive	Narrow, Limited, Restricted
Wife	A married woman considered in relation to her spouse.	पत्नी	Spouse, Consort, Partner	Husband, Bachelor, Single
Wild	Living or growing in natural conditions; not domesticated or cultivated.	जंगली	Untamed, Feral, Savage	Tame, Domesticated, Cultivated

Word	Meaning in English	Meaning in Hindi	Synonyms	Antonyms
Win	To be successful or victorious in a contest or competition.	जीतना	Triumph, Succeed, Conquer	Lose, Fail, Surrender
Wisdom	The quality of having experience, knowledge, and good judgement.	ज्ञान	Knowledge, Insight, Understanding	Ignorance, Foolishness, Stupidity
Wise	Having or showing experience, knowledge, and good judgement.	बुद्धिमान	Intelligent, Sagacious, Prudent	Foolish, Ignorant, Unwise
Withdraw	To remove or take back (something) from a particular place or situation.	वापस लेना	Retract, Remove, Extract	Deposit, Add, Insert
Witness	A person who sees an event, typically a crime or accident, take place.	साक्षी	Observer, Spectator, Onlooker	Participant, Actor, Perpetrator
Witty	Showing quick and inventive verbal humour.	विनोदी	Clever, Humorous, Amusing	Dull, Boring, Unfunny
Wizard	A person who has magical powers, especially in legends and fairy tales.	जादूगर	Magician, Sorcerer, Enchanter	Muggle, Nonmagician, Mundane
Wonder	A feeling of surprise and admiration caused by something beautiful, unexpected, or unfamiliar.	हैरानी	Amazement, Astonishment, Marvel	Indifference, Disinterest, Apathy
Wool	The soft, thick hair that grows on the bodies of sheep and some other animals.	ऊन	Fleece, Fiber, Yarn	Synthetic, Artificial, Polyester
Worry	To feel or cause to feel anxious or troubled about actual or potential problems.	चिंता	Anxiety, Concern, Distress	Calm, Serenity, Tranquility
Worth	The value equivalent to that of someone or something under consideration.	मूल्य	Value, Merit, Importance	Worthlessness, Insignificance, Irrelevance

Word	Meaning in English	Meaning in Hindi	Synonyms	Antonyms
Wound	An injury to living tissue, typically caused by a cut, blow, or other impact.	घाव	Injury, Trauma, Lesion	Heal, Cure, Recovery
Wrap	To cover or enclose (someone or something) in paper or soft material.	लपेटना	Enclose, Envelop, Package	Unwrap, Uncover, Unfold
Wrath	Extreme anger.	क्रोध	Anger, Rage, Fury	Calmness, Serenity, Patience
Wreck	The remains of something that has been severely damaged or destroyed.	तबाही	Ruin, Destruction, Devastation	Construction, Restoration, Repair
Writer	A person who has written a particular text or piece of literature.	लेखक	Author, Novelist, Scribe	Reader, Audience, Listener
Wrought	Beaten out or shaped by hammering.	बनाना	Forged, Created, Fashioned	Unformed, Shapeless, Rough
Wry	Using or expressing dry, especially mocking, humour.	तिरछा	Sarcastic, Cynical, Ironical	Straight, Direct, Genuine
Waddle	To walk with short steps and a clumsy swaying motion.	टेढ़ा चलना	Wobble, Shuffle, Hobble	Stride, March, Glide
Wager	To risk something, usually money, on the outcome of an uncertain event.	दांव	Bet, Gamble, Stake	Guarantee, Assure, Protect
Wake	To emerge or cause to emerge from a state of sleep.	जागरूक होना	Awake, Arise, Stir	Sleep, Slumber, Rest
Wallet	A small, flat pocket-sized folding case for holding money and plastic cards.	बटुआ	Purse, Billfold, Money holder	None
Wander	To travel or move around without a specific destination or purpose	भटकना	Roam, Explore, Drift	Stay, Settle, Remain
		X		
Xenophobia	Fear or hatred of foreigners or strangers.	जाति भेदवाद	Prejudice, Discrimination, Racism	Acceptance, Tolerance, Inclusiveness

Word	Meaning in English	Meaning in Hindi	Synonyms	Antonyms
Xylophone	A musical instrument consisting of a row of wooden bars of different lengths that are struck with mallets to produce musical notes.	संगीतयंत्र	Marimba, Glockenspiel, Vibraphone	None
X-ray	A form of electromagnetic radiation that can penetrate solid objects and is used in various applications, especially for medical imaging.	एक्स-रे	Radiograph, Roentgenogram, Radiogram	None
Xerophyte	A plant that is adapted to survive in dry conditions, typically having specialised structures to conserve water.	सूखे के लिए योग्य पौधा	Desert plant, Drought-resistant plant, Succulent	Hydrophyte, Aquatic plant, Moisture-loving plant
Xenon	A chemical element of the noble gas group, used in various lighting applications and in certain types of lasers.	जेनॉन	None	None
Xylography	The art or technique of printing from wooden blocks, especially for illustrations or designs.	लकड़ी की छापाई	Woodcut, Wood engraving, Xylograph	None
Xenolith	A rock fragment that becomes enclosed in a larger rock during the latter's development and solidification.	शास्त्रीय पर्वतावशेष	Inclusion, Enclave, Fragment	None
Xanthic	Relating to a yellow colour or a substance with yellow pigmentation.	पीला	Yellowish, Golden, Amber	None
Xyloid	Resembling or relating to wood; woody in nature.	लकड़ीजैसा	Woody, Timber-like, Lignified	None
Xenophile	A person who is attracted to or has a strong liking for foreign cultures, people, or customs.	परदेशी प्रेमी	Cosmopolitan, Enthusiast, Globalist	Xenophobe, Chauvinist, Nationalist

Word	Meaning in English	Meaning in Hindi	Synonyms	Antonyms
Xylograph	A wood engraving, especially one used in printing illustrations or designs.	लकड़ी की छाप	Xylography, Woodcut, Engraving	None
Xylophonic	Pertaining to or produced by a xylophone.	ज्यान्त्रिक	None	None
Xylotomy	The study or practice of cutting or preparing wood for various purposes.	लकड़ी की छेदन-भेदन	Woodworking, Timber cutting, Lumbering	None
Xylophobia	The fear or aversion to wood or wooden objects.	लकड़ी से डर	None	None
Xerography	A dry photocopying technique that uses electrostatic principles to reproduce images and text.	क्षरिकोपी	Photocopying, Electrostatic copying, Copying	None
Xenograft	Tissue or organ graft taken from one individual and transplanted to another of a different species.	जीवदान	Heterograft, Cross-graft, Allotransplantation	None
Xylose	A sugar derived from wood, straw, or other plant materials.	जटिल शर्करा	None	None
Xyster	A surgical instrument used for scraping bones, especially during surgery or dissection.	हड्डी की छिलाने के लिए सर्जिकल उपकरण	Bone scraper, Osteotome, Surgical instrument	None
Xerarch	Relating to a plant succession in a dry environment, usually starting with xerophytes.	सूखी पर्यावरण में पौधों के अनुक्रम	Dry succession, Xeric succession, Arid succession	None
Xylenol	Any of several isomeric phenols derived from xylene, used in the production of resins, solvents, and disinfectants.	जटिल वस्त्र या दूसरे वस्त्रों की सफाई के लिए विशेष या सामान्यतः इस्तेमाल होने वाला खांड	None	None

Word	Meaning in English	Meaning in Hindi	Synonyms	Antonyms
Xerostomia	Abnormal dryness of the mouth caused by a reduced flow of saliva.	मुँह की सूखापन	Dry mouth, Cottonmouth, Hyposalivation	Salivary hypersecretion, Ptyalism, Hypersalivation
Xiphias	A genus of large, fast-swimming marine fish known as swordfish.	कटार मछली	Swordfish, Broadbill, Marlin	None
		Y		
Yearn	To have an intense longing or desire for something.	आकांक्षा करना	Crave, Desire, Long	Reject, Dislike, Detest
Yacht	A recreational boat or ship used for pleasure or racing.	याच्ट	Boat, Vessel, Cruiser	Dock, Shore, Land
Yield	To produce or provide a result, profit, or amount.	प्राप्त करना	Generate, Produce, Bear	Resist, Withhold, Refuse
Yawn	To open one's mouth wide and take a deep breath involuntarily, often when tired or bored.	जमकर यातना से साँस लेना	Gape, Inhale, Sigh	Close, Refrain, Suppress
Yodel	To sing with a rapid change of pitch between the normal voice and falsetto.	योडल	Sing, Chant, Vocalize	Whisper, Mumble, Murmur
Yonder	At or in that indicated place; over there.	वहाँ	There, Far, Distant	Here, Nearby, Close
Yarn	Spun thread used for knitting, weaving, or sewing.	धागा	Thread, Fiber, Strand	Fabric, Material, Textile
Yule	Christmas or the Christmas season, especially as traditionally celebrated in Northern Europe.	यूल	Christmas, Yuletide, Noel	Non-festive, Ordinary, Regular
Youth	The period between childhood and adulthood; the state or quality of being young.	युवा	Youngness, Adolescence, Teenage	Elderly, Old age, Maturity
Yielding	Tending to give in or surrender; compliant, submissive.	आज्ञाकारी	Submissive, Pliant, Obedient	Resistant, Defiant, Inflexible

Word	Meaning in English	Meaning in Hindi	Synonyms	Antonyms
Yoke	A wooden crosspiece that is fastened over the necks of two animals and attached to the plough or cart they are to pull.	युगल	Harness, Coupling, Link	Detach, Separate, Disconnect
Yearning	A feeling of intense longing or desire.	आकांक्षा	Longing, Craving, Desire	Apathy, Indifference, Disinterest
Yards	Units of linear measurement equal to 3 feet or 0.9144 metres.	गज	Feet, Metres, Length	Inches, Centimetres, Shortness
Yesteryear	The past, especially the recent past.	पिछले वर्षों	Past, History, Bygone days	Present, Future, Tomorrow
Yummy-licious	Extremely delicious or tasty.	स्वादिष्ट	Delectable, Scrumptious, Mouthwatering	Tasteless, Unappetizing, Disgusting
Yardsman	A person who works in or operates a yard, especially a railway yard or shipyard.	यार्डस्मान	Worker, Labourer, Operator	Supervisor, Manager, Executive
Yeast	A microscopic fungus that converts sugar into alcohol and carbon dioxide, used in brewing and baking.	खमीर	Ferment, Leaven, Barm	Antiseptic, Sterilize, Disinfect
Yearbook	A book published annually that chronicles the events and achievements of a particular organisation or group during the previous year.	वार्षिकी	Annual, Almanac, Chronicle	Fiction, Novel, Fantasy
Yachtsman	A person who sails or owns a yacht, especially one who participates in yacht racing.	याच्टस्मान	Sailor, Boater, Skipper	Non-sailor, Landlubber, Non-participant
Yank	To pull forcefully or abruptly.	झटका देना	Pull, Jerk, Tug	Push, Release, Let go
Yarmulke	A skullcap worn by Jewish men, typically as a sign of religious devotion.	यारमुलके	Kippah, Skullcap, Head covering	None

Word	Meaning in English	Meaning in Hindi	Synonyms	Antonyms
Yapper	A dog that barks sharply and frequently.	भौंकने वाला कुत्ता	Barker, Noisemaker, Barking dog	Quiet dog, Silent, Mute
Yak	A large, shaggy-haired wild ox native to the Himalayas and Tibet.	याक	Ox, Bison, Buffalo	None
Youngster	A young person, typically a child or teenager.	बच्चा/युवा	Child, Teenager, Adolescent	Adult, Elder, Senior
Yell	To shout or scream loudly, typically in anger or fear.	चिल्लाना	Shout, Scream, Cry out	Whisper, Mumble, Speak softly
Youthful	Having the characteristics or appearance of youth; young-looking.	जवां	Young, Juvenile, Fresh-faced	Aged, Old, Mature
Yesternight	The night before the present day; last night.	गतरात्रि	Last night, Yesterday night, Prior night	Tonight, Next night, Future night
Yuk	An expression or sound indicating disgust or aversion.	बहुत बुरा लगना	Disgust, Revulsion, Aversion	Pleasure, Delight, Like
Yonker	A young man or boy; a youth.	युवक	Youngster, Lad, Youth	Elder, Adult, Senior
Yogi	A person who practises yoga or follows the philosophy of yoga.	योगी	Yogin, Meditator, Ascetic	Non-yogi, Non-meditator, Non-ascetic
Yawp	To utter a loud, harsh cry or shout; to yelp or squawk.	चीख़	Shout, Yell, Scream	Whisper, Mumble, Murmur
Yielder	A person or thing that yields or gives in; someone who surrenders or concedes.	हार माननेवाला (haar mannevala)	Surrenderer, Conceder, Submitter	Résister, Opposer, Defiant
Youngish	Fairly young; still in the earlier stages of life or youth.	जवान	Youthful, Junior, Adolescent	Elderly, Mature, Aged
Yodeller	A singer who uses a rapid change of pitch between the normal voice and falsetto, typically in traditional Swiss mountain music.	योडलर	Singer, Vocalist, Entertainer	None

Word	Meaning in English	Meaning in Hindi	Synonyms	Antonyms
Yelper	A person or animal that yelps; someone who makes high-pitched, sharp cries.	चीख़नेवाला	Shrieker, Cryer, Howler	Mute, Silent, Quiet
Youthfulness	The quality or state of being youthful; the characteristics or appearance of youth.	युवावस्था	Youngness, Adolescence, Juvenility	Elderliness, Maturity, Old age
Yips	A nervous condition causing a golfer to fail to strike the ball cleanly.	बाएँ-दाएँ	Jitters, Nerves, Anxiety	Calmness, Composure, Confidence
Yeasty	Having or resembling the qualities of yeast; foamy, frothy, or fermenting.	खमीरी	Fermenting, Foamy, Bubbly	Settled, Calm, Stable
		Z		
Zany	Comical, clownish, or eccentric in an amusing way.	विचित्र	Comical, Wacky, Eccentric	Serious, Sane, Rational
Zenith	The highest point or culmination; the peak or apex.	शिखर	Pinnacle, Summit, Acme	Nadir, Bottom, Low point
Zeal	Great enthusiasm or passion for a cause or goal.	उत्साह	Enthusiasm, Eagerness, Fervour	Apathy, Indifference, Lethargy
Zest	Great enthusiasm, energy, or excitement.	उत्साह	Enthusiasm, Gusto, Vigor	Apathy, Indifference, Lethargy
Zealous	Showing great passion, enthusiasm, or fervour for a cause.	उत्साही	Enthusiastic, Fervent, Dedicated	Apathetic, Indifferent, Unenthusiastic
Zephyr	A gentle, mild breeze; a soft, refreshing wind.	हल्की हवा (halki hawa)	Breeze, Gust, Air	Gale, Storm, Hurricane
Zestful	Full of energy, enthusiasm, and liveliness.	उत्साहपूर्ण	Energetic, Lively, Dynamic	Lethargic, Dull, Apathetic
Zigzag	A line or course that moves in sharp, alternating diagonal directions.	झुकावटदार	Crisscross, Winding, Meandering	Straight, Direct, Linear

Word	Meaning in English	Meaning in Hindi	Synonyms	Antonyms
Zircon	A gemstone that is often used as a substitute for diamond.	ज़िरकॉन	Diamond substitute, Substitute gem, Synthetic gem	Diamond, Precious stone, Natural gem
Zoology	The scientific study of animals, their behaviour, classification, and characteristics.	प्राणी विज्ञान	Animal biology, Animal science, Animal study	Botany, Plant science, Plant study
Zestfully	With great enthusiasm, energy, or enjoyment.	उत्साहपूर्वक	Energetically, Enthusiastically, Vivaciously	Lethargically, Indifferently, Halfheartedly
Zodiac	A belt or circle of the celestial sphere divided into twelve equal parts, each named after a constellation.	राशि चक्र	Horoscope, Astrological sign, Celestial zodiac	- none
Zen	A school of Mahayana Buddhism that emphasises meditation and intuition to attain enlightenment.	ध्यान	Meditation, Contemplation, Serenity	Distraction, Restlessness, Chaos
Zestiness	The quality of being lively, spirited, or full of flavour.	जीवंतता	Vivacity, Spirit, Gusto	Dullness, Lethargy, Blandness
Zonal	Relating to or divided into zones, areas, or regions.	क्षेत्रीय	Regional, Sectorial, Area-based	Global, Universal, Non-specific
Zanyish	Resembling or characteristic of a zany; clownish or eccentric in a humorous way.	विचित्रपूर्ण	Quirky, Eccentric, Comical	Serious, Sober, Sane
Zealot	A person who is fanatically dedicated to a cause, belief, or ideology.	पक्षपाती	Fanatic, Enthusiast, Radical	Moderate, Indifferent, Nonpartisan
Zipper	A fastening device consisting of two strips of fabric with interlocking metal or plastic teeth.	ज़िप	Fastener, Closure, Clasp	Opening, Unfastening, Unzipping
Zoom	To move or travel quickly with a buzzing or humming sound.	तेज़ी से चलना	Speed, Rush, Hurtle	Crawl, Creep, Slow down

Word	Meaning in English	Meaning in Hindi	Synonyms	Antonyms
Zygote	The initial cell formed by the fusion of sperm and egg, from which an organism develops.	जीवाणु	Fertilised egg, Embryo, Germ cell	- none
Zippy	Full of energy, lively, or quick.	जलदबाज़	Energetic, Spirited, Dynamic	Slow, Sluggish, Lethargic
Zootomy	The dissection or study of the anatomy of animals.	प्राणिरचना विज्ञान	Animal anatomy, Animal dissection, Comparative anatomy	- none
Zestily	With great enthusiasm, energy, or flavour.	उत्साहपूर्वक	Energetically, Enthusiastically, Vigorously	Lethargically, Indifferently, Halfheartedly
Zoologist	A person who studies animals and their behaviour, classification, and distribution.	प्राणिविज्ञानी	Animal biologist, Animal scientist, Animal expert	- none
Zealously	With great passion, enthusiasm, or fervour.	उत्साहपूर्वक	Eagerly, Fervently, Dedicatedly	Indifferently, Apathetically, Halfheartedly
Zooty	Stylish, fashionable, or extravagant in dress or appearance.	फ़ैशनेबल	Dapper, Snazzy, Trendy	Shabby, Plain, Unfashionable
Zoon	An animal belonging to a particular region or time period.	प्राणी	Animal, Creature, Beast	Human, Plant, Inanimate
Zither	A musical instrument consisting of a flat wooden soundboard with strings stretched across it.	ज़िथर	String instrument, Harp, Lyre	- none
Zafu	A small round cushion used for meditation, typically filled with buckwheat hulls.	ज़ाफ़ू	Meditation cushion, Zen cushion, Yoga pillow	-none
Zill	A small metallic finger cymbal used in belly dancing or as a percussion instrument.	ज़िल	Finger cymbal, Jingling cymbal, Ghungroo	- none

Word	Meaning in English	Meaning in Hindi	Synonyms	Antonyms
Zho	A colloquial term for the Chinese language.	चाइनीज़ भाषा	Chinese, Mandarin, Cantonese	-none
Zoogeography	The study of the geographic distribution of animal species.	प्राणी विज्ञानी भूगोल	Animal geography, Faunal geography, Biogeography	- none
Zeitgeist	The general intellectual, moral, and cultural climate of a particular period.	युग-चेतना	Spirit of the age, Cultural atmosphere, Collective consciousness	-
Zip	To move or close with speed or force.	ज़िप	Fasten, Close, Secure	Unzip, Open, Release
Zoster	A viral infection characterised by a painful rash with blisters, also known as shingles.	जोस्टर	Shingles, Herpes zoster, Varicella zoster	None
Zinc	A chemical element with the symbol "Zn," often used as a protective coating or dietary supplement.	ज़िंक	Metallic element, Galvanised metal, Zinc oxide	None
Zibeline	A thick, soft, lustrous fabric made from the fur of the sable or marten.	ज़िबेलिन	Sable fur, Marten fur, Faux fur	None
Zygoma	The bony arch of the cheekbone that forms the prominence of the cheek.	गाल की हड्डी	Cheekbone, Malar bone, Zygomatic bone	None
Zeppelin	A large rigid airship with a cylindrical shape, filled with gas and propelled by engines.	ज़ेपलिन	Airship, Dirigible, Blimp	None
Zinger	A witty, striking, or surprising remark or retort.	तेज़ या चमकदार टिप्पणी	Quip, Punchline, One-liner	None

Top 200 most repeated List with tricks

1. Asinine - Stupid मूर्ख

   Trick :- Asinine yaad krne ka tarika "assi me se nine marks" - 80 में से 9 मार्क्स लाने वाला मुर्ख ही होगा।

2. August- Splendid / Majestic भव्य /

   Trick :- August yaad krne ka tarika "15 August" - 15 August को हर school में शानदार प्रोग्राम किये जाते है

3. Astound= Bewilder भोचक्का

   Trick:- Astound yaad krne ka tarika "tond" - apni tond dek k mai astound ho gya

4. Adept = Skilful दक्ष

   Trick:- Adept yaad krne ka trika "depth" - जितना ज्यादा आदमी depth (गहराई) में जाकर पढ़ाई करता है ही ज्यादा दक्ष होता जाता है। वो उतना

5. Antagonist= Enemy / Opponent शत्रु / दुश्मन

   Trick :Antagonist yaad krne ka trika " goons" -goons मतलब गुंडे जो दुश्मन होते हैं।

6. Abhor = Hate घृणा करना

   Trick :- Abhor yaad krne ka trika "bore"- किसी चीज से बोर हो जाने पर हम उससे घृणा ही तो करते है।

7. Assiduous = Hardworking मेहनती

   Trick - Assiduous yaad krne ka trika "ass-donkey"- गधा जो कि बेचारा सारे दिन ही पचता रहता है मतलब की मेहनती होता है।

8. Snag = Obstruct बाधा डालना

   Trick - Snag yaad krne ka trika "snake" -अगर रास्ते में शेष नाग मिल जाये तो वो बाधा ही डालेगा

9. Elf = Gnome, Dwarf बौना

   Trick - Eif yaad krne ka trika "elephant"- एलीफैंट के सामने बाकि ओर जानवर तो बौने ही प्रतीत होते है

10. Stout = Portly, Fat मोटा

    Trick - Stout yaad krne ka trika "stomach" -jiska stomach out hoga wo mota hi hoga

11. Adipose = Corpulent मोटा

    Trick - Adipose yaad krne ka trika "आधी पोज "वो इतना मोटा है कि जब भी पोज देता है तो उसकी फोटो आधी ही आती है।

12. Ferocious = Fierce उग्र

    Trick - ferocious yaad krne ka trika "फिरकी" किम जोंग जब भी उग्र होता है तो हमे सबको पता है वो सबकी फिरकी लेता है।

13. Sober:- Serious, Grave गंभीर

    Trick - sober yaad krne ka trika "सो वो बियर" जब भी वो गंभीर होता है तो वो बियर पीकर सो जाता है।

14. Denigrate: - Criticize निन्दा करना

    Trick – Denigrate yaad krne ka trika "डेनी" movie डेनी जिसकी मूवी में हर कोई निन्दा ही करता है।

15. Saturnine:- Gloomy उदास / दुखी

Trick - Saturnine yaad krne ka trika "सैटरडे" फाइव डे वीक है फिर भी आज सैटरडे को भी बॉस ने रात को नौ बजे तक काम करवाया इसलिए मै बहुत दु:खी हुआ

16. Disavowal:- Denial मना करना

Trick - Disavowal yaad krne ka trika "D is a vowel" जब उसने कहा की D is a vowel (D एक स्वर है) तो मैने मना कर दिया क्योकि D तो व्यंजन है

17. Bizarre :– Unusual असामान्य

Trick - Bizarre yaad krne ka trika "बाजार में" बाजार में ज्यादातर असामान्य चीजे ही देखने को मिलती है।

18. Articulate : - Clear, Lucid, Distinct सुस्पष्ट

Trick - Articulate yaad krne ka trika "आरती लेट" एक बार मेरे से आरती लेट हो गयी तो मेरी मम्मी ने मुझे सुस्पष्ट करने को कहा कि आरती क्यूं लेट हुई।

19. Scrumptious :- Tasty, Delicious स्वादिष्ट

Trick - Scrumptious yaad krne ka trika "रम पीते " जब हम रम पीते है तो वो शक्कर की तरह स्वादिष्ट ही लगती है-

20. Gnome:- Dwarf बौना

Trick - Gnome yaad krne ka trika "जन्म" जब हम जन्मे थे तब बौने ही तो थे

21. Delight:- Joy खुशी

Trick:- Delight yaad krne ka trika "लाइट" जब बिजली वाले, मैच वाले दिन फुल लाइट देते है तो बहुत खुशी मिलती है

22. Dauntless:- Fearless, Bold, Brave निडर

Trick - Dauntless yaad krne ka trika "डांट less" जब बच्चों को डांट कम लगाते है तो वो निडर बन जाते है

23. Paean:- Praise, Encomium, Eulogy प्रशंसा करना

Trick - Paean yaad krne ka trika "पाई" उसने UPSC में एक बार में ही सफलता पाई इसलिए हर कोई उसकी प्रशंसा कर रहा है।

24. Lugubrious :- Dismal उदास

Trick – Lugubrious yaad krne ka trika "लुगाई+ बरस" कई बरस हो गये उसकी लुगाई को पीहर गये हुए इसलिए वो उदास ही रहता है

25. Censure:- Criticize आलोचना करना

Trick - Censure yaad krne ka trika "सेंसर बोर्ड" अगर मूवी में कोई गलत सीन आता है तो सेंसर बोर्ड उसकी निन्दा ही करता है।

26. Surly:- Bad-tempered, Unfriendly fasfas।

Trick –Surly yaad krne ka trika "सर सबकी क्लास ले ली जब सर चिडचड़े हुए तो सबकी क्लास ले ली।

27. Emerge:- Appear प्रकट होना

Trick - Emerge yaad krne ka trika "Emergency" अपने भक्तों की रक्षा करने के लिए Emergency में ही भगवान प्रकट होते है।

28. Calamity:- Disaster, Catastrophe विपति/ संकट

Trick -Calamity yaad krne ka trika "अमेठी" अब अमेठी में कोई भी विपत्ति आती है तो वहां की जनता स्मृति ईरानी जी को कॉल करती है

29. Abscond: - Run away भाग जाना

Trick -Abscond yaad krne ka trika "अब से कांड" अब से लोग कांड करके भाग जाते है।

30. Agile:-Quick, Nimble फुर्तीला

Trick -Agile yaad krne ka trika "AG = एडम गिलक्रिस्ट" एडम गिलक्रिस्ट जो कि विकेटो के पीछे हमेशा फुर्तीला ही रहता था।

31. Diligent:- Assiduous, Untiring, Hardworking मेहनती

Trick -Diligent yaad krne ka trika "दिल्ली के gent " दिल्ली के gent (पुरूष) जो की मेहनती ही तो है।

32. Inimical:- Unfriendly, Hostile दुश्मनी

Trick -Inimical yaad krne ka trika "माई का लाल" जब किसी से अपनी दुश्मनी हो जाती है तो लड़ाई होने पर अपना दुश्मन यही कहता है कि इनमें से है कोई माई का लाल जो मुझसे भीड़ सके।

33. Rapture:- Ecstasy, Bliss खुशी

Trick -Rapture yaad krne ka trika "रफ्तार" कई लड़को को गाड़ी को तेज रफ्तार में चलाने में ही खुशी मिलती है।

34. Blithe :- Happy, Joyous खुश

Trick - Blithe yaad krne ka trika "बलि चढ़ाते है" जब काली माता के बलि चढ़ाते है तो माता खुश ही तो होती है।

35. Abridge:- Shorten छोटा करना

Trick - Abridge yaad krne ka trika "bridge" एक bridge (पूल) जो की दूरी (Distance) को छोटा करता है।

36. Ample = Sufficient / more than necessary प्रचुर मात्रा में

Trick - Ample yaad krne ka trika "temple" हमारे भारत देश में प्रचुर मात्रा में मन्दिर है।

37. Arcane : - Secret, Hidden गुप्त

Trick -Arcane yaad krne ka trika "अरे कान में कह दे" अरे कान में कह दे ताकि बात Secret ही रहे कोई भी नही सुनेगा।

38. Antipathy:- Dislike नापसन्द

Trick -Antipathy yaad krne ka trika "Anti (एन्टी)" पत्नी की पति से Anti (एन्टी) हो गयी इसलिए एक-दूसरे को नापसन्द करते है।

39. Laborious:– Hardworking, मेहनती

Trick - Laborious yaad krne ka trika "लेबर (मजदूर)" लेबर (मजदूर) जो कि नरेगा में काम करते है वो मेहनती ही तो होते है।

40. Industrious:– Hardworking (मेहनती)

Trick - Industrious yaad krne ka trika " Industry" Industry में काम करने वाले लोग मेहनती ही तो होते है।

41. Tenuous :- Weak, Thin पतला /कमजोर

Trick - Tenuous yaad krne ka trika "टेनिस" टेनिस की खिलाड़ी ज्यादातर पतली / कमजोर ही होती है।

42. Sullen:– Sulky, Gloomy उदास

Trick - Sullen yaad krne ka trika "सूली" जब ईशा मसीह को सूली पर लटकाया गया था तब उनके सारे भक्त उदास हो गये थे।

43. Deleterious : - Harmful नुकसानदायक

Trick - Deleterious yaad krne ka trika "डिलीट" हमे पता है की जो भी फाइल

हमारे लिए नुकसानदायक होती है। उसे हम कंप्यूटर से डिलीट कर देते है।

44. Adamant:- Stubborn जिद्दी

Trick - Adamant yaad krne ka trika "आदमी(man)" वो आदमी हर बात पर ही अड़ जाता है मतलब कि वो जिद्दी है।

45. Supple:- Limber

Trick - Supple yaad krne ka trika "चप्पल" चप्पल जो कि लचीली ही होती है।

46. Sloppy:- Dirty मैला

Trick - Sloppy yaad krne ka trika "स्लो स्लो पी" अरे स्लो स्लो पी नही तो कपड़े गंदे हो जायेंगे

47. Asunder:- Apart अलग

Trick - Asunder yaad krne ka trika "सुन्दर" सुन्दर लडकियाँ तो वैसे ही अलग ही दिखती है।

48. Vague:- Ambiguous अस्पष्ट

Trick - Vague yaad krne ka trika "तेज वेग" हवा का जब तेज वेग आता है तो हमे चीजे अस्पष्ट ही दिखाई देती है।

49. Antiquated - Old-fashioned or outdated पुराना

Trick -Antiquated yaad krne ka trika "आंटियां कुएं" पुराने जमाने में आंटियां कुएं से ही पानी लाती थी।

50. Lethargic:- Inactive, Sluggish, Lazy सुस्त

Trick -Lethargic yaad krne ka trika " लेटा" वो सारे दिन रजाई में लेटा रहता है इसलिए वो बहुत सुस्त है

51. Recalcitrant : Disobedient अवज्ञाकारी

Trick - Recalcitrant yaad krne ka trika "केल्क्युलेटर" जो विधार्थी बार - बार मना करने के बावजूद भी परीक्षा में केल्क्युलेटर लाता है वो अवज्ञाकारी ही होता है।

52. Irk:- Irriate, Annoy परेशान करना

Trick - Irk yaad krne ka trika "इराक" इराक का सद्दाम हुसैन जो कि अमेरिका को बहुत परेशान करता था

53. Astute:- Wise, Skilled बुद्धिमान

Trick - Astute yaad krne ka trika "Science tutor" Science tutor जो कि बुद्धिमान / चतुर होता हैं।

54. Felicity:- Happiness, Bliss खुशी

Trick - Felicity yaad krne ka trika "city फैली" अगर city फैली हुई हो तो हमे बहुत खुशी मिलती है।

55. Ephemeral:- Short living क्षणिक

Trick - Ephemeral yaad krne ka trika "अफीम का नशा" अफीम का नशा थोड़े समय (क्षणिक) के लिए मजा देता है।

56. Evanescent:- Short living क्षणिक

Trick -Evanescent yaad krne ka trika "ईवा का सेन्ट" ईवा का सेन्ट जिसकी सुगन्ध थोड़ी देर के लिए ही रहती है। मतलब की क्षणिक।

57. Assiduous - Hard working मेहनती

Trick - Assiduous yaad krne ka trika "Ass" - khachcha" "Ass" - khachchar jo ki bahut mehnati hota hai, hum log ass ko samaan dhone k liye use krte hai

58. Shun -to avoid somebody or something/ किसी से दूर रहना

Trick - Shun yaad krne ka trika

"sunscreen" Sunrays ko bachen[shun] krne ke lie sun screen use karte h

59. Abstain - Refrain दूर रहना

Trick - Abstain yaad krne ka trika " अब से train" मैं अब से train से दूर ही रहूँगा क्योंकि मैने कल ही train से accident होते देखा था।

60. Amorous - Erotic , Romantic कामुक

Trick:- Amorous yaad krne ka trika "आम के रस "आम के रस वाले ऐड में कटरीना को देख कर हर कोई कामुक हो जाता है।

61. Adjourn - Delay, Postpone टालना

Trick - Adjourn yaad krne ka trika "आधे जर्नी" जब हमे पता चला की उस जगह बाढ़ आ गयी है तो हमने हमारी जर्नी को आधे रस्ते में ही टाल दिया।

62. Adore - Admire बहुत प्यार करनाआदर / सत्कार करना

Trick - Adore yaad krne ka trika " दुरी" वो दोनों हमेशा एक दुसरे से दुरी बनाकर ही रखते है इसलिए एक दुसरे से प्यार करने के साथ साथ एक दुसरे का सम्मान भी करते है।

63. Acquittal - Exoneration, Absolution Exculpation, Release रिहाई, छुटकारा

Trick - Acquittal yaad krne ka trika " एक ही कत्ल" उसने एक ही कत्ल किया था इसलिए उसकी जल्दी ही रिहाई हो गयी।

64. Adieu - Farewell अलविदा विदाई

Trick -Adieu yaad krne ka trika "एक डयू बोतल " विदाई समारोह में सबको एक एक डयू बोतल दी।

65. Avow- Acknowledge / Avouch / स्वीकार करना

Trick - Avow yaad krne ka trika "वाऊ वो " वाऊ वो लडकी इतनी अच्छी थी की मैने एक बार में उसके शादी के प्रस्ताव को स्वीकार कर लिया।

66. Admonish- Warn / Reprove चेतावनी / डांटना

Trick - Admonish yaad krne ka trika " मनीष" हम आपके है कौन मूवी में सल्लू का बड़ा भाई मनीष उसे चेतावनी देता है कि माधुरी के पीछे और कोई लगा हुआ है।

67. Alien - Foreign / Exotic विदेशी

Trick - Alien yaad krne ka trika "एलियन " एलियन जो कि विदेशी ही होते है। (पराये)

68. Arcane- Secret / Hidden गुप्त

Trick - Arcane yaad krne ka trika " अरे कान में कह" अरे कान में कह दे ताकि बात Secret ही रहे कोई भी नहीं सुनेगा।

69. Abdicate- Give up त्याग देना

Trick - Abdicate yaad krne ka trika "अब दिक्कत " अब दिक्कत महसुस हो रही है इसलिए छोड़ दे मतलब की त्याग दे।

70. Adamant - Hard / Inflexible जिद्दी

Trick - Adamant yaad krne ka trika "अड़ " वो आदमी हर बात पर ही अड़ जाता है मतलब कि वो जिद्दी है।

71. Affluent- Rich अमीर

Trick - Affluent yaad krne ka trika " fluent (धाराप्रवाह) " जिस व्यक्ति को

धाराप्रवाह अंग्रेजी बोलना आती हो वह आसानी से काफी पैसा कमाकर अमीर बन सकता है।

72. Apathy- Indifference Listlessness, Unconcern उदासीनता

Trick -Apathy yaad krne ka trika "एक ही पाठी " अगर आप बच्चो को एक ही पाठी पढ़ाओगे तो उदासीनता तो छाएगी।

73. Abortive- Unsuccessful / Fail असफल

Trick - Abortive yaad krne ka trika " अब और टीवी" अब और टीवी मत देखना वरना फिर से Fail हो जाओगे।

74. Abrogate- Cancel / Abolish / Annul निरस्त रद्द

Trick - Abrogate yaad krne ka trika "अब रो रहा है। " उसकी अपनी छोटी सी गलती की वजह से exam का form cancel हो गया इसलिए गेट पर खड़ा-ऊं ऊं ऊं -------.--. खड़ा रो रहा है।

75. Adulterate - Make impure / Corrupt / Debase

Trick - Adulterate yaad krne ka trika "Adult "बच्चा जो कि pure होता है लेकिन Adult होते होते impure हो जाता है।

76. Adroit - Skilful दक्ष निपुण

Trick - Adroit yaad krne ka trika "Android "Android जिसने भी बनाया है वो उस काम में दक्ष ही तो था।

77. Agony - Pain / Torture कष्ट पीड़ा

Trick - Agony yaad krne ka trika "आग "अगर कोई व्यक्ति आग में जल जाये तो उसे बहुत कष्ट पीड़ा होती है|

78. Assault - Attack आक्रमण करना

Trick - Assault yaad krne ka trika "ass pe salt "अगर गधा किसी जगह से जख्मी हो रखा हो और उसके ऊपर नमक डाले तो वो आक्रमण ही तो करेगा।

79. Ally - Friend मित्र

Trick -Ally yaad krne ka trika " "आली" आली जो कि सखी (मित्र) को बोलते है।

80. Allay - Calm / Pacify शांत

Trick - Allay yaad krne ka trika "Al, Al) ले, ले)lay) "जब घर में मुन्ना रोता है तो माँ उसे शान्त करने के लिए कहती है अल, अल)Al, Al) ले, ले)lay) मुन्ना शान्त हो जा।

81. Amorphous - Shapeless अनाकार

Trick - Amorphous yaad krne ka trika "एक मोर फसने" एक मोर बेचारा सकड़ी गली में फसने के कारण SHAPELESS हो गया।

82. Avert - Avoid दूर रखना बचना

Trick - Avert yaad krne ka trika " एक महिला व्रत"जब एक महिला व्रत करती है तो उसे एक दिन के लिए खाने से दूर ही रहना पड़ता है।

83. Avaricious - Greedy लालची

Trick - Avaricious yaad krne ka trika "वारिस "राजा महारानिया जो कि वारिस के लिए लालची रहते है ताकी उनकी सम्पति उनका वारिस ही खाए।

84. Autocratic - Despotic, Dictatorial Tyrannical तानाशाही शासन

Trick -Autocratic yaad krne ka trika "Auto-अकेली " जिस देश मे अकेली

रानी ही राज करती हो वहां तानाशाही शासन ही होता है।

85. Amiable - Friendly मित्रता

Trick - Amiable yaad krne ka trika "मिया बिवी " मिया बिवी के बीच - Friendly संबंध होते है।

86. Amalgamate- Combine मिलाना

Trick - Amalgamate yaad krne ka trika "अम्ल और गम " वो अम्ल और गम को मिलाकर खाता है।

87. Acme - Top RARER शिखर

Trick - Acme yaad krne ka trika "Lakme " Lakme की क्रीम जो कि बाजार में सबसे टोप पर है।

88. Abominate - Hate घृणा करना

Trick - Abominate yaad krne ka trika "बम " बम धमाका करने वाले से हर कोई घृणा करता है।

89. Accede - Agree / Consent मान लेना

Trick - Accede yaad krne ka trika "acid " अगर घर में चोर घुस आये ओर हमारे से लॉकर की चाबी मांगे तो एक बार तो हम उसको नहीं देंगे लेकिन अगर वो मुहं पर acid फेकने लगे तो हम उसे चाबी दे देंगे मतलब कि उसकी बात मान लेंगे।

90. Disavowal:- Denial / मना करना

Trick:- Disavowal yaad krne ka trika "D is a vowel " जब उसने कहा की D is a vowel (D एक स्वर है) तो मैने मना कर दिया क्योकि D तो व्यंजन है।

91. Abscond:– Run away

Trick - Abscond yaad krne ka trika " अब से लोग कांड" अब से लोग कांड करके भाग जाते है।

92. Agility:- Nimbleness, Alacrity

Trick - Agility yaad krne ka trika "एडम गिलक्रिस्ट " एडम गिलक्रिस्ट जिसमे विकेटों के पीछे बहुत फुर्ती थी।

93. Diligent:- Assiduous, Untiring, Hardworking

Trick - Diligent yaad krne ka trika "दिल्ली के gent (पुरुष) " दिल्ली के gent (पुरुष) जो की मेहनती हो तो है।

94. Spruce :- Smart, Natty बना ठना

Trick - Spruce yaad krne ka trika "स्प्रे " उसे बन-ठन कर बने रहने की आदत है इसलिए रोजाना स्प्रे लगाता है

95. Chide:- Scold डाटना

Trick- Chide yaad krne ka trika " Chide = चिड़ /"Chide = चिड़ / जब मैंने उसे सभी Friends के सामने डांटा तो वो चिड़ गया।

96. Stentorian :- Loud जोर की आवाज़ का

Trick :- Stentorian yaad krne ka trika " S= शादी, tent टेंट शादी में जो टैंट लगाने वाले आते हैं वो टैंट लगाते वक्त बहुत जोर की आवाज में बोलते हैं।

97. Clasp :- Grip मजबूती से पकड़ना

Trick :- Clasp yaad krne ka trika " Cla = कला, sp- एस पी एस पी में अपराधी को मजबूती से पकड़ने की कला होती है।

98. Kindle - Ignite जलाना

Trick - Kindle yaad krne ka trika "candle " Candle (मोमबती) जो कि जलाने के ही काम आती है।

99. Amass:- Gather Together Accumulate

इक्कटा करना

Trick - Amass yaad krne ka trika " मांस" एक मांस के टूकड़े को देखते ही गांवो में काफी सारे कुते इकट्ठा हो जाते है।

100. Aftermath :- Result / Consequence परिणाम

Trick - Aftermath yaad krne ka trika "गणित+बाद "गणित पढ़ने के बाद इस बार उसका परिणाम अच्छा आया है।

101. Absolve- Forgive / Pardon / Acquit माफ करना

Trick - अब वकिल ने केस solve कर दिया इसलिए जज साहेब ने मुझे माफ़ कर दिया।

102. Assent - Agree सहमत होना

Trick - मेरी Girlfriend ऐसा सेन्ट) Perfume लगाती है कि हर कोई उससे Agree हो जाता है।

103. Abandon - Give up / Forsake त्यागना

Trick - अभिताभ बच्चन ने पहली Don मूवी में काम करने के बाद दूसरी Don मूवी को त्याग दिया था तभी तो शाहरूख खान ने दूसरी Don मूवी में काम किया था।

104. Accord - Agreement

Trick - अगर हमें Honda Accord गाड़ी खरीदनी हो तो company के साथ कुछ समझौता करना पड़ता है।

105. Antiquarian - Ancient / Antique पुराना

Trick - 1. पुराने जमाने मे आन्टीया कुएं से पानी लाती थी।

2. पुराने जमाने मे कुवांरी लड़किया अपनी आन्टीयो के साथ कुएं पर पानी लेने जाती थी।

106. Apprehend- Apprehend गिरफ्तार करना

Trick - गिरफ्तार करते वक्त पुलिस अपराधी को यही तो कहती है कि ऊपर हेन्ड करो (हेन्डस अप)।

107. Avarice - greed लालच

Trick - वारिश के लिए हर कोई लालच रखता है।

108. Astute - Wise / Skilled बुद्धिमान

Trick - एक Science का tutor जो कि बुद्धिमान / चतुर होता हैं।

109. Acquiesce- Agree / Accept / unwillingly मान जाना सहमत होना

Trick - जब छोटे बच्चे को हम एक kiss करते है तो वो मान ही जाता है।

110. Admonition - Rebuke / Warning फटकार

Trick - जब वो मुनि से किसी बात पर अड़ गया तो उसके घर वालो ने कड़ी डांटफटकार लगायी।

111. Affront - Insult अपमानित करना

Trick - हमें कभी भी किसी अपने दोस्त की Insult किसी दूसरे व्यक्ति के सामने नहीं करनी चाहिए।

112. Apposite - Appropriate उपयुक्त

Trick - आपको वही वेबसाइट देखनी चाहिए जो आपके लिए उपयुक्त हो।

113. Abscond- Run away भाग जाना

Trick - अब से लोग कांड करके भाग जाते है।

114. Apprise / Apprize - Inform सूचित करना

Trick -15 August के दिन कई पुलिस अफसरो को अच्छे काम के लिए Prize दिया जाता है जिसके लिए उनको पहले सूचित किया जाता है।

Synonyms:- Inform

115. Assail - Attack आक्रमण करना

Trick - मिसाइल जो कि Attack करने के ही काम आती है।

116. Atrocity- Violent and cruel act / Barbarity जुल्म

Trick - मैट्रो सिटी मे ज्यादा ही जुल्म और अत्याचार होते है।

117. Assay - Evaluation / Analysis जॉचना

Trick - Essay (निबंध) को examiner ही जॉचता है।

118. Audacious - Daring / bold साहसी

Trick - योद्धा जो कि साहसी होते है।

119. Ascetic- Hermitlike / Austere सन्यासी

Trick - इसके टिका लगा हुआ है इसलिए सब उसे सन्यासी ही समझ रहे है।

120. Aspersion- Unpleasant false remarks / Calumny/ Slander/ Slanderous remarks कलंक लगाना

Trick - उसके बेटे ने भरे बाजार में उस लड़की को स्पर्श कर दिया इसलिए उस पर कलंक लग गया।

121. Apex - Top / Summit / Peak शिखर

Trick - अपेक्स बैंक राजस्थान में सबसे Top पर है।

122. Antediluvian- Antiquated पूरानी

Trick - पुराने जमाने की आन्टीया लव के चक्कर में जल्दी ही दिल दे बैठती थी।

123. Alacrity- Enthusiasm जोश

Trick - अगर किसी व्यक्ति के पास पहले कुछ भी रूपये न हो और अचानक एक लाख रूपये मिल जाये तो जोश आ जाता है।

124. Adipose- Corpulent मोटा

Trick - वो इतना मोटा है कि जब भी पोज देता है तो उसकी फोटो आधी ही आती है।

125. Aromatic- Fragrant सुगन्धित

Trick - मैं रोमान्टिक हो गया जब मेरी girlfriend सुगंन्धित सेन्ट लगा कर आयी।

126. Arraign- Indict / Accuse / Charge / Impeach / Bring a criminal charge against a person मुकदमे के लिए अदालत में लानादोषी ठहराना /

Trick - अरे Sanjay dutt को illegal तरीके से gun रखने के कारण अदालत ने दोषी ठहराया।

127. Articulate- Clear, Vivid, Lucid / Distinct सुस्पष्ट

Trick - एक बार मेरे से आरती लेट हो गयी तो मेरी मम्मी ने मुझे सुस्पष्ट करने को कहा कि आरती क्यूं लेट हुई।

128. Amity- Friendship मित्रता

Trick - अमेठी में राहुल गांधी जी के संबंध वहां की जनता से मित्रता पूर्वक है तभी तो वो वहां से हमेशा चुनावों में जीतते है।

129. Attenuate- Weakened / Very thin बहुत पतला

Trick - वो आटे की रोटी नहीं खाती है इसलिए बहुत पतली हो गई है।

130. Accumulate - Accrue इकट्ठा करना

Trick - प्रिन्सिप्ल ने टीचर्स से कहा की एक काम करो जो भी स्टूडेंट्स लेट आये है उनको एक जगह इकट्ठा करो।

131. Accolade - Praise / Laurels सराहना

Trick - उनके एक ही औलाद है इसलिए उसकी हमेशा सराहना ही करते रहते है।

132. Adversity- Misfortune, Poverty दुर्भाग्य

Trick - एक ऐसा शहर जहां वर के लिए Adv. (Advertisement) देना पड़ता हो

शादी के लिए तो ये उनका दुर्भाग्य ही होगा।

133. Adequate - Ample / Enough पर्याप्त

Trick - कुवेत देश के आधे हिस्से मे पर्याप्त मात्रा मे तेल के भण्डार है।

134. Advent- Arrival आगमन

Trick - वो आडवाणी ही थे जिनका सबसे पहले BJP पार्टी मे आगमन हुआ था।

135. Agitate- Disturb उतेजित करना परेशान

Trick - सीता - गीता मूवी में गीता, सीता को बहुत परेशान करती है।

136. Abundance - Plentifulness / Exuberance

Trick - एक-2 बूंद-से अनेक (प्रचुर) मात्रा मे धन इकट्ठा किया जा सकता है।

137. Astonish - Overwhelm विस्मित करना

Trick - आस तो किसी को नही थी उसने सारे आतंकवादियों का नाश करके सबको विस्मित कर दिया।

138. Abstruse- Obscure / अस्पष्ट

Trick - अब से true love को समझना काफी difficult मतलब अस्पष्ट है।

139. Antagonism - Antipathy / Enmity दुश्मनी

Trick - एन्टी होने पर दो लोगो के बीच दुश्मनी अग्नि की तरह फेल जाती है।

140. Agile- Quick and nimble फुरतीला

Trick - एडम गिलक्रिस्ट जो की विकेटों के पीछे बहुत ही ज्यादा फुर्तीला रहता था।

141. Acute- Sharp तीक्ष्ण कुशाग्र

Trick - पुलिस वाले बम धमाको मे एक कुते का उपयोग इसलिए करते है क्योंकि कुते मे सूंघ कर पता लगाने की तीक्ष्ण / कुशाग्र क्षमता होती है।

142. Abjure - Give up त्याग देना

Trick - 1. जब खेल में खिलाड़ी को चोट लगती है तो उसे उस समय खेल को छोड़ना ही पड़ता है।

2. अब जूरी के सामने कसम खाता हूँ कि कभी भी चोरी नहीं करूंगा।

143. Abduct- Kidnap अपहरण करना

Trick - अब अपहरणकर्ता आजकल बच्चों को ढक कर ले जाते है या फिर अगर बीस - 25 किडेसाथ मकोड़े एक- चल रहे हो और उनकाKidnap करना हो तो उन्हे ढक दे तो वो kidnap हो जायेंगे।

144. Abase - Degrade नीचा दिखानाअपमान / करना

Trick - उसने पूरे भरे मार्केट में मुझे मेरी girlfriend के सामने ऐसे कहा कि अबे इधर आ और पूरी public के सामने अपमान कर दिया

145. Abate - Reduce, Lessen कम करना

Trick - अब इसने खाना खा लिया है, इसलिए खाना कम हो गया।

146. Ablution- Washing स्नान

Trick - बॉडी लॉशन जो कि स्नान करने से पहले लगाया जाता है।

147. Apparent - Obvious / Manifest स्पष्ट

Trick - आपके माता-पिता हमेशा आपको स्पष्ट ही बोलते है कि बेटा पढ़ ले नहीं तो मेरे जैसे मजदूरी करनी पड़ेगी।

148. Gloomy : - Sad, Sombre, Morose दुखी

Trick:- Gloomy Sound of गुलामी गुलामी में आदमी उदास ही तो रहता है और उसकी जिंदगी में अँधेरा ही छाया रहता है।

149. Pillory :- Censure, Condemn निंदा करना

Trick:- जब Question का आंसर नहीं बताया तो उसे पिलर से बाँध दिया इसलिए सभी ने उस teacher की निदो

150. Lampoon:- - To criticize निन्दा करना

Trick:- Lamp = लैम्प, on = on जब मैने रूम का लेम्प ऑन ही छोड़ दिया तो पापा ने मेरी सबके सामने बहुत निंदा की

151. Detest :- - Hate, Dislike घृणा करना

Trick - De - दे, test टेस्ट जो टीचर Student को ज्यादा ही टेस्ट देते है उससे ज्यादातर Student घृणा ही करते है।

152. Ameliorate - Improve सुधारना

Trick - सब्जी मे अम्ल (खटाई) डालने पर सब्जी का स्वादimprove हो जाता है।

153. Abundant - Plentiful / Ample / Abounding प्रचुर

Trick - आंटी एक -एक बूंद पानी इकट्ठा कर करके प्रचुर मात्रा में इकट्ठा कर लेती है।

154. Aversion- Dislike घृणा करना

Trick - जब हमें चाइनीज फोन का वर्जन पसन्द नहीं आता है तो हम उससे घृणा ही तो करते है।

155. Acerbic - Bitters कड़वा

Trick - एक शराब का स्वाद कड़वा ही होता है।

156. Assiduous - Hard Working मेहनती

Trick - गधा जो की बेचारा सारे दिन ही पचता रहता है मतलब की मेहनती होता है।

157. Altruism - Generosity, Selflessness, Kindness / Unselfish परोपकारिता

Trick - उसने सारा पैसा टूरिज्म के लिए दान करके परोपकारिता का ही काम किया है।

158. Abutting

Meaning - Adjoining, Adjacent, Contiguous, Neighbouring सटा हुआ

Trick - अल्फाबेट में A से B सटा हुआ और U, T से सटा हुआ रहता है।

159. Anile - Senile, Decrepit, Old बुढ़िया के समान

Trick - जब बुढ़िया के समान उसकी उम्र हुई तो उसके नीले नीले धब्बे पड़ गये।

160. Amateurs - शौकिया

Trick - अम्मा ट्यूर पर जाने का बहुत शौक रखती है।

161. Appoint - नियुक्त करना

Trick - उसको मैंने ही अपोइन्ट किया है मतलब की नियुक्त।

162. Abusive - निन्दापूर्ण

Trick - जब उसने रात की एक बासी रोटी भी उस मेहमान को दी तो हर किसी ने उसकी निंदा की।

163. Abstemious - Abstinent, Moderate, Temperate संयमी

Trick - अब से टम्मी कम करने के लिए हमे खाने पर संयम बरतना ही पड़ेगा।

164. Absurd - Preposterous / Ridiculous बेतुका / निरर्थक

Trick - जब कोई व्यक्ति बेतुकी या निरर्थक बाते करता है तो हम यही तो कहते है कि अब मेरा सिर दर्द कर रहा है बेतुकी बाते मत कर।

165. Augment - Increase बढ़ना

Trick - जब किसी जगह आग लगती है तो बढ़ने में 1 मिनट भी नहीं लगाती है।

166. Amenable - Responsible / Accountable / Answerable/ Responsive जिम्मेदार

Trick - A=एक, men = आदमी, able= योग्य एक बच्चा जब बड़ा होकर आदमी बन

जाता है तो अपनी जिम्मेदारी निभाने के योग्य बन जाता है।

167. Anguish - Agony, Pain, Affliction, desolation पीड़ा

Trick - उसके शरीर के हर अंग अंग पर मारा गया इसलिए उसे बहुत पीड़ा हो रही है।

168. Altercation- Noisy quarrel / Wrangle झगड़ा

Trick - जब हम कई बार दर्जी के पास कपड़े Alter कराने जाते है और वो फिर से गलत कर दे तो उससे हमारा झगड़ा हो जाता है।

169. Alight- Disembark किसी वाहन से नीचे उतरना

Trick - जब रात मे हम किसी वाहन से नीचे उतरते है तो एक लाइट की जरूरत हमेशा पड़ती है।

170. Ague- Malaria

Trick - जब उसको मलेरिया बुखार हुई तो हर उसके शरीर में आग लग गयी।

171. Accrue- Accumulate / Enlarge / Increase by addition

Trick - उसने धीरे धीरे एक करोड़ रूपये जमा कर लिए।

172. Aptitude - Talent क्षमता

Trick - एप्टीट्यूड टेस्ट स्टूडेन्ट का talent (क्षमता) परखने के लिए लिया जाता है।

173. Adversary - Competitor, Rival, Opponent, Foe, Hostile. विरोधी

Trick - वो वर सारी दुनिया से अड़ने के लिए तैयार था क्योकि वो उसकी वधु के विरोधी थे।

174. Agonising- Excruciating / Distressing / Painful दुखदायी

Trick - बहुत दुःख दायी सा फील होता है जब ये सुनते है की फला फला परिवार अग्नि में जलकर खाक हो गया।

175. Advocacy- Support पक्ष का समर्थन

Trick - Advocate जिस केस को लेता है उसी पार्टी का पक्ष लेता है।

176. Adorn- Decorate सवांरना सजावट / करना

Trick - शादी के समय दुल्हन को सजाने के लिए आभूषण पहनाते है।

177. Assuage- Mollify / Placate / Palliate / Alleviate शान्त करना

Trick - जब पड़ोसी की मृत्यु हो गयी तो आंसू ही आ गये और घर वालो ने कैसे न कैसे शान्त किया कि उसका साथ इतने दिनो के लिए ही था।

178. Approbation- Approval स्वीकृति/मंजूरी

Trick - जब आप Probation period पूरा कर लेते हो तब ही जॉब को job से Approval मिलती है।

179. Accomplice- Partner in crime गुनाह के साथी

Trick - एक ऐसा क्षेत्र जहां कम पुलिस हो वहां पर गुनाह के साथी बहुत ज्यादा होते है।

180. Animosity- Active enmity शत्रुता

Trick - उस शहर में वो जानवरों की तरह लड़ते है इसलिए शत्रुता बहुत ज्यादा है।

181. Apogee- Highest point पराकाष्ठा / शिखर

Trick - बैंक पीओ जो कि post में शिखर पर है।

182. Applaud- Laud सराहना करना, प्रशंसा करना

Trick -आप तो लाड़ साहब होना इसलिए हर कोई आपकी प्रशंसा करता रहता है।

183. Artisan- कुशल कारीगर

Trick - जिस कलाकार की कला मे शान होती है वो कुशल कारीगर ही होता है।

184. Analogue- Parallel अनुरूप

Trick - अन्ना के आंदोलन मे सब लोग एक जैसे ही थे मतलब की अनुरूप थे।

185. Austere - Strict सख्त

Trick - आस्ट्रेलिया के क्रिकेटर खेल के प्रति मैदान में काफी Serious और strict रहते है।

186. Accumulated - Accrue इकट्ठा करना

Trick - प्रिंसिपल ने टीचर को कहा की आप एक काम करो जो भी स्टूडेंट लेट आया है उनको एक जगह इकट्ठा करो।

187. Accidental - Fortuitous अचानक

Trick - Accident जो कि अचानक ही होता है कभी भी जाननहीं किया बुझकर - जाता है।

188. Acquitted- Absolve, Clear, Exonerate, Exculpate अपराधमुक्त

Trick - असिस्टेंट कमांडेड ने उसे जेल से क्विट कर दिया मतलब की अपराध मुक्त कर दिया।

189. Appraise- Judge मूल्याकन करना

Trick - Company आपके काम का मूल्याकन करने के बाद ही Salary बढाती है।

190. Avenue- Way, Road, Route, Path, Street मार्ग, द्वार

Trick - उस वेन्यू पर जाने के लिए केवल एक ही मार्ग है।

191. Apparition- Spirit प्रेत

Trick - आप भुत प्रेत में विश्वास मत किया करो ऐसा साइंस कहती है।

192. Addle- Muddle, Confuse बिगाड़ना; व्याकुल कर देना; गड़ बड कर देना

Trick - उसने उस गुंडे से अडके के बहुत बड़ा पंगा ले लिया मतलब की सब कुछ बिगाड़ कर गडबड कर दी।

193. Affirm - Confirm, Assert, Declare, State, Certify, Verify दावे के साथ कहना, पुष्टि करना

Trick - कन्फर्म होने के बाद उसने दावे के साथ कह दिया कि उसने ही उसका कत्ल किया था।

194. Alleviate- Reduce, ease, relive, lessen, moderate / assuage कम करना

Trick - हम सबने खाना खा लिया है इसलिए वो कम हो गया है।

195. Amplify- Enlarge / Extend

Trick - एम्पलीफायर जो की electrical signals, का amplitude बढ़ाने के काम आता है।

196. Amend - Correct / Improve सुधारना

Trick - अमन शांति से ही भारत और पाक के बीच रिश्ते सुधारे जा सकते है।

197. Aplomb- Confidence आत्मविश्वास

Trick - अगर आप लम्बे हो तो किसी भी काम को आत्मविश्वास के साथ कर सकते हो।

198. Acquit - Exonerate, Exculpate / Free अपराध से मुक्त करना

Trick - असिस्टेंट कमांडेड ने उसे जेल से क्विट कर दिया मतलब की अपराध मुक्त कर दिया।

199. Authentic - Genuine, Legitimate असली प्रमाणिक

Trick - ऑथेंटिक न्यूज़ देता है वो मतलब की असली न्यूज़ देता है।

200. Asceticism - Abstinence, Temperance, Abstemiousness संन्यास वैराग्य

Trick - इसके टिका लगा हुआ है इसलिए सब उसे ऐसे ही समझ रहे है की उसने सन्यास धारण कर लिया है।

Confidence booster Practise sets

Question I

Directions: In this section, you will be presented with a word. Select the option that best represents a synonym (word with a similar meaning) for the given word.

1. **Agile is the synonym of:**
   a) Nimble b) Clumsy
   c) Inflexible d) Sluggish
2. **Benevolent is the synonym of:**
   a) Malevolent b) Kind
   c) Cruel d) Harsh
3. **Caricature is the synonym of:**
   a) Genuine b) Realistic
   c) Portrayal d) Cartoon
4. **Discern is the synonym of:**
   a) Perceive b) Confuse
   c) Ignore d) Overlook
5. **Eccentric is the synonym of:**
   a) Conventional b) Ordinary
   c) Quirky d) Traditional
6. **Forego is the synonym of:**
   a) Acquire b) Forfeit
   c) Possess d) Retain
7. **Generous is the synonym of:**
   a) Stingy b) Greedy
   c) Selfish d) Benevolent
8. **Haughty is the synonym of:**
   a) Arrogant b) Humble
   c) Modest d) Timid
9. **Illusion is the synonym of:**
   a) Delusion b) Reality
   c) Truth d) Authenticity
10. **Jeopardy is the synonym of:**
    a) Security b) Safety
    c) Danger d) Protection

Answers

1.	(a)	2.	(b)	3.	(d)
4.	(a)	5.	(c)	6.	(b)
7.	(d)	8.	(a)	9.	(a)
10.	(c)				

Question II

Directions: In this section, you will be presented with a word. Select the option that best represents a synonym (word with a similar meaning) for the given word.

1. **Keenness is the synonym of:**
   a) Eagerness b) Apathy
   c) Indifference d) Disinterest
2. **Laconic is the synonym of:**
   a) Wordy b) Verbose
   c) Rambling d) Concise
3. **Melancholy is the synonym of:**
   a) Happy b) Sorrowful
   c) Joyful d) Cheerful
4. **Nomadic is the synonym of:**
   a) Wanderer b) Settled
   c) Stationary d) Sedentary
5. **Overwhelm is the synonym of:**
   a) Encourage b) Underwhelm

c) Submerge d) Support

6. **Perish is the synonym of:**
   a) Prosper b) Thrive
   c) Flourish d) Die

7. **Quibble is the synonym of:**
   a) Nitpick b) Agree
   c) Concur d) Harmonize

8. **Rejuvenate is the synonym of:**
   a) Revitalise b) Drain
   c) Exhaust d) Deplete

9. **Semblance is the synonym of:**
   a) Distinction b) Difference
   c) Disparity d) Resemblance

10. **Temerity is the synonym of:**
   a) Timidity b) Audacity
   c) Shyness d) Fearfulness

Answers

1.	(a)	2.	(d)	3.	(b)
4.	(a)	5.	(c)	6.	(d)
7.	(a)	8.	(a)	9.	(d)
10.	(b)				

Question III

Directions: In this section, you will be presented with a word. Select the option that best represents a synonym (word with a similar meaning) for the given word.

1. **Unison is the synonym of:**
   a) Harmony b) Discord
   c) Conflict d) Dissonance

2. **Vivacious is the synonym of:**
   a) Boring b) Dull
   c) Lively d) Lethargic

3. **Wry is the synonym of:**
   a) Hilarious b) Humorous
   c) Serious d) Sarcastic

4. **Yield is the synonym of:**
   a) Surrender b) Resist
   c) Defy d) Withstand

5. **Lurid is the synonym of:**
   a) Mild b) Shocking
   c) Calm d) Soothing

6. **Magnanimous is the synonym of:**
   a) Stingy b) Selfish
   c) Greedy d) Generous

7. **Novice is the synonym of:**
   a) Beginner b) Expert
   c) Professional d) Veteran

8. **Penchant is the synonym of:**
   a) Dislike b) Aversion
   c) Inclination d) Detestation

9. **Revere is the synonym of:**
   a) Disrespect b) Admire
   c) Disregard d) Ignore

10. **Savvy is the synonym of:**
   a) Knowledgeable
   b) Ignorant
   c) Uninformed
   d) Naive

Answer

1.	(a)	2.	(c)	3.	(d)
4.	(a)	5.	(b)	6.	(d)
7.	(a)	8.	(c)	9.	(b)
10.	(a)				

Question IV

Directions: In this section, you will be presented with a word. Select the option that best represents an antonym (words with an opposite meaning) for the given word.

1. Hazardous is the antonym of:

a) Safe b) Dangerous
c) Perilous d) Risky

2. Gorge is the antonym of:

a) Feast b) Devour
c) Consume d) Abstain

3. Gallant is the antonym of:

a) Heroic b) Brave
c) Valiant d) Cowardly

4. Fatuous is the antonym of:

a) Foolish b) Intelligent
c) Silly d) Stupid

5. Fragile is the antonym of:

a) Sturdy b) Delicate
c) Brittle d) Frail

6. Enormous is the antonym of:

a) Immense b) Huge
c) Tiny d) Gigantic

7. Dearth is the antonym of:

a) Abundance b) Shortage
c) Scarcity d) Lack

8. Cavort is the antonym of:

a) Rest b) Frolic
c) Play d) Dance

9. Baffle is the antonym of:

a) Confuse b) Understand
c) Puzzle d) Perplex

10. Arduous is the antonym of:

a) Laborious b) Difficult
c) Challenging d) Easy

Answer

1.	(a)	2.	(d)	3.	(d)
4.	(b)	5.	(a)	6.	(c)
7.	(a)	8.	(a)	9.	(b)
10.	(d)				

Question V

Directions: In this section, you will be presented with a word. Select the option that best represents an antonym (words with an opposite meaning) for the given word.

1. Prudent is the antonym of:

a) Reckless b) Cautious
c) Thoughtful d) Wise

2. Onus is the antonym of:

a) Duty b) Release
c) Obligation d) Responsibility

3. Naive is the antonym of:

a) Innocent b) Worldly
c) Gullibled) Credulous

4. Muster is the antonym of:

a) Collect b) Assemble
c) Gather d) Disperse

5. Lurk is the antonym of:

a) Hide b) Reveal
c) Conceal d) Sneak

6. Kindle is the antonym of:

a) Blaze b) Ignite
c) Burn d) Extinguish

7. Jumble is the antonym of:

a) Disorder b) Mess
c) Order d) Confusion

8. Intricate is the antonym of:

a) Complicated b) Complex
c) Simple d) Elaborate

9. **Intense is the antonym of:**
   a) Mild b) Strong
   c) Powerful d) Extreme

10. **Hover is the antonym of:**
   a) Land b) Float
   c) Levitate d) Soar

Answer

1.	(a)	2.	(b)	3.	(b)
4.	(d)	5.	(b)	6.	(d)
7.	(c)	8.	(c)	9.	(a)
10.	(a)				

Question VI

Directions: In this section, you will be presented with a word. Select the option that best represents an antonym (words with an opposite meaning) for the given word.

1. **Zip is the antonym of:**
   a) Unzip b) Accelerate
   c) Rush d) Prompt

2. **Yearn is the antonym of:**
   a) Crave b) Desire
   c) Reject d) Relish

3. **Xenophobia is the antonym of:**
   a) Acceptance b) Tolerance
   c) Harmony d) Hatred

4. **Wreck is the antonym of:**
   a) Ruin b) Destruction
   c) Create d) Demolish

5. **Virulent is the antonym of:**
   a) Lethal b) Deadly
   c) Mild d) Toxic

6. **Unequivocal is the antonym of:**
   a) Definite b) Clear
   c) Certain d) Ambiguous

7. **Toil is the antonym of:**
   a) Labour b) Relax
   c) Work d) Exert

8. **Swindle is the antonym of:**
   a) Cheat b) Honesty
   c) Deceive d) Scam

9. **Repel is the antonym of:**
   a) Deter b) Bore
   c) Captivate d) Encourage

10. **Quaintness is the antonym of:**
   a) Modernity b) Charm
   c) Delight d) Old-fashioned

Answer

1.	(a)	2.	(c)	3.	(a)
4.	(c)	5.	(c)	6.	(d)
7.	(b)	8.	(b)	9.	(c)
10.	(c)				

Question VII

Directions: Choose the most appropriate word to fill in the blank in each sentence. Select the letter corresponding to your chosen option.

1. **The boxer faced a tough ___________ in the upcoming match.**
   a) Ally b) Teammate
   c) Opponent d) Partner

2. **The tribe used ___________ tools and techniques for survival.**
   a) Modern b) Advanced
   c) Primitive d) Sophisticated

3. **His collection of antique books was considered the ___________ of his**

library.

a) Essence b) Foundation
c) Core d) Quintessence

4. The professor provided a brief __________ of the main points covered in the lecture.
a) Recapitulation b) Chapters
c) Expansion d) Repetition

5. She was known for her __________ habits and frugal lifestyle.
a) Expensive b) Spendthrift
c) Prodigal d) Thrifty

6. The theory proposed a __________ explanation for the observed phenomenon.
a) Limited b) Common
c) Universal d) Narrow

7. There was a faint __________ of the ancient civilization in the ruins.
a) Trace b) Hint
c) Remnant d) Vestige

8. The sign provided a __________ about the potential danger ahead.
a) Caution b) Direction
c) Guidance d) Warning

9. Her vibrant energy and enthusiasm gave her an aura of __________.
a) Maturity b) Experience
c) Wisdom d) Youthfulness

10. The two houses were in close __________, just a few steps away from each other.
a) Distance b) Proximity
c) Isolation d) Separation

Answer

1.	(c)	2.	(c)	3.	(d)
4.	(a)	5.	(d)	6.	(c)
7.	(d)	8.	(d)	9.	(d)
10.	(b)				

Question VIII

Directions: Choose the most appropriate word to fill in the blank in each sentence. Select the letter corresponding to your chosen option.

1. The professor gave a __________ lecture on advanced mathematics.
a) Confusing b) Boring
c) Captivating d) Cerebral

2. The fruit basket was __________ with a variety of fresh fruits.
a) Scarce b) Limited
c) Abundant d) Sparse

3. He received an __________ supply of resources to complete the project.
a) Insufficient b) Inadequate
c) Scanty d) Ample

4. The queen decided to __________ her loyal servant with a royal title.
a) Dismiss b) Banish
c) Praise d) Bestow

5. The wind blew __________ through the open field.
a) Slow b) Lethargic
c) Briskly d) Sluggish

6. The judge appointed a __________ lawyer to handle the complex case.
a) Incompetent b) Capable
c) Skilled d) Competent

7. The ___________ doctor provided comfort and care to the patients in need.

a) Compassionate b) Apathetic
c) Cold-hearted d) Indifferent

8. They chose to ___________ in a small cottage by the lake.

a) Abandon b) Dwell
c) Migrate d) Depart

9. It took him some time to ___________ the ancient script and understand its meaning.

a) Decipher b) Encode
c) Read d) Encrypt

10. His promotion to manager ___________ his status within the company.

a) Diminished b) Lower
c) Elevated d) Reduce

Answer

1.	(c)	2.	(c)	3.	(d)
4.	(d)	5.	(c)	6.	(d)
7.	(a)	8.	(b)	9.	(a)
10.	(c)				

Question IX

Directions: Choose the most appropriate word to fill in the blank in each sentence. Select the letter corresponding to your chosen option.

1. She provided an ___________ explanation for her absence, including every detail.

a) Simple b) Concise
c) Brief d) Elaborate

2. The actor tried to ___________ surprise when he received the award.

a) Hide b) Conceal
c) Feign d) Reveal

3. He felt ___________ for the help he received during a difficult time.

a) Ungrateful b) Thankless
c) Grateful d) Inappreciative

4. The organisation followed a ___________ structure with clear levels of authority.

a) Democratic b) Hierarchical
c) Egalitarian d) Flat

5. They decided to ___________ the new policy across all departments.

a) Abandon b) Discard
c) Implement d) Remove

6. The lawyer tried to ___________ his client's actions in court.

a) Justify b) Condemn
c) Accuse d) Disapprove

7. The garden was infested with ___________ , which was difficult to eliminate.

a) Knotweed b) Ornamental
c) Blossoming d) Fragrant

8. He adjusted his ___________ pin before entering the formal event.

a) Cuff b) Collar
c) Pocket d) Lapel

9. The chef recommended to ___________ the meat in the curd overnight for enhanced flavour.

a) Dry b) Bake

c) Fry d) Marinate

10. The smell from the garbage made her feel ___________.

a) Hungry b) Appetising

c) Nauseous d) Pleasant

Answer

1.	(d)	2.	(c)	3.	(c)
4.	(b)	5.	(c)	6.	(a)
7.	(a)	8.	(d)	9.	(d)
10.	(c)				

Question X

Match the words in Column A with their corresponding meanings in Column B by writing the appropriate letter from Column B in the space provided next to the corresponding number in Column A.

Column A	Column B
1. Luminous	**a.** Complain or protest about something in a bad-tempered but typically muted manner
2. Rogue	**b.** Making a loud, confused noise; characterised by disorderly commotion or agitation
3. Grumble	**c.** In a dying or decaying state; coming to an end
4. Advocate	**d.** Emitting or reflecting light, especially in the dark; shining or glowing.
5. Nincompoop	**e.** Magnetic
6. Docile	**f.** Absolutely necessary or essential
7. Tumultuous	**g.** A dishonest or unprincipled person
8. Imperative	**h.** A foolish or silly person; someone lacking intelligence or common sense
9. Charismatic	**i.** To support or promote a cause or idea
10. Moribund	**j.** Easily taught, managed, or controlled; obedient and submissive

Answer

1.	(d)	2.	(g)	3.	(a)
4.	(i)	5.	(h)	6.	(j)
7.	(b)	8.	(f)	9.	(e)
10.	(c)				

PYQs Practise Sets:

SET-1

Directions: Choose the word which is similar in meaning to the given word.

1. Coerce -

(a) enchant (b) pressurise
(c) cajole (d) leave

2. Chronic-

(a) ordinary (b) persistent
(c) common (d) temporary

3. Garrulous-

(a) guttural (b) throaty
(c) concise (d) talkative

4. Tilt-

(a) slant (b) straighten
(c) cross (d) support

5. Inept-

(a) capable (b) fit
(c) strong (d) clumsy

6. Inarticulate-

(a) fluent (b) inevitable
(c) eloquent (d) incoherent

7. Indelible -

(a) Illegal (b) Illegible
(c) Inerasable (d) Ineffective

8. Triumph-

(a) Fight (b) Victory
(c) Attack (d) Peace

9. Entice-

(a) ensue (b) entail
(c) enrage (d) entrap

10. Dubious-

(a) certain (b) fishy
(c) loyal (d) steady

Answers

1.	(b)	2.	(b)	3.	(d)
4.	(a)	5.	(d)	6.	(d)
7.	(c)	8.	(b)	9.	(d)
10.	(b)				

SET-2

Directions: Choose the word which is similar in meaning to the given word.

1. Drag-

(a) rush (b) pull
(c) push (d) rest

2. Engulf-

(a) encroach (b) enshrine
(c) entangle (d) envelop

3. Lethal-

(a) harmless (b) healthy
(c) fatal (d) strong

4. Prevalent-

(a) unusual (b) common
(c) rare (d) different

5. Rampant-

(a) excessive (b) limited
(c) rare (d) gentle

6. Exempt -

(a) hinder (b) exclude
(c) reduce (d) prevent

7. Reticent

(a) silent (b) garrulous
(c) extrovert (d) confident

8. Fury

(a) sorrow (b) anger
(c) cruelty (d) fright

9. Precarious-

(a) abundant (b) dangerous
(c) valuable (d) premature

10. Sterile

(a) pure (b) productive
(c) barren (d) sordid

Answers

1.	(b)	2.	(d)	3.	(c)
4.	(b)	5.	(a)	6.	(b)
7.	(a)	8.	(b)	9.	(b)
10.	(c)				

SET-3

Directions: Choose the word which is similar in meaning to the given word.

1. Pensive

(a) spontaneous (b) spiteful
(c) reflective (d) tragic

2. Vindictive

(a) watchful (b) revengeful
(c) forceful (d) helpful

3. Lament

(a) distress (b) torment
(c) afflict (d) mourn

4. Repudiate

(a) renounce (b) sanction
(c) regret (d) enforce

5. Perplex

(a) surprise (b) bewilder
(c) complex (d) deceive

6. Defer

(a) dread (b) despair
(c) dictate (d) delay

7. Mammoth

(a) gigantic (b) minuscule
(c) perilous (d) magnificent

8. Taciturn

(a) phlegmatic (b) talkative
(c) reticent (d) placid

9. Exalt

(a) challenge (b) praise
(c) condemn (d) extract

10. Concise

(a) brief (b) detailed
(c) complex (d) lengthy

Answers

1.	(c)	2.	(b)	3.	(d)
4.	(a)	5.	(b)	6.	(d)
7.	(a)	8.	(c)	9.	(b)
10.	(a)				

SET- 4

Directions: Choose the word which is opposite in meaning to the given word

1. Lackadaisical

(a) weak (b) fastidious
(c) productive (d) local

2. Metropolitan

(a) defect (b) rural
(c) calm (d) urban

3. Barbarity

(a) atrocity (b) cruelty
(c) humility (d) favour

4. Vague

(a) explicit (b) abhor
(c) vogue (d) deep

5. **Abhor**
   (a) detest (b) loathe
   (c) hate (d) praise
6. **Composed**
   (a) bright (b) nervous
   (c) dull (d) calm
7. **Abysmal**
   (a) shallow (b) arable
   (c) deep (d) profound
8. **Cogitable**
   (a) credible (b) generous
   (c) incredible (d) benevolent
9. **Virtue**
   (a) defect (b) fertile
   (c) étiquettes (d) relaxed
10. **Abet**
   (a) induce (b) aid
   (c) create (d) prevent

Answers

1.	(c)	2.	(b)	3.	(c)
4.	(a)	5.	(d)	6.	(b)
7.	(a)	8.	(c)	9.	(a)
10.	(d)				

SET-5

Directions: **Choose the word which is similar in meaning to the given word.**

1. **Renown**
   (a) obscurity (b) fame
   (c) wisdom (d) conceit
2. **Devout**
   (a) revered (b) loyal
   (c) pious (d) distant
3. **Intricate**
   (a) complete (b) colourful
   (c) connected (d) complex
4. **Assist**
   (a) help (b) mend
   (c) create (d) change
5. **Adept**
   (a) skilled (b) kind-hearted
   (c) alone (d) unknown
6. **Initiate**
   (a) sign (b) slow
   (c) start (d) show
7. **Obstacle**
   (a) benefit (b) clearance
   (c) accessory (d) barrier
8. **Endeavor**
   (a) success (b) result
   (c) achievement (d) attempt
9. **Insult**
   (a) remove (b) apply
   (c) offer (d) offend
10. **Hostility**
   (a) enmity (b) sympathy
   (c) goodwill (d) friendship

Answers

1.	(b)	2.	(c)	3.	(d)
4.	(a)	5.	(a)	6.	(c)
7.	(d)	8.	(d)	9.	(d)
10.	(a)				

SET-6

Directions: **Choose the word which is opposite in meaning to the given word.**

1. **Antagonism**
   (a) latitude (b) freedom
   (c) antipathy (d) amicable

2. **Arid**
(a) dry (b) deny
(c) damp (d) reject

3. **Exodus**
(a) hope (b) alien
(c) futile (d) inflow

4. **Curtail**
(a) biassed (b) prolonged
(c) humid (d) unbiased

5. **Futile**
(a) fruitful (b) glazed
(c) unproductive (d) observe

6. **Agony**
(a) harass (b) simple
(c) pleasure (d) tad

7. **Atheist**
(a) believer (b) antagonist
(c) theist (d) repeal

8. **Gruesome**
(a) admire (b) denial
(c) attractive (d) nadir

9. **Summit**
(a) nadir (b) culmination
(c) apogee (d) zenith

10. **Gainsay**
(a) prior (b) conform
(c) dull (d) living

Answers

1.	(d)	2.	(c)	3.	(d)
4.	(b)	5.	(a)	6.	(c)
7.	(a)	8.	(c)	9.	(a)
10.	(b)				

SET-7

Directions: Choose the word which is opposite in meaning to the given word

1. **Revere**
(a) legitimate (b) affable
(c) despise (d) virtuous

2. **Ephemeral**
(a) latent (b) eternal
(c) decay (d) anterior

3. **Idiosyncrasy**
(a) ideal (b) prevailing
(c) provoke (d) earthy

4. **Dauntless**
(a) sublime (b) bold
(c) timorous (d) craven

5. **Ambiguous**
(a) apparent (b) genuine
(c) widen (d) prolonged

6. **Vendetta**
(a) active (b) appreciation
(c) evident (d) allure

7. **Beguile**
(a) rigid (b) usual
(c) robust (d) allure

8. **Benevolent**
(a) beguile (b) insolent
(c) benign (d) rural

9. **Barren**
(a) unproductive (b) local
(c) arable (d) credible

10. **Embark**
(a) commence (b) begin
(c) initiate (d) terminate

Answers

1.	(c)	2.	(b)	3.	(a)
4.	(c)	5.	(a)	6.	(b)
7.	(a)	8.	(b)	9.	(c)
10.	(d)				

SET-8

Directions: Choose the word which is opposite in meaning to the given word

1. **Ancestor**
(a) successor (b) sustain
(c) agreement (d) retain

2. **Frailty**
(a) vulnerable (b) lethargic
(c) weak (d) energy

3. **Anonymous**
(a) renowned (b) stern
(c) famous (d) relinquish

4. **Vigilant**
(a) cautious (b) modest
(c) negligent (d) humility

5. **Coherent**
(a) cacophony (b) clement
(c) kind (d) chaos

6. **Bondage**
(a) liberation (b) humble
(c) optimist (d) generous

7. **Meagre**
(a) mandarin (b) curb
(c) ample (d) dismay

8. **Narcissist**
(a) safety (b) ardour
(c) neglect (d) altruist

9. **Detest**
(a) condemn (b) scold
(c) praise (d) censure

10. **Egoist**
(a) egotist (b) humanitarian
(c) nostalgia (d) shroud

Answers

1.	(a)	2.	(d)	3.	(c)
4.	(c)	5.	(a)	6.	(a)
7.	(c)	8.	(d)	9.	(c)
10.	(b)				

SET-9

Directions: Choose the word which is opposite in meaning to the given word

1. **Dense**
(a) global (b) sparse
(c) refuse (d) love

2. **Impede**
(a) criticise (b) inflow
(c) disallow (d) hinder

3. **Catholic**
(a) parochial (b) humble
(c) hostility (d) dislike

4. **Impeccable**
(a) smooth (b) fallible
(c) respect (d) intact

5. **Exonerated**
(a) enfeeble (b) firm
(c) convicted (d) generous

6. **Lewd**
(a) bawdy (b) gesture
(c) tremendous (d) elegance

7. **Gaudy**
(a) living (b) gainsay
(c) prior (d) elegant

8. Dilettantism

(a) sobriety (b) slim
(c) odious (d) typical

9. Attenuate

(a) narrow (b) breadth
(c) pygmy (d) length

10. Ambiguous

(a) jest (b) engross
(c) apparent (d) jade

Answers

1.	(b)	2.	(b)	3.	(a)
4.	(b)	5.	(c)	6.	(d)
7.	(d)	8.	(a)	9.	(d)
10.	(c)				

SET 10

Directions: Choose the word which is opposite in meaning to the given word

1. Camouflage

(a) flaunt (b) real
(c) nervous (d) uncurious

2. Dormant

(a) fake (b) reveal
(c) stringent (d) diligent

3. Tardy

(a) slow (b) slow
(c) crawling (d) rapid

4. Conclude

(a) commence (b) end
(c) terminate (d) finish

5. Benign

(a) gentle (b) generous
(c) malicious (d) humble

6. Coherent

(a) messy (b) chaotic
(c) contend (d) alluring

7. Barbarous

(a) cultured (b) tad
(c) unethical (d) infamous

8. Boorish

(a) genial (b) rude
(c) impolite (d) detest

9. Annihilate

(a) deep (b) reject
(c) shallow (d) make

10. Clamorous

(a) dubious (b) boisterous
(c) articulate (d) quiet

Answers

1.	(a)	2.	(b)	3.	(d)
4.	(a)	5.	(c)	6.	(a)
7.	(a)	8.	(a)	9.	(d)
10.	(d)				

Chapter - Four

Phrasal Verbs

Phrasal verbs

Introduction

Phrasal verbs are special combinations of verbs and particles (prepositions or adverbs) that have unique meanings when used together. They add a lot of flavour and versatility to the English language. Let's break it down in a simple and easy manner:

Verb: A word that describes an action (e.g., run, eat, sleep).

Particle: A small word that changes the meaning of the verb when combined with it (e.g., up, off, in).

When you combine a verb with a particle, you create a new expression with a different meaning. Here are a few examples:

"Turn off" - It means to stop the operation or functioning of something. For example: "Please turn off the lights before leaving."

"Give up" - It means to stop doing or trying something. For example: "I decided to give up smoking for my health."

"Get along" - It means to have a good relationship or manage well with someone. For example: "They get along very well as roommates."

"Take off" - It means to remove or to leave quickly. For example: "He took off his jacket before entering the room." or "The plane will take off in a few minutes."

All Phrasal Verbs asked in SSC (from 2012 till date)

1. **Account for- To explain the reason for**

   Example- "Asking the government to account for its work is a trend now", PM Narendra Modi

2. **Answer for: to be answerable for (किसी गलत बात की जिम्मेदारी लेना)**

   Example - If one makes a mistake then one should be ready to answer for it.

3. **Ask after: to inquire about (किसी के बारे में पूछताछ करना)**

   Example - Rohit had to contact the branch office to ask after the delay in the process.

4. **Attend on: to serve (सेवा करना)**

   Example - We should not forget to attend on our grandparents in their old age.

5. **Back out: to choose not to do something agreed (किसी सहमत बात से पीछे हटना)**

   Example - After his father had refused him, he backed out of the picnic plan.

6. **Back up: to support (सहायता देना)**

   Example - I couldn't have solved this issue without your back up.

7. **Bear down: to press down heavily (दबाना या कुचलना)**

   Example - The snow bore down on the roof. (बर्फ़बारी ने छत पर दबाव बनाया)

8. **Blow over: to pass without harming (बिना नुकसान पहुचाये गुजर जाना)**

   Example - My headache finally blew over.

9. **Bound for: going to a destination (किसी स्थान को जाता हुआ)**

   Example - This train is bound for Chennai.

10. **Break down (of machinery) : to stop working (कम करना बंद कर देना)**

    Example - Our car broke down on the way of Udaipur. (कार ने ख़राब होने के कारण काम करना बंद कर दिया)

11. **Break down: to lose control emotionally (रोने लगना)**

    Example - The old lady broke down when heard the news of her son's death.

12. **Break into: to enter illegally (जबरदस्ती घुसना)**

    Example - Last night, some thieves broke into our neighbor's house

13. **Break out: to start (of disease or war etc.) (अचानक फैलना)**

    Example - In Southern Jaipur, the swine flu has broken out.

14. **Break up (of relationship) : to end/ separate (अलग हो जाना)**

Example - Suman and Sohan broke up after 5 year's long relationship.

15. **Bring about: to cause to happen (होने का कारण होना)**

Example - This injury on my hand brought about skin infection to my whole body. (इन्फेक्शन होने का कारण हाथ पर हुई चोट हैं)

16. **Bring down: to reduce (कम करना)**

Example - Carelessness in studies brings down the performance of students in exam.

17. **Bring up: to raise, to rear (पालन पोषण करना)**

Example - After My parent's death in an accident, I was brought up by my grandparents.

18. **Call for: to demand (मांग करना)**

Example - The Company workers called for extra wages.

19. **Call off: to cancel (रद्द कर देना)**

Example - Due to heavy rainfall, we had to call off our picnic plan.

20. **Call on: to pay a visit (जाकर मुलाकात करना)**

Example - The Rural development minister calls on rural areas every month.

21. **Call up: to recall (याद करना)**

Example - Although Tina is an atheist, she calls up God when in trouble.

22. **Carry on: to continue (जारी रखना)**

Example - After the rain had stopped, we carried on our party on the roof.

23. **Carry out: to execute (किसी कार्य को पूरा करना)**

Example - The Supervisor carried out all the instructions carefully given by Manager.

24. **Catch up (with): to stop being behind (बराबरी पर आ जाना)**

Example - Though Rajan took admission in the midsession, he caught up with his classmates in final exams.

25. **Clear someone of: to free from blame (आरोप मुक्त करना)**

Example - The Court has cleared him of all the charges leveled against him.

26. **Come about: to happen (घटित होना)**

Example - What came about last night? I had heard something.

27. **Come across: to meet by chance (अचानक मुलाकात होना)**

Example - Yesterday, while wandering in the market, I came across my old school friend.

28. **Come off : to be successful (सफल होना)**

Example - After toiling hard, Ramesh has finally come off in his IAS exam.

29. **Cordon off : to seal a place (किसी स्थान की घेराबंदी करना)**

Example - The Police cordoned off the area, where the accident took place.

30. **Count on : to depend on, to rely on (विश्वास करना या निर्भर रहना)**

Example 1 - Drishti always counts on her mother for her personal work as she is too lazy. (निर्भर रहती हैं)

Example 2 - Nowadays, it's not safe to count on strangers. (विश्वाश करना)

31. **Cut out for : to be suitable for (किसी कार्य के लिए उपयुक्त होना)**

Example - The Candidate who will be cut out for the post, will be recruited by our HR manager.

32. **Deal in : to have business of (किसी चीज का व्यापर करना)**

Example - Mr. Sinha deals in garment. (कपड़ो का व्यापर करते हैं)

33. **Deal out : to distribute (वितरित करना)**

Example - Our teacher dealt out the exam sheet.

34. **Deal with : to treat with a person (किसी से व्यव्हार करना)**

Example - My aunt deals with everyone in a very kind way.

35. **Do away with : to abolish/murder (समाप्त कर देना)**

Example - Hari was very disturbed with his family issue, he finally did away with it. (मुद्दों को सुलझा के समाप्त कर दिया)

36. **Drop in/by : to visit informally (बिना पूर्व सूचना के आ जाना)**

Example - Yesterday, Our Principal madam dropped in class.

37. **Egg on : to motivate (प्रेरित करना)**

Example - Our Parents always egg on us for a better career.

38. **Fall for : fall in love with (आकर्षित होना)**

Example - Jack fell for Jill in his early school days.

39. **Fall out (with) : to quarrel with (झगडा होना)**

Example - Yesterday, Our neighbors fell out on trivial matters.

40. **Feel like : to be excited to do something (किसी काम को करने का इच्छुक होना)**

Example - Sachin loves cricket, he feels like playing it all the time.

41. **Figure out : to understand (समझ पाना)**

Example - The manager is trying to figure out the concept of a new project.

42. **Fizzle out : to weaken gradually (क्रमश कमजोर पड़ना)**

Example - We were all excited about festivals in childhood, but the excitement has frizzled out. (त्योहारों का उत्साह धीरे धीरे कम हो गया हैं)

43. **Gain on : to come close to (प्रतियोगिता में नजदीक होना)**

Example - Although Rita was an average student in the beginning, she gained on topper of class in annual exams.

44. **Get along (with someone) : to have a friendly relationship (दोस्ताना व्यव्हार होना)**

Example - Deepika gets along well with Ranvir.

45. **Get away with : to do something illegal without being punished (गलत कम करके बिना सजा के बच के निकल जाना)**

Example - Though Rohan had committed a crime, he got away with this

46. **Get over : to have control on (किसी पर काबू होना)**

Example - Parents should be able to get over their children.

47. **Get on : to make progress (प्रगति करना)**

Example - Everyone can get on if he/ she works hard.

48. **Get rid of : to leave, to dispose of, to throw away (छुटकारा पाना)**

Example - We were so irritated with the children, so we sent them out to play and got rid of the disturbance.

49. **Get through with : to complete a task (किसी कार्य को पूरा करना)**

Example - The marketing team has got through with its assignment.

50. **Give away : to reveal the secret (रहस्य उजागर करना)**

Example - My friends were planning a surprise birthday party but one of them was so excited that he gave away the plan.

51. **Give in : to surrender (समर्पण करना)**

Example - However, The king had struggled hard but in the end, he had to give in.

52. **Give up : abandon (त्याग देना)**

Example - After watching the height of the mountain, we gave up our plan of climbing.

53. **Go about : to move from place to place (एक जगह से दूसरी जगह जाना)**

Example - Government employees go about in towns and villages for the social campaign.

54. **Go along with : to agree (सहमत होना)**

Example - My boss went along with me on the idea regarding the upcoming project.

55. **Goes by : to work accordingly (नियमानुसार कार्य करना)**

Example - Suman is a very sincere employee; she always goes by the company's policies.

56. **Go down in history : to get admitted in history (इतिहास में नाम दर्ज होना)**

Example - Gandhiji struggled hard for freedom in India so his name went down in history.

57. **Go on : to continue doing something (किसी कार्य को जारी रखना)**

Example - Even after the exam gets

postponed, Students should go on preparation.

58. Get through with : to complete a task (किसी कार्य को पूरा करना)

Example - The marketing team has got through with its assignment.

59. Give away : to reveal the secret (रहस्य उजागर करना)

Example - My friends were planning a surprise birthday party but one of them was so excited that he gave away the plan.

60. Give in : to surrender (समर्पण करना)

Example - However, The king had struggled hard but at the end, he had to give in.

61. Give up : abandon (त्याग देना)

Example - After watching the height of the mountain, we gave up our plan of climbing.

62. Go about : to move from place to place (एक जगह से दूसरी जगह जाना)

Example - Government employees go about in town and villages for the social campaign.

63. Go along with : to agree (सहमत होना)

Example - My boss went along with me on the idea regarding the upcoming project.

64. Goes by : to work accordingly (नियमानुसार कार्य करना)

Example - Suman is a very sincere employee; she always goes by company's policies.

65. Go down in history : to get admitted in history (इतिहास में नाम दर्ज होना)

Example - Gandhiji struggled hard for freedom in India so his name went down in history.

66. Go on : to continue doing something (किसी कार्य को जारी रखना)

Example - Even after the exam gets postponed, Students should go on preparation.

67. Go through : To read, to pass through a time (किसी दौर से गुजरना/ पढना)

Example1. - You are advised to go through this chapter in order to find the solution of your problem. (पढना)

Example2. - These days, Real estate business is going through inflation. (मंदी के दौर से गुजर रहा हैं)

68. Go with : to match (मेल खाना)

Example - This scarf is going with my new dress which I bought last week.

69. Hear of : to get the news about (किसी के बारे में सूचना मिलना)

Example - I was shocked when heard of his fatal accident. (दुर्घटना के बारे में सूचना मिलना)

70. Hit out : to attack verbally (आलोचना करना)

Example - Some persons are in the habit of hitting out others.

71. **Hold back : to control expression (व्यक्त करने से रुकना)**

Example - Sunita was about to say something, but suddenly she held back. (बोलते बोलते रुक गयी)

72. **Hold on : to keep something in a position**

Example - In spite of her aching shoulders, Robin held onthe rope.(कंधे में दर्द के बावजूद रस्सी को पकडे रखा)

73. **Jump at : to reach conclusion in a hurry (जल्दबाजी में किसी निष्कर्ष पर पहुचना)**

Example - John has no passions, he always jumps at. (धैर्य नही होने के कारण जल्दी में निष्कर्ष पर पहुच जाता हैं)

74. **Keep away : to maintain distance (दूरी बनाये रखना)**

Example - Childern were instructed to keep away from garbage while playing in the street. (कचरे से दूर रहने के लिए कहा गया)

75. **Keep from : to abstain from (बुरी संगत से दूर रहना)**

Example - We should keep from bad company.

76. **Keep up: to maintain in good condition/ to continue doing something (अच्छी स्थिति में रखना/ किसी कार्य को जारी रखना)**

Example1. - Sameer loves his bike, so he keeps it up. (अच्छी स्थिति में रखता हैं)

Example2. - You are doing well in a game, keep it up. (जारी रखो)

77. **Knock down : to thrust someone to the ground (धक्का मार के गिरा देना)**

Example - In the game of Kabbadi, Sushil knocked down his opponent.

78. **Lay down : to give up arms (हथियार डाल देना)**

Example - Though soldiers struggled hard in the battle, but in the end they had to lay down.

79. **Lay off : to dismiss/ to fire (छटनी करना/ नौकरी से निकालना)**

Example - In the time of recession, Companies usually lay off their employees.

80. **Lie behind : to be the real reason (वास्तविक कारण होना)**

Example - We need to explore what lies behind the increasing weight problem. (वजन बढ़ने के पीछे वास्तविक कारण क्या हैं)

81. **Live by : to earn livelihood/ to follow (कोई काम करके गुजर बसर करना/ अनुसरण करना)**

Example - My uncle lives by furniture work.(फर्नीचर का काम करके गुजर बसर करते हैं)

Example - We should live by traffic rules while on road. (यातायात के नियमो का अनुसरण करना चाहिए)

82. **Live off : to live on particular food**

(किसी खास भोजन पर रहना)

Example - Some monks live off fruits and vegetables only. (सिर्फ फल और सब्जिया ही खाते हैं)

83. Live through : to survive in difficulty (किसी अप्रिय अनुभव को झेलना)

Example - Nowadays, My family is living throughinsolvency. (कंगाली में रह रहे हैं)

84. Live up to : to reach an expected standard (उम्मीद के अनुसार होना)

Example - This project should have lived up to, but unfortunately it is not. (उम्मीद के अनुसार होना चाहिए था)

85. Look about/for : to search (खोजना)

Example 1. - I am looking about my spectacles.

Example 2.- My mother has looked for the shirt, but didn't find it.

86. Look after : to take care of something or someone (देख भाल करना)

Example - We should look after our grandparents in their old age.

87. Look down on /upon : to regard as inferior (नीची निगाह से देखना / किसी को कम आंकना)

Example - He looks down on everyone, who doesn't belong to his community.

88. Look forward to : to anticipate pleasantly (उत्सुकता से प्रतीक्षा करना)

Example - As Minal has performed well in an interview, she is looking forward to a positive response from the company.

89. Look into : to investigate (जाँच करना-खोजबीन के सन्दर्भ में)

Example - The police are looking into the case honestly.

90. Look out for : to try to find (खोजने या समझने की कोशिश करना)

Example - You need to look out for why he declined your proposal.

91. Look over : to examine (जांच करना)

Example - Teachers look over the answer sheet carefully before submitting them to the exam cell.

92. Make do with : to manage (काम चलाना)

Example - There was no juice so I had to make do with a soft drink which I generally avoid.

93. Make for : to result in/ to cause (किसी बात में सहायक होना)

Example - The low quality of service made for failure of project. (गुणवत्ता में कमी, प्रोजेक्ट के असफल होने का कारण बनी)

94. Make out : to manage to understand (किसी व्यक्ति या चीज को समझना)

Example - Manager is trying to make out the concept of a new project proposed by me.

95. Make the most of : to get maximum (पूरा पूरा लाभ उठाना)

Example - The smart person always

makes the most of every situation that comes his way.

96. **Occur to : to understand (समझ में आना)**

Example - Physics never occurs to me, however, I try a lot to understand it.

97. **Part with : to leave/ abandon (बिछड़ना / त्यागना वस्तु के सन्दर्भ में)**

Example - You need to part with your some luggage as it is creating extra load in the car.

98. **Part from : leave or separate from someone (किसी व्यक्ति से अलग होना या बिछड़ना)**

Example - Reena parted from her boyfriend after five year's long relationship.

99. **Pull off : to succeed in doing something difficult (किसी मुश्किल काम को करने में सफल होना)**

Example - It was almost impossible to convey my father for my Udaipur trip but finally we have pulled off.

100. **Pull up : to criticize (आलोचना करना)**

Example - My aunt is in the habit of pulling up others without any reason.

101. **Put across : to communicate successfully (समझोता आदि के लिए बातचीत करना)**

Example - Pakistan and China put across on the issue of their new upcoming project.

102. **Put aside : to save for future or to avoid (भविष्य के लिए बचाना या उपेक्षा करना)**

Example1. - It is always advised to put aside some money from our parents. (भविष्य के लिए बचाना)

Example2. - Rohan put aside all the bottlenecks while preparing for the IAS exam. (नजरंदाज किया)

103. **Put up with : to tolerate (सहन करना)**

Example - We should never put up with wrong doings or unsocial elements.

104. **Put forth : to request (निवेदन करना)**

Example - We had to put forth to authority to consider our application first.

105. **Put together : to put someone in trouble or to create or construct (किसी को परेशानी में डालना/ बनाना)**

Example 1. - Reena always puts together me with her pranks. (परेशानी में डाल देती हैं)

Example 2. - The manager has put together separate team for every task. (मैनेजर ने सभी कार्य के लिए अलग टीम बनायीं हैं)

106. **Put down : to suppress or criticize (दमन करना या आलोचना करना)**

Example - The mettle king put down his enemy bravely. (शत्रुओ का दमन किया)

107. **Put off : to postpone (स्थगित करना)**

Example - Karan had to put off his

holiday trip due to the busy schedule of the office.

108. Put on : to wear clothes/ gain weight (कपडे पहनना या वजन का बढ़ना)

Example - Children don't like putting on woolen clothes even in extreme winter. (भरी सर्दी में भी ऊनी कपडे पहनना पसंद नही करते)

Example - Sheela has put on so she is not able to fit in her old dresses. (वजन बढ़ गया हैं)

109. Put out : to extinguish (बुझाना)

Example - At last, the fire brigade arrived and put out the fire.

110. Put through : to make someone feel .something unpleasant (किसी को परेशानी में डालना)

Example - Seema is very childish in nature, she always puts through others.

111. Run down : to criticize / to decline (आलोचना करना / कमजोर पड़ना)

Example - Don't run down your brother in public, it will definitely annoy him. (आलोचना मत करो)

Example - Due to the low quality of service, the rating of this product has run down. (रेटिंग कम हो गयी हैं)

112. Run into (problem) : to face (समस्या में पड जाना)

Example - I just wanted to help him, but I didn't know I would run into this pathetic situation.

113. Run into : to meet by chance (अचानक मुलाकात होना)

Example - It was really unexpected to run into my old college friend in market.

114. Run over : to crush by a vehicle (वाहन से कुचलना)

Example - Yesterday, My grandmother was run over by a car in street.

115. Set about : to initiate effort (प्रयास प्रारंभ करना)

Example - Vikas is very sincere about his career, he set about his IAS exam in the graduation period.

116. Set up : to establish (स्थापित करना)

Example - Coal India has set up one of its branches in Dhanbad.

117. Sit around/about : to spend time without any activity (खाली बैठना)

Example - My brother is so careless. He neither studies nor works. He just sits around.

118. Smile on : to bless (भाग्य का किसी पर प्रसन्न होना)

Example - Destiny has smiled at Tanmay as he has cracked the exam without preparing for it.

119. See off - To take leave of

Example- I went to the station to see off my friends.

120. Stand by - To remain loyal/ to be ready

Example- I will stand by you through thick and thin.

121. Taken aback- To be surprised

Example- I was taken aback by his audacity.

122. Take after - To resemble a close, older relative

Example- He has taken after his father.

123. Take over - To take responsibility for or control of

Example- A new secretary has taken over the key post.

124. Turn down - To refuse or reject

Example- He turned down my offer.

125. Turn out (to be) - To prove to be

Example- He turned out to be a crook.

126. Wear off - To lose effect Soon

Example- The polish started wearing off .

127. Weigh down - To make anxious, to burden

Example- Men were weighed down with added responsibilities.

Top 300 MOST REPEATED Phrasal Verbs asked in SSC Exam

English	Hindi
Phrasal verb starts with 'a'	
Account for	हिसाब देना
Ask after	बारे में पूछना
Ask in	अंदर बुलाना
Answer back	मुँह लगे जबाब देना
Answer for	जिम्मेदार होना
Add to	बढ़ाना
Act on/upon	असर डालना
Add up	का योग करना
Allow for	ध्यान में लेना
Phrasal verb starts with 'b'	
Back out	पीछे हटना
Back up	समर्थन देना
Bank on	भरोसा करना
be off	चला जाना
bear out	साथ देना
beat up	खूब पीटना
blow out	फूंककर बुझाना
blow up	बर्बाद करना
break down	स्वास्थ ख़राब हो जाना
break in	बल पुर्बक भीतर जाना
break into	जबर्दस्ती घुसना
break out	फेलना
break with	आदत छोड़ना
break up	समाप्त हो जाना
bring about	उत्पन्न करना
bring under	नियंत्रण में करना
bring down	गिरना
bring out	प्रकट करना
bring up	पालन पोषण करना
build on/upon	निर्भर करना
build up	बढ़ना
bail out	जमानत देना
bring along	साथ लाना
bring forward	दिखाना

English	Hindi
Phrasal verb starts with 'c'	
call on	किसी को बुलाना
call off	वापस लेना
call up	याद करना
call for	मांग करना
call on	थोड़ी देर के लिए जाना
call out	बुलाना
call at	थोड़ी देर के लिए जाना
call back	वापस बुलाना
call down	प्रार्थना करना
care about	चिंतित होना
care for	पसंद करना
carry away	उत्तेजित करना
carry off	जितना
carry on	चलाना
cast aside	छोड़ देना
catch up with	आगे निकलना
clear off	छुटकारा पाना
clear out	चला जाना
climb down	उतरना
close down	स्थाई रूप से बंद करना
close with	स्वीकार करना
come at	पहुंचना
come back	लौटना
come down	उतरना
come in	अंदर जाना
come in for	हासिल करना
come in on	भाग लेना
come of	संतान होना
come off	अलग होना
come on	पीछे आना
come over	दूर से आना
come to	होश में आना
come up with	सामना करना
come upon	आक्रमण करना

English	Hindi
cool down	शांत होना
cry down	निंदा करना
cry out	चिल्लाना
cry up	प्रयास करना
cut away	काट केर हटा देना
cut back	घटाना
cut down	छोटा करना
cut in	हस्तछेप करना
Phrasal verb starts with 'd'	
deal in	बेचना
deal with	संबंध रखना
die away	शांत हो जाना
dig up	उखाड़ फेखना
do with	काम चलाना
draw back	पीछे हटना
draw on	पहुंचना
drink in	चूसना
drop across	अचानक मिलना
drop off	कम हो जाना
dry up	सुखना
Phrasal verb starts with 'e'	
eat up	सब खा जाना
end off	समाप्त करना
enter into	खोलना
enter on/upon	आरम्भ करना
explain away	समझाना
Phrasal verb starts with 'f'	
fade away	धीरे धीरे नजरो से गायब होना
fall away	छोड़ना
fall back	पीठ दिखाना
fall down on	असफल होना
fall for	प्रभावित होना
fall in	दरार पड़जाना
fall on/upon	आक्रमण करना
fall through	असफल होना
feel for	खोजना
feel up to	योग्य होना

English	Hindi
fill out	फूलना
fill up	पूरा भरना
find out	खोज निकालना
Phrasal verb starts with 'g'	
get about	फेल जाना
get ahead	बढ़ना
get along with	सहमत होना
get at	पहुंचना
get back	सत्ता में लौटना
get by	जिन्दा करना
get into	पहनना
get on	आगे बढ़ना
get on with something	जारी करना
get out	प्रकट करना /बहार निकलना
get over	भूलना
get round	फसा लेना
get through	सम्पर्क करना
get up	उठना
give away	वितरण करना
give in	मान जाना
give out	समाप्त होना
give up	त्याग देना
go away	चला जाना
go down	डूबना
go on	जारी रखना
go over	छानबीन करना
go through	पार करना
go up	उठना
Phrasal verb starts with 'h'	
hand down	सौंपना
hand over	दूसरे को देना
hang on	जकड कर पकड़ना
hang out	दिखाना
hold off	दूर रहना
hold on	रुकना
hold over	स्थगित करना
hunt for	खोजना
hush up	छिपाना

English	Hindi
Phrasal verb starts with 'i'	
imbue with	भरना
inquire for	किसी के बारे में पूछना
insist on	जोर देना
Phrasal verb starts with 'j'	
jump at	खुसी से स्वीकार करना
jump on/upon	हमला करना
Phrasal verb starts with 'k'	
keep back	रोक लेना
keep down	दमन करना
keep off	दूर रहना
keep on	जारी रखना
keep out	बहार रहना
keep under	दबा देना
keep up	जारी रखना
knock about	ठोकर मारना
Phrasal verb starts with 'L'	
laugh at	उपहास उड़ाना
launch out	प्रारम्भ करना
lay aside	बचत करना
lay down	स्थापित करना
lay in	जमा करना
lay on	लगाना
lay out	व्यय करना
leave off	बंद कर देना
leave over	स्थगित करना
let off	सजा न देना
let up	काम होना
lie on/upon	आश्रित होना
look after	देखभाल करना
look for	खोजना
look into	निरीक्षण करना
look on	देखना
look out	ताक में रहना
look over	छानबीन करना
look up	ढूंढ निकालना
look up to	इज्जत करना

English	Hindi
Phrasal verb starts with 'm'	
make after	पीछा करना
make away with	आत्महत्या करना
make of	समझना
make out	निकालना
make up	पूरा करना
make up for	क्षतिपूर्ति करना
meet with	अनुभव करना
move in	घर में प्रवेश करना
move on	चलना / बढ़ना
phrasal verb starts with "N"	
nose something out	सूंघ कर पता करना
note down	लिख कर रखना
nuzzle up/to	नाक रगड़ना
Phrasal verb starts with 'o'	
open with	प्रारम्भ करना
offend against	गलत करना
Phrasal verb starts with 'p'	
pass away	गुजर जाना
pass for	स्वीकृत होना
pass on	मर जाना
pass over	अनदेखा करना
pay back	चुकाना
pick off	अलग करना
pick out	छाट लेना
pick up	उठा लेना
pull down	दमन करना
pull off	सफल होना
pull in	आकर्षित करना
pull up	फटकारना
push over	गिरा देना
put aside	बचाना
put in	देना
put up	उठाना
put on	धारण करना
Phrasal verb starts with 'q'	
quarrel with	असहमत होना

English	Hindi
quest for	खोजना
Phrasal verb starts with 'r'	
read out	बोल कर पढ़ना
rub off	रगड़ कर साफ करना
run away	भाग जाना
run into	टकरा जाना
run out	समाप्त हो जाना
run over	कुचल देना
run through	उड़ा देना
Phrasal verb starts with 's'	
see about	प्रबंध करना
see off	विदा करना
see to	देख रेख करना
sell out	बेच देना
send for	बुलावा भेजना
send out	बाटना
send out	उत्पन्न करना
set about	शुरू करना
set aside	अलग रखना
set in	प्रारम्भ होना
set off	प्रस्थान करना
set for	निर्धारित करना
set out	रवाना होना
set up	खड़ा करना
set upon	हमला करना
settle up	चुकता कर देना
shake up	मिलाना
show off	इठलाना
shut down	दुकान बंद करना
shut off	बंद करना
shut up	चुप कर देना
sit down	बेठ जाना
sit up	उठ जाना
stand off	अलग रहना
stay off	दूर रहना
stay out	बहार ठहरना
step down	त्याग पत्र देना
step up	बढ़ाना

English	Hindi
stick at	जारी रखना
stop out	घर से बाहर रहना
Phrasal verb starts with 't'	
take back	वापस ले लेना
take off	उड़ान भरना
take down	लिख लेना
take off	हटाना
take over	उत्तरदायित्व लेना
take up	उठाना
tell from	अंतर करना
think of	विचार करना
think about	जांचना
think up	सोच निकालना
throw off	छुटकारा पाने में सफल होना
throw up	त्याग पत्र देना
try out	आजमाएं"
tumble over	गिर पड़ना
turn away	हटा देना
turn down	रद्द कर देना
turn on	निर्भर कर देना
turn up	उपस्थित होना
Phrasal verb starts with 'u, v'	
use up	उपभोग करना
vouch for	जिम्मेवार होना
vote down	मतदान के द्वारा हटाना
Phrasal verb starts with 'w'	
wait up	सजग रहना
wait upon	इंतजार करना
wake up	जागना
wake up to	होश में आना
walk into	फस जाना
walk off	छोड़ना
walk out	हड़ताल पर जाना
walk up	पहुंचना
wash away/out	धोकर हटाना
watch over	देख रेख करना
wind down	बंद करना
wipe out	अस्तित्व मिटा देना

English	Hindi
work off	छुटकारा पाना
work out	हल करना
work up	भड़कना
write down	लिखना
yell out	तेज चिल्लाना
zip through	तेजी से करना या पढ़ना

PREPOSITIONAL-PHRASES

Competition with (somebody)

- in a situation in which you are trying to get something that other people also want
- ऐसी स्थिति में जिसमें आप कुछ पाने की कोशिश कर रहे हैं जो अन्य लोग भी चाहते हैं
- This time I have a competition with the class topper for the first rank.

Competition for (something)

- the act or process of competing for something
- किसी चीज की प्रतिस्पर्धा करने की क्रिया या भाव
- This time it's a huge competition for the first rank.

Compliance with (a request)

- acting according to certain accepted standards
- कुछ स्वीकृत मानकों के अनुसार कार्य करना
- The company was in compliance with the various safety regulations.

Compensation for (a loss)

- the act of compensating for service, loss, or injury
- सेवा, हानि या चोट की भरपाई
- I have decided to buy a wristwatch for my sister as a compensation for her lost watch.

A Contrast between (two things)

- an obvious difference between two or more things
- दो या अधिक चीजों के बीच एक स्पष्ट अंतर
- She wore a beautiful red-black dress at the party, and the contrast between the two colours added beauty to her dress.

A Contrast to (a person or thing)

- compare in such a way as to emphasize differences.
- इस तरह से तुलना करें कि मतभेदों पर जोर दिया जाए।
- Politicians these days promise a lot of things like free electricity, free education etc., but in contrast to this, all they do is corruption.

Decision on (some case)

- a report of a conclusion regarding a case
- किसी मामले से संबंधित निष्कर्ष की रिपोर्ट
- The decision on the Ayodhya case is soon to be released.

Decision of (some dispute)

- a conclusion or resolution on a dispute reached after consideration.
- विचार के बाद किसी विवाद पर निष्कर्ष या संकल्प
- I had a great fight with my best friend, but I took decision of the fight based on

the fact that she is the only person who stood by my side when I was in need.

Decline of (an empire)

- The end of an empire
- एक साम्राज्य का अंत
- After the decline of the power of Rome, the dominant force in Asiatic commerce and navigation was Persia

Decline in (moral/ price)

- a gradual and continuous loss of strength, numbers, quality, or value.
- शक्ति, संख्या, गुणवत्ता या मूल्य का एक क्रमिक और निरंतर नुकसान
- Last time this dress was so expensive when I found it in the market. The decline in price is due to the festive sale, I guess.

Desire for (wealth)

- strongly wish for wealth.
- धन की प्रबल इच्छा।
- Those who have a strong desire for wealth and believe in their own hard work, make their way to success either by hook or by crook.

Desirous of (something)

- impelled or governed by the desire of something
- किसी चीज की इच्छा से लगाया हुआ या शासित
- We all are desirous of success.

Disgust at (something)

- Strong feeling of dislike for something.
- किसी बात से घृणा करना
- She expressed her disgust at the program by writing a letter of complaint.

Dislike to (a person or a thing)

- feel distaste for or hostility towards a person or a thing.
- किसी व्यक्ति या किसी चीज़ के प्रति शत्रुता या दुश्मनी महसूस करना
- He treated the Levellers with some severity and showed his instinctive dislike to revolutionary proposals

Distaste for (mathematics/ something)

- mild dislike or aversion for something.
- किसी चीज के लिए घृणा।
- My friend's brother hates studying but his distaste for mathematics is jaw-dropping.

Grief at (an event)

- Show intense sorrow at an event.
- किसी घटना में एक तीव्र दुःख दिखाना।
- His friends gathered to show their grief at his mother's death.

Grief for (a person)

- intense sorrow caused by the loss of a loved one (especially by death)
- किसी प्रियजन की हानि के कारण तीव्र दुःख (विशेषकर मृत्यु के कारण)
- No one can measure his grief for his mother.

Hindrance to (something)

- an obstruction to something

- किसी चीज के लिए रुकावट
- I was solving my Maths problems while my younger sister was constantly making hindrance to it by playing music and tickling me.

Abundance of (something)

- Excess of wealth
- धन की अधिकता
- He has an abundance of wealth yet he never helps the needy.

Alternative to (a method/ something)

- necessitating a choice between mutually exclusive possibilities of something
- किसी चीज़ की पारस्परिक रूप से अनन्य संभावनाओं के बीच चुनाव करना
- One should always keep an alternative to one's school dress, in case it is not ironed or washed.

Conformity with (something)

- Similarity in form or type of views
- रूप या प्रकार के विचारों में समानता
- Knowledge is of ideas and is in conformity with the necessary laws of thought.

Conformity to (a rule)

- Similarity in form or type agreement in character.
- Decisions must be taken in conformity with the company's procedures.
- If a man is thought of as under the authority of God, any transgression of or want of conformity to the law of God is defined as sin.

Compensation for (a loss)

- something, typically money, awarded to someone in recognition of loss, suffering, or injury.
- आमतौर पर पैसा, नुकसान, दुख, या चोट की भरपाई
- My friend offered to pay for lunch as compensation for keeping me waiting.

Contempt for (a person or a thing)

- किसी व्यक्ति या चीज की निंदा
- If you have contempt for someone, you can
- They held contempt for politicians.

Degradation from (something)

- The act of lowering something or someone to a less respected state.
- किसी चीज से ह्रास
- The long term danger of land degradation from irrigation and chemical fertilizers is growing.

Delight in (something)

- Happiness in doing something
- किसी चीज में खुशी
- My delight in them is as varied as my moods.

Exception to (a rule)

- person or thing that is excluded from a general statement or does not follow a rule.

- एक नियम के अपवाद
- It's always easy to, learn the rules of organic chemistry, but the exceptions to those rules are confusing.

Excuse for (a mistake)

- a reason or explanation was given to justify a fault or offense.
- गलती के लिए बहाना
- One should always focus on improving mistakes rather than making excuses for them.

Faith in (something/ something)

- complete trust or confidence in someone or something.
- किसी पर विश्वास
- Everything will be alright, have faith in god.

Familiarity with (a person/ thing)

- Close acquaintance with or knowledge of something.
- किसी व्यक्ति या वस्तु से परिचित होना
- Familiarity with books is always beneficial.

Freedom from (care/ something)

- To become free from something.
- किसी चीज से मुक्ति
- These days most of the haircare products claim to give freedom from hair fall.

Freedom of (action)

- To become free from action.
- एक क्रिया से मुक्ति
- In our school, we have the freedom of keeping mobile phones.

Glance at (a person or a thing)

- take a brief look at a picture
- When we went to the picture exhibition, we just took a glance at a portrait of a lady, that we thought is an actual lady.
- Yesterday we had a fight, that is why she passed by without glancing at me.

Glance over (a wide surface)

- examine hastily
- जल्दबाजी में जांच करना
- He glanced over the newspaper before turning it.

Gratitude for (a thing)

- Thankful for the thing
- किसी चीज के लिए आभार
- She was presented with a gift in gratitude for her long service.

Gratitude to (a person)

- Thankful to a person
- किसी के प्रति आभार
- I'll always show gratitude to my sister for preparing me for board examinations.

Hint at (something)

- To talk about (something) in an indirect way.
- अप्रत्यक्ष तरीके से किसी चीज़ के बारे में बात करना।
- I will only hint at some of the enterprises

which I have cherished.

Immersion into (something)

- Immersion is the act of dipping something in a substance, completely covering it.
- विसर्जन किसी पदार्थ में किसी चीज को डुबाने, पूरी तरह से ढकने का कार्य है।
- The first immersion into liquid air generally produced a permanent decrease in the magnetic moment.

Implication in (crime/ something)

- an occasion when you seem to suggest something without saying it directly
- एक ऐसा अवसर जब आप किसी चीज को सीधे-सीधे कहे बिना सुझाव देते हैं
- By his absence, Rachit had avoided implication in the troubles at home.

Implication on (someone)

- a charge or claim that someone has done something undesirable; an accusation.
- एक आरोप या दावा, कि किसी ने कुछ अवांछनीय किया है
- After the murder, the clear implication was on him as he's the rival and the only enemy of the Business tycoon.

Imputation against (somebody)

- A charge or claim of something undesirable against someone.
- किसी के खिलाफ अवांछनीय चीज का आरोप या दावा।
- He was suspended on the basis of so many imputations against him.

Indifference to (something)

- Lack interest in helping others
- दूसरों की मदद करने में उदासीनता
- One man says, in his despair or indifference to life, take up a handful of the earth at your feet, and paint your house that color.

Indulgence to (something)

- Allow oneself to enjoy the pleasure of a thing/ person.
- किसी वस्तु का सुख भोगना
- Recommended a moderate indulgence to his son, Prince Henry, and Charles I.

Inquiry into (circumstances/ a case)

- An official investigation of a circumstance/ case.
- एक परिस्थिति / मामले की एक आधिकारिक जांच
- This research gives insight into the theory of evolution.

Insight into (something/ somebody's characters)

- an accurate and deep understanding of something.
- किसी चीज़ की सटीक और गहरी समझ।
- This book gives insight into rural family life in 1930s Ireland.

Liking for (something/ someone)

- A feeling of fondness for something.
- किसी चीज के लिए शौकीन होना

- He hadn't developed a liking for her.

Longing for (someone or something)

- a yearning desire for someone or something
- किसी की लालसा
- It was strange sitting beside him and longing for him to come back.

Malice against (an enemy)

- किसी शत्रु के प्रति द्वेष
- A desire to harm someone
- I don't feel any malice against you for it.

Neglect of (duty)

- Fail to care for one's duty.
- कर्तव्य की उपेक्षा
- In order to be successful in life, one should never neglect the duties given to him.

Neglect in (doing a thing)

- to not give enough care or attention to people or things that are your responsibility.
- लोगों या उन चीजों पर पर्याप्त ध्यान न देना जो आपकी जिम्मेदारी हैं
- He neglected in solving maths problems hence his result was not as expected by his parents.

Nomination of (a member)

- the action of nominating a person.
- किसी व्यक्ति को नामांकित करने की क्रिया।
- He said that he should like a nomination of his son to the Charterhouse, and I gave it to him.

Nomination to (a position)

- official suggestion of someone for a position
- किसी पद के लिए किसी का आधिकारिक सुझाव
- His nomination to the post of college leader was discarded by the authority.

Opportunity for (going abroad/ doing)

- a time or set of circumstances that makes it possible to do something.
- परिस्थितियों का एक समय जो कुछ करना संभव बनाता है
- I believe it's an opportunity for educators and parents to express their frustration with the betterment of the public school system.

Precaution against (something)

- a measure is taken in advance to prevent something dangerous, unpleasant, or inconvenient from happening.
- किसी चीज के प्रति सावधानी बरतना
- Nowadays the health departments are continuously advising to take proper precautions against dengue and malaria.

Preface to (a book)

- An introduction to a book, typically stating its subject, scope, or aims.
- किसी पुस्तक के लिए प्रस्तावना
- In the preface to his friend's favorite book, he found so many things that

made the books interesting for him as well.

Preference for (something)

- a greater liking for one alternative over another or others.
- दूसरे पर एक विकल्प के लिए एक अधिक पसंद
- Now that you have passed your board exams, what is your preference for college?

Preparation for (an examination/ something)

- the action or process of preparing or being prepared for something.
- किसी चीज की तैयारी
- I asked my friend, " How's your preparation for the examination going?"

Proof against (somebody)

- evidence or argument establishing a fact or the truth of somebody.
- किसी के विरुद्ध प्रमाण
- The mother asked Sita if she has any proof against his brother that he has broken the cutlery.

Proof of (guilt)

- evidence or argument establishing a fact or the truth of guilt.
- अपराधबोध का प्रमाण
- You will be asked to give proof of your identity at the entrance of the examination center.

Quarrel with (somebody)

- A heated argument or disagreement, typically about a trivial issue and between people who are usually on good terms.
- एक तर्क या असहमति, आमतौर पर एक तुच्छ मुद्दे के बारे में और उन लोगों के बीच जो आमतौर पर अच्छे कार्यकाल पर होते हैं।
- I quarreled with my best-friend over a very minor issue, and I felt so bad for it later.

Quarrel with (something)

- take exception to or disagree with (something)
- किसी चीज से असहमत होना
- I have no quarrel with the court's verdict.

Reference to (a person or a thing)

- The act of talking about something/ someone or mentioning them.
- किसी व्यक्ति या बात का संदर्भ
- We were lost on our way to the party last night, but the reference to Google Maps helped us to reach on time.

With regard to (a matter)

- In reference to someone or something; considering someone or something.
- किसी व्यक्ति या किसी चीज़ पर विचार करना
- I am writing to you with regard to your letter of 15 March.

Relation between (things)

- the way in which two or more people or things are connected.

- चीजों के बीच संबंध
- We were asked to write the relation between normality and molarity.

Remonstrance against (somebody's conduct)

- Make a forcefully reproachful protest against somebody's conduct.
- किसी के आचरण के खिलाफ जबरदस्त विरोध करना।
- His petition of remonstrance against the proposed assessment, drawn up at the suggestion of Mr. Andrew was widely circulated and procured its defeat.

Remonstrance with (somebody)

- Objection with someone
- किसी के साथ आपत्ति
- I remonstrance with my mom as soon as I found Tinda at dinner.

Reply to (a query/ person)

- Whenever you say something in response to a query or person, you reply.
- किसी बात का जवाब देना
- Vidushi made Anjana angry while she was replying to a query from the learner.

Request for (a thing)

- To request something means to formally ask for it.
- किसी चीज़ के लिए अनुरोध
- Rohit had to go home suddenly so he requested leave from the boss.

Rivalry with (a person)

- Rivalry is the act of competing for the same thing against another person.
- किसी व्यक्ति के साथ प्रतिद्वंद्विता
- Venice, always in rivalry with the papal city, often presented itself as the new Rome.

Rival in (something)

- A rival is a competitor or contender that you want to defeat.
- दावेदार जिसे आप हराना चाहते हैं
- Shyam and Raju are best friends in college but rivals in a football field.

Share in (the property/ something)

- Assets belonging to or due to or contributed by an individual person or group.
- किसी व्यक्ति या समूह द्वारा या उसके कारण या उससे संबंधित संपत्ति।
- They are four siblings, three brothers, and one sister. And everyone's share in the property is same.

Share with (somebody)

- the allotment of some amount by dividing something
- किसी के साथ साझा करना
- My parents have asked me to share my room with my younger brother.

Trespass against (something)

- commit an offense against the law.
- कानून के खिलाफ अपराध करना।

- Even after the implementation of tough traffic rules, people are still trespassing against the rules.

Warrant for (somebody's arrest)

- a document issued by a legal or government official authorizing the police or another body to make an arrest, search premises, or carry out some other action relating to the administration of justice.
- एक कानूनी या सरकारी अधिकारी द्वारा जारी किया गया एक दस्तावेज जो पुलिस या किसी अन्य निकाय को गिरफ्तारी, खोज परिसर बनाने या न्याय प्रशासन से संबंधित कुछ अन्य कार्रवाई करने के लिए अधिकृत करता है।
- The police had a warrant against Sam for his arrest.

Wonder at (something)

- a feeling of amazement and admiration, caused by something beautiful, remarkable, or unfamiliar.
- कुछ सुंदर, उल्लेखनीय या अपरिचित के कारण प्रशंसा की भावना।
- He looked up in wonder at the tallest building in the world.

Accrue to (somebody)

- (used of interest paid on money) to be credited to an account or to a person's account.
- किसी खाते या किसी व्यक्ति के खाते में जमा होने के लिए पैसे पर दिया गया ब्याज।
- Ability to think will accrue to you from good habits of study.

Accrue from (something)

- to obtain from something
- किसी चीज से प्राप्त करना
- The advantages that might accrue from the wider distribution of cotton-growing are mainly fourfold.

Acquit (a person) in (a crime)

- To free a person from the crime or the charges of crime.
- किसी व्यक्ति को अपराध में बरी करना
- The court acquitted the innocent in stealing the gold chain.

Adapt to (something)

- Become adjusted to new conditions
- नई परिस्थितियों के अनुकूल
- She has adapted herself to college life quite easily.

Adhere to (something)

- Believe in and follow the practices of something.
- किसी चीज का पालन करना
- All drivers must adhere to speed limits.

Apologize to (someone)

- To tell someone that you are sorry for having done something that has caused problems
- किसी से माफी माँगना
- He apologized to her for his insincerity.

Apologize for (something)

- express regret for something that one has done wrong.

- किसी बात के लिए माफी
- The criminal apologizes to the justice for his wrong deeds.

Appeal to (somebody)

- A serious, urgent, or heartfelt request to someone.
- किसी से हार्दिक अनुरोध
- His appeals to his father for money were ignored

Appeal against (something)

- To raise a voice against something.
- किसी चीज़ के खिलाफ आवाज उठाना
- The prosecution may appeal against the sentence, while the defence may appeal against the conviction.

Appeal for (something)

- To request or to ask for something.
- कुछ माँगना
- Their appeal for the renovation of the classrooms was ignored.

Apply to (a person)

- be pertinent or relevant or applicable.
- किसी व्यक्ति पर लागू करना
- If you would just apply yourself to your schoolwork, you would get much better grades.

Apply for (something)

- Make a formal application or request for something.
- किसी भी चीज़ के लिए एक औपचारिक आवेदन या अनुरोध करना
- Rita was so much frustrated with his job that she applied for a job in another firm.

Borrow from (somebody)

- Take and use (something belonging to someone else) with the intention of returning it.
- किसी से उधार लेना
- I borrow a dress from my sister for tomorrow's party.

Burst into (something/ laughter or tears)

- To laud loudly.
- जोर से हँसना
- I burst out laughing when I saw their outfits.

Come after (somebody)

- To follow somebody
- किसी का पीछा करना
- I was going home after tuition classes and suddenly felt someone coming after me.

Come into (fashion)

- Of a particular style, trend, etc.
- फैशन में आना
- Denim jackets have again come into fashion.

Come by (something)

- Obtain by effort
- प्रयास से प्राप्त करना
- The crowd watch celebrities enjoying their success, but little did they know,

that came through hard work.

Commence with (a thing)

- Begin with something.
- किसी चीज़ की शुरुआत
- Our new project will be commenced with a new tagline in September.

Communicate with (somebody)

- (of two people) be able to share and understand each other's thoughts and feelings.
- किसी के साथ संवाद
- We can now communicate instantly with people on the other side of the world.

Compare (something) with (something similar)

- estimate, measure, or note the similarity or dissimilarity between similar things.
- सामान चीज़ों की तुलना
- One shouldn't compare oneself with someone else, everyone has different special qualities.

Compare (something) to (something dissimilar)

- estimate, measure, or note the similarity or dissimilarity between dissimilar things.
- आसमान चीज़ों की तुलना
- The actress is so beautiful that people compare her to the moon.

Compensate for (loss)

- To provide something good as a balance against something bad or undesirable
- नुकसान की भरपाई
- The price of the item has been reduced to compensate for a defect.

Compete with (somebody) for (something)

- Be in a state of rivalry with someone.
- किसी के साथ प्रतिद्वंद्विता की स्थिति में होना
- You will have to compete with others for this position

Complain to (somebody)

- Express dissatisfaction or annoyance to someone.
- किसी से शिकायत करना
- She complained to her parents for not giving her much attention.

Complain against (somebody)

- Express dissatisfaction or annoyance against somebody.
- किसी के खिलाफ शिकायत
- She complained about the three boys who followed her last evening, yet no action has been taken yet by the police.

Complain of/ about (something)

- Express dissatisfaction or annoyance about something.
- किसी के बारे में शिकायत करना
- The students keep complaining about the faculty but nobody listens to them.

Congratulate (somebody) on (his success)

- Give (someone) one's good wishes when something special or pleasant has happened to them.
- किसी को उसकी सफलता पर बधाई
- Everyone congratulated him on his achievement.

Condemn to (something/ a norm)

- Express complete disapproval of something.
- किसी चीज की निंदा करना
- She was condemned to hang for killing her husband.

Consult with (someone)

- Seek information or advice from (someone, especially an expert or professional).
- किसी से सलाह लेना
- I consulted my friend on whether I should prepare for banking or SSC.

Correspond with (a person)

- Have a close similarity with a person.
- किसी के साथ मेल
- Will he deny me the visits of my dearest friend, and forbid me to correspond with her?

Correspond to (something)

- Match or agree almost exactly to something.
- किसी चीज़ से बिलकुल सहमत होना या मेल खाना
- Analysis showed it to have an empirical formula that doesn't correspond to any compound that's ever been reported.

Cure of (a disease/ a habit)

- Treatment or the process of treating a disease.
- किसी बीमारी का इलाज
- She was cured of viral fever after 12 days.

Cure for (a disease)

- Relieve (a person or animal) the symptoms of a disease or condition.
- किसी बीमारी के लिए इलाज
- There's no cure for baldness.

Differ with (a person) on (a subject)

- To be unlike or distinct in nature, form, or characteristics from a person.
- किसी व्यक्ति के साथ प्रकृति, रूप या विशेषताओं के विपरीत या अलग होना।
- I differ with my friend on views towards different political parties.

Differ from (anything)

- To be unlike
- किसी चीज़ के साथ प्रकृति, रूप या विशेषताओं के विपरीत या अलग होना
- My sister and I resemble each other a lot, yet we differ from each other in so many characters and face cut is one of them.

Disapprove of (something)

- Have or express an unfavourable opinion about something.
- किसी चीज को अस्वीकार करना
- Most people disapprove of such violent tactics.

Enter a (place)

- Come or go into (a place).
- एक जगह पर प्रवेश करना
- And then we entered a beautiful historical palace.

Enter into (a new era/ a conversation/ some business/ an agreement)

- To start to take part in an official discussion or other formal activity.
- किसी आधिकारिक चर्चा या अन्य औपचारिक गतिविधि में भाग लेना
- Let's not enter into details at this stage.

Entrust (somebody) with (something)

- Assign the responsibility of something to somebody.
- किसी को कुछ करने की जिम्मेदारी सौंपना।
- Could she entrust him with her heart?

Entrust (something) to (somebody)

- Assign the responsibility for doing something to someone.
- किसी को कुछ करने की जिम्मेदारी सौंपना
- I couldn't entrust my precious things to strangers.

Escape from (somewhere)

- Run away from somewhere.
- कहीं से भाग जाना
- The prisoner escaped from imprisonment.

Excel in (something)

- Be exceptionally good at or proficient in something.
- किसी चीज में असाधारण रूप से अच्छा या कुशल होना।
- She excels in many sports.

Exchange (one thing) for (another)

- to trade one thing for another.
- एक वास्तु को दूसरी वास्तु से बदलना
- So now as I'm leaner, I'd like to exchange this dress for a smaller one.

Exchange (something) with (a person)

- The act of giving something to someone in return for something received.
- किसी प्राप्त वस्तु के बदले में किसी को कुछ देने की क्रिया।
- I loved my sister's dress more so I exchanged mine with her.

Import (goods) into (a country)

- Bring goods and services from a foreign country.
- कहीं पर कुछ आयात करना
- Most of the decorative lights are imported into India from China.

Import (goods) from (a country)

- Commodities (goods or services) bought from a foreign country
- किसी विदेश से खरीदी गई वस्तुएं या सेवाएं

- India imports a huge amount of goods from China.

Inquire of (a person)

- To ask for information from a person.
- किसी व्यक्ति से पूछताछ
- The police inquired of his neighbors if they knew where he was

Inquire about (something)

- To ask or find information about something.
- किसी चीज के बारे में जानकारी मांगना या खोजना।
- You are advised to inquire about the scheme properly before investing in it.

Interfere with (a person)

- To distrupt
- किसी व्यक्ति के साथ हस्तक्षेप
- If you interfere with their affairs, you're definitely having a bad influence.

Interfere in (something)

- To involve yourself in a situation or something when your involvement is not wanted or is not helpful.
- किसी चीज में हस्तक्षेप करना
- The most irritating kind of people are the ones who keep interfering in other's business.

Invest in (something)

- Put (money) into financial schemes, shares, property, or a commercial venture with the expectation of achieving a profit.
- किसी चीज में निवेश करना
- We should invest in our studies to get good results in the future.

Invest with (someone)

- Put (money) into financial schemes, shares, property, or a commercial venture with the expectation of achieving a profit.
- किसी के साथ निवेश करना
- I am about to invest with my sister in a very good scheme.

Jump at (an idea)

- accept (an opportunity or offer) with great eagerness.
- किसी अवसर या प्रस्ताव को बड़ी उत्सुकता के साथ स्वीकार करना।
- I'd jump at the chance of a career in defense.

Jump to (a conclusion)

- Deciding too quickly that something is true.
- बहुत जल्दी फैसला करना कि कुछ सच है
- It's never a good idea to jump to any conclusion without knowing the complete thing.

Pass from (one thing into another)

- Move or cause to move from one thing into another.
- एक चीज से दूसरी चीज में जाना
- Due to his notorious behavior, his

parents pass him from his old school to the new one.

Pass for (someone/ something)

- To be accepted, wrongly, as being a particular type of person or thing.
- किसी विशेष प्रकार के व्यक्ति या चीज के रूप में, गलत तरीके से स्वीकार किया जाना।
- He speaks the language so well he could easily pass for a French.

Pass over (something)

- To disregard; ignore; omit.
- किसी बात को अनदेखा करना
- Most of the time the candidates pass over the important instructions given before the exam.

Point at (a person)

- To extend one's finger, especially the index finger, in the direction of someone or something.
- किसी पर इशारा करना
- When asked about the girl of his choice, Tom pointed at Marry.

Point to (something)

- To indicate or signify the direction or location of someone or something.
- किसी बात की ओर इशारा करना
- The ecstatic little kid pointed to the kite in the sky.

Pray for (something)

- Wish or hope strongly for a particular outcome or situation.
- किसी चीज के लिए प्रार्थना करना
- After several days of rain, we were praying for the sun.

Pray to (god)

- Address a prayer to God or another deity.
- ईश्वर से प्रार्थना करना
- We all are praying to god for the good health of our grandmother.

Prepare for (something/ exam)

- किसी चीज की तैयारी करना
- To make oneself ready for something, like exams.
- These days I'm preparing for my upcoming CDS exam.

Prepare against (disaster)

- आपदा के खिलाफ तैयार
- To make oneself ready for something, like a disaster.
- The disaster management team has started preparing against the floods, as the monsoon is coming.

Provide for (someone/ one's family)

- To make whatever is necessary for someone available to him or her.
- किसी के लिए जो चीज़ आवश्यक है वो उपलब्ध कराना
- My dad always tries his best to provide for our family the best things.

Provide against (something)

- To make plans in order to prevent or

deal with a bad situation.

- बुरी स्थिति से बचाव या उससे निपटने के लिए योजनाएँ बनाना
- The captain of the rival team provided the plan to his team against the other team.

Provide with (something)

- To give something wanted or needed.
- किसी चीज को जरूरत या जरूरत के हिसाब से देना।
- Golu's mother provided him with snacks and chocolates on his way to school picnic.

Reconcile to (a situation)

- To resolve a situation
- किसी स्थिति को हल करना
- When they came together, they reconciled to the situation of completing targets in very less time.

Reconcile with (someone)

- Restore friendly relations with someone.
- किसी के साथ सामंजस्य बिठाना
- The two enemy brothers reconciled with each other when it came to their parents' health.

Recover from (something)

- किसी चीज से उबरना
- Return to a normal state of health, mind, or strength.
- She took too long to recover from chicken pox.

Rejoice in (something)

- Finding happiness or joy in something.
- किसी चीज में आनन्दित होना
- Rejoice in one own's success.

Rejoice at (something)

- Feel or show great joy or delight at something.
- किसी बात पर आनन्दित होना
- The children rejoiced at the arrival of Santa Clause.

Revolt against (something)

- Take violent action against something.
- किसी चीज के प्रति विद्रोह
- Consumers are in revolt against high prices.

Rule over (a country)

- Exercise ultimate power or authority over (an area and its people).
- किसी देश या छेत्र पे शासन
- BJP is ruling over most of the states in India.

Stand against (someone/ something)

- To oppose someone or something, especially in a brave or determined way.
- किसी का या किसी चीज़ का विरोध करना, विशेष रूप से बहादुर या दृढ़ तरीके से।
- You should stand against the acts you thinks are not fair.

Stand by (someone/ something)

- to support or be loyal to someone or something, or tolerate something.
- किसी के साथ या किसी चीज के प्रति वफादार होना या कुछ सहन करना
- If you stand by and let something bad happen, you do not do anything to stop it.

Stand on (someone/ something)

- To be or remain in an upright position while on top of someone or something.
- किसी के ऊपर या किसी चीज के ऊपर एक सीधी स्थिति में रहना
- You can stand the mirror on that box over there.

Think of/ about (someone or something)

- किसी के बारे में सोचना
- Intend to or refer to.
- I think of food whenever I see my favourite restaurant.

Think over

- to consider a problem or decision carefully
- किसी समस्या या निर्णय पर सावधानी से विचार करना
- I think you should think over before saying yes to anyone.

Wait at (somewhere)

- stay somewhere delay action until a particular time or event.
- किसी स्थान पर प्रतीक्षा करना
- They wait at the same place for each other every day.

Wait for (someone)

- To stay somewhere until a person arrives
- किसी की प्रतीक्षा करना
- Everyone left for the party but he kept waiting for her till she arrived.

Warn (a person) of (disaster/something)

- Inform someone in advance of a possible danger, problem, or other unpleasant situation.
- किसी चीज के लिए किसी व्यक्ति को चेतावनी देना
- The news channels are continuously warning of increased AQI levels.

Warn (a person) against (a fault/ something)

- Give someone cautionary advice about their actions or conduct.
- किसी को उसके कार्यों या आचरण के बारे में सावधानीपूर्वक सलाह देना
- Her mother warned her a lot against her clever friends yet she trusted them.

Acceptable to (a person/ someone)

- Able to be agreed on someone.
- किसी को स्वीकार्य करना
- Insincerity is not acceptable to anyone in a relationship.

Accessible to (someone)

- able to be easily obtained or used by someone.

- किसी के द्वारा आसानी से प्राप्त या उपयोग किया जा सकता है।
- The office WiFi is accessible to everyone.

Accessory to (a crime/ something)

- A thing which can be added to something else in order to make it more useful, versatile, or attractive.
- एक ऐसी चीज़ जिसे और अधिक उपयोगी, बहुमुखी या आकर्षक बनाने के लिए किसी और चीज़ में जोड़ा जा सकता है।
- He wanted fashion accessories such as scarves, handkerchiefs, bracelets, and rings as an accessory to murder.

Accomplished in (something)

- Possessed of good qualities
- किसी चीज में निपुण
- She is so accomplished in singing that whoever listens to her, becomes her fan.

Accountable to (someone)

- To be answerable to a person
- किसी व्यक्ति के लिए जवाबदेह
- I am only accountable to my parents about where I'm going and with whom.

Accountable for (something)

- Required or expected to justify actions or decisions; responsible
- किसी चीज के लिए जवाबदेह
- Shyam's parents were accountable for his wrong deeds.

Accuse (somebody) of (theft/ something)

- A claim that (someone) has done something wrong.
- किसी पर कुछ आरोप लगाना
- They accused me of being a liar.

Acquainted with (someone)

- To know someone
- किसी के साथ परिचित होना
- "Do make me acquainted with your charming daughters," said she.

Acquit (a person) of (something)

- Free (someone) from a criminal charge by a verdict of not guilty.
- दोषी न होने के फैसले द्वारा किसी को आपराधिक आरोप से मुक्त करना
- The judge acquits the innocent of all charges that had been imposed on him.

Addicted to (someone or something)

- किसी चीज का आदी
- Physically and mentally dependent on a particular substance.
- These days even little kids are so much addicted to mobile phones.

Amazed at (something)

- Greatly surprised at something.
- किसी बात पर चकित
- My friend gifted me a very beautiful bouquet that I was really amazed at it.

Ambition for (something)

- a strong desire to do or achieve

something.

- कुछ करने या हासिल करने की तीव्र इच्छा।
- Amit's ambition for his goals will take him too far on the way to success.

Ambitious of (something)

- Having or showing a strong desire and determination to succeed
- किसी चीज का महत्वाकांक्षी
- In order to be successful in life, one should always be ambitious of his goals.

Amused at (something)

- Finding something funny or entertaining.
- किसी चीज़ में खुश
- Rahul and his parents were amused at his result since he cleared the SSC CGL exam.

Angry at (a thing)

- Feeling or showing strong annoyance or displeasure at something.
- किसी बात पर तीव्र झुंझलाहट या नाराजगी महसूस करना या दिखाना।
- My mother is angry at me for skipping the dinner.

Angry with (a person)

- Feeling or showing strong annoyance or displeasure at a person.
- किसी व्यक्ति पर तीव्र झुंझलाहट या नाराजगी महसूस करना या दिखाना।
- I was so angry with my brother for breaking my favourite coffee mug.

Annoyed at (something)

- Slightly angry or irritated at something.
- किसी बात पर नाराज होना
- I am annoyed at the fact that my parents won't be at home on my birthday.

Annoyed with (a person)

- Slightly angry or irritated with a person.
- किसी व्यक्ति पर थोड़ा गुस्सा या चिढ़ होना
- She was annoyed with her brother because he keeps disturbing her whenever she tries to concentrate on her studies.

Answerable to (a person)

- Required to explain or justify one's actions to a person.
- किसी व्यक्ति के लिए जवाबदेह
- Councils should be answerable to the people who elect them.

Answerable for (something)

- Required to explain or justify one's actions for something.
- किसी बात के लिए जवाबदेह
- Whatever you study will be visible in your results and only you are answerable for that.

Anxious for (something)

- full of mental distress or uneasiness because of fear of danger or misfortune
- खतरे या दुर्भाग्य के डर के कारण मानसिक परेशानी या बेचैनी से भरा हुआ

- Parents are naturally anxious for their children.

Anxious about (something)

- feeling or showing worry, nervousness, or unease about something with an uncertain outcome.
- किसी चीज के बारे में चिंता, घबराहट या बेचैनी महसूस करना या दिखाना।
- I am extremely anxious about my upcoming exams.

Previous Year Questions:

Exercise 1

Direction: Fill in the blanks with the appropriate phrasal verb from the given options:

1. I need to ____________ my room before guests arrive.

a) clean up b) clean in
c) clean off

2. The meeting was ____________ due to bad weather.

a) called out b) called off
c) called in

3. She always ____________ early to avoid traffic.

a) sets in b) sets up
c) sets off

4. He ____________ his brother's bad behavior.

a) put up with b) put up
c) put off

5. The teacher asked the students to ____________ their homework.

a) hand over b) hand in
c) hand out

6. The company decided to ____________ a new product line.

a) bring in b) bring up
c) bring off

7. The cat ____________ the tree and refused to come down.

a) climbed up b) climbed in
c) climbed over

8. We need to ____________ the old furniture and make space for the new.

a) clear out b) clear off
c) clear up

9. She couldn't ____________ her excitement when she won the award.

a) hold on b) hold up
c) hold back

10. The children were ____________ by their grandparents during the summer vacation.

a) looked after b) looked into
c) looked up

Answers

1.	(a)	2.	(b)	3.	(c)
4.	(a)	5.	(b)	6.	(a)
7.	(a)	8.	(a)	9.	(c)
10.	(a)				

Exercise 2

Directions: **Fill in the blanks with the appropriate phrasal verb from the given options:**

1. **I need to ___________ the meeting because of a scheduling conflict.**
   a) call off b) call in
   c) call up
2. **The students were asked to ___________ their ideas for the project.**
   a) come up b) come up with
   c) come in
3. **They had to ___________ the fire before it spread to the neighbouring buildings.**
   a) put off b) put up
   c) put out
4. **The car broke down on the highway, so we had to ___________ a tow truck.**
   a) call for b) call on
   c) call out
5. **He always ___________ early in the morning to get a head start on the day.**
   a) get by b) get up
   c) get ahead
6. **The police were able to ___________ the thief after a thorough investigation.**
   a) track down b) track up
   c) track in
7. **The company decided to ___________ a new marketing strategy to attract more customers.**
   a) come up b) come up with
   c) come down on
8. **She had to ___________ her vacation plans due to unexpected work commitments.**
   a) put of b) put off
   c) put forward
9. **The teacher asked the students to ___________ the important information from the textbook.**
   a) pick out b) pick up
   c) pick on
10. **The manager called a team meeting to ___________ the project progress.**
    a) check on b) check out
    c) check in

Answers:

1.	(a)	2.	(b)	3.	(c)
4.	(a)	5.	(b)	6.	(a)
7.	(b)	8.	(b)	9.	(a)
10.	(a)				

Exercise 3

Directions: **Fill in the blanks with the appropriate phrasal verb from the given options:**

1. **She ___________ her jacket and left it at the restaurant.**

a) took off b) took over
c) took on

2. The company had to ___________ several employees due to budget cuts.
a) lay off b) lay out
c) lay down

3. I need to ___________ this book before returning it to the library.
a) look up b) look over
c) look after

4. The concert was ___________ due to bad weather conditions.
a) called off b) called up
c) called in

5. He needs to ___________ his expenses in order to save money.
a) cut back on b) cut off
c) cut through

6. The teacher asked the students to ___________ the instructions carefully.
a) go over b) go off
c) go by

7. We should ___________ a plan to address this issue.
a) come up with b) come across
c) come in

8. The children were ___________ when they saw the fireworks display.
a) taken aback b) taken in
c) taken over

9. The car broke down on the highway, so we had to ___________ help.
a) call for b) call off
c) call out

10. He needs to ___________ his shoes before entering the house.
a) take off b) take in
c) take on

Answers:

1.	(a)	2.	(a)	3.	(b)
4.	(a)	5.	(a)	6.	(a)
7.	(a)	8.	(b)	9.	(a)
10.	(a)				

Exercise 4

Directions: **Fill in the blanks with the appropriate phrasal verb from the given options:**

1. The meeting has been ___________ until next week.
a) put off b) put on
c) put up

2. She ___________ the news and couldn't stop smiling.
a) took over b) took in
c) took off

3. The teacher asked the students to ___________ their hands if they knew the answer.
a) put out b) put off
c) put up

4. The company decided to ___________ a new marketing campaign to increase sales.
a) come up with b) come across
c) come in

5. He needs to ___________ his mistakes and learn from them.

a) own to b) own up to
c) own over to

6. The children ____________ when they saw the magician perform a trick.
a) lit in b) lit off
c) lit up

7. I had to ____________ some money to pay for the car repairs.
a) shell out b) shell off
c) shell in

8. The team ____________ a great victory in the final match.
a) pulled over b) pulled off
c) pulled up

9. The dog ____________ the bone buried in the backyard.
a) dug up b) dug off
c) dug in

10. The manager asked the employees to ____________ on time for the meeting.
a) show up b) show off
c) show in

Answers:

1.	(a)	2.	(b)	3.	(c)
4.	(a)	5.	(b)	6.	(c)
7.	(a)	8.	(b)	9.	(a)
10.	(a)				

Exercise 5

Directions: **Fill in the blanks with the appropriate phrasal verb from the given options:**

1. She ____________ her old clothes to charity.
a) gave away b) gave in
c) gave off

2. The bus ____________ passengers at the next stop.
a) dropped of b) dropped off
c) dropped in

3. The students were asked to ____________ their assignments by Friday.
a) hand over b) hand out
c) hand in

4. The fire alarm ____________ when there was smoke in the building.
a) went off b) went out
c) went over

5. The manager ____________ a new policy to improve employee productivity.
a) came across b) came up with
c) came into

6. The kids ____________ the idea of going to the park.
a) jumped over b) jumped off
c) jumped at

7. He ____________ the news and couldn't believe what he heard.
a) took in b) took off
c) took over

8. They ____________ the old furniture and bought new ones.
a) got off b) got rid of
c) got into

9. The teacher ____________ a difficult concept to the students.
a) broke down b) broke off
c) broke out

10. **He ____________ a successful business after years of hard work.**

a) built up b) built in

c) built over

Answers:

1.	(a)	2.	(b)	3.	(c)
4.	(a)	5.	(b)	6.	(c)
7.	(a)	8.	(b)	9.	(a)
10.	(a)				

Exercise 6

Directions: Fill in the blanks with the appropriate phrasal verb from the given options:

1. **The students were asked to ____________ the information from the textbook.**

a) look up b) look over

c) look after

2. **Please ____________ your shoes before entering the house.**

a)take in b) take up

c) take off

3. **I need to ____________ my car at the mechanic's shop for repairs.**

a) drop off b) drop out

c) drop in

4. **The company decided to ____________ a new marketing campaign.**

a) come across b) come up with

c) come into

5. **The movie ____________ a lot of positive reviews from critics.**

a) brought in b) brought up

c) brought about

6. **He ____________ his career as a chef at a renowned restaurant.**

a) started off b) started over

c) started out

7. **The team had to ____________ their opponents in the final match.**

a) hold on b) hold off

c) hold out

8. **The meeting was ____________ due to unforeseen circumstances.**

a) called off b) called for

c) called out

9. **She ____________ the secret to her best friend.**

a) let go b) let down

c) let out

10. **The company decided to ____________ its manufacturing operations overseas.**

a) move out b) move on

c) move up

Answers:

1.	(a)	2.	(c)	3.	(a)
4.	(b)	5.	(a)	6.	(c)
7.	(b)	8.	(a)	9.	(c)
10.	(a)				

Confidence Booster Practice Sets

Exercise 1

Questions based on the given phrasal verbs. The answers are provided at the end.

1. The company was asked to ________ its sudden drop in profits.
   a) answer for b) break into
   c) account after d) back up
2. John was called to ________ his absence from work yesterday.
   a) answer for b) ask after
   c) back out d) blow over
3. Sarah called her friend to ________ her health after the surgery.
   a) back out b) ask after
   c) bear down d) break down
4. The nurse was there to ____ the needs of the patient throughout the night.
   a) ask after b) attend on
   c) blow over d) break into
5. Lisa decided to ________ of the agreement at the last moment.
   a) back up b) break out
   c) back out d) account for
6. James promised to ________ his friend during the presentation.
   a) break down b) back up
   c) bear down d) blow over
7. The weightlifter tried to ________ the heavy barbell during the competition.
   a) back up b) account for
   c) bear down d) break into
8. The argument between the siblings quickly ________ and they made up.
   a) bear down b) blow over
   c) break out d) attend on
9. The flight is ________ New York City.
   a) attend on b) break into
   c) bound for d) account for
10. The old washing machine ________ in the middle of the cycle.
    a) back out b) ask after
    c) broke down d) blow over

Answers:

1.	(a)	2.	(a)	3.	(b)
4.	(b)	5.	(c)	6.	(b)
7.	(c)	8.	(b)	9.	(c)
10.	(c)				

Exercise 2

1. Mr. Sharma ________ electronic goods at his store.
   a) deals in b) figures out
   c) falls out d) feels like
2. The teacher ________ the assignment papers to the students.
   a) feels like b) deals out
   c) eggs on d) falls for
3. The manager had to ________ a difficult customer complaint.
   a) figure out b) fizzle out

c) deal with d) drop in

4. **The government decided to ________ an outdated law.**
a) deal in b) do away with
c) fall out d) feel like

5. **Sarah decided to ________ her friend's house unannounced.**
a) deal with b) drop in/by
c) fizzle out d) figure out

6. **Mark's friends always ________ him to take risks.**
a) deal out b) egg on
c) feel like d) fall for

7. **Jane instantly ________ the charming stranger she met at the party.**
a) figures out b) feels like
c) falls for d) fizzes out

8. **Sarah ________ her best friend after a disagreement.**
a) falls out b) feels like
c) figures out d) deals with

9. **I ________ going for a walk in the park this evening.**
a) deal in b) feel like
c) drop in/by d) egg on

10. **Tom is trying to ________ the solution to the math problem.**
a) deal with b) figure out
c) fizzle out d) fall for

Answers:

1.	(a)	2.	(b)	3.	(c)
4.	(b)	5.	(b)	6.	(b)
7.	(c)	8.	(a)	9.	(b)
10.	(b)				

Exercise 3

Questions based on the given phrasal verbs. The answers are provided at the end.

1. **Get along (with someone): Which of the following best defines the phrasal verb "get along"?**
a) To make progress
b) To reveal a secret
c) To abandon something
d) To have a friendly relationship

2. **Get away with: What does the phrasal verb "get away with" mean?**
a) To complete a task
b) To surrender
c) To make progress
d) To do something illegal without being punished

3. **Get over: What does it mean to "get over" something?**
a) To throw away
b) To reveal a secret
c) To abandon something
d) To have control over something

4. **Get on: Which of the following is the closest meaning of "get on"?**
a) To make progress
b) To complete a task
c) To surrender
d) To reveal a secret

5. **Get rid of: What does the phrasal verb "get rid of" mean?**
a) To have control over something
b) To do something illegal without being punished

c) To leave or dispose of
d) To surrender

6. Get through with: Which of the following best defines the phrasal verb "get through with"?
a) To abandon something
b) To reveal a secret
c) To complete a task
d) To have a friendly relationship

7. Give away: What does it mean to "give away" something?
a) To surrender
b) To throw away
c) To reveal a secret
d) To make progress

8. Give in: Which of the following is the closest meaning of "give in"?
a) To surrender
b) To abandon something
c) To make progress
d) To complete a task

9. Give up: What does the phrasal verb "give up" mean?
a) To throw away
b) To reveal a secret
c) To have a friendly relationship
d) To abandon something

10. Go about: Which of the following best defines the phrasal verb "go about"?
a) To complete a task
b) To surrender
c) To move from place to place
d) To do something illegal without being punished

Answers:

1.	(d)	2.	(d)	3.	(d)
4.	(a)	5.	(c)	6.	(c)
7.	(c)	8.	(a)	9.	(d)
10.	(c)				

Exercise 4

1. What does the phrase "laugh at" mean?
a) To ridicule or mock someone
b) To take a break
c) To make a plan
d) To save money

2. What does the phrase "launch out" mean?
a) To ridicule or mock someone
b) To begin or start something
c) To save money
d) To look for something

3. What does the phrase "lay aside" mean?
a) To ridicule or mock someone
b) To take a break
c) To save or set aside money or resources
d) To look for something

4. What does the phrase "lay down" mean?
a) To ridicule or mock someone
b) To take a break
c) To save or set aside money or resources
d) To give up arms

5. What does the phrase "lay in" mean?
a) To ridicule or mock someone
b) To take a break

c) To save or set aside money or resources

d) To accumulate or stock up on supplies

6. What does the phrase "lay on" mean?

a) To ridicule or mock someone

b) To provide or apply

c) To save or set aside money or resources

d) To establish or establish

7. What does the phrase "lay out" mean?

a) To ridicule or mock someone

b) To take a break

c) To spend money or incur expenses

d) To accumulate or stock up on supplies

8. What does the phrase "leave off" mean?

a) To ridicule or mock someone

b) To stop or cease

c) To save or set aside money or resources

d) To establish or establish

9. What does the phrase "leave over" mean?

a) To ridicule or mock someone

b) To continue or carry on

c) To save or set aside money or resources

d) To refrain or abstain

10. What does the phrase "let off" mean?

a) To ridicule or mock someone

b) To forgive or release without punishment

c) To save or set aside money or resources

d) To complete or finish

Answers:

1.	(a)	2.	(b)	3.	(c)
4.	(d)	5.	(d)	6.	(b)
7.	(c)	8.	(b)	9.	(b)
10.	(b)				

Exercise 5.

Directions (1-10): In each of the questions, four alternatives are given for the Phrase. Choose the alternative which best expresses the meaning of the Phrase.

1. Set to

(a) Enter (b) Exhausting

(c) Start (d) Arrive

2. Hold Out

(a) Resist (b) look after

(c) discontinue (d) Donate

3. Fall in with

(a) disagree with (b) Release

(c) Agree with (d) To fall down

4. Go down

(a) Be remembered

(b) Go on

(c) Concluding

(d) Postpone

5. Round up

(a) look for (b) Arrest

(c) calculating (d) To wander

6. Take down

(a) add on (b) installing

(c) Write (d) Pursue

7. Work upon

(a) Influence (b) work hard

(c) practice (d) Learn about

8. **Turn up**
(a) disappointing someone
(b) arrive
(c) praise
(d) pretend

9. **Look up to**
(a) Respect (b) denounce
(c) praise (d) Come across

10. **Jump at**
(a) hesitant
(b) Accept happily
(c) playing
(d) To jump

Answers

1.	(c)	2.	(a)	3.	(c)
4.	(a)	5.	(b)	6.	(c)
7.	(a)	8.	(b)	9.	(a)
10.	(b)				

Exercise 6.

1. **What does the phrase "wait up" mean?**
a) To stay awake and be ready
b) To wait patiently
c) To wake up suddenly
d) To walk slowly

2. **What does the phrase "wait upon" mean?**
a) To walk quickly
b) To wait patiently
c) To wake up suddenly
d) To serve or assist someone

3. **What does the phrase "wake up" mean?**
a) To stay awake and be ready
b) To wait patiently
c) To become conscious after sleep
d) To walk with determination

4. **What does the phrase "wake up to" mean?**
a) To stay awake and be ready
b) To wait patiently
c) To become conscious and aware of something
d) To walk with urgency

5. **What does the phrase "walk into" mean?**
a) To stay awake and be ready
b) To unintentionally encounter or get trapped in something
c) To become conscious after sleep
d) To walk aimlessly

6. **What does the phrase "walk off" mean?**
a) To leave abruptly
b) To wait patiently
c) To become conscious after sleep
d) To walk slowly

7. **What does the phrase "walk out" mean?**
a) To leave a place as a form of protest or strike
b) To wait patiently
c) To become conscious after sleep
d) To walk with confidence

8. **What does the phrase "walk up" mean?**
a) To walk hastily

b) To wait patiently

c) To become conscious after sleep

d) To approach or reach by walking

9. What does the phrase "wash away/ out" mean?

a) To wait patiently

b) To remove or eliminate by washing

c) To become conscious after sleep

d) To walk quickly

10. What does the phrase "watch over" mean?

a) To guard or protect

b) To wait patiently

c) To become conscious after sleep

d) To walk with caution

Answers:

1.	(a)	2.	(d)	3.	(c)
4.	(c)	5.	(b)	6.	(a)
7.	(a)	8.	(d)	9.	(b)
10.	(a)				

Exercise 7

1. What does the phrase "read out" mean?

a) To speak aloud or recite

b) To remove by rubbing

c) To escape or flee

d) To collide with something

2. What does the phrase "rub off" mean?

a) To speak aloud or recite

b) To remove by rubbing

c) To escape or flee

d) To collide with something

3. What does the phrase "run away" mean?

a) To speak aloud or recite

b) To remove by rubbing

c) To escape or flee

d) To collide with something

4. What does the phrase "run into" mean?

a) To escape or flee

b) To remove by rubbing

c) To speak aloud or recite

d) To collide or meet unexpectedly

5. What does the phrase "run out" mean?

a) To come to an end or be depleted

b) To remove by rubbing

c) To speak aloud or recite

d) To collide with something

6. What does the phrase "run over" mean?

a) To remove by rubbing

b) To drive over or crush

c) To speak aloud or recite

d) To escape or flee

7. What does the phrase "run through" mean?

a) To speak aloud or recite

b) To remove by rubbing

c) To quickly go through or review

d) To collide with something

8. What does the phrase "write down" mean?

a) To take notes or record in writing

b) To tear apart forcefully

c) To speak in a hasty manner

d) To clean thoroughly using a cloth

9. What does the phrase "yell out" mean?

a) To shout or scream loudly

b) To write quickly

c) To walk swiftly and effortlessly
d) To look up or admire someone

10. What does the phrase "zip through" mean?
a) To move quickly and effortlessly
b) To read aloud with enthusiasm
c) To wash and remove dirt
d) To carefully examine or inspect

Answers:

1.	(a)	2.	(b)	3.	(c)
4.	(d)	5.	(a)	6.	(b)
7.	(c)	8.	(a)	9.	(a)
10.	(a)				

Exercise 8.

1. What does the phrase "pass for" mean?
a) To be mistaken for
b) To move quickly
c) To repay a debt
d) To separate or detach

2. What does the phrase "pass on" mean?
a) To skip or avoid
b) To die or pass away
c) To lend or give temporarily
d) To examine or investigate

3. What does the phrase "pass over" mean?
a) To retrieve or collect
b) To handle with care
c) To overlook or skip
d) To dismantle or destroy

4. What does the phrase "pay back" mean?
a) To provide or supply
b) To select or choose
c) To accumulate or gather
d) To repay or settle

5. What does the phrase "pick off" mean?
a) To remove or eliminate
b) To discard or throw away
c) To purchase or buy
d) To complete or finish quickly

6. What does the phrase "pick out" mean?
a) To dismantle or disassemble
b) To choose or select
c) To disperse or scatter
d) To organize or arrange

7. What does the phrase "pick up" mean?
a) To avoid or evade
b) To drop or release
c) To lift or raise
d) To inspect or examine closely

8. What does the phrase "pull down" mean?
a) To demolish or destroy
b) To lift or raise up
c) To push or thrust
d) To hold or grasp firmly

9. What does the phrase "pull off" mean?
a) To accomplish or achieve
b) To remove or detach
c) To confuse or bewilder
d) To slow down or decrease

10. What does the phrase "pull in" mean?

a) To attract or draw in

b) To push or shove

c) To release or let go

d) To delay or postpone

Answers:

1.	(a)	2.	(b)	3.	(c)
4.	(d)	5.	(a)	6.	(b)
7.	(c)	8.	(a)	9.	(a)
10.	(a)				

Exercise 9.

Match the following phrases with their corresponding meanings:

1. Goes by	(a). To control expression
2. Go down in history	(b). To attack verbally
3. Go on	(c). To match
4. Go through	(d). To continue doing something
5. Go with	(e). To get the news about
6. Hear of	(f). To read, to pass through a time
7. Hit out	(g). To work accordingly
8. Hold back	(h). To reach a conclusion in a hurry
9. Hold on	(i). To keep something in a position
10. Jump at	(j). To get admitted in history

Answers:

1.	(g)	2.	(j)	3.	(d)
4.	(f)	5.	(c)	6.	(e)
7.	(b)	8.	(a)	9.	(i)
10.	(h)				

Exercise 10.

Match the following phrases with their corresponding meanings:

1. Keep away	(a). To abstain from
2. Keep from	(b). To maintain distance
3. Keep up	(c). To maintain in good condition/ to continue doing something
4. Knock down	(d). To dismiss/ to fire
5. Lay down	(e). To give up arms
6. Lay off	(f). To thrust someone to the ground
7. Lie behind	(g). To be the real reason
8. Live by	(h). To earn livelihood/ to follow
9. Live off	(i). To search or seek
10. Look for	(j). To live on particular food

Answers:

1.	(b)	2.	(a)	3.	(c)
4.	(f)	5.	(e)	6.	(d)
7.	(g)	8.	(h)	9.	(j)
10.	(i)				

Chapter - Five

Spelling Errors

SPELLINGS ERROR

All Spellings asked in SSC EXAM

Now let's explore the most commonly encountered spellings that have appeared in various exams.

Acclaim
Accommodate
Committee
Connoisseur
Mining
Recede
Resplendent
Sanctuaries
Acoustics
Apparently
Beginning
Commit
Conscientious
Countenance
Jealous
Magnificent
Tropical
Achieve
Aggression
Approach
Beggar
Bureaucrat

Ceremony
Compassionate
Conquer
Conscience
Eloquent
Embarrass
Embarrassment
Machiavellian
Millennium
Minuscule
Miscellaneous
Privilege
Realm
Receipt
Substantive
Accommodation
Accustomed
Acquire
Advertise
Amateur
Attention
Bureaucracy

Cactus
Calendar
Celebration
Combination
Commentary
Conjecture
Deficient
Definitely
Dwelling
Eradication
Exhausted
Exhibit
Experiment
Explanation
Extract
Fallacious
Guardian
Handkerchief
Heterogeneous
Illegitimate
Irresistible
Lethargy
Maintenance
Manoeuvre
Meadow
Medieval
Milieu
Necessary
Occasion
Olfactory
Omission
Possess
Possession
Pretensions
Quarrel
Recommend
Remuneration
Repercussion
Secrecy
Secretary
Abundance
Accompany
Accomplice
Accredited
Accumulate
Achievement
Acquaintance
Acquisition
Admonition
Adventure
Aesthetic
Aggravate
Anxiety
substantiate
Arrangement
Atrocious
Audible
Autumn
Behave
Believe

Belligerent
Beneficial
Beneficiary
Benign
Blithesome
Bulletin
Business
Campaigns
Ceiling
Ceremonial
Coalition
Colleague
Commemorate
Conceit
Conscious
Contagious
Contradiction
Cooperate
Corrupt
Definite
Definition
Describe
Desiccate
Detach
Discipline
Eighth
Election
Elementary
Embankment
Esteem

Evocation
Exaggerate
Exaggeration
Exceed
Excessive
Expedition
Explain
Exuberant
Forcibly
Foreign
Foreseeable
Grammar
Grandeur
Groovy
Guarantee
Heresy
Hierarchy
Hindrance
Humanitarian
Humorous
Idiosyncrasy
Immaculate
Independence
Independent
Inevitable
Influence
Irrevocable
Jealousy
Journey
Knowledge

Leisure
License
Manipulates
Mathematics
Millennia
Mischievous
Misogynist
Moustache
Navigation
Negligence
Non-commissioned
Noticeable
Nourishment
Occasionally
Ominous
Parallel
Pernicious
Perseverance
Personnel
Prefer
Preferable
Provision
Quarrelled
Quieten
Rehabilitation
Rehearsal
Rejuvenation
Remarkable
Remembrance
Reminiscence

Remnant
Schedule
Scintillating
Sentiment
Separate
Pamphlet
Proprietor
Pandemonia
Psychology
Pantomimes
Politicians
Punctuation
Parallel
Primitive
References
Principal
Referred
Principles
Regrettable
Privilege
Relieve
Probably
Religion
Procedure
Reminisce
Proceed
Renowned
Pronounce
Repetition
Mathematics

Obstacle	Assassination
Leisurely	Et Cetera
Occasion	Buffalo
Lengthening	Potato
Occurrence	Architecture
License	Cheque (Bank)
o'Clock	Arithmetic
Lieutenant	Aggravate
Omit	Deteriorate
Lightening	Ameliorate
Omitted	Auditorium
Lightning	College
Opinion	Accumulate
Abbreviation	Conscience
Accessory	Counselor
Affidavit	Chocolate
Vice Versa	Colossal
Lieutenant	Embarrassment
Champagne	Harassment
Rendezvous	Diarrhea
Archaeology	Diabetes
Tomorrow	Encyclopedia
January	Environment
February	Ecclesiastic
Auxiliary	Differentiate
Campaign	Embroidery
Cannibal	Etiquette
Cauliflower	Councilor
Cassette	Competition
Cigarette	Grammar

Espionage
Enthusiasm
Fahrenheit
Pronunciation
Eunuch
Gonorrhoea
Garrulous
Hemorrhage
Haemoglobin
Receipt
Deceive
Hygiene
Corruption
Terrorism
Tomato
Rendezvous
Foetus
Ignominious
Jubilee
Chivalry
Mischievous

Miscellaneous
Mustache
Leisure
Massacre
Neighbour
Museum
Miraculous
Pyorrhoea
Programme
Phoenix
Pharmaceutical
Parachute
Psychiatrist
Psychology
Quotation
Quinine
Quite
Quiet
Reference
Restaurant

Let's Practice

In the following options, four words are given, and one word is misspelled. Find the misspelled word.

1. **Family-controlled companies surpass their peers because they focus on resilience, not short- term results. During economic booms, this approach leads them to forego some opportunities, but it puts them in a position of strength during downturns, when they shine.**

   a). Surpass
   b). Peers
   c). Resilience
   d). Forego

   Answer: It should be 'forgo' which means to abandon.

2. **Meanwhile, a spate of new magazines, conferences, and websites were jockying to serve an unprecedented appetite for management ideas.**

   a). Spate
   b). Jockying
   c). Unprecedented
   d). Appetite

   Answer:It should be 'jockeying'.

3. **Not only has the editorship never reverted to faculty hands, but the entire faculty editorial advisory board was disbanded and in 1994 HBR was established as a wholly owned subsidairy of Harvard University.**

   a). Editorship
   b). Reverted
   c). Disbanded
   d). Subsidairy

   Answer:It should be 'subsidiary' which means secondary.

4. **Associated with the successes- and perhaps the exccesses- of the previous generation, it didn't seem to speak to the new one. In the midst of a business world being overturned by web-based enterprises, it seemed strictly "old economy" – the preferred reading of the sitting- duck incumbent.**

   a). Successes
   b). Exccesses
   c). Overturned
   d). Incumbent.

   Answer:It should be 'excesses' which means plenty.

5. **The new operating system continually assesses the business, the industry, and the organization, and reacts with greater agility,speed, and creativity than the existing one. It complements rather than overburdens the**

traditional hierarechy, thus freeing the latter to do what it's optimized to do.

a). Continually
b). Assesses
c). Complements
d). Hierarechy

Answer:It should be 'hierarchy' which means ranks.

6. **Disparities across gender, income and other resources need to be reduced drastically as they have a direct correlation with how different income groups interact with each other. Lack of access to economic oppurtunities can lead to social unrest and divided society.**

a). Disparities
b). Drastically
c). Correlation
d). Oppurtunities

Answer:It should be 'opportunities.'

7. **Apex industry body ASSOCHAM (Associated Chambers of Commerce and Industry) has taken the initiative by choosing the theme 'India Moving Forward: Journey Towards A $5 Trillion Economy' to commemorate its 100 years and the Annual Conference on 20th December 2019.**

a). Commerce
b). Initiative
c). Trillion
d). all are correct

Answer:All are correct.

8. **The report has identified three trajectories for the next surge of economic growth – Transforming agriculture and doubling farmers income, future-ready manufacturing, levaraging technology to drive growth, other key areas identified for propelling the country's economy are Infrastructure Development.**

a). Trajectories
b). Doubling
c). Levaraging
d). Propelling

Answer:It should be 'leveraging'.

9. **Farmers need to be treated as 'agri-entreprenuers' and it is time that the existing policy framework is redesigned with transformative interventions, unconventional approaches to tackle climate change and focus on direct measures to promote farmers' welfare.**

a). Entreprenuers
b). Existing
c). Approaches
d). Tackle

Answer:It should be 'entrepreneurs'.

10. In the ensuing decades, this scepticicm of technology manifested itself in various avatars: in the 1970s, the Indian government harvested the anger of labour unions to discourage computerisation in PSUS.

a). Ensuing
b). Scepticicm
c). Manifested
d). Computerisation

Answer:It should be 'skepticism'.

Previous Year Questions:

Set 1

1. **Which of the following is the correct spelling?**
   a). Exaggurate
   b). Exaggarate
   c). Exaggerate
   d). Exagarate
2. **Choose the correctly spelled word:**
   a). Occurence
   b). Occurrence
   c). Occurrance
   d). Occurunce
3. **Identify the correct spelling:**
   a). Embarrassment
   b). Embarrasment
   c). Embarassment
   d). Embarasment
4. **Select the correctly spelled word:**
   a). Accomodate
   b). Accommodate
   c). Acommodate
   d). Accommodatte
5. **Which of the following is spelled correctly?**
   a). Privilege
   b). Privelege
   c). Privilage
   d). Privelege
6. **Identify the correct spelling:**
   a). Desparate
   b). Desperate
   c). Desperatte
   d). Desperat
7. **Choose the correctly spelled word:**
   a). Mischievious
   b). Mischevious
   c). Mischievous
   d). Mischevous
8. **Select the correct spelling:**
   a). Sepreate
   b). Sepreate
   c). Separate
   d). Separatte
9. **Which of the following is spelled correctly?**
   a). Convinient
   b). Convienient
   c). Convenient
   d). Conveneint
10. **Identify the correct spelling:**
   a). Acquaintence
   b). Acquaintence
   c). Acquaintance
   d). Aquaintance
11. **Choose the correctly spelled word:**

a). Neccessary
b). Neccessary
c). Necessary
d). Necesary

12. **Select the correct spelling:**
a). Perservere
b). Persever
c). Persever
d). Persevere

13. **Which of the following is spelled correctly?**
a). Seperate
b). Seperate
c). Separate
d). Seperrate

14. **Identify the correct spelling:**
a). Dificult
b). Difficul
c). Difficult
d). Dificult

15. **Choose the correctly spelled word:**
a). Embarras
b). Embarass
c). Embarrass
d). Embaras

16. **Select the correct spelling:**
a). Accomodation
b). Accommodation
c). Acomodation
d). Accomodation

17. **Which of the following is spelled correctly?**
a). Inconvinient
b). Inconveniant
c). Inconvenient
d). Inconvienient

18. **Identify the correct spelling:**
a). Rhythem
b). Rhythm
c). Rhytm
d). Rythm

19. **Choose the correctly spelled word:**
a). Oportunity
b). Oppertunity
c). Opportunity
d). Opporunity

20. **Select the correct spelling:**
a). Occassion
b). Occasion
c). Occassion
d). Occasionn

Answers:

1.	(c)	2.	(b)	3.	(a)	4.	(b)	5.	(a)	6.	(b)
7.	(c)	8.	(c)	9.	(c)	10.	(c)	11.	(c)	12.	(d)
13.	(c)	14.	(c)	15.	(c)	16.	(b)	17.	(c)	18.	(b)
19.	(c)	20.	(b)								

Set 2:

1. **Select the wrongly spelt word.**
   a). Wildernesses
   b). Exterminated
   c). Unmanageable
   d). Voilence

   Answer:(d) Violence (behaviour which harms or damages somebody/ something physically)

2. **Select the wrongly spelt word.**
   a). Decrease
   b). Pieceful
   c). Specified
   d). Creature

   Answer:(b) peaceful (calm and quiet)

3. **Select the wrongly spelt word.**
   a). Allowance
   b). Borrow
   c). Alottment
   d). Terrorism

   Answer:(c) Allotment (the process of giving something to somebody)

4. **Select the wrongly spelt word.**
   a). Insolence
   b). Idleness
   c). Inershia
   d). Indolence

   Answer:(c) Inertia (a lack of energy; an inability to move or change)

5. **Select the wrongly spelt word.**
   a). Friend
   b). Scenic
   c). Fiery
   d). Neice

   Answer:(d) Niece (the daughter of your brother or sister; the daughter of your husband's or wife's brother or sister)

6. **Select the wrongly spelt word.**
   a). Moisture
   b). Anxious
   c). Vishious
   d). Mimic

   Answer:(c) Vicious (cruel, immoral, or evil)

7. **Select the wrongly spelt word.**
   a). Arbitrary
   b). Cerebral
   c). Scrutinize
   d). Withdrawl

   Answer:(d) Withdrawal (moving or being moved back or away from a place)

8. **Select the wrongly spelt word.**
   a). Fatalist
   b). Perfectionist
   c). Pessymist
   d). Optimist

   Answer:(c) Pessimist (who thinks that bad things are going to happen)

9. **Select the wrongly spelt word.**

a). Virtuous
b). Profuse
c). Luxuriaus
d). Recluse

Answer:(c) Luxurious

(very comfortable; full of expensive and beautiful things)

10. Select the wrongly spelt word.

a). Electronics
b). Dielmma
c). Professional
d). Perpetuate

Answer:(b) Dilemma (a situation in which you have to make a difficult choice between two or more thing)

11. Select the wrongly spelt word.

a). Competency
b). Processing
c). Photgraph
d). Boundary

Answer:(c) Photograph (a picture that is taken with a camera)

12. Select the wrongly spelt word.

a). Incriminating
b). Unpretensious
c). Cancellation
d). Embodiment

Answer:(b) Unpretentious

(not trying to impress or appear more special or important)

13. Select the wrongly spelt word.

a). Bouquet
b). Acquarium
c). Pledge
d). Abridge

Answer:(b) Aquarium

(a glass container filled with water, in which fish and water animals are kept)

14. Select the wrongly spelt word.

a). Piety
b). Depressed
c). Sovereignty
d). Vivedly

Answer: (d) Vividly

(In a way that produces powerful feelings or strong, clear images in the mind)

15. Select the wrongly spelt word.

a). Casheir
b). Security
c). Certain
d). Imagery

Answer:(a) Cashier (the person in a bank, shop,

etc. that customers pay money to or get money from)

16. Select the wrongly spelt word.

a). Adress
b). Astound
c). Advice
d). Amount

Answer:(a) Address (particulars of a place, a formal speech, speak about)

17. Select the wrongly spelt word.

a). Camoflage
b). Comedian
c). Caravan
d). Custard

Answer:a) Camouflage (concealment by means of disguise)

18. Select the wrongly spelt word.

a). Seasonal
b). Hygeinic
c). Celestial
d). Gymnastic

Answer:(b) Hygienic (conducive to maintaining health and preventing disease by being clean)

19. Select the wrongly spelt word.

a). Lizard
b). Scorpeon
c). Chameleon
d). Caterpillar

Answer:(b) Scorpion (a small creature with a sting, similar to an insect that lives in hot, dry areas)

20. Select the wrongly spelt word.

a). Proffesser
b). Director
c). Teacher
d). Headmaster

Answer:(a) Professor (a teacher at a college or university)

Set 3

In the following questions, select the correctly spelt word from the four alternatives.

1.
- a). ferocios
- b). falssified
- c). facilitating
- d). finaliced

2.
- a). (a) inclyned
- b). (b) interfare
- c). (c) intensified
- d). (d) integrete

3.
- a). brouser
- b). bruisar
- c). beniygn
- d). benevolence

4.
- a). reprisal
- b). ratifeid
- c). resonence
- d). restrein

5.
- a). (a) distributesd
- b). (b) deteriorating
- c). (c) distresssed
- d). (d) drestic

6.
- a). humilietad
- b). hemble
- c). humanitarian
- d). horible

7.
- a). creiminated
- b). credentials
- c). cristopher
- d). cartitude

8.
- a). petulance
- a). penitrate
- a). pericede
- a). neumonia

9.
- a). abcsonding
- b). abondon
- c). adsolutely
- d). abstain

10.
- a). extreordinary
- b). exasperation
- c). extampore
- d). exonarate

Answers

1- (c)

2- (c)

3- (d)

4- (a)

5- (b)

6- (c)

7- (b)

8- (a)

9- (d)

10- (b)

Set 4

Fill in the most appropriate word from the options.

1. **The airline was unable to give us a reason for the ______________ departure delay.**
   a). indivisible
   b). invincible
   c). invisible
   d). inexplicable
2. **The president's team of advisers was unable to offer him a ____________ to the national problem.**
   a). solvent
   b). solute
   c). solution
   d). mixture
3. **We feared the enemies attack because they ______________ everything in their path.**
   a). encinerate
   b). incinerate
   c). incenerate
   d). inncinerate
4. **The company decided to ______________ their outdated equipment and invest in new technology.**
   a). upgrade
   b). upgrate
   c). uppgrade
   d). uppgrate
5. **The chef's secret ingredient ______________ the flavor of the dish.**
   a). enhansed
   b). enhanched
   c). enhanced
   d). enhansced
6. **The heavy rain ______________ the streets, causing flooding in many areas.**
   a). submurged
   b). submerjd
   c). submerged
   d). submergged
7. **The artist used vibrant colors to ______________ the beauty of the landscape.**
   a). captuer
   b). capture
   c). captore
   d). cappture
8. **The detective's keen observations ______________ the truth behind the mysterious case.**
   a). reveealed
   b). revealed

c). reavealed

d). reveled

9. **The strong winds _______________ the tree branches, causing them to sway violently.**

a). battered

b). batterred

c). batteered

d). batttered

10. **The singer's powerful voice _______________ the audience during the live performance.**

a). mesmerised

b). mezmerized

c). mesmirized

d). mesmerissed

Answers:

1- (d)

2- (c)

3- (b)

4- (a)

5- (c)

6- (c)

7- (b)

8- (b)

9. (a)

10- (a)

Set 5

Fill in the most appropriate word from the options.

1. **The marathon runner's determination _______________ him to cross the finish line.**
   a). compelled
   b). compellled
   c). complelled
   d). comppelled

2. **The summer heat _______________ the ice cream, causing it to melt quickly.**
   a). liquified
   b). liquiffied
   c). liquiified
   d). liquefied

3. **The construction workers _______________ the building materials to the construction site.**
   a). transported
   b). transpported
   c). transportted
   d). transpported

4. **The teacher's engaging presentation _______________ the students' interest in the subject.**
   a). piqued
   b). peeked
   c). peacked
   d). piqqued

5. **The politician's scandalous behavior _______________ his chances of winning the election.**
   a). dimnished
   b). diminished
   c). diminisshed
   d). diminnished

6. **The athlete's rigorous training _______________ her endurance and strength.**
   a). enanced
   b). enhanced
   c). enanched
   d). enhanched

7. **The magician's sleight of hand _______________ the audience's senses.**
   a). decieved
   b). deceived
   c). decieived
   d). decceeived

8. **The storm's strong winds _______________ the power lines, causing a widespread blackout.**
   a). dammaged
   b). damagged
   c). damaged
   d). dammaged

9. The new medication ______________ the patient's pain and provided relief.

a). alievated
b). alleviated
c). allievated
d). alleeviated

10. The skilled negotiator's persuasive arguments ______________ a favorable outcome.

a). secured
b). securred
c). seecured
d). secuured

Answers

1- (a)

2- (d)

3. (a)

4. (a)

5- (b)

6- (b)

7- (b)

8- (c)

9- (b)

10- (a)

Set 6

Fill in the most appropriate word from the options.

1. The filmmaker's creative vision ______________ a compelling story on the screen.
   a). transpirred
   b). transppired
   c). transpired
   d). trannspired

2. The brave firefighter's heroic actions ______________ lives during the rescue operation.
   a). saved
   b). savved
   c). saaved
   d). saveed

3. The chef's unique recipe ______________ a perfect balance of flavors.
   a). concocted
   b). conncotted
   c). (c) concockted
   d). (d) concoctted

4. The ________ to the throne eagerly prepared to assume their rightful place as the future ruler.
   a). hair
   b). here
   c). hear
   d). heir

5. The taxi driver quoted a reasonable ______ for the journey to the airport.
   a). fair
   b). fear
   c). fade
   d). fare

6. She ____ her bicycle along the scenic coastal path, enjoying the fresh sea breeze on her face.
   a). rode
   b). rowed
   c). robe
   d). roast

7. The wildfire's intense heat threatened to ______________ the entire forest.
   a). consumed
   b). consume
   c). consuume
   d). consumme

8. The acid spill could ______________ the metal surfaces, causing severe damage.
   a). corrode
   b). corode
   c). corroode
   d). corrodde

9. The volcano's eruption had the potential to ______________ nearby villages.

a). obliterate
b). obliteerate
c). oblitterate
d). oblliterate

10. The hacker's malicious software could ______________ sensitive data from the computer system.

a). extort
b). extortt
c). exxtort
d). exxtortt

Answers

1- (c)

2- (a)

3- (a)

4- (d)

5- (d)

6- (a)

7- (b)

8- (a)

9- (a)

10- (a)

Set 7

In the following questions, four words are given out of which one word is correctly spelt. Select the correctly spelt word.

1.
a). andulate
b). undulate
c). undulete
d). andulete

2.
a). Mutiniers
b). Mutineers
c). Muteniers
d). Muteneers

3.
a). Perverted
b). Pervirted
c). Parverted
d). Parvirted

4.
a). Blandnes
b). Blandeness
c). Blandenes
d). Blandness

5.
a). Ditheering
b). Dethering
c). Dithering
d). Detheering

6.
a). Throtled
b). Throttlede
c). Throtlede
d). Throttled

7.
a). poseses
b). posesses
c). possesses
d). posseses

8.
a). palatable
b). palateble
c). pallateble
d). pallatable

9.
a). murmuring
b). murmurring
c). murrmuring
d). murrmurring

10.
a). jukstapose
b). jaxtapuse
c). juxtapose
d). jaxtapose

Answers

1- (b)

2- (b)

3- (a)

4- (d)

5- (c)

6- (d)

7- (c)

8- (a)

9- (a)

10- (c)

Set 8

In the following questions, four words are given of which one word is incorrectly spelt. Select the incorrectly spelt word.

1.
a). Dictionory
b). Irrelevant
c). Perishable
d). Tangible

2.
a). Receeding
b). Cemetery
c). Parallelogram
d). Rehearsal

3.
a). Fabulous
b). Gorgeous
c). Heterogeneous
d). Inocuous

4.
a). Anasthetic
b). Obliterate
c). Concurrence
d). Blithesome

5.
a). Secondary
b). Sizable
c). Succumb
d). Sustanence

6.
a). Ecstasy
b). Profecient
c). Sacrifice
d). Temporary

7.
a). Colonel
b). Hypocracy
c). Offence
d). Strength

8.
a). Millionaire
b). Omission
c). Foreign
d). Proprietry

9.
a). Entrepreneur
b). Remuneration
c). Apprentice
d). Soveriegnity

10.
a). Reside
b). Revise
c). Advise
d). Demice

Answers

1- (a)

2- (a)

3- (b)

4- (a)

5- (d)

6- (b)

7- (b)

8- (d)

9- (d)

10- (d)

Set 9

1. **Which of the following is the correct spelling?**
   a). Espionnage
   b). Espionnage
   c). Espionage
   d). Espionnage

2. **Which of the following is the correct spelling?**
   a). Gramar
   b). Grammer
   c). Grammar
   d). Gramar

3. **Which of the following is the correct spelling?**
   a). Competittion
   b). Competiition
   c). Commpetition
   d). Competition

4. **Which of the following is the correct spelling?**
   a). Architecure
   b). Archtecture
   c). Architecture
   d). Architeccture

5. **Which of the following is the correct spelling?**
   a). Assasination
   b). Assassination
   c). Assasinationn
   d). Asassination

6. **Which of the following is the correct spelling?**
   a). Cigarete
   b). Cigaret
   c). Cigarette
   d). Ciggarette

7. **Which of the following is the correct spelling?**
   a). Cassett
   b). Casseette
   c). Casette
   d). Cassette

8. **Which of the following is the correct spelling?**
   a). Canibal
   b). Cannibal
   c). Canniball
   d). Canibbal

9. **Which of the following is the correct spelling?**
   a). Auxilliary
   b). Auxilliarry
   c). Auxiliary
   d). Auxilliery

10. **Which of the following is the correct spelling?**
    a). Archeology
    b). Archaeology
    c). Archaelogy
    d). Archeaology

Answers

1- (c)

2- (c)

3- (d)

4- (c)

5- (b)

6- (c)

7- (d)

8- (b)

9- (c)

10- (b)

Chapter - Six

Homonyms

HOMONYMS

Homonyms are words that have the same pronunciation or spelling but have different meanings. They can be categorized into two types: homophones and homographs.

Homophones: These are words that sound the same but have different meanings and often different spellings. Examples of homophones include:

"There" and "their"

"To" and "too"

"Flour" and "flower"

"Meet" and "meat"

Homographs: These are words that have the same spelling but different meanings, and they may or may not have the same pronunciation. Examples of homographs include:

"Bow" (a knot) and "bow" (an act of bending forward)

"Tear" (to rip) and "tear" (a drop of liquid from the eyes)

"Wind" (movement of air) and "wind" (to twist or turn)

Understanding homonyms can be challenging because they require context to determine the correct meaning. Correct usage relies on knowing the appropriate spelling and meaning for each specific context.

Homonyms can be a source of confusion and ambiguity, but they also add depth and richness to the English language.

Here are 50 homonyms, which are words that sound the same but have different spellings and meanings:

1. Air/Heir: Air refers to the atmosphere, while heir refers to someone who inherits something.
2. Ate/Eight: Ate is the past tense of "eat," while eight is the number following seven.
3. Bare/Bear: Bare means naked or without covering, while the bear is a large mammal.
4. Brake/Break: Brake refers to a device for stopping or slowing down, while break means to separate or shatter.
5. Buy/Bye/By: Buy means to purchase, bye is a shortened form of goodbye, and by indicates a method or means.
6. Cereal/Serial: Cereal refers to a type of grain, while serial relates to a series or sequence.
7. Check/Cheque: A check refers to verifying or examining something, while a cheque is a written order for payment.
8. Flour/Flower: Flour is a powdery substance used in baking, while flower refers to a plant's reproductive structure.
9. Hare/Hair: Hare is a type of animal, while hair refers to the strands that grow on the body.
10. Here/Hear: Here indicates a location, while hear means to perceive sound.
11. Knight/Night: Knight refers to a medieval warrior, while the night is the period of darkness.
12. Made/Maid: Made is the past tense of "make," while maid refers to a female servant.
13. Mail/Male: Mail relates to letters and packages, while male refers to the sex of an organism.
14. Peace/Piece: Peace means freedom from conflict, while piece refers to a part or portion.
15. Rode/Road: Rode is the past tense of "ride," while the road is a paved pathway.
16. Sea/See: Sea refers to a large body of saltwater, while see means to look, perceive or observe.
17. Tail/Tale: The tail is the rear end of an animal, while the tale refers to a

story or narrative.

18. To/Too/Two: To indicates direction or purpose, too means also or excessive, and two is the number after one.

19. Way/Weigh: Way refers to a method or direction, while weigh means to measure weight.

20. Yew/You: Yew is a type of tree, while you refers to a person being addressed.

21. Allowed/Aloud: Allowed means permitted, while aloud refers to speaking or making a sound audibly.

22. Band/Banned: Band is a musical group, while banned means prohibited or not allowed.

23. Beach/Beech: Beach is a sandy or pebbly shore by the sea, while beech is a type of tree.

24. Board/Bored: Board refers to a flat piece of wood or a group of individuals, while bored means feeling uninterested or weary.

25. Cell/Sell: Cell is a small compartment or a unit of life, while sell means to exchange something for money.

26. Chord/Cord: Chord refers to a musical note combination, while cord is a thin flexible string or wire.

27. Dear/Deer: Dear means loved or precious, while deer is an animal.

28. Fair/Fare: Fair can mean just or light in color, while fare refers to the cost of transportation or food.

29. Grate/Great: Grate means to shred or a framework of bars, while great means large or excellent.

30. Hair/Hare: Hair refers to the strands that grow on the body, while hare is a type of animal.

31. Idle/Idol: Idle means inactive or lazy, while idol refers to a revered figure or a representation of a deity.

32. Kernel/Colonel: Kernel is the inner part of a seed or grain, while colonel is a military rank.

33. Mail/Male: Mail relates to letters and packages, while male refers to the sex of an organism.

34. Morning/Mourning: Morning is the early part of the day, while mourning refers to expressing grief or sorrow.

35. Pail/Pale: Pail is a bucket, while pale means light in color or lacking color.

36. Paws/Pause: Paws are the feet of certain animals, while pause means to stop temporarily.

37. Principal/Principle: Principal refers to the head of a school or a sum of money, while principle relates to a fundamental belief or rule.

38. Rain/Reign/Rein: Rain is water falling from the sky, reign means to rule as a monarch, and rein is a strap used to control a horse.

39. Sew/So/Sow: Sew means to stitch, so indicates a result or reason, and sow means to plant seeds.

40. Steal/Steel: Steal means to take something without permission, while steel is a strong metal alloy.

41. Sun/Son: Sun is the star at the center of the solar system, while son refers to a male offspring.

42. Thyme/Time: Thyme is a herb, while time relates to the measurement of events.

43. Waste/Waist: Waste refers to garbage or squandering, while waist is the narrowest part of the torso.

44. Wood/Would: Wood is the material from trees, while would is a modal verb.

45. Road/Rode/Rowed: Road is a paved pathway, rode is the past tense of "ride," and rowed is the past tense of "row."

46. Base/Bass: Base means foundation or bottom, while bass refers to a low musical tone or a type of fish.

47. Bean/Been: Bean is a type of seed or legume, while been is the past participle of "be."

48. Bore/Boar: Bore means to drill or a dull or tedious person, while boar is a wild pig.

49. Cellist/Sellist: Cellist refers to a person who plays the cello, while sellist is a term used in trading or sales.

50. Dew/Due: Dew refers to moisture condensation, while due means owed or expected.

51. Dye/Die: Dye is a substance used to color something, while die refers to the cessation of life.

52. Flour/Flower: Flour is a powdery substance used in baking, while flower refers to a plant's reproductive structure.

53. Idle/Idol: Idle means inactive or lazy, while idol refers to a revered figure or a representation of a deity.

54. Miner/Minor: Miner refers to someone who works in a mine, while minor means someone under the age of majority.

55. Morning/Mourning: Morning is the early part of the day, while mourning refers to expressing grief or sorrow.

56. Pair/Pear: Pair refers to a set of two, while pear is a type of fruit.

57. Peal/Peel: Peal refers to a loud ringing sound, while peel means to remove the outer layer of something.

58. Pole/Polle: Pole refers to a long, slender object, while polle is a variant spelling of "poll" which can refer to voting or a person's head.

59. Rite/Right/Wright: Rite refers to a religious or ceremonial act, right means correct or a direction, and wright is a person who constructs or repairs something.

60. Suite/Sweet: Suite refers to a set of rooms or a musical composition, while sweet means pleasant or sugary.

61. Tail/Tale: Tail is the rear end of an animal, while tale refers to a story or narrative.

62. Weather/Whether: Weather relates to the atmospheric conditions, while whether introduces a choice or possibility.

63. Write/Right/Rite: Write means to inscribe or record, right means correct or a direction, and rite refers to a religious or ceremonial act.

64. Altar/Alter: Altar refers to a sacred table or platform, while alter means to change or modify.

65. Ascent/Assent: Ascent refers to the act of climbing or rising, while assent means agreement or approval.

66. Blue/Blew: Blue is a color, while blew is the past tense of "blow."

67. Cite/Sight/Site: Cite means to quote or refer to, sight refers to vision or a view, and site relates to a location or place.

68. Groan/Grown: Groan means to make a low, mournful sound, while grown is the past participle of "grow."

69. Inn/In: Inn refers to a small hotel or lodging place, while in indicates location or inclusion.

70. Naval/Navel: Naval relates to the navy or naval forces, while navel

refers to the belly button.

71. **Not/Knot: Not is a negation or denial, while knot refers to a tied loop in a cord or rope.**

72. **Pair/Pare/Pear: Pair refers to a set of two, pare means to trim or peel, and pear is a type of fruit.**

73. **Stare/Stair: Stare means to gaze or look fixedly, while stair refers to a step in a staircase.**

74. **Threw/Through: Threw is the past tense of "throw," while through means to move from one side to the other.**

75. **Vein/Vain: Vein refers to a blood vessel or a streak of a mineral, while vain means conceited or without success.**

Exercise:

Exercise 1: Fill in the Blanks

Choose the correct homonym to complete each sentence.

1. She _______________ the document on the desk. (set/sit)
2. The _______________ is ringing. (cell/sell)
3. He has a _______________ for playing the piano. (flour/flower)
4. The _______________ of the novel was unexpected. (tail/tale)
5. Can you _______________ the difference between these two colors? (see/sea)
6. We need to _______________ the meeting to discuss the new proposal. (break/ brake)
7. The _______________ told a story about a haunted house. (tail/tale)
8. She was _______________ when she heard the news. (dear/deer)
9. The _______________ is shining brightly in the sky. (son/sun)
10. They went for a walk on the sandy _______________. (beach/beech)

Answers:

1. **She set the document on the desk.**

   Explanation: "Set" is the correct word choice here, indicating the action of placing or putting something down.

2. **The cell is ringing.**

   Explanation: In this context, "cell" refers to a mobile phone. Therefore, the sentence implies that someone's mobile phone is ringing.

3. **He has a flair for playing the piano.**

   Explanation: The word "flair" refers to a natural talent or aptitude for something. It indicates that he possesses a skill or ability when it comes to playing the piano.

4. **The tale of the novel was unexpected.**

   Explanation: A "tale" refers to a story or narrative, while a "tail" is the rear end of an animal or a long, slender extension. In this sentence, "tale" is the appropriate word choice, suggesting that the story's plot was unexpected.

5. **Can you see the difference between these two colors?**

   Explanation: "See" implies the act of perceiving or visually discerning something. It is used here to inquire if the person can visually distinguish the dissimilarities between the two colors.

6. **We need to break the meeting to discuss the new proposal.**

   Explanation: In this sentence, "break" is the correct word choice, indicating the intention to pause or interrupt the meeting temporarily.

7. **The tale told a story about a haunted house.**

   Explanation: Here, "tale" signifies a narrative or story. The sentence suggests that the "tale" being referenced revolves around a haunted house.

8. She was dear when she heard the news.

Explanation: "Dear" is an adjective used to describe affection, endearment, or something cherished. In this context, it implies that the person had a strong emotional reaction upon hearing the news.

9. The sun is shining brightly in the sky.

Explanation: "Sun" refers to the star that provides light and warmth to the Earth. The sentence conveys that the sun is radiating light with intensity.

10. They went for a walk on the sandy beach.

Explanation: In this sentence, "beach" refers to a shoreline or sandy area along a body of water. It implies that they took a stroll in that particular location.

Exercise 2: Multiple Choice

Choose the correct homonym to complete each sentence.

1. The chef used _______________ to add flavor to the dish. (herbs/herds)
2. I need to _______________ this letter before sending it. (cite/site/sight)
3. The team captain gave his _______________ to proceed with the plan. (assent/ascent)
4. She _______________ the candle and made a wish. (blew/blue)
5. The _______________ of the bookshelf is made of oak. (waist/waste)

Answers:

1. The chef used herbs to add flavor to the dish.

   Explanation: "Herbs" are plants with aromatic or savory properties used for seasoning or medicinal purposes. It is the correct word choice in this context to indicate the ingredients used by the chef.

2. I need to proofread this letter before sending it.

   Explanation: "Proofreading" refers to the act of carefully reviewing and correcting errors in a written document. It ensures accuracy and clarity before sending or publishing it. "Cite" means to refer to a source, "site" refers to a location, and "sight" relates to vision. In the given sentence, "proofread" is the appropriate word.

3. The team captain gave his assent to proceed with the plan.

   Explanation: "Assent" means to give approval or agreement. It indicates that the team captain agreed to move forward with the plan. "Ascent" refers to the act of climbing or rising. In this context, "assent" is the correct word.

4. She blew the candle and made a wish.

Explanation: "Blew" is the past tense of the verb "blow." It means to produce a current of air or extinguish something by blowing. In the sentence, it indicates the action of extinguishing the candle.

5. The shelf of the bookshelf is made of oak.

Explanation: A "shelf" is a flat, horizontal surface used for holding or displaying items. It refers to the part of the bookshelf on which books are placed. "Waist" is the narrow part of the body between the ribs and hips, while "waste" refers to material that is discarded or not used. In the given sentence, "shelf" is the correct word choice.

Exercise 3:

1. I need to ________________ my keys before leaving the house. (write/right)
2. The ________________ of the movie kept the audience on the edge of their seats. (climate/climax)
3. Can you ________________ me your pen? I forgot mine. (lend/loan)
4. She wore a beautiful ________________ to the party. (gown/gone)
5. The teacher asked the students to ________________ quietly during the test. (be/bee)
6. The chef added a pinch of ________________ to enhance the flavor of the soup. (bouillon/bullion)
7. I could hear the ________________ of the waves as I walked along the beach. (sound/sound)
8. The ________________ of the crime scene remained a mystery. (site/sight)
9. She carefully ________________ the recipe to make sure she had all the ingredients. (read/red)
10. The children played in the ________________ until the sun went down. (yard/yarn)

Answers:

1. I need to right my keys before leaving the house.

   Explanation: "Right" means to correct or put something in its proper position. In this context, it means the person needs to locate or adjust their keys before leaving.

2. The climax of the movie kept the audience on the edge of their seats.

   Explanation: The word "climax" refers to the highest point of tension or excitement in a story or event. In this context, it signifies the most intense and thrilling part of the movie.

3. Can you lend me your pen? I forgot mine.

   Explanation: "Lend" means to give someone something temporarily with the expectation of it being returned. In this case, the speaker is requesting the pen for a short period.

4. She wore a beautiful gown to the party.

   Explanation: A "gown" refers to a long, formal dress. It is the appropriate term to describe the type of attire the person wore to the party.

5. The teacher asked the students to be quietly during the test.

   Explanation: "Be" is a verb indicating existence or state of being. In this sentence, it is used to instruct the students to maintain quietness during the test.

6. The chef added a pinch of bouillon to enhance the flavor of the soup.

   Explanation: "Bouillon" refers to a concentrated stock or broth used for flavoring dishes. It is the correct word choice to describe the ingredient added to the soup.

7. I could hear the sound of the waves as I walked along the beach.

   Explanation: "Sound" refers to the vibrations that travel through the air and can be heard. In this sentence, it represents the audible waves.

8. The site of the crime scene remained a mystery.

   Explanation: "Site" refers to the location or place where something significant or specific has occurred. In this context, it indicates the place where the crime took place.

9. She carefully read the recipe to make sure she had all the ingredients.

   Explanation: "Read" refers to the action of looking at and understanding written or printed words. In this sentence, it describes the activity of going through the recipe to ensure ingredient availability.

10. The children played in the yard until the sun went down.

    Explanation: "Yard" refers to an outdoor area, typically surrounding a house, where children can play.

Chapter - Seven

The Hindu Vocabulary

Hindu Vocabulary

Word	English Meaning	Hindi Meaning	Synonyms	Antonyms
Catalyst	an agent that provokes or speeds significant change or action	उत्प्रेरक (Utprerak)	Stimulus, Trigger, Propellant	Hindrance, Inhibitor, Obstacle
Adversity	difficulties or misfortune	विपत्ति (Vipatti)	Hardship, Misfortune, Tribulation	Prosperity, Success, Favorable conditions
Emulate	to imitate or follow as an example	अनुकरण करना (Anukaran Karna)	Mimic, Copy, Replicate	Diverge, Deviate, Differ
Intrepid	fearless and adventurous	निडर (Nidar)	Fearless, Bold, Courageous	Timid, Cowardly, Fearful
Benevolent	well-meaning and kind	उदार (Udaar)	Kind, Generous, Compassionate	Malevolent, Cruel, Selfish
Ephemeral	lasting for a short time	अल्पकालिक (Alpakalik)	Transient, Fleeting, Temporary	Permanent, Enduring, Everlasting
Fortitude	courage in facing difficulties	धैर्य (Dhairya)	Resilience, Bravery, Strength	Weakness, Cowardice, Timidity
Camaraderie	mutual trust and friendship among a group	सखावत (Sakhavat)	Comradeship, Solidarity, Fellowship	Discord, Enmity, Hostility
Inevitable	certain to happen; unavoidable	अपरिहार्य (Apariharya)	Unavoidable, Certain, Inexorable	Avoidable, Uncertain, Preventable
Hypothesis	a proposed explanation based on limited evidence	परिकल्पना (Parikalpana)	Theory, Assumption, Conjecture	Fact, Reality, Truth
Abdicate	to renounce or give up power or responsibility	त्यागना (Tyagna)	Renounce, Resign, Surrender	Assume, Retain, Keep
Pervasive	spreading widely throughout an area or a group	व्यापक (Vyapak)	Widespread, Prevalent, Ubiquitous	Limited, Rare, Scarce

Word	English Meaning	Hindi Meaning	Synonyms	Antonyms
Conundrum	a confusing and difficult problem or question	पेचीदा (Pechida)	Puzzle, Enigma, Dilemma	Solution, Clarity, Answer
Diligent	showing careful and persistent effort	मेहनती (Mehnati)	Industrious, Hardworking, Assiduous	Lazy, Slothful, Negligent
Eloquent	fluent and persuasive in speaking or writing	प्रभावशाली (Prabhavashali)	Articulate, Expressive, Persuasive	Inarticulate, Mumbled, Incoherent
Ubiquitous	present or found everywhere	सर्वव्यापी (Sarvavyapi)	Omnipresent, Pervasive, Universal	Rare, Limited, Scattered
Voracious	having a great appetite or desire for something	भुक्खड़ (Bhukkhad)	Insatiable, Ravenous, Greedy	Content, Satisfied, Moderate
Quandary	a state of uncertainty or perplexity	दुविधा (Duvidha)	Dilemma, Predicament, Conundrum	Certainty, Clarity, Solution
Resilient	able to recover quickly from difficulties	प्रतिरोधी (Pratirodhi)	Strong, Tough, Adaptive	Fragile, Vulnerable, Delicate
Tangible	perceptible by touch; capable of being touched or felt	स्पर्शनीय (Sparshaniya)	Touchable, Palpable, Concrete	Intangible, Abstract, Immaterial
Impeccable	faultless; without flaws or mistakes	अचूक (Achook)	Flawless, Perfect, Immaculate	Imperfect, Flawed, Defective
Exemplary	serving as a desirable model; representing the best of its kind	प्रशंसानीय (Prashansaniya)	Commendable, Admirable, Laudable	Mediocre, Average, Inferior
Prolific	producing many works, results, or offspring	उत्पादक (Utpadak)	Productive, Fertile, Creative	Barren, Unproductive, Sterile
Eccentric	unconventional and slightly strange	अद्भुत (Adbhut)	Quirky, Odd, Unconventional	Conventional, Normal, Ordinary

Word	English Meaning	Hindi Meaning	Synonyms	Antonyms
Meticulous	showing great attention to detail; very careful and precise	सूक्ष्म (Sukshm)	Thorough, Accurate, Diligent	Careless, Sloppy, Negligent
Nurture	care for and encourage the growth or development of	पोषण (Poshan)	Foster, Cultivate, Support	Neglect, Abandon, Ignore
Empathy	the ability to understand and share the feelings of another	सहानुभूति (Sahanubhuti)	Compassion, Understanding, Sympathy	Indifference, Apathy, Insensitivity
Euphoria	a feeling of intense happiness and excitement	उत्साह (Utsah)	Joy, Bliss, Ecstasy	Sadness, Misery, Desolation
Altruism	selfless concern for the well-being of others	परोपकार (Paropkar)	Selflessness, Generosity, Philanthropy	Selfishness, Greed, Egoism
Vulnerable	susceptible to physical or emotional harm or attack	आलोच्य (Alochya)	Defenseless, Fragile, Exposed	Protected, Invulnerable, Secure
Enigmatic	difficult to interpret or understand; mysterious	रहस्यमय (Rahasyamay)	Cryptic, Puzzling, Ambiguous	Clear, Transparent, Understandable
Conscientious	wishing to do one's work or duty well and thoroughly	ईमानदार (Imandar)	Diligent, Meticulous, Scrupulous	Careless, Negligent, Irresponsible
Vivacious	attractively lively and animated	जीवंत (Jivant)	Lively, Energetic, Spirited	Dull, Lifeless, Lethargic
Serenity	the state of being calm, peaceful, and untroubled	शांति (Shanti)	Tranquility, Peace, Harmony	Turmoil, Chaos, Disturbance
Exuberant	filled with lively energy and excitement	प्रफुल्लित (Prapullit)	Energetic, Vibrant, Joyful	Depressed, Dull, Lethargic

Word	English Meaning	Hindi Meaning	Synonyms	Antonyms
Imminent	about to happen; impending	सन्निकट (Sannikat)	Pending, Approaching, Close	Distant, Remote, Far-off
Tenacious	tending to keep a firm hold of something; persistent	सटीक (Sateek)	Determined, Persistent, Resolute	Weak, Indecisive, Surrendering
Melancholy	a feeling of pensive sadness, typically with no obvious cause	उदासी (Udasi)	Sorrow, Gloom, Desolation	Happiness, Joy, Elation
Inquisitive	curious or inquiring	जिज्ञासु (Jigyansu)	Curious, Interested, Nosy	Indifferent, Apathetic, Uninterested
Impartial	treating all rivals or disputants equally; fair and just	निष्पक्ष (Nishpaksh)	Fair, Unbiased, Neutral	Biased, Partial, Prejudiced
Effervescent	vivacious and enthusiastic	उत्साही (Utsahi)	Bubbly, Lively, Sparkling	Dull, Gloomy, Flat
Indomitable	impossible to subdue or defeat	अजेय (Ajey)	Unbeatable, Invincible, Unconquerable	Defeatable, Vulnerable, Subduable
Augment	to make something greater by adding to it	बढ़ाना (Badhana)	Increase, Expand, Enhance	Decrease, Reduce, Diminish
Reticent	not revealing one's thoughts or feelings readily	मौन (Maun)	Reserved, Introverted, Taciturn	Talkative, Outspoken, Expressive
Pragmatic	dealing with things sensibly and realistically	यथार्थवादी (Yatharthvadi)	Practical, Realistic, Logical	Idealistic, Impractical, Unrealistic
Innovative	introducing new ideas, methods, or concepts	नवीन (Navin)	Creative, Inventive, Pioneering	Traditional, Conventional, Ordinary
Ambivalent	having mixed feelings or contradictory ideas about something	द्विधारी (Dvidhari)	Conflicted, Uncertain, Indecisive	Certain, Definite, Resolute

Word	English Meaning	Hindi Meaning	Synonyms	Antonyms
Zeal	great energy or enthusiasm in pursuit of a cause or objective	उत्साह (Utsah)	Enthusiasm, Passion, Ardor	Apathy, Indifference, Lethargy
Plausible	seeming reasonable or probable	संभाव्य (Sambhavya)	Credible, Believable, Likely	Unlikely, Improbable, Unbelievable
Ambiguous	open to more than one interpretation; unclear or inexact	अस्पष्ट (Aspasht)	Vague, Uncertain, Cryptic	Clear, Explicit, Unambiguous
Incessant	continuing without pause or interruption	अविराम (Aviram)	Unending, Constant, Persistent	Intermittent, Occasional, Sporadic
Nostalgia	a sentimental longing or wistful affection for the past	यादें (Yaden)	Reminiscence, Longing, Yearning	Disinterest, Indifference, Unconcern
Impetus	the force or energy with which a body moves	शक्ति (Shakti)	Momentum, Drive, Boost	Halt, Inertia, Stagnation
Rendezvous	a meeting at an agreed time and place	मुलाकात (Mulaqat)	Encounter, Tryst, Appointment	Separation, Departure, Disconnection
Serendipity	the occurrence of finding pleasant or valuable things by chance	अकस्मात (Akasmat)	Fortuity, Luck, Discovery	Misfortune, Unluckiness, Bad luck
Imperative	of vital importance; crucial	आदेशक (Aadeshak)	Essential, Critical, Indispensable	Optional, Unimportant, Insignificant
Infallible	incapable of making mistakes or being wrong	अचूक (Achook)	Flawless, Perfect, Errorless	Fallible, Imperfect, Erroneous
Enthralling	capturing and holding one's attention; fascinating	मोहक (Mohak)	Captivating, Gripping, Spellbinding	Boring, Tedious, Uninteresting
Transient	lasting only for a short time; temporary	अस्थायी (Asthaayi)	Fleeting, Ephemeral, Evanescent	Permanent, Enduring, Lasting

Word	English Meaning	Hindi Meaning	Synonyms	Antonyms
Compromise	an agreement reached by making concessions	समझौता (Samjhauta)	Settlement, Conciliation, Agreement	Conflict, Disagreement, Discord
Eccentric	deviating from conventional or accepted norms	विलक्षण (Vilakshan)	Quirky, Unconventional, Offbeat	Normal, Conventional, Typical
Mitigate	to make less severe, serious, or painful	कम करना (Kam Karna)	Alleviate, Reduce, Lessen	Aggravate, Worsen, Intensify
Repudiate	to refuse to accept or be associated with	अस्वीकार करना (Asvikar Karna)	Reject, Disown, Deny	Accept, Embrace, Acknowledge
Enigmatic	mysterious and difficult to understand	रहस्यमय (Rahasyamay)	Cryptic, Puzzling, Baffling	Clear, Obvious, Transparent
Vigilant	keeping careful watch for possible danger or difficulties	सतर्क (Satarak)	Alert, Watchful, Attentive	Careless, Inattentive, Negligent
Diverse	showing a great deal of variety; very different	विविध (Vividh)	Varied, Multifarious, Heterogeneous	Uniform, Homogeneous, Similar
Novel	new or unusual in an interesting way	नवीनता (Navinta)	Fresh, Original, Innovative	Familiar, Common, Routine
Resilience	the ability to recover quickly from difficulties or adapt to change	पुनर्स्थापना (Punarsthapana)	Endurance, Toughness, Flexibility	Fragility, Vulnerability, Inflexibility
Proficient	skilled or competent in doing something	कुशल (Kushal)	Skilled, Competent, Capable	Inept, Incompetent, Unskilled
Inevitable	certain to happen; unavoidable	अपरिहार्य (Apariharya)	Unavoidable, Inescapable, Certain	Avoidable, Preventable, Uncertain
Paradigm	a typical example or pattern of something; a model	मिसाल (Misaal)	Model, Example, Pattern	Anomaly, Exception, Aberration
Prudent	acting with or showing care and thought for the future	विवेकी (Viveki)	Wise, Sensible, Judicious	Foolish, Imprudent, Reckless

Word	English Meaning	Hindi Meaning	Synonyms	Antonyms
Enthrall	to captivate or charm; to hold someone's attention completely	मोहित करना (Mohit Karna)	Fascinate, Mesmerize, Spellbind	Bore, Repel, Disinterest
Ebullient	cheerful and full of energy; enthusiastic	उत्साही (Utsahi)	Exuberant, Lively, Animated	Depressed, Gloomy, Dull
Catalyst	an agent that provokes or speeds significant change or action	उत्प्रेरक (Utprerak)	Stimulus, Trigger, Propellant	Hindrance, Inhibitor, Obstacle
Adversity	difficulties or misfortune	विपत्ति (Vipatti)	Hardship, Misfortune, Tribulation	Prosperity, Success, Favorable conditions
Emulate	to imitate or follow as an example	अनुकरण करना (Anukaran Karna)	Mimic, Copy, Replicate	Diverge, Deviate, Differ
Intrepid	fearless and adventurous	निडर (Nidar)	Fearless, Bold, Courageous	Timid, Cowardly, Fearful
Benevolent	well-meaning and kind	उदार (Udaar)	Kind, Generous, Compassionate	Malevolent, Cruel, Selfish
Ephemeral	lasting for a short time	अल्पकालिक (Alpakalik)	Transient, Fleeting, Temporary	Permanent, Enduring, Everlasting
Fortitude	courage in facing difficulties	धैर्य (Dhairya)	Resilience, Bravery, Strength	Weakness, Cowardice, Timidity
Camaraderie	mutual trust and friendship among a group	सखावत (Sakhavat)	Comradeship, Solidarity, Fellowship	Discord, Enmity, Hostility
Inevitable	certain to happen; unavoidable	अपरिहार्य (Apariharya)	Unavoidable, Certain, Inexorable	Avoidable, Uncertain, Preventable
Hypothesis	a proposed explanation based on limited evidence	परिकल्पना (Parikalpana)	Theory, Assumption, Conjecture	Fact, Reality, Truth
Abdicate	to renounce or give up power or responsibility	त्यागना (Tyagna)	Renounce, Resign, Surrender	Assume, Retain, Keep
Inquisitive	curious or inquiring	जिज्ञासु (Jigyansu)	Curious, Interested, Nosy	Indifferent, Apathetic, Uninterested

Word	English Meaning	Hindi Meaning	Synonyms	Antonyms
Impartial	treating all rivals or disputants equally; fair and just	निष्पक्ष (Nishpaksh)	Fair, Unbiased, Neutral	Biased, Partial, Prejudiced
Effervescent	vivacious and enthusiastic	उत्साही (Utsahi)	Bubbly, Lively, Sparkling	Dull, Gloomy, Flat
Indomitable	impossible to subdue or defeat	अजेय (Ajey)	Unbeatable, Invincible, Unconquerable	Defeatable, Vulnerable, Subduable
Augment	to make something greater by adding to it	बढ़ाना (Badhana)	Increase, Expand, Enhance	Decrease, Reduce, Diminish
Reticent	not revealing one's thoughts or feelings readily	मौन (Maun)	Reserved, Introverted, Taciturn	Talkative, Outspoken, Expressive
Pragmatic	dealing with things sensibly and realistically	यथार्थवादी (Yatharthvadi)	Practical, Realistic, Logical	Idealistic, Impractical, Unrealistic
Innovative	introducing new ideas, methods, or concepts	नवीन (Navin)	Creative, Inventive, Pioneering	Traditional, Conventional, Ordinary
Ambivalent	having mixed feelings or contradictory ideas about something	द्विधारी (Dvidhari)	Conflicted, Uncertain, Indecisive	Certain, Definite, Resolute
Zeal	great energy or enthusiasm in pursuit of a cause or objective	उत्साह (Utsah)	Enthusiasm, Passion, Ardor	Apathy, Indifference, Lethargy
Plausible	seeming reasonable or probable	संभाव्य (Sambhavya)	Credible, Believable, Likely	Unlikely, Improbable, Unbelievable
Ambiguous	open to more than one interpretation; unclear or inexact	अस्पष्ट (Aspasht)	Vague, Uncertain, Cryptic	Clear, Explicit, Unambiguous
Incessant	continuing without pause or interruption	अविराम (Aviram)	Unending, Constant, Persistent	Intermittent, Occasional, Sporadic

Word	English Meaning	Hindi Meaning	Synonyms	Antonyms
Nostalgia	a sentimental longing or wistful affection for the past	यादें (Yaden)	Reminiscence, Longing, Yearning	Disinterest, Indifference, Unconcern
Impetus	the force or energy with which a body moves	शक्ति (Shakti)	Momentum, Drive, Boost	Halt, Inertia, Stagnation
Rendezvous	a meeting at an agreed time and place	मुलाकात (Mulaqat)	Encounter, Tryst, Appointment	Separation, Departure, Disconnection
Serendipity	the occurrence of finding pleasant or valuable things by chance	अकस्मात (Akasmat)	Fortuity, Luck, Discovery	Misfortune, Unluckiness, Bad luck
Imperative	of vital importance; crucial	आदेशक (Aadeshak)	Essential, Critical, Indispensable	Optional, Unimportant, Insignificant
Infallible	incapable of making mistakes or being wrong	अचूक (Achook)	Flawless, Perfect, Errorless	Fallible, Imperfect, Erroneous
Enthralling	capturing and holding one's attention; fascinating	मोहक (Mohak)	Captivating, Gripping, Spellbinding	Boring, Tedious, Uninteresting
Ebullient	cheerful and full of energy; enthusiastic	उत्साही (Utsahi)	Exuberant, Lively, Animated	Depressed, Gloomy, Dull
Catalyst	an agent that provokes or speeds significant change or action	उत्प्रेरक (Utprerak)	Stimulus, Trigger, Propellant	Hindrance, Inhibitor, Obstacle
Adversity	difficulties or misfortune	विपत्ति (Vipatti)	Hardship, Misfortune, Tribulation	Prosperity, Success, Favorable conditions
Emulate	to imitate or follow as an example	अनुकरण करना (Anukaran Karna)	Mimic, Copy, Replicate	Diverge, Deviate, Differ
Intrepid	fearless and adventurous	निडर (Nidar)	Fearless, Bold, Courageous	Timid, Cowardly, Fearful

Word	English Meaning	Hindi Meaning	Synonyms	Antonyms
Benevolent	well-meaning and kind	उदार (Udaar)	Kind, Generous, Compassionate	Malevolent, Cruel, Selfish
Ephemeral	lasting for a short time	अल्पकालिक (Alpakalik)	Transient, Fleeting, Temporary	Permanent, Enduring, Everlasting
Fortitude	courage in facing difficulties	धैर्य (Dhairya)	Resilience, Bravery, Strength	Weakness, Cowardice, Timidity
Camaraderie	mutual trust and friendship among a group	सखावत (Sakhavat)	Comradeship, Solidarity, Fellowship	Discord, Enmity, Hostility
Inevitable	certain to happen; unavoidable	अपरिहार्य (Apariharya)	Unavoidable, Certain, Inexorable	Avoidable, Uncertain, Preventable
Hypothesis	a proposed explanation based on limited evidence	परिकल्पना (Parikalpana)	Theory, Assumption, Conjecture	Fact, Reality, Truth
Abdicate	to renounce or give up power or responsibility	त्यागना (Tyagna)	Renounce, Resign, Surrender	Assume, Retain, Keep
Pervasive	spreading widely throughout an area or a group	व्यापक (Vyapak)	Widespread, Prevalent, Ubiquitous	Limited, Rare, Scarce
Conundrum	a confusing and difficult problem or question	पेचीदा (Pechida)	Puzzle, Enigma, Dilemma	Solution, Clarity, Answer
Diligent	showing careful and persistent effort	मेहनती (Mehnati)	Industrious, Hardworking, Assiduous	Lazy, Slothful, Negligent
Eloquent	fluent and persuasive in speaking or writing	प्रभावशाली (Prabhavashali)	Articulate, Expressive, Persuasive	Inarticulate, Mumbled, Incoherent
Ubiquitous	present or found everywhere	सर्वव्यापी (Sarvavyapi)	Omnipresent, Pervasive, Universal	Rare, Limited, Scattered
Voracious	having a great appetite or desire for something	भुक्खड़ (Bhukkhad)	Insatiable, Ravenous, Greedy	Content, Satisfied, Moderate

Word	English Meaning	Hindi Meaning	Synonyms	Antonyms
Quandary	a state of uncertainty or perplexity	दुविधा (Duvidha)	Dilemma, Predicament, Conundrum	Certainty, Clarity, Solution
Resilient	able to recover quickly from difficulties	प्रतिरोधी (Pratirodhi)	Strong, Tough, Adaptive	Fragile, Vulnerable, Delicate
Tangible	perceptible by touch; capable of being touched or felt	स्पर्शनीय (Sparshaniya)	Touchable, Palpable, Concrete	Intangible, Abstract, Immaterial
Impeccable	faultless; without flaws or mistakes	अचूक (Achook)	Flawless, Perfect, Immaculate	Imperfect, Flawed, Defective
Exemplary	serving as a desirable model; representing the best of its kind	प्रशंसानीय (Prashansaniya)	Commendable, Admirable, Laudable	Mediocre, Average, Inferior
Prolific	producing many works, results, or offspring	उत्पादक (Utpadak)	Productive, Fertile, Creative	Barren, Unproductive, Sterile
Eccentric	unconventional and slightly strange	अद्भुत (Adbhut)	Quirky, Odd, Unconventional	Conventional, Normal, Ordinary
Meticulous	showing great attention to detail; very careful and precise	सूक्ष्म (Sukshm)	Thorough, Accurate, Diligent	Careless, Sloppy, Negligent
Nurture	care for and encourage the growth or development of	पोषण (Poshan)	Foster, Cultivate, Support	Neglect, Abandon, Ignore
Empathy	the ability to understand and share the feelings of another	सहानुभूति (Sahanubhuti)	Compassion, Understanding, Sympathy	Indifference, Apathy, Insensitivity
Euphoria	a feeling of intense happiness and excitement	उत्साह (Utsah)	Joy, Bliss, Ecstasy	Sadness, Misery, Desolation
Altruism	selfless concern for the well-being of others	परोपकार (Paropkar)	Selflessness, Generosity, Philanthropy	Selfishness, Greed, Egoism

Chapter - Eight

Root Words

VOCABULAR

I) Vocabulary Made Easy through Root Words

Word - Ambi

Meaning - Both side/Both

Ambivalent	Uncertain अनिश्चित
Ambilateral	Affecting both sides दोनों ओर प्रभावित
Ambidextrous	Able to use the right and left hands equally well दाहिनी और बायां हाथों का समान रूप से उपयोग करने में सक्षम
Ambiguous	Uncertain, unclear अनिश्चित, अस्पष्ट
Ambiguity	Uncertain, an unclear situation अनिश्चित, अस्पष्ट स्थिति

Word- Ami

Meaning - Friend

Amity	Friendly relations मैत्रीपूर्ण संबंध
Amicide	The act of killing a friend एक मित्र की हत्या करने की क्रिया
Amiable	Friendly मित्रपूर्ण
Amicable	Friendly मित्रपूर्ण

Word- Acer

Meaning- Bitter/harsh

Acrimonious	Angry and bitter गुस्से और कड़वा
Acrid	Unpleasantly bitter अप्रियतापूर्ण और कड़वा
Acrimony	Bitterness or ill-feeling कड़वाहट
Acerbic	Bitter/harsh कड़वा/कठोर
Acerbity	Bitterness/harshness कड़वापन/कठोरता
Exacerbate	Making a situation from bad to worse स्थिति को खराब से बदतर बनाना

Word- Arch

Meaning- Ruler

Archy	Denoting a type of rule शासन के प्रकार को दर्शाने वाला
Anarchy	A state without government सरकार के बिना एक राज्य
Biarchy	Government by two people दो लोगों द्वारा सरकार
Monarch	A single Ruler/king एकल शासक/राजा

Monarchy	Absolute sovereignty by a single person एकल व्यक्ति द्वारा पूर्ण संप्रभुता
Matriarch	A female head of a family एक महिला शासक
Matriarchy	Government ruled by a woman or women महिला या महिलाओं द्वारा सरकार
Patriarch	A male head of a family परिवार का पुरुष मुखिया
Patriarchy	A system of society or government in which the man holds the power. एक समाज या सरकारी प्रणाली जिसमें पुरुष शक्ति मान्य होती है

Word - Acro

Meaning - Height

Acrophobia	Fear of height ऊचाई का भय
Acrobat	Who performs spectacular gymnastic जो शानदार ताल मेल करता है
Acrophyte	A plant growing at a high altitude ऊची स्थानीयता पर उगने वाला पौधा
Acropolis	A city at a high altitude ऊची स्थानीयता पर स्थित एक शहर

Word -Cide

Meaning - Killing

Patricide	Killing of father पिता की हत्या
Matricide	Killing of mother मां की हत्या
Sororicide	Killing of sister बहन की हत्या
Regicide	Killing of king राजा की हत्या
Bovicide	Killing of cattle पशुओं की हत्या
Homicide	Killing of human मनुष्य की हत्या
Populcide	Killing of population जनसंख्या की हत्या
Genocide	Killing of race जाति की हत्या
Amicide	Killing of friend मित्र की हत्या
Fratricide	Killing of brother or comrade भाई की हत्या
Herbicide	Killing of herbs जड़ी बूटी की हत्या
Infanticide	Killing of newly born baby नवजात शिशु की हत्या
Foeticide	Killing of fetus or unborn baby अविधवंत के भ्रूण की हत्या
Insecticide	Killing of insect कीट की हत्या
Pesticide	Killing of pests कीटाणुओं की हत्या
Siblicide	Killing of siblings सहोदरों की हत्या
Filicide	Killing of children बच्चों की हत्या
Parricide	Killing of parent/close relatives माता-पिता/निकट संबंधियों की हत्या
Uxoricide	Killing of wife पत्नी की हत्या

Mariticide	Killing of husband पति की हत्या

Word - Cata/Cad

Meaning- Fall/Downward

Catastrophe	Disaster विनाश
Cataclysm	Destruction नष्ट
Cadence	Flow of words in speech or singing
Cascade	Water fall जलप्रपात
Cataract	A large waterfall/ a medical condition of eyes बड़ा जलप्रपात

Word- Clud/Clus/Claus

Meaning- Shut/Close

Recluse	One who lives a solitary life एकांतवासी
Seclude	Keep someone away किसी को दूर रखना
Occlude	Block
Seclusion	The act of shutting oneself अपने आप को बंद करने का कार्य
Conclude	To end something like "conclude the topic विषय समाप्त करें
Claustrophobia	Fear of being in closed spaces बंद स्थान में होने का डर
Claustrophobic	Person having an extreme fear of confined places सीमित स्थानों के लिए अत्यधिक डर रखने वाला व्यक्ति
Claustrophobe	A person who has claustrophobia जिसे सीमित स्थानों का अत्यधिक डर होता है

Word- Carn

Meaning- Flesh

Carnivore	One who eats flesh मांसाहारी
Carnivorous	Having characteristic of eating flesh मांसाहारी गुणवत्ता वाला
Carnage	Destruction of life जीवन का विनाश
Carnal	Related to flesh मांस संबंधी

Word - Demos

Meaning- People

Demography	Study of human population मानव जनसंख्या का अध्ययन
Demophobia	Fear of people लोगों का डर
Democracy	Government by the people जनता द्वारा सरकार
Democratic	Elected चुने गए
Democrat	One who believes in democracy लोकतंत्र में विश्वास रखने वाला

Demographist	One who studies demography जनसंख्या विज्ञान का अध्ययन करने वाला

Word- Gamy

Meaning- Marriage

Polygamy	A custom of marrying multiple people. एकाधिक व्यक्तियों से विवाह करने की प्रथा
Polygamist	A person who has more than one wife or husband at the same time. एक समय में एक से अधिक पत्नी या पति रखने वाला व्यक्ति
Bigamy	A custom of marrying someone while already married to another person. एक व्यक्ति से विवाह करने की प्रथा जबकि पहले से ही किसी अन्य व्यक्ति से विवाहित हो

Word- Melli/Molly

Meaning- Soft

Mollify	Appease/placate संतुष्ट करना
Emollient	Softening/moisturizing मुलायम करना
Mellifluous	Sweet-sounding मधुर ध्वनि
Melodious	Pleasant-sounding सुंदर ध्वनि

Word- Necro

Meaning- Death

Necrophile	Lover of dead body मृतक शरीर के प्रेमी
Necromania	Obsessed with dead bodies मृतक शरीरों में प्रवृत्ति
Necromaniac	A person who suffers from Necromania मृत्यु प्रेमी
Necrophobia	Fear of dead bodies - मृतक शरीरों का भय
Necrophobic	A person who suffers from Necrophobia मृतक भय
Necropolis	Place where dead bodies are buried मृतकों को दफनाया जाने वाला स्थान
Necromancy	Talking to the spirit of dead bodies मृतकों के प्रेत से बातचीत

Word- Mania/Maniac

Meaning- Madness

Megalomania	obsession of being powerful शक्तिशाली होने की प्रवृत्ति
Sophomania	obsession of being intelligent बुद्धिमान होने की प्रवृत्ति
Photomania	obsession for light प्रकाश के प्रति आकर्षण
Pseudomania	obsession for telling lies झूठ बोलने की प्रवृत्ति
Squandermania	obsession for spending money wastefully धन की अनावश्यक खर्च करने की प्रवृत्ति
Kleptomania	obsession for stealing चोरी करने की प्रवृत्ति
Pyromania	obsession for setting the things on fire चीज़ों को आग लगाने की प्रवृत्ति

Dipsomania	obsession for having alcohol शराब पीने की प्रवृत्ति
Bibliomania	obsession for books किताबों के प्रति आकर्षण
Ergomania	obsession for work काम करने की प्रवृत्ति
Logomania	obsession for talking बातचीत करने की प्रवृत्ति
Phytomania	obsession for collecting plants पौधों का संग्रह करने की प्रवृत्ति
Cynomania	obsession for dogs कुत्तों के प्रति आकर्षण
Theomania	obsession for God भगवान के प्रति आकर्षण
Verbomania	obsession for words शब्दों के प्रति आकर्षण
Agromania	obsession for living in isolated area एकांतवासी इलाके में रहने की प्रवृत्ति
Graphomania	obsession for writing लेखन करने की प्रवृत्ति
Monomania	obsession of a single thought or idea एक ही विचार या विचार की प्रवृत्ति
Toxicomania	obsession for poison जहर के प्रति आकर्षण

Word- Mal

Meaning- Evil/ ill, bad

Malady	A disease बीमारी
Malicious	Having bad feelings बुरी भावना रखने वाला
Malcontent	Who is dissatisfied and rebellious शरारती
Malediction	Curse अभिशाप
Malefaction	An evil deed बुरा काम
Malefactor	A person who commits a crime अपराधी
Malpractice	Bad practice बुरी रीति
Malevolence	Ill feeling द्वेष

Word- Mor

Meaning- Death

Mortal	perishable/ causing or liable to cause death विनाशी
Immortal	Who can't die अमर
Mortify	Causing great embarrassment बड़े ही शर्म की बात
Moribund	Dying stage मृत्युवीय अवस्था
Morbid	Related to death, unpleasant मृत्यु संबंधी
Morting	Killing हत्या
Morose	Ill tempered क्रोधी
Mortuary/Morgue	A place where dead bodies are kept for identification एक वह स्थान जो पहचान के लिए मरे हुए शरीरों को रखा जाता है

Word- Omni

Meaning- All

Omnivore	One who eats everything सब कुछ खाने वाला
Omnipresent	Who is present everywhere हर जगह मौजूद
Omniscient	One who knows everything सब कुछ जानने वाला
Omnipotent	One who is very powerful बहुत शक्तिशाली
Omnibus	A large vehicle एक बड़ा वाहन

Word- 'INE'

Meaning- Similar

Feline	Like cat बिल्ली जैसा
Piscine	Like fish मछली जैसा
Porcine	Like pig सुअर जैसा
Porcus	Pig सुअर
Leonine	Like Lion सिंह जैसा
Bovine	Like cattle पशु जैसा
Equine	Like horse घोड़े जैसा
Equestrian	who rides on a horse घोड़े पर सवार
Ursine	Like bear भालू जैसा
Ursus	Bear भालू
Canine	Like dog कुत्ते जैसा
Canis	Dog कुत्ता
Lupine	Like wolf भेड़िया जैसा
Lupus	Wolf भेड़िया
Serpentine	Like snake सांप जैसा
Saline	Like salt नमक जैसा
Caprine	Like Goat बकरी जैसा
Caprus	Goat बकरी
Ovine	Like sheep भेड़ जैसा

Word - Andr

Meaning- Male person/husband

Polyandry	having more than one husband एक से अधिक पति रखने वाला
Androphile	Lover of men पुरुषों का प्रेमी
Androcide	Killing of men पुरुषों की हत्या

Androcracy	Rule by men पुरुषों द्वारा शासन
Androphobia	Fear of men पुरुषों का भय
Androphobe	A person who has androphobia जिसको पुरुष भय होता है
Androphobic	Having the features of androphobia पुरुष भय की विशेषताएं रखने वाला
Androgynous	Having both male and female features पुरुष और स्त्री दोनों की विशेषताएं रखने वाला
Misandrous	Who hates men पुरुषों से नफरत करने वाला
Misandry	Hate towards men पुरुषों के प्रति घृणा

Word- Chrono

Meaning- Time

Chronology	Study of time and dating of historical events समय का अध्ययन
Chronograph	Instrument which records time समय रिकॉर्ड करने वाला यंत्र
Chronological	Related to sequence based on time or date समय संबंधी
Chronicle	An account of historical events ऐतिहासिक घटनाओं का विवरण
Chronic	Persisting for a long time बहुत लंबे समय तक बरकरार रहने वाला
Synchronous	Having same time समान समय रखने वाला
Synchronization	Happening at the same time एक साथ होने वाला

Word- Bene/Ben/Bon

Meaning- Good

Benediction	Wishing well for someone किसी के लिए शुभकामना
Beneficial	Positive result सकारात्मक परिणाम
Benefit	Advantage or Profit लाभ
Benevolent	Kind दयालु
Bona fide	In good faith, genuine अच्छी नियत से
Bonus	Tip टिप
Bon Voyage	Good trip अच्छी यात्रा

Word- Cracy

Meaning- Rule

Democracy	A government by the people जनता द्वारा सरकार
Autocracy	Government by one person एक व्यक्ति द्वारा सरकार
Plutocracy	Government by the rich धनी द्वारा सरकार
Aristocracy	Government by the nobles महाराजाओं द्वारा सरकार
Bureaucracy	Government by administration प्रशासन द्वारा सरकार

Mobocracy	Government by mob भीड़ द्वारा सरकार
Theocracy	Government by God ईश्वर द्वारा सरकार
Meritocracy	Government by talented people प्रतिभाशाली लोगों द्वारा सरकार
Necrocracy	Government that operates under the rules of the former or dead leader पूर्व नेता के नियमों के अनुसार संचालित सरकार
Gerontocracy	Government by people लोगों द्वारा सरकार
Neocracy	Government by new people नए लोगों द्वारा सरकार
Gynocracy	Government by women महिलाओं द्वारा सरकार
Ochlocracy	Government by crowd भीड़ द्वारा सरकार
Androcracy	Government by men पुरुषों द्वारा सरकार
Oligocracy	Government by a few persons कुछ लोगों द्वारा सरकार
Polycracy	Government by many people बहुत सारे लोगों द्वारा सरकार

Word- Verb

Meaning- Word

Verbose	Full of words शब्दों से भरपूर
Verbatim	being in or following the exact words शब्दांतर
Verbomania	obsession for words शब्दांतरासक्ति
Verbicide	Distortion of words शब्दों का विकृति
Verbal	Related to verb(words) मौखिक

Word- Chiro

Meaning- Hand

Chiromancy	Prediction of a person's future by reading palms हस्तरेखा ज्योतिष
Chiromancer	One who practises chiromancy हस्तरेखा ज्योतिषी
Chirographer	Who practices studies chirography हस्तलेखा शास्त्र
Chirography	Study of Handwriting; calligraphy लिखावट का अध्ययन
Chiropody	Treatment of the feet पैरों का इलाज
Chiromantic	Related to chiromancy हस्तरेखा संबंधी
Chirophobia	Fear of hands हाथों का भय
Chiropodist	One who treats the diseases of hands and feet हाथ-पैरों के रोगों का इलाज करने वाला

Word-Caco

Meaning- Bad

Cacographer	One who is bad at spelling or has bad writing अक्षर-व्यंग्य करने वाला

Cacography	Bad spelling or handwriting गलत अक्षरों का लेखन
Cacophonous	Having bad voice खराब आवाज़ होना
Cacophobia	Phobia of ugliness सौंदर्याभिभूति भय

Word-Calli

Meaning- Beautiful

Calligraphy	Beautiful handwriting सुंदर हस्तलेखा
Calligrapher	One who does calligraphy कलिग्राफी करने वाला
Callimorph	Beautiful shape or appearance सुंदर आकार
Calliphony	Beautiful sound सुंदर ध्वनि
Calliphonous	Having beautiful sound सुंदर ध्वनि होना
Callomania	Obsession for beautiful items सुंदर वस्तुओं की आक्रांति

Word- Greg

Meaning- group

Aggregate	Collection or total संग्रह
Segregate	To separate अलग करना
Gregarious	Sociable मिलनसार
Aggregation	A collection एक संग्रह
Congregate	gather into a crowd or mass एकत्रित होना
Congregation	A group of religious people धार्मिक लोगों का समूह
Segregation	Separation into groups समूहों में विभाजन

Word- Fide

Meaning- Faith

Malafide	Carried out in bad faith बुरी नियत से किया जाना
Fidelity	Faithfulness वफ़ादारी
Infidel	Unfaithful विश्वासघाती
Bonafide	In good faith अच्छी नियत से
Infidelity	State of being unfaithful अविश्वासिता की स्थिति

Word- Somn

Meaning- Sleep

Insomnia	Sleep disorder सोने की बीमारी
Somnolent	Sleepy, drowsy नींद आना
Somnific	Causing sleep नींद लाने वाला

Somnambulist	One who walks while sleeping सोते समय चलने वाला
Somnambulism	A disease of walking while sleeping नींद में चलने की बीमारी
Somniloquist	One who talks while sleeping सोते समय बोलने वाला
Somniloquism	A disease of talking while sleeping नींद में बोलने की बीमारी

Word- Sophos

Meaning- Wisdom

Sophic	Relating to or Full of wisdom ज्ञान से पूर्ण
Sophical	Related to wisdom ज्ञान संबंधी
Philosopher	A person engaged or learned in philosophy ज्ञान प्रेमी
Sophisticated	Worldly-wise (having a lot of worldly experience)

Word- Specto

Meaning- to look/ examine

Spectacular	Awesome शानदार
Introspect	Examine one's own thought अपने विचारों की जांच करना
Extrospect	Observe outside oneself अपने बाहर की जांच करना
Retrospect	To look back in the past पीछे मुड़ना
Circumspect	To look around आसपास देखना

Word- Eu

Meaning- Good

Euphoria	A feeling of intense excitement उत्कंठा
Euphoric	Elated, happy आनंदित
Euphonious	Full of pleasing sound सुस्वर
Euphony	Pleasing sound सुन्दर ध्वनि
Euphemism	To say bad things in good and sweet words मीठी बातों में बुरी बातें कहना
Eulogy	Good speech that praises someone who has died अच्छा भाषण

Word- Nov

Meaning- New

Novel	New नया
Novelty	Newness नवीनता
Novice	New corner,beginner नवीन कोना, शुरुआती
Innovate	To make something new कुछ नया बनाना
Innovator	One who makes new things नया करने वाला

Innovation	Creation of new things नवसृजन
Renovate	To restore to a good state कुछ नया फिर से बनाना
Renovation	To restore to a good state फिर से कुछ नया बनाना
De novo	Once more/over again एक बार और

Word- Syn/Sym

Meaning- Same

Symmetry	Having exactly similar parts समानांतर
Symposium	A gathering or meeting for discussion बैठक
Sympathy	The act of feeling same emotion/ pity/ sorrow for someone else सहानुभूति
Synonym	similar in meaning अर्थसम
Synchronization	At the same time समयानुसार
Synergy	Having same energy समान ऊर्जा वाला
Symphony	an elaborate musical composition for full orchestra वाद्य-वृंद रचना
Synagogue	Meeting at the same place by jews यहूदियों द्वारा समान स्थान पर मिलना
Syndicate	A body of business people working together for the same reason एक ही कारण के लिए साथ मिलकर काम करने वाले व्यापारियों का समूह

Word- Logo

Meaning- Talk/Speak

Logomania	abnormal talkativeness असामान्य बोलचालिता।
Logomaniac	Who is obsessed with words शब्दों में प्रवृत्त होनेवाला।
Logomisia	Strong dislike for some words कुछ शब्दों के प्रति मजबूत असहिष्णुता।
Logonomy	Science of words शब्दों का विज्ञान
Logophobia	Fear of some words कुछ शब्दों से भय।
Misologia	Aversion to speaking or arguing बोलने से विमुखता या अनुराग।
Neologism	Newly discovered word हाल ही में खोजा गया शब्द।
Neologist	A person who coins new words नए शब्दों का निर्माता।
Polylogy	An excessive amount of talking अत्यधिक बोलने की प्रवृत्ति।

Word- Logue

Meaning- A written or a spoken form/compilation

Catalogue	A list of items in a specific order एक विशेष क्रम में वस्तुओं की सूची
Dialogue	A conversation between two or more people दो या अधिक लोगों के बीच बातचीत
Prologue	Introduction/ preface to a poem/play/book कविता/नाटक का प्रस्तावना/प्रस्ताव
Monologue	A long speech by one person एक व्यक्ति द्वारा लंबा भाषण

Travelogue	A description of someone's travel किसी की यात्रा का वर्णन
Polylogue	A speech by several person कई लोगों द्वारा भाषण
Monopolylogue	A speech by a single of many characters in a particular play. किसी विशेष नाटक में एक या अनेक पात्रों द्वारा भाषण

Word- macro

Meaning- large

Macrocosm	the entire universe संपूर्ण ब्रह्मांड
Macro Image	a large image बड़ी छवि
Macroscopic	things that can be visible with the naked eye. आंखों से देखे जा सकने वाली चीज़े
Macroeconomics	branch of economics concerned with large scale productivity अर्थशास्त्र का शाखा
Macromania	thinking that body's parts are bigger than they are. शरीर के अंगों को अपने आकार से बड़ा सोचना

Word- magn

Meaning- large, great

Magnate	rich and powerful person धनी और प्रभावशाली व्यक्ति
Magnitude	the importance of something. किसी चीज़ का महत्व
Magnify	Magnify = increase in size or significance बढ़ाना
Magnificent	Magnificent = something wonderful or great शानदार
Magnanimous	noble and great personality उदात्त और महान व्यक्तित्व

Word- multi

Meaning- many

1) Multitude	a large indefinite number of people/ things/ aspects असीम संख्या के लोग
2) Multifarious	of many types or aspects कई प्रकार या पहलुओं का
3) Multidimensional	having many dimensions कई आयाम वाला
4) Multifaceted	having many faces or aspects कई चेहरे या पहलुओं वाला
5) Multiform	having many shapes/form कई आकार/रूप वाला

Word- mania

Meaning- madness/obsesssion

Megalomania	madness for money and fame. पैसे और प्रसिद्धि के लिए पागलपन
Kleptomania	obsession to steal चुराने की दीवानगी
Pyromania	uncontrollable desire to set things on fire आग में चीज़ों को जलाने की अनियंत्रित इच्छा
Dipsomania	obsession for alcohol शराब के प्रति दीवानगी

Macromania	obsession for huge things विशाल चीज़ों की दीवानगी
Ablutomania	Obsession for bathing and cleaning स्नान और सफाई की सनक
Bibliomania	obsession of books किताबों की सनक
Gamomania	uncontrollable desire to marry again and again बार-बार शादी करने की अनियंत्रित इच्छा

Word- nat

Meaning- born

Innate	since birth; natural जन्म से; प्राकृतिक
Naive	innocent; lack of experience मासूम; अनुभव की कमी
Native	a person born in a specified place is a native of that place. अपने जन्म से संबंधित
Natal	relating to one's birth {sounds like fetal; means birth} जन्म से पहले
Prenatal	before birth जन्म से पहले
Neonatal	relating to the infant during the first month after birth जन्म के बाद पहले महीने तक के शिशु से संबंधित
Cognate	related to a common ancestor सामान्य पूर्वज से संबंधित

Word- ped

Meaning- foot

Millipedet	having many tiny pairs of legs. बहुत सारे छोटे जोड़ों वाला
Pedestal	base on which a statue or column is mounted. मूर्ति या स्तंभ को स्थापित करने का आधार
Pedometer	instrument to measure number of steps walked कदमों की संख्या मापने का यंत्र
Biped	with two feet दो पैरों वाला
Expedition	a long journey esp far away लंबी यात्रा, विशेष रूप से दूरस्थ

Word- pel

Meaning- push, force

Repel	to move back by force or push बलपूर्वक पीछे हटना या धक्का देना
Repeal	to cancel officially आधिकारिक रूप से रद्द करना
Appeal	push a court case to a higher court. एक मुकदमे को उच्चतर न्यायालय में पहुंचाना
Propel	to push something forward कुछ को आगे धकेलना
Expel	push or force to leave किसी को धक्के मारकर या बाहर करना
Impel	push a person to do some action {oblige , exhort} किसी को कुछ करने के लिए बाध्य करना
Compel	a driving force एक गतिशील बल

Confidence Booster Practice Sets

Practice Set I

Directions: In this section, you will be presented with a word. Select the option that best represents a synonym (word with a similar meaning) for the given word.

1. Ambivalent is the synonym of:

a) Uncertain b) Indecisive
c) Doubtful d) Conflicted

2. Amity is the synonym of:

a) Friendship b) Harmony
c) Goodwill d) Camaraderie

3. Biarchy is the synonym of:

a) Dual rule
b) Co-governance
c) Two-party system
d) Joint leadership

4. Monarchy is the synonym of:

a) Kingdom b) Reign
c) Dynasty d) Autocracy

5. Acrophobia is the synonym of:

a) Fear of heights b) Height phobia
c) Vertigo d) Aerial terror

6. Genocide is the synonym of:

a) Ethnic cleansing
b) Mass extermination
c) Annihilation of a race
d) Elimination of a group

7. Herbicide is the synonym of:

a) Pesticide b) Plant poison
c) Fertilizer d) Compost

8. Filicide is the synonym of:

a) Parental killing b) Killing one's child
c) Killing d) Child-slaying

9. Cadence is the synonym of:

a) Rhythm b) Beat
c) Meter d) Musical flow

10. Exacerbate is the synonym of:

a) Alleviate b) Mitigate
c) Improve d) Worsen

Answers

1.	(c)	2.	(c)	3.	(a)
4.	(b)	5.	(a)	6.	(c)
7.	(a)	8.	(b)	9.	(a)
10.	(d)				

Practice Set II:

Directions: In this section, you will be presented with a word. Select the option that best represents a synonym (word with a similar meaning) for the given word.

1. Seclude is the synonym of:

a) Isolate b) Combine
c) Include d) Engage

2. Claustrophobia is the synonym of:

a) Hemophobia b) Acrophobia
c) Arachnophobia d) Agoraphobia

3. Carnage is the synonym of:

a) Salvation b) Massacre
c) Harmony d) Redemption

4. Democratic is the synonym of:

a) Republican b) Authoritarian
c) Totalitarian d) Liberal

5. Necropolis is the synonym of:
a) Sanctuary b) Cathedral
c) Graveyard d) Library

6. Kleptomania is the synonym of:
a) Stealing b) Giving
c) Obession d) Snatching

7. Logomania is the synonym of:
a) Talkativeness b) Silent
c) Orator d) Speech

8. Bovine is the synonym of:
a) Lupine b) Poultry
c) Reptilian d) Cow-like

9. Chronicle is the synonym of:
a) Record b) Fiction
c) Encyclopedic d) Transcribe

10. Synchronization is the synonym of:
a) Coordination b) Disruption
c) Isolation d) Fragmentation

Answers

1.	(a)	2.	(d)	3.	(b)
4.	(d)	5.	(c)	6.	(a)
7.	(a)	8.	(d)	9.	(a)
10.	(a)				

Practice Set III:

Directions: In this section, you will be presented with a word. Select the option that best represents a antonym (words with an opposite meaning) for the given word.

1. Occlude is the antonym of:
a) Reveal b) Conceal
c) Open d) Connect

2. Carnivore is the antonym of:
a) Omnivore b) Herbivore
c) Insectivore d) Frugivore

3. Democracy is the antonym of:
a) Autocracy b) Meritocracy
c) Oligarchy d) Plutocracy

4. Emollient is the antonym of:
a) Abrasive b) Softening
c) Calm d) Sleek

5. Malicious is the antonym of:
a) Sinister b) Malevolent
c) Vindictive d) Benevolent

6. Malefaction is the antonym of:
a) Felony b) Virtue
c) Misdeed d) Transgression

7. Immortal is the antonym of:
a) Mortal b) Eternal
c) Infinite d) Perpetual

8. Saline is the antonym of:
a) Aqueous b) Alkaline
c) Freshwater d) Brackish

9. Polyandry is the antonym of:
a) Polygamy b) Monogamy
c) Bigamy d) Celibacy

10. Beneficial is the antonym of:
a) Detrimental b) Advantageous
c) Favorable d) Valuable

Answer

1.	(c)	2.	(b)	3.	(a)
4.	(a)	5.	(d)	6.	(b)
7.	(a)	8.	(c)	9.	(b)
10.	(a)				

Practice Set IV

Directions: In this section, you will be presented with a word. Select the option that best represents a antonym (words with an opposite meaning) for the given word.

1. Benevolent is the antonym of:

a) Malevolent b) Generous
c) Altruistic d) Compassionate

2. Bonus is the antonym of:

a) Premium b) Reward
c) Incentive d) Penalty

3. Autocracy is the antonym of:

a) Tyranny b) Monarchy
c) Democracy d) Dictatorship

4. Gynocracy is the antonym of:

a) Androcracy b) Matriarchy
c) Equality d) Hierarchy

5. Verbatim is the antonym of:

a) Copy b) Quotation
c) Rephrase d) Writing

6. Verbal is the antonym of:

a) Written b) Oral
c) Linguistic d) Articulate

7. Cacography is the antonym of:

a) Scribble b) Typography
c) Penmanship d) Calligraphy

8. Calliphony is the antonym of:

a) Symphony b) Cacophony
c) Melody d) Harmony

9. Aggregate is the antonym of:

a) Summation b) Collective
c) Individual d) Totality

10. Segregation is the antonym of:

a) Integration b) Separation
c) Division d) Segmentation

Answers

1.	(a)	2.	(d)	3.	(c)
4.	(a)	5.	(c)	6.	(a)
7.	(d)	8.	(b)	9.	(c)
10.	(a)				

Practice Set V

Directions: In this section, you will be presented with a word. Select the option that best represents a antonym (words with an opposite meaning) for the given word.

1. Infidel is the antonym of:

a) Atheist b) Unfaithful
c) Heretic d) Devotee

2. Insomnia is the antonym of:

a) Awake b) Slumber
c) Restlessness d) Somnolence

3. Sophic is the antonym of:

a) Foolish b) Wise
c) Intelligent d) Philosophical

4. Sophisticated is the antonym of:

a) Refined b) Elegant
c) Simple d) Complex

5. Spectacular is the antonym of:

a) Mundane b) Impressive
c) Dazzling d) Extraordinary

6. Novel is the antonym of:

a) Unconventional
b) Unique
c) Innovative
d) Familiar

7. Renovate is the antonym of:

a) Refurbish b) Restore
c) Deteriorate d) Enhance

8. **Symmetry is the antonym of:**
a) Asymmetry b) Harmony
c) Balance d) Proportion

9. **Synergy is the antonym of:**
a) Unity b) Collaboration
c) Cooperation d) Discord

10. **Prologue is the antonym of:**
a) Epilogue b) Prelude
c) Introduction d) Foreword

Answers

1.	(b)	2.	(d)	3.	(a)
4.	(c)	5.	(a)	6.	(d)
7.	(c)	8.	(a)	9.	(d)
10.	(d)				

Practice Set VI

Directions: **In this section, you will be presented with a word. Select the option that best represents a synonym (word with a similar meaning) for the given word.**

1. **Monologue is the synonym of:**
a) Soliloquy b) Dialogue
c) Conversation d) Banter

2. **Macroscopic is the synonym of:**
a) Substantial b) Gigantic
c) Enormous d) Microscopic

3. **Magnificent is the synonym of:**
a) Ordinary b) Splendid
c) Mediocre d) Average

4. **Multidimensional is the synonym of:**
a) Complex b) Simple
c) Unidirectional d) Linear

5. **Pyromania is the synonym of:**
a) Incendiarism b) Arson
c) Firebug d) Ignition

6. **Innate is the synonym of:**
a) Taught b) Learned
c) Acquired d) Inborn

7. **Prenatal is the synonym of:**
a) Antenatal b) Postnatal
c) Prehistoric d) Premature

8. **Propel is the synonym of:**
a) Drop b) Push
c) Pull d) Hinder

9. **Synchronization is the synonym of:**
a) Desynchronization
b) Asynchronization
c) Coordination
d) Disharmony

10. **Theocracy is the synonym of:**
a) Governed by God
b) Democracy
c) Autocracy
d) Plutocracy

Answers

1.	(a)	2.	(d)	3.	(b)
4.	(a)	5.	(c)	6.	(d)
7.	(a)	8.	(b)	9.	(c)
10.	(a)				

Practice Set VII:

Directions: **Choose the most appropriate word to fill in the blank in each sentence. Select the letter corresponding to your chosen option.**

1. **Even though she was 87, the ________ of the family knew everything that was going on**

a) matriarch b) ruler
c) father d) patriarch

2. The ______ was captured on the CCTV camera of the shopping center.

a) redo b) matricide
c) option d) mountain

3. The government was criticized for its ________system, where power was concentrated in the hands of a few.

a) Democratic b) Oligarchy
c) Autocratic d) Plutocracy

4. He visited a __________ to get relief for his foot pain.

a) Cardiologist b) Chiropodist
c) Dermatologist d) Orthopedist

5. She was known for her __________ nature and always enjoyed socializing with new people.

a) Introverted b) Solitary
c) Reserved d) Gregarious

6. The students __________ in the library to study for their upcoming exams.

a) Disperse b) Congregated
c) Scatter d) Disperse

7. The __________ butterfly with its vibrant colors caught everyone's attention.

a) Plain b) Dull
c) Callimorph d) Unattractive

8. She visited a __________ to have her palm read and learn about her future.

a) Astrologer b) Chiromancer
c) Card reader d) Physicist

9. They had to provide __________ proof of their eligibility to participate in the competition.

a) False b) Fake
c) Bona fide d) Fraudulent

10. Her __________ remarks about men showed her biased and negative attitude towards them.

a) Misogynistic b) Misandrous
c) Inclusive d) Unbiased

Answers

1.	(a)	2.	(b)	3.	(b)
4.	(b)	5.	(d)	6.	(b)
7.	(c)	8.	(b)	9.	(c)
10.	(b)				

Practice Set VIII:

Directions: Choose the most appropriate word to fill in the blank in each sentence. Select the letter corresponding to your chosen option.

1. The river followed a __________ path through the dense forest.

a) Straight b) Curved
c) Serpentine d) Direct

2. She believed that with her new position, she would have __________ control over the company's decisions.

a) Limited b) Restricted
c) Omnipotent d) Insignificant

3. They visited the __________ to identify the deceased person.

a) Hospital b) Cemetery
c) Church d) Morgue

4. **She felt deeply ___________ when she realized she had made a mistake in her presentation.**
a) Elated b) Mortify
c) Delighted d) Amused

5. **The doctor was sued for ___________ after a surgical procedure went wrong.**
a) Malpractice b) Excellence
c) Competence d) Proficiency

6. **The witch uttered a ___________ to curse her enemies.**
a) Benediction b) Prayer
c) Blessing d) Malediction

7. **His ___________ for work often led him to neglect other aspects of his life.**
a) Laziness b) Indolence
c) Ergomania d) Relaxation

8. **The politician's ___________ led to the reckless spending of public funds.**
a) Thrift
b) Frugality
c) Squandermania
d) Prudence

9. **She suffered from ___________, an intense fear of dead bodies.**
a) Arachnophobia
b) Claustrophobia
c) Necrophobia
d) Acrophobia

10. **The singer's voice was incredibly ___________, and it mesmerized the audience.**
a) Grating b) Mellifluous
c) Harsh d) Jarring

Answers

1.	(c)	2.	(c)	3.	(d)
4.	(b)	5.	(a)	6.	(d)
7.	(c)	8.	(c)	9.	(c)
10.	(b)				

Practice Set IX:

Directions: Choose the most appropriate word to fill in the blank in each sentence. Select the letter corresponding to your chosen option.

1. **Polygamy is the practice of having multiple spouses, whereas ___________ refers to the act of having two spouses.**
a) Bigamy b) Polyandry
c) Monogamy d) Polygyny

2. **In a ___________ society, power is vested in the people, who participate in decision-making through voting.**
a) Oligarchy b) Monarchy
c) Autocracy d) Democracy

3. **After a long day, she decided to ___________ herself from the outside world and enjoy some solitude.**
a) Expose b) Seclude
c) Embrace d) Engage

4. **The volcanic eruption caused a ___________ that resulted in massive destruction and loss of life.**
a) Cataclysm b) Calamity
c) Tragedy d) Misfortune

5. **The farmer used ___________ to protect his crops from insect**

infestations.

a) Fertilizer b) Herbicide

c) Insecticide d) Pesticide

6. The act of ___________ refers to the deliberate termination of a fetus in the womb.

a) Suicide b) Homicide

c) Genocide d) Foeticide

7. The assassination of the king is ___________.

a) Monarchy b) Democracy

c) Regicide d) Aristocracy

8. An ___________ is a plant that grows in conditions of limited sunlight, such as in the shade of trees.

a) Epiphyte b) Acrophyte

c) Hydrophyte d) Xerophyte

9. The absence of a governing authority or order results in ___________.

a) Democracy b) Monarchy

c) Anarchy d) Autocracy

10. Their discussion turned ___________ as they exchanged bitter and hostile remarks.

a) Friendly b) Amiable

c) Acrimonious d) Pleasant

Answers

1.	(a)	2.	(d)	3.	(b)
4.	(a)	5.	(c)	6.	(d)
7.	(c)	8.	(b)	9.	(c)
10.	(c)				

Practice Set X:

Match the words in Column A with their corresponding meanings in Column B by writing the appropriate letter from Column B in the space provided next to the corresponding number in Column A.

Column A	Column B
Patriarch	(a) Able to use the right and left hands equally well
2. Cascade	(b) Unpleasantly bitter
3. Necrophile	(c) A male head of a family
4. Ambidextrous	(d) Killing of children
5. Cynomania	(e) Water fall
6. Meritocracy	(f) Lover of dead body
7. Filicide	(g) Obsession for dogs
8. Somniloquist	(h) Bad practice
9. Malpractice	(i) Government by talented people
10. Acrid	(j) One who talks while sleeping

Answers

Column A	Column B
1. Patriarch	(c) A male head of a family
2. Cascade	(e) Water fall
3. Necrophile	(f) Lover of dead body
4. Ambidextrous	(a) Able to use the right and left hands equally well
5. Cynomania	(g) Obsession for dogs
6. Meritocracy	(i) Government by talented people
7. Filicide	(d) Killing of children
8. Somniloquist	(j) One who talks while sleeping
9. Malpractice	(h) Bad practice
10. Acrid	Unpleasantly bitter

Chapter - Nine

Foreign Words

Foreign words

- **Ad hoc** - For a specific purpose or situation
- **Ad infinitum** - Without limit or end
- **Ad nauseam** - To a sickening or excessive degree
- **Alma mater** - One's former school, college, or university
- **Alpha** - The first letter of the Greek alphabet; often used to signify the beginning or dominance
- **Amigo** - Friend (Spanish)
- **Amour** - Love or a romantic relationship (French)
- **Bon voyage** - Have a good journey (French)
- **Bravo** - Well done or excellent (Italian)
- **C'est la vie** - That's life; accepting the ups and downs (French)
- **Carpe diem** - Seize the day; live in the present (Latin)
- **Carte blanche** - Complete freedom or authority (French)
- **Ciao** - Hello or goodbye (Italian)
- **Comme ci**, comme ça - So-so, neither good nor bad (French)
- **Cul-de-sac** - Dead-end street or situation (French)
- **Déjà vu** - The feeling of having experienced something before (French)
- **Eureka** - An exclamation of joy or discovery (Greek)
- **Fiancé/Fiancée** - An engaged man/woman (French)
- **Gestalt** - An organized whole or pattern (German)
- **Hasta la** vista - Until we meet again (Spanish)
- **Hoi polloi** - The common people, the masses (Greek)
- **In situ** - In its original place or position (Latin)
- **Joie de vivre** - Joy of living (French)
- **Karma** - The sum of a person's actions and their consequences (Sanskrit)
- **Laissez-faire** - A policy of non-interference, letting things take their own course (French)
- **Magnum opus** - A great work or masterpiece (Latin)

- **Memento** - A reminder or keepsake (Latin)
- **Nirvana** - A state of perfect peace and happiness (Sanskrit)
- **Nom de plume** - Pen name or pseudonym (French)
- **Onomatopoeia** - The formation of words that imitate sounds (Greek)
- **Panache** - Flamboyant confidence or style (French)
- **Paradigm** - A typical example or model (Greek)
- **Paparazzi** - Photographers who pursue celebrities (Italian)
- **Persona non** grata - An unwelcome or unacceptable person (Latin)
- **Quid pro quo** - A favor or advantage granted in return for something (Latin)
- **Rendezvous** - A meeting or gathering (French)
- **RSVP** - Please respond (French: Répondez s'il vous plaît)
- **Schadenfreude** - Pleasure derived from others' misfortune (German)
- **Status quo** - The existing state or condition (Latin)
- **Tabula rasa** - A clean slate or blank state (Latin)
- **Tête-à-tête** - A private conversation or meeting between two people (French)
- **Verbatim** - Word for word, exactly as written or spoken (Latin)
- **Voilà** - There it is; expressing satisfaction or completion (French)
- **Wanderlust** - A strong desire to travel and explore the world (German)
- **Zeitgeist** - The defining spirit or mood of a particular period (German)
- **Zenith** - The highest point or peak (Arabic)
- **Zest** - Great enthusiasm or energy (English)
- **Zigzag** - A pattern of sharp turns or angles (English)
- **Zombie** - A fictional reanimated corpse (originating from Haitian folklore)
- **Zoom** - To move quickly or bring into focus (English)
- **Zucchini** - A type of summer squash (Italian)
- **Café** - A small restaurant or coffeehouse (French)
- **Décor** - The style or arrangement of furniture and other elements in a space (French)
- **Éclair** - A pastry filled with cream and topped with icing (French)
- **Faux pas** - A social blunder or mistake (French)

- **Gourmet** - Relating to high-quality or exotic food and drink (French)
- **Hors d'oeuvre** - A small appetizer served before a meal (French)
- **Incognito** - In disguise or under an assumed name (Italian)
- **Judo** - A martial art that emphasizes using an opponent's strength against them (Japanese)
- **Karaoke** - A form of entertainment where people sing along to recorded music (Japanese)
- **Lingerie** - Women's underwear and sleepwear (French)
- **Macho** - Displaying stereotypically masculine characteristics (Spanish)
- **Niche** - A specialized or unique area of focus (French)
- **Origami** - The art of paper folding (Japanese)
- **Piñata** - A decorated container filled with candy, often broken during celebrations (Spanish)
- **Quiche** - A savory pie with a custard filling (French)
- **Salsa** - A spicy sauce or a style of Latin American dance and music (Spanish)
- **Tango** - A partner dance originating in Argentina (Spanish)
- **Tsunami** - A large ocean wave caused by an underwater earthquake or volcanic eruption (Japanese)
- **Utopia** - An imagined perfect or ideal society (Greek)
- **Van Gogh** - Referring to the artist Vincent van Gogh (Dutch)
- **Wannabe** - Someone who aspires to be like someone else or achieve something (English)
- **Xylophone** - A musical instrument with wooden bars played by striking them with mallets (Greek)
- **Yoga** - A physical, mental, and spiritual practice originating in ancient India (Sanskrit)
- **Zebra** - A wild animal with black and white stripes (English)
- **Zip code** - A numerical code used for postal addresses (English)
- **Zen** - A school of Buddhism emphasizing meditation and intuition (Japanese)
- **Zany** - Eccentric or comically unconventional (English)
- **Zeal** - Enthusiasm or fervor (English)
- **Zenith** - The highest point or peak (Arabic)

Confidence Booster Practice sets

Exercise 1

1. **Which phrase means "Without limit or end"?**
   A) Ad hoc B) Ad infinitum
   C) Ad nauseam D) Alma mater
2. **Which phrase means "To a sickening or excessive degree"?**
   A) Ad hoc
   B) Ad infinitum
   C) Ad nauseam
   D) Alma mater
3. **Which phrase means "One's former school, college, or university"?**
   A) Ad hoc
   B) Ad infinitum
   C) Alma mater
   D) Alpha
4. **Which phrase means "Well done or excellent"?**
   A) Bravo
   B) C'est la vie
   C) Carpe diem
   D) Carte blanche
5. **Which phrase means "Seize the day; live in the present"?**
   A) Bravo B) C'est la vie
   C) Carpe diem D) Carte blanche
6. **Which phrase means "Hello or goodbye"?**
   A) Bravo
   B) C'est la vie
   C) Ciao
   D) Carte blanche
7. **Which phrase means "So-so, neither good nor bad"?**
   A) Comme ci, comme ça
   B) Déjà vu
   C) Eureka
   D) Fiancé/Fiancée
8. **Which phrase means "Dead-end street or situation"?**
   A) Cul-de-sac
   B) Déjà vu
   C) Eureka
   D) Fiancé/Fiancée
9. **Which phrase means "The feeling of having experienced something before"?**
   A) Cul-de-sac
   B) Déjà vu
   C) Eureka
   D) Fiancé/Fiancée
10. **Which phrase means "An exclamation of joy or discovery"?**
    A) Cul-de-sac
    B) Déjà vu
    C) Eureka
    D) Fiancé/Fiancée

Answers

1.	(A)	2.	(C)	3.	(C)
4.	(A)	5.	(C)	6.	(C)
7.	(A)	8.	(A)	9.	(B)
10.	(C)				

Exercise 2

1. **Which phrase means "Until we meet again" in Spanish?**
   A) Hasta la vista
   B) Hoi polloi
   C) In situ
   D) Joie de vivre
2. **Which phrase means "The common people, the masses" in Greek?**
   A) Hasta la vista
   B) Hoi polloi
   C) In situ
   D) Joie de vivre
3. **Which phrase means "In its original place or position" in Latin?**
   A) Hoi polloi
   B) In situ
   C) Joie de vivre
   D) Karma
4. **Which phrase means "Joy of living" in French?**
   A) In situ
   B) Joie de vivre
   C) Karma
   D) Laissez-faire
5. **Which phrase means "The sum of a person's actions and their consequences" in Sanskrit?**
   A) Joie de vivre
   B) Karma
   C) Laissez-faire
   D) Magnum opus
6. **Which phrase means "A policy of non-interference, letting things take their own course" in French?**
   A) Karma
   B) Laissez-faire
   C) Magnum opus
   D) Memento
7. **Which phrase means "A great work or masterpiece" in Latin?**
   A) Laissez-faire
   B) Magnum opus
   C) Memento
   D) Nirvana
8. **Which phrase means "A reminder or keepsake" in Latin?**
   A) Magnum opus
   B) Memento
   C) Nirvana
   D) Hasta la vista
9. **Which phrase means "A state of perfect peace and happiness" in Sanskrit?**
   A) Memento
   B) Nirvana
   C) Hasta la vista
   D) Joie de vivre
10. **Which phrase means "The common people, the masses" in Greek?**
    A) Hasta la vista
    B) Hoi polloi
    C) In situ
    D) Joie de vivre

Answers

1.	(A)	2.	(B)	3.	(B)
4.	(B)	5.	(B)	6.	(B)
7.	(B)	8.	(B)	9.	(B)
10.	(B)				

Exercise 3

1. **Panache is a French word that means ________ confidence or style.**
   A) Flamboyant
   B) Reserved
   C) Timid
   D) Subdued
2. **The term "Paradigm" refers to a ________________ example or model.**
   A) Unique
   B) Peculiar
   C) Typical
   D) Extraordinary
3. **Paparazzi are photographers who relentlessly pursue _______.**
   A) Landscapes
   B) Celebrities
   C) Wildlife
   D) Art
4. **Persona non grata refers to an ________________ or unacceptable person.**
   A) Insignificant
   B) Unremarkable
   C) Unwelcome
   D) Unknown
5. **Quid pro quo refers to a favor or advantage granted ________________.**
   A) Without expectation
   B) In exchange
   C) Unconditionally
   D) Indifferently
6. **Rendezvous means a ________________ or gathering.**
   A) Formal meeting
   B) Political rally
   C) Meeting
   D) Casual conversation
7. **RSVP is an abbreviation derived from the French phrase "Répondez s'il vous plaît," which means "Please ________________."**
   A) Arrive promptly
   B) Dress formally
   C) Bring a guest
   D) Respond
8. **Schadenfreude is the pleasure derived from ________________ misfortune.**
   A) One's own
   B) Unexpected
   C) Fortunate
   D) Others'
9. **Status quo refers to the ________________ state or condition.**
   A) Changing
   B) Progressive
   C) Existing
   D) Ideal
10. **Tabula rasa refers to a ________________ or blank state.**
    A) Fulfilled
    B) Complex
    C) Colorful
    D) Clean

Answers List:

1.	(A)	2.	(C)	3.	(B)
4.	(C)	5.	(B)	6.	(C)
7.	(D)	8.	(D)	9.	(C)
10.	(D)				

Exercise 4

1. **Which phrase means "There it is; expressing satisfaction or completion" in French?**
   A) Voilà
   B) Wanderlust
   C) Zeitgeist
   D) Zenith

2. **Which phrase means "A strong desire to travel and explore the world" in German?**
   A) Voilà
   B) Zenith
   C) Zeitgeist
   D) Wanderlust

3. **Which phrase means "The defining spirit or mood of a particular period" in German?**
   A) Wanderlust
   B) Zeitgeist
   C) Zenith
   D) Zest

4. **Which phrase means "The highest point or peak" in Arabic?**
   A) Zeitgeist
   B) Zenith
   C) Zest
   D) Zigzag

5. **Which phrase means "Great enthusiasm or energy" in English?**
   A) Zest
   B) Zenith
   C) Zigzag
   D) Zombie

6. **Which phrase means "A pattern of sharp turns or angles" in English?**
   A) Zest
   B) Zigzag
   C) Zombie
   D) Zoom

7. **Which phrase means "A fictional reanimated corpse" originating from Haitian folklore?**
   A) Zigzag
   B) Zombie
   C) Zoom
   D) Zucchini

8. **Which phrase means "To move quickly or bring into focus" in English?**
   A) Zombie
   B) Café
   C) Zucchini
   D) Zoom

9. **Which phrase refers to "A type of summer squash" in Italian?**
   A) Zoom
   B) Café
   C) Zucchini
   D) Voilà

10. **Which phrase means "A small restaurant or coffeehouse" in French?**
   A) Zucchini
   B) Café
   C) Voilà
   D) Wanderlust

Answers List:

1.	(A)	2.	(D)	3.	(B)
4.	(B)	5.	(A)	6.	(B)
7.	(B)	8.	(D)	9.	(C)
10.	(B)				

Exercise 5

Match the Words:

Instructions: Match the words on the left with their corresponding descriptions on the right.

1. **Piñata ( )**
2. **Quiche ( )**
3. **Salsa ( )**
4. **Tango ( )**
5. **Tsunami ( )**
6. **Utopia ( )**
7. **Van Gogh ( )**
8. **Wannabe ( )**
9. **Xylophone ( )**
10. **Yoga ( )**

Descriptions:

A. A spicy sauce or a style of Latin American dance and music.

B. A musical instrument with wooden bars played by striking them with mallets.

C. A decorated container filled with candy, often broken during celebrations.

D. A physical, mental, and spiritual practice originating in ancient India.

E. Someone who aspires to be like someone else or achieve something.

F. Referring to the artist Vincent van Gogh.

G. An imagined perfect or ideal society.

H. A large ocean wave caused by an underwater earthquake or volcanic eruption.

I. A savory pie with a custard filling.

J. A partner dance originating in Argentina.

Answer Key:

1.	(C)	2.	(I)	3.	(A)
4.	(J)	5.	(H)	6.	(G)
7.	(F)	8.	(E)	9.	(B)
10.	(D)				

Exercise 6

1. What does the phrase "ad hoc" mean?

a) Without limit or end
b) For a specific purpose or situation
c) To a sickening or excessive degree
d) None of the above

2. What does the phrase "ad infinitum" mean?

a) Without limit or end
b) For a specific purpose or situation
c) To a sickening or excessive degree
d) None of the above

3. What does the phrase "ad nauseam" mean?

a) Without limit or end
b) For a specific purpose or situation
c) To a sickening or excessive degree
d) None of the above

4. What does the phrase "alma mater" mean?

a) Friend (Spanish)
b) Love or a romantic relationship (French)
c) One's former school, college, or university
d) None of the above

5. What does the term "alpha" signify?

a) The first letter of the Greek alphabet
b) That's life; accepting the ups and

downs (French)

c) Seize the day; live in the present (Latin)

d) None of the above

6. **What does the term "amigo" mean?**

a) Without limit or end

b) Friend (Spanish)

c) For a specific purpose or situation

d) None of the above

7. **What does the term "amour" mean?**

a) That's life; accepting the ups and downs (French)

b) Love or a romantic relationship (French)

c) One's former school, college, or university

d) None of the above

8. **What does the phrase "bon voyage" mean?**

a) Have a good journey (French)

b) Well done or excellent (Italian)

c) For a specific purpose or situation

d) None of the above

9. **What does the term "bravo" mean?**

a) Without limit or end

b) Have a good journey (French)

c) Well done or excellent (Italian)

d) None of the above

10. **What does the phrase "c'est la vie" mean?**

a) Friend (Spanish)

b) That's life; accepting the ups and downs (French)

c) Seize the day; live in the present (Latin)

d) None of the above

Answers

1.	(b)	2.	(a)	3.	(c)
4.	(c)	5.	(a)	6.	(b)
7.	(b)	8.	(a)	9.	(c)
10.	(b)				

Exercise 7

1. **vis-a-vis :**

(a) similar

(b) face to face

(c) contrary to the fact

(d) in good faith

2. **Modus operandi**

(a) successful operation

(b) unsuccessful mission

(c) mode or manner of doing a thing

(d) a clandestine operation

3. **Ad valorem**

(a) according to the-value

(b) according to utility

(c) according to cost

(d) according to demand

4. **Aide-mémoire**

(a) hearing aid

(b) without memory

(c) with sound memory

(d) notes to aid memory

5. **Ad interim :**

(a) finally

(b) ultimately

(c) unanimously

(d) in the mean time

6. **Ad infinitum :**

(a) with an end

(b) without end

(c) in the beginning
(d) at least

7. Aide :
(a) father
(b) teacher
(c) helper
(d) friend

8. Prima facie:
(a) without any evidence
(b) unceremoniously
(c) on the face of it
(d) deliberately

9. Inter Alia :
(a) among other things
(b) without other things
(c) in seclusion
(d) in great demand

10. Ad hoc :
(a) for the purpose
(b) without any purpose
(c) for ever
(d) in great demand

Answer

1.	(b)	2.	(c)	3.	(a)
4.	(d)	5.	(d)	6.	(b)
7.	(c)	8.	(c)	9.	(a)
10.	(a)				

Exercise 8

1. Mala fide
(a) in good faith
(b) in bad faith
(c) in remembrance
(d) after death

2. Ipso facto :
(a) by the very fact
(b) contrary to the fact
(c) in isolation
(d) year after year

3. 3) In toto :
(a) isolated
(b) part by part
(c) on the whole
(d) unknown

4. Viamedia
(a) extreme course
(b) right course
(c) left course
(d) middle course

5. Postmortem :
(a) medical examination after death
(b) medical examination after birth
(c) medical examination of the children
(d) medical examination of the adults

6. Lingua franca
(a) Latin language
(b) a common language
(c) an unknown language
(d) a new language

7. Ultra Vires :
(a) within one's powers
(b) in God's hand
(c) beyond one's powers
(d) beyond one's imagination

8. Locus standi :
(a) a place for dancing
(b) an exit
(c) centre of an office
(d) a place for standing

9. Per capita:
(a) per hundred

(b) per capitals

(c) per fifties

(d) per head

10. Beau Jour

(a) good times

(b) bad times

(c) A.and B.

(d) None of these

Answers

1.	(b)	2.	(a)	3.	(c)
4.	(d)	5.	(a)	6.	(b)
7.	(c)	8.	(d)	9.	(d)
10.	(a)				

Exercise 9

1. Ab initio (Latin):

(a) Initiative

(b) The initial

(c) Originality

(d) From the beginning

2. Aborigine (Latin):

(a). Originally

(b) Really

(c) From the origin

(d) Native

3. Euge (Latin, Greek)

(a) Huge

(b) Well done!

(c) Alas!

(d) Perfect!

4. Dei gratia (Latin):

(a) Thankfully

(b). I am grateful

(c) By the grace of God

(d) Thank you

5. Coup d'etat (French):

(a) Sudden overthrow of a government

(b) Capture

(c) Rebellion

(d) Statehood

6. Boutique (French):

(a) Beauty

(b) Bazaar

(c) A shop

(d) Bouquet

7. Eureka!/Meureka! (Greek):

(a) Amazement

(b) I have found!

(c) Attack!

(d) Disappointment

8. Magnum opus (Latin

(a) Magnification

(b) Horrible

(c) Terrific

(d) A great work

9. Bona fide (Latin):

(a) Good faith

(b) Good night

(c) Bonus

(d) Benefit

10. Au Contraire (French):

(a) Contradiction

(b) On the contrary

(c) Controversy

(d) On one's contribution

Answers

1.	(d)	2.	(b)	3.	(b)
4.	(c)	5.	(a)	6.	(c)
7.	(b)	8.	(d)	9.	(a)
10.	(b)				

Exercise 10

1. **Fade (French):**
(a) Insipid
(b) Improper
(c) Disgusting
(d) Failed

2. **Bonhomie (French):**
(a) Good home
(b) A homely place
(c) Good/friendly nature
(d) A fine house

3. **Prima facie (Latin):**
(a) Primal face
(b) Primitive man
(c) Main facilities
(d) At first sight

4. **Par excellence (French):**
(a) To a degree of excellence
(b) Beyond excellence
(c) Beyond any doubt
(d) Far from excellence

5. **Mon ami (French):**
(a) My love
(b) My aim
(c) My friend
(d) Happy mind

6. **R.S.V.P. (Respondez si'l vous plaet) (French):**
(a) Respond as soon as possible
(b) Reply if you please
(c) Reply is a must
(d) Reply through a letter

7. **Sine die (Latin):**
(a). A fixed day
(b) A signed document
(c) A sin
(d) Without an appointed day

8. **Vice-versa (Latin):**
(a). Assistant
(b) The vice officer
(c) An evil deed
(d) The terms being exchanged

9. **Vis-a-vis (French):**
(a) In exchange
(b) Face-to-face
(c) Tate-A-tate
(d) Side-by-side

10. **Beneficiare (French):**
(a) Benefits
(b) Bonus
(c) Donor
(d) Beneficiary

Answers

1.	(d)	2.	(c)	3.	(d)
4.	(a)	5.	(c)	6.	(b)
7.	(d)	8.	(d)	9.	(b)
10.	(d)				